FEMINIST CHRONICLES

P9-CKO-848

24⁹⁵
12⁵⁰

FEMINIST CHRONICLES
1953-1993

TONI CARABILLO
JUDITH MEULI
JUNE BUNDY CSIDA

WOMEN'S GRAPHICS
LOS ANGELES

Designed by Toni Carabillo.
Cover Design by Garry Burrell & Toni Carabillo

Library of Congress Cataloging-in-Publication Data

Carabillo, Toni
    Feminist chronicles, 1953–1993 / Toni Carabillo, Judith Meuli and
June Bundy Csida.
        p. cm.
    Includes bibliographical references and index.
    ISBN 0-9634912-0-2 (Soft Cover) ISBN 0-9634912-1-0 (Hard Cover)
        1. Feminism--United States--History--Chronology.   I. Meuli,
Judith. II. Csida, June Bundy. III. Title.
HQ1420.C37   1993
305.42 ' 0973--dc20   93-12500
                                                                              CIP

5 3 4 5 6-98 97 96 95

Attention: Schools and Businesses

Women's Graphics books are available at quantity discounts with
bulk purchase for educational, business, or sales promotional use.
For information write: Special Sales Department, Women's Graphic Communications, 1126 Hi-Point Street, Los Angeles, California,
90035.

TABLE OF CONTENTS

Acknowledgements

A number of people, aside from the authors, have made significant contributions to the creation of this book.

The first pass at creating the chronology on which the *Feminist Chronicles* is based was begun in 1980, when volunteers then working on the *National NOW Times* assembled a draft covering 1966-1979.

Those volunteers included Marj Jensen, Bonnie Sloane, Mary Margaret Smith, Gloria Windell, and Bede Urich, as well as *Chronicle* authors Carabillo and Meuli.

Long-time feminist activist David Dismore helped develop and enlarge the chronology by entering the original typewritten draft and hundreds of new entries into a data base on a PC, a major technological advance that became available to us in 1981.

Dolores Alexander, NOW's first executive director, now a copy editor at *People* magazine and a friend since 1969, volunteered to take vacation time to come to California and copy read the manuscript for which we are deeply grateful. The project was longer than her vacation so any remaining errors are ours, not hers.

Another friend and colleague, Peg Yorkin, has been involved in the process of getting the computer-generated book into print–in the contemporary printers' lingo "from disk to film"—and participated in the many production decisions.

No one has been a more enthusiastic supporter of the project as a tool for educating future feminist generations and as a resource for feminist writers as well as the media than Eleanor Smeal, president of the Feminist Majority.

She has given generously of her time and knowledge, tirelessly reading one draft after another and contributing ideas and information to ensure its comprehensiveness and accuracy. We have been allies and often writing partners in the feminist movement and friends for some 20 years now, yet we still marvel at how much she gives of herself and how rich her contributions are.

v

INTRODUCTION

These *Feminist Chronicles 1953 – 1993* are actually excerpted from a larger work in progress, the *Feminist Chronicles of the 20th Century.*

This larger work documents the feminist movement primarily in the United States from the turn of the century national convention of the National American Woman Suffrage Association, (NAWSA), when Susan B. Anthony retired as president and turned the organization over to the younger Carrie Chapman Catt, to "the present," which may well be the year 2000.

Both *Chronicles* dramatize the ever-on-going, day-by-day, year-by-year effort of feminist women to improve the lives and status of all women and to empower them as equal players in the world's affairs. This book documents not just the work of highly visible leaders who became famous but the efforts of the thousands of women (and sometimes men) whose names never became familiar, and without whom there would have been nothing that could be labeled a national movement.

What becomes obvious is that for the prominent and the unknown, advances have required extraordinary persistence, commitment, and faith in a vision of what might be that transcends the many near misses and defeats and the incredible backlash such efforts seem to inspire.

The format of the chronology, unlike a narrative history, makes it easier to recognize and track the multiple issues that were being pursued simultaneously across the country. Though the media might picture it otherwise, the feminist movement has never really narrowed its focus to a single issue.

The *Chronicles 1953-1993* use the National Organization for Women (NOW) justifiably as the organizing focal point of the movement in these years.

Though there was a slowly awakening consciousness among the young women of the New Left and Peace movements, in SNCC and the SDS, in the 60s, it was in fact the founding and organizing of NOW that became the public kickoff of the revitalized movement of these last three decades.

Though Women's Liberation groups emerged and flourished across the country for a few passionate years—for example, Radical Feminists, Redstockings, Witch—they lacked national coordination, goals, an accepted leadership, and, not the least, an effective fundraising mechanism. Many disappeared; others became service organizations, dedicated to providing assistance to women in a single area, such as battered women's shelters.

Many other organizations, old and new—the National Woman's Party (NWP), the Business and Professional Women (BPW), the American Association of University Women (AAUW), the League of Women Voters(LWV), the National Association for the Repeal of Abortion Laws, later the National Abortion Rights Action League (NARAL), the National Women's Political Caucus

(NWPC)—nurtured the movement and its successes and shared in its failures. But NOW has remained—as NAWSA and the National Woman's Party before it—central to its existence and vitality.

The press has written many premature obituaries for the feminist movement of these decades. But then NOW (which seems to be uniquely capable of the task) organizes a march in Washington to which hundreds of thousands come, giving visible proof that feminism lives and flourishes in numbers always superior to its opposition. And the obituary becomes merely another expression of the opposition's wishful thinking or disinformation.

The feminist movement and NOW are no longer the novelties on which the media continue to practice pack journalism, as they did in the early years. And perhaps with the exception of the massive marches, NOW itself is not always as militantly visible.

But on one day in October on opposite coasts, NOW was there for women in two different cases reported respectively in the *New York Times* and the *Los Angeles Times.*

In Newark, New Jersey, members of Essex County NOW were seated in a courtroom monitoring the case of four high school football players charged with sexually assaulting a mentally impaired young woman with a baseball bat, a broom handle and a stick, and forcing her to perform masturbation and fellatio in the basement of the home of two of the boys. As defense lawyers argued that the woman was the aggressor, the Essex County NOW Coordinator charged that "this is a second gang rape" of the victim.

In Newport Beach, California, five women, current and former employees of the police department, charged the police chief and a police captain with rape and sexual harassment. Defense lawyers described the women as employees who had a grudge because they had been disciplined. The Bayview Chapter of NOW released a statement declaring, "Every woman in Orange County should be outraged when charges of this magnitude are dismissed by city-paid attorneys as 'frivolous.' It is not surprising that women are reluctant to come forward when, as in the case of Anita Hill, the accuser is portrayed from the outset as mentally unstable or as a 'disgruntled employee.'"

As the *Chronicles* demonstrate, NOW Chapters remain ubiquitous across the country as the watchdogs of women's rights on a broad agenda of issues—not only in the big cities but also in the suburbs, in the small towns and in the countryside, in fact, wherever sex discrimination or misogyny surfaces. And women who have never been involved in any movement organization and who never called themselves feminists, who find themselves at wit's end in a crisis, call NOW for help.

Its national leadership in Washington, D.C., often moving in advance of colleagues in other generally like-minded women's organizations and even over their resistance, have often framed the new issues and set the tone and pace of the movement at the next cutting edge.

The fact is, if the National Organization for Women were to collapse and disappear, it would be taken as a signal of the end of this era of feminism.

Thankfully, the era has not ended.

Furthermore, the emergence of the Feminist Majority in 1987, a new, lean organization unencumbered by structural layers or an internal political process, has provided the movement with a fresh source of ideas and initiatives. Concentrating on the acquisition of power for women, the Feminization of Power Campaign crisscrossed the country beginning in 1987, jump-starting a process that climaxed in the so-called Year of the Woman in 1992. Rather than begging men to address the issues and needs of women, the feminist movement shifted its emphasis to taking power itself. The timing was right. Some 685 women's organizations in the late '80s endorsed the concept.

EMILY's List, launched in 1985 to raise early political money for Democratic pro-choice women through a technique long-used informally by the "boys," became the first political action committee to "bundle" money for candidates. Through bundling, EMILY's List could maximize women's political power by legally directing more than the federal political action committee's limitation of $5,000 per candidate. By 1992, EMILY's List had successfully raised $6 million for the presidential election and tens of thousands of dollars each for some targeted feminist candidates. So successful was the technique that it was instantly copied: pro-choice Republican women formed the "WISH List."

The spontaneous reaction to the Anita Hill/Clarence Thomas hearings by millions of women showed that the feminist movement still packed a mighty wallop throughout the country at both the grassroots level and on the asphalt streets of the inner cities. So mighty was the reaction to an all-white male Judiciary Committee's insensitive handling of Professor Hill's sexual harassment charges that it became a major contributing factor to the 1992 Congressional wins for women. All leading feminist organizations reported massive gains in fund raising, membership, and support immediately after the hearings.

Not only did the Anita Hill reaction attest to the strong pull of the feminist movement among women to its existing formal organizations, but it also resulted in the spinning off of new, nonhierarchical organizations reminiscent of the late 1960s. In New York City, the Women's Action Coalition (WAC), formed in the wake of the hearings, was reporting hundreds of women in attendance weekly at meetings. Its founders, Mary Dorman, a lawyer, Ann Philbin, a curator, and Deb Kass, a visual artist, were stirred to activism by what they witnessed of the televised hearings. WAC soon spread to other cities.

But perhaps nowhere is the current strength of feminism more noticeable to the power establishment than in pop culture. The 1991 movie *Thelma and Louise* struck such a chord among women, and took men by such surprise, that it made the cover of *Time* magazine. To this day, *Thelma and Louise* T-shirts are a brisk seller to feminist women.

In 1992-1993, Susan Faludi's *Backlash* and Gloria Steinem's *Revolution From Within*, both best-sellers, showed not only the tremendous popularity of feminism but also that it was still cross-generational in its appeal. And nowhere was the movement more radical than among its very young members, as evidenced in the music of the Riot Girls and the all-women rock bands. In the '70s, the anthem for women was the consciousness-raiser of Helen Reddy's "I Am Woman." For the '90s, the lesser-known but prophetic anthem is feminist Kay Weaver's "Take The Power."

As we go to press, a headline in the *Washington Post* reads, "Sisterhood of the Hill: Shaking Up the Place." In the spirit of Anita Hill, African-American women more than doubled their numbers in 1992 in Congress, led by the only African-American in the U.S. Senate, Carol Moseley-Braun, and in the House of Representatives, veteran lawmaker Cardiss Collins and the youngest of the group, Cynthia McKinney. All are being seen and heard as they take on the right- wing, antiwoman Congressional neanderthals led by Senator Jesse Helms and Representative Henry Hyde.

As we near the beginning of the 21st century, the feminist movement, dedicated to equality for women and a more just society, has firmly grasped the vision that to achieve its goals, women must become at least 50% of the decision-makers of our nation and world.

In the vernacular of the day, from a prophetic anthem by Annie Lennox, "Sisters Are Doin' It for Themselves."

—Los Angeles, August 1993

PART I

"... a passion for the possible."

A serigraph by Corita Kent has been hanging on the wall of my room for so many years that it's easy not to really see it or react to its message any more. But as I became absorbed in the re-creation of NOW's early years, I found myself again registering the words on it—a quote from William Sloane Coffin:

" . . . . hope, as opposed to cynicism and despair, is the sole precondition for new and better experiences. Realism demands pessimism but hope demands that we take a dim view of the present because we hold a bright view of the future; and hope arouses as nothing else can arouse . . .

...a passion for the possible."

Toni Carabillo

Awakening from the '50s

The peculiarly passive obsession with security as the ultimate happiness, the compulsive conformity of life styles (engendered at least in part by the virulent anti-communism of McCarthyism in odd combination with the Eisenhower era's pacifying blandness), and the pervasive apathy of most of the '50s was replaced in the 1960s with an extraordinary and even reckless social energy and political activism.

First Blacks, then other racial minorities, students, the New Left, peace protesters, and finally women, emerged one by one as forces demanding social change.

Each group became inflamed with a passion for the possible.

The momentum of the feminist movement of the earlier decades of the 20th century had waned in the post-World War II decades. Though work for women's rights actually continued by core organizations, it had become almost an underground resistance to a nearly overwhelmingly negative media blitz that insisted on proclaiming the death of feminism and on writing its obituary as it celebrated the happy suburban housewife.

As early as 1946, Doris Stevens, a long-time militant suffragist with the National Woman's Party, wrote to a friend, wondering "if those who were living at the beginning of the last Dark Ages. . . knew the darkness had descended!"[1]

However, hope for a revival of feminist momentum in the United States was stimulated in part by a curious series of events.

On August 26, 1957, (the uncelebrated 37th anniversary of the woman's suffrage amendment to the U.S. Constitution), the Soviet Union announced it had successfully tested an intercontinental ballistic missile. On October 4, it launched Sputnik I, the first "man-made" space satellite, and on November 3, Sputnik II, which carried a live dog.

This demonstration of a challenging superiority in space technology spurred what was immediately termed "the space race" between the U. S. and the Soviet Union.

The demands in the United States for a skilled and educated work force escalated to the point where even women—who, along with minorities, constituted the tra-

WE SHALL OVERCOME

DON'T TRUST ANYONE OVER 30

EVEN PARANOIDS HAVE REAL ENEMIES

I AM A HUMAN BEING do not fold, spindle or mutilate

ditional reserve labor force summoned forth in national emergencies—were worth serious consideration.

Prelude and Precursors

In 1957, the National Manpower Council (NMC) at Columbia University published its study, *Womanpower, A Statement by the National Manpower Council with Chapters by the Council Staff*. It was a comprehensive look at the experience of women in the labor force, their employment needs, and the implications of both for education, training, and public policy.[2]

This NMC analysis called women "essential" and "distinctive" workers and recommended that the Secretary of Labor establish a committee to review "the consequences and adequacy of existing Federal and state laws which have a direct bearing on the employment of women. " But this suggestion was not acted upon by the Eisenhower Administration.

In 1959, three landmark books on women were published: *A Century of Struggle* by Eleanor Flexner, the first professional history of the 19th century women's movement, which contained an implicit call to arms; *A Century of Higher Education for American Women* by Mabel Newcomer, which disclosed that the relative position of women in the academic world was in decline; and *Women and Work In America* by Robert Smuts, which drew attention to the fact that "the picture of women's occupations outside the home between 1890 and 1950 had changed in only a few essentials."

By 1961, President John F. Kennedy, elected on a platform that committed him to achieve an American victo-

ry in the space race, was open to pressure to establish a President's Commission on the Status of Women.

The pressure came from a variety of sources and was successful for a variety of reasons.

Esther Peterson, Assistant Secretary of Labor and director of the Women's Bureau, the highest ranking woman in the Kennedy Administration, wanted such a commission. Along with equal pay legislation, it had long been on the agenda of labor movement women and it was in that movement that Peterson's working career had been concentrated.

Women's organizations, notably AAUW and BPW, had been proposing a similar idea. They found a champion in Eleanor Roosevelt, who backed the proposal when she met with Kennedy at the White House after his election.[3]

The establishment of the Commission may also have been regarded by Kennedy as an expedient way to pay off his political debts to the women who had supported his campaign but were bitterly disappointed with his dismal record of appointments of women to his Administration.

There was also a desire to have Eleanor Roosevelt, the most respected woman in the country, associated with the Kennedy Administration. Roosevelt had only reluctantly supported JFK's presidential candidacy after her first choice, Adlai Stevenson, lost the nomination.

Her acceptance of the appointment as the chair of the Commission accomplished that. More importantly, however, was its symbolic impact.

In many ways, Eleanor Roosevelt's extraordinary political life was the bridge between the end of the drive for the right to vote in 1920 and the revitalization of the feminist movement in the United States in the 1960s. If she was a late supporter of woman's suffrage, once awakened and aware, there was no issue significant for women that did not concern her. Inspired by Carrie Chapman Catt and allied with her social feminist friends, she worked through the League of Women Voters and the Democratic Party to empower women politically and economically—as, in fact, she had empowered herself.

Already in ill health, Mrs. Roosevelt's role in the actual work of the Commission was limited: she conducted meetings of the Commission, signed many of its letters, served as adviser, and made herself available for purposes of publicizing the Commission. She died on November 7, 1962, a year before the report of the Commission was completed.

The Commission set up seven study committees on education and counseling, home and community services, women in employment, labor standards, security of basic income, women under the law, and women as citizens. Two special consultations were also organized by the Commission on "the problems of Negro women" and "the portrayal of women in the mass media."

The Commission met only eight times in the two years of its existence. As a consequence, the Women's Bureau and the hired staff of the Commission were very influential in steering its direction, most notably in dealing with the proposed Equal Rights Amendment (ERA), which Peterson and the labor-dominated Women's Bureau had long opposed, largely because of its anticipated impact on protective labor legislation for women. It was, in fact, Peterson who succeeded in removing—for the first time since 1944—a plank supporting a constitutional amendment from the 1960 Democratic Party platform.

Debate over the ERA had torpedoed previous efforts at such a commission. Peterson was determined that the Commission would, once and for all, kill the proposal for such a constitutional amendment by taking a different approach to the problems of discrimination facing women. She contended that "specific bills for specific ills" was the more effective approach.

Alice Paul, the aging leader of the National Woman's Party(NWP), who had originated the idea for the amendment in 1923, had good reason to be cynical about the Peterson approach: the NWP had tried the "specific bills" approach, literally framing hundreds of bills, but had succeeded in passing only a few. She had devised the Equal Rights Amendment to the Constitution as a way of wiping out all discriminatory laws in one stroke. Now she was convinced that the Commission had been set up to block its passage and expected that opponents would persuade Congress to delay any action on it until the Commission issued a report. She was right.[4]

On the day the Commission released its report, October 11, 1963, Esther Peterson wrote a thank you letter to Senator Carl Hayden for his help in immobilizing the ERA in Congress. She described his rider to the Equal Rights Amendment, which nullified its intent, as "an indispensable safeguard" against its passage. She asked him to continue attaching it in the event the ERA was introduced in Congress again.[5]

In terms of sheer attention focused on women, however, 1963 was certainly a banner year.

The Feminine Mystique

The "pervasive limitations" narrowing women's choices of roles that would be cited in the Commission's report were essentially those that Betty Friedan described polemically in and as *The Feminine Mystique*, published in February 1963, which rapidly hit the best seller lists with three million copies sold.

Friedan participated in the Commission's special consultation on the portrayal of women in the mass media.

Friedan also documented the fact that there was a substantial reservoir of educated women, remote from the labor force, that remained untapped precisely because "the feminine mystique" required their compulsory isolation in suburban homes with an almost mandatory 2.3 children and a largely absentee husband, uniformed in a gray flannel suit and preoccupied with upward mobility on a corporate organization chart.

Essentially, Friedan argued for the right of the wife and mother to pursue an identity and a career of her own.

The Commission published its report, entitled *American Women*. Far from a radical feminist document in its recommendations, it did describe many of the problems confronting women, including a desperate need for child care and the fact that "one of the most pervasive limitations is the social climate in which women choose what they pre-

pare themselves to do."

But the Commission's discussions, as well as the report itself, were racked by ambivalence between a commitment to women's traditional role of motherhood and its desire for equal opportunity for women in employment and in public life.

As an entity created and, in many respects, manipulated by members of the Kennedy Administration, the report steered a cautious course to avoid making controversial proposals that might prove an embarrassment to the President.

The report attempted to finesse the issue of the ERA by proposing that the Fifth and Fourteenth Amendments already provided women with Constitutional equality and all that was required was judicial clarification through test cases. It was a tactic that worked–for a time.

The report also recommended:

•the end of blatant sex discrimination in government employment (where agency heads could still specify the preferred sex of applicants to fill any job);

•an Executive Order to encourage Federal contractors to end sex discrimination;

•consideration of women "of demonstrated ability and political sensitivity" for appointment to policy-making positions;

•the improvement and extension of protective labor laws to men, in the meantime retaining legislation limiting maximum hours of work for women [*Author's note*: thus retaining a barrier preventing women from earning higher overtime pay];

•that restrictions that set maximum limits

upon weights women were allowed to lift (which barred able women from many higher paying jobs) did not take account of individual differences and should be replaced by more flexible regulations;

•continuation of the prohibition against home work, but permitting some flexibility for clerical, editorial, and research part-time work for women "during years of intensive homemaking;"

•passage of laws establishing the principle of equal pay for comparable work;

•a widow's benefit under Social Security be equal to the amount her husband would have received (but made no recommendations for changes in the Social Security system for married women workers who paid the tax but received no more than wives who made no payments);

•paid maternity leave or comparable insurance benefits for women workers;

•that educational institutions accommodate to the patterns of women's lives by offering part-time study, financial aid, and flexible academic and residency requirements so that women who followed the traditional role could reenter the labor force when their children had grown;

•programs to help women prepare for their special role by teaching child care, family relations, nutrition, family finances, and "the relation of individuals and families to society" (with no recommendation of such a program for men and boys);

•and (ambivalently) imaginative counseling programs to "lift aspirations beyond stubbornly persistent assumptions about 'women's roles' and 'women's interests' and result in choices that have inner authenticity for their makers."[6]

Release of the report made the front page of the *New York Times*, was covered by the Associated Press, and given a segment on NBC's "Today Show." It also elicited editorial comments in newspapers around the country. *The Wall Street Journal* may have set the tone for all child care legislation that would be proposed for many years to come with its comment on the Commission's recommendation for day care, terming it "a tinge collectivist." [7]

The task of the Commission was completed with publication of its report and, in the year following its release, the government distributed 83,000 copies. (In 1965, Scribner's published another edition, edited by Margaret Mead, which went on sale in the nation's commercial bookstores). However, on November 1, 1963, the Interdepartmental Committee on the Status of Women and the Citizen's Advisory Council were established by President Kennedy's Executive Order—one of the last two he signed—to "insure the work begun by the Commission would be continued."[8] Catherine East was named as Executive Secretary of both groups.

East was a confirmed member of an informal feminist underground in Washington, D.C., composed largely of women who had long careers in government service and were painfully aware of the limitations that had been placed on those careers by rampant sex discrimination in Federal employment.

Another earlier development also insured that the effort begun by the President's Commission would continue and spread. As early as November 1962, the National Federation of Business and Professional Women's Clubs told Esther Peterson that it wanted to initiate a campaign to pressure the governors of every state to appoint state commissions based on the model of the President's Commission. They wanted and got, with Peterson's intercession, President Kennedy's endorsement of the plan. The first state commission was appointed by the Governor of Washington in February 1963 and by 1967, every state had established one. [9]

The appointments to these commissions almost inevitably assembled as a group the "best and brightest," most politically active women in each state, eventually creating a new and potentially powerful national network of the like-minded, committed to advancing the status of women.

The Equal Pay Act of 1963

Even as the Commission was being established, Peterson launched another initiative—a campaign for equal pay legislation—and in March 1961, hired Morag Simchak, then a lobbyist for the United Rubber Workers, to head the operation. Rep. Edith Green (D-OR) authored and introduced the bill in the House.

The proposed legislation was endorsed at the first meeting of the President's Commission on the Status of Women on February 13, 1962. In a subsequent press conference, Eleanor Roosevelt expressed the Commission's belief that unequal wages for comparable work were "contrary to the concept of equality and justice in which we believe."[10]

Efforts to pass equal pay legislation had begun in 1945 but had failed time after time under both Democratic and Republican Administrations. All of the early proposals for this legislation and the Commission's own report used the language "comparable work," [11] but as in contemporary debates over comparable worth legislation, opponents argued that "comparability" was simply impossible to determine.

This time, compromise language was offered by Rep. Katherine St. George (R-NY) so that the key clause was amended to read, "equal pay for equal work." The House actually passed this bill by voice vote and without any vocal opposition, but it died in the Senate in a snarl of parliamentary procedure that could not be resolved before adjournment.

The business community, however, stunned and aroused by its passage through the House, had also begun mounting an opposition campaign and was ready when a new effort to pass the legislation began in the next session of Congress.

Over the opposition of the Chamber of Commerce and a number of corporate executives who testified against it, the bill passed both houses of Congress in May 1963. It amended the Fair Labor Standards Act and prohibited discrimination on the basis of sex in the payment of wages for equal work on jobs requiring equal skill, effort, and responsibility, which were performed under similar working conditions; prohibited employers from lowering men's wages to achieve this goal; it exempted wage differentials based on seniority, merit, or piece rate; it prohibited unions from attempting to negotiate wage differences based on sex; but it exempted from coverage executive, administrative, and professional employees, including teachers and academic administrative personnel in educational institutions.

President Kennedy signed the bill into law on June 10, 1963, in a ceremony in his office attended by Peterson, Simchak, and representatives of many of the women's organizations that had worked so hard for its passage.[12]

It had taken 18 years to achieve this victory and, for the first time, the Federal government was asserting the right of women to be employed on the same basis as men.

Even as the debate on equal pay legislation was occurring, for eight months in 1963, a Senate Subcommittee on Employment and Manpower [sic], was investigating "the impact of technological change upon the work force, our communities and our industries." Its report, published in April 1964, disclosed the fact that a sleeper revolution of women had in fact been underway throughout the '50s: women (most of them married) had been quietly moving into the nation's work force in massive numbers and constituted its largest increase.

According to the report, "Women, particularly those in the older age groups, accounted for an unexpectedly large part—nearly 60%—of labor force growth during the 1950s."

Rossi's Immodest Proposal

The American Academy of Arts and Sciences also sponsored a conference on "The Woman In America" in October 1963, assembling a preeminent roster of women and men from academic and professional fields, including historians, sociologists, psychologists and psychiatrists.

The ubiquitous Esther Peterson was there and presented a paper on "Working Women," documenting the reasons women worked outside the home and the inequities that beset them. In perhaps her boldest statement, Peterson declared: "I cannot agree with those who would raise the moral issue concerning whether or not a mother should work outside the home. Surely the question here is one which she, in counsel with her family, must settle on an individual basis. It is an area in which she has every right to exercise her freedom of choice. If the decision is that she should work, then the tenets of our democratic way of life dictate that her choice be respected and she have the same opportunities and rights afforded the male worker. Actually, we have, in my opinion, moved beyond that point in history where a woman has to choose between a home and a career. Today, she can have both—often at different intervals in her life, sometimes simultaneously."[13]

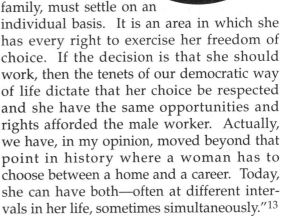

But the landmark paper of this conference, entitled "Equality Between The Sexes: An Immodest Proposal," was presented by sociologist Alice Rossi.

In this iconoclastic essay, Rossi pointed out what the conservative psychoanalysts and sociologists of the post-war period had chosen to ignore: that "for the first time in the history of any known society, motherhood has become a full-time occupation for adult women. . . . women in all strata of society except the very top were never able to be full-time mothers as the 20th century middle class American woman has become. These women were productive members of farm and craft teams along with their farmer, baker or printer husbands and other adult kin. Children either shared in the work of the household or were left to amuse themselves; their mothers did not have the time to organize their play, worry about their development, discuss their problems."

Rossi made it quietly clear that her proposal was really immodest: "By sex equality I mean a socially androgynous conception of the roles of men and women, in which they are equal and similar in such spheres as intellectual, artistic, political and occupational interests, complementary only in those spheres dictated by physiological differences between the sexes. This assumes the traditional conceptions of masculine and feminine are inappropriate to the kind of world we can live in in the second half of the 20th century." [14]

The Civil Rights Act of 1964

Lyndon Johnson, who succeeded to the Presidency after John Kennedy's assassination in late November 1963, had expressed strong support of the Commission on the Status of Women when he was Vice President. Now, anxious to demonstrate his commitment to completing Kennedy's unfinished agenda and transfer JFK's popularity with key constituencies to himself, he initiated efforts to win the support of women's organizations for his Administration.

One initiative, particularly pleasing to Party-affiliated women, was the appointment of more women to his Administration. Though he did not appoint a woman to his Cabinet, by 1968 he had appointed 52 women, (compared with 30 serving in 1963), a significant number of them in positions that were firsts for women. He named Esther Peterson to serve as his special assistant on Consumer Affairs in addition to her post as Assistant Secretary of Labor.

Peterson voluntarily gave up the directorship of the Women's Bureau, and Johnson replaced her with Mary Dublin Keyserling. Keyserling, an economist who had been active in the Democratic Party and with the National Consumers League, believed strongly that women workers required special protective legislation—a philosophical commitment that would put her in conflict with many other activist women and women's organizations that had begun to see them as restricting opportunities for promotion and higher wages.

In June 1963, Rep. Emmanuel Celler (D-NY), who had long opposed the Equal Rights Amendment, had introduced an omnibus civil rights bill, primarily directed at protecting Blacks and other racial, religious, or ethnic minorities against discrimination in voting, access to public education, employment, public accommodations, and in Federally-assisted programs. After 22 days of hearings, the House Judiciary Committee, chaired by Cellar, had reported the bill out favorably on November 20, 1963, just two days before President Kennedy's assassination in Dallas, Texas.

In December, 1963, the National Council of the National Woman's Party passed a resolution calling for an amendment to the Civil Rights bill to prohibit discrimination based on sex and protesting that, as the bill stood, it "would not even give protection against discrimination because of 'race, color, religion, or national origin' to a White Woman, a Woman of the Christian Religion, or a Woman of United States origin." [15]

As radical as National Woman's Party members appeared in the campaign for suffrage, there was strong inclination among many of its well-to-do members to a conservatism that abhorred interference in private enterprise, mirrored the racism of the majority of Americans and, even in the 1950s, led some of them to support Senator Joseph McCarthy's anticommunist crusade.

The reality was that racism and ethnic and religious bigotry were pervasive in American life and few organizations—whether composed of women or men—were free of all traces.

It was also true that white, male politicians promoted prejudice by making minority groups compete against each other in the pursuit of civil and economic rights that should have been theirs as a birthright. The temptation to exploit a backlash to advance one's own group would be hard to resist, given the frustrations that blocked civil rights movements.

With the Civil Rights bill headed for debate on the floor of the House, members of the National Woman's Party contacted Rep. Howard W. Smith (D-VA), chairman of the House Rules Committee, to suggest that a ban against sex discrimination be included in the legislation. Smith, a Southern archconservative who was also a longtime sponsor of the Equal Rights Amendment, told them he expected such an amendment to be offered on the floor, but did not commit to do it himself. Though he opposed the Civil Rights bill, he apparently agreed that if it was going to pass it should cover sex discrimination as well so that women would have the same rights as Blacks.

During Committee hearings, Smith questioned Cellar about the absence of a provision banning sex discrimination and said he would correct the omission.

On January 26, on the television show, *Meet The Press*, lifelong feminist May Craig, a member of the White House press corps and a regular on the show, questioned Smith about whether he would amend Title VII of the legislation to ban sex discrimination. (Craig had also long made it a practice at Presidential press conferences to query the incumbent President on what he had done for women lately).

"Well, maybe I would," Smith replied. "I'm all strong for women, you know."

"Amendment on the floor?" Craig persisted.

"I might do that, " Smith replied. [16]

Both Congresswomen Martha Griffith (D-MI) and Katherine St. George (R-NY), strong supporters of the ERA, had by now decided to back the amendment but to let Smith introduce it. They knew that Smith's sponsorship of the amendment, as part of a Southern strategy designed to defeat the entire bill, would guarantee the votes of 100 or more Congressmen from the deep South, who would otherwise vote against a feminist measure.

On February 8, 1964, Smith introduced the amendment to add the word "sex" to the provisions of Title VII of the Civil Rights Act. The debate that followed has been characterized as "Ladies' Day in the House."

Though Smith later denied he was insincere in introducing the amendment, Griffiths has said that it was Smith himself who told her he had proposed the amendment as a joke. The fact that he began his own arguments in its favor by reading a letter from a woman complaining that the 1960 Census had reported 2,661,000 "extra females" in the U.S. and asking that he introduce legislation to remedy the shortage of men for women to marry certainly set the tone. [17]

His reading of the letter brought down the house and, though Smith had to repeatedly ask for quiet, he concluded, "I read that letter just to illustrate that women have some real grievances."

Cellar, the leader of the coalition handling the bill, responded in kind: "I can say as a result of forty-nine years of experience—and I celebrate my fiftieth wedding anniversary next year—that women, indeed, are not in the minority in my house. . . . I usually have the last two words, and those words are, 'Yes, dear.' "

On a more serious note, he also quoted Esther Peterson, who insisted that adding sex to the Civil Rights bill would "not be to the best advantage of women at this time."

Liberals in Congress were reluctant to add the sex provision to the Civil Rights Act because they feared it would endanger its chances of passage, jeopardizing this historic opportunity to advance the civil rights of Blacks. For them it was, as it had been with passage of the 14th Amendment in 1866 which also excluded women, once again "the Negro's hour." Many conservatives were blind or indifferent to discrimination against women or believed that such discrimination was reasonable to protect women's traditional role.

But, as the ribaldry of the debate swelled among the male representatives, it seemed to betray not a patriarchal gallantry but a deep-rooted contempt for women. And regardless of the many reservations expressed by some of the women representatives, every Congresswoman but one abruptly rallied to support the amendment in defiance of party discipline.

Martha Griffith, who had planned to support it and had come prepared, rose to point out that the laughter of the men at the introduction of the amendment only underscored women's second class citizenship. The bill as written, she said, would leave white women without the protection it would provide Black women. The main function of protective labor laws for women, she said, was to protect men's rights to the best paying jobs. She ended her speech declaring that a white man's vote against the amendment was a vote against his wife, his widow, his sister, and his daughter.

Only Rep. Edith Green continued to oppose it, but not without a feminist awareness, as her statement indicated.

"As the author of the Equal Pay bill, I believe I have demonstrated my concern and my determination to advance women's opportunities," she said. "But I do not believe this is the time or place for this amendment. At the risk of being called an Aunt Jane, if not an Uncle Tom, let us not add any amendment that would get in the way of our primary objective. . . . For every discrimination I have suffered, the Negro woman has suffered ten times that amount of discrimination."

The Southern strategy backfired and on

DOWN WITH MALE CHAUVINIST PIGS

February 8, 1964, the prohibition against sex discrimination passed by a vote of 168 to 133. As the teller announced the vote count, a woman's voice from the gallery cried, "We made it! God bless America!"[18]

The provision stayed in Title VII of the version of the whole Civil Rights Act that passed the House two days later by a vote of 290 to 130. It's worth noting that every man who had spoken in favor of the sex discrimination amendment, except Rep. Ross Bass (D-TN), voted against the Civil Rights Act.

The National Woman's Party, which had already been lobbying intensely for passage of the amendment, now set up an emergency committee to work on keeping it in the Senate version of the bill. Pauli Murray, a Black woman attorney and one-time protegé of Eleanor Roosevelt, wrote a forceful "Memorandum in Support of Retaining the Sex Amendment," which the lobbyists of the Business and Professional Women, by then also actively campaigning, distributed to members of the Senate.

The Administration also dropped its opposition to the amendment in order to expedite passage of the same version of the bill in the Senate. On June 17, the Senate, in fact, passed a substitute bill, with the sex discrimination provision included, by a vote of 76-18. Two weeks later, on July 2, the House adopted the Senate version by a better than two-thirds vote. On the same day, President Johnson signed the bill into law.

By coalescing with the reactionary Southern strategists, and in the absence still of a widespread national women's rights movement, a handful of feminists had succeeded in pulling off a major political coup.

But the struggle was far from over.

Trivialization Takes Its Toll

The existence of the Citizen's Advisory Council on the Status of Women and the mushrooming State Commissions on the Status of Women kept the pressure on for change. Between 1963, when the President's Commission released its report, and 1965, many states made changes in the laws affecting women in the work force, largely as a result of the activities of state commissions and a resurgence of activism of existing women's organizations. Some of the changes:

•six states enacted minimum wage laws that applied to both women and men and nine states extended the coverage of the laws to men;

•eleven states made the laws limiting the hours women could work more flexible, and three repealed them altogether;

•six states adopted laws to give women overtime pay for work in excess of a specific number of hours;

•nine states enacted equal pay laws, bringing the total number of states with such a provision to 35;

•local community services to homemakers became more widespread;

•four states amended jury service provisions that discriminated against women;

•three states amended laws that restricted a woman's right to dispose of her own property;

•several states eliminated the difference in the age at which women and men could marry;

•a number of states began to bolster child support laws.[19]

But more significant than any of these efforts was the fact that in 1964 the Citizen's Advisory Council on the

Status of Women and the Interdepartmental Committee on the Status of Women began holding national conferences of the state commissions in Washington, D.C. The first meeting, on June 12, 1964, was attended by 83 representatives from 31 state commissions. By the second conference, on July 28-29, 1965, there were 400 representatives from 44 states. These conferences were attended also by cabinet members, other Federal agency heads, and President Johnson himself.

Women from all over the country were mingling in workshops and expanding their knowledge beyond the boundaries of their individual states on a whole range of topics affecting women's everyday lives: minimum wage laws, equal pay, daycare, public employment, special educational and counseling programs for women, media treatment of women and women's issues, vocational guidance, labor standards, income maintenance, community services, women in public life, educational and employment opportunities.

The conferences expedited the creation of a new, national network. They provided a forum for an expression of women's rising expectations for correcting the injustices they all now saw as limiting the lives and opportunities of women. Passage of the Civil Rights Act of 1964 had raised these expectations even higher.

On June 1, 1965, the Senate confirmed President Johnson's five appointees to the Equal Employment Opportunity Commission (EEOC), the agency charged with enforcing Title VII's provisions. Franklin D. Roosevelt Jr. was named Chair and Luther Holcomb, Vice Chair. The other Commissioners were Richard Graham, Samuel C. Jackson and Aileen Clarke Hernandez, the only woman—as she termed it, "a 20% nod to more than 50% of the population."[20]

As a black woman with a Hispanic-American surname (even if acquired by a marriage that ended in divorce), with a background in the civil rights and trade union movements and fresh from a job as Assistant Chief of the California Fair Employment Practices Commission, Hernandez was well-qualified for the appointment.

The law required that the EEOC begin operations on July 2, 1965, and with the Commissioners now in place, there was a scramble to assemble a staff. It turned out to be the first indication, as Hernandez put it, "that the Commission was not planning to be an example to industry of the meaning of 'equal opportunity employer.'"[21] No women were included in the top appointments (Civil Service Grades 16, 17, and 18), and, in fact, none were hired over Grade 12.

The new commissioners began preparing themselves for their work by reading hundreds of pages of documents, prepared by consultants, to orient them to the duties of the EEOC. Hernandez found that there were "only limited references to sex discrimination—all of which suggested minimal attention to the entire subject."[22]

Even as they were setting up, there was a drumbeat in the press that continued the trivialization of the sex amendment that had begun in the Congressional debate. On June 22, 1965, the *Wall Street Journal* ran an article that asked readers to picture "a shapeless, knobby-kneed male 'bunny' serving drinks to a group of stunned businessmen in a Playboy Club" or a "matronly vice-president" chasing her male secretary around a desk. The personnel office of a large airline was quoted asking, "What are we going to do now when a gal walks into our office, demands a job as an airline pilot and has the credentials to qualify?" The manager of an electronic company employing only women worried aloud about having to provide "equal opportunity" to men: "I suppose we'll have to advertise for people with small, nimble fingers and hire the first male midget with unusual dexterity [who] shows up." And a government official said the EEOC would be lenient in enforcing the prohibition against sex discrimination "if the women's groups will let us get away with it."[23]

Hernandez noted that "Commission meetings produced a sea of male faces, nearly all of which reflected attitudes that ranged from boredom to virulent hostility whenever the issue of sex discrimination was raised. The message came through clearly that the Commission's priority was race discrimination—and apparently only as it related to Black *men*."[24]

"There was such insensitivity to sex discrimination," she said, "that a major meeting with employers in California was arranged at a private club which barred women—even though I was scheduled to accompany the Chairman to the meeting."[25]

In August 1965, while it was really still pulling itself together, the EEOC was diverted into planning and executing the White House Conference on Equal Employment Opportunity as its public debut. According to Hernandez, "Of the 75 people listed as speakers and panelists, only nine were women, and six of the nine were on the panel dealing with sex discrimination. Of the 14 people who were either chair or vice chair of a session, I was the only woman. Many of the women who attended were infuriated at the cavalier manner of Commission members and staff concerning the importance of sex discrimination cases. The conference may well have underscored," Hernandez concluded, "in the minds of some of the participants, the need for an outside, activist organization to force the Commission to pay serious attention to the problems facing women in the job market."[26]

Though the majority of the Commission may have been reluctant to deal with sex discrimination, one third of the complaints that began to flow in were filed by women, putting pressure on the Commission for some decisions.

The initial complaints coming from women were concentrated in three areas: newspaper help wanted ads that were segregated by sex in separate sections; state protective laws that had the effect of discrimi-

A MAN OF QUALITY INSISTS ON EQUALITY

SHARE POWER NOW

Trust in God SHE will provide

nating against women in employment; and bona fide occupational qualifications (BFOQ) for the job of flight attendant, for example, whether being female, single and under 32 to 35 were really essential qualifications.

No Women Need Apply

The first of these issues to surface was the sex-segregated help wanted advertising.

Title VII of the Civil Rights Act read: "It shall be an unlawful employment practice for an employer . . . to publish or cause to be . . . published any notice or advertisement relating to employment . . . indicating any preference, limitation, specification, or discrimination, based on race, color, religion, sex, or national origin" except where a BFOQ existed.

The Commission had no second thoughts about ruling that a job ad specifying race would violate Title VII but convened a special 17 member committee (13 men and four women, 10 of whom represented newspapers or advertising agencies) on August 18, 1965, to consider the sex question. Composed disproportionately of business interests, this committee quickly concluded that want ads segregated by sex in newspapers did not violate Title VII.[27]

But even as these deliberations were still in process, the supposedly liberal press, kept up the drumbeat of trivialization. "Why," asked the *New Republic*, "should the mischievous joke perpetrated on the floor of the House of Representatives be treated by a responsible administrative body with this kind of seriousness?"[28]

At first, the EEOC itself split 3-2 in favor of ruling that sex-segregated help-wanted ads did violate Title VII, with Richard Graham, Aileen Hernandez, and Sam Jackson in the majority and Commission Chair, Franklin Roosevelt Jr., and Vice Chair, Luther

Holcomb in the minority. But then Jackson changed his vote and the Commission issued its ruling on Sep-tember 22, 1965, that sex-segregated advertising was permissible. All that was required was for the newspaper publishers to print a disclaimer in a prominent place:

> "NOTICE: many listings in the 'male' or 'female' columns are not intended to exclude or discourage applications from persons of the other sex. Such listings are for the convenience of readers because some occupations are considered more attractive to persons of one sex than the other. Discrimination in employment because of sex is prohibited by the 1964 Federal Civil Rights Act with certain exceptions. . . .Employment agencies and employers covered by the Act must indicate in their advertisement whether or not the listed positions are available to both sexes. . . . In the absence of such a statement in the advertisement, readers may assume the advertisers prefer applicants of a particular sex. . . ."[29]

As Hernandez pointed out, "the Commission's tortuous reasoning was in marked contrast with a guideline proposed by the Wisconsin Industrial Commission in the same month which stated simply: 'It shall be deemed a discriminatory practice because of sex to designate help-wanted columns 'male' and 'female' except where the exclusive employment of one sex is in positions where the nature of the work or working conditions provide valid reasons for hiring only men or women.'"[30]

On October 12, the National Council of

Women of the United States held a conference attended by some 300 women from across the country at the Biltmore Hotel in New York City on Title VII and the EEOC. Both Dr. Pauli Murray, professor of law at Yale University and a member of the President's Commission on the Status of Women, and Franklin D. Roosevelt Jr., chair of the EEOC, were speakers.

In his speech, Roosevelt defended his agency's policy of permitting sex-segregated help-wanted ads, saying that enforcement of the law to protect women against employment discrimination had to proceed "gradually." He pointed out that in introducing the amendment, Rep. Howard Smith had wanted to create "ridicule and confusion." The last minute introduction of the amendment meant no Congressional hearings had been held, so it had no legislative history, Roosevelt contended.

Murray flatly declared that the EEOC's policy on job advertising was a violation of Title VII and a product of subtle opposition to the new law.

"If it becomes necessary to march on Washington to assure equal job opportunities for all," Murray said, "I hope women will not flinch from the thought."

One of those who read the news coverage of this event in the *New York Times* the following morning was Betty Friedan; she made immediate telephone contact with Dr. Murray, establishing one of the many historic linkups that led to a re-emergence of an overt feminist movement in the U.S.

Murray had still more to say and she did so in collaboration with Mary Eastwood, then employed in the Office of Legal Counsel in the Department of Justice. Together they wrote an article, published in December 1965, in the *George Washington Law Review*,

entitled, "Jane Crow and the Law: Sex Discrimination and Title VII." At the outset they declared, "That manifestations of racial prejudice have been more brutal than the more subtle manifestations of prejudice by reason of sex in no way diminishes the force of the equally obvious fact that the rights of women and the rights of Negroes are only different phases of the fundamental and indivisible issue of human rights."[31]

Among the points they made in reviewing the legal discriminations against women was that ". . . great scientific and social changes have already taken place, such as longer life span, smaller families, and lower infant death rate, with the result that motherhood consumes smaller proportions of women's lives. Thus, the effects of sex discrimination are felt by more women today.

"We are entering the age of human rights," they wrote. "In the United States, perhaps our most important concerns are with the rights to vote and to representative government and with equal rights to education and employment. Hopefully, our economy will outgrow concepts of class competition, such as Negro v. white, youth v. age, or male v. female, and, at least in matters of employment, standards of merit and individual quality will control rather than prejudice."[32]

In January 1966, historian Dr. Carl N. Degler, who had participated in the American Academy of Arts and Science Conference in 1963 with Alice Rossi, further developed his ideas for a

WOMEN TRY HARDER & GET PAID LESS

new symposium in Dallas, Texas entitled, "American Women in Social and Political Affairs— Change and Challenge."

In this presentation, he declared, "We have to restructure the attitudes of women as well as men as to what is the proper place of women in society; we have to broaden the expectations of young women; we have to expand our conception of what a woman may become. As a society we have to act as if we believe that women are entitled to careers as well as to babies and husbands. This is not to say that every woman will want a career or will even have one. But if the paths are to be kept open for those who do and if we are to make maximum use of the talents of women, then we have to abandon the prevalent notion that a girl must choose between a career and marriage. And even for those young women who do elect not to take a job or pursue a career when they marry, they should know that in the modern life-pattern of American women raising a family is, in fact, not a lifetime job."[33]

Aileen Hernandez circulated copies of this paper to her colleagues on the EEOC in the hope of enlarging their vision.

In the meantime, however, the second issue surfaced at the EEOC—the discrimination against women that resulted from state protective legislation.

". . . In A Class By Herself"

The major types of state laws regulating the employment of women were: laws prohibiting the employment of women in certain occupations, such as in bars and mines;

maximum hour laws that women could work; minimum wage laws for women; laws prohibiting the employment of women during certain hours of the night in certain industries; laws limiting the weights women could lift on the job (from a low of 15 pounds in Utah to 35 pounds in Michigan); and laws requiring special facilities for women employees such as chairs and restrooms.

The U.S. Supreme Court case that provided the legal precedent for the passage of a mushrooming number of these laws by the states was *Muller v. Oregon* in 1908. The Oregon law had limited the number of hours women could work and had been hailed by trade unions, some of which had originally pushed to have the law cover both men and women.

In upholding the Oregon law, the U.S. Supreme Court's decision declared ". . . women's physical structure and the performance of maternal functions place her at a disadvantage in the struggle for subsistence. . . [her physical well-being] becomes an object of public interest and care in order to preserve the strength and vigor of the race. . . [she] is properly placed in a class by herself, and legislation designed for her protection may be sustained even when like legislation is not necessary for men and could not be sustained."

EQUAL PAY FOR EQUAL WORK

Being in "a class by herself" however was being perceived by many women in the work force less as a protection than as a major obstacle to better job opportunities and higher pay, including the higher rates paid for working overtime. And the EEOC began receiving an increasing number of complaints filed by women that raised the issue of the conflict between Title VII and these state laws.

On November 22, 1965, the Commission released the guidelines covering these complaints: "The Commission will not find an unlawful employment practice where an employer's refusal to hire women for certain work is based on a state law which precludes the employment of women for such work, provided that the employer is acting in good faith and that the law in question is reasonably adapted to protect women rather than to subject them to discrimination. . . ."

In his comments at the press conference at which the guidelines were released, EEOC Chair Roosevelt said the Commission could not assume Congress intended to strike down state legislation, though "study demonstrates that some of this legislation is irrelevant to the present day needs of women." However, he went on to say that until the laws were revised, the Commission "will consider qualifications set by state laws or regulations to be bona fide occupational qualifications and not in conflict" with Title VII.

Coffee, Tea or Me

The third issue to surface during the first year of the EEOC's operations involved the entire airline industry. Flight attendants—then called "stewardesses"—filed an escalating number of complaints charging that the airlines were violating Title VII by hiring only women for that job, by discharging them if they married, and by firing or grounding them when they reached the age of 32 or 35.

On October 25, 1965, Judith Evenson filed a sex discrimination complaint against Northwest Airlines because it required women, but not men, to sign an agreement to resign after they got married.

Aileen Hernandez, the decision commissioner on this complaint, found "reasonable cause" that Evenson was the victim of sex discrimination and directed a Commission conciliation team to attempt to restore her to her job, in spite of her marriage, and get her back pay for the period since she had been discharged by Northwest.

The conciliation effort failed and Northwest and other airlines petitioned the EEOC for a public hearing on their request for a BFOQ exemption for the position of flight attendant.

At the first hearing on May 10, 1966, and for months afterward, the airlines attempted to make their case that being female was essential to the job. They did so primarily by citing surveys that indicated a customer "preference" for young, unmarried women as flight attendants.

In the meantime, on March 27, 1966, the *New York Times* reported that a spokesperson for the EEOC had said that the EEOC was moving carefully on sex discrimination issues because of the absence of legal precedent, out of its concern for upsetting protective labor legislation and because "it did not want this area to interfere with its main concern, racial discrimination."

Then, a month later on

April 27, the majority of the EEOC buckled completely under pressure from newspaper publishers and advertisers and amended its guidelines to lift even its mild requirements, essentially permitting the advertising of jobs in sex-segregated columns.

Reaching the Boiling Point

On May 19, Michigan Congresswoman Martha Griffiths challenged the guidelines in a letter to the EEOC that declared, "I assume you will agree that the heading 'white' or 'Negro' or 'Protestant' would be prohibited by the statute, and therefore I have difficulty seeing how advertisements under the headings of 'male' or 'female' could be in compliance with the very clear prohibitions of Section 704(b). . . I am convinced that advertising columns labeled by sex. . . is most pernicious because it reinforces prejudicial attitudes limiting women to the less rewarded and less rewarding types of work."

Luther Holcomb, then serving as Acting Chairman of the EEOC because Roosevelt had resigned to run for governor of New York, responded by letter, contending, "Column headings do not prevent persons of either sex from scanning the area of the jobs-available page."

On June 20, Griffiths took to the floor of Congress to castigate the Commission for its approach to sex discrimination issues, characterizing it as "nothing more than arbitrary arrogance, disregard of law, and a manifestation of flat hostility to the human rights of women." She termed its ruling on sex-segregated want ads as a "peak of contempt."

"I would remind them," she said, "that they took an oath to uphold the law, not just the part of it that they are interested in."

To Holcomb, in particular, she responded pointedly, "I have never entered a door labeled 'Men,' and I doubt that Mr. Holcomb has frequently entered the women's room."

Catherine East, now serving as the Executive Secretary of both the Interdepartmental Committee on the Status of Women and the Citizen's Advisory Council on the Status of Women, fanned the growing dissatisfaction with the EEOC's handling of sex-discrimination complaints by seeing that copies of Griffiths' speech were distributed to the delegates of the state commissions assembled for the third annual conference of Commissions on the Status of Women on June 28 in Washington, D.C.

Presiding at the conference were the small hierarchy of women then prominent in government, mostly from the Department of Labor and the Women's Bureau. These included Esther Peterson, Mary Keyserling, heading the Women's Bureau, and Marguerite Gilmore, chief of the Bureau's field division.

Margaret Hickey, public affairs editor of the *Ladies' Home Journal*, who had been on the President's Commission and was also just retiring as chair of the Citizen's Advisory Council, actually conducted many of the conference sessions.

Hickey was, in reality, one of the only women in the leadership of the conference who was a free agent; most of the others were subordinates in the male-dominated

Department of Labor and members of the political administration then in power. They were subject to discipline as well as instructions from its upper echelons. Their leeway for encouraging or even entertaining expressions of dissent with administration policies was obviously minimal.

Even the state commissioners in attendance could be subject to intimidation or reprisal. Many came freshly aware of what had happened to the Illinois Commission on the Status of Women, which had been established with funding of only $10,000 for its activities. (Many commissions in other states had to fund themselves). The year after the Illinois Commission succeeded in getting and equal pay act passed in the state, it lost its funding in the state budget.

The Dissidents Assemble

However, among the conference attendees were a core of willing dissidents. For them, hope coupled with frustration had aroused an impatient passion for what at last seemed possible. Tolerance for any new frustration was at an all-time low.

Betty Friedan attended this conference as a writer/observer, and has indicated she arrived already persuaded of the need for a civil rights organization to represent the interests of women.

She had, Friedan wrote, "followed closely the valiant efforts of Richard Graham and Aileen Hernandez as Equal Opportunity Employment Commissioners to enforce the prohibition against sex discrimination in employment" and she had "learned how seriously handicapped they were by the absence of support or pressure from organizations who would speak out on behalf of equality for women as the Civil Rights Movement had done for Negroes. The leaders of a number of major women's organizations told me that they could not or did not wish to speak out in protest against sex discrimination or press for serious enforcement of the law on behalf of women, for fear of being called 'feminist.' " [35]

During this same period, EEOC Commissioners Richard Graham and Aileen Hernandez were "privately suggesting the need for an organization to speak on behalf of women in the way civil rights groups had done for Blacks."[36]

The Darling of the Bureau

"I still remember running into Dorothy Haener [of the United Automobile Workers] and Pauli Murray on the escalator the first morning at the Washington Hilton," Friedan wrote, "and agreeing, somewhat less than enthusiastically, that we would invite to my hotel room that night anyone we met who seemed likely to be interested in organizing women for action."[37]

After hearing Kay Clarenbach, head of the Wisconsin Commission on Women, give what Friedan described as "a biting talk on how far from equality the very terms were in which the status of women was being discussed,"[38] she invited Clarenbach to the meeting. According to Friedan, her co-conspirators were horrified, describing Clarenbach as "the darling of the Women's Bureau."[39]

Clarenbach's status with the Department of Labor's Women's Bureau

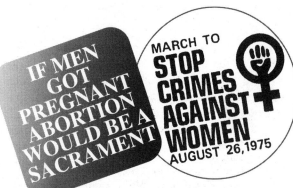

probably was cause for concern among the more militantly-minded women because of the prominence of representatives from the Women's Bureau in the machinery of the conference and the relatively "conservative" reputation of the Bureau itself.

Because of the Bureau's origins in the trade union movement, it tended to reflect the traditional male-dominated biases of unions. Many union women were all too painfully aware that the unions had never been a dynamic force for opening job opportunities to women on an equal basis with men. Unions had a long history of opposition to the ERA because it threatened protective labor legislation for working women, which unions favored, though they depended on independent trade union negotiation and action to advance the rights of working men. Unions had in fact provided testimony opposing the inclusion of sex discrimination in Title VII of the Civil Rights Act.

The Legendary Meeting

Some 15-20 women assembled in Friedan's hotel room, among them: Catherine Conroy of the Communication Workers of America, from Wisconsin; Inka O'Hanrahan and Rosalind Loring from the California Commission on the Status of Women; Mary Eastwood from the Department of Justice in Washington, D.C. ; Dorothy Haener, Pauli Murray, Kay Clarenbach and, of course, Betty Friedan.

What happened in the now legendary hotel room meeting has been variously described by several of the participants. At a dinner honoring the founders of NOW at the 1971 national conference in Los Angeles, Dorothy Haener presented one account, excerpted here:

"The whole concept of the need in this country of an NAACP for women was really brought to me by women who worked in the Labor Department. One in particular, a Black friend of mine, made it very clear that what the women in this country really needed was an NAACP for women. And frankly, that night in Betty's hotel room, when it almost didn't come off because there were some women there who said, 'Do you really think we need another women's organization?' and I can recollect . . . that the session which up until then had been very productive, completely erupted and we really had a kind of all-out shouting match. And Betty ended up by opening the door and saying to one woman, 'You know, this is my room and my liquor and you're perfectly free to say anything you please, but you're not going to use my room and my liquor while you're doing it.' And so, after she had left, some of us tried to smooth things over. And in the process of smoothing things over, we came up with the idea of allowing that group that thought they could just work within the establishment to try the following day to get a motion on the floor to reappoint Richard Graham, who had done such a wonderful job for women on the Equal Employment Opportunity Commission. Now those of us who were in the know knew that [President] Lyndon Johnson didn't intend to reappoint him because he was doing a job for women and because, really, we had such a terrible time trying to make Title VII anything but the standard cocktail hour joke in Washington about [Playboy] bunnies. And so we said, 'Well, let them try.' "[40]

Another participant, Nancy Knaak, then a member of the Wisconsin Commission on the Status of Women and dean of women at the River Falls campus of the University of Wisconsin, who also became a founder of NOW, remembered it somewhat differently in an account written in 1973:

> "On the second night of the conference, I crossed paths with Kay Clarenbach in the hotel lobby. There was to be a meeting in Betty's room, she said, and I ought to come. I had no idea why there was to be a meeting, and was reluctant to appear without an invitation, but Kay assured me that it was quite an informal affair and the gathering a random one . . . .
> "The meeting began at a late-ish hour . . . perhaps 10:00 p.m. Though I did not count the house, it was my impression that 15 or 20 women were crowded into all available space, and I considered it fortunate to find a swatch of wall against which I could lean while sitting on the floor from a vantage point which required peering over two beds towards Betty and Kay who somehow were ensconced on chair or stool. Some of the women were drinking, but because the choice was limited and because I was a sort of unintended guest, I found a paper cup and settled for plain water.
> "The discussion seemed to have just gotten underway. No clear leadership had been established, but the main conversants were Betty, Kay, and Pauli Murray. They seemed to think there was a need for still another kind of structure which could effectively meet women's needs as the

earnest souls present at the conference weren't going to be able to. I was slow to offer an opinion, the evidence seeming to be that this was no random group at all. Rather, I had a hunch that several of the folk there might well have had a preliminary meeting for which the agenda for this one had already been outlined. This impression was confirmed when the acronym of NOW was so quickly proposed. Though Betty takes credit for it, and my own recollection may be inaccurate, I think it was Kay who suggested such a label–and several quickly gave assent. (Betty says she wrote the letters on a napkin earlier in the day: perhaps Kay was merely introducing the notion for her. But whatever else, it was Kay who said more than once that the objectives of such an organization would include bringing women into 'full participation in the mainstream of American society'. . . and in full partnership with men.' If credit for those phrases is ever due, it has to be accorded Kay and not Betty.")[41]

"This discussion was interesting, wide-ranging, and passionate," Nancy Knaak remembered.

Rosalind Loring's recollection was that much of the conversation was about how angry most of the women present were at what was happening at that conference and what they could do to change the way it was being conducted. The feeling was that the Women's Bureau staff was "sit-

ON OCTOBER 29, 1975

Alice doesn't!

...ting on them and not letting them make strong enough statements about what they expected the Federal government to provide in the way of services, legislation, support, etc. Mary [Keyserling] was trying to keep it low key because there were other people there from the Department of Labor—male, more senior people, or higher-up-the-echelon people."[42]

"It became clear," Loring recalled, "that while all of us in the room were very uncomfortable with the way the conference was being conducted, because I really agreed with Betty—it *was* arbitrary—I guess the difference was in how we thought it should be handled."[43]

The ostensible cause celebre—what they wanted from the conference—seems harmless enough in retrospect: passage by the conference of the Commissions of a resolution calling for the enforcement of Title VII by the EEOC and for the reappointment of Richard Graham (his term expired July 2) as an EEOC Commissioner. Had they been permitted to pass this resolution, it might have convinced at least some of the dissidents that the existing mechanisms—the combination of state commissions and federal agencies—could be useful in advocating the interests of women.

"Finally," according to Knaak, "it was Pauli Murray who seemed to have a course of action to suggest." Knaak recalled Murray beginning to outline an organizational plan, speaking from notes on a large, yellow legal pad. At about this point, as she remembers it, Knaak interrupted to offer

"the benefits of my great wisdom."

Bathroom Politics

Loring's recollection was that when Knaak spoke, it wasn't in disagreement. "She was really asking League-like questions, such as, 'Have we really explored all the alternatives? Have you told Mary [Keyserling] how you feel about this? Have we exhausted all the channels?'"

"Betty, however, was not pleased," Knaak remembered. "By the time I'd all but concluded. . . Betty was visibly annoyed, a response which grew in intensity. Finally, she interrupted my lecture to ask, 'Who invited *you*?' She said more, but what I really heard was Kay's quick assertion that it had been she who'd done so, and that I somehow had a right to be where I was. 'Get out! Get out!' Betty shouted.

Knaak can't remember what verbal response, if any, she made, but Loring recalled that she replied, "I will not. I'm having too good a time!" Knaak remembered feeling "entitled to disagree . . . it seemed to be justified in a fluid situation."

> "So I was not about to get out. In fact, had it taken a herd of camels, I'd not have moved from my uncomfortable spot if I could have helped it. Voices were raised in my defense–Kay's and others–not on the grounds that I'd said anything worth considering, but purely on the matter of the right to speak, invited or not. Betty noted the conflict, saw my failure to leave, and she thereupon stomped to the bathroom, entered, slammed its door, and noisily snapped the lock. What a pickle. Perhaps I really didn't belong in that room . . . . [But] I also considered Betty's demonstration to be childish, so I decided to wait her out. If I had to leave before she would come out of

the bathroom, then, by gum, she could stay in there all the rest of the night.

"What Dorothy Haener later described as 'some of us tried to smooth things over' occurred then–and not after my departure. We lowered our voices, I retreated from the certainty of my stance, and the meeting continued. It had lost some of its momentum: after all, our hostess was locked in her bathroom! But discussion was quieter, arguments modified, and we did move on to other considerations. I timed it on my watch: Betty returned to the group after a 15-minute period of isolation, ignored my presence, and gradually resumed her role as an important participant. And in awkward concession, I remained until she seemed sufficiently distracted by the business at hand, so that I could inch toward the exit and leave, generally unnoticed."[44]

Symbol of Constancy

"Among the limited legends of NOW," Knaak commented, "the woman 'thrown out who never returned' has been a sort of symbol of constancy of those who remained. That I am still among the membership does make me feel a bit subversive sometimes."

". . . I have regret that I am still that legendary woman. She serves a purpose, I suppose, in showing that there was deviation within the charmed circle, but I'm really rather tired of being her. I was there. I cared a whole lot. And I'm still among the people who consider justice for all human beings to be a worthy goal."[45]

Friedan identified Clarenbach as among

those who resisted the idea of forming a new organization. Knaak's memory is that no one really opposed the idea and there was general agreement that it had to be done. Her recollection was that part of the plan agreed on that night was to meet again at lunch the next day to further develop the idea and recruit more support before they all had to leave for home.

Knaak remembered that while it was agreed that Clarenbach would make another formal attempt at getting the conference leadership to accept the resolutions, no one expected her to succeed. It would just be one last confirmation that "we were not going to be allowed to move" and a new organization was necessary.

Some Not Ready

Loring's recollection was that she and a friend, who was also present at the hotel room meeting, shared the same reaction and weren't as ready as some of the others "to go all the way." But their objection was not to the idea of forming an organization (they both joined NOW later), but to "the tone of voice" which she remembered as uncomfortably "strident."

"It sounded to us more energized than the occasion called for," Loring said. "In fact, now that I look back on it, I am sure that that much energy wasn't caused just by that conference. That was a catalyst. But there was a lot of feeling building in a lot of women then and, depending on their other experiences, they were more–or less–ready."[46]

Friedan recalled, ". . . they left, in what I felt was sanctimonious disapproval of me for suggesting anything so radical as an inde-

A Woman Without a Man is Like A Fish Without a Bicycle

She Who Laughs, Lasts

GOD CREATED WOMAN IN HER OWN IMAGE

Jesus was a feminist

pendent organization. And Pauli Murray, the Black scholar who'd triggered me first, and my indefatigable friends from the Washington underground, and Dorothy Haener from UAW and I just looked at one another and shrugged, 'Women—what can you expect?' "[47]

The next day, as expected, the leaders of the conference—Hickey, Peterson and Keyserling—ruled the Clarenbach resolutions "out of order" because the participants in the conference were not really official delegates and "government commissions cannot take action against other government departments." What they were really saying was that they did not want resolutions being passed at the conference that would embarrass or criticize its sponsor—the Johnson Administration—an angered Clarenbach reported back to Friedan and the others who had been at the meeting the night before.

With time running out on the conference, about 15 of the "dissidents" gathered at several tables during the final formal conference luncheon and under the very noses of the conference's leadership planned the formation of the new organization.

The recollections of another founder, Gene Boyer, of Beaver Dam, WI, provides some of the ambience of those now historic moments:

> "My own memories of those fateful days at the National Conference of Commissions on the Status of Women in Washington are still very vivid," she wrote in 1971, "although I was among the 'lesser lights' attend-

ing the event as chairwoman of one of the two municipal commissions on the status of women which existed at that time. . . .

> "I was at a nearby luncheon table, straining to overhear the heavily whispered conversation, but the word about 'getting organized to take action' was soon buzzing around the conference, and I knew I wanted to be part of it. There were allusions to 'reaching the grass roots' which struck a respondent note in me. Why, I had grass roots hanging out of my ears. Perhaps more than any other woman there, I was aware of the undiscovered hordes of frustrated feminists buried alive in the small, dusty corners of our nation. . . .

> "For me, the most exciting moment was just before we all ran off to catch our planes when a few of us gathered in a small meeting room to start the ball rolling. Catherine Conroy pulled out a five-dollar bill from her wallet and, in her usual terse style, invited us to 'put your money down and sign your name.' NOW was a reality, and I think we all felt somehow we had participated in a significant beginning."[48]

What the women had agreed upon, sitting at those tables during the luncheon and at the second quick gathering before they left for the airport, was documented in a memorandum of record by Analoyce E. Clapp, dated June 29, 1966:

> "In a hurried gathering on the final day of the Third National Conference of the Commissions on the Status of Women . . . 28 women met to set up a temporary organization for this purpose:
> "'To take action to bring women into full participation in the mainstream of American society *now*,

assuming all the privileges and responsibilities thereof in truly equal partnership with men.'

"These agreements were arrived at in informal manner:

"1. That Kathryn Clarenbach act as temporary chairman.

"2. That members join as individuals; it will be a voluntary organization, speaking only for ourselves.

"3. That the group be called the National Organization for Women (N.O.W.).

"4. That NOW will recommend action in the areas of equality for women.

"5. That we begin with the assumption that we will not have unanimity on all questions.

"6. That NOW will be an action organization for the advancement of women into equal participation in the whole spectrum of American life.

"7. That each member contribute $5 per month toward the expenses of the organization. The ultimate financing will be decided later.

"8. That NOW keep in touch with all similar groups, both action and non-action groups.

"9. That a telegram be sent to each of the EEOC Commissioners urging them to rescind the Commissions ruling that help-wanted ads again be labeled *Male* and *Female*.

"These agreements came after a discussion of the ruling that government commissions cannot take action against other departments. It was felt that this was the time for action in this field. That the problem cannot be tackled through existing apparatus was confirmed by talking with Margaret Hickey, retiring chairman of the Citizen's Advisory Council on the Status of Women, Mary Keyserling, director of the Women's Bureau of the Department of Labor, and Marguerite Gilmore, Chief Field Division,

Women's Bureau, U. S. Department of Labor.

"Everyone agreed that in forming NOW, there be no implied criticism of any existing group or conference, but rather a realization of the limitations of various organizations. Further, an organization is needed that can supply nationwide pressures on an immediate basis, an organization that will identify the problems (in the field of equal rights) and relay the information to other interested organizations.

"Recruiting of membership will continue until August 1, 1966, when the charter list will be closed. [Clarenbach recommended this date be extended to September 1, according to a footnote].

"Simple rules of operation will be set up by mail and phone.

"An executive committee may be selected by the chairman to help her in any way necessary.

"There was agreement on three areas of immediate concern:

"1. Jury participation

"2. Title VII (Civil Rights Act of 1964)

"3. Newspaper ads."

The telegrams agreed upon were sent to the Commissioners and read:

"We respectfully urge the Equal Employment Opportunity Commission to rescind its ruling permitting employment advertisements in newspapers under separate help-wanted male and help-wanted female column headings and to adopt in its place the language recommended by Representative Martha Griffiths,

DISARM RAPISTS

which appears in the Congressional Record for June 20, 1966."

It was signed by the 28 women and was so temperate in tone that it hardly sounded like a clarion call to revolution.

But the dissidence actually went beyond just the 28 women. In the Title VII workshop, 80 of the representatives to the conference voted for a resolution anyway that demanded that President Johnson reappoint Richard Graham to the EEOC. There was also a discussion of protective labor legislation in which some union women joined other conference participants in criticizing the laws. One participant reported that this discussion "created the impression that labor is either divided or no longer concerned about these labor standards."

"Justice Delayed. . ."

Aileen Hernandez who (although a speaker at the conference) had not been present either in Friedan's hotel room or at the lunch the next day, was continuing her own struggle within the EEOC in a worsening environment. The Commission's chairman, Franklin D. Roosevelt, Jr., who had not distinguished himself as a champion of women's rights, had resigned in May 1966, and the Johnson Administration had named no successor. Richard Graham had not been reappointed to the Commission and had left as scheduled on July 2. This left the EEOC with only three functioning commissioners to deal with the mushrooming piles of new complaints pouring in for action and earlier ones as yet undecided.

On August 25, 1966, the General Counsel's office finally submitted two draft opinions on the BFOQ requested by the airline

industry for the job of flight attendant, one opinion supporting and one opposing the grant of an exemption.

Hernandez had been pressing for the Commission to act for months, and sometime in June "had gone to the White House" with her concerns about the entire performance of the Commission, the slowness of the Administration in naming Commission replacements and the high turnover in the support staff, which, in her opinion, clearly signaled a burgeoning morale problem.

On September 6, immediately after reviewing the General Counsel's two opinions "and making minor revisions in the proposed finding that sex was not a BFOQ for the flight attendant position (which was the recommended decision of the General Counsel)," she dispatched the following compelling memorandum to all the remaining other Commissioners and to relevant staff members:

> "Cases have been pending before us since November of 1965. New cases are being filed each month and will continue to be filed until the decision is reached. It is still valid to remind ourselves that 'justice delayed is justice denied.'

> "This Commission has both long-range and short-range responsibilities. In the short range, we are required by law to make determinations on cases before us—to assess whether or not the charging party has been discriminated against because of race, color, national origin, sex or religion. We have no right to determine that we will not be as forthright in attacking one kind of discrimination as we are in attacking another kind. I confess that I am basically oriented to eliminating the centuries old discrimination against Negroes, but I cannot close my eyes to the obvious

inequities of treatment of other groups in our society. If we are to win our fight for equality, we have to do it by erasing *all* irrelevant barriers to advancement. Therefore, in our short-range responsibility, we must seek to eliminate discrimination as we find it–without regard to whether sex cases should have lower priority than race cases *or* religious cases *or* national origin cases. Our law does not provide for such priorities. The rigid time limits imposed on us require that we dispose of cases within 60 days. It is appalling to realize that we are approaching the one-year mark since some of the airlines cases were filed with us. Such callous disregard for the charging parties and the respondents is difficult to condone. I cannot help but wonder when that disregard will extend to other areas of our jurisdiction.

Attitudes are significant in determining action. I am well aware that there is a difference of opinion within this agency as to the extent and kind of discrimination against women. I don't think there is any difference of opinion on the fact that there is discrimination. That brings me to our long-range responsibility–assuming the role of attitude-changer. We have been somewhat successful in changing the attitudes on the race, religion and national origin questions. The more than 20 years of work by state and local FEPC's, by civil rights organizations, religious groups and Federal government have changed behavior and have begun to change attitudes. The old 'accepted' roles of the Negro in American society are neither accepted or acceptable today. We have broken out of the 'conventional wisdom' on the race question because that wisdom was challenged by those who rejected its obvious inequities. There are obvious inequities in the role of women in our society and the 'conventional wisdom' is strong. Congress has given us the responsibility, by law, to find and eliminate those inequities based on sex. We have the responsibility to change attitudes, deep though they may be, which limit the opportunity for women to seek their full potential. Just as in race, we can start the change in attitude by forcing a change in behavior. Implicit in this request for a BFOQ are all the limiting stereotypes (benevolent or gallant as they may appear) which dictate the second class status of women workers. By rejecting this BFOQ, I think we will have begun the long uphill road to equality of opportunity for women and will indicate that our Commission recognizes the multiple roles women may and should play in our society.

"I am disappointed that we have chosen to vacillate on this issue on the specious argument that we are not completely informed. I do not believe that there has been a single issue before this Commission which has been so fully aired. Because of this, I urge that the decision be made as rapidly as possible so that justice can be done–to our complainants, our respondents and to our integrity as a Commission. *I request that the matter be set for the agenda on the first day in the first week of October that all members of the Commission can be present.*" [49]

Resignation

A few weeks later, President Johnson finally appointed a new chair of the EEOC, Stephen Shulman, and on September 23, the EEOC's General Counsel submitted finished drafts of the two

positions on the BFOQ. But the meeting of the commission on October 1 that Hernandez had requested did not occur. On October 4, she fired off another memo requesting action, but the decision-making session was again delayed.

"Finally," Hernandez declared, "in frustration over the inaction on this issue and other cases which had drifted on for more than a year in spite of the time requirements of Title VII, I submitted my resignation on October 10 to become effective November 10."[50]

On October 28, 1966, legal counsel for the airline industry wrote to the new chairman of the Commission requesting new hearings on the BFOQ request for airline attendants, citing the changed composition of the Commission.

This time Commissioner Jackson fired off a memo to the new chairman of the EEOC, declaring, "I'm shocked at the effrontery of the Air Transport Association's request for a re-hearing in the airline stewardesses cases. . . . Our Commission has 92 cases pending that involve this question, as well as the request for a BFOQ finding by Northwest Airlines. . . . Indeed, some airlines have already changed their policies as a result of their anticipation of the Commission decisions. The Commission has had a hearing. We have transcripts of the hearing, as well as numerous briefs by Commissioners and by all parties concerned, and exhibits, surveys, Commission decisions, etc. as a basis for making a decision on the question."[51]

Jackson urged the Chairman to let the Commission make its decision and then those unhappy with it "could exercise their right to challenge the decision in the appropriate Federal court."[52] He asked that it be the first item on the agenda for November 1. However, it was scheduled for November 9, one day before Hernandez's resignation was to take effect.

Getting NOW Together

While this was all taking place within the EEOC, a temporary steering committee consisting of Kay Clarenbach (its chair who was given the authority to appoint such a committee), Dorothy Haener, Esther Johnson, Pauli Murray, Inka O'Hanrahan, Betty Talkington and Caroline Ware was engaged in laying the groundwork for the new organization.

Friedan seemed conspicuous by her absence from this committee, considering her pivotal role in NOW's conception. In her book, *It Changed My Life*, Friedan made a brief allusion that may provide a clue: "I started out suspicious of Kay as an agent of the Women's Bureau, and she surely saw me as a wild New York radical."[53]

There are additional hints of an underlying conflict among the activist founders suggested by Hole and Levine, early researchers of the movement: "In spite of the general agreement on the 'main purpose' of NOW, it should be remembered that at this point in time, Friedan's avowed feminist position coupled with her flamboyant and combative personal style had made her extremely controversial and, in some corners, greatly feared. Several observers have interpreted the sudden urgency to organize the new action group 'on the spot,' even before the Conference had adjourned, as an attempt

CAPITOL MARCH for ERA

June 6, 1982
TALLAHASSEE

"FAILURE IS IMPOSSIBLE"

to circumvent Friedan, and keep control of any new women's group in less militant hands. Apparently the endeavor to keep NOW firmly within the 'establishment' continued over the summer as charter members were being recruited. While Friedan and the 'East coast contingent' tried to interest feminists and potential feminists in joining, the 'Midwestern and Western contingents' strove to attract more conservative members, reportedly through the recruiting efforts of Women's Bureau staff members in the Midwest. In addition, it was only after a certain amount of haggling between the East and Midwest factions that the formal organizing conference was scheduled to be held in the East."[54]

Since Hole and Levine did not attribute these observations to their source, it's impossible to evaluate their validity. Even if such difference really existed between the East and Midwest/West, they did not seriously impede progress. It also seems highly unlikely that Clarenbach was any government bureau's agent and most likely that differences in the personal style of an academic woman from a Midwestern university (she was director of Continuing Education at the University of Wisconsin, very prominent and highly regarded in her own milieu) and a Manhattan-based, media-oriented celebrity-author (Friedan) of a best-seller, (even one who had been born in Peoria, IL), were real, natural, replicated to greater or lesser degrees among other founding members, and that only time and experience in working together could bridge or exaggerate them.

In any case, membership recruiting, even if it was competitive, went on, and by Octo-

ber, some 300 women and men had become charter members; the organizing conference was scheduled for October 29-30 in Washington, D.C. and by October 26, a slate of nominees for national officers and board members had been prepared.

The slate offered the following nominees as officers: Chairman of the Board, Kathryn Clarenbach; President, Betty Friedan; Executive Vice President, Aileen Hernandez ("*Subject to nominee's acceptance, following the effective date of her resignation as Commissioner of the EEOC"*); Vice President, Richard Graham; and Secretary/Treasurer, Caroline Davis (from Michigan and director of the Women's Department of the United Automobile Workers).

The slate made clear that, sometime before October 29, consideration had been given to some elements of the structure of the new organization. Certainly a very pragmatic appraisal had been made of the skills of the principals, specifically Clarenbach and Friedan.

Friedan was a public figure already and her name had national recognition value that would be a critical asset in attracting the attention of the media. She also came with a built-in constituency—the hundreds of thousands of women who had already read her book and who would flock to hear her impassioned speeches. But she had absolutely no experience or natural skill in organizing and no patience for the bread-and-butter work it would take to build an organization. Despite her long tenure as president of the fledgling organization—four years—and the fact that the by-laws required the

president to preside at national conferences, she never learned to chair an orderly meeting, small or large.

Kay Clarenbach, though widely known and highly respected in Wisconsin and much of the Mid-west, especially in the academic community, and in more limited circles in Washington, D.C., was not naturally media-oriented, but she had all the other experience and skills that Friedan lacked. The reality is that without her the mechanisms for making the organization functional might not have been constructed soon enough for it to survive. She also attracted a significant portion of NOW's membership that Friedan's name alone would not have drawn, and they came with skills comparable to her own. The role she played–and her tenure in office was as long as Friedan's—has nowhere yet been adequately described or appreciated.

The division at that time of the top leadership between a chair of the board and a president was clearly an astute stroke.

The fact that both Clarenbach and Caroline Davis, the Secretary/Treasurer, had offices and staff that could be pressed into service to assist them with the development and processing of basic organizing materials and functions was also an enormous asset.

Nominating Hernandez as Executive Vice President—though it was to have major repercussions yet to be described—was another organizing coup. She brought with her not only an enormous range of skills, but experience from the Black civil rights move-

ment, trade union organizing, government service and—despite her resignation as EEOC commissioner—connections and credibility in government as well as industry and labor that she could and ultimately did use time and again to advance NOW's purposes.

There's no question that as a national celebrity, Friedan was able to recruit as working members a far different set of women than the academics, government service, union, and professional women from the East, Midwest, or West could have attracted. However, many of us who later read the news story about NOW's formation might not have been so quick to join without the impression of stability and the different kind of prestige the names of Clarenbach and Hernandez conveyed.

The Few Seemed Many

When the organizing conference of NOW opened in the John Phillip Sousa Community Room of the *Washington Post* building in the nation's capital, there were actually only about 30 of the 300 charter members present, though many of us who joined later long had the impression the whole 300 had been in attendance. NOW's flair for making the few seem many apparently began with this first formal meeting.

According to Friedan's account, Clarenbach was not present, though if this had any political significance it has never been alluded to, and the likelihood is that a university commitment prevented her attendance.

The slate of officers was elected as originally nominated, including Clarenbach as chair of the Board. Hernandez was also elected *in absentia*, though Anna Arnold Hedgeman agreed to serve as Acting Executive Vice President until her consent to take the office could be obtained.

The board of directors that was elected

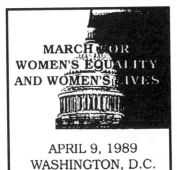

MARCH FOR WOMEN'S EQUALITY AND WOMEN'S LIVES

APRIL 9, 1989
WASHINGTON, D.C.

included some names already familiar, others that soon would be, and a few that apparently served with NOW only briefly.

In alphabetical order, NOW's first board included:

Coleen Boland, president of Transport Workers Union Local 550 (the flight attendant's union);

Inez Cassiano, who had to resign the following March because she took a position with the EEOC;

Catherine Conroy of United Automobile Workers (UAW);

Dr. Carl N. Degler, historian;

Sister Mary Austin Doherty, Alverno College;

Dr. Elizabeth Drews;

Muriel Fox, vice president of Carl Byoir public relations firm;

Betty Furness, then more famous as a television personality than as the consumer affairs expert she later became;

Dorothy Haener, of UAW;

Jane Hart, militant advocate for women, including the involvement of women in the space program, and wife of Senator Philip Hart;

Anna Arnold Hedgeman, professionally a social worker with a long career in government service;

Phineas Indritz, a Washington, D.C. attorney;

Reverend Dean Lewis, prominent Presbyterian church leader;

Inka O'Hanrahan, clinical biochemist, lifelong feminist, active in many women's organizations;

Graciela Olivarez, attorney;

Dr. Patricia Plante;

Eve Purvis;

Sister Mary Joel Read, Alverno College;

Charlotte Rowe;

Dr. Alice Rossi, Goucher College;

Dr. Vera Schletzer;

Edna Schwartz;

Dr. Gretchen Squires, physician; and

Herbert Wright.

Looking at NOW's first officers and board members more analytically, they consisted of seven university professors or administrators; five state and national labor union officials; four federal and local government officials; four business executives; four who had served or were serving on state commissions on the status of women; in addition to one M.D., seven held Ph. D.'s; four were men; three were in religious vocations.

Six vacancies on the board remained after the first elections were over, which were to be filled from "regions and groups not yet reached, notably the business community and the South."

A major task of the conference was the adoption of a "Statement of Purpose." Friedan reported in a memorandum to members issued shortly thereafter that it "was debated and approved sentence by sentence, by the 32 men and women attending the conference. . . ."

At the Founders' Dinner at NOW's 1971 national conference, public credit for much of the writing of the Statement of Purpose was given to Pauli Murray.

A Passionate Concern

The NOW Statement of Purpose adopted by the conference addressed a far wider spectrum of the population than the narrow segment of middle and upper class, college-educated, largely suburban women with whom Friedan had been concerned in *The Feminine Mystique.* It addressed broader concerns than most state commissions had yet addressed; and certainly implied that more radical solutions might be needed than any proposed by the President's Commission.

It rang—and still does—with a passionate concern for "the worldwide revolution of human rights now taking place within and beyond our national borders." It pointed out with a sensitivity few Caucasian women had yet acquired that Black women were "the victims of the double discrimination of race and sex" and two-thirds were employed "in the lowest paid service occupations."

It recognized that "women's problems are linked to many broader questions of social justice" and that "their solution will require concerted action by many groups." It unequivocally declared that "human rights for all are indivisible" and pledged "to give active support to the common cause of equal rights for all those who suffer discrimination and deprivation." It called upon "other organizations committed to such goals to support our effort toward equality for women."

It was and remains in many ways a timeless document, almost elastic enough to encompass the enlarged agenda of women's issues that emerged in the next 10 years.

According to Friedan's report, the conference also "approved targets for action for six task forces to be set up by the executive board to address themselves to Equal Opportunity in Employment; Education to Full Potential; Social Innovations for Equal Partnership Between the Sexes; New Image of Women; Equal Political Rights and Responsibilities; and a War for Women in Poverty. The exact scope, title, priorities of targets and strategy for each task force will be worked out by its members, with the approval of the Executive Board."

"We debated virtually every comma of our Statement of Purpose," Friedan added later in her report, "but were not divided on any of its substance nor on the targets for action to which we committed ourselves in setting up the task forces."

It was apparently easy for the organizing conference to decide on Washington, D.C. "for NOW national headquarters," but though there was agreement on the basic principles to be contained in NOW's Constitution, it had not been possible to complete the task at the conference. A Constitution Committee was established to incorporate these principles in a draft which was to be presented to the Executive Board for submission to the membership.

Parenthetically, Friedan explained, "This will be, in effect, our third try at a Constitution to mesh NOW's specific needs and the democratic will of its members. Previously, the Steering Committee and the National Organizing Conference were not able to agree on draft constitutions mod-

I WASN'T BORN DEMOCRAT, REPUBLICAN, OR YESTERDAY

eled after other organizations such as the American Veterans Committee, the American Civil Liberties Union, and national labor unions, nor did we want to model ourselves after women's organizations whose constitutions preclude the action to which we are dedicated. The structure we have now agreed upon," she wrote, "gives the basic power to the membership as a whole, in annual national conferences, which will decide major policy and elect board and officers–with provisions to prevent domination by any one group or region, to provide representation for those unable to attend, and to insure continuity. Between such conferences, the national board of 35, including the five national officers, will be free to act, meeting every three months; between its meetings, the five officers will be free to execute agreed policy. It was agreed that NOW will basically function as a national organization of individual members, with provisions, however, for setting up local chapters where desired."

Plan For Action

The conference approved immediate action on efforts to get enforcement of Title VII. It also authorized the board to set up a legal committee (which soon consisted of the extraordinary history-making team of Marguerite Rawalt, Mary Eastwood, Carruthers Berger, and, somewhat less actively, Phineas Indritz) to first take action on behalf of the airline attendants and a California case that offered the possibility of resolving the conflict between Title VII and the so-called protective labor legislation.

At the first meeting of the new board immediately after the adjournment of the conference, it was decided that meetings would be sought with President Johnson, the current Chair of the EEOC, the Attorney General and the head of the Civil Service Commission.

It was, all in all, what soon came to be regarded as a typical NOW conference. In the original document mailed to the charter membership in 1966 as a report on the conference, Friedan wrote: "We wasted no time on ceremonials or speeches, gave ourselves barely an hour for lunch and dinner. . . kept going until we had to vacate our meeting room . . . met in Task Forces over breakfast. . . Throughout, in order to accomplish what we did, we had to keep our eyes on the clock, and keep pushing ourselves and each other on with it. At times we got very tired and impatient, but there was always a sense that what we were deciding was not just for now 'but for a century.'

"Shortly before we adjourned Sunday afternoon. . . we shared a moving moment of realization that we had now indeed entered history. Pauli Murray passed on to us a medallion that had been handed down to her by one of the survivors of the battle for the vote for women in America half a century ago—a woman who had been imprisoned, and starved herself in protest in a jail near where we were meeting. And Alice Rossi recalled that exactly 100 years ago, two British women took the first petition for the vote for women to the British Parliament— and did not know how to get it inside except by hiding it in the bottom of a cart of apples being taken in for the members to eat. We suddenly realized the confidence and courage we must all now share—to confront the complex unfinished business of the revolution they started so long ago, to launch this new movement for full equality for all women in America, in truly equal partnership with men.

"So NOW begins. . . ."

Telling The World

The conference had been closed to the press so the participants could be free to hammer out policy and structure with no holds barred. But now it was time to tell the world that a revolution had begun.

Friedan had met Muriel Fox while giving an address to American Women in Radio and Television (which Fox then headed), on the image of American women in radio and television. Fox had scribbled a note then, "If you ever start an NAACP for women, count me in." Friedan remembered the contact some weeks before the conference, had contacted her, and Fox had been as good as her word: she had come.

"The night after we adopted the Statement of Purpose in Washington," Friedan wrote in *It Changed My Life*, "Muriel Fox, and a half-dozen women economists and lawyers stayed up till five a.m. running off NOW's first press releases on Senator Hart's mimeograph machine, and taking them by hand to the newspaper offices."

All of the principals who provided NOW with incredibly vigorous leadership in its early years were now in place save one: Hernandez.

The "unauthorized gesture," as she has described it, of nominating and electing her Executive Vice President, even though it had been qualified with the phrase, "subject to her consent," on the slate and in the first press releases and news stories that ran about NOW's formation had serious consequences.

Charge of Impropriety

The EEOC decision on sex as a BFOQ for the job of flight attendant was finally scheduled to be made on November 9, 1966, the day before Hernandez's resignation became effective. On November 8, by hand delivery, the airlines directed a letter to each commissioner, challenging the propriety of their making any decision in view of the press announcement of Hernandez's "imminent employment in an executive capacity by an organization which has already publicly advocated an adversary position in respect to an issue now *sub judice* before the Commission" and demanding that "she refrain in the few days remaining of her official tenure from participating further in any Commission action with respect to that issue."

An emergency meeting of the Commission was called in response to the letter and, when asked if she wished to disqualify herself, Hernandez was "emphatic in my decision to participate as scheduled. . . ." The Commission held the decision session on November 9 and voted, but the Air Transport Association sought, and was granted, a restraining order forbidding the Commission to issue its decision "until the propriety of my (Hernandez) participation was determined by the court."

Affidavits were subsequently taken from Hernandez when she arrived in California after leaving the Commission, and from Betty Friedan, as president of NOW. On February 27, 1967, the judge ruled in favor of the airlines and the commission was ordered not to release its decision.

Rather than appeal, the Commission decided to make a new determination. As a result, the Commission did not make a decision until February 23, 1968—27 months after the first cases were filed and nearly a year after the restraining order—when it finally decided that "sex is not a bona fide occupational qualification for the position of flight cabin attendant."

Fulfillment of a Dream

Hernandez did not accept the vice presidency of NOW until March of 1967, but in the interim she wrote to Clarenbach, "In many ways, NOW represents for me the beginning of the fulfillment of a dream I have long had that the women of the United States and the many racial and ethnic minorities which face similar discrimination would unite in their common cause. I was, therefore, delighted to see the Statement of Purpose reflect this same idea. I am wholeheart-

edly in support of NOW . . . ."

For every one of these women, so prominent in the first days of the movement, there were hundreds of others in towns and cities across the country who responded to that Statement of Purpose as the first brief words appeared in newspapers around the country.

The announcement of NOW's formation did not make the front pages. It was often buried pretty far back in a much-abbreviated version of the press release that had been issued. The *Washington Post*, in whose building it had been born, gave the story five inches. The *Los Angeles Times* was more generous with 12.

And yet, we found the story and responded, because, brief though it may have been, it aroused in us that same passion for the possible.

So we joined, and became ourselves carriers of that contagious passion, inflaming still others. Feminism became epidemic across the United States, and the rest is our history.

PART II

FEMINIST CHRONICLES
1953 — 1993

USING THE CHARTS

The charts are divided into three major sections: **Events, Issues,** and **The Backlash.**

Events lists the major public events that constituted the context in which the feminist movement operated.

The seven **Issues** are essentially among those that the President's Commission on the Status of Women first explored and the founders of NOW specifically chose to pursue.

A particular issue, for example, **Education,** is listed only if there is a relevant item on the page, though the item, because of space problems, may not be lined up exactly on a line with the label. It is possible to track the developments in any one of the seven categories just by checking this list.

Backlash describes the activities of the opposition to the movement, tracking the rise of the so-called New Right and Christian Right, along with the more traditional opponents of feminism including the Old Right in the form of such organizations as the John Birch Society and the Roman Catholic Church, a long-time foe, .

This format, which reports the small separate actions as well as major events of the movement, also makes it possible to use the names of many of the women and men across the country who made things happen wherever they were. What they chose to do, in fact, raised the consciousness of the entire country and made this a national movement.

We think it is important that they be recognized. Unlike the leaders who were sometimes (though not always) compensated by becoming public figures and given opportunities for financial rewards through writing books or going on the lecture circuit, these people often radically changed their lives in order to do what they could to advance the cause with no thought of rewards beyond the satisfaction of doing what they saw needed to be done.

—The Authors

YEAR	1953	1954	1955
U. S. President	Dwight D. Eisenhower		
NOW President			

EVENTS	*The Second Sex* by French feminist writer Simone De Beauvoir, was published in the United States. The phrase "women's liberation" later adopted by the more radical wing of the feminist movement, was first used in this book.	The U.S. Supreme Court ruled that race-segregated schools violated the 14th Amendment, striking down the concept of "separate but equal." President Dwight Eisenhower signed the Congressional Resolution altering the words of the U.S. Pledge of Allegiance by changing the phrase "one nation indivisible" to "one nation, under God, indivisible."	Rosa Parks kept her seat in the front of a bus in Montgomery, AL, and was arrested. On the first day of her trial, Blacks began a boycott of the city's buses. (12/01) Peru granted voting rights to women. (09/07)

ISSUES

Lifestyles

Economic

Religion

Media

Political

1953	1954	1955
For the 20th successive year, the Connecticut State Senate debated retention of a law forbidding the use of contraceptives by both married and unmarried women. (04/18) The Kinsey report on *Sexual Behavior in the Human Female* was published. The study was based on interviews with 8,000 women. Jacqueline Cochran was the first woman to pilot a plane faster than the speed of sound, flying an F-86 Saber jet at 760 miles per hour over Rogers Dry Lake at Edwards Air Force Base in CA. In World War II, Cochran had been the first woman to ferry a bomber to England. Playwright Clare Boothe Luce, former member of Congress (1943-47), was appointed Ambassador to Italy, the first woman to represent the U.S. in a major diplomatic office. (03/03) Doriot Anthony Dwyer, descendant of Susan B. Anthony's brother, was appointed first flute in the Boston Symphony Orchestra–a male preserve. Oveta Culp Hobby, who organized and directed the Women's Auxiliary Army Corps (WAC) during World War II, became the first Secretary of Health, Education and Welfare. (05/11) Eleanor Roosevelt publicly allied herself with the National Federation of Business and Professional Women (BPW) by shifting her original stand on the Equal Rights Amendment (ERA) to favor complete equality. Katherine St. George of New York, the ERA's congressional sponsor, sought to put the bill on the first docket before the 83rd Congress. (01/02)	"Father Knows Best" premiered on television, creating the mythical image of the American family. Contraception pioneer Margaret Sanger, the first woman to address the Diet, Japan's parliament, urged Japanese women to practice birth control. (04/15) Women volunteers participated in the first experimental trials on humans of oral contraceptives developed by Dr. Gregory Pincus at the Worcester Foundation for Experimental Biology, Shrewsbury, MA. The research project was being financed by Katherine Dexter McCormick, who, in 1904, had been the second woman to graduate from MIT. General Electric hired Ronald Reagan as the host on "The General Electric Theater" and to do plant tours promoting free enterprise. As his movie acting career faded, Reagan had switched to television and had been the host for three years on "Death Valley Days" sponsored by Borax. Eleanor Roosevelt and Lorena Hickok published *Ladies of Courage*, a tribute to women in American politics. It also contained a chapter that urged women to enter politics and offered concrete advice on how to get started. Two women destined to be powerful advocates for women's rights in Congress, Edith Green (D-OR) and Martha Wright Griffiths (D-MI), were elected to the U.S. House of Representatives. (11)	"Not so long ago," said a writer in a *New York Times* feature, girls were expelled from college for marrying; now girls feel hopeless if they haven't a marriage at least in sight by commencement time. . . . The well-known statistical fact that males are fewer than females in this country tends to push each girl into a desire for early marriage." The federal minimum wage was increased by the U.S. Congress from 75 cents an hour to $1. (08/12) The first male nurse was commissioned by the U.S. Army. (10/06) Women were accepted, by vote, as ministers in the U.S. Presbyterian Church. (01/23) Mrs. Sheldon Rubbins became the first female cantor in the history of Judaism. (08/02) Lucille Ball's character on "I Love Lucy," the TV comedy show watched by millions, gave birth to Little Ricky, and by continuing to do the show throughout her pregnancy, and by letting her pregnancy show on the screen, Lucille Ball proved by example that women need not give up their careers. The character "Lucy" often tried to subvert her husband's refusal to "permit her" to go out to work. Mary McLeod Bethune, noted Black educator, died at the age of 80. With the support of Eleanor Roosevelt, she became the first Black woman to officially advise a U.S. President. Franklin D. Roosevelt appointed her Negro Affairs Director in 1939. In 1935, she became the founder and first president of the National Council of Negro Women (NCNW). (05/18)

The Backlash	Phyllis Schlafly did research for Senator Joseph McCarthy at the height of the "McCarthy era," which lasted from 1950-54. Praised by *Better Homes and Gardens* for not attempting "to become an intellectual," First Lady Mamie Eisenhower was glowingly depicted in the *Woman's Home Companion* as "no bluestocking feminist." (07)	The American Security Council was founded. The "Army-McCarthy" hearings before the Senate Permanent Investigations Subcommittee captured a television audience of 20 million off and on for nearly three months.	Adlai Stevenson's address to the Smith College graduating class urged the women not to define themselves by any profession and to participate in politics through the role of wife and mother.

YEAR	1956	1957	1958
U. S. President	Dwight D. Eisenhower		
NOW President			

EVENTS

1956	1957	1958
Martin Luther King emerged as the key Black civil rights leader. The U.S. Supreme Court ruled that segregation on buses violated the Constitution.	The Soviet Union launched Sputnik, the first space satellite. President Eisenhower ordered troops to Little Rock, AR, to keep order during school desegregation.	Pope Pius XII died and Pope John XXIII succeeded him. According to a Gallup Poll, Eleanor Roosevelt was the most admired woman in the United States.

ISSUES

Lifestyles

1956	1957	1958
Actress Grace Kelly married Prince Rainier of Monaco–the favorite fairy tale of the 50s.	Althea Gibson was the first Black to win the All England title in tennis at Wimbledon.	The Hula Hoop was a national fad for 25 million Americans who paid $3 for the hip swiveling experience.

Education

Economic

Religion

Media

Political

1956	1957	1958
Autherine Juanita Lucy, 26, became the first Afro-American ever admitted to a white public school or university. In less than a week she was suspended because her presence incited violence from a white mob. (02/20) The number of women in the work force had jumped from 8.5 million in 1947 to almost 13 million this year. Reka Hoff, a lawyer, responded to an attack by Sloan Wilson on "The Woman in the Gray Flannel Suit," asserting that career women were forced to keep justifying themselves: "If unmarried, their career is designated a 'substitute' for marriage; if married, their career is designated a 'substitute' for motherhood; if a mother, their career brands them as selfish and neglectful." Hoff declared that although she was a member of a minority group as a career woman, she was neither "neurotic" nor the "compulsive half-woman" Sloan Wilson had written about. *Life* magazine published interviews with five male psychiatrists who believe female ambition was the root of mental illness in wives, emotional upsets in husbands and homosexuality in boys. *The Organization Man* by William Whyte was published. Marilyn Monroe was 20th Century-Fox's biggest box office attraction. President Eisenhower was the first president to conduct a televised news conference. *Peyton Place* by Grace Metalious was a best-seller.	The National Manpower Council (NMC) at Columbia University published its study, *Womanpower*, a comprehensive look at the experience of women in the labor force, their employment needs, and the implications of both for education, training and public policy. The NMC analysis called women "essential" and "distinctive" workers and recommended that the Secretary of Labor establish a committee to review "the consequences and adequacy of existing federal and state laws which have a direct bearing on the employment of women." The committee was not established and no study was undertaken by the Labor Department. Senator John F. Kennedy won the Pulitzer Prize for *Profiles in Courage*. An award-winning series of articles in the *New York Post* documented the existence of an unwritten ban on contraceptive counseling in New York City's public hospitals sustained by the pervasive power and influence of the Catholic Church. In the minutes of a meeting of Secretary of Labor James P. Mitchell's Policy Committee, it was noted that on the ERA, "Pres. for it–but not quite." It was also noted, "Secretary will fudge." (02/04 & 04/22) The Civil Rights Act of 1957 established the Civil Rights Commission and allowed the Justice Department to bring suit on behalf of Blacks denied their right to vote.	When the city commissioner of hospitals in New York ordered the chief of obstetrics at King's County General Hospital not to fit a diaphragm for a diabetic Protestant mother of three children, who had already had two Caesarean section deliveries, the story of the unwritten ban on contraceptive counseling broke in the newspapers again. While the Catholic archdiocese and Catholic organizations of both doctors and lay people defended the ban, the policy, based on the doctrines of one religious denomination, was publicly condemned by almost everyone else. Non-Catholic religious groups and many medical, civil liberties and civic organizations demanded that the policy be revoked. A new policy was instituted that recognized contraceptive measures as proper medical practice, though it was condemned by the Catholic archdiocese as "an immoral practice." In succeeding years, the same battle had to be fought and won in other cities throughout the United States over the bitter opposition of the local Catholic archdiocese. Marion E. Kenworthy (1891-1980) became the first woman president of the American Psychoanalytic Association. In 1930, she was Columbia University's first female psychiatry professor. John Kenneth Galbraith's book *The Affluent Society* tied inflation and recession to the materialistic public and the tired policies of timid leaders.

The Backlash

1956	1957	1958
The first lobotomy in the U. S. was performed at George Washington (DC) University Hospital on a 63-year old woman. The controversial operation was looked upon by some surgeons as a cure for the "mad housewife" syndrome. (09/14)	The Ku Klux Klan (KKK) opened its membership to Roman Catholics, a group it formerly targeted.	The John Birch Society was organized by Robert Welch. (12/09) Phyllis and Fred Schlafly set up the Cardinal Mindszenty Foundation to "educate the world about communism."

YEAR	1959		
U. S. President	Dwight D. Eisenhower		
NOW President			

EVENTS	Pope John XXIII called for an ecumenical council. (01/25) Alaska became the 49th state. (01/03) and Hawaii became the 50th (08/21).	Students for a Democratic Society (SDS) was organized. Tom Hayden, later a California legislator, was one of three key founders.	During his Presidency, Eisenhower named 28 women to Senate-confirmed posts, topping Truman's total of 20.
ISSUES Lifestyles	The Barbie Doll was introduced by Mattel. She was invented by Ruth Handler who later invented the first breast prosthesis for mastectomy patients.	Searle pharmaceutical company filed its application with the FDA to license "the pill" as a contraceptive.	Although available for decades, it was not until this year that the American Medical Association (AMA) finally sanctioned birth control.
Education		The University of Minnesota set up a revolutionary program to encourage older women to get college degrees. It may have resulted from the fact, finally noted, that women had more than 40 years to live after their youngest children entered school.	*Therapeutic Abortion: A Problem in Law and Medicine* by Professors Packer and Campbell, writing on "the abortion problem," noted that many non-clandestine abortions were performed to protect a woman's health as opposed to her life, which was not a valid reason under most existing abortion laws. Further, a vast abortion black market was thriving throughout the United States with an estimated million or more abortions a year performed and with between 5,000 and 10,000 women dying as a result.
Economic	The National Aeronautical and Space Administration (NASA) selected the first seven candidates for astronauts–all men.		
Media	*Century of Struggle* by Eleanor Flexner, the first history of the U. S women's movement written by a professional historian, was published– with an implicit call to arms.	*The Status Seekers* by Vance Packard examined the country's class system and noted that a college education was the wedge dividing white and blue collar workers.	*A Century of Higher Education for Women* by Mabel Newcomer reported that although the proportion of women among college students had increased in the U.S. to 47% in 1920, by 1958, it had dropped to 35.2%. Fewer than 10% of doctorates were awarded to women, compared with one in six in 1920 and 13% in 1940. Five women's colleges had in fact closed, 21 had become co-educational and two had become junior colleges. Three out of five women attending co-educational, colleges were taking secretarial, nursing, home economics or education courses; the percentage of women receiving professional degrees had not been as low since before World War I.
Legal	The American Law Institute's Model Penal Code included a section on abortion law reform. In addition to saving the life of the pregnant woman, it proposed that abortion be justified when there was a substantial risk to the physical or mental health of the woman, for congenital defects, and when the pregnancy resulted from rape or incest.		
Political	The U.S. Senate confirmed Claire Boothe Luce as ambassador to Brazil (04/28) but she resigned (05/01) because of a relentless one-man campaign against her appointment by Senator Wayne Morse. Morse described her as "unqualified" and "emotionally unstable" though some thought the attacks were because she was married to Henry Luce, editor-in-chief of *Time, Fortune* , and *Life*..	Indira Gandhi, 41, only daughter of Prime Minister Jawaharlal Nehru, was elected President of the Congress Party in India. (02/02)	
The Backlash	Pat Robertson began "The 700 Club" on his TV station. Robertson, who advocated a Bible-based, "pro-family" agenda, was later supported by the Coors family, which contributed money and time to advance his ministry.		

YEAR	1960
U. S. President	Dwight D. Eisenhower
NOW President	

EVENTS

Four Black freshmen from North Carolina's Agricultural and Technical College were refused service at a Woolworth's lunch counter in Greensboro. Within weeks the tactic of sit-ins had been taken up by 50,000 people across the South. The sit-ins and picketing resulted in riots in some major cities and in numerous arrests. (02/01))

The U-2, an American spy plane piloted by Francis Gary Powers, was shot down by the Soviet Union, disrupting a Big Four Summit Conference. (05/26)

John F. Kennedy defeated Richard Nixon in one of the closest Presidential elections in U.S. history. It was also the first election in which television played a crucial role in the form of four nation-wide debates between the candidates. Kennedy was the youngest President elected and the first Roman Catholic. (11/09)

ISSUES

Lifestyles

The Food and Drug Administration (FDA) approved the contraceptive pill (Enovid and Norlutin) for use. The pills were expected to be on the market early the next year and a month's supply was estimated to cost $10 to $15.   (05/11/60)

Education

New York University presented its 1960-61 "outstanding alumna" Gallatin Award to Florence Ellinwood Allen (1884-1966). She was the first woman on the U.S. Court of Appeals (1934) and the first female to serve on a general court (1920). She won the office of common appeals court judge against nine male opponents in 1920 and was the first woman elected to the Ohio Supreme Court in 1922.

Religion

According to a report in the official Soviet newspaper, *Izvestia*, while women were only 45% of the labor force, the majority of Soviet Union's professionals were women. There were 110,000 women scientists, 233,000 women engineers and 300,000 women physicians. Some 85% of all medical personnel were women. (01)

Legal / Political

As the legislative representative for the Industrial Union Division of the AFL-CIO, Esther Peterson headed an alliance to prevent the Democratic convention from endorsing the Equal Rights Amendment in its 1960 platform. Testifying before the Platform committee on behalf of 24 national organizations, Peterson said that real equality required measures that distinguished between women and men and that "specific bills for specific ills" would be the better approach to remedying discrimination on the basis of sex. (07/06)

The U.S.'s grande dame of etiquette, Mrs. Emily Post, died in New York at the age of 86. Actually a proponent of common sense in manners, her first best-seller, *Etiquette*, was published in 1922. (09/25)

Over 53% of female college graduates held jobs and both husband and wife worked in over 10 million homes, an increase of 333% over 1940. The proportion of wives at work had doubled from 15% in 1940 to 30% in 1960. Mothers of children under 18 comprised almost a third of all women workers; 40% of all women over 16 held a job. Female employment was increasing at a rate four times faster than that of men. However, women's average earnings in 1960 were less than 60% of men's, as compared with 65% in 1950. And in the sales field, women's wages were only 40% of salesmen's, while female clerks made 44% of their male counterparts.

Award-winning radio-TV journalist Pauline Frederick was the first woman to act as a radio network anchor for a Presidential convention.

Mrs. Sirimavo Bandaranaike was sworn in as Prime Minister of Ceylon (now the Republic of Sri Lanka), the first woman premier of a modern parliamentary government. She also served as Foreign Minister and Minister of Defense. The socialist Sri Lanka Freedom Party that she led to an overwhelming victory in the polls had been led by her husband, who was assassinated in 1959. (07/26)

The Student Non-Violent Coordinating Committee (SNCC) was formed by a group of Southern Black college students. Their goal was to end segregation in the South through voter registration drives, sit-ins and marches. College students in the North also began to organize and picketed stores whose Southern branches had segregated facilities. The young women who went South to work alongside men in the fight for Black civil rights slowly became aware that they were second-class citizens in a movement to wipe out discrimination.

Contraception was practiced as often by Catholics as by couples of Jewish and Protestant faiths, according to a Texas survey. (06/21)

Margaret Leech (1893-1974) won the Pulitzer Prize for history for *In the Days of* (U.S. President William) *McKinley*, making her the first woman to win the history Pulitzer twice; her first win in 1942 was for a Civil War book, *Reveille in Washington*.

Harper Lee's *To Kill A Mocking Bird*, a moving saga about Southern bigotry, became a best-seller and won a Pulitzer Prize. A Broadway dramatization (retitled *All the Way Home*) of Ms. Lee's book later won another Pulitzer for drama in 1961.

Senator Margaret Chase Smith and Lucia Marie Cormier, a six-term member of the Maine House of Representatives, participated in the first all-female race for the U.S. Senate. Republican incumbent Smith won. (11)

The Backlash

Young Americans for Freedom (YAF) was founded. Alumni of YAF include William F. Buckley, a founder; Richard Viguerie, right-wing direct mail guru; Howard K. Philips, head of the Conservative Caucus; and John T. (Terry) Dolan, who headed the National Conservative Political Action Committee (NCPAC).

According to the first synod, or diocesan ecclesiastical council convened in Rome by Pope John XXIII, women in Rome with bare arms or wearing male clothing would be denied the sacraments. (01/24)

YEAR	1961
U. S. President	John F. Kennedy
NOW President	

EVENTS

The Soviet Union won the race to put a man in space. (04/12)

The invasion of the Bay of Pigs in Cuba by anti-Castro exiles supported by the United States was a fiasco. (04/25)

A wall dividing East and West Berlin was erected by East German soldiers to stop the flight of refugees—some 2,000 a day—from the Communist dominated sector. (08/20)

Left to right: Margaret Mealey, William Schnitaker, Eleanor Roosevelt, Rep. Edith Green and President Kennedy.

President Kennedy (at Eleanor Roosevelt's request) established the President's Commission on the Status of Women by Executive Order 10980. Its charge was to review women's progress and make recommendations for constructive action on employment, social insurance, tax laws, federal and state labor law and legal treatment. (12/14)

ISSUES

Lifestyles

The first oral contraceptive –"The Pill"–became available.

Education

The University of Georgia, Atlanta, GA, was ordered to admit its first two Black students. One of them was Charlayne Hunter-Gault. After enduring a barrage of jeers, rocks and burning effigies, Hunter-Gault graduated in 1963 and became the first Black staffer at *The New Yorker* magazine. By the '90s she would be the acclaimed national correspondent for "The MacNeil/Lehrer Newshour" on TV's Public Broadcasting Service

Economic

A voluntary affirmative action program called "Federal Plans for Progress," for all contractors doing business with the federal government, was initiated.

Religion

The Roman Catholic Church decided to permit female religious (nuns) or school girls to read the epistle of the Mass, but only in a religious community, at a Mass where only women were present, or at a school Mass.

Media

Jacqueline Kennedy, 31, was a new kind of First Lady: aloof, glamorous, multilingual and dedicated to the arts. Utilizing a staff of 40, headed by her social secretary Letitia Baldrige, a Republican, she set out to make the White House "a showcase of American art and history" with an ambitious plan to restore the building's original furnishings. She also sought counsel from Eleanor Roosevelt on the role of the First Lady.

Janet Graeme Travell, who cared for President Kennedy after his 1955 spinal operation, was appointed White House physician, the first woman to hold the post. During the twenties (1927-29), she was a New York City Police Department ambulance surgeon.

Aviator Jerrie M. Cobb was the first woman to pass all the tests to become an astronaut. Jane Hart, later a NOW National Board member from 1966-1968 and the wife of Senator Philip Hart (D-MI), was also one of 13 women who passed the physical tests to become astronauts in the early days of the space program. NASA subsequently announced it would not send women into orbit and implied that there was medical data showing women were less tolerant of physical stress than men.

The Peace Corp was created by President Kennedy. Among the thousands of idealistic women and men sent to help underdeveloped countries was Ann Moore. As a result of her experiences during a West African tour, she invented the Snugli child carrier. Later she patented a personal carrier for portable oxygen supplies. (03/01)

Former Governor of Texas Miriam A. "Ma" Ferguson died. Ferguson's husband, who had been impeached as governor and who had disapproved of the women's rights movement, campaigned for her election under the slogan, "Two governors for the price of one." Another slogan reflected their opposition to the Ku Klux Klan: "A Bonnet or a Hood." Mrs. Ferguson was elected in 1924, but defeated in 1926 and 1930. She won re-election again in 1932 but ended up fourth in the Democratic primary in 1940. (06/25)

Wilma Rudolph set a women's record in the 100-meter dash of 0:11:2. (07/19)

President Kennedy appointed Esther Peterson to head the Women's Bureau . As Assistant Secretary of the Department of Labor, Peterson also had charge of the Bureau of Labor Standards, the Bureau of Employees' Compensation and the Employees' Compensation Appeal Board. Her position meant she made policy decisions that affected male as well as female workers. With her labor union background Peterson sought to implement the long-standing agenda of union women: equal pay legislation, a national commission on women, and opposition to the Equal Rights Amendment.

Painter Grandma Moses, who had been a farm worker most of her life until her primitive paintings of rural America caught the public's fancy in the 1950s, died in Hoosick Falls, NY, at the age of 101. (12/13)

Edith Wilson, widow of President Woodrow Wilson, died in Washington, D.C. at the age of 89. Mrs. Wilson had been described at the "First Woman President" because of the position of power she occupied after her husband suffered a paralyzing stroke during his second term in 1919. She and his aides essentially ran the executive office, secluding the President from public view. (12/28)

Eleanor Roosevelt, the first U.S. delegate to the United Nations (1945-51), was reappointed to the U.N.

Political

The Backlash

Women held 2.4% of all executive positions in the Kennedy Administration, the same percentage they held under the two previous presidents, Truman and Eisenhower. Kennedy was the first President since Herbert Hoover to have no women in his cabinet. Kennedy made only 10 appointments of women, requiring Senate confirmation, to policy-making executive and judicial positions. For the same time period Truman made 15 and Eisenhower made 14. Even Emmanuel Celler, the powerful chairman of the House Judiciary Committee, who persistently blocked the Equal Rights Amendment, had urged Kennedy to make appointments of women as a way of elevating their status. Washington, DC reporter Nan Dickerson deemed Kennedy a "male chauvinist" who believed "it ridiculous to pay (women) the same as men." India Edwards, a prominent fundraiser for the Democratic Party, said Kennedy looked upon women as "nothing but sex objects." (09/21)

43

YEAR	1962
U. S. President	John F. Kennedy
NOW President	

EVENTS			
	An American, John Glenn, orbited the earth three times in the spacecraft, Friendship 7. (02/20) The U.S. Supreme Court in the case of *Engel v. Vitale* ruled that the recitation of a prayer written by a state agency for use in the public schools violated the establishment clause of the First Amendment. (06/25)	Students for a Democratic Society (SDS) issued a manifesto, *The Port Huron Statement*, calling for participatory democracy to overcome a sense of powerlessness in society. Tom Hayden drafted the statement. (07) Marilyn Monroe, 36, was found dead in her home in Los Angeles, an apparent suicide. (08/05)	President John Kennedy and Russian Premier Nikita Khrushchev faced off over missiles in Cuba. (10/22-10/28)

ISSUES

Lifestyles

Education

Economic

Religion

Media

Television celebrity Sherry Finkbine, the married mother of four children, and pregnant with her fifth, discovered that Thalidomide, the sleeping pill she had been using, was responsible for an epidemic in Europe of extensive and crippling fetal deformities. Her obstetrician-gynecologist recommended a therapeutic abortion. Concerned that other pregnant women might be taking the same drug, Finkbine told her story to a reporter friend, but after the news story appeared, the hospital where her abortion was to be performed canceled her appointment. Her case became a cause celebre, with opponents of abortion making death threats against her and her other children. The FBI was brought in to protect her. Because of all the publicity, she was denied a visa to go to Japan for the abortion and finally had the abortion in Sweden, where she was told afterward that the fetus was so deformed it would never have survived.

Two of the networks (CBS and NBC) telecast First Lady Jackie Kennedy's historical "A Tour of the White House with Mrs. John F. Kennedy." The 60-minute program was both a rating and a critical success. (02/14)

Chinese-born physicist Chien-Shiung was the American Association of University Women's 1962 Woman of the Year. In 1964, Wu, who received her Ph.D. physics degree from Berkeley, would be acclaimed as the first female winner of the National Academy of Sciences' Comstock Price.

Twenty-eight percent of businesses polled in a 1962 study regarded a woman's appearance and "sex appeal" as a "must" job qualification in sales and service industries, particularly for airline stewardesses.

Pope John XXIII set up the Pontifical Commission on the Family. Birth control was one of the major issues it was charged with studying.

Washington reporter Marianne Means received the New York Newspaper Women's Club Front Page Award. She was the first woman reporter to cover the White House full time (1961-65). In 1963, she would write about those years in a book titled *The Woman In The White House.* Means would go on to become a lawyer in 1977.

Nineteen-year old Barbra Streisand made her Broadway debut in a supporting role and stopped the show with a solo spot, "Miss Marmelstein," in the Harold Rome musical, *I Can Get It For You Wholesale.*

"How Nice to be a Pretty Girl and Work in Washington" was the title of an article in *Life* magazine.

Eleanor Roosevelt, the most extraordinary woman of the 20th century, died on November 7.

Eugenie Moore Anderson was appointed U. S. envoy to Bulgaria. America's first female ambassador to a Communist country was the first U.S. woman to serve as an ambassador (to Denmark) in 1949.

Future Nobel Prize co-winner for Medicine (1988) Dr. Gertrude Elion discovered Imuram, a drug that helped prevent rejection in kidney transplants. It was just one of Elion's many contributions to the treatment of cancer and viruses. Elion would go on to patent 45 vital drug treatments–many in collaboration with Dr. George Hitchings–and, as of 1992, was the only woman in the Inventors' Hall of Fame.

Rachel Carson's book, *Silent Spring,* attacked the careless use of pesticides and revived interest in ecology.

The Backlash

Christian fundamentalists Mel and Norma Gabler of Longview, TX, began reviewing textbooks and testifying before the state textbook committee to block the adoption of books they found objectionable. Because Texas purchases as much as 5% of all textbooks in the country, the Gablers had enormous impact beyond their

own state. They supported the teaching of Biblical creationism, opposed sex education, and wanted a return to "traditional values."

A *New York Times* article paid the country's new First Lady a backhanded compliment: "It is now all right for a woman to be a bit brainy or cultured as long as she tempers her intelligence with a 't'rific' girlish rhetoric." (01/20)

YEAR	1963		
U. S. President	John F. Kennedy		Lyndon Johnson
NOW President			

EVENTS	The civil rights struggle in Birmingham, AL, intensified as 1,000 Blacks were arrested after a protest march against the state's segregation policies. The Kennedy Administration sent in federal troops. (05/18) Soviet Cosmonaut Valentina Tereshkova, the first woman in space, orbited the earth 45 times in tiny Vostok 6. (06/16-19)	President Kennedy visited the Berlin Wall and told a crowd of 150,000, "Ich bin ein Berliner." (06/26) Some 200,000 Freedom Marchers demonstrated in Washington, D.C. and heard Martin Luther King Jr.'s "I have a dream . . ." speech. (08/28)	President John F. Kennedy was assassinated in Dallas, TX. Vice President Lyndon Johnson was sworn in at the Dallas airport with Jackie Kennedy at his side. (11/22)

ISSUES			
Lifestyles	Eight-year-old Nancy Lotsey joined the New Jersey Small-Fry League–the first girl to participate in organized all-boy baseball games. Her superior pitching and batting skills enabled her team to win the League Title.	*The Feminine Mystique* by Betty Friedan became a best-seller. Debunking the myths that women, particularly housewives, were totally fulfilled by marriage and motherhood, Friedan said it was time for women "to stop giving lip service to the idea that there are no battles left to be fought for women in America."	Illegitimate births among American teenagers were up 150% since 1940.
Economic	A Senate Subcommittee on Employment and Manpower reported that women accounted for 60% of the growth of the labor force in the 1950s. Irene Otillia Galloway, director of the Women's Army Corps (1953-57), died at the age of 55. She was European Command staff director for four years (1948-52) and was named commandant of the WAC Training Center in 1952. (01/06)	After 20 years, the Equal Pay Act was passed by the U. S. Congress, amending the Fair Labor Standards Act to provide equal pay for equal work without discrimination on the basis of sex. Bills to achieve this goal were first introduced in Congress in 1943. (05/28)	The advent of the "pill" generated considerable coverage in the media. CBS won an Albert and Mary Lasker Foundation Medical Journalism award for its "CBS Reports" TV program on "Birth Control and the Law." And the *Chicago Daily News* was awarded a Pulitzer Prize for the Most Disinterested (sic) and Meritorious Public Service Rendered by a U.S. Newspaper. The Service? "Calling attention to the issue of providing birth-control services in the public health programs of its area." (05/06)
Religion	Two remarkable actresses won Academy Awards this year for playing two remarkable women in *The Miracle Worker*. The best actress Oscar went to Anne Bancroft for her brilliant portrayal of Helen Keller's teacher and mentor, Annie Sullivan, who taught Keller, a wild six-year old deaf mute, to communicate with the world via sign language and, finally, speech. Child actress Patty Duke won a supporting player Oscar in the role of Helen Keller. (03)	*The Time Has Come: A Catholic Doctor's Proposals to End the Battle Over Birth Control* by Dr. John Rock, a Catholic who did breakthrough research on the contraceptive pill, was published. It was perceived as a head-on challenge to the Roman Catholic Church's prohibition against artificial birth control.	Alicia Patterson, publisher, founder and editor of *Newsday* in New York for 23 years, died at the age of 57. (07/02)
Media		Barbara Tuchman won a "best non-fiction" Pulitzer Prize for her 1962 best-seller, *The Guns of August*, about World War I. In 1937, she covered the Civil War in Spain for *Nation* magazine. Another Pulitzer Prize, for best book on U.S. history, went to Constance McLaughlin Green for *Washington, Village and Capital, 1800-1878*. (05/06)	Sociologist Alice Rossi presented a paper at the American Academy of Arts and Sciences conference entitled, "Equality Between the Sexes: An Immodest Proposal." (10)
Legal			
Political	Federal Judge Sarah Tilghman Hughes (1896-1985), the first (and so far, the last) woman to swear in a U.S. President (Lyndon Johnson), worked her way through law school by working as a Washington, D.C. policewoman. In the 1930s, the avowed feminist served two terms in the Texas House of Representatives and successfully sponsored a bill whereby women were finally allowed to serve as Texas jury members.	Maria Goeppert-Mayer was the first American woman to win a Nobel Prize for physics (for her work on the shell structure of atomic nuclei) and the second woman of any nationality to receive the award. Marie Curie was the first in 1903. (12/10)	The report of the President's Commission on the Status of Women, entitled *American Women*, was published, documenting pervasive sex discrimination and the absence of support systems for women's changing lives. Among many recommendations, it called for a clarification of the legal status of women under the Constitution by the U. S. Supreme Court. (10/11)

The Backlash	In the proceedings of the University of California Medical Center's conference on "The Potential of Women," Edmund W. Overstreet, a gynecologist, commented jokingly, on women's capacity to live longer than men: "When you come right down to it, perhaps women just live too long! Maybe when they	get through having babies they have outlived their usefulness." In *The Feminine Mystique* (pgs. 151-52), Betty Friedan quoted Lynn White, the male president of California's women-only Mills College, who considered women non-creative and thought they should primarily be educated to become wives	and mothers. "Why not," asked White, "study the theory and preparation of a Basque paella . . . an authoritative curry. . . even such simple sophistications as serving cold artichokes with fresh milk?"

45

YEAR	1964
U. S. President	Lyndon B. Johnson
NOW President	

EVENTS

The Civil Rights Act of 1964 was passed by Congress and signed by President Johnson. It included in Title VII a prohibition against discrimination in employment on the basis of sex as a result of action by Congresswoman Martha Griffiths (D-MI) and in an attempt by Southern members of Congress to block its passage. (07/02)

The 24th Amendment to the U.S. Constitution was ratified, ending the poll tax.

The Beatles arrived for their first tour of the United States. (02/07)

President Johnson submitted a proposal to Congress for a $1 billion "War on Poverty." (03/16)

Lyndon Johnson was elected President and Hubert Humphrey Vice President in a landslide victory over the Republican ticket headed by Senator Barry Goldwater. (11/03)

ISSUES

Lifestyles

Between 1964 and 1966 there was an epidemic of rubella, commonly known as German measles and documented since the 1940s as the cause of deformities if contracted by a pregnant woman in the first 16 weeks of pregnancy. Hearings were held on a therapeutic abortion bill introduced in California by Anthony Bielenson. Among those testifying in favor of the bill were the American Association of University Women (AAUW) and the Unior Chamber of Commerce (Jaycees). Testimony against the bill came predominantly from an array of Catholic organizations, convincing those in favor of liberalizing abortion laws that opposition was largely religious.

Geraldine Mock of Germany was the first woman to complete a solo flight around the world. (04/16)

From their apartment windows in a middle class Queens, NY, neighborhood, 37 people witnessed the murder of Kitty Genovese and did nothing to help her. (03/27)

Education

Dr. Mary Steichen Calderone founded the Sex Information and Education Council of the U.S. (SIECUS) to promote understanding and acceptance of human sexuality. (07/08)

Fifteen women "auditors" were invited to attend sessions of the Roman Catholic Church's Ecumenical Council (Vatican II), which had convened October 11, 1962. (09/23)

Religion

Rep. Howard W. Smith, in a "southern strategy" to defeat the Civil Rights Act, moved to add "sex" to one of its provisions. After heated debate, the House of Representatives voted to pass the amendment, which added the word "sex" to the discriminatory bans of race, color, religion, and national origin in Title VII of the bill. (02/08)

Margaret Chase Smith, the first woman to be elected to both the U.S. House and the Senate, was also the first woman to run for the Presidential nomination of a major party. She declared her candidacy in January and received 27 delegate votes at the Republican Convention in San Francisco, more than anyone else except the GOP nominee, Senator Barry Goldwater. (07/13-18)

Economic

May Craig, life-long feminist member of the White House press corps and regular on "Meet the Press," asked Rep. Howard W. Smith of Virginia during the television show if he would put equal rights for women in Title VII. "Well, maybe I would," Smith replied. Craig persisted, asking, "Amendment on the floor?" And Rep. Smith said: "I might do that." (02)

The first National Conference of State Commissions on the Status of Women was held in Washington, DC, sponsored by the Citizen's Advisory Council and the Interdepartmental Committee. Twenty-four state commissions were represented by 73 delegates. Eight of the states without state commissions also sent delegates. (06/12-13)

By the end of the year, 33 states had established Commissions on the Status of Women and at the federal level, an Interdepartmental Committee on the Status of Women and a Citizen's Advisory Council were established by Executive Order to follow up on the report of the President's Commission.

Media

Rachel Carson, 56, the author of *Silent Spring,* died. (04/14)

Sidney Poitier was the first Black to win an Oscar for Best Actor. Actress Hattie McDaniel won an Oscar for Best Supporting Actress in 1939.

Political

While the phenomenal Marie Sklodowska Curie was the first woman to win a Nobel Prize (1911) in chemistry, British crystalographer Dorothy Crowfoot Hodgkin became the second female to receive that honor for determining the molecular structure of Vitamin B_{12} and penicillin.

Lady Astor, the first woman ever to sit in the British House of Commons, who kept her seat for 25 years through seven consecutive elections, died just before her 85th birthday. She had retired from office at age 65 after a political career in which she advanced the interests of women and children. (05/02)

The Senate Judiciary Subcommittee on Constitutional Amendments reported favorably on the ERA. (09/12)

The Backlash

At a Student Non-Violent Coordinating Council (SNCC) staff meeting, Ruby Doris Smith presented a paper on "The Position of Women in SNCC." SNCC leader Stokley Carmichael declared, "The only position for women in SNCC is prone."

Phyllis Schlafly wrote and self-published *A Choice, Not An Echo* to support Barry Goldwater as the Republican Presidential nominee. In the March 1960 issue of the John Birch Society Bulletin, Robert Welch, the organization's founder, described her as "a very loyal member of the JBS."

YEAR	1965
U. S. President	Lyndon B. Johnson
NOW President	

EVENTS

Malcolm X was assassinated. (02/21)

25,000 demonstrators for civil rights marched from Selma, AL, to the state capitol in Montgomery, challenging the state to end racial discrimination in voting rights and segregation. (03/28)

15,000 students marched in Washington, protesting the war in Vietnam. (04/17)

U.S. forces, previously in Vietnam only as military advisers, were authorized for combat for the first time. (07/08) President Johnson sent 50,000 more troops to Vietnam. (07/28)

Medicare became law. (07/30)

At the first White House Conference on Equal Employment Opportunity, Title VII of the Civil Rights Act was dubbed "the bunny law" as a result of a discussion on whether Playboy Clubs would have to hire male bunnies. (08)

The Watts Riots erupted in Los Angeles. (08/15-20)

ISSUES

Lifestyles

The Second National Conference of State Commissions on the Status of Women was held, attended by 322 participants representing 44 state commissions. The six remaining states without state commissions also sent representatives. (07/28-30)

Economic

Equal Employment Opportunity Commissioners (EEOC) were appointed to oversee enforcement of the Civil Rights Act. Aileen Hernandez, a future president of NOW, was the only woman appointed to the Commission. Franklin D. Roosevelt Jr. was named chair.

A survey of women graduates at Stanford University (CA) found that 70% planned not to work at all when their children were under age 6, and only 43% intended to work full time even after their children were over 12. A survey of 1972 graduates would show a considerable change in views. (06)

Religion

The St. Joan's Alliance, a British-based Catholic lay women's organization, established a U.S. branch to campaign for women's equality in the Catholic Church. (02/21)

The EEOC issued its first set of guidelines for employers on state protective legislation. The State laws could be interpreted as a Bona Fide Occupational Qualification (BFOQ) exception to Title VII, provided the employer acted in "good faith" and that the laws effectively protected rather than discriminated against women. The EEOC did not define what constituted "protection" or "discrimination." (12/02)

In *Griswold v. Connecticut*, a state law banning the provision of contraceptives to married couples was struck down by the U.S. Supreme Court, which declared that "the right to privacy" implicit in the Bill of Rights guaranteed access to birth control for married couples. The majority opinion was written by Justice William O. Douglas. A second concurring opinion written by the now-retired Justice Arthur J. Goldberg, and joined by Chief Justice Earl Warren and Justice William Brennan, Jr., grounded the right to privacy in the Ninth Amendment and said that the rights enumerated in the first eight amendments were not an exhaustive list. Wrote Goldberg: "The Ninth Amendment simply shows the intent of the Constitution's authors that other fundamental personal rights should not be denied such protection or disparaged in any way simply because they are not specifically listed in the first eight constitutional amendments." The right to privacy became the basis for striking down abortion laws in *Roe v. Wade* in 1973. (06/07)

Media

Casey Hayden and Mary King, women active in SNCC, wrote a paper on the role of women in the movement. The paper was attacked by male radicals. It was published as a two-part article, "Sex and Caste," in *Liberation*, (April, December issues, 1966).

Dr. Pauli Murray addressed the National Council of Women of the United States at the Biltmore Hotel in New York. Aware of the EEOC conflicts over the sex-segregated "help-wanted" ads in the newspapers, and with Franklin D. Roosevelt, Jr., chair of the EEOC present, Murray declared, "If it becomes necessary to march on Washington to assure equal job opportunities for all, I hope women will not flinch from the thought." (10/12) The *New York Times* headline: "PROTEST PROPOSED ON WOMEN'S JOBS; YALE PROFESSOR SAYS IT MAY BE NEEDED TO OBTAIN RIGHTS." This coverage of the event prompted Betty Friedan to immediately telephone Murray, establishing an important feminist link-up. (10/13)

Legal

Frances Perkins, the first woman ever to serve in a President's cabinet, died at age 83. Perkins was appointed Secretary of Labor by President Franklin Delano Roosevelt in 1933, serving for 12 years. Among the social legislation she championed was the Public Works Administration, the National Recovery Act (NRA) and the Social Security Act. (05/14)

Political

Dr. Pauli Murray and Mary O. Eastwood published an article in the *George Washington Law Review* entitled, "Jane Crow and The Law," a comprehensive examination of women's legal status under the Constitution and the implications of Title VII of the Civil Rights Act. (11)

The Backlash

As the movement for liberalized contraception and abortion laws gained momentum, the Catholic Church began to organize Right to Life groups.

The Education Research Institute was established by the American Conservative Union as a research arm. It sponsored the National Journalism Center

to train young right-wing writers with the hope of placing them in professional positions as news reporters. The Institute is a recipient of grants from the Adolph Coors Foundation.

At the Students for a Democratic Society (SDS) conference, a discussion of "women's issues" elicited "storms of ridicule and

"The New American Female, Demi-feminism Takes Over" by Marion K. Sanders in *Harper's* magazine (July) argued that "an unoppressed minority of the most discussed sex do not feel sorry for themselves–and wish their self-appointed champions would find something else to fret about."

YEAR	1966
U. S. President	Lyndon Johnson
NOW President	Betty Friedan

EVENTS

At the Third Annual Conference of Commissions on the Status of Women in Washington, D.C., the failure of the EEOC to enforce Title VII of the Civil Rights Act prompted the formation of NOW. Twenty-eight women contributed $5 each to help fund its organization. (06/28-29)

Betty Friedan, Kathryn Clarenbach and Anna Arnold Hedgeman.

The founding conference of NOW was held in Washington, D.C. Betty Friedan was elected president and Kay Clarenbach, chair of the board. Aileen Hernandez (subject to her consent–she was not present), executive vice president; Richard Graham, vice president; and Caroline Davis, secretary-treasurer. (10/29-30)

ISSUES

NOW Founding Membership 28
NOW Startup Budget $140

Economic

Flight attendants filed complaints under Title VII on industry policy requiring them to quit if they got married, pregnant or reached the age of 32-35. The airlines asked the EEOC to rule that sex was a BFOQ (Bona Fide Occupational Qualification) for the job of flight attendant.

The EEOC issued guidelines that approved sex-segregated "Help Wanted" classified ads. (04/22)

Religion

Pope Paul VI received the report of the Pontifical Commission on the Family. Though the results weren't leaked until nine months later, theologians voted 64-4 that Catholics should be permitted to use artificial contraception as a form of "generous and prudent parenthood," Only four conservatives (one of whom became Pope John Paul II), in a separate minority report, condemned contraception as "intrinsically evil." (08)

Legal

In *White v. Crook,* a three-judge federal court declared an Alabama law that excluded women from state juries to be unconstitutional. (02/07)

A poll by the Field Research Corporation indicated that only 25% of the population favored very restrictive abortion laws, while 65% favored liberalizing them. (07)

Political

Margaret Sanger, champion of birth control, died in Tucson, AZ, just a few days short of her eighty-eighth birthday. (09/06)

Equal Employment Opportunity Commission (EEOC), established by the Civil Rights Act to implement Title VII and its prohibition against discrimination in employment based on race, color, religion, sex, or national origin, stated it had no authority to rule on the conflict between Title VII and state protective legislation and the courts would have to resolve the issue. (08/19)

EEO Commissioner Aileen Hernandez urged the entire Commission to accept the recommendation of the General Counsel and issue the finding that sex was not a BFOQ for the position of flight attendant. (09/06)

Almost immediately after its founding conference, NOW petitioned the EEOC for public hearings on its advertising guidelines, threatened the Commission with a *mandamus* action to compel enforcement of the prohibition against sex discrimination, demanded the appointment of at least two women as EEOC Commissioners, initiated a campaign to persuade President Johnson to extend Executive Order 11246 (prohibiting discrimination by federal contractors) to include women, and demanded the EEOC show its own commitment to ending sex discrimination by appointing qualified women to its top staff.

Aileen Hernandez submitted her resignation as EEOC Commissioner, effective November 10, ". . . in frustration over the inaction on this issue [flight attendants] and other cases which had drifted on for more than a year in spite of the time requirements of Title VII." (Under Title VII, cases were supposed to be disposed of in 60 days). (10/10)

NOW Membership 300
NOW Annual Budget $1500

To refine its policies and establish its specific goals, NOW set up seven Task Forces: Family Life, Education, Employment, Media, Religion, Women in Poverty, and Women's Legal and Political Rights. (10/29-30)

NOW 's Legal Committee, chaired by Marguerite Rawalt and including Carruthers Berger, Mary Eastwood and Phineas Indritz, was authorized to take action on behalf of the airline stewardesses and the case of *Velma Menglekoch v. the California Industrial Welfare Commission* in which Menglekoch charged loss of wages and promotional opportunity because she was denied the right to work overtime under California protective legislation applicable only to women. (This had been one of the first complaints received by the EEOC and had been referred to Hernandez to decide; she found "reasonable cause" to believe Menglekoch was discriminated against by her employer's adherence to state law. The Hernandez decision on the case had been held up pending discussion by the full Commission, which determined, on a split vote, not to decide the case. (10/29-30)

Romania substituted a restrictive abortion law for one allowing abortion on request. (10)

Five NOW officers and 35 members filed a formal petition with the EEOC for hearings to amend the regulations on classified job advertising that permitted segregating the ads on the basis of sex. (12/19)

The Backlash

The Los Angeles Archdiocese hired the firm of Spencer-Roberts to organize Right-to-Life groups in California.

The *National Observer* published a front page feature article entitled, "Women Are The Next Great Issue For Civil Rights," (quoting Friedan), by Mark R. Arnold. The article began:

"Warning to all American husbands: the days of male supremacy are numbered. Your wives, victimized and degraded by a double standard in law and custom, have found a new champion. It is NOW–the National Organization for Women–a militant new women's rights movement envisioned as becoming a mass-

based pressure group capable of fulfilling the dream of emancipation of womanhood held out by the Nineteenth Century suffragettes." The article concluded, "it remains to be seen whether great numbers of women will rally to NOW's call to arms." (12/26)

YEAR	1967		
U. S. President	Lyndon Johnson		
NOW President	Betty Friedan		

EVENTS

Massive anti-Vietnam War demonstrations in Washington.

Blacks rioted in Cleveland, Newark, Detroit.

The National Organization For Women (NOW) was formally incorporated in Washington D.C. The initial registered office of the corporation was 1629 K Street, NW, Suite 500. (02/10)

At the American Medical Association's (AMA) annual meeting, the House of Delegates voted to support therapeutic abortions under three circumstances: when the pregnancy threatened the physical or mental health of the woman; when the infant might be born with a disabling physical deformity or mental deficiency; or if the

pregnancy resulting from rape or incest threatened the mental or physical health of the mother. (06)

In New York, 22 Protestant ministers and rabbis opened the Clergy Consultation Service on Abortion to refer women to doctors in the U.S., Puerto Rico and later London for safe in-office abortions.

ISSUES

Lifestyles

NOW campaigned for a Presidential Executive Order to ban discrimination in federal employment and by companies doing business with the government.

Economic

At a Civil Rights Act Enforcement Meeting with Acting Attorney General Ramsey Clark and John W. Macy, chairman of the Civil Service Commission, the NOW delegation insisted, "Any administration-supported bill which prohibits discrimination based on race, color, religion or national origin is not true to its full democratic potential–unless it also prohibits discrimination based on sex." The NOW delegation pressed for enforcement of Title VII. (01/09-12)

At a press conference in Washington, D.C. led by NOW President Betty Friedan, NOW expanded its demands to include Federally-aided child care centers for working mothers and a full income tax deduction of child care costs. Friedan also said, ". . . we want more than lip service to woman power and token appointments of a few women to special posts outside the mainstream of promotion and decision-making." (01/12)

At the NOW National Board Meeting in Chicago, IL, by-laws were adopted by the Board incorporating the revisions specified by the October 1966 National Conference. These by-laws provided for the establishment of chapters. The Task Forces established by the Board at this meeting were: Equal Opportunity of Employment; Legal and Political Rights; Education; Women in Poverty; The Family; Women and Religion. Task Force position papers were approved on Employment, Legal & Political Rights, Women in Poverty, and Image of Women. The appointments of Standing Committees and Task Force Chairmen (sic) were announced as follows: Legal Committee, Marguerite Rawalt; Finance Committee, Ti-Grace Atkinson; Membership, Inka O'Hanrahan; Public Relations, Muriel Fox; Special Committee for Constitutional Protection (to evaluate need for ERA), acting chair, Betty Friedan; Employment, Dorothy Haener; Legal and Political Rights, Jane E. Hart; Family, Alice Rossi; Education, Helen Schleman; Women & Religion, Elizabeth Farians; Image of Women, Patricia H. Trainor; Poverty, Dr. Anna Arnold Hedgeman. (02/22-23)

Kathy Switzer became the first woman to run the Boston Marathon. She entered as K. Switzer, and her gender was not discovered until after the race had begun. An official tried to tear her number off her back, but was bumped out of the way by a hefty male runner whom she later married and divorced.

Colorado became the first state to liberalize its abortion law authorizing abortion when pregnancy resulted from rape or incest, endangered a woman's physical or mental health, or was likely to result in the birth of a child with severe mental or physical defects. It required the abortion be performed in a licensed hospital and only after a panel of three doctors had unanimously given approval. (04/25)

Similar bills liberalizing abortion laws were passed in North Carolina and California where Governor Ronald Reagan finally signed it into law though he had originally told Republicans to oppose it after consulting with Roman Catholic Cardinal James Francis McIntyre.

Media

This Week magazine published a major article by Thomas J. Fleming, "Sex and Civil Rights" which described the thrust of NOW's program as well as the dismal status of American women including the fact that "a doleful 89% of all working women earn less than $5,000 a year. Only 1.4% have an annual income of more than $10,000." (03/19)

Legal

The U.S. Supreme Court upheld a Florida statute which provided that no female would be called for jury duty unless she had registered to be placed on the jury list (*Haupt v. Florida*).

NOW was officially incorporated in Washington, DC. (02/10)

Political

Senator Eugene McCarthy introduced the Equal Rights Amendment (ERA) in the Senate. He had 37 co-sponsors for S. 3567. (03/13)

NOW and other women's organizations spurred the EEOC to hold hearings on protective labor legislation that kept them out of higher paying jobs.

New York Chapter of NOW filed notarized complaint with New York Human Rights Commission on the discriminatory effect of sex-segregated job advertising in the city newspapers. (05/02)

The Backlash

Phyllis Schlafly established the Eagle Trust Fund & the Eagles Are Flying organization after she was defeated in a run for the presidency of the National Federation of Republican Women, as liberals tried to recapture their party from the Right Wing. She also began publication of *The Phyllis Schlafly Report.*

A San Jose, CA, police officer became the first to challenge California's Therapeutic Abortion Law when he asked the State Supreme Court to block the abortion of his estranged wife. He argued that the law was unconstitutional because "it breaches the right to have children." He contended that

he was suffering "great mental distress because of the threat of being deprived of the care, comfort, society and companionship" of the fetus. (12/06)

49

YEAR	1967		
U. S. President	Lyndon Johnson		
NOW President	Betty Friedan		

EVENTS	Presidential Executive Order 11375 amended E. O. 11246 to prohibit sex discrimination in employment by the federal government and by contractors doing business with the government–a NOW victory! (10/13)	At its second national conference, NOW adopted passage of the Equal Rights Amendment (ERA) to the Constitution, the repeal of all abortion laws, and publicly-funded child care as goals of the organization in a "Bill of Rights for Women." NOW was the first national organization to endorse the legalization of abortion. The United Auto Workers (UAW)	withdrew its support of NOW over the ERA and its members withdrew from NOW's board. (11/18-19)

ISSUES Lifestyles Economic Media Legal Political	**NOW Members 1035** **Treasury $826.69** EEOC hearings were held in Washington, D.C. on protective labor legislation, sex-based discrimination in advertising and pension plans. The hearings were the result of the petition filed in December 1966 by the NOW Legal Committee, urging that the discriminatory guidelines on sex-segregated classified advertising in newspapers be rescinded, and that the EEOC substitute clear and unequivocal guidelines suggested by Congresswoman Martha Griffiths. (05/02-03) An article entitled, "Buyer's Market" in *Time* Magazine discussed the unemployment rate of 3.7% and pointed out that opportunities for women now included such male-stereotyped jobs as plumbers and cab drivers. (05/19) An article in the *Los Angeles Times* was entitled, "Working Wives Crying–all the way to the bank."(05/14) A feature article in the *Wall Street Journal* was headlined, "Women's Groups Fight Last Vestiges of Bias on Job, Before the Law." The story began: "Shades of the suffragettes! The ladies are up in arms again. They're demanding equal rights." (05/22) An adverse court decision was handed down in the *Thelma Bowe et al v. Colgate Palmolive Co.* by the U.S. District Court Southern District Indiana. The court upheld the company policy regulations under which women factory workers were confined to lower paid "finishing" jobs on the ground that it is proper to "protect" women from jobs requiring the lifting of more than 35 pounds. (06/30)	The radical women's group in New York (later called the New York Radical Women) was formed. This was an important "seed bed" group of the more radical branch of the women's movement. It introduced the "consciousness raising" techniques to further the women's movement. (10/31) New York NOW picketed the *New York Times* to protest sex-segregation of job advertising. This first picket line for the New York Chapter was organized by Carol Perlys and Dolores Alexander. Dressed in old-fashioned costumes, the NOW demonstrators protested the old-fashioned policies of the *Times*. Leaflets explaining the protest were distributed. The demonstration was featured on television news shows and even the *New York Times* felt obliged to report the story with a photograph (on an inside page). (08/30) NOW filed the appeal in the case of *Bowe v. Colgate Palmolive* in which a group of women at the Colgate plant in Indiana were laid off when the company refused to permit them to exercise their seniority to claim jobs involving lifting beyond the state maximum of 35 pounds. A Federal District Court had found in favor of the company practice. (07/30) The NOW Board of Directors, meeting in Madison, WI, voted unanimously to approve the formation of the Legal Defense and Education Fund and authorized NOW officers to set it up. (09/17) The National Conference for a New Politics (NCNP) held its nationwide meeting of new left groups in Chicago. A strong women's rights plank was ignored by the conference and as a result, the Chicago women's group began to meet regularly. (08/31-09/04)	At its post-national conference press briefing, NOW announced its support for Cindy Judd Hill, a music teacher, in her fight with a Pennsylvania school district. Hill was deprived of sabbatical study pay and later fired after she gave birth to a baby while on sabbatical leave obtaining her master's degree. She had fulfilled all the requirements of her leave and received the degree, but had taken off one week to have the baby. (11) President Johnson signed public law 90-130 which retained combat limitations but allowed women in the Armed Forces equal promotion and retirement rights, and removed the 2% restriction on the number of women who could serve in the armed forces. (11/08) The National Federation of Business and Professional Women's Clubs (BPW), with membership of 170,000, charged both subtle and overt discrimination against women in many fields; it cited state protective labor laws as the major cause. (10/20) NOW held simultaneous demonstrations at EEOC field offices across the country. The demonstration sites included New York, Washington, D.C., San Francisco, Chicago, and Atlanta, and emphasized the EEOC's failure to end sex-segregated job advertising. Demonstrators in San Francisco (in above photo) included national NOW Treasurer Inka O'Hanrahan, Vice President Aileen Hernandez, Del Martin and Phyllis Lyon. (12/14)

The Backlash	*McCall's* magazine carried the Clare Booth Luce column "Without Portfolio" on "Is It NOW or Never for Women?" a rather snide commentary in which Luce remarked, "It is difficult. . . to share NOW's indignation about the so-called overall 'inferior' status of women in economic and social life." The	column concluded: "Husbands, praise your wives! And marvel at how quickly they stop complaining about discrimination." (04)	

YEAR	1968		
U. S. President	Lyndon Johnson		
NOW President	Betty Friedan		

EVENTS

"Women's Liberation" groups began to emerge around the country as a spin-off of the male-dominated student movement.

The United Nations inaugurated the International Year of Human Rights. (01/01)

Three Black students were shot to death and 30 wounded by police on the campus of South Carolina State College in Orangeburg. (02)

Walter Cronkite, breaking a code of neutrality among major newscasters, opposed the Vietnam War in a national television broadcast. (03/06)

Martin Luther King was assassinated in Memphis, TN. (04/05)

It took 1000 police officers to end the week-long student takeover of Columbia University. (04/30)

Robert F. Kennedy was assassinated in Los Angeles.(06/05)

ISSUES

Lifestyles

At the opening of Congress, a coalition of women's peace groups (5000 women) called the Jeanette Rankin Brigade, demonstrated against the Vietnam war. The New York Radical Women staged a "Burial of Traditional Womanhood" in a first action by radical women to raise the consciousness of their anti-war activist sisters. This was the first use of phrase "Sisterhood is Powerful." (01/15)

New York NOW demonstrated for abortion law repeal. Among the chapter demonstrators was Kate Millet carrying a sign that read, "Nobody should legislate my rights to my body." (02/29)

NOW chapters around the country demonstrated at facilities that denied admittance or service to women as a public accommodations issue.

Economic

EEOC hearings in New York City were picketed by New York NOW when NOW was refused permission to testify or take part in final round table discussion concerning "Discrimination in White Collar Employment" that included representatives from the finance, insurance, communications, banking industries and 100 major corporations with headquarters in New York City. (01/15)

The EEOC finally ruled that sex was not a BFOQ for the job of airline flight attendant. (02/03)

NOW filed a writ of mandamus against the EEOC to require it to make a determination on the formal petition NOW had filed on the sex-segregation of help-wanted advertising in newspapers. On the strength of the EEOC promise to perform more expeditiously, the court dismissed the case. (02/12)

Muriel Siebert became the first woman to have a seat on the New York Stock Exchange. The seat cost $445,000 plus a $7515 initiation fee.

Twelve Trans World Airlines flight attendants filed a complaint with the EEOC against the airline for sex discrimination. The complaint alleged that TWA maintained two classifications for flight cabin attendants: purser and hostess. Both had the same duties but men as pursers made from $2500 to $3500 more a year. (04)

Religion

Media

Caroline Bird's *Born Female, The High Cost of Keeping Women Down* was a feminist best-seller.

The first independent radical women's newsletter: "Voice of the Women's Liberation Movement," was written and published in Chicago. By 1971, there were over 100 women's movement journals, newsletters and newspapers throughout the country. (03)

The *New York Times Magazine* ran the article "The Second Feminist Wave," by Martha Weinman Lear. (03/18)

The Church and The Second Sex by Mary Daly was published.

Notes From the First Year, a collection of writings and reports on radical feminism, was published. Also published was a position paper, "Toward a Female Liberation Movement" (called the Florida Paper) by Beverly Jones and Judith Brown.(06)

Legal

NOW attorney, Sylvia Roberts took the case of *Weeks v. Southern Bell* on appeal. Weeks had been denied a promotion because of a state law that prohibited women from lifting 30 pounds or more on the job. (02/14)

In *U.S. ex. rel. v. Robinson*, the Federal District Court struck dawn the Connecticut statute requiring longer prison sentences for women than for men as unconstitutional. (02/28)

Political

The federal Citizen's Advisory Council issued four task force reports on Health and Welfare, Social Security and Taxes, Labor Standards and Family Law Policy; the Family Law Policy report recommended repeal of abortion laws. (04)

NOW President Betty Friedan appointed a special committee consisting of Jean Witter, Ti-Grace Atkinson and Muriel Fox to plan a major campaign for enactment of the Equal Rights Amendment in the 91st Congress. Mary Eastwood and Caruthers Berger wrote the rationale for its adoption.

CONSTITUTIONAL EQUALITY FOR U. S. WOMEN

The Backlash

YEAR	1968
U. S. President	Lyndon B. Johnson
NOW President	Betty Friedan

EVENTS

At the Democratic Convention in Chicago police and students rioted; Hubert Humphrey was chosen as the Democratic nominee for President. (08/26-29) Republicans held their convention in Florida and chose Richard Nixon. (08/5-9)

More than 200 women from 37 states and Canada convened in Chicago for the first national Women's Liberation Conference. (11/28-30)

The Women's Equity Action League (WEAL) was formed as a spin-off from NOW by women who did not want to deal with the issue of abortion but did want to actively work for equal opportunity for women in education and employment. (12/01)

ISSUES

Lifestyles

A *New York Times* story disclosed the fact that Ti-Grace Atkinson, a member of NOW's National Board, had involved herself in the Valerie Solanis case. Solanis shot Andy Warhol and was the author of the "S.C.U.M. (Society for Cutting Up Men) Manifesto" A newspaper photo identified Atkinson as representing NOW at the Solanis trial. Solanis' attorney was Flo Kennedy, another member of New York NOW and a nominee for the NOW National Board. Some national officers and board members and members of New York NOW objected to the unauthorized association of NOW's name in defense of a woman who advocated and used violence. In the furor within NOW that followed, Atkinson maintained neither she nor Kennedy had represented themselves as connected with NOW. (06/14)

Economic

NOW Annual Budget
$7,079.82

The EEOC ruled 3-2 that it violated the Civil Rights Act for employers to place separate male and female "Help Wanted" ads in newspapers, except where sex was a bona fide occupational qualification. (08/05)

NOW called its first boycott of Colgate-Palmolive products and demonstrated for five days in front of the company's New York City headquarters on Park Avenue. Anselma Dell'Olio and Barbara Love of New York NOW led the action with picket signs that read "Down the Drain With Ajax," "The White Knight Is A Dirty Old Man" and "Cold Power Versus Woman Power." One of the days featured a "flush in," where New York NOW members poured Colgate products into a real toilet. (09/05)

Dr. Naomi Weisstein delivered her paper " 'Kinder, Kuche, Kirche' As Scientific Law: Psychology Constructs the Female" at the American Studies Association meeting at UC Davis (CA). The paper was widely distributed in the women's movement. (10/26)

In *Rosenfeld v. Southern Pacific Company,* the federal district court ruled that Title VII superseded California protective labor laws that restricted women from working overtime and from lifting weights in excess of the prescribed limit. The case was considered a landmark advance for women's rights. Southern Pacific appealed the decision. (11/22)

NOW member Shirley Chisholm became the first Black woman elected to the House of Representatives. After the 1968 elections, 10 women were serving in the House and one in the Senate; the 1968 Census indicated that women were 53.3% of the population of the United States. (11/04)

Women's Liberation groups, joined by members of New York NOW, targeted the Miss America Beauty Contest in Atlantic City. This was the event from which the myth of "bra-burning" feminists was created by the press, distorting the early image of the movement. In fact, there was an ordinance against burning anything on the Atlantic City Boardwalk, which the demonstrators observed. (09/07)

Four New York City newspapers – *the New York Times, Post, Daily News and Village Voice*– integrated their Help Wanted advertisements. (12/01)

NOW protested the exclusion of women as astronauts from the space program. Nita Ladewig, president of the Northern California Chapter of NOW, initiated correspondence with NASA that continued for six months, also protesting the exclusive use of the names of masculine gods for the space ships. NASA maintained it had yet to find women who qualified either as pilots or scientists. (12/27-68-05/26/69))

At its Third National Conference, NOW committed to launch a campaign to outlaw public accommodations discrimination based on sex, initiate a nationwide boycott against United Airlines because of its "men only" executive flights, and work for the amendment of the Social Security Act to provide insurance coverage for the wife as an individual rather than as a dependent of her husband. (12/06-08)

Media

Members of New York NOW again picketed the *New York Times,* this time for a week, urging the end of sex-segregated job advertising. They chanted: "The New York Times is a sex-offender!" (07/22-26)

Legal

Political

The Pennsylvania Supreme Court, acting on an appeal filed by NOW attorneys Marguerite Rawalt and Phineas Indritz, voided the state's Muncy Law, which required longer prison sentences for women than for men convicted of the same crime. In *Pennsylvania v. Daniel,* NOW's attorneys argued it was discriminatory to sentence women up to 10 years for the same crime for which men could only receive a four-year sentence. (07/01)

The Backlash

Though most Catholics had expected approval of the pill, the Pope's encyclical *Humanae Vitae,* again forbade the use of artificial methods of birth control and voluntary sterilization. The encyclical was not proclaimed an infallible document. (07/29)

The American Newspaper Publishers Association (ANPA) and the Washington *Star* filed suit in federal court challenging the authority of the EEOC to issue its regulation eliminating sex-segregated classified job advertising and charging compliance with the regulation would hurt job seekers, employers and newspapers. (09/30)

Richard Viguerie set up his fundraising firm, RAVCO, using lists he acquired from the Goldwater campaign.

YEAR	1969		
U. S. President	Richard M. Nixon		
NOW President	Betty Friedan		

EVENTS

President Nixon issued Executive Order 11478 which required Affirmative Action programs in Federal employment. (08/08)

The "Chicago Seven" were found not guilty of plotting to incite a riot at the 1968 Democratic Convention. (02/28)

The United States landed two astronauts on the moon: "That's one small step for man, one giant leap for mankind." (07/20)

For one brief weekend, the Woodstock Nation, consisting of some 400,000 people, existed to hear the Who, Jefferson Airplane, Jimi Hendrix, the Band and Janis Joplin. (08/17)

When New York City Police entered the Stonewall Inn to harass gay patrons, they fought back and the modern gay and lesbian rights movement began. (06/28)

ISSUES

Lifestyles

New York NOW's Abortion Committee formed New Yorkers for Abortion Law Repeal (NYALR), an independent statewide organization that has been characterized as the first abortion law repeal group whose philosophy was based entirely on a radical feminist analysis of the issue. NYALR campaigned against any restrictions on a women's access to abortion or any form of birth control. It also campaigned against passage of "reform" abortion laws. (01)

Education

The first national conference on abortion laws convened in Chicago and decided to establish the National Association for the Repeal of Abortion Laws (NARAL). Lawrence Lader was the first chair. NOW's representatives included: Betty Friedan; Lucinda Cisler, East Coast Chair of NOW's National Abortion Committee; and Lana Phelan, West Coast Chair. Friedan spoke on abortion as "A Woman's Civil Right." (01/14-16)

Economic

NOW Chapters were involved in efforts to establish women's studies courses at universities in California, Michigan and at newly co-educational Princeton University.

Marlene Dixon, an Assistant Professor of Sociology, was fired from the University of Chicago for alleged radical teachings and being female. Her dismissal precipitated public demonstration in her support of both women's liberation groups and the radical student groups. (01)

Legal

The U.S. Court of Appeals ruled in favor of the EEOC Guidelines prohibiting sex-segregated help wanted advertising and denied the appeal of the American Newspaper Publisher Association (ANPA). (01/24)

The radical feminist group Redstockings was formed. The group practiced a formalized concept of consciousness raising and declared its principles in a document called "The Bitch Manifesto." (02)

BILTMORE MEN'S BAR

NOW proclaimed "Public Accommodations Week" and there were national actions at "men only" restaurants and bars and public carriers across the country including: New York City, Syracuse, Cochester (CT), Pittsburgh, Washington, Atlanta, Chicago and Los Angeles. The assumptions behind policies like this were that women were not involved in business. Further, that unescorted women in bars were there for only one purpose: soliciting men for prostitution. In the Call to Action, Karen DeCrow, the national coordinator of the action, pointed out that Title II of the Civil Rights Act of 1964 forbade discrimination against anyone on the basis of race color, religion, or national origin in places of public accommodation but did not exclude discrimination on the basis of sex. Yet, she wrote, "the most basic right of all may be the right to equal treatment in places of public accommodation." Among the places picketed during the year were the Oak Room at the Plaza Hotel in New York by New York NOW, Stouffers Grill in Pittsburgh by Pittsburgh NOW, the Polo Lounge of the Beverly Hills Hotel in Los Angeles by Los Angles NOW. (02/09)

Members of Redstockings disrupted an abortion law reform hearing of the New York State legislature when the panel of witnesses turned out to be made up of 14 men and one nun. Like NOW, the group demanded the repeal, not reform, of all abortion laws. (02/13)

The first accredited women's studies course appeared in the spring curriculum of Cornell University in New York State as a result of efforts by the recently formed Cornell-Ithaca Chapter of NOW. (03)

NOW's National Board established a Sports Task Force with its first objective to integrate the Soapbox Derby. (03/29)

Dolores Alexander, formerly a prize-winning reporter for *Newsday* (a Long Island daily newspaper), began work as NOW'S first National Executive Director (at half her previous salary). It was an act of faith since the best estimate of the balance in the national treasury was something under $600. Her job was to encompass membership processing, public relations, national correspondence and fundraising (also for the purpose of raising her own salary). National headquarters of NOW were to be housed in one room of her two-bedroom apartment in New York. This entailed moving NOW's possessions—one desk, a stationery storage cabinet, and one four-drawer filing cabinet and the records it contained—from Washington, D.C. to New York. This was accomplished by Alexander and Jean Faust, then President of New York NOW, in a station wagon borrowed from Muriel Fox. (02/10-13)

The Backlash

Accuracy In the Media (AIM) was set up as the Right Wing's watch dog on "liberal bias" in the media.

The FBI initiated an investigation of the women's movement for possible subversive activity, though verification of this investigation did not come until 1977, when information about the surveillance was disclosed by an inquiry under the Freedom of Information Act. (01)

CLICK!
(CONSCIOUSNESS RAISED)

YEAR	1969
U. S. President	Richard M. Nixon
NOW President	Betty Friedan

EVENTS

Canada passed an omnibus crime bill that legalized abortion and homosexuality. (05/14)

Los Angeles NOW member Judith Meuli designed "The Brassy," the woman's symbol with the equality sign across the circle. The original version was hand-welded of brass rod. (03)

After 60 years, the journalism society Sigma Delta Chi decided to admit women to membership. (11)

The largest anti-war demonstration in Washington, D.C.'s history occurred when 250,000 people marched in the capital. Another 200,000 gathered in Golden Gate Park in San Francisco. (11/15)

TRW featured NOW member and mathematician Poppy Northcott in its ads to tell the world of the key role she played in the Apollo mission control center.

ISSUES

Lifestyles
Education
Economic
Religion
Media
Legal
Political

In what NOW designated as "Freedom for Women Week," members demonstrated at the White House on Mother's Day for "Rights, Not Roses." Other demonstrations occurred in Chicago, Albuquerque and Los Angeles. (05/04-11)

Sylvia Roberts

It was a major NOW victory when the U.S. Court of Appeals (Fifth Circuit) ruled in *Weeks v. Southern Bell* that the weight-lifting rule for women violated Title VII of the Civil Rights Act. NOW attorney Sylvia Roberts had used as evidence the example of a typewriter that Weeks, as a secretary, was required to lift, though it weighed more than the 30-pound limit being used to bar her from the job of switchman. ((03/04)

Sexual Politics, A Surprising Examination of Society's Most Arbitrary Folly, by Kate Millet, a historical and cultural analysis of sexism written originally as a doctoral thesis, became a widely debated and quoted best-seller. Kate Millet was an active member of New York NOW.

The logo that became the trademark of National NOW was designed by Ivy Bottini, a founder of the New York Chapter of NOW and a graphic designer, at the request of Aileen Hernandez, a national vice-president of NOW. Bottini also designed the logo for the National Women's Political Caucus, founded in 1971. (03)

NOW celebrated a victory in the *People v. Belous* case when the state supreme court found California's 100 year-old abortion law unconstitutional. Dr. Leon Belous, a member of NOW, had insisted on defending himself on constitutional grounds against the charge of making illegal abortion referrals. (09/05)

After considerable pressure from NOW and other women's rights groups, public hearings were held on the Department of Labor's proposed sex discrimination guidelines to be issued to implement Executive Order 11375. (08/04-06)

The EEOC issued another set of guidelines declaring that state protective laws that applied only to women were in direct violation of Title VII of the Civil Rights Act. (08/19)

The National Coalition of American Nuns was founded to support the civil rights and anti-war movements and to pressure for women's equality within the Catholic Church. (07)

Dr. JoAnn Evansgardner and other members of Pittsburgh NOW started their own press, KNOW, Inc., under the slogan, "Freedom of the press belongs to those who own the press." KNOW published the first articles and reprints for a burgeoning women's studies movement.

NOW won a victory in the *Colgate-Palmolive* case when the Appeals Court ruled that any weight-lifting test must be applied to all employees, male and female, and forbade separate male/female seniority lists. The Court also ruled any union contracts restricting jobs women could bid on were illegal and awarded back pay to the women. (09/26)

The first Women's Caucus in a professional society was established in the American Sociological Association led by NOW charter member Dr. Alice Rossi. (09/03)

The Columbia University (NY) Women's Liberation group published a lengthy report on the status of women faculty at Columbia. The data revealed that 24% of all doctoral degrees were awarded to women (the highest in the nation); but the percentage of women professors with tenure was only 2%. (09)

The first accredited women's law course was taught at New York University Law School.(09)

San Diego (CA) State College offered a 10-course program of women's studies, believed to be the first full program and most comprehensive in the country at the time. (10)

Pittsburgh NOW filed charges of sex discrimination against the *Pittsburgh Press* because of the paper's continued use of sex-segregated "Help Wanted" ads. (10)

The highly-acclaimed children's television program, "Sesame Street," drew sharp criticism from feminists for its stereotypical portrayal of women and girls. As a result of the protest, some changes were made by the show's producers. (09)

NOW attorney Faith Seidenberg filed suit in *Seidenberg v. McSorley's Old Ale House*, asserting women's right to public accommodations. (11/13)

The First Congress to Unite Women, initiated by NOW was held in New York City. The coalition conference of over 500 feminists in the northeast region was coordinated and chaired by New York NOW President Ivy Bottini. The conference was closed to men and the media. The workshop reports and the conference resolutions represented a fusion of moderate and radical feminist interests. There were at least three other similar regional conferences in San Francisco, Los Angeles, and Chicago. (11/21-23)

The Backlash

The *Bulletin* of the John Birch Society called for the establishment of an "organized, nationwide, intensive, angry and determined opposition to the now mushrooming program of so-called sex education in the public schools." The Birchers believed sex education was part of the "overall Communist design." The Birch Society's

local Movement to Restore Decency (MOTOREDE) Committees, the Oklahoma-based Christian Crusade headed by the Rev. Billy James Hargis, and the American Education Lobby, another right wing group, led the attack that erupted in 34 states and targeted The Sex Information and Education Council (SIECUS). (01)

"A Matter of Simple Justice," a report by President Nixon's Task Force on Women's Rights and Responsibilities, was transmitted to the President, but the report was not released publicly until the following year because of its "militant tone." (12/15)

YEAR	1970
U. S. President	Richard M. Nixon
NOW President	Aileen Hernandez

EVENTS

Aileen Hernandez was elected President and Wilma Scott Heide, chair of the Board, at NOW's Fourth National Conference in Des Plaines, IL. During a two-hour "farewell address," retiring president Betty Friedan called for a "Women's Strike for Equality" on August 26–a surprise proposal to other national officers sitting on the dais, including the incoming president, Hernandez. (03/20)

The Women's Heritage Calendar and Almanac, the forerunner of many feminist calendars and datebooks to come, was produced and published by Toni Carabillo, Sylvia Hartman, Judith Meuli, Louise Ramsdell, Cathy Timlin and Lenore Youngman—all NOW activists—and went on sale at NOW's National Conference. (03/20)

ISSUES

Lifestyles

United Airlines halted its "men only" executive flights between New York and Chicago, which NOW had protested as a form of sex discrimination in public accommodations. (01/14)

Education

NOW opposed the appointment of G. Harrold Carswell to the U.S. Supreme Court, the first time an appointment to the court was ever challenged on the basis of sexism. Betty Friedan, testifying for NOW, cited the case of *Mrs. Ida Phillips v. Martin Marietta* in which Carswell ruled in favor of the company's refusal to hire a woman with pre-school age children, while hiring men with pre-school age children. (01/28)

Economic

Religion

Inka O'Hanrahan

NOW founder and national treasurer Inka O'Hanrahan died on January 15, 1970. A clinical biochemist, she owned and directed her own laboratory in San Francisco until she suffered a first heart attack in 1969. She was vice chairman of the California Commission on the Status of Women (1965-67) and lectured in the U.S. and Europe on the status of women. She organized the Northern and Southern California Chapters of NOW.

Media

Legal

NOW staged a large demonstration at the Los Angeles Hall of Justice to protest prosecution of doctors who performed abortions. (02/11)

A Hawaii law allowing abortions for all women who had been residents of the state for 90 days went into effect. (02/11)

Political

Pressure from Los Angeles NOW persuaded Congressman Tom Reese (D-CA) to support the appointment of 16-year-old Monica Mortz as a page in Congress. Historically, only boys had been permitted this opportunity. (02/05)

NOW Membership 3033
NOW Annual Budget $38,000

About 20 NOW members, led by Wilma Scott Heide and Jean Witter, disrupted the Senate hearings on the 18-year-old vote to demand hearings on the Equal Rights Amendment. At a signal from Heide the women rose, and unfolded posters they had concealed in their purses. Committee chair Birch Bayh disclosed later that this demonstration prompted the hearings on the ERA held later in the year. (02/17)

Sisterhood Is Powerful, An Anthology of Writings from the Women's Liberation Movement edited by Robin Morgan, and *A Dialectic of Sex, The Case for a Feminist Revolution* by Shulamith Firestone, were published.

Forty-six editorial staff members of *Newsweek* filed formal charges of sex discrimination against the magazine. (03/16)

The NOW Legal Defense and Education Fund was formally incorporated in Washington, D.C. (03/16)

NOW filed sex discrimination charges against Harvard under Executive Order 11375. $3 million dollars in government contracts were delayed for two weeks until the university agreed to submit personnel information on its women employees and students to investigators. (03/25)

More than 300 women attended a Professional Women's Caucus, organized by NOW's Dr. JoAnn Evansgardner and Doris Sassower, an attorney and former president of the New York Women's Bar Association. They decided to formally organize their Caucus and work for women's rights, child care and to initiate women's studies courses and programs. (04/11)

More than 100 women from 10 women's liberation groups, including New York NOW, invaded the offices of the *Ladies Home Journal's* executive editor, John Mack Carter, and conducted an 11-hour sit-in with him and senior editor Lenore Hershey. They protested the image of women portrayed by women's magazines and the status of women working on the magazines. (03/18)

Ten women invaded the CBS Annual Stockholders meeting in San Francisco to protest media distortion of women's role in commercials and programming. (04/15)

The New York State Senate gave final legislative approval to a bill removing all restrictions on abortion during the first six months of pregnancy. (04/10)

At the first statewide AFL-CIO Women's Conference in Wisconsin, 200 women convened to discuss the status of women in unions. Contrary to their union's policy, they endorsed passage of the ERA and opposed state protective legislation. (03/07)

The Backlash

The National Right to Life Committee was established by the Catholic Church to try and block the liberalization of abortion laws.

YEAR	1970
U. S. President	Richard M. Nixon
NOW President	Aileen Hernandez

EVENTS

As a prelude to the Women's Strike for Equality on August 26, New York NOW members, led by chapter president Ivy Bottini, organized a demonstration at the Statue of Liberty. They draped over a railing an enormous banner, which they had carried over to the island in sections, which read, "WOMEN OF THE WORLD UNITE!" (08/10)

WOMEN OF THE WORLD UNITE!

Four students were killed and 10 were wounded when National Guardsmen opened fire on students demonstrating on the Kent State University campus against the American invasion of Cambodia.(05/18)

ISSUES

Lifestyles

Diane Crump became the first woman jockey to ride in the Kentucky Derby. (05/03)

Education

NOW established a Federal Compliance Committee to press for enforcement of federal equal opportunity laws for women. The Committee was specifically charged to develop a program and procedures for filing sex discrimination complaints with the Office of Federal Contract Compliance (OFCC) and the EEOC. (05/02)

Economic

NOW chapters in California lobbied for a bill introduced in the California Legislature to permit girls to work as newspaper deliverers at the same age as boys. Existing state law allowed boys to begin delivering newspapers at age 10 and girls at age 18. (04/15)

Religion

In Detroit, women of NOW's Ecumenical Task Force burned part of the newly released Roman Missal, which restricted the right of women to be lectors at Catholic Mass. (04/19)

The 147 women on the editorial staff of *Time* magazine filed a formal sex discrimination complaint with the New York State Division of Human Rights against the corporation's four magazines: *Time, Life, Fortune* and *Sports Illustrated*. (05/04)

Legal

The logo that became the trademark of NOW was designed by Ivy Bottini, a founder of the New York Chapter of NOW and a graphic designer, at the request of Aileen Hernandez. She also designed the logo for the National Women's Political Caucus founded in 1971.

Political

Alaska repealed its existing abortion law when the state's legislature voted to over-ride the governor's veto by 41-17. 04/30)

The Canadian House of Commons was forced to adjourn for nearly an hour while guards removed young women who had chained themselves to seats in the public galleries to dramatize a demand for a liberalized abortion law. (05/11)

Women's Equity Action League (WEAL) filed charges of sex discrimination under EO 11375 against the entire college and university system of the state of Florida.(05/25)

A model affirmative action plan, the first ever written to conform to Office of Federal Contract Compliance (OFCC) requirements, was published by NOW and submitted to the Labor Department to be used for all colleges and universities. The plan was written by Dr. Ann Scott, chair of NOW's Campus Coordinating Committee and a member of the faculty at SUNY's University of Buffalo, NY. (05/14)

Time magazine reported that less than half of U.S. women were now full-time homemakers. In 1957, 57% of all women were homemakers full time; in 1970 the figure was only 48.4%. (05/11)

NOW won its public accommodations case in *Seidenberg v. McSorley's Old Ale House*. The U. S. Supreme Court ruled that sex discrimi-nation had no foundation in reason and violated the equal protection clause of the 14th Amendment. However, the court limited the impact of the decision by applying it only to situations where women had been denied the right to enter a public accommodation "under sufficient control of the state." (05/26)

The biennial conference of the American Civil Liberties Union adopted a strong policy recommendation supporting women's rights. (06/07)

Congress initiated the first federal family planning program, Title X of the Public Health Services Act.

A survey of some of the most highly educated men and women in the nation showed that 60% of the men and 43% of the women believed that a woman's major role should be as a wife or mother. The survey was conducted by the American Association of University Women. (06)

U.S. House hearings on education discrimination, for which NOW had long agitated, were finally held. The first such hearings in U.S. history, they resulted in 1,250 pages of testimony. (06/07)

NOW filed a blanket sex discrimination complaint with the OFCC under Executive Order 11375 against 1,300 corporations charging they had all failed to file affirmative action plans for hiring women. (06/25)

The editor of the *Washington Post* issued a staff memorandum on guidelines for reporting about women and women's issues, stipulating that reporters avoid words such as "brunette," "cute," "divorcee," etc., unless the same kinds of words also were used about men. (06/03)

A three-judge federal panel said that the Texas abortion laws were unconstitutional because they infringed on the fundamental right of single or married women to choose whether or not to have children. The suit was brought by a pregnant single woman, a married couple and a doctor facing two criminal abortion charges. (06/17)

The Backlash

At the Democratic Party's Committee on National Priorities, Rep. Patsy Mink (D-HI) urged that a high priority be given to establishing women's rights. Dr. Edgar F. Berman, a long time friend of presidential-aspirant, Hubert H. Humphrey, declared that women were incapable of holding important decision-making jobs because

they were subject to "raging hormonal imbalances" as a result of their menstrual cycle and meno-pause. The outraged protests of NOW and other feminist groups forced Berman to resign from the Committee. (04/30)

Happiness of Womanhood (HOW) was organized at Kingman, AZ, by Jacquie Davison and three friends as an anti-women's liberation movement group. The League of Housewives was also affiliated with HOW. (07)

YEAR	1970
U. S. President	Richard M. Nixon
NOW President	Aileen Hernandez

EVENTS

On the 50th anniversary of the 19th Amendment giving women the right to vote, NOW organized the "Women's Strike for Equality." There were demonstrations and rallies in more than 90 major cities and small towns in 42 states. Some 50,000 women marched on Fifth Avenue in New York and across the country more than 100,000 women were involved. (08/26)

After the elections,13 women were members of Congress–12 in the House and one in the Senate. This was the largest number of women to serve in Congress since 1960 and, in a change from a traditional pattern, none of the women who ran for Congress were widows trying to fill seats vacated by the death of their husbands. (11/03)

ISSUES

LifeStyles

After prolonged lobbying by New York NOW, the city passed a bill banning sex discrimination in public accommodations, believed to be the first law of its kind in any major city in the country. (07/21)

Education

Economic

NOW conducted demonstrations in 14 cities against the National Association of Manufacturers & Department of Labor closed-circuit television conference on equal opportunity to protest the exclusion of guidelines on sex discrimination from the Labor Department's "Order 4," which required affirmative action plans for minorities only. The next day, the Secretary of Labor promised to set up a group to develop guidelines on women. (07/31)

Religion

NOW President Aileen Hernandez and NOW member U.S. Representative Shirley Chisholm testified in support of the ERA before the U.S. Judiciary Subcommittee on Constitutional Amendments. The last Senate hearings on the ERA had been held in 1956. (05/05)

Rep. Martha Griffiths (D-MI) successfully filed a discharge petition to get the ERA out of the House Judiciary Committee, where it had been held for years by Rep. Emmanuel Celler. It was only the eighth time in 20 years that this rarely used parliamentary tactic had been used successfully. (06/11)

Media

Political

The first U.S. Circuit Court of Appeals declared a Massachusetts law forbidding the sale of contraceptives to unmarried adults was unconstitutional. (07/13

Additional courses on the role and history of women began to emerge on campuses like Cornell, Princeton, Vassar, the University of Florida, State University of New York at Buffalo, University of California at Los Angeles (UCLA), and others.(09)

The first suit under the Civil Rights Act of 1964 to secure equal job rights for women was filed against Libbey Owens Ford and United Glass and Ceramic Workers of North America and local union #9 of Toledo OH. (07/20)

The first suit filed by the Labor Department under the 1963 Equal Pay Act was filed on behalf of men to equalize the pay of order-takers at McDonald drive-ins where young men were being paid less than older women employees. (08)

An "inside study" (anonymously authored) of "Sexism on Capitol Hill" documented discrimination against women on Congressional staffs. Of the 990 Senate staffers earning $12,000 to $31,000, nearly three-fourths were men. (09/15)

More than 200 nuns, priests and lay persons met in Garrison, NY, to discuss the meaning for religion of the feminist movement. (11/12)

The Federal Communications Commission (FCC) issued a ruling requiring affirmative action in hiring by radio and television stations, but deliberately excluded women from coverage. NOW began a series of protests. (08)

The Female Eunich by Germaine Greer was published.

The Equal Rights Amendment was passed by the U.S. House of Representatives by a vote of 350-15. (08/10)

A press conference in New York headed by Gloria Steinem, Ti-Grace Atkinson, Flo Kennedy, Sally Kempton, Susan Brownmiller, Ivy Bottini and Dolores Alexander expressed "solidarity with the struggle of homosexuals to attain their liberation in a sexist society." It was provoked by the *Time* magazine article that sought to discredit Kate Millet because of her bisexuality. (See below). NOW's president, Aileen Hernandez, sent a statement deploring *Time's* "sexual McCarthyism." (12/17)

AT&T held a press conference in New York City to express its outrage at the EEOC charges of discrimination, claiming it had been a leader in hiring minorities and that women were "eligible for and were actually working in" all kinds of jobs, except those requiring climbing power poles or descending into "manholes." (12/12)

NOW was a party to the petition filed by the Equal Employment Opportunity Commission (EEOC) with the Federal Communications Commission (FCC) to deny AT&T a rate increase on the grounds that the company practiced "pervasive, system-wide, and blatantly unlawful" discrimination in the employment of women, Blacks and the Spanish-surnamed. Seven percent of all discrimination complaints filed with the EEOC were against AT&T– more than any other company. (12/10)

Heads of seven Catholic nuns' organizations met with seven Catholic bishops at a meeting of bishops in Washington, D.C., declaring they wanted a stronger voice in policy matters and more varied job opportunities, including pastoral responsibilities. (11/17)

Under pressure from women, the National Press Club in Washington, D.C., long a traditional male bastion, voted to admit women members. (12/14)

The Backlash

The media generally dismissed the events of August 26, 1970 as a "flop," trivializing the women's movement and stereotyping its advocates as ugly man-haters and left-wing radicals.

Billy Graham called feminism "an echo of our overall philosophy of permissiveness" in an article in the *Ladies Home Journal*.

He claimed that women didn't want to be "competitive juggernauts pitted against male chauvinists" and that the role of wife, mother, and homemaker was the appointed destiny of "real womanhood," according to the Judeo-Christian ethic. (11)

Time magazine did a cover story on Kate Millet, declaring that she was probably discredited as a spokesperson for the feminist movement because she had admitted her bisexuality. (12/08)

YEAR	1971
U. S. President	Richard M. Nixon
NOW President	Aileen Hernandez

EVENTS

The U.S. Supreme Court held a two-hour hearing on its first-and key-abortion case. Although the case did not involve a woman's right to control her own body, it had the potential for abolishing abortion laws of 39 states which allowed abortion "when necessary for the preservation of the mother's health." In the Washington, D.C. ruling, then on appeal to the Supreme Court, Federal District Judge Gerhard Gesell held that the city's 1901 abortion law was unconstitutionally vague because it did not tell physicians what constituted the "health" of the mother. Similar constitutional challenges were being brought in Colorado, Indiana and New Jersey. In Ohio, a federal tribunal ruled that the state abortion laws were constitutional. Federal courts returned decisions favorable to existing abortion-control laws in Minnesota, Missouri, Louisiana, Iowa, Vermont and Massachusetts. (01/12)

LEGALIZE ABORTION

ISSUES

LifeStyles

NOW made the attainment of child care legislation the priority issue of the year.

New York Radical Feminists held a "Speakout on Rape." Women told about their experiences and analyzed societal assumptions about rape. (01/24)

Economic

NOW President Aileen Hernandez expressed NOW's outrage to the President of Southern Bell at the continued harassment of Lorena Weeks, warning that NOW had committed itself to a national action campaign against Southern Bell and AT&T. (01/18)

Media

NOW petitioned the Federal Communications Commission (FCC) to have women included in affirmative action programs for radio and television as a condition for renewal of their broadcast licenses. (01)

The U.S. Supreme Court ruled in the case of *Phillips v. Martin Marietta* that employers cannot refuse to hire women solely because they have small children unless fathers of small children are also denied employment. But on this first ruling on a Title VII case, the Court sent it back to the lower court for hearings on whether Phillips could be denied a job because of bona fide occupational qualifications. (01/25)

Religion

Legal

The U.S. Ninth Circuit Court of Appeals ruled that a "substantial constitutional issue" was involved in the case of *Mengelkoch v. Industrial Welfare Commission of California*. NOW attorneys had been involved in this case since 1966, arguing that the state protective laws covering women in fact violated women's constitutional rights under the 14th Amendment. The Court of Appeals remanded the case to the district court for decision. (01/11)

The Fayetteville (NC) Chapter of NOW held a press conference at which wheels were presented to two girls, Deborah Boisseau and Sandra Sosa, who were the first to break the sex barrier for the Soap Box Derby Grand Prix. Chapter President Carol Forbes, Deborah's mother, initiated the action against the National Soap Box Derby when the two girls were refused entrance locally. In an out-of-court settlement, the rules limiting the Soap Box Derby to boys were abolished by Derby Officials and Chevrolet. Any child 11-15 became eligible to compete. (03/29)

Lorena Weeks was finally given the switchman's job she sought but was then subjected to harassment on the job. A supervisor in her area told workers to treat her "just like any nigger" and co-workers began calling her "Switch Bitch." Her union, Communications Workers of America (CWA) condemned the use of the term "nigger" but dismissed "Switch Bitch" as "humorous office camaraderie." (03/04)

The *Pittsburgh Press* and *Post Gazette* were given 30 days to end the sex segregation of their "Help Wanted" classified ads. The state court ruling was the first in the country on the legality of sex classified job advertising and was handed down in response to an appeal by the *Pittsburgh Press* of an order from the Pittsburgh Human Rights Commission directing the newspaper to comply with the city ordinance forbidding sex discrimination in employment practices. Both the rulings by the commission and the court were victories for Pittsburgh NOW which had first initiated action against the Press in 1969 and continued to exert pressure until the court decision. The court ruling was appealed by the *Pittsburgh Press*. (03/25)

NOW staged demonstrations at local telephone companies in 15 cities across the country, protesting AT&T's discriminatory practices toward women in hiring, promotions, fringe benefits and executive appointments. The demonstrations also protested Southern Bell's handling of the Lorena Weeks case. NOW chapters in Boston, New York, Pittsburgh, Bethlehem, (PA), Miami, Chicago, Huntsville,(AL), Milwaukee, Youngstown, (OH), St. Louis, New Orleans, Albuquerque, Houston, Los Angeles and Seattle participated in the action which was coordinated nationally by Dr. JoAnn Evansgardner of Pittsburgh NOW. (03/29)

Ti-Grace Atkinson was physically attacked by Patricia Buckley Bozell (William F. Buckley's sister) in response to Atkinson's criticism of the Catholic Church's attitudes towards women. Atkinson, was a former president of New York NOW.

The Chicago Chapters of NOW and the ACLU filed complaints with the EEOC against five Chicago daily newspapers which persisted in printing sex-segregated "Help Wanted" ads. (04)

The Backlash

Beer tycoon Joseph Coors sent his aide, Jack Wilson, to Washington, D. C. to investigate projects that he might support that advanced his very conservative views. Coors met Paul Weyrich when Weyrich was a press aide to Senator Gordon Allot of Colorado. Weyrich became Coors unofficial agent in Washington.

From 1971 to 1974, Coors contributed funds to organizations that were not as effective as Coors and Weyrich envisioned. They established Analysis and Research, Inc. in Washington, D.C. as a political research entity. (01/15) The group failed to attract other supporters.

YEAR	1971
U. S. President	Richard M. Nixon
NOW President	Aileen Hernandez

EVENTS

The National Women's Political Caucus (NWPC) was organized at a conference attended by some 2,000 women; 40% of the attendees were NOW members. The objective of the Caucus was to field women candidates, to influence both parties to support women, and to organize women at the state and local levels, based on the development of local caucuses. Among the orga-

nizers were Bella Abzug, Gloria Steinem, Shirley Chisholm and Betty Friedan. (07/10)

President Nixon ordered limits on the freedom of military physicians to perform abortions on military bases by requiring them to observe the laws of the states in which they were based. (04/03)

NOW's Legal Defense and Education Fund (NOW LDEF) received tax-exempt status from the Internal Revenue Service. (05/24)

ISSUES

LifeStyles

President Nixon announced his opposition to abortion at any time during pregnancy based on his "personal and religious beliefs." (04/03)

Education

NOW conducted a write-in campaign to the New York Legislature for a child care tax deduction. (03/31)

The New York NOW Chapter published a 55-page, "Report of Sex Bias in the Public Schools." (04/21)

Economic

NOW urged the Department of Health, Education and Welfare (HEW), to require goals and time-tables for women graduate students on the grounds that acceptance to graduate school is a pre-condition for employment at that level. The issue was referred to the Department of Labor which decided against their inclusion. (04)

In a class-action suit the Professional Women's Caucus sued every law school in the U.S. receiving federal funds because of discrimination against women. (03/26)

Legal

New York NOW formed a "Baby Carriage Brigade" for a demonstration in support of Elizabeth Barrett, a widow who was fighting in the U.S. tax courts defending her right to deduct child care expenses. Their slogan: "Are Children As Important As Martinis?"

Political

A U.S. House subcommittee opened hearings on the Equal Rights Amendment, the first hearings in that legislative body since 1948. (03/24)

A Louis Harris poll found that 42% of women "favor efforts to strengthen and change women's status in society" while 43% opposed those efforts. Among Black women, the poll showed 62% approved and only 20% opposed. (05/20)

Twenty days after NOW's nationwide demonstration, Southern Bell surrendered when the U.S. District Court ordered the company to pay Lorena Weeks $30,761 in back pay and made the job title of switchman effective from April 24, 1966. Bell attorneys signed the order which also provided Weeks with pension credits. The U.S. Circuit Judge who signed the court order was Griffin B. Bell, who became U.S. Attorney General in 1976. (04/19)

Speaking before more than 300 corporate personnel executives at the first conference on "Equal Pay and Promotion: Corporate Affirmative Action Programs for Women Employees" sponsored by the Urban Research Corporation of Chicago, NOW's National President Aileen Hernandez disclosed that NOW planned to file suit against the Secretary of Labor, the Secretary of Defense, and the Director of the Office of Federal Contract Compliance (OFCC) for not enforcing Executive Order 11246, as amended – *unless* they met the July 30 deadline for issuing regulations on sex discrimination and guidelines for affirmative action goals and timetables for federal contractors. Doris Wooten of the OFCC, who spoke later , declared that the OFCC "had every intention" of making the deadline. (05/13-14)

Los Angeles NOW adopted a resolution declaring lesbianism a "legitimate concern of feminism" after a series of "rap" meetings at the Los Angeles NOW Center extending over some months in which both gays and straights participated. (05/18)

NOW filed charges with the U.S. Department of Labor under Executive Order 11246 and 11375 against the U.S. public school system, elementary and secondary, to draw attention to the denial of equal opportunity in employment for women teachers. The complaint pointed out that 78% of all elementary school principals in the U.S. and 96% of all secondary school principals were male, though men constituted only 15.4% of the elementary teachers and slightly over 50% of the secondary level teachers, while women were 67.6% of all public school teachers. (Teachers and school administrators were specifically exempted from coverage of the Equal Pay Act of 1963 and Title VII of the Civil Rights Act of 1964). (05)

At a NOW national board meeting, Western Regional Director Shirley Bernard, Aileen Hernandez, Wilma Scott Heide and PR Vice President Lucy Komisar.

Three young women–Julie Price, Paulette Desell and Ellen McConnell–were finally approved as pages for the U.S. Senate by unanimous vote. They had been nominated by Senators Percy, Javits and Harris in December and January, but the Senate's sergeant-at-arms had refused to swear them in until the Rules Committee directed him to do so. (05/13)

The Backlash

Father Michael Collins, pastor of St. Barbara's Church in Santa Ana (CA) urged his Democratic parishioners to switch parties because of the California Democratic Party's position on abortion. A few days later, a Roman Catholic assemblyman, Joe A. Gonsalves, a fellow opponent of abortion law liberalization, nevertheless strenuously objected to this fusion of church and state.

YEAR	1971
U. S. President	Richard M. Nixon
NOW President	Wilma Scott Heide

EVENTS

At the National NOW Conference in September, Wilma Scott Heide was elected President and Muriel Fox, chair of the National Board. The conference passed historic resolutions on lesbianism "as a legitimate concern of feminism," voluntarism, and the double oppression of minority women. (09/03-06)

The 26th Amendment to the Constitution, giving 18-year-olds the right to vote, was ratified. (06/30)

In Washington, D.C., more than 7,000 people demonstrating against the Vietnam War were arrested. (05/03)

The U.S. Supreme Court by a vote of 6-3 said the the *N.Y. Times, Washington Post* and other newspapers could resume publication of *The Pentagon Papers*, a secret study of the U.S. involvement in the Vietnam War. (06/30)

ISSUES

LifeStyles

During Congressional hearings on discrimination against women, Rep. Martha Griffiths (D-MI) testified that in Virginia in 1970, 21,000 women and no men were turned down for admission to state schools. (09)

Education

NOW protested the Department of Health, Education and Welfare's (HEW) handling of individual complaints of discrimination against universities under Executive Order 11246 and its lack of communication with women's groups though it maintained full communication with academic institutions. NOW was invited to comment on HEW's proposed policy guidelines for affirmative action for the universities. (06)

Economic

Media

Legal

The California Court of Appeal ruled that a woman could obtain an abortion in any licensed California hospital if her doctor judged the operation was required to preserve her physical and mental health. The court's 2-1 decision struck down the the 1967 California Therapeutic Abortion law's requirement that every abortion receive advance approval by a hospital committee of physicians. (07/22)

The ERA in its original form (without a series of amendments that NOW and other women's organizations had been working to oppose) passed the House of Representatives by a vote of 354-23. (10/12)

Political

Led by Pennsylvania NOW chapters, Pennsylvania added a state ERA to its constitution by a large margin in a statewide referendum. (05)

NOW Annual Budget $42,000

Dr. David Harris, speaking to the annual meeting of the American Public Health Association, said that the maternal death rate in New York City had been cut by half since the state's abortion law was liberalized. (10/12)

By a vote of 50-32, the U.S. Senate approved an $18 billion higher education bill, but turned back an attempt to bar sex discrimination in public undergraduate and graduate school admissions, ruling that the amendment was "not germaine." (09)

NOW launched a campaign against National Airlines' offensive advertising campaign: "I'm Cheryl, Fly me to Miami." New York NOW picketed National's advertising agency. (10)

The first of a flood of books on women's issues began to appear, including *Sexual Politics* by Kate Millet, *Revolt of the Second Sex* by Julie Ellis, *The Bold New Women* by Barbara Allen Wasserman, which included Vivian Gornick's moving essay, "The Next Great Moment In History Is Ours," and *Woman Power, The Movment for Women's Liberation* by Celestine Ware. American photographer Diane Arbus, 48, died. (07/26)

Photographer Margaret Bourke-White died of Parkinson's disease. For three decades, she photographed the historic events, people and places ranging from the Dust Bowl, to the horrors of Buchenwald. (08/27)

NOW initiated a campaign in support of the Mondale-Javits Comprehensive Child Care Act. The legislation called for a new national child development pro-gram costing $7 billion annually within several years. It's pas-sage by Congress initiated a behind-the-scenes battle at the White House where then Budget and Management Director, George P. Schultz (later Reagan's Secretary of State), urged Nixon to veto the bill. (11/01)

Success finally crowned NOW's two-year campaign to have sex discrimination included in the guidelines for Federal contractors when Secretary of Labor J. D. Hodgson finally issued Revised Order #4. It required Federal contractors to devise and implement affirmative hiring and promotion programs with goals and timetables for women. (12/02)

As NOW testified at FCC hearings on an AT&T request for a rate increase, the EEOC filed a 23,000- page report with the FCC charging that AT&T was "without doubt the largest oppressor of women workers in the U.S." (12/01)

By unanimous decision, the U.S. Supreme Court found in *Reed v. Reed* that an Idaho law giving arbitrary preference to men as executors of estates could not be allowed to "stand in the face of the 14th Amendment" and was unconstitutional. This was the first time the Supreme Court invoked the 14th Amendment to overturn a distinction based on sex, but the Court clearly stopped short of making all laws incorporating sex bias "inherently suspect" as if had on racial issues. Feminist attorney Ruth Bader Ginsburg argued the case before the U.S. Supreme Court. (11/22)

The Backlash

The synod of Roman Catholic Bishops recommended that Pope Paul establish a pontifical commission on the role of women in church and society. (11)

In New York, a Roman Catholic law professor and abortion opponent was appointed guardian for a fetus in order to prevent its abortion. (12/04)

President Nixon vetoed the Comprehensive Child Care Act which NOW and a coalition of feminists and child care advocates had lobbied, nursed, and coerced through Congress. In his veto message, written by Pat Buchanan, Nixon described it as "the most radical piece of legislation to emerge from the 92nd Congress" and said it would

"commit the vast moral authority of the national government to the side of communal approaches to child-rearing" and "would lead to the Sovietization of American children." (12/09)

YEAR	1972
U. S. President	Richard M. Nixon
NOW President	Wilma Scott Heide

EVENTS

President Nixon made his historic visit to Red China, the first visit ever made by a U.S. President to that country. (02/28)

Dr. Juanita Kreps was elected the first female governor of the New York Stock Exchange. (02/20)

Rep. Shirley Chisholm was the first Black woman to run for the U.S. presidency in the primary of one of the two major parties. She was endorsed by NOW and NOW members worked to organize her campaign in many states.

The Equal Rights Amendment passed the U.S. Senate by a vote of 84-8 and was sent to the states for ratification–a major victory for NOW, Business and Professional Women (BPW), the National Woman's Party and other feminist organizations. (03/22)

ISSUES

LifeStyles

The American Civil Liberties Union (ACLU) allocated $32,000 for a project on women for the first time in its history. A program on women was arranged for the Board by a Director, Faith Seidenberg, who was a past vice President of NOW. Chairone and later President of NOW, Wilma Scott Heide, participated in the presentation. One of the functions of the project was to assemble information on unjust laws against women and other unfair practices. (01)

Education

Economic

Vermont's abortion law was invalidated by the state's Supreme Court in the case of *Beecham v. Leahy*. (01)

Michigan NOW demanded $91 million in back pay for Michigan Bell employees, the wages they lost because of sex discrimination. (01/20)

Media

Ms. Magazine, made its debut in a preview issue with Gloria Steinem as editor and Pat Carbine as publisher.

The FCC granted NOW's petition that affirmative action programs for women be a condition for the renewal of a station's broadcast license. The new guidelines followed a NOW proposal which required stations to file specific affirmative action programs with the FCC on the employment of women. (02/04)

Legal

In *Eisenstadt v. Baird,* a Massachusetts statute restricting the distribution of contraceptives to unmarried persons was invalidated by the U.S. Supreme Court as a violation of the rights of single persons under the equal protection clause of the 14th Amendment. (03)

Political

200 NOW chapters
Membership – 5800

The Florida Supreme Court overturned its old abortion law and gave the state legislature 60 days to pass a new one. The legislature passed one which made the principal criteria the woman's physical and mental health, grave physical deformity or mental retardation of the fetus, or in the case of rape or incest. (02/14)

In a well-publicized national media action against AT&T, local chapters of NOW across the country presented a lump of coal in a Christmas stocking –the traditional holiday gift for naughty children–to local Bell System affiliates because of their failure to end sex discrimination in company policies and practices. (01/03)

The U.S. Census Bureau revised 52 sexist job titles under NOW pressure.

The Connecticut Liquor Control Commission revoked the liquor license for Mory's, the tavern celebrated in the "Whiffenpoof Song," because the tavern refused to serve women. The action was filed by attorney Kathryn Emmet on behalf of Yale faculty members, students, alumni, and five women. (01/31)

New Jersey's abortion law was struck down by a three judge federal district court on grounds it was unconstitutionally vague and contravened the First, Ninth, and Fourteenth Amendments. (02)

The League of Women Voters endorsed the ERA after a campaign led within the League by NOW President Wilma Scott Heide and NOW activists within the League's leadership. The endorsement came after the Senate vote sent the amendment to the states for ratification.

Following early NOW efforts, the EEOC issued guidelines stating that pregnancy and related disorders must be treated the same as other temporary disabilities, allowing pregnant employees to be granted leaves of absence and entitlement to reinstatement without loss of seniority and other benefits when they returned to work. (03)

The Rochester (NY) Junior Chamber of Commerce chapter, second largest in the nation, was suspended by the national organization for admitting women to its membership. The chapter had 750 members, of which 4 were women. (02/25)

The Equal Employment Opportunity Act of 1972 passed Congress. This law empowered the EEOC to take legal actions in federal courts to enforce Title VII of the Civil Rights Act of 1964, an enlargement of the EEOC's power that NOW had lobbied for intensively. (03/24)

A U.S. District Court in Pennsylvania ruled that a fetus is not a "person" or "citizen" within the meaning of the Fourteenth Amendment or the Civil Rights Act, and therefore not entitled to the legal rights and protections they confer. The case was *McGarvey v. Magee-Women's Hospital.* (03)

Two presidential candidates, Rep. Shirley Chisholm (D-NY) and Senator George McGovern (D-SD) refused invitations to attend the Gridiron Club's annual dinner on April 8 because the prestigious journalism club excluded women from membership. "Gentlemen of the Gridiron Club," replied Ms. Chisholm in a statement, "guess who's not coming to dinner!" (02/23)

The Backlash

For the first time, Phyllis Schlafly attacked the Equal Rights Amendment in her newsletter, *The Phyllis Schlafly Report,* and formed a new organization called "Stop ERA." (02)

The Catholic Bishops Committee for Pro-Life Activities was established.

Judge Francis X. Smith served an injunction on New York Municipal Hospitals, barring them from performing abortions. The injunction had been sought by Robert Byrn, bachelor law professor and chairman of the New York Right to Life group who had earlier persuaded Judge Lester Holtzman to appoint him guardian of all four to 24 week old fetuses. (01/05)

In an effort to take over the organization, Coors funded the Robert Schuchman Foundation. The Schuchman board balked at Coors' plans for lobbying and political action, fearing they would lose their tax exempt status.

61

YEAR	1972
U. S. President	Richard M. Nixon
NOW President	Wilma Scott Heide

EVENTS

Alabama Governor George Wallace survived an assassination attempt made as he spoke at a presidential campaign rally, but a bullet wound in the spine would confine him to a wheelchair for life. The gunman, Arthur Bremer, was seized moments after firing the shots. (05/16)

MY CONSCIOUSNESS IS FINE — IT'S MY PAY THAT NEEDS RAISING

In a 5-4 decision, the U.S. Supreme Court ruled that the death penalty as usually enforced represented cruel and unusual punishment and was therefore unconstitutional. (06/29)

A jury in California found Black activist Angela Davis not guilty of murder, kidnapping and conspiracy charges. (06/04)

ISSUES

Lifestyles
Economic
Education
Media
Political

Fewer than one out of every 25 women graduating from Stanford University (CA) in June, 1972, expected to be a full-time homemaker in 1977, according to a survey released by the university. This contrasted sharply with a survey from 1965 when 70% of Stanford women planned not to work at all when their children were under six, and only 43% intended to work full time when their children were over 12. Only 3% of the 1972 grads planned to stop working when their husband finished school, and only 7% said they would stop work to raise children. Only 18.5% of the women mentioned the role of wife and mother as part of their main activities in the next five years. (06)

Joseph Lash won the Pulitzer Prize National Book Award for *Eleanor and Franklin.* (04/13)

NOW filed a petition to deny the license renewal of WABC-TV, New York, because of discrimination against women. This was the first petition filed solely on behalf of women and was also the first to charge Fairness Doctrine violations throughout all programming and commercials. (05/01)

As a result of reforms that encouraged state delegations to include women, members of minority groups, and young people, women were 40% of the delegates at the Democratic Party's convention in Miami Beach, FL, triple the 13% present in 1968 and constituted a large voting bloc. The convention was one of the most open and truly representative in U.S. history. (07/10-13)

Mother Courage, the first feminist restaurant in America opened its doors at 342 West 11 Street in New York City's Greenwich Village. The owners were two activists, Jill Ward, an organizer of the 1970 Women's Equality March on 5th Avenue, and Dolores Alexander, a former reporter and executive director of NOW. For the next five years, the restaurant served as a kind of salon for feminists from around the world. ((05)

Ann Arbor, MI, passed legislation outlawing discrimination based on sexual orientation in the areas of employment, housing, and public accommodations. (07)

In a major victory for NOW and other feminist groups, Congress passed the Education Amendments of 1972, including Title IX, introduced by Rep. Edith Green (D-OR), which prohibited sex discrimination in educational institutions that receive federal funds. If an institution did not comply with the law, the government might delay awards of money, revoke current awards, or debar institutions from eligibility for future awards. Also, the Department of Justice might bring suit at HEW's request. Title IX applied to all schools: kindergartens, pre-schools, junior and community colleges, four-year colleges, universities and graduate and professional schools and private institutions if they accepted federal funds. Exemptions were made for religious organizations to the extent that anti-discrimination provisions conflicted with their religions' tenets and for military schools training individuals for the U.S. military. (06/23)

For the first time, women became floor reporters at political conventions, as Catherine Mackin of NBC and Elizabeth Drew of Public Television covered the Democratic Convention. (07/10-13)

The Equal Pay Act of 1963 was extended to cover executive, administrative and professional personnel, a goal that NOW and other feminist organizations had sought. (07/01)

NOW's work in showing that women were either omitted or stereotyped in school textbooks began to have results. A leading publisher of textbooks, Scott Foresman and Co., published a booklet entitled *Guidelines for Improving the Image of Women in Textbooks.* "Sexism," the booklet stated, "refers to all those attitudes and actions which relegate women to a secondary and inferior status in society. Textbooks are sexist if they omit the actions and achievements of women, if they demean women by using patronizing language, or if they show women only in stereotyped roles with less than the full range of human interests, traits, and capabilities."

The second issue of *Ms. Magazine* went into the mail at one dollar a copy and offered essays by Kate Millet and Angela Davis, fiction by Alice Walker. (07/15)

NOW and the Urban League filed a class-action suit against General Mills for sex and race discrimination. (07/26)

Pittsburgh NOW chapters led by JoAnn Evansgardner, Ellie Smeal, and Kathy Bonk threatened to challenge the license renewals of area TV stations and were successful in reaching a negotiated settlement with them on women's employment and programming. (08/01)

Four NOW chapters and other feminist groups filed a second major petition to deny the license renewal of WRC-TV in Washington, D.C. (08/21)

At the Republican Party Convention in Miami, women were 30% of the delegates, nearly double the 17% they comprised in 1968. (08/22)

The Backlash

Midge Decter, high priestess of neo-conservatism and wife of Norman Podhoretz (described as a "mandarin general in the neo-conservative camp"), produced a diatribe against the feminist movement in a book entitled, *The New Chastity and Other Arguments Against Women's Liberation.*

The American Jewish Committee addressed a letter to the candidates of both parties asking for their position on racial, sexual and ethnic "quotas." (08)

Mounting a defense by going on the offensive and seeking to exploit the American Jewish Committee's position to his own political advantage, President

Nixon attacked Democratic Party reforms in his acceptance speech at the Republican Convention. He triggered a backlash against statistical targets for the inclusion of women, Blacks and other minorities in affirmative action programs in American industry, labeling them with the perjorative code word "quotas" rather than "goals." (08/23)

YEAR	1972
U. S. President	Richard M. Nixon
NOW President	Wilma Scott Heide

EVENTS

Richard Nixon was re-elected in a landslide–60.7% of the vote–against Democrat George McGovern, whose complaints about a break-in at Democratic National Committee offices in the Watergate were ignored. (11/08)

SUPPORT THE E.R.A.

"Equality of rights under the law shall not be denied or abridged by the United States or by any State on account of sex"

By the end of the year, 22 states had ratified the Equal Rights Amendment: (in alphabetical order) Alaska, California, Colorado, Delaware, Hawaii, Idaho, Iowa, Kansas, Kentucky, Maryland, Massachusetts, Michigan, Nebraska, New Hampshire, New Jersey, New York, Pennsylvania, Rhode Island, Tennessee, Texas, West Virginia and Wisconsin.

ISSUES

Education

AT&T and the General Services Administration (GSA) held a press conference to announce a "sweetheart" agreement that amounted only to a promise by AT&T to employ and promote more women and minorities. NOW Legislative Vice President Ann Scott interrupted their press conference to attack the agreement, reading aloud and distributing a press release listing the agreement's deficiencies. (09/20)

Economic

NOW, the NAACP, the Mexican American Defense Fund and the Women's Legal Defense Fund filed a formal protest with the Office of Federal Contract Compliance about the AT&T/GSA agreement because, among other deficiencies, it made no provisions for award of back pay, provided no goals or timetables and perpetuated the Bell System's discriminatory wage transfer policy that would continue to penalize women and minorities.(10/02)

Religion

Women theologians called for the "castration of sexist religion" at the largest and most prestigous gathering of biblical scholars in history, the American Academy of Religion, meeting at the Century Plaza hotel in Los Angeles. Dr. Mary Daly, noted Catholic theologian of Boston College, told a seminar of women that historic sexist religion had led to patriarchal institutions whose teachings had amounted to "a gang rape of our minds." (09/02)

Media

Legal

Detroit NOW announced the successful settlement reached with WXYZ-TV, the Detroit ABC-owned and operated station that provided for improvements in the employment of women, prime-time programming directed at feminist issues and goals, and a Woman's Advisory Council to the stations. The station also agreed to prohibit sexism in its overall programming.(09/07)

Political

NOW President Wilma Scott Heide, Legislative Vice President Ann Scott, and Dr. Sally Hacker, coordinator of NOW's National Task Force on AT&T, met with AT&T President Robert D. Lilley and Vice President for Human Resources Development David Easlick to discuss NOW's objections to the AT&T/GSA agreement. In one exchange during the meeting, President Lilley said that the corporation had a firm position on the issue of back pay that amounted to "an emotional hang-up." Ann Scott responded, "So do we." (10/25)

Mandatory pregnancy leave statutes, regulations, and policies were challenged in several cases. Those which were successful were: *Doe v. Osteopathic Hospital of Wichita, Inc.* 333 F. Supp. 1357 (Kansas); *Bravo v. Board of Education*, 345 F. Supp. 155 (Illinois); *Heath v. Westerville Board of Education*, 345 F. Supp. 501 (Ohio); *La Fleur v. Cleveland Board of Education*, 465 F. 2nd 1184 (Ohio); *Pocklington v. Duval County School Board*, 345 F. Supp. 438 (California); *Williams v. San Francisco Unified School District 340*, F. Supp. 438 (California); *Robinson v. Rand*, 340 F. Supp. 37 (Col-

Six states had Equal Rights Amendments to their state constitutions on their ballots. All six states voted to adopt the amendment. In Maryland, the vote was 2-1 in favor; in Hawaii, 6-1; New Mexico, 2-1; Colorado, 3-1; and Texas, 4-1. In Washington, the ERA was 10,000 votes behind before the absentee ballots were counted. After they were counted, the state ERA passed by 3,000 votes! (11/07)

For the first time, a girl won a local Soap Box Derby. Upon winning, she apologized.

National NOW initiated action against sexism in elementary school textbooks. *Dick and Jane as Victims*, issued by New Jersey NOW Task Force, was a 78-page booklet that used 15 of the most widely-employed series of readers as sources to analyze the sex-role stereotyping pervasive in school books. (12/07)

A two-part story line in which TV's "Maude" (Bea Arthur), a 47-year old grandmother, found herself with a late-life, pregnancy and opted for abortion was shown on CBS. Produced by Norman Lear, "Maude's Dilemma" was carried by all but two of CBS' nearly 200 affiliates. It attracted some 7,000 letters of protest. (11/14-21)

Elizabeth Holtzman (D-NY) defeated anti-ERA, anti-feminist Emanuel Celler. She and 14 other women were elected to the U.S. House of Representatives (nine were incumbents). (11/02)

In 1970 New York NOW members had marched to the Brooklyn apartment of Rep. Emanuel Cellers to ask him to hold hearings on the Equal Rights Amendment.

The Backlash

Jesse Helms (R-NC) was elected to the U.S. Senate.

Pope Paul VI, spurning appeals from cardinals and feminist groups alike, barred women from even the smallest formal role in the ministry of the Roman Catholic Church. In a *motu propio* (a decree by his own hand), the Pope ruled that though women could continue to read the Bible during Mass and perform some altar ser-

vices, as local needs required, they could never claim that performing such duties was a right. "In accordance with the venerable tradition of the Church," he wrote, "installation in the ministries of lector and acolyte is reserved to men." (09/14)

YEAR	1973
U. S. President	Richard M. Nixon
NOW President	Wilma Scott Heide

EVENTS

For the first time in 24 years, the U.S. Senate had no women members. Sen. Margaret Chase Smith of Maine, who had served since January 3, 1949, was defeated in her re-election bid in November 1972. (01/20)

Justice Harry A. Blackmun wrote the decision in *Roe v. Wade* (see below) legalizing abortion. He was appointed to the U.S. Supreme Court by President Nixon, a third choice after two previous nominees, Clement Haynsworth and Harrold Carswell, failed to be confirmed by the Senate due to a successful campaign by civil rights groups. (01/22)

An official cease-fire agreement was signed in Paris effectively ending the U.S. role in combat in the Vietnam War. An end to the military draft was announced on the same day. (01/27)

ISSUES

Lifestyles

NOW won the first sex discrimination complaint against a university: *Johnson v. U. of Pittsburgh.*

Education

NOW began a campaign across the country for enforcement of Title IX which had been passed in June 1972. The Office of Civil Rights and HEW had delayed time after time in preparing guidelines for the enforcement of Title IX in schools. (01/01)

Economic

In another coordinated national action to keep public pressure on AT&T, NOW chapters all over the country presented their local Bell System affiliates with a "bill" for $4 billion in back wages that NOW calculated its employees had lost as a result of discrimination. (01/03)

Media

In a small park across the street from the U.S. Supreme Court, NOW members, dressed in judicial robes, conducted a mock session of the Court. The skit dramatized what the Court would be like if it were composed exclusively of women interpreting the laws that applied to men's lives. The NOW justices were: Jo Ann Evansgardner, Roberta Benjamin, Muriel Fox, Jacqui Ceballos, Wilma Scott Heide (as Chief Justice), Karen De Crow, Nola Claire, Dorothy Haener and Toni Carabillo. (02/16)

Legal

Political

At its national convention, the YWCA voted to lobby for the ERA, reversing a position the 2.4 million member organization had held for 48 years.

A U.S. Supreme Court decision in *Roe v. Wade* declared invalid all state laws that restricted abortion in the first three months of pregnancy, grounding the decision on the right to privacy. According to the Court, the decision in the first trimester of pregnancy was to be left to the woman and her doctor. During the second trimester of pregnancy, the states could regulate the abortion procedure only in a manner reasonably related to the states' interest in protecting the health of the woman. In roughly the third trimester, after viability of the fetus, the states could regulate or even prohibit abortion except when necessary to save the life or health of the woman. On the same day, in *Doe v. Bolton*, the Court struck down procedures required by statute that created unnecessary obstacles for a woman who sought an abortion. (01/22)

AT&T signed a $38 million agreement with the Department of Labor and EEOC, the largest job discrimination settlement in the nation's history. It provided that AT&T and its 24 operating companies make one-time lump-sum payments totaling $15 million to 15,000 workers the EEOC found were victims of "pervasive and systemic" discrimination. An additional $23 million per year was allocated for wage adjustments aimed at elevating women and minority males to equal standing with white males in similar jobs. It also provided for new hiring practices aimed at getting more men as operators and clerks and more women into outside craft jobs, and a broadening of management opportunities. (01/18)

Eight women were selected by the Navy for flight training, in a test program to assess the feasibility of assigning women to flying duties. (01)

NOW protested Jaycees' sexism at the Tulsa, OK, headquarters of the Junior Chamber of Commerce. NOW stated that while the Jaycees purport to develop leadership in community service, its membership is limited to men, which wrongly utilizes its tax-exempt status and consciously violates the law and spirit of the American commitment to equality. (02/19)

The NOW Task Force on Sexuality and Lesbianism was established two years after the NOW membership, at its national conference in Los Angeles, adopted a resolution stating that "a woman's right to her own person includes the right to define and express her own sexuality and to choose her own lifestyle."

Emily Howell of Denver became a second officer for Frontier Airlines, flying Boeing 737 jets. She was the first woman pilot employed in that capacity by a regularly scheduled commercial airline. In June 1973, Bonnie Tibursi became the first female pilot with American Airlines when she began her three-year training program for co-pilot duties. (02)

NOW protested a dinner honoring former Reps. Celler and McCullock, who had opposed civil rights for women of all races, opposing Title VII of the 1964 Civil Rights Act and the Equal Rights Amendment in Congress. NOW's position was that even though these men had had relatively good records pertaining to civil rights for Blacks, racism and sexism are still closely related, although each issue has unique dimensions.(01/29)

The Backlash

On the West coast, Helen Andelin, author of a book called *Fascinating Womanhood* (originally published in 1963), which was used by the Mormon Church as a kind of handbook to train its women as "domestic goddesses," emerged as a spokeswoman against the Equal Rights Amendment and the feminist movement.

The National Committee for a Human Life Amendment was established.

The Society for a Christian Commonwealth, a conservative Catholic lay organization, called for the excommunication of Justice William Brennan, Jr. for his pro-choice views in the *Roe v. Wade* decision. (01/26)

Joseph Coors funded the formation of The Heritage Foundation, later to become the "think tank" of the Reagan Administration.

Lottie Beth Hobbs founded the Pro-Family Forum in Texas, an anti-abortion, anti-ERA group. Hobbs was also a vice president of the Eagle Forum.

YEAR	1973
U. S. President	Richard M. Nixon
NOW President	*Wilma Scott Heide*

EVENTS

Anne Armstrong was appointed by President Nixon to the Cabinet as counselor to the President, the first woman to hold such a position. One of her duties was to coordinate the appointment of women to federal posts. (02/01)

The U.S. House of Representatives appointed its first female page. (05/31)

President Nixon, in his human resources message to Congress said the administration "will continue" to support ratification of the [Equal Rights) amendment ". . . so that American women. . .need never again be denied equal opportunity." However, the administration did not go all out for ratification, because of an alleged fear that if the White House pressed

aggressively for ratification, it might generate more opposition to the amendment on the ground that the President was overstepping his authority. The White House limited its support to some telephone calls, telegrams, and an occasional speech by an administration figure, such as Jill Ruckelshaus. (03/01)

ISSUES

Lifestyles

Economic

Religion

Legal

Political

NOW voted at the 6th National Conference to support workers in the Farah boycott, and the farm workers' iceberg lettuce boycott. In other actions at the conference in Washington, D.C., NOW established a Task Force on Rape, and a Task Force on Older Women. Resolutions called for a $2.50 minimum wage, decriminalization of prostitution, and divorce law reform. Theme of conference, "Tomorrow Is NOW," was also the title of the last book written by Eleanor Roosevelt. NOW voted at the national conference to "condemn the policies of the Nixon administration as not being in the interest of minorities." Members voted resolutions calling for changes in welfare programs, and the establishment of a Committee on Women in Poverty. (02/16-19)

NOW action: "I Gave Blood for the ERA" Day. A resolution of the NOW National Board recommended that NOW chapters and members have a "Blood For The Equal Rights Amendment" day in their communities and sell their blood to raise money to help finance the campaign to pass the ERA. Persons unable to do so were urged to donate $10 to the "Blood for the ERA Fund." Chapters all over the country participated in the action. (02/05)

The U.S. Government Printing Office agreed to accept "Ms." as an optional title for women in government publications. (02)

NOW chapters in New York City joined 1,000 demonstrators at the New York HEW headquarters to protest proposed federal regulations that would end day care for many recipients. (03/07)

Arkansas formally adopted as a state policy the availability of "all medically acceptable contraceptive procedures, supplies and information. . . through legally recognized channels to each and every person desirous of the same, regardless of sex, race, age, income, number of children, marital status, citizenship or motive." (03/07)

Physicians could legally prescribe contraceptives to unwed, unemancipated minors without parental consent, according to an opinion issued by the Attorney General of Missouri, John Danforth. (03/09).

Corrine C. (Lindy) Boggs of Louisiana was elected to the House of Representatives to fill the vacancy caused by the death of her husband, Hale, who was missing and presumed dead in a plane crash in Alaska. (03/21)

The U.S. Supreme Court, in the *Frontiero v. Richardson* decision, ruled that denial of benefits to military husbands was unconstitutional. The court determined that because Frontiero was denied employment benefits under regulations different from those applicable to her male peers, the statute was discriminatory. Sharon Frontiero, an Air Force officer, had sought increased quarters allowances and medical and dental benefits to cover her husband, benefits which automatically went to male officers for their spouses. Ruth Bader Ginsburg argued the case before the Supreme Court. (05/14)

NOW's Task Force on Rape began a campaign to redefine it as a crime of violence against women and to change some of the laws dealing with rape and trials for rape.

The Bank of California settled a lawsuit by NOW and minority groups charging sex and race discrimination. The bank agreed in federal court to a plan by which women and minorities would constitute a majority of its management positions by 1982. The bank also agreed to establish a $225,000 educational development fund to benefit women and minorities. (05/02)

Pope Paul VI appointed 15 women from 13 nations as charter members of a temporary pontifical Commission on Women in the Church and Society. Debbie Schellman, 21, an art student from Atlanta, was the only American member. Although it was announced that a majority of the commission members would be women, American feminists later complained that only 10% of the group's 26 members were female, and they criticized the selection of Schellman. It was announced before the Commission's first meeting in November 1973 that they would not deal with birth control, priesthood for women, or other "doctrinal" issues. In March 1974, the Pope extended the life of the commission to January 1976, to continue it through 1975, the United Nation's Year of the Woman. (05/03)

More than 300 women from 27 countries attended the International Feminist Planning Conference in Cambridge, MA which was organized and sponsored by NOW. The goal of the planning Conference, organized by National Board member Patricia Burnett, was to build an international feminist movement and to organize a full-scale international feminist conference in 1975. (06/01-04)

The Backlash

The National Council of Catholic Bishops warned that Catholics who undergo or perform an abortion "place themselves in a state of excommunication." (02/13)

Eighty six hundred delegates of the Southern Baptist Church in Portland, OR, met at their 116th annual meeting and passed a resolution espousing male

superiority. It read in part: "Man was not made for woman, but the woman for the man. Woman is the glory of man. Woman would not have existed without man." (06)

The National Council of Catholic Women reaffirmed its stand in opposition to the Equal Rights Amendment at its convention in New Orleans. (10)

Education Research Analysts was incorporated as a non-profit. Run by Mel and Norma Gabler out of their Texas home, its purpose was to search textbooks for signs of unpatriotic, anti-Christian or anti-family sentiments and protest the books use before the state textbook committee. Joseph Coors provided funding. 65

YEAR	1973
U. S. President	Richard M. Nixon
NOW President	Wilma Scott Heide

EVENTS

Women's Equality Day, conceived by NOW, and introduced in Congress by Rep. Bella Abzug (D-NY), was confirmed by Congress and the President. Feminist groups took to the parks and streets across the country to celebrate the 53rd anniversary of Women's Suffrage. They also promoted a boycott of Farah Pants because of its discriminatory practices. (08/26)

Billie Jean King defeated Bobby Riggs in a tennis match billed as "The Battle of the Sexes" in the Houston Astrodome. The match was set up after Riggs claimed that even an over-the-hill man could beat any championship class woman. King defeated Riggs in straight sets in the five-set match which was televised nationally. (09/20)

ISSUES

Lifestyles

The United States Tennis Association announced the U.S. Open would award equal prize money to women and men. (07/19)

A Women's Hall of Fame was established at Eisenhower College, Seneca Falls, NY. The first 20 inductees included suffragist Susan B. Anthony, author Pearl Buck, American Red Cross founder Clara Barton, aviator Amelia Earhart, artist Mary Cassatt, poet Emily Dickinson, actress Helen Hayes, singer Marian Anderson, former Sen. Margaret Chase Smith, humanitarian Helen Keller, and former First Lady, Eleanor Roosevelt. (08)

The Coast Guard quietly did away with its regulations requiring separate bathrooms for men and women aboard ships. A spokesman for the Coast Guard confirmed that separate heads no longer are required as long as privacy is maintained. The move apparently was aimed at letting more women work on oceanographic ships. (09/05)

Economic

The first inter-union conference of trade union women was held in Chicago, a pre-cursor to the formation of the Coalition of Labor Union Women (CLUW) (06/30; see also 03/23/74)

Columbia (SC) NOW filed sex discrimination charges with EEOC against the state and the Governor, for discrimination in employment in state jobs. (09/14)

Media

Singer, songwriter Helen Reddy won a Grammy Award for the hit record "I Am Woman," the first explicitly feminist song to become a gold record and unofficial anthem of the feminist movement. It was estimated that seven out of 10 record buyers were women. (07)

NOW chapters demonstrated against the Little League World Series in Pennsylvania. Pittsburgh NOW filed a charge of sex discrimination against the city because Little League games were scheduled in public parks. Pittsburgh had a city ordinance which prohibited sex discrimination in public accommodations. Essex County, NJ, NOW filed charges against the New Jersey Little League, which resulted in hearings by the state's Division on Civil Rights. (08/25)

Members of New York NOW raised a banner with the words "Woman Power" over the public gallery of the American Stock Exchange. They said they were protesting "male domination of the Wall Street empire." (08/23)

Religion

Margaret A. Haywood was elected the first female moderator of the United Church of Christ. An associate justice of the Superior Court of the District of Columbia, she became the first black woman to head a major U.S. denomination. (06/23)

As a result of a campaign against the show organized by the U.S. Catholic Conference, 39 CBS stations refused to carry the re-run of a "Maude" episode in which the 47- year old character finds herself pregnant and eventually opts for abortion. Not one corporate sponsor bought commercial time and there were some 17,000 protest letters.. NOW organized protest campaigns in cities where anti-abortion groups had forced cancellation of the Norman Lear -Bud Yorkin TV show. The episodes attracted 41% of the available audience and CBS estimated that as many as 65 million people watched at least one of the episodes, either first-run or in the re-run. (08/21)

Lorraine K. Potter of Warwick, RI, a minister of the American Baptist church, became the first woman chaplain in the U.S. Air Force and the second woman chaplain in U.S. military history. She was assigned to Lackland AFB, TX. (09)

Conservative Judaism ruled that women could be counted along with men in making up the minimum number for congregational worship. (09/10)

Legal

After a five-year campaign by NOW, and three and a half years of litigation of the NOW complaint, a U.S. Supreme Court ruling prohibited sex-segregated employment advertisements. (06/21)

Political

Doris Wright, a New York NOW Advisory Council member, and Lori Sharpe, New York NOW member, were instrumental in founding the National Black Feminist Organization. (08/15)

Cardiss Collins of Chicago was elected to fill the vacancy in the U.S. House of Representatives caused by the death of her husband, George. She was re-elected in 1974 for a full term. (06/05)

A three judge panel ruled that Louisiana's law which required that women register their desire to serve on a jury with the clerk of court was unconstitutional. (08/31)

NOW participated in forming a 13-member Women's Coalition for the 21st Century, as an alternative to the American Bicentennial Commission which NOW President Wilma Scott Heide described as "undemocratic, political, commercial and anti-feminist." (09/10)

The Backlash

Sen. Jesse Helms (R-NC) introduced an amendment to the Foreign Assistance Act, which prohibited the use of funds for abortion services or research, and for abortifacient drugs and devices (which included menstrual extraction and IUDs). This amendment passed the Senate unanimously. There were no women Senators. (10/02)

A Superior Court Judge in Montesano, WA, ruled that Carol & Delores Darrin and Kathy Tosland, who had won starting positions on the Wishkah High football team could not play. The Washington Interscholastic Activities Association ruled that if Wishkah coach John Clark let the girls play on his team, he would

have to forfeit the game and the school would be subject to sanctions. The girls, supported by the ACLU, challenged the ruling but lost. (10/10)

YEAR	1973
U. S. President	Richard M. Nixon
NOW President	Wilma Scott Heide

EVENTS

Betty Friedan met with Pope Paul VI, who told Friedan: "We want to express our gratitude and appreciation for all you have done for the women of the world." He gave her a medallion of his likeness, and she gave him the women's equality symbol known as the "Brassy," created by NOW National Board Member from Los Angeles, Judith Meuli. (10/24)

The Watergate scandal unfolded throughout the year as Judge John Sirica sentenced the burglars (03/23); top White House aides had to resign (04/30); and the Senate Judiciary Committee conducted televised hearings (05/17); Vice President Agnew also resigned to avoid charges of income tax evasion; Senator Gerald Ford replaced him. (10/12)

ISSUES

Lifestyles

In her new book, *Beyond God the Father*, Dr. Mary Daly outlined a proposed theology for the women's movement, rejecting the symbolic male divinity of Christianity. She called herself a "post-Christian feminist." (10)

Education

A New Jerry court ruled the Little League in New Jersey must admit girls. The ruling followed a suit in which Judith Weis and Essex County NOW helped to refute testimony by Little League witnesses who claimed girls were not physically able to play baseball with boys. There were reports that the Little League intended to appeal the decision to the U.S. Supreme Court. (11/07)

Economic

The Essex County` (NJ) NOW chapter filed charges of sex discrimination against 13 school systems in Essex and Hudson Counties for maintaining sex-segregated courses in home economics and industrial arts classes. Charges were filed in the New Jersey Division of Civil Rights. (11/03)

Religion

NOW organized support for the "Three Marias" jailed in Portugal for writing a feminist book. In its first international action, NOW chapters in Houston, New York, Washington, D.C., Eastern Massachusetts and Los Angeles had demonstrations at Portugese embassies and consulates in their cities. Similar protests were held the same day in France, Belgium, Sweden, Germany and England. The protest actions and petitions were effective in drawing attention to what was considered the first international feminist cause celebre. The Portugese government suddenly postponed the trial of the Marias in a delaying tactic calculated to relieve public pressure and discourage further demonstrations. (The Three Marias were acquitted in 1974.) (07/03)

Media

The September issue of *MS.* suggested that NASA was a male chauvinist bastion that barred qualified women from competing for positions as astronauts.

The New Woman's Survival Catalog was published. Edited by Kirsten Grimstad and Susan Rennie, the book was a directory of women's activities nationwide with emphasis on the various efforts being made to free women from male-dominated social attitudes and over-dependence on men. It contained practical information on divorce, managing money, how to file a job discrimination complaint, and other data intended to help women realize their growing expectations.

Legal

Political

The AFL-CIO reversed its stand opposing the ERA and endorsed its ratification after a campaign led by Ann Scott, NOW Vice President Legislation. (10/26)

365 NOW Chapters, NOW Membership 15,000

Demonstrations against the steel industry were initiated in cooperation with the NOW National Compliance Task Force, chaired by Lynne Darcy, by Chicago NOW and Southwestern Pennsylvania NOW Chapters, when it was learned that the steel companies' plan to correct job discrimination within the industry did not include women. (12/10-14)

NOW Vice President-Public Relations, Toni Carabillo, presented extensive testimony to the National Association of Broadcasters (NAB) Television Code Review Board and the Radio Code Review Board on the image of women and the women's movement in the media and proposed revisions to the codes prepared by Joan Nicholson, National Coordinator of NOW's Image of Women Task Force and Whitney Adams, National Coordinator of NOW's FCC Task Force. The revisions were aimed at establishing stricter guidelines for broadcasters in portraying women in programming and advertising. Joyce Snyder, of New York NOW, was instrumental in arranging NOW's participation in the NAB Code conferences. The NAB Television Code Review Board agreed to the "thrust and spirit" of NOW's changes to the television code and NAB also agreed to revisions of its Radio Code as proposed by NOW. In addition, NAB distributed copies of Toni Carabillo's presentations to all stations subscribing to the radio and television codes. (10/11 & 11/02)

Eight more states–Connecticut, Minnesota, New Mexico, Oregon, South Dakota, Vermont, Washington and Wyoming–ratified the ERA during the year, bringing the total to 30.

The Backlash

The Pacific Legal Foundation was set up by the California Chamber of Commerce to protect business and industry from what they termed costly government regulations, such as affirmative action.

Using the Pacific Foundation as a model, the legal network for the radical right was enlarged with the establishment of the National Legal Center for the Public Interest; Joseph Coors provided funding and served on its board of directors. The National Legal Center began setting up regional legal groups which ultimately included the Connecticut Legal Foundation; the Southeast Legal Foundation; the Mid-America Legal Foundation; and the Mountain States Legal Foundation.

Sexual Suicide by George Gilder, a diatribe against the feminist movement, was published. In it Gilder asserted, "Women domesticate and civilize male nature. They can destroy civilized male identity merely by giving up the role."

67

YEAR	1974
U. S. President	Richard M. Nixon
NOW President	Karen DeCrow

EVENTS

At the Seventh NOW National Conference in Houston, Karen DeCrow was elected president and Judith Lightfoot, chair of the board. Resolutions were passed calling for the impeachment of President Nixon and another calling for the resignation of NASA's administrator because of unfair practices in hiring and promotion of women and minorities and asking for an investigation of NASA's equal employment opportunity program. (05/25-27)

In *Geduldig vs. Aiello* the Supreme Court ruled that excluding pregnancy coverage from the list of compensable disabilities under the California Disability plan did not constitute sex discrimination .

ISSUES

Lifestyles

Columbus, OH, passed an ordinance outlawing discrimination based on sexual orientation in the areas of employment, housing, and public accommodations. (01)

Education

Over 1,000 women attended a New York State Conference on Marriage and Divorce at the Commodore Hotel, New York City, billed as the first such conference in the world. It was sponsored by the New York State Chapters of NOW, with the assistance of the New York State Women's Unit of the Governor's Office in planning the conference. (01/19-20)

Economic

NOW members picketed the U.S. Jaycees national headquarters. Among the picketers was NOW President Wilma Scott Heide, who noted, "The Jaycees accept public funds and public tax advantages yet deny membership to women." (02/14)

Lenore Hershey became editor of the *Ladies Home Journal*. She was only the second woman to hold this position in the magazine's 90-year history. The magazine's top jobs had always been held by men. NOW had earlier protested to the magazine for its stereotyping of women and its insensitivity to the real problems facing women of all ages and occupations. (01)

Media

San Diego (CA) TV station KCST agreed to change its hiring practices after San Diego NOW filed a petition charging discrimination against women. (03)

Mory's Tavern, celebrated in "The Wiffenpoof Song" lost its liquor license because it discriminated against women, a practice it had employed since 1861. The Supreme Court ruled that Mory's failed to meet the legal definition of a club. (02/26)

Legal

Some 1,000 colleges and universities were offering women's studies courses and over 80 had full-fledged women's studies programs, some offering bachelor's degrees in this area of study. A few offered master's degrees in Women's Studies. NOW had earlier formed the Committee to promote Women's Studies. (06)

In the first industry-wide race and sex discrimination settlement, steel companies settled with the Labor Department to give approximately $56 million in back pay and wage adjustments to 386,000 workers in the steel industry. The NOW National Compliance Task Force and several NOW Chapters in Chicago and Southwestern Pennsylvania had previously initiated actions to improve the status of women in the steel industry. In one negotiation session between Pennsylvania NOW and officials of U.S. Steel Co., the officials stated that management policy was to award fringe benefits differ-entially on the basis of sex. When NOW representatives pointed out that this was prohibited by Title VII of the Civil Rights Act, one company officer said, "The law is absurd." (04/15)

After 30 years of covering Washington for United Press International (UPI), Helen Thomas was named White House reporter for UPI. It was the first time a woman had held such a position. (03/05)

Political

Physicist Virginia Carter, Los Angeles NOW President, made a major career switch, and, working with Norman Lear, went on to become the producer of an award-winning documentary.

NOW's National Conference paid special tribute to the Women's Airforce Service Pilots (WASP). The WASP flew 50 million miles during World War II and 38 lost their lives on duty. They received no military benefits and even their burial expenses were paid by their families. The event was part of a campaign to help them win military status from the Defense Department. (05/25-27)

In the second settlement in 16 months involving AT&T, the company signed a $30 million consent decree with the EEOC providing back pay and wage adjustments to management employees who were victims of sex discrimination. AT&T and its 24 operating companies agreed to equalize starting salaries for men and women and guarantee that both sexes would receive equal pay in promotions. It provided that AT&T make one-time lump sum payments totaling $7 million to 7,000 Bell System employees who were discriminated against under the Equal Pay Act of 1963. (05/30)

The Backlash

The "March for Life" was organized for the first time by Nellie Gray with strong backing from Catholic organizations such as the Knights of Columbus.

The U.S. Coalition for Life was set up.

Joseph Coors provided the funds for Paul Weyrich to organize the Committee for the Survival of a Free Congress; Richard Viguerie became the organization's direct mail fundraiser.

Howard W. Phillips and Richard Viguerie established The Conservative Caucus.

YEAR	1974
U. S. President	Richard M. Nixon
NOW President	Karen DeCrow

EVENTS

The first U.S. woman police officer to be killed in the line of duty was Gail Cobb, 24, a Black member of the District of Columbia Metropolitan Police Department, shot pursuing a holdup suspect into a down-town parking garage. The National Association of Chiefs of Police estimated there were 6,694 women among the nation's 266,839 full-time police officers. (09/20)

Forty-three states and the District of Columbia provided unrestricted Medicaid payments for abortions during the first trimester. Thirty-nine states and the District of Columbia paid for all legal abortions under their Medicaid plans. Five of these states did so voluntarily, five by court orders to do so. Two more states provided unrestricted funds for first trimester abortions, while an additional two states had consultation requirements in all three trimesters. (10)

ISSUES

Lifestyles

Proposed guidelines for compliance with Title IX (still too weak), were finally released by HEW for public comment, two years after passage of the legislation and only after much pressure from NOW and other concerned organizations. (06/11)

Education

NOW, in coalition with other women's organizations, helped defeat a proposal by the National Collegiate Athletic Association to narrow the scope of Title IX of the Education Amendments of 1972 by entirely omitting sports from its coverage. (06/11)

Economic

Settling another complaint by NOW and minority organizations, Bank of America agreed to pay $10 million in compensatory salary increases to its women employees, and promised to increase its proportion of women officers from 31% to 40% by the end of 1978, with 5.1% at top management levels. Included as well was a provision for a $3 3/4 million trust fund for self-development programs for women employees, for management training, education, travel, and sabbaticals. (05/31)

Media

Julia Phillips won an Oscar from the American Academy of Motion Picture Arts and Sciences for "The Sting." This was the first Oscar won by a woman as a movie producer. She shared the award with her husband and Tony Bill. Altogether the film won seven Oscars. (04)

Legal

The U.S. Supreme Court ruled against women receiving disability pay for pregnancy leave in a California case stating that "There is no risk from which men are protected and women are not," even though men received compensation for disabilities resulting from vasectomies and prostatectomies. (06/17)

Political

NOW sued the Democratic Party in several states for sex discrimination.

NOW National Board member John Clegg, one of Los Angeles NOW's first male members, died of Hodgkinson's disease while still in his twenties. His wife, Jean Stapleton (not the actress) was L.A. NOW President in the mid-seventies.

Alfred, NY, passed gay rights anti-discrimination ordinance. (05)

St. Paul, MI, passed a gay rights anti-discrimination ordinance. (07)

NOW LDEF won a $90,000 grant for a project to monitor enforcement of Title IX in elementary and secondary schools. (08)

After the first suits were brought by NOW in 1973, Little League Baseball, Inc., a federally chartered organization, announced that girls would be eligible to compete in its 9,000 leagues on an equal basis with boys. At the time of the organization's "voluntary" decision there were 57 lawsuits pending against the Little League because of its "boys only" policy, many of them instituted by chapters of NOW around the country. And Pennsylvania NOW had picketed its

Hearings were held by a Subcommittee of the House Armed Services Committee on a bill which would admit women to the Service Academies. Ann Scott, NOW's vice president/Legislation, testified for the organization in support of the admission of women. (07/16)

The state Council of Massachusetts NOW sponsored a Conference on Rape. Among the 300 people attending from all over the state were medical and legal professionals, legislators, jurists, police and past and potential victims. Massachusetts NOW called for the immediate establishment of a state commission on rape, support for women's groups already working on this crime and for legislative reform. Two bills were submitted to the state legislature, strongly supported and assisted by NOW. (06/22)

In an atmosphere of both celebration and conflict, eleven women, including one NOW activist Betty Bone Schiess, were ordained as the first female priests of the Episcopal Church by four bishops challenging the denomination's rules and practices as well as 2,000 years of male dominance of the Christian priesthood. (07/29)

Catholic nuns adopted a resolution calling upon their church to ordain women as priests. The resolution, approved by about 600 nuns, came at a leadership conference made up of most of the women in top posts in Catholic religious orders. The National Leadership Conference of Women Religious thus became the most prestigious body to call for the ordination of women. (08/29)

RAPE (How to Avoid It And What To Do About It If You Can't), written by Los Angeles NOW members June Bundy Csida and Joseph Csida hit the stands. It was the first book-length, feminist treatment of the shocking facts about the under-reported, under-prosecuted crime against women.

The Fair Housing Act of 1968 was extended to prohibit discrimination based on sex, in addition to the previously prohibited grounds of race, color, religion, and national origin. (08/02)

The Backlash

Militant anti-feminists stormed the speaker's podium of the Michigan House to protest a committee's refusal to rescind ERA. "We'll get rid of the gun control proposal and then I'll blow every one of your heads off," shouted Mrs. Linda Van Steenis. Twenty militants screamed, shook their fists, and then attacked the legislators.

Sergeants-at-arms were called into the chamber to disperse the women and protect the legislators. (07/14)

Textbooks censors Mel and Norma Gabler convinced the Texas State Board of Education to amend the Textbook Proclamation to promote the teaching of creationism. They also filed

163 objections to 10 reading books up for adoption. Seven of the books were rejected and the Texas Board of Education required extensive changes in the the eighth book.

YEAR	1974	
U. S. President	Richard M. Nixon	Gerald Ford
NOW President	Karen DeCrow	

EVENTS

Under a new law signed by Governor Ronald Reagan, any California retail store could sell condoms, but sale by vending machines was still prohibited. In 1973, Ronald Reagan vetoed a bill easing restrictions on the sale of prophylactics because he believed "indiscriminate access to prophylactics would not be in the public interest." (09/26)

Prodded by the threat of impeachment, President Richard Nixon resigned, the first American President in history to do so. (08/08) He was succeeded by Vice President Gerald Ford who later chose Nelson Rockefeller as his Vice President. (08/20) Subsequently, President Ford issued an unconditional pardon for all crimes Nixon may have committed in office. (09/16)

ISSUES

Education

The Educational Equity Act, for which NOW and other feminist organizations had campaigned, passed Congress. The act authorized the Secretary of HEW to develop non-sexist curricula and non-discriminatory vocational and career counseling, sports education, and other programs designed to achieve equity for all students regardless of sex. (08/21)

Economic

In an attempt to portray men and women primarily as people and not as members of opposite sexes, McGraw Hill Book Company issued its "Guidelines for Equal Treatment of the Sexes" to be used in its new books, textbooks, and educational films. NOW from its beginning had filed complaints and protests directed toward publishers for their sexist material, particularly in school books. (09)

NOW filed suit against the city of Chicago for employment discrimination. (11/18)

Religion

Fresno (CA) NOW filed formal petitions to deny the license renewal applications of KMJ-TV and KFSN-TV with the FCC as well as an informal objection to the license renewal of KJEO-TV. The action was taken after negotiations with station management failed to produce agreement with the chapter's recommendations. The challenges were made on the station's failure to: 1) employ women for other than clerical jobs, 2) adequately ascertain needs of women in its service area, and 3) broadcast programs dealing with women's issues. (11)

Media

Legal

Following a suggestion of President Ford, Mary Louise Smith became Chair of the Republican National Committee. A member of the National Women's Political Caucus (NWPC), she was co-chair of the party at the time of her appointment and had a long record of service to the GOP. (09)

Political

The Equal Credit Opportunity Act passed Congress. Equality in credit was a 1972 NOW resolution. The Act covered all agencies which regularly extended credit to individuals, banks, finance companies, department stores, credit card issuers and government agencies. A woman's income or savings had to be counted as equal to a man's in determining eligibility for credit. Credit history of "family accounts" had to be extended to women as well as men. No one could be refused credit on account of sex or marital status. (09/28)

President Gerald Ford, met with women's groups after pressure from NOW and other women's groups for almost two years to secure such a meeting. It was the first time a president of NOW had been invited to the White House. NOW President Karen DeCrow and the presidents of 16 other women's organizations met with Ford for 58 minutes. (09)

The constitutional right to privacy includes the decision whether or not to become pregnant and applies equally to single and married people, a three judge federal district court held in striking down a Wisconsin statute which prohibited the sale of contraceptives to unmarried persons. (11/26)

Eighteen women were elected to the U.S. House of Representatives, an increase of two in spite of the retirement of three female incumbents: Edith Green (D-OR), Martha Griffiths (D-MI) and Julia Butler Hansen (D-WA), and the departure of Ella Grasso (D-CT) who was elected Governor of Connecticut. Grasso became the first woman to be elected governor without having followed her husband into the office. None of the three women nominated by major parties for the U.S. Senate were elected. (11/05)

The National Education Association and four feminist groups (NOW, WEAL, the Federation of Professional Women and American Women in Science) filed a class action lawsuit accusing the government of failing to enforce federal laws banning sex discrimination in education. The organizations sought an order directing the Department of Health, Education and Welfare (HEW), and the Department of Labor to withhold millions of dollars in federal funds from colleges, universities, and public school systems if they discriminated against women teachers and students. (11/26)

The U.S. Court of Appeals for the Ninth Circuit held that the Church Amendment (which permitted institutions receiving federal assistance to refuse to perform sterilizations or abortions on "conscience" grounds) was constitutional, and represented "the government's neutrality in the face of religious differences. The case was *Chrisman v. Sisters of St. Joseph of Peace.* (11/21)

The Gridiron Club voted to admit women, after 89 years as a male-only club. The club, an association of journalists, was well-known for its "roasting" of political figures in Washington, D.C.(12)

By the end of the year, three more states, Maine, Montana, and Ohio, had ratified the ERA, bringing the total to 33.

The Backlash

The National Conservative Political Action Committee, (NCPAC), was established, headed by John T. (Terry) Dolan, a former member of Young Americans for Freedom. NCPAC became the Right's tool for political terrorism.

ALEC, the American Legislative Exchange Council was set up with funds from the Scaife Foundation. The foundation's funds came from the Mellon family. ALEC opposed ratification of the Equal Rights Amendment.

YEAR	1975		
U. S. President	Gerald Ford		
NOW President	Karen DeCrow		

EVENTS

President Ford signed an executive order which established a National Commission on International Women's Year. The government allocated $350,000 to finance the Commission; both Australia and Canada allocated $2 million. During the signing ceremony, President Ford urged the ratification of ERA in 1975. (01/10)

The Vietnam War ended–after 14 years and 56,559 American dead. (01/10)

The first attempt to stop Medicaid abortion funding was defeated. (01)

Margaret Thatcher, 49, was elected leader of Britain's Conservative Party, the first woman to serve in that capacity. (02/11)

ISSUES

Lifestyles

NOW's Older Women Task Force chair, Tish Sommers, coined the phrase "Displaced Homemaker" and defined the problems besetting such women, in the January Older Women Task Force newsletter. (01)

Ann London Scott 1929-1975

Ann Scott, NOW Vice President Legislation, died of cancer on February 17. Scott was a founder of the Buffalo (NY) Chapter of NOW and was elected to the National Board of NOW in 1970. She served as Vice President Legislation from 1971 until her death. She left her work as teacher, scholar and poet at the State University of New York to open NOW's legislative office in Washington, D.C.

Tulsa (OK) NOW filed with EEOC against ten restaurants which refused to hire women in the evenings when the tips were better.

At a meeting with HEW Secretary Caspar Weinberger and 13 national women's groups–including NOW LDEF's PEER project–Weinberger suggested that he preferred to leave final Title IX decisions to the courts and implied that once final regulations were issued, HEW would avoid making policy decisions in order not to "prejudge" the court cases. In February, the group sent him a letter charging him with "clear abdication of HEW's legal responsibility to enforce" Title IX, maintaining that "the statute directs the Executive Departments providing federal educational aid, not the courts, to enforce the law." (01/21)

Education

The Rochester, (MN) NOW chapter filed a class action suit against Sears with the EEOC for firing five full-time saleswomen who Sears said were dismissed as part of cutbacks forced by the poor economy. The saleswomen and NOW believed they were let go because they were near retirement and pension benefits; four of the five were over 55 years old and the fifth was nearing a major boost in profit-sharing benefits.

Economic

Atlanta NOW filed suit with EEOC against three banks– C & S Bank, First National, and Trust Company of Georgia– for sex discrimination in hiring, promotion and training after the chapter had conducted a seven-month study of employment conditions.

Media

The NOW Media Task Force testified against a five year funding of the Corporation for Public Broadcasting (CPB) because of its poor record on women. Testifying before the Communications Subcommittee of the House, Kathleen Bonk, Task Force Chair, also testified against nominees of President Ford to CPB Board of Directors who were up for Senate approval, especially the nomination of Joseph Coors, VP of Coors Brewery, founder of TVN, a politically conservative news service, and a supporter of reactionary causes.

U.S. Circuit Court of Appeals for D.C., in an extraordinary move, ordered the FCC to take action after two and a half years of delay on claims by NOW that WABC-TV (NY) and WRC-TV (DC) were guilty of sex discrimination in programming and employment. The FCC was ordered to act within 60 days or provide the court with a clear statement of the FCC's reason for further delay. The court also dismissed a motion made by the FCC which would have imposed highly technical procedural rules on the petitioner. (01/24)

Legal

The Washington Supreme Court ruled in the case of *Washington v. Koome* that the requirement that an unmarried minor under 18 who is seeking an abortion have the consent of a parent or guardian violated due process and equal protection principles. The Court ruled that it encumbered the minor's right to choose abortion and it discriminated between pregnant women in terms of their right to obtain an abortion. (01/17)

The U.S. Supreme Court ruled that it was unconstitutional for states to deny women equal opportunity for jury service, thus striking down by a vote of 8-1 a Louisiana statute which automatically excluded any woman from jury service unless she applied for it in writing. (01/21)

Political

At a press conference arranged by NOW and Men for ERA in Washington, D.C., NOW President, Karen DeCrow, TV's "M.A.S.H." star Alan Alda, Democratic Party Chair Robert Strauss, and the representative of Republican Party Chair Kathy Plowman expressed strong support for the 1975 campaign to pass the ERA. (02/30)

The Freedom of Information Act became law. NOW began an investigation into government documentation of NOW activities and members by Secret Service, IRS, CIA, Civil Service Commission, FBI, Department of Justice and others. (02/01)

The Backlash

The National Right to Life PAC was organized.

Phyllis Schlafly organized the Eagle Forum. In addition to opposition to the ERA, the organization, which Schlafly described as "the alternative to women's lib," offered a broad agenda that ranged from support of voluntary school prayer, to opposition to busing, federally-funded child care, abortion support of "law and order" and a strong national defense.

Gun Owners of America was established. H.L. Richardson, former John Birch Society staff member and a California state senator , organized Gun Owners of California.

The first anti-ERA editorial appeared in a Mormon publication, the *Church News*. (01/11)

71

YEAR	1975
U. S. President	Gerald Ford
NOW President	Karen DeCrow

EVENTS

The United Nations' World Conference on International Women's Year was held in Mexico City. The conference was attended by representatives of member governments and its official purpose was to consider a 10-year UN World Plan of Action. The plan developed covered education, employment, population control, child marriages, etc., but it did not agree on a general condemnation of sexism, nor did it include the right of women to control their own bodies. Nothing in the plan was legally binding on any country and each nation was left to work out the details in its own way. Another conference, called the Tribune, was put together by a small committee of NGO's (non-government organizations) and was structured in panels and workshops in order to contain the feminists who poured in from around the world; estimates exceeded 7,000. (06/23-07/04)

ISSUES

Lifestyles

The first national conference on rape was held at University of Alabama. Tuscaloosa NOW Rape Task Force coordinator Mary Ann Largen worked with the University's Center for Correctional Psychology to set up the conference, and many task force members were speakers at the conference. (01/20-22)

Education

Title IX regulations barring sex discrimination in intercollegiate athletics and broadening opportunities for women were signed by HEW Secretary Caspar Weinberger and sent to President Ford. (02/28)

Lt. Col. Grace King, dismissed in 1975 as WAC Commander in Virginia for feminist activities, was reinstated. King, NOW's top military advisor, testified many times at Congressional hearings.

Economic

Denver NOW filed a complaint with EEOC & OFCC & U.S. Air Force charging sex discrimination against Martin-Marietta.

Religion

Bishop Leo T. Maher of the Roman Catholic Diocese of San Diego, CA, issued an order denying communion to Catholics who were "members of pro-abortion groups such as the National Organization for Women." The pastoral letter, which was read or distributed at every Mass in the 512,000-member diocese the following Sunday, singled NOW out for its "shameless agitation" in favor of abortion and stated NOW members were not to receive the sacraments. (04/08)

Legal

Political

"The day after the November elections, we said we'd be #34, and we did it!" declared Anita Wasik, NOW State Coordinator for North Dakota. The North Dakota House voted 52-49 for the ERA. The Senate had passed the ERA two weeks before, 28-22. (02/28)

Legislation to assist Displaced Homemakers, developed by Tish Sommers and Laurie Shields of the NOW Task Force on Older Women, was introduced in California. (04/10)

Sommers and Shields

About 350 persons attended a demonstration to protest an order by San Diego Roman Catholic Bishop Leo Maher denying communion to Catholic members of NOW who advocate abortion. At least a dozen San Diego NOW women wearing conspicuous NOW buttons were denied Communion at St. Brigid's Church in Pacific Beach CA, site of the demonstration, after they told the parish priest they did not support the church's anti-abortion views. Other demonstrations included pickets from the Pro-Abortion League in front of St. Joseph's Cathedral in downtown San Diego, and 50 pickets from Women in Law demonstrating in front of the University of San Diego's Immaculata Chapel. (04/13)

NOW's national Secretary Charlene Suneson was notified by the IRS that "So long as your support of a political candidate is not the primary activity of your organization, it will not jeopardize your exempt status under section 501(c)4. (03/31)

Florida NOW sponsored the ERA People's Parade in Tallahassee. One of the marchers, Madine Steele, was suspended from her teaching position for participating in ERA activities. (04/14)

According to a survey conducted by the Working Women United Institute, sexual harassment was widespread; over 70% of respondents reported experiencing it at least once, and the incidence of harassment was found to cut across age, economic, marital, and experience categories, although waitresses and clerical workers were more likely to be harassed than women in other job categories. The survey also reported that 56% of the reported cases involved some form of physical harassment, and that one-third of all reported incidents carried some variety of negative repercussions (further harassment, firing, etc.) with them. (05)

AT & T agreed to pay an additional $2.5 million to about 2,500 employees, mostly women, because AT & T had not met its agreed 1973 intermediate targets for ending job discrimination. (05/03)

In *Weinberger v. Wiesenfeld*, a case argued before the U.S. Supreme Court by Ruth Bader Ginsburg, the Court held unconstitutional the Social Security provision that gave widows with minor children monthly benefits based on their deceased husbands' contributions but denied similar benefits to widowers with minor children.

A Utah law, requiring divorced fathers to support sons until age 21 but daughters until only 18, was ruled unconstitutional by the U.S. Supreme Court in an 8-1 decision. Justice Harry Blackmun wrote "No longer is the female destined solely for the home and the rearing of the family and only the male for the market place and the world of ideas. Women's activities and responsibilities are increasing and expanding." Justice William Rehnquist was the only dissenting vote. (04/15)

The Backlash

Maurine Startup, Mormon mother of 11 and grandmother of 32, launched a petition drive to rescind California's ratification of the ERA. Joining her was her own mother. Both agreed that the 19th amendment was "unnecessary" and took the same attitude toward the ERA. (05/11)

In California, the Coalition of Christian Citizens announced a referendum drive aimed at repealing newly enacted legislation legalizing all private sex acts between consenting adults. They hoped to block the law from taking effect by gathering 312,404 signatures to put the issue on the June 1976 primary election ballot. One of the Coalition founders was State Senator H.L. Richardson.(05/19)

The Roman Catholic Archdiocese of Philadelphia severed its support of the city's 8,000 church-sponsored Girl Scouts in protest of a planned series of sex education workshops in which scouts would discuss birth control and abortion.

YEAR	1975
U. S. President	Gerald Ford
NOW President	Karen DeCrow

EVENTS

Eleanor Smeal & Karen DeCrow

At the Eighth NOW Conference in Philadelphia in October, in a bitterly contested election, Karen DeCrow was reelected president and Eleanor Smeal was elected chair of the board. Candidates of their Majority Caucus slate won a dominant majority on the executive committee and board of directors. Resolutions were passed calling for a constitutional convention to amend NOW's by-laws and on ERA ratification. (10/24-27)

ISSUES

Lifestyles

Lansing (MI) NOW achieved one of its highest legislative priorities for 1975 when the Michigan House passed one of the country's most progressive housing acts. The House substitute for Senate Bill 13 amended the Fair Housing Act of 1968 to prohibit discrimination in the renting, leasing or selling of real estate based on sex, marital status, age, or handicap.(05/28)

Education

Congress passed legislation opening the U.S. military academies to women. NOW pushed for a September 1976 effective date. (05/20)

Economic

Chicago NOW demonstrated at the Sears stockholders meeting and, through public embarrassment, forced Sears to put the question of affirmative action on its agenda.(05/19)

Capitol Hill NOW filed the first formal complaint of sex discrimination under the Comprehensive Employment and Training Act of 1973.

Religion

Mothers' Day of Outrage brought 4,000 pro-choice demonstrators to the Vatican Embassy in Washington, D.C. The action was called by the Eastern Region of NOW to publicize the amount of money the Catholic Church had spent to enforce compulsory pregnancy. (05/11)

Media

Legal

NOW chapters in Missouri held a symbolic ERA vigil on the steps of the Capitol building in Jefferson City. Action originated with and was approved by the Missouri State Conference. (05/21)

Political

The American Psychological Association removed homosexuality from its list of mental disorders.

Except for contact sports, schools and colleges getting federal aid were required to give boys and girls equal access to physical education classes and facilities, decreed Health, Education and Welfare (HEW) Secretary Caspar Weinberger. "Equal education opportunity for women is the law of the land and it will be enforced," he said. (06/02)

HEW announced plans for its Office of Civil Rights to stop investigating individual complaints within 90 days and to concentrate instead on identifying patterns of discrimination in higher education. In 1969, HEW received 14 complaints but in 1974, it received 444. (06/03)

New York NOW and Queens (NY) NOW sponsored an Older Women's Conference with 19 workshops and featured NOW's Older Women Task Force Chair Tish Sommers, Representative Bella Abzug, and actress Viveca Lindfors. (06/07-08)

A sex discrimination suit filed with the New Jersey Division of Civil Rights against WBRW radio by Somerset County NOW was settled, with "probable cause" found for discrimination .

Despite tremendous community pressure, Kiwanis International members voted for the third straight year to ban women from membership in the organization and revoked the charters of two U.S. chapters which had admitted women. (06/24)

Joanne Little was acquitted, and a precedent was set for the right of self-defense of rape victims. Many NOW members had raised money for her defense and NOW had publicly supported her. (08/15)

NOW Labor Task Force Coordinator Sara Nelson met with the U. S. Justice Department on the Karen Silkwood cover-up, and urged them to reopen the investigation. Four men represented the Justice Department, and told the NOW representative that Karen Silkwood might have been a "kook"and suggested the reason NOW members raised concerns about the unsolved aspects of the case was because they "watched too much television."(08/26)

NOW called all members to the streets to protest against violence against women and to "claim the night and the streets as ours." Deborah Hart, Coordinator of the first "Take Back the Night" action, also called for vigils in memory of "our sisters who have died in the streets." (08/26)

NOW sponsored "Alice Doesn't Day" women's strike. (10/29)

"Shoulder to Shoulder," a brilliant documentary series by Midge Mackenzie on the militant suffrage movement in Great Britain led by Emmeline Pankhurst, was broadcast on Public Television. (10)

At year's end, only one state, North Dakota, had ratified the Equal Rights Amendment, for a total of 34.

The Backlash

Brigham Young University (BYU) in Utah ran large newspaper advertisements explaining why it intended to ignore some of the Federal regulations issued under Title IX, which the Mormon Church considered unconstitutional. BYU contended that six of the rules violated the constitutional right to freedom of religion. (10/18)

Bishop Bernardin of the U.S. Conference of Catholic Bishops met with President Ford, HEW Secretary Weinberger and officials of the State Department to urge the President to produce a Constitutional amendment and to continue the prohibition against U.S. aid for abortion services abroad. (06/19)

At its national conference, U.S. Catholic Bishops adopted a Pastoral Plan calling for citizen's lobbies by congressionaldistrict on a national scale to oppose abortion and lobby for an amendment to the Constitution to overturn the U.S. Supreme Court decision in *Roe v. Wade* legalizing abortion. (11/24-27)

73

YEAR	1976
U. S. President	Gerald Ford
NOW President	Karen DeCrow

EVENTS

NOW adopted the Women's Bicentennial Medallion as a fund-raiser for the ERA ratification campaign. It was designed by Judith Meuli and Toni Carabillo(01)

The Senate agreed to NOW's demands for hearings in the death of Karen Silkwood, Kerr-McGee nuclear plant employee. The 28-year-old mother of three had been killed in a suspicious auto accident November 13, 1974, as she traveled to meet a *New York Times* investigative reporter. The Senate, however, referred the hearings to Rep. John Dingell's House Subcommittee on Energy & Environment. (04/26)

ISSUES

Lifestyles

Redbook magazine surveyed sexual harassment in the work-place. Replies from 9,000 young women (in their 20s and 30s) showed that 90% thought the problem was "serious." (01)

NOW opened its new Action Center in Washington, D.C., and projected its first $1 million budget. (01/05)

NOW established a national Task Force on Battered Women/Household Violence. Del Martin and Nancy Kirk-Gormley chaired. (02)

More than 1,500 women participated in the New York City NOW chapter "Walk Against Rape" through Central Park. (03)

Education

The national NOW board recommended that the NOW LDEF provide legal and financial support for Mary Jo Risher in her custody suit. Dallas County (TX) NOW launched a national fundraiser for the lesbian mother's case.(01/24-25)

NOW slapped a sex discrimination charge on the Southern EEOC regional director. (02/03)

An Arizona poll of registered voters, commissioned by the Arizona Republican Party at a cost of $15,000, was buried in a safe when it was discovered that Pima County residents favored ERA by 3 to 1 and Maricopa County residents wanted ERA by a 2-1 margin. (03)

NOW formed a Task Force on Feminism in Rural America.(03)

Mt. Pleasant (MI) NOW chapter filed a Title IX complaint with HEW when school officials tried to fill two administrative jobs by recruiting only among the current Mt. Pleasant district administrative staff – all white males. (03/07)

Battered Wives by Del Martin, former National Board member of NOW and coordinator of NOW's Task Force on Household Violence, was published. It was the first major report on this widespread form of violence against women.

Economic

Religion

Pope Paul VI cautioned women to be on their guard against movements for equality that run the risk of "masculinizing" and "depersonalizing" them. Vatican observers said the Pontiff's remarks were aimed at women's liberation movements allegedly advocating divorce, abortion, and promiscuity. (01/31)

When Judy K. Hartwell, 29, of Belleville, MI, was acquitted of murdering her husband, the case resulted in a "landmark" ruling for the sexual rights of women. She had claimed self-defense from a sexual attack and in giving the case to the jury, the judge instructed them that "A married woman is not compelled by law to submit, against her will, to sexual contact with her husband which she finds offensive." Although not binding on subsequent cases, it marked the first time a Michigan judge ever had made such a ruling regarding the marital relations of men and women. (03)

Media

A Georgia ERA rally of thousands received media coverage of only one UPI photo, which distorted the purpose of the rally. NOW protested to UPI.(01/11)

Virginia NOW sponsored a 100-mile walk for the ERA. Fourteen walkers covered the entire route. (01/09-14)

Circulation of *Do It NOW*, NOW's national newsletter reached 70,000. (01)

Legal

The South Dakota House defeated a recision attempt, 37-33. Intensive NOW effort, in coalition with the League of Women Voters and the AAUW, was key to the victory. (01/30)

Political

NOW targeted Florida, Illinois, Indiana, Missouri, Nevada and South Carolina for ERA action at a national strategy meeting in St. Louis, MO. (01/03-04)

Non-ratification of the ERA at this point in time set the dubious record for being the constitutional amendment taking the longest time to be ratified. The 19th Amendment on women's suffrage was ratified in 15 months, and the 26th Amendment, giving 18-year-olds voting rights, was ratified in four months. (02/25)

NOW president Karen DeCrow and Phyllis Schlafly debated the ERA at Yale University. DeCrow won the debate 32-20. (02/22)

ERAmerica opened headquarters in Washington, D.C. (02/25)

The Backlash

Roman Catholic Bishop Leo T. Maher of the San Diego Diocese openly admitted that the proposed amendments to the Constitution would bestow personhood at fertilization and would outlaw the Intra Uterine Device (I.U.D.). He asserted that women who used I.U.D.'s would be regarded as "murderers." (01/28)

Anti-abortion candidate Ellen McCormick was certified by the Federal Election Commission to receive matching funds for her presidential campaign. The vote was 4-1, with FEC Vice Chairman Neil Staebler dissenting on grounds that many of her contributions were made payable to the Pro-Life Action Committee and may not have been intended for a Presidential campaign. (02/25)

The mayor of Stamford, CT, proclaimed "Right to Life Day." NOW prepared a strong protest for the February 27 National Mayors' Conference. (01/22)

YEAR	1976
U. S. President	Gerald Ford
NOW President	Karen DeCrow

EVENTS

The U.S. Supreme Court ruled that states cannot require a woman seeking an abortion to get consent from her husband or force all single girls under 18 desiring an abortion to get permission from a parent. The decision struck down a 1974 Missouri law, but upheld a provision requiring a woman to give her written consent before the operation can be performed.

The vote on the spousal consent requirement was 6-3 (Burger, White and Rehnquist voted with the anti-choice minority). The vote on the parental consent requirement was 5-4 with Stevens joining the three opposed to abortion. (06/30)

ON OUR WAY TO ILLINOIS

ISSUES

Lifestyles

The U.S. Supreme Court ruled 6-3 that states could impose criminal penalties for a homosexual act– even though it was between consenting adults, in private. The ruling upheld a lower Federal Court decision in a Virginia case. (03/29)

Education

The nation's first Displaced Homemakers Center opened at Mills College in Oakland, CA. Tish Sommers, coordinator of the NOW Task Force on Older Women, was the founding director. (05)

Economic

The Hawkins-Humphrey Employment/Growth bill was "marked up" with only one of NOW's 10 recommendations adopted. Discrimination against married women was deleted. (04/27)

Religion

The National Organization for Women asked the Internal Revenue Service to audit all Roman Catholic Dioceses, the National Conference of Catholic Bishops and the U.S. Catholic Conference, charging that its tax-exempt dollars were being used to create "an anti-abortion political network." (04)

Media

No states ratified the fourth year of ERA, but five recision efforts were defeated in 1976. (03/22)

Legal

The U.S. Supreme Court ruled that workers who could prove they were denied jobs because of illegal discrimination were entitled to retroactive seniority and related benefits. The landmark 5-3 decision was the Court's first ruling on the highly controversial issue of seniority vs. affirmative action. Although the case (*Franks v. Bowman Transportation Co.*) involved race discrimination, feminists agreed the ruling would apply to women as well, because it was brought under Title VII of the Civil Rights Act. (03/24)

Political

President Ford vetoed a child care bill, saying it would cause "unwarranted Federal interference" in states' rights and cost the taxpayer too much. The standards established in the vetoed legislation would have required a minimum number of adult workers to care for children between the ages of six weeks and six years at child day care centers. The Day Care Services Act would have provided financial aid to child care centers and funding to hire welfare mothers to staff them. (04/06)

PEER, a project of NOW's Legal Defense & Education Fund, charged 40 states and Washington D.C. with violating federal requirements for ending sex bias in education under Title IX, which had been passed in 1972. Complaints were filed with HEW. (05/10)

ABC offered Barbara Walters a $1 million per year, five year contract to co-host the news with Harry Reasoner–a pairing later doomed by Reasoner's sexism. (04/20)

A suit filed by the Vermont Caucus for the Family (VCF) against the Governor's Commission on the Status of Women was dismissed by Superior Court Judge Stephen B. Martin. The anti-ERA Caucus, suing in its capacity as a representative of tax-payers, asked for an injunction preventing Commission members from further participation in activities supporting the Equal Rights Amendment and opposing the VCF's movement to rescind ERA in Vermont. But Assistant Attorney General Greg Studen argued that the Commission, as a branch of the Governor's Office, was empowered to take stands on controversial issues and had as much right to do so as the governor. (05)

Maryland NOW supported, with lobbying and testimony, a state Displaced Homemakers (DH) Bill. NOW called for a national act to be signed by President Carter by Mothers Day 1977. Earlier, Florida was the second state to pass a DH bill, though its center had not yet opened. Seven other states had filed bills, and five states had drafted Displaced Homemaker bills. Laurie Shields, coordinator of NOW's Task Force on Older Women, traveled to many of these states to organize support for their passage. (05)

California NOW joined Women Against Violence Against Women (WAVAW) in protesting "snuff" movies and an offensive Rolling Stones billboard on Sunset Strip. The billboard was whitewashed over. (06)

NOW's organizing for an ERA rally brought 16,000 supporters to Springfield, IL. Delegations from the Eastern region came on the NOW "Freedom Train." (05/15-16)

At the 1976 National Democratic Convention in New York, Ellie Smeal, Karen DeCrow, Alice Cohan, Jean Conger, Lillian Ciarrochi, Arlie Scott and Gloria Allred waged a successful campaign for equal division of representation between women and men. (07/15)

The Backlash

An anti-abortion bill that redefined a "person" as "a human being from the moment of fertilization and implanta-tion" was signed into law by Louisiana Governor Edwin Edwards. Had the law survived court challenge, it could have led to the filing of murder charges against physicians, medical support staff, and

women seeking abortions– a fact admitted by the author, Senator E. Edwards Barham. (09)

Presidential candidate Jimmy Carter was jostled by shouting anti-abortion demonstrators as he tried to shake hands in a crowd outside his hotel in Scranton, PA. (09/07)

Orrin Hatch, the hand-picked candidate of the New Right, with no record of public service in Utah, was elected to the U.S. Senate, defeating a three-term incumbent. Richard Viguerie was his fundraiser and he received funding and support from key right-wing groups, as well as a $6,000 donation from Joseph Coors. (11/02) 75

YEAR	1976
U. S. President	Gerald Ford
NOW President	Karen DeCrow

EVENTS

Jimmy Carter won the presidential election, defeating incumbent President Gerald Ford with 50.08% of the vote. (11/02)

Massachusetts voters approved a state ERA by 60-40 margin. Colorado voters rejected repeal of their state ERA, which had been in effect since 1972. (11/02)

A Harris Poll (taken in late October of 1,720 voters) showed support for the U.S. Supreme Court abortion decision was 60-31; ERA support (shared by Carter and Ford) was 65-27, and

Catholic support for legalized abortion was 52-39. (11/02)

The U.S. Supreme Court ruled, in a suit against General Electric Co. (GE v. Gilbert), that employers could exclude pregnancy from sickness and accident disability insurance plans without violating federal prohibitions against sex discrimination. (12/07)

ISSUES

Lifestyles

U.S. District Judge Gerhard Gesell upheld the right of the Air Force to dismiss Sgt. Leonard Matlovich for being gay. Despite his decision, Judge Gesell implored the Air Force to change their regulations. "The time has come or may be imminent when the military services must address the problem of homosexuality. Public attitudes are clearly changing, moving more in the direction of tolerance," he said. (07/16)

Education

Florida NOW filed a sex discrimination suit against the Florida State Department of Education. (09)

Economic

The Vatican said it was studying the subject of the ordination of women as priests but warned that this did not mean that a change was foreseen. A brief announcement said the study simply dealt with the form to present the traditional doctrine of the Roman Catholic Church on the subject. (06/28)

Do It Now, NOW's national newsletter, was converted to a monthly tabloid newspaper, renamed the National NOW Times. (08)

Media

In California, 200 ERA supporters walked 200 miles from Salinas to Sacramento. (08/17-26)

NOW By-Laws Conference was held at Overland Park, KS. (10/09-11)

Legal

Mary Lynn Myers, a NOW national board member from Pierre, SD, and Sue McGee, a Seattle, WA, NOW member were among 17 White House Fellows for 1976-77. (09/01)

Political

The National Republican Convention endorsed the so-called Human Life Amendment by placing it in its Platform. (08)

Reform Judaism leaders announced a proposed glossary for prayer books and worship services that substituted non-sexist language for masculine terms. It was prepared by the New York task force within the 1.1 million member Union of American Hebrew Congregations, the Reform branch of Judaism. (09)

The Episcopal Church, meeting in Minneapolis/St. Paul, officially recognized ordination of 15 women as priests, including the very first, Jacqueline Means, and Rev. Betty Bone Schiess, a Syracuse, NY, NOW member, who had formed a feminist parish. (09/16)

A seven-week NOW vigil at the White House for the ERA was begun. It was inspired by the suffragists of 1917-1918, and reminded the hordes of summer tourists of the continued fight for the ERA. The vigil lasted each day from 7 a.m. to 11 p.m. (07/05-08/28)

State ERAs were defeated in New York by 400,000 votes and narrowly in New Jersey after a massive campaign of deception and misrepresentation against it by the John Birch Society, Schlafly's Stop ERA, and, for the Catholic Church, the Knights of Columbus and parish Holy Name Societies. Pro-ERA forces spent only an estimated $25,000 on the New York ERA Campaign and only $8,000 in the New Jersey campaign. (09)

According to the Harris Poll, 65% of Americans approved of the ERA with only 27% opposed. (11/04)

The Washington Post reported that a study by the Post and Harvard University's Center for International Affairs showed that men were as supportive of feminist goals as women. Strongest feminist support came from people aged 18-30. Among those 45 or older, only 39% of the men and 25% of the women chose careers and jobs over family and home life as primary goals for women. (09/28)

United Air Lines settled a three-year-old job bias suit for $1 million and established hiring goals and ratios for women and minorities. (04/30)

A strong majority of delegates, representing the American Catholic Church at the first National Call to Action Conference in Detroit, endorsed the Equal Rights Amendment. The recommendation of the Conference called upon the Church to "commit significant economic resources and personnel, especially in social action agencies and offices, to achieve speedy ratification of the ERA." It further recommended that special efforts be made in those states that had not yet ratified the amendment. (11)

A study by students at the University of Houston, TX, showed that the major difference in ERA activists–pro and anti–was in religious activity. Of the 154 anti-ERA women studied, 66% belonged to fundamentalist churches compared with only 4% of the 156 pro-ERA activists. Pro-ERA women were found to be of higher socio-economic status, younger, urban, suburban, with secular religious views. (09)

The Backlash

The First Presidency of the Mormon Church issued its first formal anti-ERA statement. Women were entitled to additional rights, but "the Equal Rights Amendment is not the answer." (10/22)

A "taxpayer" suit was filed that tried to dissolve the California Commission on the Status of Women. The group initiating the suit called itself "Women's Committee for Responsible Government." (11/17)

Harper's magazine published "Requiem for the Women's Movement" by Veronica Geng. It was among many "requiems" the media would produce – prematurely. (11)

YEAR	1977
U. S. President	Jimmy Carter
NOW President	Karen DeCrow

EVENTS

NOW president Karen DeCrow delivered a Women's State of the Union Address in Washington, D.C. (01/13)

NOW's new bylaws were reported as ratified after mail ballots were counted. The new bylaws provided for paid officers, a delegate system and modern, streamlined management. (01/29)

The Tenth National Conference of NOW in Detroit, MI, elected Eleanor Cutri Smeal as its new president by an overwhelming majority. Among more than 20 resolu-

tions, the delegates authorized the creation of a NOW ERA Strike Force to make the ratification effort a national campaign and and pledged an all-out fight for ratification of the ERA; the establishment of a NOW Political Action Committee; and voted to join the boycott of J.P. Stevens, the second largest textile manufacturer in the country. (04/22)

ISSUES

Economic

Marjorie Wyngaarden, a NOW Coordinator, and other NOW activists won a three-year battle with AT&T for dual phone book listings for husbands and wives without an extra charge. Ms. Wyngaarden had taken her case to the AT&T shareholders, the Public Utilities Commission, the Securities Exchange Commission and the FCC. (01/11)

Religion

Jacqueline Means, a 40-year-old nurse and prison chaplain, became the first woman officially admitted to the priesthood in the Episcopal Church in America. (01/01)

Media

Legal

An 18-page declaration prepared by the Sacred Congregation for the Doctrine of the Faith, and personally approved by Pope Paul VI, flatly ruled out the admission of women to the priesthood of the Roman Catholic Church because women lacked a "natural resemblance which must exist between Christ and His Minister." (01/28)

Political

The Virginia Senate came within one vote of ratifying ERA. The vote was 20 to 18 in favor of ratification, but the rules required a majority of the 40-member Senate, or 21, for passage. (01/27)

In New Hampshire, efforts by NOW helped to defeat an attempt to abolish the state's ERA. Women's groups throughout the state responded to the NOW alert with legislative testimony, phone calls and letters to counteract the misinformation circulated by New Hampshire's branch of the Eagle Forum and the State Commission on the Status of Women. (02/15)

Indiana became the 35th state to ratify the ERA, despite frantic last-minute efforts by Phyllis Schlafly and her supporters to kill the amendment. The ratification followed intensive action on the part of national NOW, directed by NOW's Chair of the Board, Eleanor Smeal, and Indiana NOW under the leadership of state coordinator Sue Errington, capped by a huge ERA rally January 9 in a raging blizzard. NOW members kept vigil in the Capitol rotunda during the entire voting process. (01/18)

The ERA was ratified in the Nevada Senate by the tie-breaking vote of Lt. Gov. Bob Rose after a parliamentary maneuver devised by NOW Chair Eleanor Smeal. Since a pro-ERA vote in the Assembly was regarded as a foregone conclusion, ERA backers celebrated. (02/08)

The Nevada Assembly rejected the ERA by a vote of 24-15. Eleven of the 24 negative votes were cast by Democrats pledged to support their party's platform. They had run for office as pro-ERA candidates, used pro-ERA people as campaign workers, accepted contributions from pro-ERA individuals and organizations, and some had even voted in favor of ERA when it passed the Assembly in 1975. The vote switch was attributed to unprecedented pressure from the Nevada Legislature's Mormon Bishops who held key positions in the state's power structure. (02/11)

NOW Membership 53,500
NOW Annual Budget $1,373,524

The NOW National Board approved an economic sanctions campaign against unratified states at its meeting in Ft. Lauderdale, FL. Also approved was participation in the J.P. Stevens boycott. (02/19)

Joe Smith, chair of the board of Elektra-Asylum (EA) records, met with representatives of California NOW and Women Against Violence Against Women (WAVAW) in response to the group's growing boycott of Warner, Atlantic and EA record covers that used women in subservient poses. Smith agreed that such depictions should not be part of EA's normal artistic standards and promised to meet with his counterparts at Warner and Atlantic records to "discuss the situation." (02)

With three states already having voted recision of ERA (Idaho, Tennessee, and Nebraska), the Justice Department informed President Carter's counsel that in the Department's opinion, recision was illegal and unconstitutional. (03)

Two NOW members studying law at Whittier College in California, Catherine Timlin and Alice Bennett, proposed to NOW national board members Judith Meuli and Toni Carabillo that NOW seek an extension of the deadline for ratification of the ERA from Congress based on the fact that the Constitution imposed no time limit for the ratification of amendments. The idea was passed on to Eleanor Smeal. (03/11)

The Backlash

Anita Bryant reported that she was "divinely" inspired to testify against a proposed Dade County (FL) ordinance prohibiting discrimination against homosexuals. (01)

In a unanimous decision, the Seventh Circuit Court of Appeals in Chicago ruled that

the activities of the National Commission on the Observance of International Women's Year could not be challenged in Federal court by members of Stop-ERA. In their suit against the commission, the plaintiffs – represented by Fred Schlafly – alleged that federal funds were being spent for lobbying activi-

ties. The court agreed that the commission had engaged in a variety of activities pursuant to its broad Congressional mandate, but that none of these activities were shown to harm the plaintiffs' interests. (02/24)

YEAR	1977		
U. S. President	Jimmy Carter		
NOW President	Karen DeCrow	Eleanor Smeal	

EVENTS

Alice Paul, militant suffragist and author of the Equal Rights Amendment, died at the age of 92. Of her lifetime dedication to achieving equality for women she once said, "I always thought once you put your hand on the plow, you don't remove it until you get to the end of the row." (07/09)

The first House hearings on the Hyde Amendment prohibiting the use of Medicaid funding for abortion were held. (06/17)

The U.S. Supreme Court ruled that neither the Constitution nor federal Medicaid law required the government to pay for abortions that were not medically necessary. Commenting on this decision, President Carter made his famous "life is not fair" statement. (06/21)

ISSUES

Education

At the New York Chapter's Tenth Anniversary dinner at the Biltmore Hotel, Ellie Smeal was seated next to N.Y. Rep. Elizabeth Holtzman (who had replaced longtime ERA foe Emmanuel Celler in Congress) and outlined the idea of extending the ERA deadline to her. Holtzman, an attorney, sat on the House Judiciary Committee. She was fascinated with the idea and offered her help instantly. (03/12)

An equally divided U.S. Supreme Court upheld a decision approving sexually separate public high schools for academically superior boys and girls in the case, *Vorcheimer v. Philadelphia.* (04/19)

Joanie Caucus, the runaway housewife made immortal in the comic strip *Doonesbury,* "graduated" from Law School. (05/21)

Economic

Vermont was the site of the first International Woman's Year (IWY) state meeting in preparation for the National Women's Conference. More than 1,000 men and women braved cold and snow to attend and pass resolutions supporting ERA, affirmative action, scholarships for older women students, and others. Forty-five percent of those attending had never before attended a meeting on women's rights. (02/26)

Timlin and Bennett delivered their paper on the extension of the deadline for ratification of the ERA to Carabillo and Meuli. They located Smeal in Tallahassee working on the doomed ratification campaign in Florida. The paper was mailed to her on March 31. About this time, Smeal discussed the concept of the extension with Jean Witter, another longtime NOW member who had been a leader in the campaign for ratification by Congress in the early 70s and who had also gone on to become an attorney. Witter wrote the first extensive and validating legal memorandum on the concept, which was presented to Elizabeth Holtzman. (03/30)

Religion

Los Angeles NOW became one of the plaintiffs in the huge class-action suit filed against Hughes Aircraft Company for sex discrimination in employment and hiring. Hughes was one of the largest employers in Southern California. (04)

NOW's Task Force on Women and Religion published a pastoral letter and sent it to every Roman Catholic bishop and newspaper in the country, urging the church hierarchy to "purge itself of sexism and related forms of idolatry" or "forfeit its right to a serious hearing on the great social and moral issues of our day." The letter also admonished the bishops to petition the Pope for ordination of gays and the recognition of reproductive freedom. (04/24)

The U.S. Army announced it was restoring the Medal of Honor to Dr. Mary Edwards Walker, a front-lines Civil War surgeon and the only woman among 3,000 medal winners in American history. (06/10)

Games Mother Never Taught You, (Corporate Gamesmanship for Women) by Betty Lehan Harrigan was published.

By a vote of 56-to-42, the Senate voted to forbid the use of public funds to pay the cost of elective abortions for the nation's poor, except where the woman's life may be endangered. (06/29)

Legal

In Salinas, CA, Inez Garcia, who had become a feminist symbol of a woman's right to self-defense, was acquitted of second-degree murder after a retrial for killing the man who stood guard while a second man raped her. (03/04)

By a vote of 201-to-155, the House voted for the Hyde Amendment, which prohibited the use of federal money for Medicaid abortions. (06/29)

Political

California NOW began a boycott of Nevada because of its refusal to ratify the Equal Rights Amendment. In addition to NOW, California Women Lawyers asked lawyers in California to stay out of Nevada and called on attorney's groups not to schedule meetings there. (03/05)

The Florida Senate voted against ERA ratification 21-19. Chair of the NOW Board, Eleanor Smeal, who participated in NOW's ratification campaign in Tallahassee, noted that it was two long-time supporters who made a last-minute switch to the opposition that blocked ratification, following the Nevada pattern. (04/13)

The American Association of University Women adopted a resolution directing that regional conventions not be held in states that had not ratified the Equal Rights Amendment. (06/29)

The Backlash

By a margin of more than two to one, the Dade County (FL) ordinance prohibiting discrimination on the basis of sexual preference was repealed in the referendum vote, following intense public agitation against the ordinance by Anita Bryant and her group, Save Our Children. (06/07)

Life Advocates was formed in Texas by a Phyllis Schlafly associate, Margaret Hotze.

The Life Amendment PAC was established by Roman Catholic activist Paul Brown.

The National Pro-Life PAC was set up in Chicago by Father Charles Fiore and Peter Gemma.

Mormons attempted to take over IWY in Ellensburg, WA. Mormon men with walkie-talkies instructed their women on which meetings to attend and how to vote. (07/08)

The Consumer Alert Council, an anti-union, pro-business group, was set up and headed by Barbara Keating.

YEAR	1977
U. S. President	Jimmy Carter
NOW President	Eleanor Smeal

EVENTS

The National Women's Conference in Houston, TX, chaired by Bella Abzug, adopted a National Plan of Action to be submitted to the President and Congress. NOW's President, Eleanor Smeal, was on the 45 member Commission and led the effort to include gay rights in the plan of action. Some 20,000 women attended the conference. Ten years before, the Second Nation-

al Conference of NOW had endorsed the ERA and a wom-

an's right to abortion in a landmark "Bill of Rights for Women." The plan of action adopted by the Houston Conference–and approved by more than 80% of the delegates attending–with only a few additions (that in the intervening years NOW had also already adopted) echoed the NOW "Bill of Rights" proposed

(Continued next page)

ISSUES

Lifestyles

Janet Guthrie became the first women to race in the Indianapolis 500. After the race she publicly thanked her parents "for not bringing me up thinking I couldn't do something because I was a woman." (05/31)

Economic

U.S. District Judge Harry Pregerson certified as a class action a lawsuit filed against KNXT, Los Angeles, and CBS by a former female writer and producer who alleged the station and network discriminated against women in employment. Melinda Cotton alleged in the suit that the station discriminated against women with respect to hiring, job placement, promotions, salary and other conditions of employment. (08/29)

Legal

Rep. Elizabeth Holtzman received the first of a series of opinions from the Congressional Research Service of the Library of Congress concurring in the opinion of the Timlin-Bennett paper and the Witter memorandum that it was indeed within the power of Congress to extend the ratification deadline. (04/28)

Political

Wisconsin Judge Archie Simonson, who described the rape of a 16-year old girl in a high school stairwell as a "natural reaction" by a gang of boys, was defeated in a recall election and replaced by Moria Krueger, the first female judge elected in Dane County history after an intense NOW campaign. (09/07)

Calling the Social Security System, "one of the worst example of institutionalized sexism in our society," NOW president Eleanor Smeal testified before the House Subcommittee on Social Security in support of legislation which would remove the need for a dependency test and establish a system by which homemakers would have their own individual social security records not linked to spousal accounts. (07/21)

The Air Force graduated its first 10 women pilots. (09/02)

The U.S. Civil Rights Commission accused the FCC of issuing rosy "window dressing" reports on the progress of women and minorities in TV. Screen Actors Guild findings showed that employment for women and minorities in the entertainment industries was worse than two years previously. (08)

Four thousand people, representing 60 national organizations, commemorated the 57th anniversary of the ratification of the 19th Amendment, giving women the right to vote, with a precision march down Pennsylvania Avenue to the White House. Marchers demanded that President Carter take an active and vigorous part in the effort to gain ratification of the ERA. The idea of the march as a tribute to Alice Paul was conceived by the NOW Executive Committee the day following her death and NOW organized the march. This was the first ERA march. (08/26)

Southwest Council Pennsylvania NOW Walkathon

On Women's Equality Day, ERA Walkathons throughout the country raised $150,000 for the NOW ERA Strike Force. (08/29)

The Wichita, KS, Commission passed a gay-rights bill by a 3-2 vote. The bill prohibited discrimination on the basis of sexual or affectional preference and marital status in the areas of employment, housing and public accommodations.(09/06)

NASA chose the first women as astronaut candidates.

NOW President Eleanor Smeal testified in support of the Labor Law Reform Act of 1977 before the House Education and Labor Subcommittee on Labor-Management Relations. The proposed legislation guaranteed that workers would be able to attain rights denied them due to inadequacies in existing laws. Smeal said: "Women, concentrated in the lowest paying, unorganized occupations, have the most to gain through collective bargaining." (09/08)

In his Labor Day message, AFL-CIO President George Meany declared: "The organizations formed by wealthy white businessmen in the South who opposed civil rights in the 1960's are now deep into a campaign of anti-unionism in that region the same is true of the women's movement. Scratch an opponent of the ERA and you will find an advocate of the so-called `right to work' laws, which are clearly anti-union." (09/05)

The Backlash

Approximately 14,000 Mormon women and men crowded the International Women's Year (IWY) Conference in Salt Lake City. They voted down all proposals including ERA and world peace. (06/24)

The IWY conference in Hawaii was taken over by anti-ERA Mormons. An anti-ERA slate was elected to go to Houston for the IWY meeting. (07/09)

The ACLU asked the Rhode Island Supreme Court to overturn a lower court ruling that a married woman must use her

husband's last name. The appeal resulted from a ruling in which Superior Court Judge Thomas Needham said that the state Registry of Motor Vehicles could force a woman to use her husband's surname on her driver's license, even if she was divorced. (12/08)

YEAR	1977
U. S. President	Jimmy Carter
NOW President	Eleanor Smeal

EVENTS

a decade earlier. The "radical" goals advanced by NOW in 1967 had by 1977 become the national objectives of the majority of American Women. The Conference was attended by Coretta Scott King, widow of Martin Luther King, and the wives of three U.S. Presidents– Rosalyn Carter, Betty Ford, and Ladybird Johnson.

A Roper Poll conducted a week before the conference revealed that only 19% of the general public felt that their views were represented by Phyllis Schlafly, almost the same percentage as anti-delegates, indicating that the Plan of Action passed by the delegates in Houston truly represented the will of the majority. (11/18-20)

ISSUES

Lifestyles

Education

Economic

Religion

Media

Legal

Political

HJ 638 calling for a seven-year extension of the deadline for ratification of the ERA was introduced in the House of Representatives by Rep. Elizabeth Holtzman (D-NY). (10/20)

Rosie Jiminez, 27, a single mother with a five-year-old daughter and a scholarship student six months away from receiving her teaching credential, died in agony from septicemia after an illegal abortion, the first known victim of the Hyde Amendment blocking Medicaid funding for abortion. (10/03)

The Project of Equal Education Rights (PEER) of the NOW Legal Defense and Education Fund charged that the Department of Health, Education and Welfare was allowing school districts all over the country to continue discrimination based on sex, despite a 1972 law prohibiting such practices. (11/07)

World War II women pilots– the WASPs – were finally granted veterans' benefits by an act of Congress after 34 years of seeking veteran status. About 800 surviving women pilots were affected by the new law. (11/03)

At the opening of the hearings on the ERA extension resolution, the Justice Department advised Congress that it had the right to extend the deadline for ratification of the ERA or, for that matter, any other amendments. Furthermore, according to the Justice Department, "the extension would not give rise to any right of recision and furthermore, Congress cannot give to the states a right to rescind by any means short of amending Article V of the Constitution." (11/02)

James M. Thompson, majority leader in the Virginia House of Delegates, was defeated by pro-ERA Republican challenger Gary Myers after an intensive NOW-directed campaign. (11/08)

The head of the Carter administration Task Force on Alternatives to Abortion, Connie J. Downey, disbanded the group after concluding that the only real alternatives were "suicide, motherhood, and, some would add, madness." (11/26)

The United Auto Workers, AFL-CIO, announced its plans to support the convention boycott of states that had not ratified the ERA, joining nearly 70 other national organizations. As a result of the campaign spearheaded by NOW, convention bureaus in such previously popular locations as Miami, New Orleans, Chicago, Atlanta, Las Vegas and St. Louis were counting revenue losses in the tens of millions of dollars. (12/01) The Missouri legislatures refusal to ratify the ERA cost St. Louis an estimated $1.1 million in lost convention business. (12/13)

Pope Paul VI agreed to halt, retroactively, the automatic excommunication of divorced and remarried Catholics in the U.S.A. The action was taken in response to the near unanimous request for the change made by the American Catholic bishops at their semi-annual meeting in May 1977. (11/09)

In the first year in which women were eligible to become priests in the Episcopal Church, over 90 took advantage of the option.

The U.S. Supreme Court ruled in *Satty v. Nashville Gas Company* that pregnant employees could be denied sick pay. It also ruled unanimously that seniority rights could not be taken away from women who were on leave to give birth to children. (12/06)

After NOW won in the 1976 elections, removing anti-ERA state legislators and replacing them with ERA supporters, women were robbed of ERA victories with key vote switches in Nevada, North Carolina and Florida.

A number of cities passed laws banning anti-gay discrimination in 1977. They were: Wichita, KS; Tucson, AZ; Iowa City, IA; Champaign, IL; and Aspen, CO. (12)

Quebec, Canada passed legislation outlawing discrimination based on sexual orientation in the areas of employment, housing, and public accommodations. (12)

After nearly five months of bitter debate and painstaking negotiations in Conference Committee, the House of Representatives and the Senate reached a "compromise" on wording to restrict access to elective abortions by poor American women who rely on Medicaid funds for their medical care. Said NOW President Eleanor Smeal, "The final resolution is totally unacceptable. Even though the Senate conferees were strong enough to win wording that will assure Medicaid funds for at least a third of those who need them, it leaves hundreds of thousands of women with no choice." (12/07)

After nearly a year of trying to reach a settlement with the Citizen's National Bank of Wilmar, MI, to correct discrimination in salaries, opportunity for promotion and union representation, eight women employees went out on strike. It was the beginning of a bitter, grueling and ultimately losing three-year struggle by the women, who came to be known as the "Wilmar 8." Director Lee Grant portrayed their struggle in a documentary film. (12/16)

The Backlash

Anti-feminists at IWY National Woman's Conference in Houston, TX, led by the ubiquitous Phyllis Schlafly, were only 20% of the delegates. Most resolutions adopted were passed by 90% of the delegates, indicating splits in the unity of the opposition, though one, on Equal Credit, passed unanimously. During one of her press confer-

ences about why she and her followers opposed establishing shelters for battered women, she said, "It's just beyond me how giving a wife who's been beaten an 'R & R' at taxpayers expense is going to solve her problem. . . . She needs a divorce lawyer and she can get that through the legal aid society." (11/18-20)

YEAR	1978
U. S. President	Jimmy Carter
NOW President	Eleanor Smeal

EVENTS

The U.S. government said that it would finance abortions for poor women who were victims of rape and incest if the incidents were reported to the proper authorities within 60 days. The ruling was by Joseph Califano, a personal opponent of abortion, and head of the Department of Health, Education and Welfare (HEW).(01/26)

NOW's National Board voted unanimously to declare a State of Emergency on the ERA, committing almost all the organization's resources to the state ratification campaigns and a national campaign to win a seven year extension of the ratification deadline (HJ Res 638), an action without precedent in NOW's history. NOW President Eleanor Smeal explained to the

Board that evidence in recent months made it clear the ERA had become a political football, and that ratification had been sabotaged in 1977 state campaigns by "backroom power brokering." (02/26)

ISSUES

Lifestyles

Two hundred and fifty-two women employees of the U.S. Department of Energy won more than $6 million in back pay in a major job discrimination suit. The amount was the largest judgement ever obtained against the U.S. government in such a case. (01/14)

Education

Carl Rubin, a Federal District judge in Dayton, OH, called the Title IX regulation as it related to contact sports unconstitutional, and ordered that the Ohio High School Athletic Association change its rules to allow physically qualified girls to participate with boys in interscholastic contact sports. (02)

Economic

The Equal Rights Amendment was killed for the 1978 Georgia legislative session in a unanimous Senate committee vote which a woman legislator labeled "history in the unmaking." (01/16)

Media

"Who Remembers Mama?" a documentary about displaced homemakers in the Dallas/Fort Worth area, was broadcast on KERA-TV, Dallas, TX. (01/11)

Legal

NOW LDEF voted to appropriate funds to establish an ERA litigation program focusing on suits brought in states which had added an ERA to their state constitutions. (01/29)

NOW activist Marianne Fowler, a longtime Democratic worker in Virginia, was stripped of her party responsibilities – including Treasurer of the Alexandria, VA, Democratic Committee – as punishment for her support of Republican Gary Myers, a pro-ERA candidate. Myers had defeated anti-ERA leader Democrat Jim Thompson for the State Senate. Two other women members of the Committee resigned immediately in protest. (01)

Political

NOW Annual Budget
$2,020,953

Four thousand demonstrators, including NOW President Eleanor Smeal and Virginia NOW members, marched to the state Capitol in Richmond, to demand passage of the ERA in the Virginia legislature. Organized by LERN, a coalition of Virginia labor groups, it was the largest pro-ERA march ever held in the state. (01/22)

The Missouri House reversed itself and voted to exclude rape victims from collecting money for abortions under a bill that would compensate other victims of violent crimes. (02/03)

The South Carolina State Senate voted 23-18 to table the ERA ratification bill. Three legislators tipped the balance from victory to defeat when they switched votes from "aye" to "nay" on the morning of the roll call. (02/07)

Adopting the theme of "No Turncoat Will Return," the NOW Political Action Committee (PAC) announced the goal of targeting key races in unratified states. (02/24)

The District of Columbia government banned payment of expenses for any of its employees attending conventions in states that have failed to ratify the Equal Rights Amendment. It was the first such action taken by a major U.S. city. (02/01)

A House subcommittee heard testimony from experts that violence occurs between family members more often than it occurs in any other setting except armies in war and police during riots. More than 1.8 million wives are beaten every year by their husbands, most of them at least twice, the experts stated. (02)

In *Lemons v. City and County of Denver*, a U.S. District court judge ruled against nurses who claimed their jobs were undervalued, saying the idea of comparable worth was "pregnant with the possibility of disrupting the entire economic system of the United States."

Jean Marshall Clark, Virginia NOW State Coordinator and a registered lobbyist, being arrested.

Despite strong public support, including a poll showing 59% state electorate support for ERA, the Virginia House Privileges and Elections Committee defeated the ERA before it got a chance to be heard by the full House. NOW activists Marianne Fowler and Jean Marshall Clark (Virginia NOW Coordinator) were arrested on charges of civil disturbance during the chants of protest which followed the vote. NOW President Smeal commented "I have never seen such behavior on the part of the police. I think they (Fowler and Clark) were targeted." (02/09)

The Backlash

Literature describing lesbian love-making was distributed in the Kentucky House by opponents of the Equal Rights Amendment, outraging some legislators and bringing demands for an investigation. Carol Maddox, a member of Stop ERA, said she had assembled the material in booklet form and had it distributed to

support her argument that passage of the ERA would encourage lesbians to advertise their sexual preferences, which she said were immoral.(02/11)

The Concerned Women's Clinic in Cleveland, OH, an abortion facility, was attacked by an arsonist wearing a delivery uniform and carrying a plastic

bag of gasoline. He set fire to an operating room while an abortion was in process, temporarily blinding a technician and forcing evacuation. The facility suffered $30,000 in damage and was forced to close. (02/15)

YEAR	1978		
U. S. President	Jimmy Carter		
NOW President	Eleanor Smeal		

EVENTS

The U.S. Department. of Labor's Women's Bureau released statistics which indicated that women continued to receive less than their fair share of the economic pie.

In the second year of women's eligibility for the Rhodes Scholarship, 12 of 32 American college student recipients were women.

After a national referendum, by a vote of 160 to 148 in the Senate, Italy adopted the most liberal abortion law in Europe. (05/17)

Pope Paul VI endorsed a campaign of Italian bishops to use excommunication to fight Italy's new law legalizing abortions. (06/07)

President Jimmy Carter announced the appointment of

Bella Abzug and Carmen Votaw, president of the National Conference of Puerto Rican Women, to be co-chairs of his 40-member National Advisory Committee for Women. Judy Carter, his daughter-in-law, was named Honorary chair. NOW President Eleanor Smeal was among those appointed to the Committee. (06/21)

ISSUES

Lifestyles

The Columbia (SC) chapter of NOW picketed *Playboy* magazine's photograph sessions at the Carolina Inn. NOW member Janet Elsinger said the picketing was to protest sexual exploitation of women. (04/06)

Education

Kentucky Lt. Gov. Thelma Stoval, acting for Governor Julian Carroll out of state on vacation, vetoed a resolution to rescind the ERA passed by the state legislature. "Sixty four percent of the people of Kentucky are for ERA," Stoval explained. (03/20)

Economic

Religion

The Equal Employment Opportunity Commission (EEOC) released its findings that Associated Press (AP) was guilty of violating federal laws prohibiting discrimination against women and minorities in its employment practices. (04/14)

Media

The Louisiana Supreme Court let stand a state law that called the husband "head and master" and said he could make all the decisions about the property he shared with his wife. By a 4-3 vote, the court reversed a judge who said the law was unconstitutional because it assumed that husbands were smarter than wives. The case involved a husband who had taken out a second mortgage on the family home over the objections of his wife, who was the breadwinner. Her name was Selina Martin. (04/10)

Legal

Political

According to a report by NOW's Project on Equal Education Rights (PEER), from June 1972 to October 1976 HEW managed to resolve a total of 179 complaints covered under Title IX–one out of every five filed. Two and three year delays were not uncommon, and the average wait on a case was 14 months. In 3/4 of the cases the government took on, HEW staff never even visited the school district charged. In more than four years after the bill's passage HEW had independently investigated a grand total of 12 of the country's 16,000 school districts. Overwork wasn't the explanation. For each staff investigator on the payroll, HEW received fewer than two complaints per year. The real problem, according to PEER was indecision over whether to enforce the law. (04)

San Francisco Mayor George Moscone–with gay Supervisor Harvey Milk at his side–signed into law a landmark gay rights ordinance that prohibited discrimination in employment and housing because of sexual orientation. (04/11)

Bayh, Holtzman and Edwards

Don Edwards (D-CA) subcommittee chair of the House Judiciary Committee, and Rep. Elizabeth Holtzman (D-NY) in the House and Senator Birch Bayh (D-IN), chairman of the judiciary subcommittee on the Constitution, the chief Senate sponsor of the Equal Rights Amendment, introduced resolutions that would extend by seven years the deadline for ratifying the amendment. (05/17)

NOW President Ellie Smeal was among several distinguished spokespersons urging a Senate subcommittee to act favorably on the Susan B. Anthony dollar coin. Smeal's testimony was strong and to the point about the need for using a real woman instead of "Miss Liberty" or some other mythical figure on the coin. Said Smeal: "Susan B. Anthony was an active participant in the great social change movements of her time. She expended her life's energy in the fight for the causes of freedom, justice and equality – a fight which goes on today. It is important that we recognize and pay suitable tribute to her work." (06)

More than 30 prominent Chicago-area Catholics announced the formation of a new organization called the Illinois Catholic Committee for the ERA. (06/05)

Despite opinion polls showing 73% of the American Catholic population in support of reproductive freedom and 68% in favor of ERA, the administrative committee of the National Conference of Catholic Bishops unanimously rejected a proposal for endorsement of the ERA as a separate issue from abortion. (06)

NOW's LDEF received a grant from *MS*. Foundation to carry on and expand its program to increase the number of women judges in the U.S. judiciary system. (06)

Although the Illinois House of Representatives voted 101-64 for ERA, the measure failed ratification by six votes because five Black male, pro-ERA representatives from Chicago failed to cast their votes as a protest on another issue. (They later switched their votes back). The 107th victory vote was expected to come from any one of a number of fence-sitters. (06/07)

The Backlash

Missouri Attorney General John Ashcroft and Nevada Attorney General Robert List filed suit in Federal District Courts against NOW, alleging violations of the Sherman Antitrust Act in NOW's coalition boycott of unratified states. The Nevada suit charged that the boycott had injured the state's tourist business. (02/27)

The city council of Akron, OH, voted 7 to 6 to institute severe restrictions on the operation of abortion clinics in Akron, including several procedural restraints clearly designed to harass and frustrate the operation of the clinics. Pro-choice advocates in Ohio uniformly declared the provisions of the ordinance were a "blatant

attempt to intimidate women who seek abortions." (02/28)

Violence against reproductive choice clinics continued as the Emma Goldman Clinic in Iowa City was fire-bombed following intensive picketing by anti-abortionists. (06/14)

YEAR	1978
U. S. President	Jimmy Carter
NOW President	Eleanor Smeal

EVENTS

The U.S. Supreme Court threw the concept and practice of affirmative action into doubt in its *Bakke* decision, upholding the general principles of affirmative action but striking down specific quota systems in higher education admission programs. Legal experts could not predict what impact the decision would have on affirmative action programs in other areas. (06/28)

Naomi James, second woman in history to circumnavigate the globe by herself, discovered she would be ineligible for admission to the Circumnavigators Club because she was a woman. (07)

Pope Paul VI died (08/06)and was succeeded by Albino Cardinal Luciani who chose the name, Pope John Paul I. ((08/26) Pope John Paul I died 33 days later (09/29) and there are those who suspect he was murdered to keep him from pursuing changes at the Vatican Bank and in the Church's position on birth control. He was succeeded by John Paul II, the former Karol Cardinal Wojtyla, a conservative and the first non-Italian in 455 years. (10/23)

ISSUES

Lifestyles

NOW's presence was felt in cities across America on Gay Freedom Day. In San Francisco, where some 240,000 people gathered to commemorate the day, the California NOW banner was cheered by spectators. NOW President Smeal addressed the crowd and emphasized NOW's commitment to fight the right-wing forces behind the anti-gay, anti-feminist backlash. In New York, Kay Whitlock, chair of NOW's Lesbian Rights Committee, addressed a crowd of 85,000 gay rights supporters. (06/25)

Thirteen thousand people watched 3,700 participants march in the eighth annual Gay Pride Parade on Hollywood Boulevard in Los Angeles (CA). The theme of the rally was "Stop the Briggs Initiative." (07/02)

Attorneys for 10 Los Angeles Mexican-American women who underwent sterilization procedures at USC Medical Center announced they would appeal the decision dismissing their suit against the doctors who performed the operations. The women claimed, after the procedures were done, that they had been forcibly performed without proper consent, since the release papers were signed when the women were in active labor. The judge dismissing the case, Jesse Curtis, failed to see the point as relevant. (07/08)

The Concerned Children of Congress, composed of the daughters of members of Congress began actively lobbying for passage of the ERA. (08)

Arriving not by hundreds or thousands, but by the tens of thousands, over 100,000 women and men of all ages and races marched down Constitution Avenue to the D.C. Capitol steps to deliver their message: the people of America want ERA and they want the extension! The NOW-organized march halted traffic and eclipsed the entire Capitol Mall in a sea of purple, gold, and white (the old suffragist colors). Marchers struggled through 95 degree heat to hear NOW President Smeal and other celebrity speakers congratulate them on their perseverance and dedication to ERA. (07/09)

Economic
Religion

NOW took out a full-page signature ad in the *New York Times* urging passage of legislation to extend the deadline for the ERA. (06/22)

Media

Climaxing three years of intensive lobbying by Massachusetts NOW members, the Massachusetts Displaced Homemakers Act was signed into law by Governor Michael Dukakis. NOW activists had spent all three years in full-time consciousness-raising in the state legislature to convince the lawmakers of the need for financial protection for women who were without income after years of providing unpaid household services for their families. (07/26)

The model for the commemorative medallion of the July 9 march was NOW LDEF President Muriel Fox who wore a period costume and carried the march flag.

More than 6,000 NOW members from 20 states from Alaska to New York descended on Washington D.C. to lobby on "Must Do Day" for the Senate to schedule its vote on the bill to extend the deadline for the ERA.(10)

Legal

The obnoxious "head and master" law in Louisiana, which made all Louisiana wives de jure slaves of their husbands, was voted out of existence by the Louisiana Senate, 36-2. (07)

Political

The Illinois House came within two votes of giving ERA ratification the required 3/5 majority. (06/22)

The Backlash

Thea Rossi Barron, chief lobbyist for the National Right to Life Committee, resigned to protest the growing collaboration between the anti-abortion movement and the right-wing. (09)

The formation of Concerned Women for America (CWA), a "pro-family" organization, was begun by Beverly LaHaye, wife of pastor Timothy LaHaye, the founder and president of Family Life Seminars. The LaHaye's conducted those seminars and authored several books on marriage together. Timothy LaHaye was also the founder of the San

Diego (CA) Christian Unified School System and Christian Heritage College. To swell its membership total, CWA adopted the practice of counting as members anyone who contributed money to the organization or signed petitions..

YEAR	1978
U. S. President	Jimmy Carter
NOW President	Eleanor Smeal

EVENTS

In the closing hours of the 95th Congress, passage of the Pregnancy Discrimination Bill overturned the U.S. Supreme Court decisions in *Gilbert vs. G.E. (1976) and Satty vs. Nashville Gas Co.* (1977). Both decisions had approved discrimination against "pregnant people," the former in the payment of disability benefits for women recovering from childbirth and the latter in denying women the use of their earned sick leave for hospitalization and recovery from childbirth. The hard-won victory was the result of a two-year massive campaign by NOW and a coalition of labor, feminist, and pro-choice groups. (10/15)

In San Francisco, Mayor George Moscone was shot to death in his office at City Hall, and a few minutes later gay Supervisor Harvey Milk was also shot and killed. Dan White, who had recently stepped aside as a Supervisor but then sought to withdraw his resignation and remain in office, surrendered to the police, and was booked on two counts of murder. Dianne Feinstein became the city's mayor. (11/27)

ISSUES

Education / Economic / Religion / Media / Legal / Political

In a victory for NOW and other feminist organizations, the House voted 233 to 189 to extend until June 30, 1982, the ratification deadline for the Equal Rights Amendment. (08/15) The U. S. Senate voted 60-36 to extend the deadline a few months later. (10/06) However, the extension voted was only half of the seven years that had been requested in the original bill–a compromise that doomed the ratification effort.

Rep. Elizabeth Holtzman's (D-NY) bill, protecting the privacy of rape victims in Federal trials by preventing cross examination into their prior sexual experience, was passed by the U.S. Congress. NOW had lobbied for passage of the legislation. (10/06)

The Second Annual ERA Walk raised $170,000 nationwide in pledges for the NOW ERA Strike Force. (08/26)

In a mood of celebration because of passage of the extension, the First NOW Bi-Annual Issues Conference (under NOW's new by-laws) was held in Washington, D.C. The Conference took action in many areas, including extension of the State of Emergency on ERA; a position against sterilization abuse; an inclusive statement on labor; development of a comprehensive reproductive rights campaign; adoption of the Homemakers' Bill of Rights; opposition to the Briggs initiative in California; support for D.C. voting representation; and recognition of the special problems of rural women and women in nursing homes. (10/05-08)

Feminists "held their own" in the 1978 elections, with neither dramatic gains or losses. Improvements were seen in statehouse elections, where the percentage of women rose from seven to 11%. Six women were elected to Lieutenant Governorships. But the representation of women in Congress dropped to 17, down two from 1976. (Yvonne Burke ran unsuccessfully for Attorney General of California and left her Congressional seat and Barbara Jordan retired). Nancy Kassebaum, the daughter of Alfred Landon, was elected the only woman Senate member. NOW's analysis: women remain tokens in the nation's political houses. (11)

U.S. District Judge Constance Baker ruled that women sports writers had a constitutional right to enter the locker room of the New York Yankees after a game to conduct interviews. The judge ruled that the policy of total exclusion of women from the Yankee locker room did not violate the players' right to privacy, but did deprive women sports writers of their rights to equal protection of the laws. (09/24)

Federal Judge Ellen Burns denied Yale University's request for dismissal of the suit *Price vs. Yale University,* charging the institution with sex discrimination based on sexual harassment of students. (11/29)

Dr. Margaret Mead, 76, anthropologist expert on primitive cultures, died of cancer. (11/06)

Golda Meir, Israel's first woman Prime Minister from 1969-1974, died at the age of 80. (12/08)

Four thousand Catholics, mostly women, marched on the streets of Baltimore, MD, calling for admission of women to the priesthood prior to attending the Women's Ordination conference. (11/10-12)

Lee Anne Schreiber was appointed sports editor of the *New York Times.* She headed a staff of 50 reporters, as well as took overall charge of the Sunday sports section and Sports Monday. She was the first woman to hold that position. (11/09)

NOW's National Board voted unanimously to join the legal brief being prepared by NOW's LDEF in the U.S. Supreme Court case of *Massachusetts v. Feeney,* the challenge to the state's veterans-preference hiring guidelines. (12)

At their midterm Conference in Memphis, TN, the Democratic Party's Executive Committee responded to 10 years of lobbying by NOW and other feminist organizations by voting to require that half the delegates to the party's 1980 national convention must be women. (12)

As the year closed, NOW's boycott of unratified states had gained the support of 321 organizations (compared to 66 in January) and 35 cities and counties (compared to one municipality 12 months before). (12)

The Backlash

Californian's voted in favor of Proposition 13, a referendum measure that cut property tax revenue by $7 billion. The measure was part of a conservative backlash against "excess government spending." (06/06)

Nine adults and four juveniles were arrested after they invaded the offices of the Hillcrest Abortion Clinic and Counseling Service in Washington, D.C. and refused to leave.

The Institute for Educational Affairs (IEA) was set up to fund right-wing campus newspapers, known as the Collegiate Network, and received financial support from Coors. The Coors Corporation also bought ads in all the Collegiate Network papers.

YEAR	1979
U. S. President	Jimmy Carter
NOW President	Eleanor Smeal

EVENTS

By a 6-3 vote, the U.S. Supreme Court declared unconstitutional a Pennsylvania law that required a doctor performing an abortion to choose the abortion method most likely to save the life of a fetus that might be old enough to survive outside the womb. The decision was rendered in the case of *Colautti v. Franklin*, with Justices Blackmun, Brennan, Stewart, Marshall, Powell and Stevens voting pro-choice, and White, Burger and Rehnquist voting anti-choice.(01/09)

NOW Membership-100,000

ISSUES

Education

Economic

Legal

Political

NOW, AAUW, PEER, WEAL, and the League of Women Voters began a campaign to counter a strong lobbying effort against Title IX, directed towards Congress by approximately 300 universities and colleges to exempt revenue-producing sports from Title IX guidelines. (01)

A so-called "null and void" resolution challenged the right of Congress to extend the ratification deadline and declared that if the ERA had not been ratified by the required number of states by the original deadline of March 22, 1979, then South Dakota's ratification of the ERA was "null and void." Most legal experts viewed the tactic, developed by opponents of the ERA, as unconstitutional. Support came primarily from a South Dakota Right-To-Life group. The state's NOW members became the core group of a statewide effort to defeat the resolution, led by State Coordinator Ronda Mason and State Legislative Coordinator Beverly Hills-Meyer. National NOW activists, Jennifer Klindt, Ruth Whitney and Debbie Erb went to South Dakota to assist with the campaign. They were among 35 NOW members from 16 states that National NOW recruited in 24 hours to help in the face of increasing recision threats in the embattled states. Like many members in these states, these activists took time from their jobs and families to organize, manage phone banks, work on vote counts, and generally roll up their sleeves to do whatever needed to be done. They became involved in every state where there was major recision or ratification activity. Among those who volunteered to fight recision efforts in 13 states were Patty Donaldson, Gloria Sackman Reed, Dixie White, Barbara Murrin, Zelle Andrews, Christie Klein, Dorothy Sales, Audrey Ghiazzoni and Barbara Davis. (01)

On the sixth anniversary of the landmark decision by the U.S. Supreme Court on abortion, Eleanor Smeal, national president of NOW, invited leaders of both sides of the issue to a meeting on February 15 to discuss the formation of a comprehensive reproductive health program to seek ways to lessen the need for abortion, to reduce the incidence of unwanted pregnancy, and to end the polarization and violence surrounding the abortion issue. (01/22)

Declaring that "the Social Security system as it now stands is institutionalized sexism at its worst," President Eleanor Smeal presented NOW's testimony before the Department of Health, Education and Welfare Social Security Advisory Council in Washington, D.C. Appearing on a panel with leaders of other women's organizations, Smeal led off the presentations with an impassioned statement on the plight of older women in this country, citing the failure of the Social Security System to provide a "measure of security in old age for the majority of our senior citizens." (01/04)

The AFL-CIO canceled plans to hold a convention in October in Miami Beach, citing the failure of Florida to ratify the ERA. (01/08)

As a result of a suit by New York NOW against the New York City Waterfront Commission, more than 100 women received temporary work permits from the New York Harbor Commission and were set to become the first women dockworkers in that city's history.(01)

Sue Von Lackum took a leave of absence from IBM to work for NOW during the drive to ratify the ERA. (01)

The Wyoming Senate, by a vote of 16-13 voted to postpone indefinitely Senate Joint Resolution 1, thus rejecting a move to rescind its ratification of the ERA. (01/17)

For the second time in a week, Miami Beach lost a major convention because of Florida's failure to ratify the ERA. Al Shanker, President of the American Federation of Teachers, (AFT) announced that his organization had decided to hold its 1982 meeting of 2,500 delegates in Honolulu, rather than in Miami as originally planned, because of Florida's failure to ratify the ERA. (01/13)

Johnson County/Iowa City (IA) NOW and other groups joined in helping Firefighter Linda Eaton fight sex discrimination at work. Eaton's request to be allowed to nurse her infant son, who would be brought by a family member to the firehouse during her personal time, was denied by the Firechief. The denial was reinforced by Iowa City officials who threatened to take disciplinary action if any breast feeding took place at the fire house. (01/22)

NOW launched a new National ERA Campaign for ratification and against illegal recisions. The campaign was designed to involve NOW members and thousands of other ERA supporters in ratified and unratified states. ERA action teams were set up in ratified states to focus on the prevention and defeat of any attempts to rescind in addition to maintaining a national pressure campaign on targets specified by an alert system. Meanwhile, campaigns in unratified states were set up to win three more states before the extended deadline for ratification. (01/01)

The Backlash

Former Catholic seminarian Joseph Scheidler of Chicago, IL, formed the Pro-Life Action League and began abortion clinic invasions.

American Life Lobby was formed and headed by Roman Catholics Judy Brown and husband Paul Brown, formerly of the National Right to Life Committee. The American Life Lobby opposed *both* abortion and artificial contraception.

A firebomb destroyed the Bill Baird Abortion Clinic in Hempstead, Long Island, NY. The clinic was believed to be the first in the United States. (02/15)

85

YEAR	1979
U. S. President	Jimmy Carter
NOW President	Eleanor Smeal

EVENTS

Bella Abzug was summarily fired as chair of the National Advisory Committee for Women after a 90-minute meeting with President Carter, who objected to the Committee's press release issued ahead of the meeting criticizing some of his policies. Her co-chair Carmen Votaw, committee member Eleanor Smeal, President of NOW, and 26 of 40 other members resigned in protest. (01/12)

A Lou Harris poll showed 57% support for ERA nationally. The poll was done for ABC news. (02/19)

The first of the Susan B. Anthony dollar coins was struck at the San Francisco Mint. (02/02)

ISSUES

Lifestyles / Economic / Media / Legal / Political

After NOW President Eleanor Smeal called for a dialogue to discover any interests in common with anti-abortion groups, 60 representatives from 30 groups, (10 anti-choice and 20 pro-choice), met in Washington, D.C. Smeal chaired the five-hour meeting. Leaders attending included: Karen Mulhauser, National Abortion Rights Action League; Faye Wattleton, Planned Parenthood; Edie Van Horn, United Auto Workers; Dr. Mildred Jefferson, Right to Life Crusade; Thea Rossi Barron, former lobbyist for the National Right to Life Committee; and Sean Morton Downey, Life Amendment PAC. Despite the attempt to have a reasonable dialogue, three members of People Expressing a Concern for Everyone (PEACE) disrupted the press conference with displays of so-called pickled fetuses. (02/15)

"Females constitute 27.7% of the U.S. population. Half of them are teenagers or in their 20's. They wear revealing outfits, jiggle a lot, but don't do much else. More than a third are unemployed or without any identifiable pursuit or purpose. Most others are students, secretaries, homemakers, household workers or nurses. For everyone who's in law enforcement, at least two are criminals." That's the composite portrait television drama painted of the American woman, according to a study released by the U.S. Commission on Civil Rights. (02/15)

A suit filed by Lakeland & Morristown, NJ, NOW in 1975 on behalf of eight employees and all other affected female employees of the Mennen Company of Hanover, NJ, which charged the company with discrimination against women in hiring, promotions, compensation, and other terms and conditions of employment, was finally settled out of court. (02)

Virginia legislature passed the Family Protection Act, a domestic violence intervention measure which was the primary legislation supported by West Virginia NOW. (03/10)

The charges of trespass, disorderly conduct and assault against Virginia NOW ERA activists Jean Marshall Clark and Marianne Fowler were finally dropped. ACLU represented Clark and Fowler against the charges stemming from the activists' forcible removal from the Virginia state capitol after the defeat of an ERA resolution in February, 1978. ACLU also filed suit on behalf of two Mississippi NOW members who were ordered to remove an ERA poster from the capitol rotunda. The state was forced to allow the Pro-ERA demonstrations to continue. (03)

Judge Elmo B. Hunter ruled in Kansas City, MO, that NOW had not violated provisions of the Sherman Antitrust Act in promoting the boycott of the 15 states that had failed to ratify the ERA. After more than three months of deliberation, Hunter ruled that the parties had stipulated that the sole purpose of the boycott was ratification of an Amendment to the Constitution. The participants were not moved by any anti-competitive purpose." The ruling was handed down 51 weeks after Missouri, the first of three plaintiffs, filed against NOW. (02/21)

The state of Mississippi again refused to enter the 20th century by defeating a resolution calling for the state to finally ratify the 19th Amendment giving women the right to vote. The Magnolia State was the single holdout among several states which, although late, finally added their names to the ranks of ratified states. Shortly thereafter the ERA was, not surprisingly, defeated in a Mississippi Senate Committee. (03)

The United Mine Workers, following the lead of the AFL-CIO, said that it was cancelling a planned fall convention in Miami because Florida had not approved the Equal Rights Amendment. (04/25)

North Dakota Citizens for the ERA, an alliance which included NOW, AAUW, BPW, Common Cause, The League of women Voters, North Dakota Presswomen, and the Home Economics Association, defeated a "null and void" bill after previously defeating a recision attempt.

Rochester (MN) NOW voted to establish a task force for equal treatment of women and children in the news media and to establish a special fund to carry out the work of this task force. The decision was made at a meeting with Wisconsin attorney Priscilla MacDougal who was in Rochester to advise NOW on its case pending with the Rochester Human Rights Commission against the Rochester Post-Bulletin. NOW charged the newspaper with sex discrimination because the Post-Bulletin refused to identify a woman by her own name in the birth announcement of her child. The Post-Bulletin routinely used only the father's name in the announcement. (03)

A woman is not morally unfit to practice law because she lives with a man who is not her husband, the Virginia Supreme Court ruled unanimously. Bonnie C. Cord, a 34-year-old lawyer for the Energy Department in Washington, DC, was denied permission by a state trial judge in 1978 to take the Virginia bar examination when he learned that Cord was not married to the man with whom she shared a house. The Supreme Court said that Cord's domestic arrangement had no rational connection with her fitness to practice law. (04/20)

The Backlash

Paul Weyrich formed the Religious Roundtable under Ed McAteer as the Right Wing counterpart of the liberal National Council of Churches. McAteer later arranged a meeting between Jerry Falwell, Weyrich and Howard Phillips, who set Falwell up as media spokesman for the organization they had devised: The Moral Majority. Weyrich also provided the organization's first executive director, Robert Billings.

A new lobby, Christian Voice, opened in Washington, DC, and promised an intense anti-gay campaign in Congress. (03/19)

YEAR	1979
U. S. President	Jimmy Carter
NOW President	Eleanor Smeal

EVENTS

The Women Airforce Service Pilots (WASP's) of World War II finally received military status from the Defense Department after almost 35 years. Although the WASP's flew over 60 million miles in wartime service from 1942 to 1944, they were considered "civilians" by the military, meaning that neither they nor their families were ever eligible for military retirement or educational benefits. Thirty eight of the women died in the line of duty and the government did not even pay to send their bodies home. (05/22)

ISSUES

Lifestyles

Economic

Religion

Media

Legal

Political

In the name of deregulation, Lionel Van Deerlin (D-San Diego, CA), chair of the Communications Subcommittee of the House introduced the Communications Act of 1979, HR 13015, legislation to wipe out public rights to fairness, equal time, news and public affairs, community ascertainment, equal employment standards, the license renewal process and other safeguards. In the past, NOW used these rules and regulations of the Federal Communications Commission (FCC) to challenge television and radio licenses or to negotiate agreements with local broadcasters on programming for and employment of women. The results were the increased coverage of feminist issues on news and public affairs programming and the improvement in minority and female hiring practices. (03)

Colorado NOW scored a significant victory when a State Senate Committee defeated a bill that would have cut off all State funding for abortion services and referrals. The vote was 10-4. The victory came on the heels of Colorado NOW's massive organizing effort against the proposed funding cut off. Peg Ackerman, immediate past Colorado State NOW Coordinator, and Barbara Malsch Chase, newly elected state coordinator, became aware of a major assault being mounted against Medicaid funding for abortion during the `79 legislative session. "We vowed to make use of the organizing tools Colorado NOW had developed during the battle for the ERA extension," said Ackerman. There were five phone banks and the Chair of the Senate Appropriations Committee alone received over a 1,000 public opinion messages opposing the funding cutoff bill. (04)

Some 250 people paid from $100 to $1,000 each to attend the ERA "Homestretch Campaign" reception at the Beverly Hilton in Los Angeles, co-hosted by Dorothy Jonas for the Los Angeles Chapter and the San Fernando Valley Chapter of NOW to raise funds for NOW's National ERA Strike Force. Among the ERA-supporting celebrities who attended and/or sponsored the event were: Frances and Norman Lear, Joan Hackett, Maureen Reagan, Lily Tomlin, Alan Alda, Marsha Mason, Neil Simon, Patty Duke, John Astin, Polly Bergen, Helen Reddy, Jeff Wald, Jean Stapleton, Mary Lasker and Joan Palevsky. (03/24)

Dorothy Jonas

Jean Stapleton

Norman Lear, Frances Lear, Eleanor Smeal, Joan Hackett and Maureen Reagan.

Promising a "unified, massive campaign," NOW President Eleanor Smeal led a major leadership news conference to mark the beginning of the extended period for ratification of the ERA. Representatives of 66 pro-ERA groups were on hand at the conference, which was Coordinated by NOW and ERAmerica. (03/22)

NOW President Ellie Smeal testified before the House Subcommittee on Retirement Income and Employment of the Select Committee on Aging. Smeal challenged the Subcommittee to develop and enact a Homemakers' Bill of Rights. Smeal told the Subcommittee, "The woman in midlife, as portrayed by society is a myth. . . . The harsh reality is that women in mid-life, whether married, divorced, widowed, or single, find that their opportunities for employment and economic security are severely limited, and their futures precarious and uncertain .[See Documents section for complete text of Homemaker's Bill of Rights.] (05/07)

Charging that Congressional Budget Committees are "going the President one better in abandoning human need considerations," Ellie Smeal, President of NOW, urged Congress to appropriate Fiscal Year 1980 funds for human needs programs at least at current policy levels. In testimony before the HEW/Labor Subcommittee of the House Appropriations Committee, Smeal focused on CETA, AFDC, Social Security, and reproductive health programs. Citing public opinion polls that showed that the vast majority of Americans want "value for their tax dollars, but not drastic cuts that would create hardship and unemployment for the disadvantaged," Smeal called on Congress to "consider the needs of the people" in its deliberations on the FY 80 Budget. (04)

The United Steelworkers union said it would move its 1980 convention from Las Vegas to Los Angeles because Nevada had not ratified the Equal Rights Amendment. (05/11)

The Backlash

ERA opponent Phyllis Schlafly, at a cocktail dinner at the Shoreham-Americana hotel in Washington, D.C. on March 22, the original deadline for ERA ratification, declared, "It's all over." Guests entered by passing a wreath of yellow and white mums with a black ribbon across it bearing the words "Rest in Peace - ERA." (03/22)

The "Pro-Family" movement began forming as an alliance of Right Wing groups. With Connie Marshner, head of the Family Policy Division of Paul Weyrich's Free Congress Research and Education Foundation, they drafted the "Family Protection Act," as a smokescreen for a range of social and political goals. Senator Paul

Laxalt (D-NV) introduced the bill in Congress.

YEAR	1979		
U. S. President	Jimmy Carter		
NOW President	Eleanor Smeal		

EVENTS

In a major decision, the U.S. Supreme Court ruled that an individual has the right to bring a private lawsuit to uphold the anti-discrimination provisions of Title IX. NOW's LDEF had filed an amicus curiae brief in the suit. Because of the decision, individuals need not go through HEW (a cumbersome process) to file suit. The effect was expected to encourage institutions to bring themselves into compliance with Title IX more quickly. (05/14)

Tens of thousands of demonstrators walked from New York's Christopher Street to Central Park to commemorate the 10th anniversary of the "Stonewall Riot," which many consider to be the beginning of the gay rights movement. (06/24)

Dan White, convicted of killing San Francisco mayor George Moscone and gay Supervisor Harvey Milk, was given the incredibly lenient sentence of seven years, eight months after a defense of temporary insanity resulting from eating too many Twinkies. He was convicted only of voluntary manslaughter the least possible offense in his case. (05/21)

ISSUES

Lifestyles

The family of Karen Silkwood was awarded $10.5 million in a landmark decision, when Kerr-McGee Corp. was found liable for Silkwood's plutonium contamination. Eleanor Smeal, NOW President, proclaimed "This victory is in honor of Karen Silkwood, who broke the stereotype that women on the job will tolerate exploitation." The campaign led by Sara Nelson, coordinator of NOW's Labor Task Force, kept the Karen Silkwood case alive. (05/18)

Lily Tomlin with her mother.

Economic

Los Angeles NOW held its second annual Mother's Day Champagne Brunch, with special guests Lily Tomlin and her mother; actress Jean Stapleton; Lorne and Nancy Greene; and School Board member Kathleen Brown Rice. The event emphasized the message that mothers need the Equal Rights Amendment and recognition of the economic value of their work - not just flowers and candy for a day. (05/13)

Legal

A federal appeals court found that the employment practices of the Los Angeles Police Department before 1973 did violate civil rights laws: the LAPD had maintained separate gender-based job classifications. The appeals court also found that the "unisex" system adopted by the Department July 1, 1973, had not been shown to justify its discriminatory impact. The system required that all officers–men and women–meet a height requirement of at least 5 feet 7 inches, later lowered to 5 feet 6 inches. (05)

Final action on a Montana nullification bill was taken by the House when it voted 59-30 to accept the Judiciary Committee's "do not pass" recommendation. State and national NOW people led by Gloria Sackman Reed (PA NOW) were responsible for setting up the Montana phone bank operation which was credited with major impact on the successful outcome.

Thanks to hard lobbying by NOW and many other feminist organizations, the New Orleans (LA) City Council voted unanimously to endorse the ERA and to urge the Louisiana legislature to ratify. The final vote was solidified, according to observers, by the contrast in behavior between ERA supporters and members of Stop-ERA, who stormed the Council meeting, grabbed microphones and screamed at Council members. (06/07)

For the fourth time, the Florida House voted in favor of ratifying the ERA. The vote was 65 - 53. (05/17)

Political

Opponents of ERA defeated the measure in the Florida Senate 21-19. The defeat was achieved by a few key Senators, among them Guy Spicola, (who had voted for ERA in 1973, 1975, and 1977), and Pete Skinner, (who voted against ERA in 1975, but for it in 1977). The switch-voting made it clear that ERA had been a political trading item in Florida for years. Vote-switching first surfaced in 1977 in the ERA campaigns in Nevada, Florida and North Carolina. (05/24)

Representative John Burton (D-CA), chair of a House Select Committee on Aging, announced his support of a "Homemakers' Bill of Rights" at the second day of hearings on the problems of women in midlife. Burton responded to the urgings of NOW through its President, Ellie Smeal, that such legislation was absolutely mandatory to ensure that women working in the home would have financial security in their own names and in the events of widowhood or divorce. (06)

NOW joined forces with the Department of Defense in testifying before a Congressional Committee against restrictions on abortion funding for military personnel and their dependents. (05/22)

More than 300 ERA supporters attended a NOW fundraising reception in Washington, D.C., to launch the National ERA Ratification Campaign. Senator Edward Kennedy addressed the function, speaking forcefully in support of ERA. NOW President Eleanor Smeal promised to take the ratification battle to the college campuses, to make young people aware of their stake in ERA as future fathers and mothers, and members of the business world. (06/25)

The Backlash

Idaho et al v. Freeman was filed in federal District Court in Boise, ID, by the states of Idaho and Arizona to challenge the constitutionality of the ERA extension and to seek validation of a state's power to rescind a prior ratification. The presiding judge was Marion J. Callister, a Regional Representative in the hierarchy of the Mormon Church. (05/09)

Perhaps the most offensive turnaround in the Florida campaign was committed by Sen. Vernon Holloway, who had promised the results of a straw poll from his constituency would be decisive in how he voted on the issue. His constituency responded in favor of ERA by 2 to 1, yet Holloway voted "no." (05/24)

Massachusetts Governor Edward J. King appointed two anti-choicers to head a new state Commission on the Status of Women. The old panel was fired for criticizing his rejection of a one-time 6% cost-of-living bonus to welfare families. (06/25)

YEAR	1979		
U. S. President	Jimmy Carter		
NOW President	Eleanor Smeal		

EVENTS

A green light was given by the U.S. Supreme Court to private, voluntary affirmative action which promotes the hiring and advancement of women and minorities in traditionally segregated job categories, when it ruled in the case of *U.S. Steelworkers of America and Kaiser Aluminum v. Weber*. (06/27)

A critical abortion decision was reached by the U.S. Supreme Court 8-1 in *Belliotti v. Baird*, in which they overturned a Massachusetts law that required parental consent or judicial approval for a minor to obtain an abortion. The decision invalidated large segments of anti-abortion ordinances in states such as Louisiana, Kansas and Ohio, but 1980 was expected to

see a flurry of introductions of more restrictive state legislation. (07/02)

The Department of Justice filed a Motion to Disqualify Judge Marion J. Callister on the basis of his high position in the priesthood of the Mormon Church. (08/21)

ISSUES

Lifestyles

Education

Economic

Religion

Media

Legal

Political

A study prepared by the Harvard-based Project on Human Sexual Development found that many men agreed that they should help with housework and child care, even though most didn't follow through. Even in households where the woman had a full time job, in less than 3% did the father do most of the household tasks, and only in 12% were the tasks shared equally. (07/17)

The U.S. Supreme Court struck a severe blow to equity for women when it upheld the Massachusetts law granting veterans an absolute, lifelong preference in state government jobs. Since the Massachusetts law was among the most extreme, the Court's ruling implicitly upheld the constitutionality of veteran's employment preference statutes in all states and in the federal government. NOW had filed an amicus brief in the case (*Massachusetts v. Feeney*) arguing that the preference had the effect of discriminating against women. (06/05)

NOW President Ellie Smeal and Phyllis Schlafly debated on the popular Phil Donahue TV show before 5,000 people in the St. Louis (MO) Civic Arena. (07/11)

The national NOW board, at its meeting in Denver, voted to enter an amicus curiae brief in the Pennsylvania *Roe v. Casey* Medicaid funding case, and in the *Minnesota v. Continental Can Co.*, where NOW LDEF was listed as attorney. (07/28-29)

According to *U.S. News and World Report*, "Women, who not many years ago were fighting city hall as outsiders, now are moving in and taking over." They went on to cite the fact that 750 women mayors out of approximately 18,800 municipal governments was the basis for the statement. Since that was less than 4%, the "take-over" didn't seem imminent. (07)

New York NOW members expressed their disapproval of a Tiffany's ad promoting the store's Brides Registry Service by wearing bridal veils along with street clothes, and handing out leaflets to passers-by explaining the legal rights of wives in New York State. Among other things, the Tiffany ad asserted that the three most important decisions a woman had to make concerned "her silverware. . . her china. . . her crystal." (06/16)

In an unprecedented move the city of Los Angeles barred J.P. Stevens Co. from doing business with the city. NOW's Southwest Regional Director Mary Margaret Smith testified against Stevens at public hearings documenting the company's long history of discrimination agains women and minorities. The company was termed an "irresponsible bidder" by L.A.'s Board of Public Works for its persistent failure to comply with the city's affirmative action and equal employment opportunity ordinances. (06/26)

NOW chapters throughout the country raised over $180,000 for the ERA in Walkathons on Women's Equality Day.(08/25-26)

The National Women's Hall of Fame was dedicated in Seneca Falls, NY, 131 years after the convening of the First Women's Rights Convention by Elizabeth Cady Stanton and Lucretia Mott in the same village. The first 20 selections, chosen in 1973, included: Jane Addams, Marian Anderson, Susan B. Anthony, Clara Barton, Mary McLeod Bethune, Elizabeth Blackwell, Pearl Buck, Rachel Carson, Mary Cassatt, Emily Dickinson, Amelia Earhart, Alice Hamilton, Helen Hayes, Helen Keller, Eleanor Roosevelt, Margaret Chase Smith, Florence Sabin, Elizabeth Cady Stanton, Helen Crooke Taussig and Harriet Tubman. The three 1976 honorees were Abigail Adams, Margaret Mead and Mildred "Babe" Didrikson Zaharias. (07/21)

Male strongholds persisted in the nation's schools, according to a study made by the Project on Equal Education Rights (PEER) of the NOW Legal Defense and Education Fund. A PEER study, "Back-to-School Lineup: Where Girls and Women Stand in Education Today," reported on female participation in three traditionally male areas of school life: top-level school administration, vocational courses leading to higher-paying jobs traditionally held by men, and interscholastic athletics. (09/04)

Twenty four out of 61 female crew members aboard the USS Norton Sound were accused of lesbianism. NOW Chapters rallied in their defense. (08)

The Minority Women's Leadership Conference held in Washington, D.C. was sponsored by the NOW Minority Women's Committee. "Racism and Sexism—A Shared Struggle for Equal Rights," was the theme of the conference. (08/25)

The Backlash

The National Catholic Conference of Bishops and the U.S. Catholic Conference,went to court in Washington, D.C., seeking to delete the provision of the Pregnancy Discrimination Act which said that employers only had to provide medical coverage for abortions when the life of the woman was endangered. The Bishops

contended that the provision violated the Church's First Amendment Rights as well as those of employers who held religious, moral, or ethical objections to abortion. The EEOC agreed not to enforce the abortion coverage provisions until the case was decided. The Catholic Bishops delayed passage of the Pregnancy Discrimi-

nation Act when it was before Congress in 1978 by their insistence on an amend-ment to the bill that would have empowered employers to discriminate against women who had abortions not only in benefits, but also in hiring, promotions and other incidences in employment. (06)

89

YEAR	1979
U. S. President	Jimmy Carter
NOW President	Eleanor Smeal

EVENTS

"Pornography is a Feminist Issue" was the message to Times Square smut merchants, as more than 5,000 feminists and friends assailed the sex shops, peep shows and pornographic movie houses among "Fun City's" 42nd Street. The demonstration, sponsored by New York City's "Women Against Pornography" group, drew college students and feminists from several states, and local members of unions, theater groups and neighborhood associations. The marchers chanted "Two-Four-Six-Eight, Pornography is woman-hate," and "Clean it up/Shut it down,/ Make New York a safer town." (10/20)

ISSUES

Lifestyles

Margaret Sanger with her sons.

Education

NOW National, State and Chapter events honored Margaret Sanger, feminist pioneer in the fight for reproductive rights, on the 100th anniversary of her birth. These events marked a major step-up in visible national action for reproductive rights and pro-choice.(09/14)

Economic

Religion

The women of California's State Assembly got in some feminist jabs at their male counterparts when they brought in a muscle man for an introduction of the type usually reserved for beauty queens. "Mr. Golden Bear, 1979" was dressed in shorts and a tank top, and introduced by Assemblywoman Maxine Waters (D-Los Angeles). (09/10)

Media

Texas NOW staged a creative demonstration when over 70 members participated in two locations at highways leading from Texas into the unratified states of Arkansas and Louisiana. Members stationed themselves on the highways into Louisiana near Orange, TX, and into Arkansas near Texarkana. Sample Burma Shave-style messages: "Equal Rights Amendment–Entering Louisiana/ We sadly regret/ Women there do not have/ Equal rights yet/ Don't spend in Louisiana/ Until ERA is ratified there." And

Legal

"Welcome to Texas/ Isn't it great/That now you are in/An Equal Rights state/ Spend in Texas–Ratified in 1972." (09)

Political

Quad Cities (IL) NOW sponsored a "Take Back the Night" rally with approximately 150 persons participating. Those in attendance marched five miles from the Rock Island County Courthouse to Lincoln Park and back, carrying candles, flashlights and picket signs.(09)

Sister Mary Theresa Kane, a high-ranking leader of American nuns, publicly challenged Pope John Paul II to reconsider his stand against women becoming priests. The unprecedented action occurred in Washington D.C. when Sister Theresa introduced the Pontiff at a prayer service for 5,000 nuns in the National Shrine of the Immaculate Conception. (10/07)

According to a study released by the Screen Actors Guild, men were over-represented and women and minorities under-represented on TV network programming. The study was based on 1,365 prime time and Saturday morning programs from 1968 - 1978. They also observed that programming was dominated by males, masculine values and questions of power, with women's concerns depicted as marriage, romance and the family. (10/29)

Thirty-four national women's magazines dedicated a portion of their issues to the ERA in the month of November. (11)

"NOW More Than Ever" was the theme of the National NOW Conference held in Los Angeles with 3,000 members attending. The persistent concern of the conference was the nearness of the cut-off date for ratification of the ERA (June 30, 1982). Smeal was re-elected president along with her team of officers: Sandra Roth, Secretary; Jane Wells-Schooley, Vice President Action; Judy Goldsmith, Executive Vice President; and Alice Chapman, Treasurer. (10/05-06)

The Department of Health, Education, and Welfare found that the Duval County (FL) School District was not in compliance with the regulation implementing Title IX of the Education Amendments of 1972. The district was notified that of the eight charges levied against the school system by Jacksonville (FL) NOW on December 13, 1977, three were sustained in their entirety and three were being analyzed further for their discriminatory effects on women employees and students. (11/07)

Running through the city streets of Los Angeles and neighboring communities, over a course last used for the 1932 Olympic marathon, Beverly Shingles of New Zealand outdistanced a pack of 56 competitors and won the first annual 20th Century Fox Los Angeles Women's Marathon. However, the Women's Marathon was not scheduled as an event in the 1984 Olympic Games. Conservative forces on the International Olympic Committee maintained that women were not physically suited to running the 26-mile marathon. (11/03)

Seventy nine members of the House of Representatives filed a motion to intervene in the Idaho court case which challenged Congressional authority in extending the time period for ratifying the ERA. The Idaho suit was filed by the states of Idaho and Arizona. (11/15)

The Backlash

In *Idaho et al v. Freeman*, the suit challenging the ERA extension, Judge Callister issued an order denying the Department of Justice's Motion to Disqualify himself, thereby refusing to withdraw from the case. (10/04)

Arsonists set several fires in a Rockville, MD, abortion clinic, and stole $1000 worth of medication. (09/07)

The American Life Lobby and the central New York Right to Life Federation initiated a nationwide boycott of United Airlines, contending that the company had made a $7,000 donation to Planned Parenthood. The donation was actually from employees of United Airlines, and not a corporate gift. (09/17)

YEAR	1979
U. S. President	Jimmy Carter
NOW President	Eleanor Smeal

EVENTS

The NOW National Board, at its December meeting in New York City, voted unanimously to recommend to the NOW Political Action Committee (NOW/PAC) that it oppose the nomination and re-election of President Jimmy Carter. The recommendation was unanimously passed by the PAC the same weekend. The primary factors in the decision were that

President Carter with Presidential Assistant Midge Costanza

the President had failed to use the power of his office effectively for ratification of the ERA; that significant and substantial ground in the area of reproductive rights was lost during his administration; and that to remain silent was to support the President by covering up the inadequacy of his performance. (12)

ISSUES

Lifestyles

More than 2,000 community, business, labor, academic and government leaders met in New York City to participate in the NOW Legal Defense and Education Fund's National Assembly on the Future of the Family to find practical and workable solutions to the problems being encountered in the rapid transition to a society of "non-nuclear-family" families. (11/19)

Economic

The National March for Lesbian and Gay Rights attracted over 100,000 marchers to Washington, D.C.. It was the first national march for gay rights. Experienced march organizers were assigned by NOW President Eleanor Smeal to help stage the event. (10/14)

Religion

The New Testament "points toward the admission of women to priestly ministry" said a task force of Roman Catholic biblical scholars after concluding a three year study for the Catholic Biblical Association of America. "While male leaders may have been more prominent and numerous in the early church, and while women's activities may have been somewhat limited by what was culturally permissible, many roles which ultimately were associated with the priestly ministry were evidently never restricted to men," the report said. (12)

Media

Legal

A two-and-a-half year war on lurid album covers depicting violence against women culminated in a public renunciation of such promotional tactics by Warner Communications, Inc. (WCI). "The WCI record group opposes the depiction of violence against women or men on album covers and in related promotional material," WCI President David H. Horowitz said in a joint statement issued by WCI and Women Against Violence Against Women. (11/08)

Political

Sonia Johnson, founder of Mormons for the ERA, was tried by the Church of the Latter Day Saints for the "crime" of supporting the ERA. NOW activists on both coasts called attention to her plight by bearing witness through vigils and by appearing on radio and television to spread the truth about the issues involved in Johnson's trial and banishment from the Mormon Church. In Los Angeles, 125 NOW members and friends from Oxnard to Orange County gathered in front of the Mormon Temple in West Los Angeles in a silent vigil. Many members wore gags to symbolize the attempt to silence Johnson by the male hierarchy of her church. In an emotional ceremony, Mormon Christine Chapman burned her baptismal certificate in front of the TV cameras. Johnson's supporters also surrounded the church where Sonia Johnson was on trial in Virginia. (12/01)

Twenty-eight women, charging that IUDs had lacerated their uterine walls and caused infection, filed lawsuits totaling $140 million against the makers of the Dalkon Shield. (12/20)

NOW members demonstrated in the rain outside the White House to protest the Carter Administration's inaction on the issue of disqualification of Judge Marion J. Callister, the high-ranking member of the hierarchy of the Mormon Church who was presiding over the Idaho case challenging the ERA extension and seeking validation of recision. The protest also was directed at the President's 30-minute "showcase" multi-issue meeting with some 18 leaders of women's groups. NOW had initiated the meeting with the President for the sole purpose of discussing the Idaho suit, the Callister disqualification and the Administration's plans to win ERA ratification in 1980. (12/13)

Eleanor Smeal, President of NOW, testified before the Washington, D.C. hearings of the White House Conference on Families. (12/01)

NOW began a "pilot project" with three objectives: to analyze equal opportunity programs at broadcast stations in at least three states, to examine the role of women in station ownership, and to assume a major role in promoting the production and syndication of public affairs programs dealing with women's issues. The project was conceived and carried out largely by Kathy Bonk, NOW Task Force Coordinator in media reform. (12)

NOW activists defeated ERA recision efforts in 13 states. (12)

The Backlash

Anti-ERA activist Phyllis Schlafly testified against proposals to split earning credits for Social Security evenly between husbands and wives, including in the event of divorce, claiming "anti-family forces" were behind the proposed changes. Social Security Commissioner Stanford G. Ross testified that "a program that basically views women as dependents in lifelong marriages is out of step with reality." (11/01) NOW President Eleanor Smeal testified in favor of the changes and pointed out that Social Security perpetuated in retirement the sex discrimination that women faced in the job market. (11/02)

Sonia Johnson, 43, a fifth-generation Mormon and mother of four, was excommunicated from her church. Convicted by a three-man Bishops Court on the charge of "apostasy," Johnson now faced–according to the tenets of her own faith–eternal separation from her family for her work for equal rights for women. (12/05)

91

YEAR	1980
U. S. President	Jimmy Carter
NOW President	Eleanor Smeal

EVENTS

A new community property law became law in Louisiana, depriving Louisiana husbands of their status as "head and master" of the household. (01)

A federal judge ruled in *McRae v. Harris* that imposing severe restrictions on Federal funding of medically necessary abortions was unconstitutional. Judge John F. Dooling, Jr. of the

Federal District Court in Brooklyn, NY, struck down the Hyde Amendment, which had cut off most federal funding of abortions. (01/15) [See Supreme Court reversal (06) page 94]

For the first time the nation's federal courts were ordered to provide equal job opportunities to racial minorities and women. The U.S. Judicial Conference, a self-governing agency of the federal court system, issued the order along with its opinion that it was "inappropriate" for any judge to belong to an organization that "practices invidious discrimination." (02)

ISSUES

Lifestyles

Despite massive lobbying by NOW and other organizations in Sacramento, CA, AB-1, the proposed legislation that would have outlawed employment discrimination against gay men and lesbians, was kept from reaching the California Assembly floor. The bill was thus dead for the year. (01/14)

The National ERA Outreach Campaign launched a special NOW ERA Campus Campaign project. ERA campus organizers and local activists began traveling to various colleges and universities around the country to organize campus Action Teams on the ERA. (01)

A bill to create a Women's Rights Historical Park in Seneca Falls, NY, was introduced in the U.S. Congress. The Elizabeth Cady Stanton Foundation backed passage of the bill, which was proposed following a study by the National Park Service. (02/05)

Education

Thirty-three percent of all high school athletes were female–a 600% increase since the early 70's, according to figures supplied by the Women's Sports Foundation. The increase was the direct result of the feminist movement, and the increased funding was a result of the passage of Title IX, for which NOW fought.

Economic

Religion

Members of Detroit NOW picketed their local station during the 1979-80 campaign.

Fifty-five women and men in Washington, D.C. participated in a silent protest of the Catholic Church's refusal to admit women to the priesthood on the third anniversary of the Vatican declaration against the ordination of women. Participants included NOW President Eleanor Smeal, Treasurer Alice Chapman, former National Secretary Jean Conger, and former Virginia Assistant Coordinator Audrey Ghizzoni. Accusing the church of sexism, the protesters, wearing blue arm bands, stood in a "witness for justice" demonstration during a mass held at St. Matthew's Cathedral. Similar demonstrations were conducted on the same day in Boston, Chicago, Hartford, CT; Providence, RI; New York City, and Albuquerque, NM. (01/27)

NOW announced that it supported the inclusion of women in the proposed draft registration. "If there is to be registration," said Eleanor Smeal, NOW President, "it must include women. Let's face it—women are an established part of the modern military. We are a key part of the trained and trainable pool of young people required to operate today's military, which is more in need of brains than brawn.... NOW is against the registration of both young men and young women because it is a response which stimulates an environment of preparation for war. But if there is a draft, it must include women." (02/08)

Media

"Three's A Crowd," a suggestive TV game show was picketed by NOW chapters and other groups across the country because it implied intimate relations between secretaries and their bosses. Its cancellation by both KNXT and KNBC in Los Angeles was hailed as a victory by Los Angeles Working Women and Los Angeles NOW. (01/15)

Political

Missouri NOW rallied forces for hearings held on the Equal Rights Amendment in the Missouri Senate. Supporters came from all parts of the state to hear testimony from a wide range of ERA proponents including Margaret Bush Wilson, National Chair-person of the NAACP; Michael Mc Auliffe, Bishop of the Catholic Diocese of Jefferson City, MO; Charles Curry, business leader; Mary Ann Sedey, Missouri ERA Coalition; and Duke McVey, representing Labor. Thesupporters of ERA exceeded 1,000 and they outnumbered the opposition 4-to-1. The ERA was passed out of the Senate Committee 4-3 the next day. (01/15)

California NOW members "blitzed" the convention of the California Democratic State Central Committee, contributing to Senator Kennedy's "straw poll" victory over President Carter and California Gov. Brown. National Board member Shelly Mandell of Los Angeles led the contingent. (01/18-20)

Legal

Colorado NOW sent a check for $25,902.77 for deposit to the National NOW-ERA Fund. It represented National's share of their Walkathon receipts.(01/07)

Feminist Ruth Bader Ginsburg, the first female tenured professor at Columbia University School of Law and the former director of the Women's Rights Project of the ACLU, was nominated by President Carter for a judgeship on the U.S. Court of Appeals for the District of Columbia. (01)

The Backlash

Right-to-Lifers victimized an innocent Rhode Island couple, Linda and Brian Grimes, whose only chance ever to have children was in out-of-uterus conception (the advance pioneered in England two years ago). Under pressure from Right-to-Lifers the Norfolk Clinic at Eastern Virginia Medical School, where Linda was undergoing

tests, was forced to halt the program. (01)

Father William R. Callahan, founder of Priests for Equality, and a strong supporter of the ordination of women in the priesthood in the Roman Catholic church, was silenced and transferred by his Jesuit superior in Rome. (01)

About 45,000 largely Roman Catholic anti-abortionists rallied in Washington to protest the Supreme Court decision in *Roe v. Wade* in 1973 with the so-called "March for Life," organized by Nellie Gray. Parochial school children swelled the line of march as always, with the Knights of Columbus serving as parade marshals. (01/22)

YEAR	1980
U. S. President	Jimmy Carter
NOW President	Eleanor Smeal

EVENTS

The Eighth Circuit Court of Appeals upheld the right of NOW to urge others to boycott states which had failed to ratify the Equal Rights Amendment. The decision, which came two years and one month after NOW was first sued by the state of Missouri and its Attorney John Ashcroft, affirmed the February 28, 1979, ruling of Judge Elmo C. Hunter that

NOW's activities were a political expression protected by the First Amendment. (03/28)

L. to r., Attorneys Donna Kohansky and John Vanderstar and NOW liaison on the case, National NOW Secretary Sandra Reeves Roth.

ISSUES

Economic

Although President Carter claimed to be a staunch supporter of the Equal Rights Amendment, he made it clear that he did not support the economic boycott of unratified states. A two-week old Energy Department policy, initiated by Secretary John Sawhill, to hold department meetings and events in ratified states whenever possible was reversed. (02/13)

Terry Korn of Tucson (AZ) NOW was the 1979 winner of the Walkathon medallion award for the most money raised by an individual in last year's Walkathons for ERA. Terry collected $1,410 in 144 separate pledges. The temperature on the day that Terry joined the approximately 100 walkers in Tucson was 102 degrees. (02)

Religion

Television station KOVR in Sacramento, CA, announced that it was being bought by the Outlet Company. The San Joaquin (CA) NOW chapter used the transfer of license as an opportunity to negotiate with the prospective owners and to enhance the employment opportunities for women and local public affairs programming. (02)

Media

NOW chapters in more than 30 cities around the country worked with local broadcasters and community leaders to promote the CBS movie *The $5.20 an Hour Dream.* Early estimates were that more than 25 million people watched the film. (02)

Legal

ERA ratification was defeated in the Virginia Senate when Senator John Chichester used a conflict of interest rule to abstain from voting. The vote was 20 for, 19 against. Constitutional amendments must pass by a majority of the 40 elected senators. Chichester admitted he was using the conflict of interest rule to keep the resolution from passing. Had the vote been 20 to 20, Charles S. Robb, acting as Lt. Governor, could have broken the tie. (02/12)

Political

Fifty corporate leaders announced that they would actively participate in a national business council to work for the ratification of the Equal Rights Amendment. Organized by the League of Women Voters and actress-businesswoman Polly Bergen, the National Business Council for ERA was headed by co-chairs William Agee, Polly Bergen, and Coy Eklund. (02/12)

In *International Union of Electrical, Radio and Machine Workers v. Westinghouse,* a federal circuit court found a pattern of deliberate wage discrimination by Westinghouse.

Mid-Suffolk (NY) NOW's ERA Committee marked Valentine's Day 1980 by selling 700 carnations to students and faculty on the campus of the local State University with the profits earmarked for the ERA Ratification drive. ERA Committee chairperson Dee Quit reported that all purchasers expressed their strong support of ERA. An ongoing ERA fund raiser by this chapter was its "Raise Dough for the ERA" project. Bread made by chapter members was sold at monthly meetings and at local conferences. The ERA Committee's major fundraiser was a dinner, co-sponsors of which included other NOW Chapters, Long Island labor unions and educational groups. Congresswoman Elizabeth Holtzman (D-NY) was the keynote speaker. (02/14)

The U.S. Supreme Court ruled unanimously that husbands or wives could, if they chose, testify against their spouses in Federal criminal trials. The decision overturned a 22- year old Supreme Court precedent that had in effect preserved for the spouse who was on trial a veto over the decision of the other spouse to offer incriminating testimony. The decision came in the case of *Trammel vs. U.S.,* No. 78-5705. (02/27)

London women gave notice to Parliament of their feelings on the debate raging in the House of Commons regarding proposed tightening of Britain's 13-year-old liberal abortion laws. Thousands of women battled police, who had to call in reinforcements; parliamentary officials evicted a group of young women who held a banner reading: "Women will not obey your bill." When evicted, the protesters continued to stand outside and chant: "Not the church, not the state, women must decide our fate." (03)

Houston, Bay Area, Huntsville, and Galveston (TX) NOW members and others demonstrated at the Texas State Conference for Youth and Single Adults of the Mormon Church, which was held at the University of Houston on March 1. The demonstration protested the all-male hierarchy of the Mormon Church, the nationwide campaign by the church to prevent ratification of the ERA, and the excommunication of Sonia Johnson. (03/01)

In a precedent-setting decision, the Iowa Civil Rights Commission unanimously ruled that Iowa City discriminated against Firefighter Linda Eaton by attempting to prevent her from breast feeding her son at the fire station during her personal time. The Commission ordered the city to pay Eaton $26,442 in attorneys' fees, $2,000 in compensatory damages for emotional distress, and $145 back pay for days she was suspended for breast feeding. (03/20)

A thousand Hispanic and non-Hispanic feminists gathered for the First National Hispanic Feminist Conference. The conference of Hispanic feminists was the brain child of Sylvia Gonzales, project director of the conference and co-chair of NOW's Minority Women's Committee. (03/28-31)

The Backlash

An article by Phyllis Schlafly in the New Orleans *Times-Picayune* attacked the Domestic Violence Prevention and Services Act (S. 1843) for increasing the federal bureaucracy. The legislation provided $10 million in the federal budget for domestic violence service for 1981. A group calling themselves "The Right Women" were reported to have set up a telephone campaign urging the bill's defeat. (02/11)

A group of fundamentalist ministers went to the White House with 70,000 signatures on petitions opposing extending the provisions of the Civil Rights Act to homosexuals. (03/21)

By a vote of 5,679 to 4,461, the American Psychiatric Association voted to rescind its ERA boycott policy on the pretense of avoiding involvement in political issues. (04)

93

YEAR	1980
U. S. President	Jimmy Carter
NOW President	Eleanor Smeal

EVENTS

Over 90,000 supporters of the Equal Rights Amendment converged on Chicago's Grant Park for what was called the largest march in Chicago's history and the largest gathering in support of the ERA ever in the state of Illinois. Marchers came from every state of the union and represented over 300 organizations and delegations. The mas-

sive event was conceived and coordinated by NOW. Mayor Jane Byrne , the first woman mayor of Chicago, addressed the crowd, together with Jessie Jackson, Ellie Smeal, TV celebrity Phil Donahue, and Marlo Thomas. See below. (05/10)

ISSUES

Lifestyles

Hollywood celebrities, Southern California NOW activists, and ERA supporters gathered by the hundreds at the Los Angeles Century Plaza Hotel for the 1980 Women of Courage and Feminist Achievement Awards. The event, chaired by Los Angeles NOW Treasurer and Fundraising Chair Dorothy Jonas and emceed by actress Joan Hackett, was a sellout. It included the

Economic

performance of an original script, "Women of Courage," created for the event. (03/30)

Norman and Frances Lear with NOW President Ellie Smeal.

Media

At a press conference confirming the "death" of Edith Bunker, Norman Lear, who originated the beloved character some 10 years ago on "All In The Family," and Frances Lear, who had been campaigning for the liberation of the Edith Bunkers of the world since the early 60's, announced the establishment of the Edith Bunker Memorial

Legal

Fund for the ERA and Women's Rights. The press conference took place in New York City. In Edith's memory, Tandem Productions (the company owned by Lear and Bud Yorkin), donated $500,000 to establish the Fund as a project of the NOW LDEF to be used in pursuit of ratification

Political

of the ERA. The gift earmarked $40,000 for the NOW LDEF and $100,000 for the NWPC. (04/10)

A protest from members of Missouri NOW changed the ads, which ran in St. Joseph on the radio and on billboards, and introduced the First Western Bank's new automated 24-hour teller machine as "Mary Anne." It included slogans like, "What You Do With Mary Anne After Hours Is Your Business" and "Mary Anne Will Make Your Nights Nicer." The bank was deluged with phone calls and letters and apologized for the ads' offensiveness. (04)

Seattle-King County (WA) NOW members began regular weekly demonstrations in support of the ERA at a newly built Mormon temple in Bellevue, WA. (05)

Nearly two months after the U.S. Civil Rights Commission found that Linda Eaton had been the victim of discrimination by the Iowa City Fire Department, Eaton resigned her post, citing physical and verbal harassment on the job and an incident in which a piece of her fire fighting equipment had been tampered with. The Commission's finding, awarding $28,000 in damages, fees, and wages to Eaton, was still under appeal by the Iowa City Fire Department. With Eaton's resignation, the department lost its only female fire fighter. (05/13)

Greater Champaign Area (IL) NOW produced its own television show entitled "Women Here and NOW," which was aired twice a month over the public access channel of the local Cablevision. Each program examined a different concern of the women's movement, such as: women's music, violence against women, reproductive rights, and women's legal rights. (05)

Northern Virginia NOW celebrated its tenth anniversary and honored its founding mother, Flora Crater, by proclaiming her "First Feminist of Virginia." Northern Virginia NOW members and its president, B. Ann Kleindienst, were joined by many friends–including many of "Crater's Raiders" who helped successfully lobby Congress for passage of the ERA in 1972. (05/04)

Citing "participation in homosexual acts," the U.S. Navy initiated dismissal action against eight female crew members of the U.S.S. Norton Sound docked in Long Beach, CA. California NOW's Lesbian Rights Task Force Chair, Johnnie Phelps, protested what she termed the "harassment" of the Navy women. (05/15)

The Ninth Circuit Court of Appeals granted NOW's motion for a stay in the proceedings of the ERA Extension/Recision lawsuit and stopped the action in that case until it decided NOW's appeal of Judge Marion J. Callister's decision that NOW could not be a party in that suit. NOW had twice been denied a stay of proceedings by Judge Callister. (05/14)

In devastatingly cruel terms, a five-man majority of the U.S. Supreme Court denied indigent women the means to obtain abortions through their government-provided health care. In *McRae v. Harris* and *Zabaraz v. Williams*, the Court held that denial of Medicaid funds for medically necessary abortions by federal and state governments did not violate the Constitution. (06)

After intense daily lobbying by thousands who went to Springfield to urge passage of the ERA, it was defeated by one vote. The ERA received 106 votes but the three-fifths majority required in Illinois needed 107 votes. (06)

The Backlash

High ranking officials of the Mormon church funneled thousands of dollars into the 1978 Florida elections in an effort to defeat pro-ERA legislators, a recent investigation by the *Miami Herald* alleged. The *Herald* claimed that Mormon officials directed funds to four candidates, financed a statewide advertising blitz, and paid for

printing and distributing 425,000 leaflets. (04)

Friends for Life, a Chicago-based anti-abortion organization, reportedly fired its director and co-founder, Joseph Scheidler, for his "guerrilla tactics" against abortion. Scheidler claimed he resigned. He founded a new group called The Pro-Life Action League. (06)

YEAR	1980
U. S. President	Jimmy Carter
NOW President	Eleanor Smeal

EVENTS

Abortion foes were dealt a stunning defeat in the Toledo, Ohio, primary. The election, which saw the defeat of an "Akron style" anti-abortion ordinance by a 2-to-1 margin, was the culmination of more than a year's work by NOW and other local activists for abortion rights. (06/03)

At the 1980 Democratic Convention, despite heavy Carter opposition and without official Ted Kennedy support, Ellie Smeal led a NOW delegation and like-minded feminist delegates in a fight to pass the strongest ERA and reproductive rights planks in political history. Women, for the first time at any party convention, were 50% (49.23% to be exact) of the voting delegates.

And the 50-50 representation made a difference on women's issues. When it came to women's rights, Carter and Kennedy delegates alike voted for the feminist positions, denying Democratic National Committee resources to candidates opposed to the ERA and supporting Medicaid funding of abortions for poor women. (08/11-14)

ISSUES

Lifestyles

The White House Conference on Families ended its three-day Eastern regional meeting by endorsing abortion rights (383-202), the ERA, non-discrimination against homosexuals (292-291), national health insurance, and a guaranteed annual income for poor families–at a minimum of about $13,000 a year for a family of four. (06/07)

The second White House Conference on Families, composed of delegates from 13 Midwest and Southern states, endorsed the ERA and narrowly defeated a resolution calling for a constitutional amendment outlawing abortion from the moment of fertilization. The delegates also approved a definition of families which excluded homosexual relationships, and denounced "secular humanism." (06/21)

San Francisco (CA) NOW organized a picket and demonstration in front of the Pacific Stock Exchange on the anniversary of women's suffrage. Six members chained themselves to pillars located in front of the exchange. Nancy Foster, the chapter's administrative vice-president, maintained that "not one of the *Fortune* 500 corporations openly supports the Equal Rights Amendment." (08/26)

Education

The Minnesota Supreme Court handed down a landmark decision that held an employer responsible for sexual harassment of female employees by male co-workers in the case of *Continental Can v. Minnesota*, the first case to focus on such harassment by co-workers. The court strongly affirmed the right of women workers everywhere to be free of sexual harassment in the workplace, whether committed by bosses, supervisors or co-workers. (06/06)

Economic

In Detroit, 12,000 ERA supporters in a NOW-organized march shouted "Keep it in the platform ... ERA." The mile-long route, which wound past the convention center and site of the Republican National Convention, was filled with marchers, dressed in the traditional suffrage white, who protested the removal of the ERA from the Republican platform. (07/14)

On the 60th Anniversary of Women's Suffrage, Nannie M. Johnson, 73, was among those protesting the removal of the ERA from the party's platform at Republican National Committee Headquarters in Washington, D.C. (08/26)

Media

The Women's Committee of the Directors Guild released statistics showing that of the 7,332 movies released by major American studios between 1949 and 1979, only 14 were directed by women. They also noted that of the 65,500 hours of prime-time TV drama since 1949, only 115 hours were directed by women, and 35 of those were directed by one woman– Ida Lupino. (06/20)

Almost one year after its first effort to participate in the ERA extension/recision lawsuit, NOW was granted the right to intervene and fully participate in the historic case. On August 15, 1980, the Ninth Circuit Court of Appeals ruled that NOW could intervene in the suit, thereby overturning the earlier decision of federal district court Judge Marion J. Callister to bar NOW's participation in the case. (08/15)

Thousands of NOW members and supporters walked in the fourth annual National Walk for the ERA. The Walks were designed to raise funds for the ratification campaign and to show the widespread public support for the amendment. The success of the event was outstanding, raising over $200,000 for the ERA. (08/23-24)

Legal

Political

For the ninth year in a row, the Equal Rights Amendment became a political football in the Illinois legislature when two previously committed pro-ERA Republicans voted "no," making the total votes in favor 105. Unlike most states in which a majority rules, a total of 107 votes, or three-fifths of the Illinois House, were needed to pass federal Amendments. (06/18)

The Rules Committee of the Democratic Party, meeting at the Mayflower Hotel in Washington, D.C., adopted two charter amendments proposing equal division between women and men in all national official Democratic Party bodies and state central committees. The amendments were presented for approval to the Democratic National Convention. NOW Vice President Jane Wells-Schooley led the NOW effort at the session while NOW organizer, Molly Yard, a member of the Rules Committee, was floor manager. (07/08-09)

West Virginia NOW tried a swimathon.

The Backlash

Christian Voice, a new right-wing lobbying group based in Washington, D.C. rated members of the U.S. House and Senate on the "morality" of their votes and flunked 57 House members and 27 Senators. Their choices for "Moral Zeros," as the group termed them, were fascinating: they included Baptist Minister, William Gray (D-

PA), a graduate of Princeton Theological Seminary; Presbyterian elder Senator John Glenn (R-OH); and several other mainstream members of Congress who also served their various religions in official positions. (07)

A directive issued by the National Conference of Catholic

Bishops prohibited the performance of tubal ligations in Catholic hospitals even in cases where the woman's life was threatened were she to become pregnant. The procedure had been performed in some Catholic hospitals when a woman's life was endangered. (07)

95

YEAR	1980
U. S. President	Jimmy Carter
NOW President	Eleanor Smeal

EVENTS

In the spirit of total mobilization, the NOW National Conference, held in San Antonio, voted overwhelmingly (by a margin of 2 to 1) to extend the terms of the officers and board members one year so that the internal elections would not interrupt the momentum of the final days of the ERA ratification drive. (10/03-05)

Ronald Reagan was elected President. However, for the first time since passage of the 19th Amendment, women voted differently than men in a Presidential election. And they did so mostly on the basis of women's issues. According to all of the exit polls, women voted for Reagan significantly less than men did. The *New York Times*/CBS News Poll reported that 8%

fewer women (46%) voted for Reagan than did men (54%). The December 1980 post-election issue of *NOW Times*, NOW's national newspaper, carried the story under a banner headline: "Women Vote Differently Than Men . . . Feminist Bloc Emerges in 1980 Elections" by Eleanor Smeal. This was the first article to note , define and name the "Gender Gap." (12)

ISSUES

Lifestyles

Economic

Ronald Reagan suddenly reopened the Equal Rights Amendment controversy by pledging efforts to enforce existing laws against discrimination against women. If elected, the Republican Presidential candidate said, "I would appoint a liaison with the governors of the 50 states to see that the states eliminate laws that discriminate against women. At the same time, I would appoint someone to supervise the 19 laws passed during the past 20 years in the federal government to eliminate unfair discrimination, to see if they are being enforced and to see if there are additional laws we need." But Reagan remained adamantly opposed to the Equal Rights Amendment, contending that the measure "will take out of the hands of elected representatives the problems of discrimination and put them in the hands of the courts. And who knows what decisions will be made there?" (09/23)

Legal

Minnesota NOW member and lesbian rights activist Karen Clark won a primary race for a seat in the Minnesota House of Representatives from a south Minneapolis district. The race was for an open seat vacated by a woman who was running for the Minnesota Senate. It was a genuine victory for gay rights: Karen won by a 2-to-1 margin in spite of efforts toward a negative campaign because of her lifestyle and lesbian rights activism. (09/09)

Religion

Media

Political

Louisiana NOW announced the defeat of the abortion/divorce bill in the Louisiana legislature. The bill would have given automatic grounds for divorce to any man whose wife had an abortion. Even an abortion for health reasons would have found the wife at fault. Louisiana NOW fought hard to prevent passage of the bill. The State Senate passed it but, when it went to the House, Representatives Diana BaJoie, Mary Landrieu, and Margaret Lowenthall led the fight to defeat it. (09)

An information clearinghouse, containing national data on Equal Rights Amendment litigation, was announced by Phyllis N. Segal, legal director of the NOW Legal Defense and Education Fund (LDEF). The ERA Impact Clearinghouse included comprehensive information about legal cases filed under state equal rights amendments. The information was compiled as part of the ERA Impact Project being carried out by the NOW LDEF and the Women's Law Project of Pennsylvania. (09/30)

Lee Remick, Colleen Dewhurst and Patty Duke starred in *The Women's Room*, an intense TV drama about women's life choices based on the best-seller by Marilyn French. (09/14)

The U. S. Supreme Court refused to hear the appeal brought by the state of Missouri on the ERA Boycott. The court's decision to let the Eighth Circuit Court of Appeals decision in NOW's favor stand ended the two and one half year battle in the courts as to whether NOW's actions in organizing and promoting the boycott of unratified states was a violation of the Sherman Anti-Trust Act. (10/06)

Bay Area NOW and Houston (TX) NOW coordinated a "Family Day for the ERA" Rally on the steps of Houston's City Hall. The purpose of the rally was to educate the public on candidates' positions on the ERA, to emphasize that the ERA would strengthen family life and to demonstrate the importance of the homemaker's contribution to the family. (11/02)

Chanting, singing and waving banners, about 25 people who supported ERA began demonstrating at the Church of Jesus Christ of Latter-Day Saints' just completed Seattle Temple. Two women chained themselves to the iron gates, which had been locked to keep non-Mormons from the grounds. (11/15)

Ten Connecticut women became the first in the country awarded a license for a television station. (11)

Baton Rouge (LA) NOW was successful in having the NARAL documentary, "So Many Voices: A Look At Abortion In America," shown on WAFB-TV in Baton Rouge. The station had previously shown an anti-abortion program sponsored by the Catholic diocese and other church groups. When the chapter reminded them of their obligation to present balanced programming, the station donated the time for the NOW-sponsored film. (11/29)

In a pilot project, the Los Angeles Chapter of NOW, working for only a few weekends and evenings in November and December before the holidays temporarily interrupted the campaign, collected more than 10,000 signatures on a petition addressed to President Ronald Reagan in support of the Equal Rights Amendment. (12)

The Backlash

In a press conference, Richard Viguerie, direct mail wizard of the Right; Paul Weyrich of the Committee for the Survival of a Free Congress; John Terry Dolan of the National Conservative Political Action Committee (NCPAC); and Howard Phillips of the Conservative Caucus detailed their legislative agenda for the next two

years. They called for the defeat of SALT II, increased defense spending, massive tax cuts, a balanced budget, passage of the Family Protection Act, cuts in federal health and human services programs, and passage of the Human Life Amendment (HLA). (11/05)

A Gallup Poll conducted just after the November 1980 election showed that only 40% of Americans had ever heard of the Moral Majority, and only 26% felt they knew enough about the group to make an informed judgment about it. Of the 26% who knew enough about it to judge, half disapproved, and a little under a third approved.

YEAR	1981
U. S. President	Ronald Reagan
NOW President	Eleanor Smeal

EVENTS

Washington D.C. was the scene of more than the Presidential

Inauguration. Thousands also came to the city to remind President Reagan of the continued and determined support for the Equal Rights Amendment. Two days of ERA actions preceded the one at the Inauguration itself. (01/20)

President Reagan endorsed a proposed Human Life Bill (HLB), the latest step in a series of attempts by anti-abortion foes to undermine the 1973 U.S. Supreme Court decision which legalized abortion. Reagan also endorsed the most extreme "paramount" version of the Human Life Amendment (HLA), a constitutional amendment which would ban abortion, the IUD, and some forms of the birth control pill. (02)

ISSUES

Lifestyles

Education

Economic

Media

Legal

Political

The Human Life Bill (HLB) was introduced in the Senate by Jesse Helms (R-NC) as S. 158, and in the House by Henry Hyde (R-IL) as H.R. 900. NOW opposed both bills at hearings held before the Senate Judiciary Subcommittee on Separation of Powers. (01/19)

NOW launched a nationwide woman-to-woman campaign aimed at stopping the so-called Human Life Amendment. NOW chapters across the country scheduled leaflet campaigns, neighborhood walks and other efforts to get people to realize that if passed, the HLA would not only prohibit all abortions, but would also ban the use of some contraceptive pills and IUDs. (01/22)

Albuquerque (NM) NOW thought of a unique way to counteract the anti-choice group's "parade of roses" campaign on the anniversary of the U.S. Supreme Court's decision legalizing abortion. The anti-choice group always gave red roses to individual members of New Mexico's state legislature. This year in addition to their annual demonstration, NOW members and members of the New Mexico Coalition for Abortion Choice gave state legislators bud vases which were stamped with the word "choice," designed and executed by Albuquerque Chapter President Jenny White. (01/22)

San Francisco (CA) NOW had Ed Asner of "The Lou Grant Show," former Congressperson Bella Abzug and Mormon Sonia Johnson speak at their very successful Sixth Annual Day in the Park for Women's Rights. "Equality Shall Not Be Silenced" was the theme and more than 15,000 people attended the rally at Golden Gate Park. (02)

Milwaukee (WI) NOW's Task Force on Gender Equity in Education checked for compliance with Title IX when the Milwaukee Public School System joined the Milwaukee Suburban Conference Athletic Association. They investigated seven school systems with which the Milwaukee schools would compete in the association's athletic events. (02)

San Fernando Valley (CA) NOW found that their HLA information booth was one of the most popular attractions in the Sherman Oaks Fashion Square as people waited in line, at times five and six deep, to sign the STOP HLA petitions and to receive information. (03)

Tucson (AZ) NOW members, dressed in suffragist costumes, marched in Tucson's Fiesta de los Vaqueros Rodeo Parade carrying a "Votes 1920, ERA 1982" banner. They were joined by members of the Southern Arizona Coalition for the ERA. (03)

Employment discrimination against women in pay, hiring, promotion, training, and termination were the charges of the Honolulu (HI) NOW chapter to the Federal Communications Commission (FCC). Honolulu NOW asked the FCC to deny the license renewal of Shamrock Broadcasting Company for television station KITV, an ABC affiliate. (01)

Los Angeles (CA) NOW opened 1981 with a new service for members: Issues Briefing Sessions held each month on the Equal Rights Amendment and on the misleadingly named Human Life Amendment (HLA). The meetings were designed to equip members with all of the knowledge on issues that a speaker's bureau training would provide, minus the concentration on formal speech making. (01)

Rocky Mountain, Arapahoe, and Ft. Collins (CO) NOW chapters were instrumental in defeating two state legislature bills that sought to define a fetus as a person, one of which would have changed the definition of "child" to "a person from the time of conception to 18 years of age." The chapters inundated the Colorado House Judiciary Committee with POMs, phone calls and letters, held a "Never Again" demonstration on the capitol steps, packed the hearing room with NOW members, and identified all pro-choice people with "Never Again" stickers. In addition, NOW members presented testimony against the bills. The victory was especially significant since it represented one of the first defeats for a "redefinition" bill. (03/01)

Johnson County/Iowa City (IA) NOW and members of other feminist organizations picketed the film *Dressed to Kill* when it was shown on the University of Iowa campus. Approximately 100 men and women participated in the silent picket each night the film was shown. Leaflets were distributed which stated NOW's position against films using violence toward women as "entertainment." (03)

The Second Stage by Betty Friedan was published accusing feminists of distorting the goals of the movement by disparaging men, marriage and the family. Activists, besieged by the backlash, fighting for the lost causes of child care, homemakers rights and the ERA, felt betrayed.

At the request of NOW and on the strength of the Missouri decision in NOW's favor, Judge Roger D. Foley dismissed all charges brought against NOW by the state of Nevada. The dismissal brought to an end three years of defense by NOW against charges that it violated anti-trust laws in promoting the boycott of states which had not ratified the Equal Rights Amendment. (03)

The Backlash

The Mormon Church dropped its trespassing charges against members and supporters of Mormons for ERA who were arrested November 17. The "Bellevue 21" had chained themselves to the gates of the new Mormon Temple in Bellevue, WA, near Seattle. (01/12)

The Heritage Foundation's *Mandate for Leadership*, released two weeks after Reagan's election victory, was used as a guide by his Administration. At the end of the first year, more than 2,000 of its specific recommendations had been adopted.

San Francisco (CA) NOW joined a picket line at the University of San Francisco to protest the appearance of Congressman Henry Hyde and Nellie Gray, a leader of the "right to life" movement. More than 600 people picketed. (03/17)

YEAR	1981
U. S. President	Ronald Reagan
NOW President	Eleanor Smeal

EVENTS

Almost 25% of the female employees at the United Nations (UN) reported that they had been sexually harassed and pursued for sexual favors in return for a promotion or other job benefit according to the Ad Hoc Group of Equal Rights for Women, based at the U.N. Most vulnerable were lower income level women, many of whom were on visas that permitted

them to stay in the U.S. only if they worked at the U.N. (03)

Kathryn Sullivan, NASA astronaut who had flown higher than any other woman, and Sylvia Earle, who had dived deeper than any other human, added to their list of achievements their unprecedented–and totally unexpected–admission to the previously all-male Explorers

Club. Two members of the Board of Directors immediately predicted that 300 members might resign as a result of the vote. "You have no idea how strongly some men feel about this," said one board member. (03)

ISSUES

Lifestyles
Education
Economic
Religion
Media
Legal
Political

Honolulu (HI) NOW and over a dozen other organizations joined forces on Opening Day of Hawaii's Legislature by releasing thousands of brightly colored balloons, each bearing a pro-choice message. The balloons were inflated and distributed in the open-air rotunda of Hawaii's beautiful Capitol Building. Anti-choice advocates annually bus hundreds of people to the Capitol for the occasion. (03)

Florida NOW Boycott Committee members returned to their posts at the entrance to Disney World, Orlando, FL, after winning a legal battle with the opposition. The controversy arose when Disney officials and local authorities insisted that NOW members needed a permit for "commercial advertising" while picketing along this particular site. (03/31)

Lincoln (NE) NOW sponsored a three-mile run for the ERA. The $5 registration fee for each runner went to National NOW's ERA fund. (03/31)

In response to Judge Marion Callister's second refusal to disqualify himself as the presiding judge in the ERA extension/recision lawsuit, the National Organization for Women petitioned the Ninth Circuit Court of Appeals to reverse this decision. The petition, in the form of a request for writ of mandamus, was filed in the Appellate Court.(03/06)

San Diego (CA) NOW sponsored a demonstration aimed at stopping the San Diego Unified Port District Board of Commissioners from granting the Playboy Club a lease until the year 2003. (03/17)

The North Dakota legislature defeated three anti-choice resolutions and joined New Mexico, Wyoming, Montana, and Arizona as the fifth state in a month to reject repressive reproductive measures. The successful votes represented a major victory for the pro-choice movement, particularly at a time when the right wing had mounted a nationwide campaign to restrict reproductive freedom. (03/10)

NOW members gathered at the National NOW Action Center for a pilot training program for the Mormon Missionary Project. The trainees were from New Jersey, Pennsylvania, California, Illinois Virginia, West Virginia, Indiana, and Utah. Feminist missionaries were being trained and sent to Utah for a door-to-door ERA education program and as a non-violent protest of the Mormon Church's systematic blocking of ERA ratification in Utah, Nevada, Arizona, Missouri, Virginia and Florida. (04/04)

San Diego (CA) NOW distributed pro-ERA brochures outside of San Diego area Mormon Churches. About 200 of the brochures, "The ERA is a Moral Issue," written by Mormons for the ERA, were distributed by the chapter. (04/05)

New York NOW held a May 3rd brunch on the lawn of the University Club, NYC, to protest the club's policy of excluding women. "All the business that gets conducted at these stag clubs is simply too important to exclude women," said Sheila Feiger, President of NOW-NYS. (05/03)

Indianapolis (IN) NOW observed Secretary's Day by distributing "rose notes" to women being taken to lunch by their bosses. The card front featured a long-stemmed red rose. Inside the message read "For every $1 a man earns, women earn 59 cents. You're worth more than 59 cents." Stuffed in the card were NOW's "Dollars and Cents Feminism" pamphlet and a membership application. (04/22)

Boston (MA) NOW's campaign against discrimination at a local television station resulted in changes in employment practices at the station. In February, Boston NOW asked viewers to turn off the station in order to lower its ratings and reduce its profits. As a result, when the chapter pointed out discriminatory practices at the station, women's salaries were upgraded and some women received raises. At least one woman was promoted to management, and a female reporter hired at the end of February began anchoring weekend broadcasts. (05)

Over 5,000 women listed the ratification of the Equal Rights Amendment as their number one "message to President Reagan," in a poll sponsored by *Glamour* magazine and reported in their May issue. Thirty three percent of respondents picked ERA as their top concern out of 19 possible categories; second choice was women's right to a safe, legal abortion, chosen as top concern by 13% of the respondents. (05)

The Backlash

To the acute embarrassment of Georgia Republicans, the leader of the Ku Klux Klan's Invisible Empire in West Georgia said that three of its chapters had "hung up their robes" because the Reagan administration was expected to do the Klan's job in Washington. The Klan endorsed the Republican Party platform–an endorsement

immediately disowned by GOP officials. (03)

President Reagan said that a constitutional amendment banning abortion would not be necessary if Congress determined that a fetus was a human being, because it would already be protected by the 14th Amendment. (03/06)

George Gilder's book, *Wealth and Poverty*, was published and became a handbook of the Reagan Administration. In it, he repeated his *Sexual Suicide* theory on the necessity for women's subservient role, as well as expounding on the virtues of supply side economics.

YEAR	1981
U. S. President	Ronald Reagan
NOW President	Eleanor Smeal

EVENTS

The National Academy of Sciences declared that the question of when human life begins was not a scientific one and that the proposed bill by Jesse Helms and Henry Hyde to define life as beginning with fertilization "has no scientific validity." (04/28)

The Reagan Administration dropped the judicial selection process inaugurated by former President Carter, which had dramatically increased the number of women judges named to the bench since 1976. The new policy marked a return to the traditional policy of recommendation by Senators or, in everyday parlance, a return to the "old boy" net-work method of appointing the friends of Senators, normally men. (05)

NOW President Eleanor Smeal testified against proposed cuts in Social Security by the Reagan Administration, charging, "The net effect. . . is to create massive holes in the safety net for the aged poor women in this country." (06/03)

ISSUES

Lifestyles

New Orleans (LA) NOW staged a two-day demonstration at the Hilton and Rivergate Convention Center to protest the American Psychiatric Association's convention in an unratified state. ERA Task Force members carried signs, distributed leaflets, and maintained a booth inside the center where Task Force people sold "ERA Yes" buttons. (05)

Education

ERA activist Alan Alda quietly donated $11,000 to help buy and preserve the home of women's rights leader Elizabeth Cady Stanton. The National Park Service announced that Alda's contribution was part of a drive

Economic

to raise the $43,000 needed to organize a Women's Rights Historical Park in Seneca Falls, NY, as authorized by Congress in December, 1980. (06)

Media

NOW President Eleanor Smeal announced at a Los Angeles luncheon that former First Lady Betty Ford would be the National Honorary Chair of the ERA Countdown events, and Alan Alda would serve as Co-chair. (06/10)

Legal

Women scored an important legal victory when the Minnesota Supreme Court ruled that the U.S. Jaycees is a public accommodation, prohibited by state law from excluding women from full membership on the basis of their sex. The NOW Legal Defense and Education Fund filed the amicus brief on behalf of Minnesota

Political

NOW. (05/08)

Tens of thousands of ERA supporters all around the country joined with NOW President Eleanor Smeal and ERA Countdown Honorary Co-Chairs Betty Ford and Alan Alda to kick off the ERA Countdown Campaign. In rallies numbering over 170, in 42 states, ERA supporters again gathered in the traditional green and white for a day of stirring speeches, music, and proclamations from mayors and governors, with green-and-white balloons filling the skies. Major rallies were held in Washington, D.C., Springfield,IL; Denver, CO; Los Angeles; Boston; and New York City. (06/30)

In the last session of their State legislature, Alaska NOW finally succeeded in passing legislation nicknamed "Mini-Title IX." The bill, which had been lobbied for years by Alaska feminists, provided that discrimination on the basis of sex was prohibited in all areas related to employment at all educational levels, including opportunities for advancement, counseling and guidance services in public education, recreational and athletic activities, course offerings, and textbooks and instructional materials. (07)

Philadelphia (PA) NOW's immediate past president, Lillian Ciarrochi, left her job to work full time for the ERA in Florida and become part of the team coordinating ratification efforts. (09)

NOW opened ERA Countdown Campaign Offices in St. Louis, MO; Tulsa,OK; Oklahoma City, OK; Tallahassee, FL; Miami, FL; Springfield, IL; Chicago, IL; Fayetteville, NC; and Raleigh, NC. The pace of the entire Countdown Campaign was accelerating daily. All local and state ERA Countdown offices established phone banks, message brigades, missionary projects, and generally maintained a massive outreach to their communities. (08)

NOW President Ellie Smeal traveled to several unratified states, key districts, and cities on a speaking tour and ERA Countdown organizing drive. The response from the standing room-only audiences was so enthusiastic that at each stop record numbers of people signed up for ERA campaign work. (08)

Linda Furney, Ohio NOW President, drove the Ohio "Stop HLA Caravan" into the Knox County Fairgrounds on opening day to help build momentum for activities during the week and to draw attention to the NOW booth. Booth exhibits included information on the ERA, teenage pregnancy, battered women, the HLA, sexual harassment, abortion, and women's economic status. (09)

Syndicated columnist Beverly Stephens reported that there was a growing "backlash" of articles in newspapers and magazines that essentially advocated that women leave their careers for the joys of motherhood and home. Said Stephens, "Perhaps it reflects wishful thinking that women will eliminate the problems involved in adjusting to equality by going back home. In any case, it's beginning to look like selling women out is as sure a path to the best seller list as a fad diet." (09)

The Backlash

Dr. Willard Cates, chief of abortion surveillance at the Centers for Disease Control in Atlanta, GA, was to have testified before the Senate Judiciary Subcommittee that legalized abortions had reduced abortion-related disease and death among American women and significantly reduced the incidence of teen-age marriages

and out-of-wedlock births. His anti-choice superiors, including HHS Secretary Richard S. Schweiker, replaced Cates at the hearing with another official, Dr. Carl W. Tyler, who presented a three-page report omitting most of the favorable effects of legalized abortion described by Cates. (05/20)

Senator Orrin Hatch (R-UT) introduced a new anti-abortion constitutional amendment (S.J. Res 110) that would give the Congress and the states concurrent authority to restrict or prohibit abortion. (09/21)

YEAR	1981
U. S. President	Ronald Reagan
NOW President	Eleanor Smeal

EVENTS

In a 6-3 ruling in *Rostker v. Goldberg*, the U.S. Supreme Court upheld the constitutionality of an all-male draft registration as passed by Congress. The majority opinion, written by Justice William H. Rehnquist, declared that, under the constitutionally authorized powers to raise an army, Congress was not required to "engage in gestures of superficial equality." (06/25)

President Reagan nominated Sandra Day O'Connor, 51, to fill the seat on the U.S. Supreme Court vacated by Associate Justice Potter Stewart. (07/07) NOW President Eleanor Smeal testi-fied in favor of her appointment. O'Connor was sworn in by Chief Justice Warren Burger, the 102nd Supreme Court Justice and the first woman on the court. (09/25)

ISSUES

Lifestyles

In a move hailed by women's rights leaders as a major breakthrough on "comparable worth," Gov. Edmund Brown, Jr. signed a bill for which California NOW had lobbied, ordering the California state government to compare the work of women employees with that of men for purposes of "improving and equalizing" pay for women. (09/24)

Education

Covering 27 colleges in 5 weeks, the ERA Countdown Campus Campaign moved through the colleges and universities of northeastern United States from Wellesley to Mount Holyoke to Quinnipiac College to Yale to Rutgers to Bryn Mawr on a whirlwind tour, with rallies, speeches, and recruiting tables. (09)

Economic

Deborah DeBare of Brown University and Jennifer Jackman and Deborah Davis-Anthonyson, both of Smith–who said ratification of the ERA was more important than going to college, and Tamar Raphael, suspended their studies to work for passage of the ERA, launching NOW's ERA College Campus Project. (10)

Michigan NOW began an organizing effort to remove Judge Donald Halstead, a Juvenile Court Judge in Kalamazoo, MI. Halstead ruled against allowing an abortion for an 11-year-old girl who was pregnant by her mother's boyfriend, who had physically abused both the girl and her 10-year-old-sister. (10)

Media

Legal

ERA activists in Illinois, Florida, and Oklahoma were energized by the dedicated campaign work done by Betty Ford, Esther Rolle, and Marlo Thomas. (10)

Political

The National Organization for Women and the American Public Health Association (APHA) were the only groups to testify against the confirmation of Dr. C. Everett Koop for U.S. Surgeon General. (10/01)

The "Last Walk for ERA," one of the largest fund-raising efforts held on behalf of the Equal Rights Amendment, raised close to a million dollars, more than tripling the proceeds from ERA Walks in any of the previous four years. One of the largest events was in Los Angeles, which combined a parade of 12,000 on the Avenue of the Stars in Century City, led by Betty Ford, Maureen Reagan Los Angeles chapter president Toni Carabillo, and an array of celebrities, with a feminist fair and walkathon in which 5,000 participated raising $300,000 for the national campaign. Los Angeles NOW Vice President Jane Guthrie was coordinator of the day, Susan Van Trees and Barbara Rose organized the Fair, and Cooper Zale coordinated the Walk. (08/22)

ERA was at its highest support level in history, with solid majorities in every population category in the country. A Gallup poll survey showed that 63% of Americans "who have heard or read about the ERA" supported it and 32% opposed it. In previous Gallup surveys conducted since 1975, ERA support never exceeded 58%. (08/09)

Teams of activists canvassing in towns and cities across the country recruited thousands of new members to the ERA Message Brigade on National Message Brigade Day. (10/01)

The Senate Judiciary Subcommittee on Constitution, chaired by Senator Orrin Hatch (R-UT), held hearings during October and November on the "Human Life Amendments" pending before the Senate, including Hatch's "Legislative Authority Amendment." Thirty-six witnesses, only four of them women, testified during the seven days of hearings. (10)

Former First Ladies Betty Ford and Lady Bird Johnson, NOW President Ellie Smeal, and other nationally prominent speakers addressed a cheering crowd of 3,000 at a "Call to the Nation's Conscience," on the final day of the NOW National Conference. The ERA rally was held on the steps of the Lincoln Memorial. (10/12)

Los Angeles NOW officers Sally Rosloff and Susan Van Trees headed for Florida by car to work in the ERA Countdown Campaign in that state. (11/16) Other members, like Marnie Delaney, an advertising executive, quit their jobs to take subsistence salaries working in the Countdown Campaign office in Los Angeles.

New York (NY) NOW raised funds for the ERA ratification campaign through profits from an art exhibit and sale. More than 40 artists, including Louise Nevelson, Claes Oldenburg, Betty Parsons, Diane Keaton and Chuck Close donated art which went on sale at the Zabriskie Gallery in New York City. (11)

The Backlash

The Reagan Administration announced plans for the most sweeping rollbacks to date on federal anti-discrimination regulations, the effect of which was to undo twenty years of progress for women. Promising a step-by-step improvement in women's rights, instead the Administration delivered an unprecedented assault on advances for women, ranging from proposals to ease job bias regulations affecting 30 million American employees to weakening guidelines that protected women from sexual harassment, and undermining protections against sex discrimination in educational institutions. (07)

The nation's Catholic Bishops closed ranks and united behind a Constitutional Amendment proposed by Senator Orrin Hatch (R-UT), which would overturn *Roe v. Wade* and give each state the right to recriminalize abortion. (11/18)

YEAR	1982
U. S. President	Ronald Reagan
NOW President	Eleanor Smeal

EVENTS

According to a poll conducted by *The Daily Oklahoman*, 44% of Oklahomans said they favored ERA, 39% opposed it, and 15% said they weren't sure. However, when read the text of the ERA, support soared to 80.6%. (01)

Nine years after the U.S. Supreme Court decision on abortion, 75% of Americans opposed a constitutional amendment that would allow Congress to ban abortions, according to an Associated Press/NBC News Poll. Only 19% favored it, 6% weren't sure and 77% said they agreed with the statement, "The decision to have an abortion should be left to the woman and her physician." (01/20-21)

ISSUES

Education

A report released by the National Advisory Council on Women's Educational Programs showed that in the nine years since Title IX, a federal statute which prohibited sex discrimination in federally funded educational institutions, was enforced, the number of females in inter-scholastic high-school sports increased by 527% to almost one third of the total. And female athletic scholarships increased impressively, from 1% of the total in 1972 to 22% in 1982. The report also called attention to much slower progress in jobs for women in education and continuing serious inequities in funding of women's sports in college. (01)

Religion

Economic

A Superior Court judge ruled that the Westarms Mall, the largest mall in Connecticut, must permit members of NOW to gather signatures for ERA in the enclosed courtyard of the shopping area. (01/04)

Legal

In Oklahoma, the ERA Campaign was set back by a negative 27-21 vote in the state Senate. An analysis of ERA votes showed that all 11 Republicans in the state Senate voted against the Amendment. Although a majority of Democrats voted "yes," two-thirds of those who were up for election in 1982 voted against the ERA in fear of the far right wing. The NOW Oklahoma ERA Campaign decided to dig in and fight on. "I don't accept the ERA vote as a loss; we simply haven't won yet!" was Alan Alda's message to thousands of ERA supporters in Oklahoma during a speaking tour through targeted rural districts. Alda, co-chair of NOW's Countdown Campaign, reminded overflow crowds in eastern Oklahoma that the next phase of the Oklahoma Campaign was to target districts of the State House and Senate members who voted "no." (01)

Political

Los Angeles (CA) NOW activist David M. Dismore pedaled east from the Santa Monica Pier on a coast-to-coast bike-a-thon to raise funds and generate publicity for the Equal Rights Amendment. In 148 days (92 on the road) the "adventure of a lifetime for the cause of the century" covered 4,482 miles, generated $3,000 in pledges and received coverage in 50 local newspapers as Dismore crossed the country, then circled Florida's perimeter, arriving in Tallahassee for the second time the day before an ERA rally. (01/09)

A Lancaster, WI, Circuit Court Judge, William Reinecke, outraged state residents with his remarks in the case of a five-year-old girl who was the victim of sexual assault by 24-year-old Ralph Snodgrass of Gays Mills. "I am satisfied we have an unusually sexually permissive young lady," said Reinecke, "and he did not know enough to refuse. No way do I believe Mr. Snodgrass initiated the sexual contact." Reinecke referred to the child as "the aggressor" in the assault. Nearby NOW chapters assisted parents in the local area to organize a petition drive to recall the judge. (01)

Low pensions–or the total lack of them–were the main cause of women's poverty, according to Karen Ferguson of the Pension Rights Center. Ferguson offered the sobering statistics that though 85% of married women outlive their husbands, only 9% of them receive any corporate pension dollars. (01)

Philadelphia (PA) NOW sent over 400 postcards to the governors of the targeted unratified states during the past two months. All of the governors responded that they support the ERA but needed to receive more mail. Philadelphia's goal was to send 1,000 cards a week as the campaign intensified. (01)

The Georgia House rejected the ERA on a 116-57 vote. This vote marked the ERA's first appearance before the Georgia House in eight years. (01/20)

Although encountering more difficulty than men in winning first assignments and still receiving smaller paychecks, women in the Protestant clergy were adjusting with success to their new roles, according to a Ford Foundation study. The report noted that the total percentage of women in the once all-male world was now 22%. (01)

Illinois NOW members focused on Governor Jim Thompson and Speaker George Ryan as part of the Republican Project of NOW's Countdown Campaign. Members tried to persuade Governor Thompson to take a more active role in ratification efforts and Ryan to allow a vote on changing Illinois' 3/5 rule. They also began a door-to-door campaign in Du Page County. (01)

The NOW National Board and the NOW-NJ Board joined civil rights organizations in opposing alleged intimidation tactics of the National Ballot Security Task Force, a project of the Republican National Committee. The Task Force, led by John A. Kelly, a Republican National Committee employee, was charged with using off-duty police and sheriff's officers to patrol only Black areas of Trenton and Newark during the November state elections. (01)

The Backlash

Planned Parenthood (PP) was cleared of suspicion of using federal money to finance abortions or pro-abortion lobbying in an audit by the Department of Health and Human Services. PP Director Faye Wattleton protested to Health and Human Services Secretary Richard Schweiker –a foe of reproductive choice–that the "unprecedented series of audits" represented an abuse of the power of government by those philosophically opposed to abortion. (01)

According to several outspoken opponents of "test tube babies," the "right to life" did not extend to them. Since they were not conceived in a womb, they had no souls. That was the essence of objections lodged against the in vitro fertilization program at Eastern Virginia Medical School (which had reported its first birth). (01)

101

YEAR	1982
U. S. President	Ronald Reagan
NOW President	Eleanor Smeal

EVENTS

Former Presidents Jimmy Carter and Gerald Ford issued a joint statement urging ratification of ERA. (01/18)

The U.S. Supreme Court ruled 6-3 in the case of *North Haven Board of Education v. Bell* that the law barring sex discrimination by schools and colleges receiving Federal funding covered not only the students but also the employees of those institutions. The decision was written by Justice Harry A. Blackmun and joined by Sandra Day O'Connor, William J. Brennan, Thurgood Marshall, John Paul Stevens, and Byron White. (05/17)

In the final month of the decade long drive to ratify the Equal Rights Amendment, NOW President Eleanor Smeal charged that the insurance industry was among the "vested interests" in an "invisible lobby" that had worked to defeat the amendment. Other industries want to preserve cheap labor pools and ". . . we know the insurance companies have been working state by state to block any bans on sex discrimination in rates and benefits," Smeal said. (06/01)

ISSUES

Lifestyles

Wisconsin became the first state in the nation to pass a law that prohibited discrimination against homosexuals in all areas regulated by the state, including both public and private employment, housing and public accommodations. In a formal ceremony, Republican Governor Lee Dreyfus signed the Gay Rights Bill and presented the pen to the author of the measure, State Representative David Clarenbach (D-Madison). (02/25)

Education

Economic

According to a book entitled *Somebody Has To Do It* by Penney Kome, the average employed woman with children did 30 hours of housework in addition to her paid job.

Religion

Lynchburg (VA) NOW picketed Jerry Falwell as Thomas Road Baptist Church and were joined by Virginia NOW officers, other Virginia chapters of NOW, and Mormons for ERA in protesting Falwell's stand on ERA and women's issues. (04/25)

Media

Los Angeles NOW sponsored a tribute dinner for actress Esther Rolle who campaigned for the ERA in her home state of Florida and in other unratified states. (04/24)

Legal

Political

The North Carolina NOW ERA Countdown Campaign, led by Terry Schooley, began a major push for ratification. The TV ads, door-to-door canvassing, action team phone-banking for constituent mail and constituent visits, a speaking tour by NOW President Ellie Smeal, and a massive rally in Raleigh were all aimed at building the climate for ratification. All polls showed solid support for ERA among North Carolinians. (04)

Eleanor R. Spikes
1936 – 1982
Eleanor Spikes, 46, partner in the firm of Hernandez Associates, a civil rights and women's rights activist and former coordinator of the the Minority Women's Task Force of NOW, died on April 3, after a long, courageous battle against cancer. In 1975 Spikes assisted the first group of women to enter and successfully complete training as full-service police officers in the San Francisco Police Department in a year-long project funded by the Mayor's Criminal Justice Planning Council. She was a co-founder of the Black Women Organized for Action in San Francisco and served on local boards of Planned Parenthood and the YMCA.

Over a quarter of a million door-hangers were distributed by ERA activists in Florida during the last critical months of the ERA Countdown Campaign. The door hangers told the recipients exactly where their state legislator stood on ERA and urged them to get involved in the ratification drive by using the "postcard" portion of the door-hanger to send a message to that legislator. (04)

A group of women gathered in Springfield, IL, to begin a fast for ratification of the Equal Rights Amendment. The women who participated were Zoe Ann Amanda, Dina Bachelor, Mary Barnes, Mary Ann Beall, Sonia Johnson, Shirley Wallace and Maureen Fiedler. (05/18)

A poll of North Carolinians showed that the Equal Rights Amendment was favored by a majority of 61-30, but anti-ERA Senators met in the legislature's chapel and, after offering a prayer "to justify use of a chapel for a political meeting," the 27 took a "solemn pledge" to kill the ERA by tabling it when it came up before the North Carolina Senate. The next day, the Senate voted to table the ERA 27-23. All 10 Republicans in the North Carolina Senate voted to table. Of the 40 Democrats, 23 voted against the tabling and 17 voted for it. (05/19)

The number of one-parent families headed by divorced women grew 181% between 1970 and 1981, from 956,000 to 2,700,000. In the same period, one-parent families headed by women separated from their husbands grew from 1.1 million to 1.6 million.

As thousands of ERA supporters gathered in Tallahassee, the Florida House voted 60-58 in favor of ratification, but the Senate voted 22-16 against it. At the conclusion of the vote, angry supporters chanted, "We'll remember in November!" (06/21)

The day after the Florida vote, the ERA came to a vote in the Illinois House where it was rejected by a vote of 103 for to 72 opposed. The three-fifths requirement of 107 votes meant that the Amendment fell short by four votes. The entire Illinois campaign revolved around the efforts to change the three fifths to a majority vote. House Speaker George Ryan would not even allow the question of majority rule to come to the floor of the House. The Amendment was further blocked by Governor Jim Thompson, self-styled ERA supporter, who, in fact, also refused to support the majority rule. (06/22)

The Backlash

Reagan's Education Department asked Attorney General William French Smith for permission to revoke rules banning discrimination in the employment practices of schools and colleges receiving federal aid.

The Federal agency charged with enforcing Affirmative Action proposed new regulations that would cripple enforcement if adopted. The regulations, issued by the Office of Federal Contract Compliance Programs, virtually killed the effectiveness of back pay awards as a remedy for discrimination and outlined goals that were absurdly low for bringing more women into the construction trade. (05)

YEAR	1982
U. S. President	Ronald Reagan
NOW President	Eleanor Smeal

EVENTS

On June 30, 1982, the Equal Rights Amendment fell three states short of ratification. Business in general and the insurance industry in particular had opposed it. Most revealing: 75% of women state legislators in the four key states but only 46% of the men voted to ratify; only 55% of Democrats voted for it; and 75% of Republicans voted against it.

Women's Equality Day, 1982, the first since a handful of legislatures blocked the ERA, was the day NOW's PACs launched a $3 million fundraising drive for the fall state and congressional elections. Some 65 PAC/ WOMAN Walkathons were held nationwide with the largest in Washington, D.C., Los Angeles, and San Francisco, each with more than 1000 walkers. (08)

ISSUES

Lifestyles

NOW marked the end of the ERA Count-down Campaign on June 30, 1982, with a protest demonstration in Lafayette Park across from the White House. Thousands of ERA Countdown Campaign workers flew in from all over the country to participate. Rallies were also held in other major cities. NOW President Ellie Smeal vowed to flood the tickets with pro-ERA women in Florida and Illinois. The NOW Equality PAC recruited candidates, turning the drive for ERA into a massive political movement for women. (06/30)

Record breaking numbers of women filed to run for office in Florida as a part of the tidal wave of political activity after the Florida ERA vote in late June. As of the last day to file in the state legislative races, 81 women had declared as candidates. Twenty women were running for the 40 member Florida Senate, and 61 women were running for the 120 member Florida House. All state legislative seats were up for election by order of the Florida Supreme Court. (06)

Education

NOW Membership – 225,000
Annual Budget – $9,050,000
NOW PAC – $1,700,000

Women who raised families and worked outside the home had a lower incidence of high blood pressure and heart ailments despite the popular notion that such dual roles produce anxiety and stress, according to a report in *Science Digest* magazine. According to the author of the report, Georgetown University Medical School physiologist Estelle Ramey, the women were healthier because of the reduced stress afforded by the sense of security a salary brings in an era of high divorce rates. (09/01)

NOW, the ACLU, and the National Lawyers' Guild prepared a joint defense team to represent 10 women and two men sailors accused by the U.S. Navy of homosexuality while serving aboard the submarine tender U.S.S. Dixon, docked in San Diego, CA. (09)

Economic

Legal

Ohio NOW chapters and other pro-choice and equal rights groups transformed themselves into "Ladies Against Women" and organized a rally when Phyllis Schlafly spoke in Cleveland. Sporting hats and white gloves for the occasion, about 75 women gathered at the club where Schlafly spoke. They waved signs reading "Suffering Not Suffrage," "Sperm Are People Too," "You're Nobody Until You're Mrs. Somebody." (07)

Birmingham (AL) NOW launched a full-scale billboard campaign for reproductive freedom. The chapter raised $4,000 from private donations and bought space for 13 billboards which were placed throughout the city. The billboards pictured a couple in bed with a second man dressed in a business suit sitting between them. The caption on the sign read, "Pregnancy Is Personal Not Political! Keep Your Senator Out Of Your Bedroom!" (07)

Political

The Minnesota State Chapter of NOW, represented by the NOW Legal Defense and Education Fund, filed an amicus curiae brief in an action before the U.S. Court of Appeals for the Eighth Circuit charging the U.S. Jaycees with discrimination against women in its membership policies. The NOW brief was filed in response to the U.S. Jaycees' challenge to a ruling by the Minnesota Supreme Court that the organization had violated the state's ban on sex discrimination by denying full membership to women.

The California Title IX signed into law by Governor Jerry Brown, and actually more comprehensive than the Federal Title IX, outlawed sex discrimination in any program or activity of an educational institution receiving any state financial assistance. It covered participation in programs or activities, financial assistance, athletics and employment, and set rules regarding pregnancy and related conditions and also required the use of instructional materials which provided a balanced view of women and men. The concept of a California Title IX bill originated with Phyllis W. Cheng of the Educational Task Force of the Los Angeles NOW chapter and was backed by California NOW and 26 other organizations. (09/16)

Chicago NOW announced a dollars and cents victory over sex discrimination in Chicago. Both Carson Pirie Scott and Company and Marshall Field and Company changed their discriminatory clothing alteration policies in response to complaints filed by Chicago NOW activists with the Illinois Department of Human Rights on March 17, 1981. The stores' former policies made women pay for alterations which men received free of charge. (09)

The Backlash

The Department of Education, through the Justice Department, took steps to limit its enforcement responsibilities under Title IX of the Education Amendments of 1972, Title VI of the Civil Rights Act of 1964, and section 504 of the Rehabilitation Act of 1973. In the case of *Grove City College v. Bell,* pending before the U.S.

Court of Appeals for the Third Circuit, the Justice Department argued that Guaranteed Student Loans did not constitute "Federal financial assistance" as defined in Title IX and Title VI. If guaranteed student loans were excluded from the definition of Federal assistance, over 300 postsecondary schools would be free to discriminate on the basis of

race, national origin, sex, and handicap. (05)

In their 21st annual protest, Mel and Norma Gabler, the Texas textbook censors, filed almost 600 pages of protests with the Texas Textbook Committee. (06/24)

YEAR	1982
U. S. President	Ronald Reagan
NOW President	Judy Goldsmith

EVENTS

When members of the National Association of Women Judges met in New York, they handed down an impromptu judgment on the Reagan Administration. The verdict: Guilty of short-changing women on Federal court appointments. The Reagan Administration had racked up just four women on its list of 84 federal court appointees.

Judy Goldsmith, NOW Vice President-Executive, was elected to a three year term as President at the 15th annual NOW Conference in Indianapolis, IN, October 8-10. Other new officers included: Barbara Timmer, Vice President-Executive; Mary Jean Collins, Vice President-Action; Kathy Webb, Secretary; and Alice Chapman, re-elected Treasurer. (10/10)

ISSUES

Lifestyles

Illinois NOW chapters joined together in front of the Chicago Bulls' ticket office in downtown Chicago to picket against Quintin Dailey, the basketball club's number one draft choice who was convicted of assaulting a University of San Francisco nursing student in her dormitory room. (10/30)

Economic

Sexual harassment would no longer be "condoned or tolerated" in the United States Navy, according to an order by Vice Chief of Naval Operations Admiral William N. Small. Small ordered commanders to crack down on sexual harassment with "swift and appropriate disciplinary action."(11/12)

Media

Political

Past NOW President Ellie Smeal was voted fourth most influential woman in America by newspaper editors across the country, according to the *World Almanac*. Out of a possible 133 votes from both female and male editors, Smeal received 53 votes. Sandra Day O'Connor, the first female U.S. Supreme Court Justice, placed first in her first year on the list with 81 votes. She was followed by Katherine Graham, chair of the board of the *Washington Post* Company, and Billie Jean King, tennis star. Following Smeal with 52 votes each were Gloria Steinem, publisher of *Ms.* Magazine and Phyllis Schlafly. Other women who received influential honors included: Carol Burnett, Jane Byrne, Sarah Caldwell, Mary Cunningham, Chris Evert-Lloyd, Millicent Fenwick, Ellen Goodman, Katharine Hepburn, Barbara Jordan, Jeane Kirkpatrick, Ann Landers, Sylvia Porter, Nancy Reagan, Brooke Shields, Beverly Sills, historian Barbara Tuchman, Abigail Van Buren, Barbara Walters, and physicist Rosalyn Yalow. (11)

The Gender Gap–the difference in male/female voting patterns–had a significant impact on races nationwide in the 1982 elections. According to exit polls, 53% of women voted Democratic as opposed to 47% going Republican; the figures for men were exactly reversed. The Gender Gap appeared in every part of the country, in varying patterns and degrees, affecting state legislator, Congressional, and gubernatorial elections. This election resulted in a doubling of the number of women in the Florida senate. In 1977, the Florida senate had only one women; in 1982, four women served; and in 1983, nine women sat in the Florida senate. The number of women in the Florida House was also increased by 50%. Of the 23 Florida Senators who voted "no" on the ERA, 10 did not return. Eight of the 10 were replaced by pro-ERA Senators. A count in the Florida Senate showed 23 pro-ERA legislators, a winning majority. In an impressive showing in Illinois, out of 79 NOW/ EQUALITY/ PAC supported legislative races, 68 of the candidates won. In the Illinois Senate, as in the Florida Senate, the number of women doubled, from four to eight. Of the eight, seven were pro-ERA. The Illinois House also switched by a substantial margin from a Republican majority to a Democratic majority. In Illinois, as a result of the election, there were 36 pro-ERA legislators in the Senate and 75 pro-ERA legislators in the House. These gains meant that there were enough votes to meet even the 3/5 voting requirements of the Illinois legislature. In the North Carolina state legislature, NOW/ EQUALITY/ PAC supported 35 races, and won 26. In Congress, an initial analysis showed women's rights issues gained approximately 21 seats in the House of Representatives. (11)

Baltimore NOW staged an "IT PAYS TO BE A MAN" march to highlight the inequities of the wage gap between women and men in various occupations such as waiter, clerical worker, and physician. As participants in the 2nd annual Charles Street on Parade event, Baltimore NOW members carried placards and handed out 500 flyers containing statistics on the wage gap and also distributed NOW membership applications and invitations to their next chapter meeting. (11/20)

In A Different Voice, Psychological Theory and Women's Development by Carol Gilligan was published.

Ellie Smeal, Alan Alda, and Betty Ford were honored at a tribute dinner sponsored by Los Angeles NOW. At the dinner, attended by 500 people many of whom had worked in the Countdown Campaign, Smeal was presented with a plaque which read "Thank you for never giving up or giving in." Other well-known individuals who received NOW Medallion Awards for their part in the Countdown Campaign were: Arlene Alda, John Astin, Patty Duke, Maryedith Burrell, Virginia Carter, Rosemary Chiaverini, Midge Costanza, Harlan Ellison, Mike Farrell, Joan Hackett, Valerie Harper, Carole Hemingway, Allan Jonas, Linda Kelsey, Judge Joan Dempsey Klein, Linda Lavin, Caroline Mc Williams, Joan Palevsky, Esther Rolle, William Schallert, Jean Stapleton, Loretta Swit, Trish Van Devere and Robert Walden, plus National Board members Mary Margaret Smith and Shelly Mandell and State Coordinator Ginny Foat. The tribute dinner was coordinated by Los Angeles NOW Vice President Marnie Delaney. (11/11)

The Backlash

The *New York Times Magazine* published an article entitled "Voices From The Post-Feminist Generation by Susan Beletin kicking off the myth that the "post-feminist" era had begun. (10/17)

The Moral Majority, which collected $134,000 to fight to keep gay speakers out of Minnea-

polis, MI, schools and then spent the money elsewhere, again sought funds nationally to oppose homosexuality. (11/24)

More and more women's "classics" were joining the "dangerous" list of books targeted by the Radical Right's book-banning arm. Among the titles challenged: *Our Bodies, Ourselves; Memoirs of An Ex-Prom Queen;*

Growing Up Female In America; and even Marlo Thomas' *Free to Be You and Me.* To fight back against the anti-book trend, the American Library Association and the American Booksellers Association joined forces, declaring a "dangerous volumes" week; targeted books were featured prominently in library and bookstore windows. (11)

YEAR	1983
U. S. President	Ronald Reagan
NOW President	Judy Goldsmith

EVENTS

The ERA was reintroduced in the U.S. House of Representatives as H.J. Res. 1 by Democratic Party leadership (without consultation with organizations supporting ERA), with 210 sponsors that rose quickly to 232. In addition, four non-voting members of Congress from the District of Columbia, Guam, Puerto Rico, and the Virgin Islands signed on as co-sponsors. For the ERA to pass the House, 290 votes were required. (01/03)

Representative Ted Weiss (D-NY) reintroduced the Gay Civil Rights Bill in the 98th session of Congress. The bill, HR 427, would amend key sections of the Civil Rights Act of 1964 so that discrimination on the basis of "affectional or sexual orientation" would be prohibited. The prohibition would pertain to the areas of housing, employment, and public accommodations. In the Senate, Senator Paul Tsongas (D-MA) introduced a similar bill. (01/03)

ISSUES

Lifestyles

Greater Rochester (NY) NOW started a reward fund to help find and arrest suspected rapists. The chapter started the fund because of the increasing number of rapes in the city including a recent case which involved a 67-year old woman who was sexually attacked in a church. (01)

Education

Pennsylvania NOW participated as *amicus curiae* on behalf of three young women challenging the sex-based admission policy of Philadelphia's Central High School. The women wanted to complete their high school education at Central because Central, which at the time admitted only males, offered the best academic education of Philadelphia's public schools. The lawsuit was brought under the Pennsylvania Equal Rights Amendment as well as the 14th Amendment of the Constitution. (01)

Economic

Legal

Santa Barbara (CA) NOW and the National Women's Political Caucus arranged speaking engagements and fundraisers to aid a TV newscaster who lost her job because she was deemed "too unattractive, too old and not deferential enough to men." Christine Craft, a 38-year old former Kansas City, MO, news anchor, then working at station KEYT in Santa Barbara, CA, filed a $1 million lawsuit against KMBC, ABC's Kansas City affiliate. The suit sought back pay, lost benefits, attorneys fees and recovery of the job. (01)

Media

Legal

Political

NOW Annual Budget – $4,200,000

United (MN) NOW (Minneapolis/ St. Paul) waged a campaign urging city bus riders to "Speak out against the threat to reproductive rights." The chapter's Reproductive Rights Committee, chaired by Sheila Knox, raised $750.00 and placed over 100 12" x 24" signs in the area's mass transit buses. The signs urged readers to contact their Congress members and speak out against the anti-abortion bills circulating in Congress. (01)

Farm women of the 80's remained full partners in their family businesses, according to a report issued by the U.S. Department of Agriculture. "Farming is usually a family affair, shared. . . by husbands and wives," said the survey of 2500 women farmers and 570 men. On livestock farms, the report said, two-thirds of farm wives help herd and milk dairy cows; 37% participate in plowing, cultivating and planting. (01)

More than 63% of respondents to a *Glamour* magazine survey still supported a federal Equal Rights Amendment, and even more –70% – felt abortion was a matter of personal choice. These opinions were combined with a disapproval of premarital sex (by 51%) and a reiteration of strong personal commitments to raising a family (90%)– but 84% believed that a woman need not marry and have children to be fulfilled. (01)

The Republicans got the bad news in a 12-page memo prepared by Ronald H. Hinckley, a special assistant in the White House Office of Planning and Evaluation. He concluded that women had a far lower opinion of President Reagan than men did, that a Gender Gap had helped Democrats in the November election, and that it "could prove dangerous for Republicans in 1984." (01)

In a settlement that marked a significant victory for women, a national insurance company agreed to decrease women's disability insurance rates to equal those of men in Pennsylvania. The settlement ended a discrimination suit filed four years before against Massachusetts Indemnity and Life Insurance Company by Ellen Starer. Starer, represented by the Women's Law Project and the NOW LDEF charged that the sex-based rates were unconstitutional under the state's Equal Rights Amendment. The settlement to avoid trial suggested that the surcharges for women were "based on stereotype rather than supported by facts," commented Judy Goldsmith, president of NOW. (01/06)

The Los Angeles docks expected an influx of women working as new members of the Longshoremen's Union and the Marine Clerks union, as the result of a settlement of a two-year, class action sex discrimination suit brought by the Center for Law in the Public Interest. The Unions agreed that 315 of the next 900 dockworkers hired would be women. Marsha Kwalwasser of the Center noted that dock workers could expect to earn up to $40,000 per year. (01)

In an amicus curiae brief filed before the U. S. Supreme Court, NOW and other women's groups urged the Court to uphold an order protecting minority hiring goals in Boston's Police and Fire Departments. The case, *Boston Firefighters Union, Local 718 v. Boston Chapter, NAACP* and companion cases, arose because the City had announced a program of layoffs that, as originally planned, would have drastically reduced Black and Hispanic representation in those departments. (02/00)

The Backlash

Both Senators Orrin Hatch (R-UT) and Jesse Helms (R-NC) reintroduced their anti-abortion legislation in the 98th Congress, but the major concern in the Senate was a proposal to return the abortion issue to the states. Senator Hatch reintroduced the Human Life Federalism Amendment as it was approved by the Senate Judiciary Committee in 1982. (01)

Health & Human Services (HHS) Secretary Richard Schweiker announced his intention to implement the "squeal rule" that required the nation's 5,000 federally funded family planning clinics to notify parents of requests by their daughters under age 18 for contraceptives, including birth control pills, diaphragms, or intrauterine devices. Schweiker said that Marjory Mecklenberg would become director of all HHS family planning programs. Mecklenberg, the former head of an anti-abortion group, initiated the parental notification concept.(01/10) **105**

YEAR	1983
U. S. President	Ronald Reagan
NOW President	Judy Goldsmith

EVENTS

A federal judge permanently barred the Department of Health and Human Services from implementing the "squeal rule" requiring government funded clinics to notify parents when teenagers seek prescription contraceptives. He said the regulation would cause irreparable harm by deterring sexually active adolescents

from visiting family planning clinics. (02/14)

The Duarte (CA) Rotary Club, known as the Ex-Rotary club since their suspension for admitting women, lost its five year battle against sexism. Los Angeles Superior Court Judge Max F. Deutz, basing his ruling solely on California law, refused

to reinstate the club in Rotary International or to sanction the decision to include women members. (02/08)

ISSUES

Economic
Education
Religion
Legal
Political

As a result of a coalition effort led by women in both houses of the legislature, Montana became the first state to ban sex discrimination in all types of insurance. The new law applied to auto, life, medical expenses, disability and old age income insurance. To get this landmark legislation passed, NOW state coordinator Dee Adams worked with State Senator Pat Regan, Representative Jan Brown, the bill's sponsor; and House speaker Dan Kemmis. She also represented NOW on the board of the Women's Lobbyist Fund, which coordinated legislative and grassroots activity by NOW chapters statewide; women's networks from several cities; Business & Professional Women (BPW); Montana Lesbian Coalition, Montana Women's Political Caucus; ERA Council; Pro-choice and Planned Parenthood. Other organizations supporting the legislation were AAUW, LWV, ACLU, Montana Federation of Teachers, Montana Education Association, Montana Democratic Women's Clubs, Montana Senior Citizens Association, and Low Income Senior Citizens Association. Although resistance to the legislation by the insurance industry was intense, it escalated after enactment of the law. (03/04)

Delaware mothers had a much better chance to collect child support payments thanks to tough new legislation initiated by NOW. Under the new law a non-custodial parent's wages would be attached automatically in new cases of court-ordered support payments. The court would put the wage attachment on hold for as long as payments were timely and regular. (03/06)

The 1983 Economic Equity Act, which contained proposals to reform discriminatory practices in insurance, pensions, tax policy, child support enforcement, day care, and federal regulations, was formally introduced in Congress. NOW endorsed the package, which had 91 cosponsors in the House and 20 in the Senate. (03/14)

A report by the Bureau of the Census showed that women were going to college in ever-increasing numbers, expanding their enrollment lead over men. In just 12 years the ratio of women to men students had changed dramatically, from 74 women per 100 men in 1972, to 108 women for every 100 men in 1981. (03/20)

Long Beach (CA) NOW prepared a flyer to be distributed to local teenagers explaining the exact implications and effects of the "squeal rule" or Parental Notification Law. The flyers not only explained the law, but encouraged teenagers to discuss birth control and sexual activity with their parents if that was possible. They emphasized responsibility on the part of the teenager in deciding to engage in sexual activity and gave information on where to go for help if they couldn't discuss these problems with their parents. (04)

A poll of editors of Roman Catholic newspapers and magazines found that 49.5% thought the church should ordain women to the priesthood and 39.6% were opposed. (04)

Connecticut NOW won a significant court decision establishing the right to permanently petition in the Westarms Mall, one of the state's largest shopping malls. The decision was based on the right to free speech guaranteed by the state, not the federal, constitution. (03)

Montgomery County (MD) NOW, joined by other activists from Virginia and Maryland, drew media attention and sent reverberations through the insurance industry when they publicly protested a closed session on sex discrimination in insurance. The incident occurred at the spring meeting of the National Association of Insurance Commissioners (NAIC) in Baltimore. (04)

Porter County and La Porte County (IN) NOW assisted a group of Indiana waitresses in forming the National Association of Waitresses to lobby and negotiate for their rights. The waitresses were opposing a new IRS taxing regulation requiring restaurant owners to report 8% of gross sales for taxing purposes on employees' tip income. Some employers were reportedly withholding the difference between the 8% figure and reported tips from employees' paychecks, regardless of the amount of tips the employee earned. As a result, some waitresses were receiving paychecks with a net earning of less than one dollar per hour, and, in a few cases, zero earnings. (04)

Utah NOW sponsored a candle-light vigil at Temple Square in Salt Lake City. The purpose of the vigil was to reaffirm NOW's determination to continue the fight for women's equality and to protest the Church of the Latter Day Saints' involvement in ERA politics. (04/02)

NOW announced plans to hold its 1984 convention in Miami Beach (FL), ending a six year boycott over Florida's failure to ratify the ERA. Miami Beach officials, who complained that the boycott cost the city $20 million in convention cancellations, hailed the development. (05/09)

The Backlash

President Reagan's nominee for the Corporation for Public Broadcasting (CPB) board of directors, Henel Marie Taylor, was a director of Phyllis Schlafly's Eagle Forum and a contributor to the Christian Broadcast Network and Moral Majority. (02)

A new Right wing group called "Renaissance Women" was organized with Nina May as its chair.

The insurance industry, launched a multi-million dollar media campaign to oppose legislation that would outlaw sex discrimination in insurance. Umbrella groups representing

major insurance companies placed full page ads in newspapers across the country, concentrating on major national papers and those in the home districts of House and Senate Committee members. (05)

YEAR	1983
U. S. President	Ronald Reagan
NOW President	Judy Goldsmith

EVENTS

Months after the defeat of the ERA, which opponents warned would make women subject to the draft, the Department of Defense (DOD) offered a little-noticed proposal that would make women eligible for the draft for the first time in American history as part of the plan to begin registering medical people again. The DOD proposed amending the old "Doctor's Draft" codes by "striking out 'males' and inserting in place thereof 'persons.'" Among the "persons" the DOD had in mind were female doctors, nurses, physical therapists, pharmacists, etc. between the ages of 18 1/2 and 46. Though anti-ERA forces had said this could only happen if the ERA became part of the Constitution, there never was any guarantee that women couldn't be drafted. The U.S. Supreme Court decision that approved an all-male draft didn't outlaw drafting women; it just left the decision up to Congress. (03)

ISSUES

Lifestyles

Education

Economic

Media

Legal

Four major organizations of physicians and nurses joined the U.S. Supreme Court debate over abortion, urging the Justices to declare unconstitutional the Akron, OH city ordinance . The four organizations filing the brief were the 235,000 member AMA; the American College of Obstetricians and Gynecologists, which represents 90% of the specialists in those fields, and its Nurses Association; and the American Academy of Pediatrics. (06/15)

NOW's National Day of Protest against the insurance industry's opposition to equality for women resulted in over 50 insurance pickets from coast to coast. Hundreds of NOW activists successfully sent a message to their communities, from Santa Fe, NM, to New York City; sex discrimination in insurance, as in anything else, hurts women. Legislation that would outlaw sex discrimination in insurance (HR 100 in the House and 5. 372 in the Senate) was strongly supported by NOW because it would require insurance rates to be based on factors other than sex, and women would benefit economically. (06/08)

The Hatch Amendment (Senate Joint Resolution 3) fell 18 votes short of the two-thirds majority needed to pass a constitutional amendment. By a vote of 50 to 49, the Republican-dominated Senate rejected the amendment, which read, "A right to abortion is not secured by this constitution." Senator Jesse Helms (R-NC) voted "Present," saying that the amendment failed to recognize "the unborn child's inalienable right to life." (06/28)

A new study on auto insurance rates by the National Insurance Consumer Organization (NICO) confirmed NOW's claim that sex discrimination in insurance cost women over $1 billion a year, and destroyed the insurance industry's threat that sex neutral rates required by H.R. 100/S. 372 would end price "breaks" for women. (7/25)

Former NOW President Eleanor Smeal began publication of the *Eleanor Smeal Report*, a twice monthly insiders report on the feminist movement. (06/10) She also celebrated the official opening of her consulting firm, Eleanor Smeal and Associates. (06/17)

The U.S. Supreme Court stood firmly behind its 1973 abortion decision and ruled 6 - 3 that government could not interfere with this "fundamental right" of women unless it was clearly justified by "accepted medical practice." The court struck down laws, similar to those in 22 states, that required hospitals, rather than clinics, to perform abortions after the first three months of pregnancy. They also invalidated an Akron, Ohio ordinance requiring a 24 hour waiting period and elaborate "informed consent" procedures before an abortion could be performed, and special "decent burial" rules for disposal of the fetus afterward. (06/15)

Physicist Sally Ride became the first American woman to travel in space. Ride served as a mission specialist when the space shuttle Challenger, which also carried four male astronauts, was launched on its second flight. (06/18-24)

Middlesex County (NJ) NOW helped a local Medical Care Center that was under siege by anti-abortion groups by providing an escort service for patients. Coordinator Debra Sabourin told the press, "Our reason for being here is to get the patients inside safely. We think a woman who walks in should not have to walk in alone. She should have a friend." (08)

The last all-male school in the Ivy League became co-educational when Columbia College enrolled women for the first time in its 229 year history. (08)

Los Angeles (CA) NOW aired its new cable show, a half hour news show, called "Women NOW" which gave updates on feminist issues via Communicom Access Channel and Valley Cable. The first program included a discussion of the Insurance Equity Act with Sally Rosloff, Los Angeles NOW President. (07)

Former Representative Robert E. Bauman, a "New Right" Republican from Maryland, and past president of the American Conservative Union, announced at the American Bar Association convention that he would actively lobby for Federal legislation to protect homosexual men and women from discrimination. Bauman, once a rising star of the Right, lost his bid for re-election in 1980 after being arrested on a morals charge—soliciting sex from a teenage boy. (08/02)

The Backlash

After 10 years of weekly anti-abortion pickets and protests, an arsonist got into the second story of the Hillcrest Clinic in Norfolk, VA, and used kerosene to set fire to the offices. The Vice President of the Virginia Society of Human Life told the press that "we rejoice" at the news of the fires. Damages totalled approximately $140,000. The clinic was forced to install a security and alarm system costing $3,500. (05/26)

The Women's Electoral Lobby of Perth, Australia, reported that Phyllis Schlafly had been visiting the Eastern Australia states. Her purpose: to undermine the ratification of the "U.N. Convention on the Elimination of All Forms of Discrimination Against Women." (06)

107

YEAR	1983
U. S. President	Ronald Reagan
NOW President	Judy Goldsmith

EVENTS

NOW activists defeated almost all of the anti-abortion bills introduced in state legislatures this year. In the 1983 legislative sessions nearly 100 bills were introduced but fewer than 20 passed.

The United States Coast Guard unequivocally took the stand that women must be completely integrated into the Coast Guard. Policy officially stated, "It is not considered a practical matter to remove women from those Coast Guard cutters which might be assigned combat missions when operating with the Navy. Coast Guard women are an integral part of the crew and would be in various positions of responsibility. . . . The removal of these key personnel on short notice would weaken our military readiness capability and have major operational impact on some units." (09)

ISSUES

Lifestyles

Christine Craft, who said she was demoted on a television news program because her employer considered her "too old, unattractive and not deferential enough to men" was awarded $500,000 in damages ($375,000 in actual damages and $125,000 in punitive damages) by a jury in Kansas City, MO. (08/08)

Education

Polls showed that the Gender Gap increased dramatically in August, while President Ronald Reagan committed a series of blunders that seemed certain to alienate women even further. A Gallup Poll released August 10 showed only 34% of women supporting Reagan, compared to 51% men. In the previous month, support for Reagan from men had dropped 1% while support from women plummeted 8%. The 17 point gender gap was the largest ever recorded by a Gallup poll. (08/10)

In a landmark decision, Judge William Marutani of the Pennsylvania Court of Common Pleas ruled that Philadelphia's Central High's exclusionary admissions policy violated the federal Constitution and the state constitution's Equal Rights Amendment. The judge's order that Central High open its doors to female students marked the end of Central High's 147-year tradition of providing education to young men only. Pennsylvania NOW had participated in the suit on behalf of the girls. (08/30)

Economic

Media

Illinois NOW in coalition with the Illinois House Rape Study Committee and the Coalition of Women Against Rape, wrote and lobbied through the Illinois legislature a comprehensive sexual assault bill. According to Anne S. Courtney, President of Illinois NOW, "The law encompasses all types of sexual assault committed by force or threat of force by both sexes against victims of both sexes and all ages; it defines assault in terms of the defendant's behavior rather than the victim's state of mind." (08)

Legal

San Diego (CA) NOW organized more than 500 demonstrators to protest President Reagan's appearance in San Diego before a group of Republican women. Los Angeles NOW rented a bus to enable a group of Los Angeles activists to participate in the demonstration. ((08/26)

Political

TAKE THE POWER

In 1971 there were 362 women state legislators, in 1983 there were 992. There were only seven women mayors of cities with more than 30,000 population in 1971, representing only 1% of the total. In 1983 there were 76 women mayors. The number of women in congress had doubled since 1971, though still miniscule. There are 24, two in the Senate and 22 in the House (4.3%), compared to 11 women in Congress in 1971. (09)

Representative Patricia Schroeder (D-CO), chair of the Subcommittee on Civil Service of the House Committee on Post Office and Civil Service, released a report comparing mid-term appointment records for Presidents Reagan and Carter. The report contained several shocking facts. Despite his promise to cut the size of government, Reagan made significantly more political appointments than Carter: 14% more full time Presidential appointments; 44% more to boards and commissions; and he more than doubled the number of Senior Executive Service positions (from 1,438 jobs to 2,978 jobs). The Schroeder report pointed out that "although Reagan had 30% more [total] appointments, he appointed 18% fewer women." The report revealed that the White House claim of 1,200 female appointments to executive level positions shrank to 88 under close inspection. Overall, Reagan appointed 14.6% women, Carter 22.4%. (09/20)

President Reagan finally unveiled a major component of his much-touted and long-secret "Equal Rights Amendment alternative" two weeks after NOW filed a Freedom of Information Act request demanding disclosure of Justice Department documents identifying sex discriminatory laws in the Federal code. The Third Quarterly Report of the Attorney General's Gender Discrimination Agency Review identified 140 federal laws that contained gender-based distinctions. Reagan released the report with recommendations to correct 47 of the discriminatory statutes. Assistant Attorney General William Bradford Reynolds admitted that the recommendations were "inconsequential" and "cosmetic." NOW President Judy Goldsmith called Reagan's proposals "painfully inadequate." (09)

The Backlash

Reagan's Department of Education dismissed or reassigned all five women in the Women's Educational Equity Act Program. Five mid-level male employees would reportedly keep their jobs with the program. According to the project's director Leslie Wolfe, the program would be "Downgraded into a tiny section under a branch under a division under the office that administers the block grants." (08)

More than 20 anti-abortion spokesmen lined up against Planned Parenthood in an effort to have it ruled ineligible for the government's version of the United Way. In an emotional meeting before the eligibility committee of the Combined Federal Campaign, the anti-abortion groups said Planned Parenthood failed to meet financial and other criteria. (08/31)

YEAR	1983		
U. S. President	Ronald Reagan		
NOW President	Judy Goldsmith		

EVENTS

The ERA failed by six votes to get a 2/3 majority in the U. S. House. The vote was 278-147. Six Democratic and six Republican co-sponsors voted against the ERA. (11/15)

In a landmark wage discrimination case, a Federal district judge ordered the State of Washington to pay an amount estimated at $838 million in immediate raises and back pay to women. Judge Jack Tanner ended three months of legal dispute in the case with this message to many women who worked for the state: "You win." The pivot of the case was the "comparable worth" of the jobs in categories filled mostly by women and those in categories filled mostly by men. The judge based his decision on studies commissioned by the state, beginning in 1974, that showed women in predominantly female jobs were paid 20 to 30% less than men in jobs considered to be of equal value. (12/01)

ISSUES

Economic

At the 1983 NOW National Conference in October all six Democratic presidential candidates pledged that they would consider a woman as vice president during a forum featuring presidential hopefuls Senators Alan Cranston, John Glenn, Gary Hart, Ernest Hollings, former Senator George Mc Govern, and former Vice President Walter Mondale. Their presence was recognition of both the political stature of NOW and the growing power of the Gender Gap. The NOW Conference pledged to "work to strengthen the ticket by advocating a woman committed to women's rights issues as the candidate for vice president." Delegates also voted overwhelmingly for NOW/PAC to endorse a presidential candidate for 1984. In December, the PAC endorsed Mondale. (10/00)

Joan Hackett
1934-1983

Joan Hackett, 49, critically acclaimed actress and NOW activist, died of cancer in California on October 8. An Oscar nominee in 1982 and winner of a 1982 Golden Globe Award for her role in the film, "Only When I Laugh," Hackett became increasingly active in the ERA ratification campaign. She worked at many ERA fundraising events and made radio and television appearances as a ERA proponent. Hackett inscribed her photo in the 1979 NOW National Conference program book with this message: "NOW is the most consistent organization for me to contribute my energy and support. I am grateful for the courage and tenacity of all the women involved." NOW representatives at her funeral included Toni Carabillo, Judith Meuli, and Sally Rosloff. (10)

Dozens of NOW chapters across the country participated in a "National Day of Protest" against Allstate Insurance for employment discrimination. A major class action lawsuit charging Allstate with violations of the Equal Pay Act and Title VII of the 1964 Civil Rights Act was filed by two Northeast Indiana (Fort Wayne) NOW leaders, Sue Thomas and Sharon Stewart, Allstate sales agents who found that despite sales records that were superior to their male peers, the men were paid $9 -$10,000 more per year. Thomas's and Stewart's discrimination complaint was joined with a nine-year old class action Title VII suit filed in California. (11/16)

Religion

Twelve hundred Roman Catholic women gathered in Chicago to express their frustration with Pope John Paul II's conservative policies on feminist issues and to seek ways to expand women's rights and role in the church. The "Woman Church Speaks" conference was the first major gathering of an emerging coalition of activist Catholic women's groups. (11/12-13)

In a parliamentary maneuver designed to prevent amendments to the ERA, Tip O'Neill and the Democratic House leadership brought the ERA to the floor under a suspension of the House rules. Under this procedure no amendments were allowed and each side had only 20 minutes for debate. Once again, as in the state legislatures, some Representatives pledged to support the ERA voted "no," including 14 co-sponsors–just enough to make the Amendment fall short of the required 2/3 vote by six votes. The vote was along Party lines with 84% of Democrats voting for it while only 32% of the Republicans did so. (11/15)

Political

More than 500 activists attended a conference where they explored the Gender Gap and how it could affect the outcome of Kentucky's statewide elections as well as the 1984 state legislative session. NWPC National Chair Kathy Wilson keynoted the session sponsored by the Kentucky Commission on Women and the AAUW with 35 co-sponsoring women's civil right and other progressive groups. Women registered to vote outnumbered men in Kentucky by 64,000. (10/01)

Western Electric Co., Inc. and nearly 3,000 female employees agreed to a $7 million settlement of a sex discrimination lawsuit, and a federal judge approved the accord. (11/17)

A New Jersey task force on sex discrimination in courts said that women were treated unequally both as lawyers and in judges' decisions. (11/21)

The House of Representatives voted unanimously to require states to withhold tax refunds from delinquent parents with children on welfare, and allowed them to withhold such refunds from delinquent parents whose children were not on welfare. It also enabled states to put liens on the real and personal property of those in arrears, and to report delinquent payments exceeding $1,000 to credit bureaus. (12/00)

The Backlash

Pope John Paul II called on United States bishops to promote "natural" family planning — the so-called rhythm method of periodic abstinence—and repeated his condemnation of artificial birth control. Surveys showed that nearly 80% of Catholic women in the United States use contraceptives. ((09/24)

Eagle Forum leader Phyllis Schlafly dragged out all her old objections to the ERA in testimony before the House Subcommittee on Civil and Constitutional Rights. She also unveiled a new brochure entitled "The ERA-Gay-AIDS Connection," carrying the parade of horribles she alleged the ERA would cause to a new and irresponsible extreme. (10/20)

Hawley Atkinson, the top elected official in Maricopa County (Az) said he wouldn't resign despite the furor created by his "facetious" remark that homosexuals should be used to replace animals in medical experiments. (12/08)

109

YEAR	1984		
U. S. President	Ronald Reagan		
NOW President	Judy Goldsmith		

EVENTS

Rep. Mary Rose Oakar, (D-OH), introduced a bill to require the Federal government to pay its male and female employees equally for comparable work saying: "For too long, women have been paid at a lower rate than men even though their jobs have been of comparable worth . . . Positive steps must be taken at the national level." (01/23)

In a 6-3 decision in *Grove City College v. Bell* , the U. S. Supreme Court accepted the Reagan Administration position that Title IX banned sex discrimination only in the specific programs within an educational institution that directly received Federal funding. The Nixon, Ford, and Carter Administrations had all interpreted Title IX to prohibit dis-

crimination in the entire institution if it received any Federal financial aid. NOW President Judy Goldsmith joined Representative Patricia Schroeder (D-CO) and Claudine Schneider (R-RI) in denouncing the ruling and pledging to immediately pass legislation that would mandate a broad interpretation of Title IX. (02/28)

ISSUES

Lifestyles

Hundreds of lesbian rights activists and supporters traveled from across the country to Milwaukee, WI, for the 1984 NOW Lesbian Rights Conference. Mandated by the 1982 NOW Conference, the meeting focused on the theme of power and politics in 1984. (01/20-22)

Education

In an overwhelming vote, the U. S. House of Representatives registered its opposition to Reagan's position on Title IX of the 1972 Education Act. Title IX prohibits sexual discrimination in "any education program or activity receiving federal financial assistance." Since its enactment in 1972, the law had applied to the entire institution. Reagan favored a narrow interpretation which would limit application to the specific program receiving the funding. (01)

Economic

Massachusetts NOW created opportunities to promote public discussion on sex discrimination in insurance and worked on legislation, in cooperation with other organizations, with the state attorney general's insurance division, and other relevant agencies. The legislation, a comprehensive ban on sex discrimination in both existing and future insurance contracts, failed to pass in 1983, but was introduced again in 1984. (01)

Why and How Women Will Elect The Next President by Eleanor Smeal, former president of NOW, written with Kathy Bonk and Toni Carabillo, was published, and provided the basic explanation of the Gender Gap, the phenomenon which Smeal had first identified in the 1980 election. (01/26)

Media

Political

Throughout the January 22nd weekend, in recognition of the 11th anniversary of the U. S. Supreme Court decision legalizing abortion, NOW chapters nationwide picketed Republican Party offices to protest President Reagan's anti-abortion leadership. Nearly 75 actions across the country sent a strong message to the public which was highly critical of Reagan's assault on women's right to decide when and whether to have children. (01/22)

NOW's Vice President for Action, Mary Jean Collins, and California NOW President Sandra Farha testified before the state's Senate Insurance Committee in support of a bill to ban sex discrimination in life insurance and annuities, and described the unique situation in California. In the past, many states such as California had put specific language permitting sex discriminatory prices and payouts in life insurance and annuities into insurance codes. Title VII bans this in payroll deductions so the state changed only this. (01)

Lexington Area (MA) NOW targeted nine major U.S. corporations as part of a campaign to end sexism in advertising. Women in Media Task Force Chair Susan Shapiro said the task force had developed a rating system which classified female images in advertising from very offensive ("sex object-victim") to desirable ("independent woman"). Portrayal of women as independent, confident, competent, with a sense of self-worth not dependent on a man or a clean house was the category that Lexington Area NOW encouraged advertisers to use. (02)

Illinois NOW members greeted Reagan with a picket when he arrived in his hometown of Dixon, IL, to celebrate his birthday. (02/06)

Walter F. Mondale, Democratic candidate for President, endorsed the federal lesbian and gay rights bill, S. 430 during a Susan B. Anthony reception sponsored by NOW in Washington, D.C.. (02/15)

Wyoming NOW and Natrona County (WY) NOW co-sponsored a conference on sexual assault which included workshops on the practice of polygraph tests for rape victims, sexual violence against women and self defense. The conference ended with a "Take Back the Night" march through downtown Casper. The Natrona County NOW Task Force on Sexual Assault also released a report called "Polygraph: The Second Assault" which detailed findings of interviews with law enforcement and court officials, hospital employees and women's advocates that substantiated the case for ending the use of the polygraph test on rape victims. (01)

More than two thirds of the women responding to a February *Women's Day* survey said they favored the ERA; four out of five believed in a woman's right to choose abortion, 75% favored a nuclear freeze, 60% favored federally subsidized day care, and more than half supported affirmative action programs. The survey, which elicited more than 115,000 responses, making it the largest response ever to a survey appearing in a single issue of a magazine, showed continued strong support for a woman Vice Presidential candidate. Seventy two percent of respondents said that they would vote for a woman for President. (02)

The Backlash

Joseph M. Scheidler, director of the Pro-Life Action League, a new breed of anti-abortion fanatic, published a book entitled *Ninety-Nine Ways to Close the Abortion Clinics*. The book gave tips on various tactics designed to intimidate and terrorize women entering clinics. He boasted that complications increased 4-5% for patients on

days when they protest outside. (02)

The anti-abortion group calling itself the "Army of God" reportedly claimed responsibility for a fire that gutted the Hillcrest Clinic in Norfolk, VA, for the second time, and threatened to destroy other clinics if abortions continue. (02/17)

Shortly after midnight, a fire ripped through a Prince Georges County, MD, office building, causing $70,000 worth of damage to the Prince George's Reproductive Health Services Clinic. The incident marked the third fire-bombing of an abortion clinic within the preceding six weeks. (02/29)

YEAR	1984		
U. S. President	Ronald Reagan		
NOW President	Judy Goldsmith		

EVENTS

A Federal judge ruled that the government must pay women in the U.S. Civil Service system the same as men with the same duties and responsibilities, regardless of where they were located. (04/03)

Declaring it the "patriotic duty" of Romanian women to bear four children, President Nicolae Ceausescu announced "stern measures" against abortion to be enforced by the police. Married women had to undergo monthly pregnancy tests at their work-places, and had to have a medical explanation for "persistent non-pregnancy."

Written confirmation from a doctor was required if a woman suffered a miscarriage. Should the pregnancy police decide a woman had lied about the termination of a pregnancy, she faced a year in prison. Women who did not fulfill their child quotas were rarely promoted, and could lose their jobs. (05/31)

ISSUES

Lifestyles

Education

Media

Economic

Political

Bucks County (PA) NOW was part of a coalition of community leaders and feminists that turned out more than 300 demonstrators for a candlelight vigil at Bucks County Community College in Newtown, PA. The rally was organized to show support for the ERA and to protest the appearance of Phyllis Schlafly who spoke against the ERA. (02/22)

Los Angeles (CA) NOW's media task force had a preview screening of vignettes from six new episodes of TV's "Cagney and Lacey." Over 100 members paid $20 each to enjoy the special presentation and the panel discussion that followed. Both series stars Sharon Gless and Tyne Daly were panelists along with Barney Rosenzweig, Executive Producer; Peter Lefcourt, Producer; Barbara Corday, Co-Creator; and Patricia Knelman, Associate Producer. (03/12)

NOW chapters from Connecticut to Oregon expanded the Women's Truth Squad on Reagan to include leafleting, rallies, and voter registration, as well as pickets of Reagan's appearances. "President Reagan is Trying to Bench Your Daughter" was the title of a leaflet on Title IX that Salem (OR) NOW distributed at girls high school basketball games. Oregon NOW leaders conducted statewide Truth Squad "Action Team Trainings" that supplied information on Reagan's record and offered skills training in such areas as public speaking and voter registration. Chapters in Connecticut, California, New York, Maryland, North Carolina, and other states also engaged in registration activities. (03)

NOW President Judy Goldsmith sent a telegram to President Reagan, demanding that he immediately order the FBI and the Department of Justice to launch a full-scale investigation into the recent wave of anti-abortion terrorism. Neither the telegram nor follow-up phone calls to the Justice Department brought any response. Within a week, another clinic, this time in Washington state, was fire bombed. (03/02)

CBS Entertainment announced that "Cagney and Lacey" and "Kate and Allie" - two prime time television programs with strong female leads - would return in the fall. NOW members across the country wrote letters and organized activities to promote "Cagney and Lacey." In response to massive viewer protest of the show's cancellation in 1983, CBS renewed the series on a trial basis for seven episodes in the spring. Both "Cagney & Lacey" and the new "Kate & Allie" did very well in the ratings, consistently ranking in the top 15 network programs. ((04/30)

Fourteen years after NOW and the Women's Legal Defense Fund filed charges of sex discrimination in pay and promotions against Giant Foods, Inc. with the Equal Employment Opportunity Commission (EEOC), a $246,000 settlement was reached. The complaint was filed on behalf of 10 female bakery department managers, and was expanded to a class action lawsuit which involved several hundred women, whose share of the settlement ranged from hundreds to thousands of dollars in back pay. (04)

Broward (FL) NOW sponsored a "Motherhood by Choice" march and rally in Hollywood, FL. The Chapter protested the increasing attacks on reproductive freedom by the legislative process and individual cases of harassment and violence. (05/12)

Los Angeles (CA) NOW's Education Task Force held an "Equity in Science" competition, designed to honor women in science and public education. Co-chairs Joannie Parker and Connie Williamson invited all the high schools in the Los Angeles Unified School District to submit the names of their outstanding science teacher and their outstanding young woman science student. (05)

San Joaquin (CA) NOW members celebrated Professional Secretaries Week by passing out flowers with the attached cards: "Raises not Roses, Comparable Worth." Flowers were distributed to over 200 office workers during the noon hour and were also presented to the Stockton (CA) City Council and the San Joaquin County Board of Supervisors along with an invitation to attend a comparable worth workshop. (04/23)

The New York NOW Women's Truth Squad on Reagan, braving pouring rain and whipping winds, picketed the President when he addressed the Women in Business Ownership Conference `84 luncheon at the Grand Hyatt Hotel. Several NOW women attending the conference distributed leaflets inside. (04/05)

The Backlash

Incidents of violence or harassment of clinics reported to the National Abortion Federation (NAF) totaled 123 in 1983. Within the first ten weeks of 1984, such incidents numbered 59. (03/02)

Two men entered a Birmingham, AL, clinic during office hours and told a counselor, "We're going to take care of this place." While one man prevented her from calling for help, the other ran through the facility destroying operating machines and birth control devices with an industrial-sized sledge hammer. (05/12)

The insurance industry spent at least $66,400 in West Virginia during the year lobbying the Legislature not to pass a unisex insurance law. (06)

YEAR	1984	
U. S. President	**Ronald Reagan**	
NOW President	**Judy Goldsmith**	

EVENTS

The top midshipman in the U.S. Naval Academy's class of 1984 was a woman, the first to graduate at the head of the class at a service academy since women were admitted in 1976. Kristine Holdereid, of Woodbine, MD, completed her four years in the Academy with a grade point average of 3.88 out of a possible 4.0. Class standing at the Naval Academy was based on both academic grades and marks in military performance. (05/15)

Europe's last bastion of male supremacy at the ballot box crumbled when the men of Liechtenstein decided– somewhat reluctantly – to give women the right to vote in national elections. (07/01)

ISSUES

Lifestyles

Education

Economic

Media

In a White House picket, NOW President Judy Goldsmith called on Reagan to cease his "irresponsible and inflammatory anti-abortion, anti-woman rhetoric." By repeatedly comparing abortion with murder, infanticide, slavery, and the Holocaust, Reagan only "encourages the fanatics to step up the violence," said Goldsmith. She told reporters at the picket, "If Reagan persists in calling American women murderers, he must accept responsibility for the violence that is occurring." (03/22)

Streisand and Jane Fonda

Barbra Streisand accepted NOW's 1984 Woman of Courage Award at the Beverly Wilshire Hotel in Los Angeles. The award was presented to Streisand by Judy Goldsmith, NOW President, at a tribute dinner sponsored by the Los Angeles NOW Education Fund. Jane Fonda was the MC for the event. (06/06)

A month after telegrams, phone calls, and a White House picket by NOW demanding an end to anti-abortion violence and harassment, Justice Department officials finally agreed to meet with NOW President Judy Goldsmith and NOW Vice President-Action Mary Jean Collins. In their two meetings with Justice Department representatives, Goldsmith and Collins called upon the Reagan Administration to fulfill its responsibility to enforce the Federal Civil Rights Laws. But the Assistant Attorney General for the Criminal Division and officials of the Civil Rights Division claimed that they were powerless to stop the persistent civil rights violations occurring nationwide against women exercising their constitutional right to choose abortion. (05)

In Washington, D.C., NOW members joined with several hundred other women and men running and rallying against Reagan. The Gender Gap Run and Rally was the kick-off event for the "Gender Gap Action Campaign," a project of the Woman's Trust, chaired by Eleanor Smeal. The object of the Campaign was to unite peace and women's rights advocates behind the effort to stop the Reagan revolution. (06/12)

As opponents of abortion rights escalated their terrorist activities at health clinics throughout the summer and fall and violent incidents escalated both in number and in the nature of the attack, more and more NOW chapters across the country began providing escort service for women entering clinics to protect them against harassment.

New Jersey NOW, along with about 100 members of other groups, rallied in front of the New Jersey Statehouse in support of a bill to end sex discrimination in the salaries of state workers. (08)

The U.S. House of Representatives passed the Federal Pay Equity and Management Improvement Act of 1984 (HR 5680), by a 413-6 vote. Representative Mary Rose Oakar's (D-OH) bill would require the office of Personnel Management to fund a private consultant to study the Federal government's pay classification system. The study would determine the extent of sex-based wage discrimination. (06/28)

In the four months preceding the 11/06 election, NOW members registered more than 250,000 new voters and NOW President, Judy Goldsmith spoke in 21 states.

Political

Polls showed that the Gender Gap continued to loom large and threaten President Reagan's reelection. *New York Times/ CBS News* and *Washington Post/ ABC News* polls taken in April and May continued to show that 10-15% fewer women than men approved of the job Reagan was doing, and supported his bid for re-election. (06)

The 1984 National NOW Conference, in Miami Beach, FL, urged Presidential candidate Walter Mondale to select a woman as his Vice-Presidential running mate. NOW passed a resolution, authored by Eleanor Smeal, saying if a woman was not on the ticket, NOW would take the nomination to a floor fight at the Democratic convention. (06/30)

Abortion rights opponents in six states tried to get referenda prohibiting state funding for abortions on the ballot in November. Five of the targeted states — Massachusetts, Oregon, Washington, Colorado, and Michigan — all provided state aid for abortions; only Arkansas already prohibited such funding. The attempt succeeded only in: Washington, Colorado and Arkansas. (07/04)

The Backlash

Anti-abortion leaders in Washington state expressed surprise at the news that one of their most ardent followers, a 29 year old roofer named Curtis Beseda, had been indicted for one of the four arson attacks on abortion clinics in the state. Before the indictment, anti-abortionists had claimed that they could not be held respon-

sible for perpetrating or encouraging acts of violence. (06)

In an alarming escalation of the violence, the headquarters of the National Abortion Federation (NAF) in Washington, D.C., were bombed. While investigators were in the NAF building, they discovered a second bomb, which would have completely

destroyed the building had it exploded. (07/04) Planned Parenthood of Annapolis, MD, was bombed. (07/07) The Cypress Fairbanks Clinic in Houston, TX, was bombed. (08/20) Both the West Loop Clinic and the Women's Outpatient Clinic in Houston were fire bombed. (09/07)

YEAR	1984		
U. S. President	Ronald Reagan		
NOW President	Judy Goldsmith		

EVENTS

The U. S. Supreme Court, in a 7-0 decision, ruled that the Jaycees could be forced to admit women as full members by the Minnesota Public Accommodations law. (07/03)

Rep. Geraldine Ferraro (D-NY) became the first woman in American history to be chosen as the nominee for Vice President on a major party ticket

after a year-long campaign by women's groups for a woman Vice Presidential candidate. From the start, the Catholic hierarchy denounced her for her pro-choice stance. (07/20)

The Republican Reagan/Bush ticket won the 1984 election in a landslide attributed to rising confidence in the economy of the country. (11/06)

The Santa Clara County Board of Supervisors unanimously adopted the concept of pay equity for County employees. (12/11)

ISSUES

Lifestyles

Anti-abortion demonstrators harassed Vice Presidential candidate Geraldine Ferraro on the campaign trail. (Fall)

The U. S. Supreme Court, citing a lack of federal jurisdiction, let stand a California Court of Appeal ruling that enabled the California Commission on the Status of Women to lobby for women's political issues. The court's action ended eight years of legal suits initiated by the "Women's Committee for Responsible Government," a coalition of anti-ERA and anti-abortion groups, to prevent the commission from lobbying for "radical feminist" causes. In the original suit filed in 1976, the Committee objected to the Commission's use of taxpayer funds to promote what they saw as ideological causes. The Committee contended that the Commission's public statements and publications on the ERA were "feminist government propaganda," and therefore attempted to have the Commission dismantled. (11)

NOW President Judy Goldsmith joined the ranks of national leaders protesting the segregationist apartheid policies of South Africa. Goldsmith was arrested along with Congressman Louis Stokes (D-OH) and Evelyn Lowry, president of the Southern Christian Leadership Conference Women, for demonstrating within 500 feet of an Embassy. (12/11)

Education

The U. S. House of Representatives overwhelmingly passed the Civil Rights Act of 1984 (HR 5490/5 2568) by a vote of 375-32, but the legislation was killed in the Senate, 53-45. The bill was introduced to overturn the U.S. Supreme Court's decision in *Grove City v. Bell.* As a result, there was no comprehensive legislation to prevent federally subsidized discrimination based on sex, race, age, or disability. (10/02)

Economic

In an important application of its anti-abortion and population control policies, the Reagan Administration told the major international family planning agency that it would lose all U.S. funding January 1, 1985. Bradman Weerakoon, secretary general of the International Planned Parenthood Federation, said that the loss of $17 million in federal funding would have "a very damaging effect" on the agency's programs in 119 nations. (12/12)

Religion

Twenty-four Roman Catholic nuns were singled out for punishment by the Vatican because of their public support for freedom of choice. The nuns signed their names to an ad published by Catholics for Free Choice in the *New York Times.* The ad was signed by nearly 100 lay and religious Catholics. It announced that "a diversity of opinions regarding abortion exists among committed Catholics" and called for "discussion of this diversity of opinion within the Church." (10/07)

Political

EQUAL PAY FOR EQUAL WORK

The NOW LDEF filed an amicus brief on its own behalf and on behalf of NOW in a landmark pay equity case in support of the American Federation of State, County, and Municipal Employees. The case, *AFSCME v. State of Washington,* was on appeal to the U. S. Supreme Court of Appeals for the Ninth Circuit. The District Court in Washington (see 11/83) held that the state had discriminatorily underpaid state employees in female dominated jobs by failing to pay them their full evaluated worth. Worth had been determined in a job evaluation study undertaken at the state's request. (11)

The Federal Government issued a nationwide warning to abortion clinics and medical offices of a potential for violence January 20-22. The warning was delivered by the Bureau of Alcohol, Tobacco and Firearms to the Washington offices of the National Abortion Federation. They would not say if they had specific knowledge of threats. (12/28)

Legal

NOW and the NOW Legal Defense and Education Fund (LDEF) filed a $2 million lawsuit against Mutual of Omaha, the largest provider of individual health and disability insurance in the country. The class action suit, filed in the District of Columbia Superior Court, charged sex discrimination in Mutual's pricing of health and disability insurance. (08/16)

In an historic decision with far-reaching implications, the Pennsylvania Supreme Court ruled that the state Equal Rights Amendment prohibited insurance companies from basing auto rates on sex. The decision, *Hartford Accident & Indemnity Co. v. Insurance Commissioner,* represented the first time any state's highest court had directly applied a state ERA to sex discrimination in insurance. (11)

The Backlash

The Clear Lake Women's Center in Webster, TX, was torched. (09/09)
The Birth Control Institute in San Diego, CA, was fire bombed. (09/13)
The Planned Parenthood clinic in Marietta, GA, which provided no abortion services, was fire bombed. (09/20)

In another indication of the widening target of terrorist attacks, Supreme Court Justice William Brennan, author of the 1973 *Roe v. Wade* decision legalizing abortion, received a death threat from the "Army of God." (10)

In Wheaton, MD, there were two separate bomb attacks. (11/19)

Three Pensacola, FL, clinics were bombed within 15 minutes of each other. Dr. William Parmenter, whose clinic was one of those destroyed, said he was quitting. He could not find temporary space or the liability insurance to re-open. (12/25)

113

YEAR	1985
U. S. President	Ronald Reagan
NOW President	Judy Goldsmith

EVENTS

A "classic male sexist charge" was U.N. Ambassador Jeane Kirkpatrick's response to a remark by her White House opponents that she was "too temperamental to hold higher office." In addressing the Women's Forum, a group of New York business and political women, Kirkpatrick stated that "sexism is alive in the U.N., in the U.S. government, in Ameri-can politics–where it is bipartisan–but it's not unconquerable." (01)

The Reagan Administration's projected 1986 budget again placed a disproportionate share of the budget burden on those who could least afford it. The budget as introduced would transfer $30 billion from domestic spending to the military. The proposed cuts would adversely affect such programs as education, health, housing, nutrition, employment, and training. (02/04)

ISSUES

Lifestyles

Education

Economic

Legal

Political

In 1979, only five states–Oregon, Iowa, Nebraska, New Jersey and Delaware–had statutes permitting the prosecution of husbands who raped their wives. Since 1979– and the growth of the feminist movement–new laws or court decisions made marital rape a criminal offense in 18 additional states and the District of Columbia. In 1985, 15 more states were considering similar statutes.

In a major victory for the lesbian and gay community, the U.S. Supreme Court let stand a lower court decision striking down an Oklahoma law that permitted the firing of teachers for speaking in favor of lesbian and gay rights. [*National Gay Task Force (NGTF) v. Oklahoma Board of Education*.] (01)

Montana activists engaged in a fierce battle to defend their state's comprehensive law prohibiting sex-based rates in all lines of insurance from legislative sabotage. Insurers had won a two and one half year delay in its effective date, October 1, 1985, "to allow time to prepare new rates and tables." Insurers were using the time to lobby the legislature to weaken or repeal the law. (01)

Sixty-two years after it was first presented, the Equal Rights Amendment was reintroduced in Congress on the first day of the legislative session. Peter Rodino (D-NJ), Patricia Schroeder (D-CO), Don Edwards (D-CA) and Hamilton Fish (R-NY) sponsored the ERA in the House, where it was designated HJ Res. 2. On the Senate side, the Amendment was introduced by Edward Kennedy (D-MA) as SJ Res. 2. (01/03)

The New York Court of Appeals revoked the state's "marital exemption" law, finding "no rational basis for distinguishing between marital rape and non-marital rape." Under that ruling, husbands found guilty of raping their wives could receive the same sentence as anyone convicted of rape – two to eight years in jail. An amicus brief to abolish the marital rape exemption was filed by New York City NOW and New York State NOW in the case, *People v. Mario Liberta*. (01)

A survey of college campuses found that women students continued to be the victims of both subtle and blatant sexual discrimination on many campuses. The study, "Out of the Classroom: A Chilly Campus Climate for Women?" was conducted by Bernice R. Sandler and Roberta M. Hall of the Project on the Status and Education of Women. (01)

The Hotel and Motel Trade Council filed charges of "blatant and deliberate sex discrimination" against 11 of New York City's largest hotels. New York City NOW President Jennifer Brown joined the Trades Council at their press conference announcing the lawsuit and commented, "These hotels don't charge women less for sleeping in a bed, so why should they pay less for making it?" 4,000, mostly female, hotel room attendants were paid $14 less per week than male housekeeping attendants for essentially the same work. This wage discrimination resulted in a $730 yearly pay differential. (01/09)

NOW Chapters all over the country conducted around-the-clock vigils in 30 abortion clinics in 18 states to guard against potential violence over a weekend when federal officials had warned that they expected attacks to occur. The NOW Chapters continued all year providing escort services for patients entering clinics through crowds of harassing, anti-abortion pickets. (01/17)

Pennsylvania auto insurers drew on industry-wide support to overcome the historic ruling by the state Supreme Court that sex-based auto insurance rates were "unfairly discriminatory" and illegal under the Pennsylvania ERA. The industry strategy called for delaying implementation of the ruling while they built public relations and media campaigns to misrepresent the Pennsylvania ERA as hurting women. (01)

Greater Youngstown NOW and Trumbull County NOW (OH) commemorated 12 years of abortion rights with a candlelight vigil. The vigil took place at the same time that many chapters nationwide were celebrating the anniversary of a woman's right to have an abortion and protesting abortion clinic terrorism. Kate Pfister Brennan, chapter president of Greater Youngstown NOW, spoke out for a woman's right to abortion on an Ohio news show presenting a discussion of the issue. (01/22)

Striking clerical and technical workers at Yale University won a victory in their fight for pay equity. The Yale contracts represented the first successful conclusion of a pay equity organizing drive involving a major private sector employer. NOW President Judy Goldsmith joined Connecticut NOW and State Coordinator Gayle Brooks in supporting this effort. (01/23)

The Backlash

A factually inaccurate and highly emotional anti-abortion video entitled *The Silent Scream*, prepared and narrated by Dr. Bernard Nathanson, was released. (01/22)

The six-week lull in abortion clinic bombings that surrounded NOW's National Vigil for Women's Lives ended abruptly when the Women's Clinic of Mesquite, TX, was set on fire. Because of high winds, the fire destroyed an entire shopping center in the Dallas suburb, and two firefighters were injured fighting the blaze. (02/22)

Police in Bridgeport, PA, arrested 51 anti-abortion demonstrators from nine states after the protesters stormed an abortion clinic and occupied examination rooms, offices, and waiting areas. Forty eight of those arrested were physically carried from the Womens Medical Center building, and three more outside were charged with disorderly conduct. (02/22)

YEAR	1985
U. S. President	Ronald Reagan
NOW President	Judy Goldsmith

EVENTS

The National Committee on Pay Equity released a national poll showing very high public awareness about the problem of wage-based discrimination. Of those surveyed, 69% believed that women were not paid as fairly as men for the work they did, and 79% supported pay equity as a solution. (02/12)

The Equal Employment Opportunity Commission (EEOC) charged with enforcing laws against discrimination in employment, said it would no longer represent entire classes of employees who might have been subject to discrimination; instead, it planned to focus on cases of individuals who had to prove that bias directly affected them at their jobs. (02/13)

Mikhail Gorbachev succeeded to leadership of the Soviet Union. At age 54, Gorbachev was the youngest man to take charge in the country since Stalin and represented a new generation. (03/13)

ISSUES

Lifestyles

NOW's "Lesbian and Gay Rights `85" project broadened its focus to include efforts to pass lesbian and gay rights legislation in New York state as well as in New Jersey.(02)

Education

The Civil Rights Restoration Act, restoring Title IX's ban on sex discrimination in federally-funded education, was reintroduced in the 99th Congress. The legislation was necessitated by the U.S. Supreme Court's decision in *Grove City College v. Bell*, which virtually gutted Title IX as legislative protection against sex discrimination in education. (01/24)

Economic

Religion

Before approximately 300 members of the Washington, DC press corps, NOW President Judy Goldsmith accused the anti-abortion leadership of "moral bankruptcy" and of pursuing an anti-abortion campaign based on "emotional manipulation, willful deception, vicious harassment, threats and outright terrorism" at a hard-hitting debate on the video, *The Silent Scream*, with Moral Majority President Jerry Falwell, sponsored by the Nation Press Club. (02/12)

Political

The Senate Foreign Relations Committee voted to reverse a Reagan Administration ban on U.S. funding for organizations that included abortion in their overseas population control programs. (03/27)

Wilma Scott Heide
1921-1985
Wilma Scott Heide, 64, third national NOW President, died of a heart attack in Norristown, PA. Heide was president of NOW from 1971 to 1974 and Chairone of the Board and National Secretary prior to that. One of the founding forces of the feminist movement, Heide had just completed a book entitled *Feminism for the Health of It* and a biography focusing on feminist ethics. entitled *A Feminist Legacy*. Heide was a driving force in the *Pittsburgh Press* case that ended sex-segregated help wanted ads and she led the action that finally won hearings on the ERA in the Senate. During her presidency, NOW played a key role in the passage of ERA through Congress, pressured the EEOC to act on sex bias cases, waged a campaign against AT&T's discriminatory policies that ended with a $38 million settlement for employees, and played a major role in making affirmative action programs a requirement for federal contractors. (05/08)

Young, unmarried women were most frequently the target of the estimated 1.5 million rapes or attempted rapes which took place between 1973-1982, the Justice Department said, in a report that it conceded "underestimated" the crime. (03/24)

In Ohio, Governor Richard Celeste submitted a budget request to the state legislature which included $9 million for pay equity adjustments for state workers in 1986-7; that figure represented only 1.5% of the general revenue fund's state payroll. Marcia Miller, Ohio NOW Board member and Study Director of the Ohio Pay Equity Advisory Committee, reported that the 1984 initial study documented a 13% overall wage gap between female and male state employees. (03)

A study by the Potomac Institute in Washington, DC, found that women and minorities made significant progress toward equal opportunity in the work force during the 1970's. That progress was in large part due to affirmative action and adoption of affirmative action by private industry - a method for achieving equality under fire from the Reagan Administration. (03/20)

As a result of extensive efforts by NOW, the National Association of Attorneys General adopted a resolution calling the harassment of abortion clinic patients and staff "illegal" and requested that the Justice Department investigate anti-abortion activities as violations of Federal Civil Rights law. The resolution affirmed NOW's position that federal, state, and local law enforcement must take responsibility for ending anti-abortion terrorism. (03/23-25)

Supporters of Montana's pioneering 1983 law, that applied the state's constitutional ban on sex discrimination to all types of insurance, successfully withstood the full force of the national insurance industry's campaign to repeal the law. The Senate Judiciary Committee by a vote of 7 to 3 rejected the House bill to repeal it. The final action in the industry's effort to modify the law came with a vote to reconsider which failed by 24 to 26. (04)

The Backlash

Legislation intended to give civil rights protection to fetuses was introduced in the U.S. Senate by Orrin Hatch (R-UT). (03/25)

The Birth Control Institute, a San Diego, CA, abortion clinic, was bombed the second time in six months. The San Diego NOW chapter responded swiftly by organizing a four-night

vigil at Womancare, another local clinic, to protect it. (03/16)

An unemployed gardener was arrested on suspicion of felony arson in connection with the March 16 firebombing of an abortion clinic. The bombing, which caused more than $10,000 damage, was the clinic's second in seven months. (03/30)

The California Coalition for Traditional Values launched a massive direct mail campaign to defeat AB-1, homosexual rights legislation that would prohibit job discrimination based on sexual orientation. (04/12)

115

YEAR	1985	
U. S. President	Ronald Reagan	
NOW President	Judy Goldsmith	Eleanor Cutri Smeal

EVENTS

In a 6-3 vote, the U.S. Supreme Court struck down an Alabama law that permitted a daily one-minute period of silent meditation or prayer in public schools. The Court thus reaffirmed its insistence that "government must pursue a course of complete neutrality toward religion." (06/04)

Ellie Smeal was reelected national president of NOW at the 1985 National Conference in New Orleans on a platform that called for action and visibility, including back to the street demonstrations and marches. "It's time to put a lot more heat on the right wing and the reactionary policies of the right wing," said Smeal after her victory. "I intend to raise a little hell." (07/19/21)

ISSUES

155,000 NOW Members
$5,100,000 Annual Budget

Lifestyles

A controversial bill to require most unmarried minors to get parental consent before having abortions was narrowly approved by the Senate Health and Human Services Committee. (05/15)

Education

At Nairobi, Kenya, "Forum `85," a 10-day conference of non-governmental organizations as well as the U.N.-sponsored Decade for Women conference, ended the officially sponsored decade for women. The 12,000 attendees at the Forum identified religious fundamentalism and fundamentalism as a philosophy as diametrically opposed to feminism. The official conference, with 2,100 delegates from 160 countries, produced a document, "Forward Looking Strategies," a plan of action for the years 1986- 2000, emphasizing legal, educational, and employment rights for women. (07/10-26)

Religion

Six installments of "Doonesbury" that satirized *The Silent Scream* were allegedly "too controversial to be distributed" according to a Universal Press Syndicate official. (05/25)

A national march in Washington D.C. and "Witness for Women's Lives" rallies, there and in 13 cities across the country, organized by NOW protested the Catholic hierarchy's opposition to abortion and contraception. The events also protested the fact that the National Conference of Catholic Bishops was holding the Civil Rights Restoration Act hostage, lobbying for an anti-abortion amendment to the bill. (06/08)

Christa McAuliffe, 36, a high school teacher in Concord, NH, was chosen to be the the first "average citizen" in space. The eldest of five children, McAuliffe married her high school sweet-heart, Steve, a lawyer, in 1970, had two children and originally studied to be a historian, but was lured to teaching in the early '70s. She taught courses in law and economics and one on "The American Woman." Asked how it felt to have been chosen for this program, McAuliffe replied, "I'm still kind of floating. I don't know when I'll come down to earth." She told another interviewer later that the space flight didn't scare her. "I really see the shuttle as a safe program." (07/19)

Tish Sommers
1914-1985
Tish Sommers, 71, who told us all, "Don't agonize–organize!" died at her home in Oakland, California on October 18, after a six-year resistance to the inroads of cancer. Sommers chaired NOW's National Task Force on Volunteerism until 1973, the year she completed a book entitled, *The Not So Helpless Female,* an activists handbook for social change. She chaired NOW's National Task Force on Older Women from 1973 to 1980, when with her associate on many of the displaced homemakers projects, Laurie Shields, she founded OWL (Older Women's League), which focused exclusively on the problems of older women.

Media

Pauli Murray
1917-1985
The Rev. Dr. Pauli Murray, 74, lawyer, writer, teacher, poet, civil rights activist, Episcopal priest, and founder of NOW, died of cancer at her home in Pittsburgh. Dr. Murray became a priest in 1977, was admitted to the bar in 1945, and had been a civil rights activist since 1940.

A federal appeals court in St. Louis, MO, overturned a $325,000 jury award to Christine Craft. The jury had found that a station in Kansas City, MO, had engaged in fraud and sex discrimination. (06/28)

Legal

NOW and NOW LDEF filed a $20 million dollar class action lawsuit against Metropolitan Life Insurance Company, the largest life insurance company in New York state, charging sex discrimination against women in life insurance and disability income insurance policies. (10/09)

Political

Emily's (Early Money Is Like Yeast) List, to raise early political money for Democratic pro-choice women candidates, was founded by Ellen Malcolm. (12)

Cecily Coleman and the ABC network reached an out of court settlement in a $15 million suit charging sexual harassment. The settlement was rumored to be around $500,000. (07/02)

Responding to the plight of married and divorced women whose financial health was being decimated by unfair marital property laws, NOW President Ellie Smeal appointed Dorothy Jonas to chair the new NOW Task Force on the Rights of Women in Marriage. Together with her daughter, Bonnie Sloane, Jonas launched a campaign to win improved legal protection over the rights of non-managing spouses. (11)

The Backlash

The restructured U.S. Commission on Civil Rights, packed with Reagan appointees, rejected as "profoundly and irretrievably flawed" the concept of pay equity by a vote of 5-2. (04/11)

Thomas Eugene Spinks, one of three men accused of bombing 10 abortion clinics in Washington, Maryland, Virginia and Delaware, pleaded guilty to conspiracy and malicious destruction. (05/04)

The Reagan Administration, d pressured by the fundamentalist new right, mounted a major attack on family planning in the rest of the world. In a break with long-established policy, the Agency for International Development agreed to fund groups that promote *only* natural family planning in underdeveloped countries. (07/08)

Ninth Circuit Court of Appeals Judge Anthony H. Kennedy reversed a federal district court decision granting back pay for wage discrimination to Washington State employees. (09)

YEAR	1986
U. S. President	Ronald Reagan
NOW President	Eleanor Smeal

EVENTS

Astronaut Judith Resnick and teacher Christa McAuliffe died with five male crew members in the explosion of the spacecraft, Challenger, as millions of Americans watched on television. (01/28)

Corazon Aquino was inaugurated as the first woman President of the Philippines. (02)

The largest march for women's rights in U.S. history occurred on March 9th in Washington, D.C. The March for Women's Lives, called and coordinated by NOW, to keep abortion and birth control legal drew 125,000 in D.C. One week later (03/16) a companion march in Los Angeles attracted 30,000 (the largest march in Los Angeles since 1968) in a driving rain

and thunderstorm. There were a total of eight such marched for women's lives in 1986–in D.C.. Los Angeles, Denver (some 5,000; the largest march in Denver's history); Harrisburg, PA; Trenton, NJ; Boston; Seattle, WA; and Portland, OR.

Simone de Beauvoir, philosopher and author of *The Second Sex*, died at age 78. (04/14)

ISSUES

Lifestyles

NOW had demonstrations in support of the *Roe v. Wade* decision in 97 cities nationwide. Pro-choice demonstrations and events included rallies, speak-outs, marches, benefit lunches and dinners ranging from New York to Los Angeles. Some of the largest rallies with estimates near 1,000 were in New York City in Bryant Park and Boston where the rally filled the Church of the Covenant. (01/22)

Economic

Pay equity settlements continued in 1986. The largest award was to 35,000 employees of Washington State in female dominated jobs who on April 1 began to receive $41 million in pay equity salary adjustments. In a July ruling (*Bazemore et al. v. Friday, et al*), the U.S. Supreme Court affirmed two essential pay equity concepts: (1) past practices of discrimination can be used to analyze current systems of pay, and (2) statistical evidence is permissible. The decision would encourage more pay equity cases. In November, clerical workers won a pay equity settlement of $5.75 million from the State of Connecticut.

Religion

Media

Mary Ann Sorrentino, Executive Director of Planned Parenthood in Rhode Island, was notified that she had been excommunicated by the Roman Catholic Church for her pro-abortion activities. (01/22)

Legal

The U.S. Supreme Court ruled unconstitutional an Indianapolis ordinance authored by Catherine MacKinnon and Andrea Dworkin, that had defined pornography as discrimination against women. (02)

Political

The Right-to-Life movement showed signs of losing steam. To mark the 13th anniversary of *Roe v. Wade*, the anti-abortion march on Capitol Hill , estimated at only 35,000 by police, featured President Reagan's pledge (via a telephone hook-up from the White House): "I'm proud to stand with you in the long march for the right to life." There were 40 arrests, mostly stemming from an attempted sit-in by anti-abortion militants at the Hillcrest Women's Surgi-Center, two miles from the Capitol. According to D.C. police estimates, the demonstration was much smaller than previous years' events. Even more stunning, the anti-abortion march scheduled for May 1st in D.C., which its organizers had promised would be larger than the NOW march, was cancelled. In June, Vice President George Bush cancelled a previously scheduled appearance at the National Right to Life Convention. (01/22)

Christine Craft lost her four-year lawsuit against Metromedia when the U.S. Supreme Court denied a writ of certiorari. TV anchorwoman Craft had previously been awarded more than $300,000 by two different juries. The lone dissent to the decision came from the only woman on the Court, Justice Sandra Day O'Connor. (03/04)

The Handmaid's Tale, a novel by Margaret Atwood, described life in what was once the United States, but which became a theocracy. Called the Republic of Gilead, it reacted to social unrest and a sharply declining birth rate by taking the Book of Genesis literally with bizarre consequences, particularly for women. (02)

The Charleston (WV) NOW Chapter staged a "Back Alley" rally to recall the days before the January 22, 1973, *Roe v. Wade* ruling. The rally was scheduled three days before the state's House Constitutional Revisions Committee had scheduled a public hearing on a proposed amendment to bar abortions in the state except when needed to save the life of the mother. "We're going into an alley because we want to remind ourselves and the public of the harsh reality faced by women before *Roe v. Wade*," said Nahla Nimeh-Lewis, local NOW action vice president. "Then, illegal abortion was the leading killer of pregnant women in the U.S." (01/21)

After 13 years of litigation and a lack-luster performance by the Reagan Administration's Employment Opportunity Commission (EEOC), a federal district judge in Chicago dismissed the $20 million sex discrimination case against Sears. The Reagan Administration's EEOC, headed by Clarence Thomas, had not made a secret of the fact that they really wanted to lose the case. (02/03)

Bishop Anthony Bevilaqua of Pittsburgh decreed that women couldn't have their feet washed on Holy (Maundy) Thursday because no women had their feet washed at the original Last Supper. (03/27)

Bias against women in the New York State court system was so pervasive that "they are often denied equal justice," according to the New York Task Force on Women in the Courts' 3l3-page report which concluded "gender bias against women litigants, attorneys and court employees is a pervasive problem with grave consequences." The report was issued by the 23-member panel appointed by the state's Chief Judge after a two year study. (04/22)

The Backlash

Jerry Falwell announced he was disbanding the Moral Majority as a subsidiary of the Liberty Federation. Falwell, admitting he was having trouble fund-raising on abortion and pornography, decided to go international, with the initial targets of shoring up "the democracies" of Ferdinand Marcos, South Africa, and the Contras. (01)

An abortion clinic was damaged in Toledo, OH, by a fire that federal investigators attributed to arson, the third Ohio clinic hit by arsonists in a week. "The only statement we're making is that it appears to be arson," said Robert Stellingworth of the federal Bureau of Alcohol, Tobacco, and Firearms. Two other Toledo abortion clinics reported bomb

threats and city police put them under surveillance. (01/01)

The Cincinnati (OH) City Council passed a "fetal burial" ordinance requiring the "humane" disposal of aborted fetuses. Akron, OH, approved a similar fetal disposal law in 1983 but the U.S. Supreme Court ruled it was too vague. (01/08)

YEAR	1986
U. S. President	Ronald Reagan
NOW President	Eleanor Smeal

EVENTS

Gro Harlem Brundtland, an active women's rights advocate, became Prime Minister of Norway for the second time in six years. (05)

The U.S. Supreme Court, 5-4, in *Thornburgh v. American College of Obstetricians and Gynecologists* overturned a Pennsylvania law designed to discourage women from seeking abortion, marking the first time that the Court explicitly stated "A woman's right to make that choice freely is fundamental." (06/11)

In a 5-4 decision the Court ruled against the right to privacy for gay men and lesbians in *Bowers v. Hardwick*, thereby upholding a Georgia statute which criminalized consensual sodomy. The concept guaranteeing the right to privacy – the basis of the *Roe* and *Thornburgh* decisions – survived with only a one vote margin, and the reasoning by which it could be vitiated is all laid out in the *Hardwick* decision. (06/30)

Exhibiting a not to be believed degree of sexism, President Ronald Reagan's Chief of Staff Donald Regan asked rhetorically if the women of America were prepared to give up their diamond jewelry to impose sanctions against South Africa. (07)

ISSUES

Lifestyles

More than 33% of U.S. medical school students are women, up from 9% in 1969, according to the Association of American Medical Colleges. (04)

Education

NOW chapters across the country joined picket lines in support of the Independent Federation of Flight Attendants' strike against TWA. Carl Icahn, chairman of TWA, had demanded greater concessions by the flight attendants because, he said, their jobs were a source of "extra income" and they didn't have families to support.(04/12)

Economic

Roman Catholic religious orders were between $2.5 billion and $3.5 billion short of funds to finance even modest retirement programs for aging nuns and brothers, forcing some orders to sell property or seek public assistance for retiring nuns, said Msgr. Daniel Hoye of the National Conference of Catholic Bishops. (05/31)

Religion

Media

A *Newsweek* poll showed 56% of all women considered themselves feminists; 71% believed the movement had helped them; only 4% considered themselves anti-feminist. (03/31)

A University of Michigan survey released in May showed significant growth in support for the women's movement since 1977. (05)

Legal

NOW President Eleanor Smeal announced that the organization would file civil suits in federal courts against the attackers of abortion clinics, charging violation of federal anti-racketeering and anti-trust laws and for personal damages. Smeal said the first suit would be filed in Pensacola, FL, against the six people who invaded The Ladies Center. (04/02)

Political

Facing rising costs, declining membership, and imminent passage of a bill by the City Council which would have *required* them to admit women, the Union League of Philadelphia voted to permit women to become members. (05)

NOW President Eleanor Smeal was banned from speaking on the Campus of the Catholic University of America(01/22). Subsequently, Smeal was banned from speaking at Catholic DePaul University. (04) She eventually spoke off-campus for Catholic University students, and on-campus at DePaul (05/12) after students and faculty waged a successful protest.

General Mills gave a sixth makeover to *Betty Crocker*, transforming her from a traditional homemaker to a well-dressed, 30ish, career woman. (05)

The third edition of Arthur Janson's *History of Art*, the standard college art history textbook, incorporated female artists for the first time. (05)

The *New York Time's* finally adopted usage of the title "Ms." (06)

NOW filed suit in Wilmington, DE, under the Sherman Antitrust and Clayton Acts asking a nationwide injunction against anti-abortion leaders who had been traveling around the country organizing harassment, invasions and violence at clinics where abortions were performed. A principal defendant named in the suit was Joseph Scheidler, head of the Chicago-based Pro-Life Action League and author of *Closed: 99 Ways to Stop Abortion*. The suit also named John Ryan of St. Louis, MO, and Joan Andrews of Newark, DE as well as the Pro-Life Action League and the Pro-Life Direct Action League. According to the National Abortion Federation, there were 224 reported acts of violence in 1985 against clinics throughout the country. (06/10)

The University Club of Pasadena, CA, voted to admit women after 60 years of men only. The last two eating clubs at Princeton University integrated after losing a seven-year old lawsuit. Rotary Clubs in California integrated after losing a unanimous decision before the California Supreme Court. Rotary International planned to appeal to the U.S. Supreme Court.

Kiwanis International rejected admission of women members for the 11th year in a row. A federal district judge ruled it must integrate. The case was pending before the U.S. Supreme Court. (06)

NOW's Woman of Achievement award was presented to Oprah Winfrey at the National conference in Denver. Winfrey held the conferees spellbound with her rendition of the famous Soujourner Truth "Ain't I A Woman" speech. The First Lady of Greece and President of the Women's Union, Margaret Papandreou and Rep. Patricia Schroeder were keynote speaker at the conference. A few blocks away from the NOW Conference, the National Right To Life Committee held its annual meeting addressed by Sen. Robert Dole, Pat Robertson and Rep. Jack Kemp. A number of anti-abortion protesters were arrested when they tried to disrupt the NOW March for Women's Lives of 5,000 people to a rally at the Capitol. (06/13-15)

The U. S. Supreme Court affirmed for the first time in *Meritor Savings Bank v. Vinson*, that sexual harassment on the job is sex discrimination and a violation of Title VII of the Civil Rights Act of 1964. In two other rulings, the Court reaffirmed the legality of affirmative action to remedy past discrimination. (06/19)

The Backlash

Six invaders, including Joan Andrews and John Burt, stormed into The Ladies Center in Pensacola, FL, damaging equipment and injuring two women at the center, one of whom was the local NOW chapter president. The same clinic was bombed twice in 1984. Police arrested the intruders, half of whom witnesses said had to be carried out. Joan Andrews was later given a prison term for her role in the invasion. At the time of the invasion, Joe Scheidler was present on the lawn of the clinic. (03/27)

A large pipe bomb ripped a 10-foot hole in the front of a clinic in Wichita, KS. (06/10)

A Lesser Life, The Myth of Women's Liberation in America, Sylvia Hewlett's anti-feminist treatise, was published by William Morrow with an unusual 200,000 advance hardcover copies printed.

YEAR	1986
U. S. President	Ronald Reagan
NOW President	Eleanor Smeal

EVENTS

William Rehnquist was confirmed as Chief Justice of the U.S. Supreme Court and Antonin Scalia as Associate Justice. Both held radical positions against legal abortion, affirmative action, and other basic women's rights. (08)

The U.S. Supreme Court agreed to decide whether states could require girls under 18 years old who seek abortions either to wait 24 hours after the doctor has notified their parents of their plans or to obtain a judicial exemption from the notification requirement. (09)

NOW led the campaign for the Vermont Equal Rights Amendment referendum, which was defeated narrowly after Schlafly forces alleged a connection between ERA and AIDS. (11/04)

The National NOW Board moved to establish "NOW Foundation, Inc." a 501 (c)3 foundation.

ISSUES

Lifestyles

In the first all-girl final of the Soap Box Derby, Jo Sullivan, 13, won the race and Rhonda Smith came in second. Since 1971, when the Derby integrated, girls won six times.

Education

Patricia McGowan Wald, 57, moved up to Chief Judge of the U.S. Court of Appeals for the District of Columbia. Wald became the first woman to preside over the D.C. Court and only the second woman to be elevated to Chief Judge in any circuit. (07)

Representatives Patricia Schroeder (CO) and William Clay (MO) introduced the Family and Medical Leave Act of 1986 that would guarantee 26 weeks of unpaid medical leave for a serious health problem, including pregnancy, and 18 weeks of unpaid parental leave to either parent. (08/01)

As women outnumbered men on college campuses, the American Council on Education found that female freshmen attitudes had shifted since 1966: the number of potential business majors had jumped from 11% to 24% while probable humanities majors had dropped from 25% to 7.3%. (09)

As Harvard University celebrated its 350th Anniversary, only 54, or 7%, of the 787 tenured faculty were women. Forty-two percent of the undergraduates were women. (09)

Religion

The fate of two Notre Dame nuns, Barbara Ferraro and Patricia Hussey (who in 1984 both signed two *New York Times* ads asserting there was a diversity of views among Catholics on abortion and also spoke at the NOW March for Women's Lives), remained undecided by the Vatican, with expulsion from their order a continuing threat.

Another victim of Pope John Paul's crackdown on liberal Catholics, Archbishop Raymond Hunthausen of Seattle announced that the Vatican had stripped him of his authority in several areas, including the liturgy, ministry to homosexuals, moral issues in church medical facilities, marriage annulments, the training of new priests, and dealings with priests who have left the ministry. (09/06)

Women constituted more than 15% of the mayors and city council members in the 2,858 cities with populations of more than 10,000 and in the 297 cities with under 10,000 population, according to a study released by the National League of Cities. The study showed that women sat in the mayors' seats in 17 of the 176 cities with populations of over 100,000. Mayor Kathy Whitmire of Houston, TX, headed the list of women at the top of city hall.

Economic

NOW's National Conference in Denver, CO, adopted a resolution supporting reform of marital property laws in the 50 states, including a fiduciary duty between spouses and equal ownership/management rights over marital property. (06/13-15) In California, a bill initiated by NOW Task Force Chair Dorothy Jonas requiring open financial disclosure between husband and wife took effect. However, the bill's original high standard of fiduciary duty (with stiff penalties for its breach) did not survive the amending process, robbing the new law of much of its impact.

NOW LDEF filed a lawsuit against Jacksonville Shipyards on behalf of welder Lois Robinson, charging sex harassment stemming from the pictures of nude women and the sexual slurs that pervaded the work environment. (09)

In *Steele v. FCC*, the Federal Communications Commission, declaring its initial ruling unconstitutional, asked the U.S. Court of Appeals to remand its women/minority preference policy back to the agency. The outcome could be the withdrawal of a seven-year FCC policy to advance minority and women's ownership in the broadcasting industry. (09)

Legal

Political

NOW President Ellie Smeal testified before the U.S. Senate Committee on Judiciary to oppose the nomination of Justice Rehnquist as Chief Justice of the Supreme Court. (07/31)

NOW President Ellie Smeal, testified against the confirmation of Judge Antonin Scalia as an Associate Justice of the Supreme Court. Only a handful of American leaders testified against Scalia, who was confirmed by the full Senate by a 100-0 vote despite his opposition to minority rights, abortion, and women's rights. (08/06)

Pennsylvania NOW filed a lawsuit with the state Insurance Commissioner against the five top insurers in Pennsylvania charging the use of sex-biased flat insurance rates was sex discrimination in auto insurance pricing. (09/23)

The Backlash

The Vatican revoked the authorization of Rev. Charles E. Curran, a major liberal theologian, to teach theology at Catholic University of America. Curran, a popular lecturer at the university in Washington, had argued that the Church's opposition to divorce, birth control, homosexual acts, and abortion should not be absolute. (08/19)

The *Stamford* (CT) *Advocate* ran a front-page, Valentine's Day report on the results of a survey done by three sociologists based at Harvard and Yale, estimating that single, white, college-educated woman at 30 had a 20-to-1 chance of getting married. The article generated a storm of stories in the media. Jeanne Moorman and Robert

Fay of the Census Bureau, using more recent data, issued different figures (over the interference of the Reagan Administration): women at 30 had a 66 to 1 chance at marriage; at 40, a 23-to-1. The media ignored the new study. (02)

119

YEAR	1986
U. S. President	Ronald Reagan
NOW President	Eleanor Smeal

EVENTS

NOW celebrated its 20th Anniversary with a benefit gala, produced by Peg Yorkin, in Los Angeles' Dorothy Chandler Pavilion with the largest array of celebrities and media personalities (over 100) ever assembled for women's rights. The two-hour show, directed by Anne Commire, was both a serious and humorous look at women's lives over the past 20 years through the use of archival film, film essays, short landmark anecdotes read by the celebrities, and musical numbers. The landmark events were based on the 20-year chronology of NOW's history by Toni Carabillo and Judith Meuli. The show, which kept an audience of 3,000 cheering, was videotaped and released in shortened form as a videocassette. (12/01)

ISSUES

Lifestyles

NOW Annual Budget: $6,300,000
NOW PAC – $450,000

Education

Twenty-three NOW Founders met in Washington, D.C. for the 20th anniversary of the founding of NOW in October, 1966. (10)

Only 11.4% of all professors were women; 23.5% were associate professors and 37.3% were assistant professors. Many of these women were grouped in the traditional fields of the humanities and home economics.

Economic

The 20-year-old United Airlines lawsuit was finally resolved when a U.S. district court judge approved a $37 million back-pay settlement for 1,725 flight attendants and the reinstatement of 475 attendants. (10/07)

Congress enacted into law six of the 22 provisions of the Economic Equity Act, including pension rights for military spouses, private pension reforms, child care services for low-income, first-time college students, continued health insurance coverage for widows, divorced spouses and their children, an increase in the tax deduction for single heads of households, and an increased tax credit for low-income families.(10)

Legal

Political

Congresswoman Mary Rose Oakar's (D-OH) Pay Equity Bill, Congresswoman Patricia Schroeder's (D-CO) Family and Medical Leave Act, and the Civil Rights Restoration Act were blocked.

Possibly the first report on RU-486 was issued by a World Health Organization (WHO) official, Dr. Jose Barzelatto, director of WHO's program on human reproduction, who noted that if a woman wished to avoid pregnancy after intercourse, or if she had missed a menstrual period and believed she might be pregnant, a single pill would initiate menstruation, sweeping the egg cell out of her system. (10/19)

In the State ERA referendum in Vermont, a campaign led by NOW, final CBS exit polls showed a significant 11-point Gender Gap, with 56% of women voting for the Vermont ERA and only 45% of men voting in its favor. There was NO Gender Gap in exit polls for the anti-abortion referenda. (11/04)

The Gender Gap—the margin of difference between men's votes and women's votes—was extremely important in the 1986 elections. According to exit polls, in 11 U.S. Senatorial races women's votes elected the Democratic senatorial candidate while men supported the losing Republican candidate. The Gender Gap elected the first Democratic Majority in the U.S. Senate since 1980.

The Boulder (CO) City Council passed an ordinance making it illegal for abortion clinic demonstrators to come within four feet of clinic patients. The "buffer-zone" ordinance, possibly the first of its kind in the nation, passed after a public hearing at which only one person opposed it. (10/22)

Congress approved stricter federal rape laws. The single crime of rape was now replaced by four gradations; penalties were based on the severity of the crime; and the marital rape exemption was abolished. (10)

Anti-abortion forces failed to obtain the necessary number of signatures to qualify measures for the ballot in California and Washington State. All four (RI, MA, OR, AR) anti-abortion state measures that did qualify were defeated. (11/04)

NOW president Ellie Smeal and other civil rights groups organized by FairTest met to strategize on how to make SAT tests less biased. FairTest contends the standardized tests typically refer to males and male experiences about twice as often as they refer to females and female experiences. (12)

When American Airlines Flight 412 from Washington, D.C., touched down at Dallas-Fort Worth International Airport at 8:52 a.m. , it did so without a man in the cockpit. The landing marked the first time in American history–and possibly in commercial aviation history– that an all-female flight crew was in command of both the cockpit and the cabin of a Boeing 727 jetliner. The crew, all of whom wore red roses in their lapels as they were greeted at the gate by some 150 passengers and spectators, consisted of Capt. Beverly Bass, co-pilot Terry Claridge and flight engineer Tracy Prior. Six weeks earlier, Bass became the first woman to win her captain's stripes for a commercial airline. Most women who flew in the cockpit had reached only the rank of co-pilot or flight engineer. (12/29)

Democrat Barbara Mikulski was elected to the U.S. Senate from Maryland, joining the only other woman member, Nancy Kassebaum, (R-KS). (11/04)

The Backlash

Shortly after 1 a.m. EST, a bomb exploded in the waiting room of a midtown Manhattan clinic—the Eastern Women's Center— blowing out windows and injuring two pedestrians who were struck by flying glass. The clinic was licensed by the state and advertised birth control services, pregnancy testing and abortions. (10/29)

Terry Dolan, co-founder and long-time head of the National Conservative Political Action Committee (NCPAC) died of AIDS. Gay baiting had been a favorite tactic of NCPAC used against progressive candidates for office. Despite the revelation about Dolan, it continued to be a right-wing tactic against the feminist movement. NCPAC helped fund the Stop ERA Campaign in Vermont that used an ERA/AIDS Connection brochure as a scare tactic. (12/28)

YEAR	1987		
U. S. President	Ronald Reagan		
NOW President	Eleanor Smeal		

EVENTS	NOW's The Court Watch Project compiled Reagan's judicial appointment record for 1987: the U.S. Senate confirmed 43 Reagan appointees to the federal bench–33 judges to district courts and 10 judges to the courts of appeals. Of these, 41 were white males, one was a white female, and one an Asian male. By the end of 1987, Reagan appointed and the Senate	confirmed 325 federal judges: 278 were white males, only 29 were females, a mere five were black, and none were Hispanic. The PTL or "Pearly-Gate" Scandal erupted: the Rev. Jim Bakker resigned his ministry after revelations of a sexual liaison began to discredit the electronic ministries. PTL members had contributed $100 million a year. (03/20)	Sounding the death knell for male-only clubs, the U.S. Supreme Court held, 7-0, a California anti-discrimination in public accommodation's law applied to Rotary Clubs. This ruling, following the 1984 Court ruling that the Jaycees were subject to state anti-discrimination laws, was too much for male-only clubs. U.S. Rotary, Lion, and Kiwanis Clubs all decided to admit women. (03)
ISSUES Lifestyles Economic Media Legal Political	The U.S. Supreme Court, in *California Federal Savings and Loan v. Guerra* upheld a California law requiring employers to grant a new mother up to four months unpaid disability leave as well as job security. In rejecting a conflict between the California law and the federal law, Justice Thurgood Marshall stated the federal Pregnancy Discrimination Act was a "floor beneath which pregnancy disability benefits may not drop–not a ceiling above which they may not rise." NOW's position in this case was widely misreported in the press. NOW favored the California law and the federal Pregnancy Discrimination Act which it had helped pass and liked the court decision. Days later the Court also upheld a Missouri law which disallowed pregnancy as a reason to be awarded unemployment compensation and said the Missouri law did not violate Federal Unemployment Compensation which forbids discrimination on the basis of pregnancy. (01/13) In *People v. Stewart*. the San Diego, CA, Municipal Court considered criminal charges against a woman, Pamela Rae Stewart, whose baby was born brain dead. The prosecutor argued that the woman's failure to get timely medical care, among other things, constituted criminal non-support under California law. California NOW, San Diego County NOW, and the NOW Legal Defense and Education Fund (LDEF) filed an amicus brief in support of Stewart. NOW argued that the statute under which Stewart was charged had been consistently applied in California as a financial child support statute; application of the law in this manner violated the constitutional rights of pregnant women; and that the use of the law in this manner undermined the doctor-patient relationship by forcing doctors to avoid giving specific medical advice for fear their patients might not follow it. The case was dismissed. (01)	A resolution sponsored by Rep. Barbara Boxer (D-CA) in the House and Sen. Orrin Hatch (R-UT) in the Senate designating March as "Women's History Month" passed both houses of Congress without debate.(01) Randa Haines, director of the 1986 film, *Children of A Lesser God*, becomes the first American woman ever to be nominated by the Directors Guild of America as best director of a motion picture. (01) Empowered by dramatic victories in the 1986 elections, major national women's groups, including NOW, presented to Congressional leaders a shared agenda which sought not only to stem the recent erosion of civil and economic rights for women, but also to press for major gains in both areas. The shared agenda called for prompt passage of the Civil Rights Restoration Act, a Federal pay equity bill, the Family and Medical Leave Act, welfare reform proposals, an increase in the minimum wage, full Federal funding for reproductive health care for all women, legislation providing affordable and accessible child care, dependent care and reintroduction of the ERA in Congress during the Bicentennial of the Constitution. The legislative agenda included only those issues on which there was a consensus. Each participating organization also had other priority issues specific to its own agenda. NOW's legislative agenda also included lesbian and gay rights and a reduction in military spending as priority issues. The 16 organizations endorsing the agenda all participated in the Council of Presidents in Washington, D.C. and included the American Association of University Women (AAUW), Business and Professional Women (BPW), and the National Women's Political Caucus (NWPC), as well as NOW. (01/15)	In a victory for American women, a landmark sex discrimination settlement decree was filed in federal court in New York City, ending 10 years of litigation by female clerical employees of the Sumitomo Corporation of America, a U.S. subsidiary of a multinational Japanese trading company. In two class action suits under Title VII, (*Avagliano v. Sumitomo Shoji America, Inc. and Incherchera v. Sumitomo Corporation of America*), female employees charged Sumitomo with sex discrimination and preferential treatment for male Japanese nationals and American males in positions above the clerical level. Under terms of the decree, female employees, including past employees, were to receive cash payments up to $6,000. Sumitomo would spend at least $1 million during the next three years on a series of career development programs for women. The company would also be required to establish standard U.S. job titling and job description systems and, based on the systems, Sumitomo would increase its annual aggregate payroll for women employees by 16.5% over its present payroll. This case settled the question that foreign owned companies must abide by Title VII of the Civil Rights Act of 1964 forbidding sex discrimination. (01/08) Dulles Area (VA) NOW picketed the office of Air France in downtown Washington, DC, to protest the airline's personnel policies. Air France had been charged with sex harassment in a suit filed by a female employee who contended she was paid less than her male colleagues for doing the same job and was told her job status could improve if she granted sexual favors. (03/13)
The Backlash	Anti-abortion terrorists launched another clinic attack at the Northern Illinois Women's Center in Rockford, resulting in minor damages estimated at $300 and the arrest of David Holman, 57, a high school janitor who was charged with arson. (01/06)	The Eastern Women's Center, located on the fifth floor of a building that houses business offices, was the target of an arson attempt resulting in the charring of the outside of an office building adjacent to the clinic. This was the second attack on the Manhattan clinic which was bombed in the early hours of October 29, 1986, injur-	ing two pedestrians and sending glass flying onto the street below. (01/13)

YEAR	1987
U. S. President	Ronald Reagan
NOW President	Eleanor Smeal

EVENTS

For the first time in history a feminist political party, The Women's Alliance of Iceland, won 10% of the popular vote and the balance of power. Party officials set as their price for joining either a right-center, or a left-center coalition to form a government as higher pay for women and improved social services. (04/26)

Feminist Nancy Pelosi defeated 13 Democratic opponents in the special Congressional election in San Francisco, CA, by capturing 36% of the vote. Pelosi was considered a sure victor in the run-

off to fill the seat left vacant by the death earlier in the year of Congresswoman Sala Burton. (04/10)

ISSUES

Lifestyles

Faced with an organized assault from a coalition of New Right organizations and the national business community on the Family and Medical Leave Act, National NOW launched "The Great American Mother's Day Write-In" as a counter-campaign to push for Congressional passage of this bill. NOW President Eleanor Smeal testified on behalf of all women's groups for the Medical Leave Act and asked for paid leave. (04)

Education

In an historic first case for women, *Johnson v. Transportation Agency Santa Clara County*, (CA), the U.S. Supreme Court upheld in a solid 6-3 decision a voluntary affirmative action plan which permitted an employer to take into consideration as one factor, in making promotions, the sex of a qualified applicant. The media widely misreported that the Court ruled in this decision that a more qualified man could be passed over by a less qualified woman. In fact, the woman in this case was as qualified and had more experience than the man suing. This case was only a small step forward for women since it involved a clear case of prior job sex-segregation and a very weak affirmative action plan. There had never been a woman in the skilled crafts positions of this transportation agency. The *Santa Clara* decision marked the fifth time in a row the Supreme Court had repudiated the Reagan Administration's arguments that affirmative action plans were reverse discrimination against white males. (03/25)

Economic

Media

Legal

NOW President Eleanor Smeal spoke at the Peace March in Washington, D.C. which drew some 75,000 people to stop U.S. intervention in Central America and to fight apartheid in South Africa. (04)

Political

The American College of Obstetricians and Gynecologists reported that for the first time, first-year female residents in obstetrics and gynecology outnumbered men. (05)

Edith Green
1910-1987
Edith Green, former school teacher, member of Congress (D-OR) for 10 terms (1954-1974), principal author of Title IX – federal legislation banning sex discrimination in federally-funded educational programs – and sponsor of the 1963 Equal Pay Act, died on April 21 in Oregon.

The National Museum for Women in the Arts opened in Washington, DC. Conceived by Wilhelmina Holladay and funded with broad-based individual and corporate support, the museum was intended to be a place for works by women artists to be seen, acknowledged and enjoyed. (04)

Some 150 people took part in the "Memphis March Against Rape" in conjunction with the Mid-South Regional Conference. According to the 1986 FBI Uniform Crime Report, the South had the highest incidence of rape with Tennessee first among the states. (04)

FairTest, the National Center for Fair & Open Testing concluded that sex-bias in standardized tests, including the SAT and the PSAT, deprived female students of National Merit Scholarships and other academic opportunities. Although girls tended to earn better grades than boys in both high school and college, the organization found that boys won a disproportionate number of Merit Scholarships. NOW President Ellie Smeal endorsed the new study and pointed out that the failure of standardized tests to accurately predict girls' academic performances denied them access to competitive universities and opportunities for special college preparatory programs. (04/16)

NOW convened the first national conference on Women of Color and Reproductive Rights to a standing room only audience of over 400 women and men at Howard University in Washington, DC. Key women of color organizations that participated included: Women of All Red Nations, the National Black Women's Health Project, the Organization of Pan Asian American Women, the National Institute for Women of Color, and the Alliance Against Women's Oppression. (05/15-17)

Pennsylvania NOW et al v. State Farm et al, revealed the anti-consumer marketing strategies behind auto insurers' rating practices. Pennsylvania NOW President Deborah Sieger, First Pittsburgh NOW President Phyllis Wetherby, and four individual plaintiffs accused the defendant auto insurers of violating both the Insurance Rate Regulatory Act and the Pennsylvania ERA. (05)

Seventy-five percent of Americans surveyed in a *New York Times*/CBS News poll said that they supported the ERA, an increase of 21% since 1982. (05)

The Backlash

Phyllis Schlafly formed a new group called the Coalition for Teen Health, advocating abstinence from sexual activity until marriage. (03)

The Vatican's 1987 document, "Instruction on Respect for Human Life in Its Origin and on the Dignity of Procreation," condemned artificial fertilization, surrogate motherhood, sperm and embryo banks, etc. addressed Catholics worldwide and called for the passage of legislation. (03)

Oliver North addressed Concerned Women for America on the need for aid to the Contras. (09)

YEAR	1987	
U. S. President	Ronald Reagan	
NOW President	Eleanor Smeal	Molly Yard

EVENTS

Organized by NOW and the National Association for Girls and Women in Sport, the Torch Run for Equality from Washington, DC, to the NOW Conference in Philadelphia dramatized the fact that on the 200th anniversary of the U.S. Constitution, women still did not enjoy full legal rights under the Constitution. (07/16)

Molly Yard was elected President of NOW together with her whole team of Sheri O'Dell,

Action Vice President, Patricia Ireland, Executive Vice President, and Kim Gandy, Secretary, by substantial margins. The NOW conference gave the exploratory Presidential campaign of Rep. Patricia Schroeder, (D-CO) a strong send-off, gathering $350,000 in pledges during a half hour of exciting fundraising. (07/19)

ISSUES

Lifestyles
Education
Economic
Religion
Media
Legal
Political

The number of pay equity settlements increased in 1987. According to the National Committee on Pay Equity, Pennsylvania nurses won a $16 million (for 3,000 nurses) out-of-court settlement in its sex discrimination suit against Pennsylvania– believed to be the largest pay equity award in the history of nursing; the Oregon legislature passed a $22.6 million pay equity adjustment for 8-9,000 (out of 41,000) state workers; the Connecticut legislature appropriated $11 million for pay equity adjustments; the Tennessee Valley Authority reached a collective bargaining agreement as a result of a law suit for $5 million in pay equity adjustments. In all of these actions the settlements were pushed by labor unions.

In San Francisco, Mayor Dianne Feinstein agreed to a $34.5 million comparable-worth settlement on both race- and sex-based wage discrimination which affected 12,000 workers as a result of passage of a local referendum.

Ms. magazine celebrated its 15th anniversary. (07)

The Writers Guild of America West reported that TV and movie producers discriminated against women, members of minority groups and writers over 40 years old. The 200-page study, based on data from 1982 to 1985, also found that women were most likely to be employed by the networks in the lowest-paying jobs, such as daytime serial writers and children's programming. (06)

The Maryland State Senate voted 27-20 to repeal that state's statute which made sodomy a crime. The legislation was referred to the House of Delegates. Maryland NOW took the lead in calling for the repeal effort and was instrumental in forming the Maryland Committee for Personal Privacy, a statewide advocacy group.

The first and second place winners in the Westinghouse Science Talent Search were for the first time both young women: Louise Chia Chang, 17, and Elizabeth Lee Wilmer, 16.

In *New York State Club Association. Inc. v. The City of New York*, the U.S. Supreme Court upheld as constitutional a New York City ordinance placing sharp limits on male-only clubs. The ordinance provided that private clubs with more than 400 members, which regularly serve meals and regularly receive payment from or on behalf of non-members in furtherance of trade or business, could not discriminate on the basis of race, sex or other invidious grounds in regard to membership.(06)

President Reagan nominated Judge Robert Bork of the U.S. Court of Appeals for the D.C. Circuit to be an Associate Justice on the U.S. Supreme Court, to replace retiring Justice Lewis Powell. Reagan described Bork as "the most prominent and intellectually powerful advocate of judicial restraint." Bork, an ardent opponent of the legalization of abortion in *Roe v. Wade*, was immediately opposed by leaders of women's organizations, including NOW President Eleanor Smeal. (07/01)

A three-judge panel of the D.C. Court of Appeals upheld a D.C. Superior Court order forcing a Caesarean section operation on Angela Carder, a 27-year old woman terminally ill with cancer at George Washington University Hospital, against her wishes, against her family's wishes, and against the advice of her physician's and that of the hospital's obstetrics staff. She died two days later; so did the fetus. (06)

Massachusetts NOW, led by Jennifer Jackman, launched a statewide drive for local pay equity studies, and the cities of Boston and Cambridge passed model pay equity ordinances.

Basing its decision on the state's ERA, the Washington State Supreme Court ruled that all money, scholarships and the number of players for women's and men's sports at Washington State University must be split by an equitable formula based on enrollment. The case was brought in 1979 by 53 coaches and athletes. (08)

Thirty-thousand Washington State workers received the second installment of a pay equity increase – the first installment paid was in July, 1986. (07)

The National Women's Political Caucus celebrated its 16th anniversary at its biennial convention in Portland, OR. (08/20-23)

During Pope John Paul's visit to the U.S., crowds were sparse at many sites. Feminists (including Eleanor Smeal, Molly Yard, Patricia Ireland, Sheri O'Dell, Jeanne K.C. Clark and Frances Kissling) were arrested at a demonstration at the Vatican Embassy, Washington, DC – proclaiming "women's right's are human rights." Demonstrations were coordinated by NOW and Catholics for a Free Choice. (09)

The Backlash

The Reagan Administration's "comprehensive" anti-abortion legislation, officially entitled the President's Pro-Life Bill of 1987, was introduced in the House by Congressman Henry Hyde (R-IL). The bill declared Congress's opposition to the U.S. Supreme Court's *Roe v. Wade* decision legalizing abortion; made permanent the Hyde

Amendment prohibition on the use of Medicaid funds and other federal health program funds for abortion services; prohibited the awarding of Title X funds to organizations such as Planned Parenthood that offered abortion services, counselling and referrals for abortion, or advocated f abortion rights. (03/19)

123

YEAR	1987
U. S. President	Ronald Reagan
NOW President	Molly Yard

EVENTS

The Fund for the Feminist Majority (FFM), an organization committed to empowering women, was founded by Eleanor Smeal, past president of NOW; Peg Yorkin, theatrical producer; Toni Carabillo, past national NOW Vice President; Judith Meuli, past national board member of NOW; and Kathy Spillar, past president of the Los Angeles Chapter of NOW. (07/08)

Eleanor Smeal launched FFM's Feminization of Power campaign and National Tour to inspire unprecedented numbers of feminist candidates to run for public office. The tour, produced by Peg Yorkin, traveled to Los Angeles, San Francisco, Dallas, Houston, Cincinnati, Columbus, Cleveland, Pittsburgh, Philadelphia, Boston, Miami and throughout Florida–a total of 29 cities. (10/14)

ISSUES

Lifestyles

A Harris poll showed opposition to a Constitutional amendment banning abortion had increased by seven points since 1986 and stood 62% opposed versus 33% in favor. The Harris poll and *New York Times*/CBS polls (May, 1987) showed ERA support was at a record high of 75%. The Harris poll revealed that an amazing 84%-14% majority supported pay equity measures for women while 68%-25% supported federal affirmative action laws in employment. (07)

Education

Sex discrimination "is alive and well in America's schools," and educators were doing little or nothing to combat it, according to the report issued by the Project on Equal Education Rights (PEER) of NOW's Legal Defense and Education Fund. The 36-page report called "The Heart of Excellence: Equal Opportunities and Educational Reform," pointed out that "How schools treat women and girls is not even considered in evaluating the effectiveness of schools." (09/29)

Economic

The Project on Equal Education Rights (PEER) of the NOW Legal Defense and Education Fund presented its annual "Silver Snail" and "Golden Gazelle" awards to 18 national and local people and institutions for particularly sluggish or exemplary behavior in the field of education. (09)

The Executive Committee of the Defense Advisory Committee on Women in the Services reported that in the Pacific, "abusive behavior," and "blatant sexual harassment continue to exist in both the Navy and Marine Corps." (09)

Media

Ms. magazine was sold for an undisclosed price to an Australian media group, John Fairfax Ltd. The new owner published 80 magazines and 53 newspapers in Australia but had only recently entered the U.S. market. Profits from the sale went to the *Ms.* Foundation for Education and Communication, Inc. Both Editor Gloria Steinem and Publisher and Editor-in-chief Patricia Carbine planned to leave those positions but continue as consultants. (09/24)

Legal

Representative Patricia Schroeder (D-CO), after spending the summer exploring her chances of winning the Democratic nomination for President, announced that she would not become a candidate in 1988. Schroeder had raised an encouraging amount of money in her brief run–nearly half a million dollars; she had qualified in the requisite number of states for federal matching funds were she to become an announced candidate; and her test direct mail fundraising efforts showed a high potential for raising the necessary funds. Wherever she traveled during her exploratory campaign, she drew large sometimes larger than expected crowds and struck a deep, responsive chord in the electorate. Her superior experience and vast knowledge of issues made her stand out as much as her gender. Significantly, the polls had her running third and indicated an extremely high "trust" factor among voters.(09/28)

Political

The National Gay and Lesbian Rights March drew 500,000 to Washington, DC. More than 5 times the size of the 1979 lesbian and gay rights march, it was ignored by Congress a few days later when it passed repressive Helms and Dannemeyer amendments restricting AIDS spending. NOW facilitators aided the march and NOW President Eleanor Smeal spoke. (10)

A *Times-Mirror* survey conducted by Gallup disclosed that feminists (women's rights supporters) were a majority. The study found feminists to be 51% of the electorate while only 31% were Republicans, 44% Democrats, 34% liberals, and 45% conservatives. (09)

Sen. Howard Metzenbaum (D-OH) once again led the fight to keep an anti-abortion amendment off the District of Columbia's appropriation legislation. He made it clear to his right-wing colleagues that he was prepared to review the history of some 470 anti-abortion bills and amendments that had been introduced in the Senate since he took office in 1976 unless the anti-abortion amendment to the D.C. appropriations bill was tabled. The motion to table passed 60-39, the largest vote to date on this recurring amendment. (10/01)

Queen Elizabeth II amended the statutes of the Most Noble Orders of the Garter and Thistle to permit non-royal women (like non-royal men) to be accepted in this highest of her nine appointed chivalric orders. (11/25)

The Backlash

A Maryland Court ordered Charlotte Fedders, ex-wife of former Securities and Exchange Commission official John Fedders, to share the proceeds of her book, *Shattered Dreams*, with her former husband. The domestic-court official found that Ms. Fedders was equally responsible for the break-up of their marriage, even though her husband had repeatedly beat her throughout their marriage. (10)

Jerry Falwell called it quits as leader of the Moral Majority. According to major polls, a Falwell political endorsement had a negative impact on a political candidate's campaign even in Falwell's native Virginia and in his hometown. (11/03)

YEAR	1987
U. S. President	Ronald Reagan
NOW President	Molly Yard

EVENTS

The Robert Bork nomination to the U.S. Supreme Court,was defeated 58-42 in the U.S. Senate after an intense campaign by women's rights and civil rights groups. NOW President Molly Yard testified against the appointment and organized opposition to it from coast to coast. (10/23)

Wall Street had its worst day in its entire history when the stock market plunged 508 points, a loss in value nearly double that of the 1929 "crash." (10/19)

President Reagan nominated Judge Anthony Kennedy of the U.S. Court of Appeals for the Ninth Circuit in his third attempt to appoint a replacement for Justice Lewis Powell. NOW President Molly Yard

declared the organization's opposition to Kennedy's nomination, citing his decisions in cases concerning comparable worth and the right to privacy as well as his membership in men-only clubs. (11/11)

ISSUES

Lifestyles / Education / Economic / Religion / Media / Legal / Political

Southwest Indiana NOW forced the Evansville, IN post office to eject an anti-abortion group which the post office had allowed to use lobby space for fundraising. At the invitation of the local postal authorities, the group was wrapping and mailing packages for the general public and charging a fee for their services. (11/30)

The Air Force struck down the last restriction on the assignment of women officers to nuclear missile crews and authorized mixed teams for duty in underground launch control centers. The new policy, effective on January 1 ended the requirement that women must be teamed with other women on the two-person crews that served at the controls of long-range Minuteman and MX nuclear missiles. (12/09)

The Navy announced that it would open a wide range of new jobs to women and would increase efforts to combat sexual harassment against female sailors. The new assignment policy would open about 10,000 posts aboard logistics ships and some aircraft to enlisted women and officers, but was designed to keep women out of combat. The Navy study that preceded these changes, also disclosed that sexual harassment was the most common complaint from women sailors. (12/22)

President Reagan nominated Judge Douglas Ginsburg to fill the vacancy on the U.S. Supreme Court after Bork was rejected. (10/29) Ginsburg withdrew as the nominee after public disclosures that he had smoked marijuana. (11/07)

The U.S. Supreme Court let stand a Seventh Circuit Court of Appeals ruling unconstitutional an Illinois parental notification in abortion law. (12/14)

A national "Jobs with Justice" march and rally was held in Nacogdoches, TX, to support food service workers at Stephen F. Austin University in their fight for non-discriminatory hiring and promotion practices at the college. Jobs with Justice was a national coalition of 15 labor organizations, NOW and groups such as the NAACP and the Southern Christian Leadership Council. Speakers at the rally included National NOW Vice President-Executive Patricia Ireland. (12/12)

Lawrence Lader's new book, *Politics, Power, And The Church*, published by Macmillan, accused the Catholic hierarchy of a determined campaign to destroy the "wall of separation" between church and state and erode the 200-year tradition of American pluralism embedded in the First Amendment. He produced an exhaustive analysis of the bishops' intrusion into politics on issues ranging from destruction of abortion rights to combating equality for homosexuals, from forcing prayer into the classroom to diverting public funds to benefit parochial schools. Lader defined the power structure built by Catholic conservatives and Fundamentalists, which blocked the Equal Rights Amendment and depicted this alliance as the most dangerous force in American politics today. He cited evidence of how the Catholic hierarchy had used vast amounts of tax exempt money to back political candidates favorable to its stands and to attack candidates opposed to them, violating federal law.

Political victories for women included the election of the first women mayors of Houston, TX, Annette Strauss, Corpus Christi, TX, Betty Turner, and Charlotte, NC, Sue Myrick; the first Black woman mayor of Hartford, CT, Carrie Saxon-Perry; and re-election of Mayor Kathy Whitmire of Houston, TX. (11/03)

As in 1986, 1985, and 1984, Rep. Rose Mary Oakar's (D-OH) pay equity bill, Rep. Patricia Schroeder's (D-CO) Family and Medical Leave Act (FMLA), and the Civil Rights Restoration Act were blocked. The FMLA moved out of the House committee only after it was severely compromised. The Equal Rights Amendment was introduced as was the "Act for Better Child Care Services of 1987." The latter was the first comprehensive child care legislation to be introduced in Congress since the 1971 legislation vetoed by Nixon.

The U.S. Fourth Circuit Court of Appeals reversed a lower court ruling that had declared the National Democratic Party's equal division rule unconstitutional in *Bachur v. Democratic National Party et al.* The equal division rule, for which NOW had fought successfully in the 70s, required voters to allocate their votes on the basis of the sex of the candidates running for convention delegate. Voters were required to vote for equal numbers of male and female delegates. NOW and The Fund for the Feminist Majority as well as NWPC had filed an amicus brief arguing that the equal division was a legal affirmative action measure designed to remedy discrimination against women in the Democratic Party. (12/29)

For the second year, South Palm Beach County (FL) NOW visited the women's jail on Christmas morning bearing gifts for each inmate. Two-thirds of the women at the jail were awaiting trial, unable to make bail. The visit was part of an on-going effort to improve conditions at the county jail. Thanks to chapter action, there were now sufficient beds and mattresses so women were no longer sleeping on the floor and were being admitted to GED classes, to the drug treatment and mental health programs, which were what most of them needed. (12/25)

The Backlash

The family that gave Coors beer to the U.S. public also brought the New Right and the Reagan "Revolution" by supporting them with donations from the Adolph Coors Foundation, which was giving away $3.4 million annually. The Heritage Foundation, which served as the Think Tank for Reagan,

was founded in 1972 with the help of Coors money and still receives $100,000 annually from Coors. The foundation also gave $10,000 to Accuracy in the Media, $100,000 to the Free Congress Research and Education Foundation; $30,000 to the Washington Legal Foundation; $15,000 to Morality in the Media–all anti-feminist right

wing organizations. The Coors Foundation's Vice Chairman Joseph Coors also admitted giving $65,000 of his own money to help the Nicaraguan Contras.

YEAR	1988
U. S. President	Ronald Reagan
NOW President	Molly Yard

EVENTS

Canada's high court ruled that a Canadian 1972 anti-abortion law restricting abortion violated a woman's right to control her body.(01)

Over President Reagan's veto, Congress finally passed the Civil Rights Restoration Act (CRRA) for which NOW had been fighting. It reversed the U.S. Supreme Court's 1984 *Grove City* decision and restored full coverage of Title IX provisions prohibiting sex discrimination in education by recipients of federal funds. The Act also restored full coverage of statutes prohibiting discrimination based on minority status, disability, or age. The CRRA included the Danforth Amendment under which federal funds recipients may, but need not, pay for abortion benefits or services but are prohibited from penalizing any individual who seeks a benefit or service related to a legal abortion. (01)

ISSUES

Lifestyles

Education

Economic

Media

Legal

Political

A favorable ruling for Sears, Roebuck and Co. in the case charging sex discrimination in hiring and promotion (and in which NOW had been involved) was upheld by the U.S. Seventh Circuit Court of Appeals, Chicago. Sears' defense was based on the argument that stark statistical disparities between Sears' employment of' men and women derived not from Sears' discrimination based upon sex but from women having different interests than men and preferring less competitive jobs, even when such jobs pay significantly less. Two feminist historians testified for opposing the sides in the case: Rosalind Rosenberg testified for Sears and Alice Kessler-Harris testified for the women plaintiffs. The Equal Employment Opportunity Commission, under Clarence Thomas, did not take the case to the U.S. Supreme Court. (01)

The Louisiana High School Athletic Association decided girls could play competitive contact sports with boys if there were no girls' teams. The old rules of the Association allowed only mixed doubles in tennis. The change allowed Melanie Dube, 17, to play on the boys' soccer team at her New Orleans High School where she hoped college recruiters woulf see her and offer a college scholarshiip. (01/29)

The April Gallup poll indicated a significant Gender Gap with more women showing a clear preference for the Democratic Party's eventual Presidential nominee and men's votes evenly divided. By summer the Gender Gap had become a gender gulf providing a huge lead in public opinion polls for Michael Dukakis. But by September, a Louis Harris poll showed the gender advantage among women had been reduced to a marginal 2%. Dukakis did not campaign on Gender Gap issues. (01)

In a first for the country, a Boston Licensing Board rule went into effect prohibiting clubs serving food and liquor for commercial purposes from treating women and men differently. The rule outlawed such practices as separate dining and/or drinking areas for women. Failure to comply could lead to penalties such as loss of food and liquor licenses. (01)

American Demographics magazine released important statistics, including: 50% of new mothers returned to jobs within one year of giving birth (a 60% increase since 1976); in 1986, women age 30-34 were the only group to record a fertility rate increase; the percentage of female high school graduates exceeded male high school graduates for the first time in 1985; and the Bureau of Labor Standards predicted that between 1986-2000 women would account for two-thirds of labor market growth (02)

It was the 25th anniversary of the publication of *The Feminine Mystique*, the book by Betty Friedan that helped launch the revitalization of the women's rights movement. (02)

The U.S. Supreme Court ruled unanimously that although state judges were immune from lawsuits concerning their judicial rulings and acts, they could be sued for alleged discrimination in their administrative and employment decisions, reversing the decision of the U.S. Court of Appeals for the Seventh Circuit in *Forrester v. White.* (01)

NOW held a memorial service in Washington, D.C. for Angela Carder, coerced by a court order to undergo a Caesarean while she was terminally ill with cancer, over the objections of her own doctors, her husband and her parents. Both she and the fetus died. The memorial service was attended by Carder's parents and was followed by a candlelight processional to George Washington University Hospital where a memorial wreath was placed to protest the hospital's actions in seeking the court order. (02/21)

Lambda Delta Lambda, a lesbian sorority, was officially recognized by University of California at Los Angeles (UCLA). It was the first Greek-letter system gay sorority or fraternity to be approved by a university. (02)

National NOW's Annual Susan B. Anthony fundraising event at the beautiful French Embassy in Washington, D.C. drew more than 300 guests including 10 international feminists. Countries represented included Australia, Eritrea, Thailand, the Philippines, Indonesia, Korea, New Guinea, and England. (02/15)

In Washington, D. C., Judge Charles Richey detailed remedies for the successful plaintiffs in a case against the U.S. Information Agency, (USIA) found in 1984 to have had hiring practices which discriminated against women in six job categories. The USIA had to notify more than 4,400 women originally denied employment that they might be entitled to back pay, preferential hiring, and retroactive promotions. (01)

The Backlash

An extensive article in the March issue of *Regardie* magazine revealed in lurid detail the depth of National Conservative Political Action Committee, (NCPAC) leader Terry Dolan's deception. Though he had used gay-baiting as a favorite NCPAC tactic, Dolan's own homosexuality was revealed only after his death from AIDS.

The article described the protection provided by the gay male community to him and to others, even those who publicly engaged in anti-gay rhetoric and actions. The article, entitled "Fear and Self-Loathing on the Far Right," described the group of conservative gay men who tolerated and often advanced the gay-bashing so pervasive in Far Right circles. The closet right-wing gays, collectively known as the "Lavender Bund" to other gays, served, in the words of Ellen Hume, the article's author, "to help the church and state to ostracize homosexuals and establish the nuclear family as the only acceptable way of life." (03)

YEAR	1988
U. S. President	Ronald Reagan
NOW President	Molly Yard

EVENTS

The fashion industry's attempt to revive the mini-skirt was a maxi-disaster in 1988. Though a minority of trend-conscious women did buy some of the short skirts, the vast majority stopped buying all together, resulting in a sharp drop in fall and winter sales to the lowest level since the 1982 recession. (03)

France became the first Western nation to approve the use of RU-486, the abortion pill. It would be available in family planning centers and was expected to reduce by 50% the 150,000 surgical and suction abortions performed each year in France. (10)

Benazir Bhutto was sworn in as the first woman to lead an Islamic country, Pakistan. She announced a program to end restrictions on women and promised maternity leave, equal pay for equal work and a minimum wage. (12/02)

ISSUES

Lifestyles

Susan Butcher won the 1,158 mile Anchorage to Nome, AK, Iditarod sled-dog race and became the first person to win the race three consecutive years. (03)

Education

Honda of America Manufacturing Inc. and the Equal Employment Opportunity Commission (EEOC) settled a Title VII class action systemic discrimination case for $6 million. The agreement included seniority adjustments for 370 women and Blacks who applied for jobs with Honda between 1983-86. (03)

Economic

A report by the National Commission on Working Women noted that only seven of 43 leading roles in the fall 1987 TV shows were held by women; moreover, 19% of the new shows had no female characters. Women over 40 got even shorter shrift from TV writers, producers, and executives according to figures supplied by the Screen Actors Guild. Only 10% of all TV and feature film roles were filled by women over 40. In 1983, 8% of all TV and feature film roles were filled by women over 40. (02)

Religion

Media

The Rev. Pauli Murray, Episcopal priest, feminist lawyer, author, granddaughter of a slave, and one of the founders of NOW, received posthumous recognition for her autobiography, *Song From A Weary Throat* as one of the recipients of the 1988 Robert F. Kennedy Book Award. (03)

Legal

Political

The Fund for the Feminist Majority introduced a new campaign symbol at the Boston Feminization of Power event–the 5% button–a white 5% on a bright raspberry background, referring to the fact that only 5% of the members of Congress were women. (03/28)

Pennsylvania's Commonwealth Court ruled that a 1986 Pennsylvania law allowing the use of gender in determining rates for automobile insurance violated Pennsylvania's Equal Rights Amendment. The State Insurance Commissioner announced her intention to apply to all types of insurance the ruling requiring non-gender based rate-making. (04)

President Reagan issued an executive order deleting gender references from the official code of conduct for military service personnel. Naval Reservist Stephanie Ann Augustine had urged the change in a 1985 letter to the Department of Defense. (04)

At the California Democratic Party Convention in Palm Springs, CA, feminists led by NOW activists Kathy Spillar, Don Cannon, Lucienne Renni, and Shelly Mandell successfully added a plank to the 1988 State Party Platform committing the party to equal representation for women in elected and appointed office. Spillar was also the National Coordinator of the Fund for the Feminist Majority. The amended platform read: "The California Democratic Party is committed to equal representation for women in local, state and national elected and appointed office. To achieve equal representation for women in elected and appointed office, the California Democratic Party is pledged to affirmatively recruit and support women candidates, to achieve parity in endorsements in Democratically-held seats, and to provide training and resources to women candidates." (03/18-20)

FairTest (National Center for Fair and Open Testing) charged that women and people of color were denied their fair share of college scholarships because of persistent bias in the standardized tests used to award more than $23 million of financial aid annually. (04)

The U.S. Catholic Bishops issued the first draft of a pastoral letter addressing women's concerns, labeling sexism a sin and stating that a sexist attitude should weigh against a candidate for the priesthood. The letter also called for further study on the question of ordaining women as priests. The draft was to be under discussion until at least November, 1989, at which time, if approved, it would become part of the church teachings. (04)

Mathilda Publishing Inc., headed by Editor Sandra Yates, bought *Ms.* magazine from Fairfax Publications Ltd. Fairfax put the magazine up for sale after purchasing it for $10 million in 1987. (05)

Haffer v. Temple University was settled with an agreement requiring that the women's athletic budget be in proportion to the percentage of athletes who are women. The agreement ended an eight-year-old Title IX lawsuit, litigated by the National Women's Law Center, against the Philadelphia university and stated that women athletes were entitled to comparable treatment in participation, expenditures, promotion, and scholarship. (06)

The Backlash

Phyllis Schlafly led a Baby Buggy Brigade in front of the Dirksen Senate Office Building In Washington, DC, "to protest the Dodd-Kildee day-care bill." In the usual excess of rhetorical gibberish the Eagle Forum's press release claimed that ". . . our legislators are attempting to use babies as pawns in a political power grab to establish a

federal vote-buying bureaucracy. . . ." (03/14)

"Operation Rescue," organized by Randall E. Terry of Binghamton, NY, staged a series of demonstrations in New York City. Participants physically blockaded entrances to abortion clinics, health care facilities and doctors' offices, to force the

clinics to close their doors, and attempted to intimidate women from seeking abortions. Over 1,500 arrests of demonstrators were made. (05)

Hundreds of anti-abortion protesters staged "Operation Rescue" blockades in Atlanta, GA, coinciding with the Democratic Convention. (07)

127

YEAR	1988
U. S. President	Ronald Reagan
NOW President	Molly Yard

EVENTS

Republican George Bush was elected President, and Dan Quayle Vice President, winning 40 of the 50 states, in one of the most negative campaigns in U.S. history. All the major exit polls showed a clear Gender Gap of 7% with men favoring George Bush and women essentially dividing their votes evenly between Bush and Dukakis. (11/08)

NOW revealed that "the anti-abortionists were pursuing a strategy organized by a five-member steering committee of the Pro-Life Action Network (PLAN), a group which, since at least 1984, had trained extremists in clinic invasions, sit-ins, and other illegal tactics." According to NOW, the all-male steering committee of PLAN included Joseph Scheidler from Chicago, IL, John Ryan from St. Louis, MO, Andrew Burnett from Portland OR. Peter Lennox from Atlanta, GA and Randall Terry from Binghamton, NY. (12)

Pope John Paul issued an apostolic letter "On the Dignity of Women." The letter narrowly defined a woman's role in the church and society, listing women's two vocations as "virginity and motherhood." (09)

ISSUES

Lifestyles

The American Bar Association's House of Delegates approved a resolution recognizing that the "persistence of both overt and subtle barriers denies women the opportunity to achieve full integration and equal participation in the work, responsibilities and rewards of the legal profession . . . ." The resolution called upon members to eliminate these barriers. (08)

Education

The issue of comparable worth surfaced on Capitol Hill when a study of 25 House committees found two-thirds of the female congressional staffers earned less than $40,000, while three-fourth of the male staffers made more. (08/05)

Economic

Congress passed the Women's Business Ownership Act, extending protection of the Federal Equal Credit Opportunity Act to applications by women for commercial credit. The Act also created a National Women's Business Council to serve as an advocate for women who deal with government agencies. (10)

Religion

Rev. Barbara Harris was elected the first female Bishop of the Worldwide Anglican Communion, breaking 454 years of a male-only tradition. Rev. Harris, who is Black, was scheduled to become the next suffragan bishop of Massachusetts. (09)

Legal

The U.S. Courts of Appeal for the Sixth and Eighth Circuits disagreed on the Constitutionality of parental notification statutes for minors seeking abortion. The Sixth Circuit invalidated an Ohio statute primarily because of the cumbersome judicial procedure for bypassing the parental notification requirement. A Minnesota scheme requiring a minor to notify both parents or submit to a judicial bypass procedure was upheld by the Eighth Circuit Court. (08)

American women brought home Olympic medals in archery, basketball, cycling, diving, equestrian events, gymnastics, rowing, swimming, synchronized swimming, tennis, track and field, volleyball and yachting. (09)

More than 20% of lawyers were women and 80% of those entered the field since 1970. An ABA commission reported that "opportunities in the legal profession remain less available to women at all levels than their male colleagues." (08/10)

The $2.5 billion Act for Better Child Care (ABC Bill) died when Senate Democrats failed to end a Republican filibuster. The Act would have improved the quality of child care centers and provided assistance to low-income parents paying for child care. (10)

Becky Bell
1971 – 1988
Becky Bell was the first teen-age victim of an abortion law that required her to get her parents consent for an abortion, or ask permission from a judge in the state of Indiana. Unwilling to disappoint her parents by telling them and aware that judges in Indiana were not giving permission, Becky sought an illegal abortion and died as a result of a massive infection on September 16.

A jury found G.D. Searle Co. liable for negligence in distribution of the Copper-7 intrauterine device (IUD). The plaintiffs in the case were awarded $8.75 million–the largest award to date in a Copper-7 case. (09)

In Michigan, anti-abortion forces won (58%-42%) a referendum banning the use of state funds for abortion. In Colorado, pro-choice forces lost a referendum to reverse such a ban by a 60%-40% margin. Both the Michigan and Colorado referenda were put on the ballot by pro-choice forces (to restore Medicaid funding in Colorado after a 1984 referendum loss and to keep medicaid funding in Michigan after a legislative loss). In Arkansas, anti-abortion forces succeeded (52%-48%) in amending the state constitution to define life as beginning "at conception." If Roe v. Wade were reversed, the Arkansas constitutional amendment would immediately be invoked to make all abortion illegal in Arkansas. (11/08)

By the end of 1988, the Office for Civil Rights of the Department of Education had received over 1,000 complaints against colleges and universities for discriminatory health services and insurance plans. (12)

Women went from 12.1% of statewide elected offices to 13.6%. The percentage of women state legislators went from 15.6% to 17%. But women remained just 5% of the members of Congress. (11/08)

The U.S. Supreme Court declined to review Conn v. Conn, leaving intact an Indiana state court decision denying a husband's right to block his estranged wife from having an abortion. (11)

For the fourth straight Congressional election, the Gender Gap advantage among women was key for Democrats and provided the gain for Democrats in the Senate. In three Senate races, Joseph,Lieberman (D-CT), Richard Bryan (D-NV), and Herbert H. Kohl (D-WI), the majority of women supported the winning Democrat and the majority of men supported the losing Republican. (11/08)

Media

Political

The Backlash

The American anti-abortion movement tried to pressure the French manufacturer of RU-486 to remove it from the market and Groupe Roussel Uclaf agreed to stop marketing it. The French Minister of Health ordered the company to resume sales, stating "from the moment government approval of the drug was granted, RU-486 became the moral property of women. . . ." (10)

Two days after the Presidential election, the U.S. Justice Department filed a brief in Webster v. Reproductive Health Services asking the U.S. Supreme Court to use the case as an opportunity to overturn Roe v. Wade. In a joint press conference, NOW president, Molly Yard and Ellie Smeal, president of the Feminist Majority, denounced the move, noting the Administration waited until after the election to slip in the controversial brief. (11)

YEAR	1989
U. S. President	George Bush
NOW President	Molly Yard

EVENTS

A Gallup poll of opinions on the effectiveness of groups, conducted nationwide involving 1,000 adults, between February 28 and March 2, showed that NOW was viewed favorably by 71% of the poll respondents, just behind the American Cancer Society, the League of Women Voters, and the Planned Parenthood Federation of America. NOW was equally popular with men and women, although Blacks viewed it more favorably than whites–90% favorable compared with 68% favorable. (03)

The Guerrilla Girls, anonymous demographers of the New York City art world's treatment of women artists, released a study revealing the percentage of women represented by 33 famous New York City art galleries. They found that works by women in the galleries totaled 16%, compared to 49.2% of bus drivers who were women, 48% of sales people and 43% of managers. In non-traditional jobs such as truck driving and welding, women totaled 17% and 4%, respectively. (04)

ISSUES

Lifestyles

The Family and Medical Leave Act was reintroduced in the U.S. Senate (S. 345) and the House of Representatives (H.R. 770). The Act mandated the provision of unpaid employment leave for birth, adoption, and serious illness in the family. (02)

Education

Felice Schwartz, president of Catalyst, proposed in an article in the *Harvard Business Review* that employers should separate women into "career-primary" and "career and family"–the "Mommy Track"– categories and treat them accordingly, with the former groomed for top-level positions and the latter restricted to mid-level positions with shorter hours and possibly part-time jobs. Feminist critics immediately pointed out that this proposal would ghettoize women workers and violate anti-discrimination laws. (01)

Catharine MacKinnon, a leading feminist legal scholar, was offered a tenured position at the University of Michigan Law School after teaching at seven law schools in the past decade. Ms. MacKinnon was instrumental in defining sexual harassment as a legal wrong and had developed a controversial civil rights bill addressing pornography. The dean of the Michigan Law School said, "I think a lot of people initially feel threatened by her ideas. . . . But as you look at what she's written, the force of her scholarship and the quality of her mind become more and more apparent." (02)

Mary Daly, "post-Christian" radical feminist theorist, was again denied full professorship at Jesuit-run Boston College. In 1969, the school had originally granted her tenure, then reversed itself after 1,500 students in its nearly all-male student body protested. Daly, the author of *Beyond God The Father* and *Gyn/Ecology*, was regularly also denied yearly salary increases, and was paid less than the $33,800 average salary of Boston College assistant professors even though she held the rank of associate professor. (03)

Martin Klein of Long Island, NY, was empowered by a judge to authorize an abortion for his comatose wife, Nancy Klein. Complete strangers, anti-choice advocates, had gone to court to prevent the abortion. Mr. Klein, with the support of his wife's parents and her doctors, sought the abortion to improve Nancy Klein's chances for recovery. (02)

The House of Representatives voted 216-206 to allow the use of federal money to fund abortions for poor women who become pregnant from rape or incest. The House also voted to approve the District of Columbia budget that included provisions to fund abortions for poor women. Both bills were vetoed by President Bush.

Economic

Religion

Elizabeth Koontz
1920-1989
Elizabeth Koontz, who served as the first African-American president of the National Education Association and as director of the Women's Bureau in the U.S. Department of Labor, died at age 69. (01)

Catherine Conroy
1920-1989
Catherine Conroy, a member of President Carter's Advisory Commission for Women and a founder of the National Organization for Women, died of cancer at age 69 in Milwaukee,WI. Conroy held a variety of positions in both the labor and women's movement. She helped organize the Chicago, Milwaukee and Wisconsin NOW Chapters. She also helped found the Wisconsin Women's Network. (02/20)

Media

Legal

Canada opened all military jobs, except submarine operations, to women by abolishing laws barring women from combat positions. (02)

The Nevada Supreme Court Gender Bias Task Force issued its report, "Justice for Women," which concluded that "in Nevada, as elsewhere, women suffer injustices at the hands of the legal system." The findings of this task force were consistent with reports issued by similar task forces in New Jersey (1984), New York (1986) and Rhode Island (1987). (01)

Pennsylvania NOW conducted a statewide campaign holding Governor Robert Casey responsible for non-enforcement of automobile insurance laws requiring proportioning prices to costs. The campaign accused him of hiding the fact that all women were being overcharged. (02/09)

Political

The Equal Rights Amendment was reintroduced in the U.S. House of Representatives and the Senate as H.J.R. I. (01)

In the case *Parrillo v. Parrillo* , the Supreme Court of Rhode Island affirmed a lower court ruling that prohibited a woman from having her boy friend stay overnight when her three children were present. Although no evidence of harm to the children was presented, the judge ruled that the visits were not conducive to the children's well-being. The restriction had been sought by the woman's former husband. (03)

Backlash

Catholic clergy and fundamentalist ministers were highly visible among the Los Angeles Operation Rescue (OR) demonstrators. Most of the organizing around OR was through the Catholic and fundamentalist Protestant churches. Cardinal O'Conner of New York endorsed Operation Rescue, and Archbishop Roger Mahoney of Los Angeles supported the OR organizers, permitting Archdiocese staff to be actively involved in the Los Angeles "rescue." (02/11)

YEAR	1989
U. S. President	George Bush
NOW President	Molly Yard

EVENTS

Abortion rights supporters over 600,000 strong marched for abortion rights and equality. Organized by NOW, it was the largest single march ever in Washington, D.C. history. (04/09)
Marching in solidarity one week later 300,000 Italians crowded the streets of Rome and stormed the Vatican to protest the latest efforts to repeal the country's 1978 law that legalized abortion. (04/15)

Another Reagan Administration scandal surfaced in the Department of Housing and Urban Development. (06/11)

Tiananmen Square massacre by Chinese soldiers ended the student democracy movement in China.(06/05)

ISSUES

Lifestyles

NOW Membership – 165,000
NOW Annual Budget – $11,000,000
NOW PACS – $220,000

Laurie Shields
1922-1989
Laurie Shields, co-founder of the Older Women's League and the Displaced Homemakers Network with Tish Sommers, died at age 67 of breast cancer. Shields had headed NOW's Task Force on Displaced Homemakers. (03/03)

The so-called "Day of Rescue" fell far short of predicted turnout numbers and was met by feminist counter-demonstrators at nearly every turn. Operation Rescue (OR) organizers had predicted that there would be upwards of 5,000 arrests in 70 cities, but police reported a much smaller number of arrests, 1,396 in 15 cities. One of the largest feminist standoffs came in Inglewood, CA, where forces organized by the Feminist Majority, NOW, Planned Parenthood, California Abortion Rights Action League (CARAL), ACLU and California Association of Business and Professional Women, beat OR to the clinic and commandeered the doors, allowing all patients to keep their appointments. No arrests were made since the crowd was controlled by security guards hired by the clinic rather than by the police. NOW's Project Stand Up for Women also organized activists in Boston, Washington, D.C., Detroit, and New York. In Brookline, MA, several hundred feminists controlled the clinic's doors and surrounded the opposition with abortion rights signs. The Greenbelt Maryland feminist forces also outnumbered anti-abortion demonstrators. In Woodbridge, NJ, feminists beat Operation Rescue to the targeted clinic. The antis then attacked a clinic in Shrewsbury, NJ, where feminists also countered them. Once again, no arrests were made. No arrests were made in Pittsburgh either, where police arrived early and took control of the doors, allowing patients to enter the clinic. In Albany, NY, a demonstration spread out along a busy downtown street near a Planned Parenthood office, as feminists lined one side of the street and the antis the other. Feminists also mobilized at a clinic in Rochester, but no attacks occurred. In Dallas, six members of the Ku Klux Klan joined the Operation Rescue protest. (04/29)

A woman jogger was raped and beaten by a gang of teenage boys in Central Park, New York City. Although many interpreted the incident as being racially motivated, women's groups pointed to the obvious fact that the brutal and dehumanizing attack was a sexual assault by men against a woman. (04/19)

A Food and Drug Administration (FDA) advisory committee voted unanimously to recommend approval of Norplant, a long-acting contraceptive, that protects a woman from pregnancy for up to five years when implanted under the skin. Final FDA approval was expected early in 1990. (04)

NBC aired *Roe v. Wade*, a movie based on the anonymous plaintiff (played by Holly Hunter), her lawyer, and the 1973 abortion rights case. Several anti-choice groups threatened sponsors of the program with a consumer boycott. The real Jane Roe, Norma McCorvey, began to speak out about her case, attending the march for reproductive freedom in Washington, D.C., and the U.S. Supreme Court argument in *Webster v. Reproductive Health Services*. (05)

The chairs and staff directors of 23 state Supreme Court task forces on Gender Bias in the Courts convened at the National Center for State Courts for the first National Conference on Gender Bias in the Courts to discuss data collection, judicial education and the long-term implementation of necessary reforms. (04)

In Philadelphia, U.S. Senior District Judge Clarence Newcomer ruled that lawyers of pro-choice groups were entitled to collect $71,000 in legal fees from Operation Rescue, including one-third of that sum from OR leader Randall Terry. (05/02)

Economic / Media / Legal / Political

Supporters of abortion rights in the House of Representatives introduced the Freedom of Choice Act, which would put the principles of *Roe v. Wade* into Federal law. It stipulated that "a state may not restrict the right of a woman to choose to terminate a pregnancy (1) before fetal viability or (2) at any time, if such termination is necessary to protect the life or health of the woman."

Eleanor Smeal, Peg Yorkin, Toni Carabillo and Katherine Spillar of the Fund for the Feminist Majority produced a video, *Abortion: for Survival,* that dramatized the need to keep abortion legal worldwide. It was created as a powerful response to *The Silent Scream* and was shown across the country on the Turner Broadcasting System. (04)

NOW Legal Defense and Education Fund and National Abortion Rights Action League submitted an *amicus curiae* brief on behalf of over 3,000 women and their supporters in the *Webster v. Reproductive Health Services* case before the U.S. Supreme Court. The brief included excerpts from letters written by women and friends of women who had experience with abortion, both pre- and post- *Roe v. Wade.* (04)

Backlash

RU-486, the French "abortion pill" was viewed by anti-abortion forces as the ultimate threat to their movement and they scrambled to find ways to keep it out of this country though it had promising treatment potential for breast cancer, Cushing syndrome, endometriosis, and other serious illnesses. National Right to Life Committee, through its publications, launched a disinformation campaign denying RU-486's other medical applications, and a new lobby group with the curious name of Robins, Carbide, Reynolds Fund (RCR Fund) threatened a worldwide campaign against Hoechst, the firm that produces the pill.

Governor Robert Casey of Pennsylvania signed a package of anti-choice legislation. Provisions of the law included a 24-hour waiting period for abortions, spousal notification, and a ban on abortions performed after the 24th week of pregnancy. (11)

YEAR	1989		
U. S. President	George Bush		
NOW President	Molly Yard		

EVENTS	Delegates to the NOW's national convention in Cincinnati, OH, passed proposals calling for an expanded bill of rights for women for the 21st century and a study by NOW leaders to explore the creation of an independent political party. (07) The U.S. Supreme Court, in a 5-4 decision in *Webster v. Reproductive Health Services,* upheld a	Missouri statute that said that human life began at conception, barred the use of public funds for abortion, prohibited abortions at public health facilities and required physicians to test for fetal viability after the 19th week of pregnancy. The provisions had been held unconstitutional by the U.S. Court of Appeals for the Eighth Circuit. (07/03)	The U.S. Supreme Court significantly reinterpreted Title VII and Section 1981 of the Civil Rights Act of 1866 with decisions in *Wards Cove Packing Co. v. Atonio* and *Patterson v. McLean Credit Union* making it much more difficult for employees to win suits challenging sex and race discrimination in the workplace. (06)
ISSUES Lifestyles Education Economic Media Legal Political	Peoria (IL) NOW was successful in its efforts to have its city implement two new state laws lobbied through the state legislature by NOW. One involved enabling a woman to charge her husband with sexual assault and the other permitted her to testify and seek redress for assault because interspousal immunity was eliminated under the Domestic Violence Act. In *Price Waterhouse v. Hopkins,* the U.S. Supreme Court ruled 6-3 that employers had the burden of proof when charged with discrimination by an employee, shifting the burden of proof to the employer in discrimination cases, once the employee had presented evidence of biased treatment. The case concerned the failure of the Price Waterhouse accounting firm to promote Ann Hopkins to partner, despite the fact that she had brought more business to the firm than any of the other (all male) partnership candidates considered in the same year. (05/01) The Maryland Special Committee on Gender Bias in the Courts published a report stating "Gender bias exists in the courts of Maryland, and it affects decision making as well as participants." Maryland's Chief Justice appointed the Select Committee on Gender Equality to implement the recommendations for reform. (05) In *Mansell v. Mansell*, the U.S. Supreme Court held that military personnel could deny their ex-spouses a share of their veteran's retirement pay by converting a portion of their pension (divisible marital property) into non-divisible disability payments. The decision was expected to relegate many military ex-spouses, predominantly women, to poverty. (05/31)	Wisconsin's Edgewood College persevered with plans to honor feminist Kathryn Clarenbach during their commencement ceremony despite Catholic Church censure. Bishop Cletus O'Donnell of the Madison, WI, Catholic Diocese severed all ties with the school. Clarenbach was one of NOW's founders and one of the most respected feminist leaders in the state. The award recognized Clarenbach's work in promoting equal opportunities for women in higher education. (05/13) U.S. District Court Judge Aubrey E. Robinson, Jr. completely vindicated NOW in a lawsuit filed against the organization by the Federal Elections Commission (FEC) in 1987. The FEC acted against NOW on a complaint lodged by the National Conservative Political Action Committee (NCPAC). The FEC argued that NOW's mailings on abortion, equal pay for women, and the Equal Rights Amendment for 1984 membership solicitations were "blatant electioneering" and violated FEC laws. According to the decision, the mailings were political speech protected by the First Amendment and did not violate federal elections laws. (05/11) Women in Madrid, Spain, rallied in the streets to denounce sexist rulings in two court cases. In one ruling, the judge attributed an office manager's sexual harassment to biological urges arising because of a woman clerk's short skirt. In the other case, two rape suspects were acquitted because of the victim's sexual history and her implicit assumption of the risk of being sexually assaulted when she accepted a ride from the suspects. Pressure from women's groups resulted in Spain's Congress passing legislation to eliminate the loopholes in the penal code that made the rulings possible. (05)	A study by the National Gay & Lesbian Task force reported 7,248 incidents of violence against gays in 1988. (07) A sample of reading lists of nearly 500 high schools was evaluated by the Center for the Learning and Teaching of Literature at the State University of New York. The survey showed that only one of the 10 most frequently assigned books was written by a woman, and only two works by authors of color were on the extended list of the 53 most frequently assigned titles. (06) **WOMAN POWER** **TOO GOOD TO WASTE** Massachusetts released a study of its court system that found that "Gender Bias existed in many forms throughout the Massachusetts court system." The Chief Justice appointed a Committee for Gender Equality to implement the study commission's findings. (06) **MEN CAN STOP RAPE** Representatives of the Feminist Majority, Ellie Smeal and Peg Yorkin, met in Paris with Andre Ullman and Emile Beaulieu of Roussel Uclaf to discuss RU-486. (05/26-28)
Backlash	In what came to be known as the Montreal (Canada) Massacre, Mark Lepine, 25 and unemployed, gunned down 14 women engineering students at the University of Montreal Engineering School, after shouting, "You're women, you're going to be engineers. You're all a bunch of feminists. I hate feminists." Lepine wounded 13	other people, nine of whom were women, and finally killed himself. His three-page suicide note also listed 15 prominent Quebec women as "enemies." The Canadian feminist movement pointed out that this was not an isolated event. Women students in Montreal had recently held a "Take Back the Night" march protesting vio-	lence against women which some male engineering students had ridiculed. (12/06)

YEAR	1989		
U. S. President	George Bush		
NOW President	Molly Yard		

EVENTS

The East German government opened its borders and the Berlin wall was torn down. (11/10)

President George Bush vetoed a bill approved by the U.S. House and Senate that would permit the use of Medicaid funds to pay for abortions for poor women who were victims of "promptly reported" rape or incest. (10)

James Florio of New Jersey and L. Douglas Wilder of Virginia won gubernatorial races in their states. Both Florio and Wilder campaigned as pro-choice candidates in races where the issue of abortion was seen as pivotal. (11/06)

ISSUES

Lifestyles

Education

Economic

Religion

Media

Legal

Political

Dr. Elizabeth Morgan, imprisoned in a Washington, D.C. jail since August 1987 on civil contempt charges in a wrenching child custody fight, was finally released after Congress passed and the President signed into law a bill that would limit to 18 months the time that judges in the District of Columbia could incarcerate a person on civil contempt. Morgan had accused her ex-husband, Dr. Eric Foretich, of sexually abusing their daughter, Hilary, and refused to allow an unsupervised visit with him ordered by D.C. Superior Court Judge Herbert Dixon. Morgan sent the child into hiding, and Judge Dixon jailed her for contempt. After her release, Morgan vowed to continue to keep Hilary in hiding until Foretich was stripped of parental rights. NOW activists across the country had lobbied for months on behalf of the "Morgan bill," and National NOW had been involved in the effort to free Dr. Morgan for more than a year. (09/25)

The U.S. Circuit Court of Appeals for the Ninth Circuit upheld the city of San Francisco's agreement on hiring and promoting all women and minority men in the Fire Department. The plan had been challenged by the Firefighters Union Local 798 on the claim that the plan violated the rights of white men. (12)

Japanese women united in a rare political effort to oust Prime Minister Sousuke Uno, who was accused of an affair with a geisha. They forced his resignation, and his successor, in an unprecedented action, named two women to his cabinet. (07/02)

While rallying support in California for a strong new marital fiduciary bill with penalties, Dorothy Jonas and Bonnie Sloane of the NOW Task Force on the Rights of Women in Marriage locked horns with California Appellate Court Justice Donald King. King was a powerful family law judge and consistent opponent of pro-women bills. King's aggressive lobbying tactics against the bill failed in the legislature, where it passed with overwhelming support. However, King persuaded Governor Deukmejian to veto the bill.

Dorothy Jonas

Bonnie Sloane

Rosabeth Moss Kanter was named editor of the *Harvard Business Review*, the first woman to hold the position. Ms. Kanter announced that, as editor, she would not have published Felice Schwartz's "Mommy Track" article, which appeared in the January/February issue, because of flawed scholarship and lack of data. (12)

A federal district court upheld a U.S. Labor Department regulation that lifted a 40-year ban on homework in five industries. The International Ladies Garment Workers Union and two other unions had filed suit, claiming that the regulation did not have adequate safeguards to prevent the violation of laws pertaining to minimum wage, child labor, maximum work hours and safety conditions in the often exploitative home work environment. (12)

Running as a Democrat in an overwhelmingly Republican district, California Assemblywoman Lucy Killea was victorious in her first effort to move up to the State Senate. Her success in the special election was due in part to the fact that three weeks before the election, Bishop Leo T. Maher announced he was denying Killea Communion because of her outspoken support of abortion rights. The election sent a message to the hierarchy of the Catholic Church and to the Republican Party. It also gave pro-choice forces in the California Senate a 21-19 vote edge. (12/05)

The National Law Journal released the results of a survey of women partners and associates in large law firms. Among the results: 60% of the respondents had experienced unwanted sexual attention; 64% felt that men had a better opportunity to obtain management positions; and 49% felt that men were more likely to be promoted. (12)

Time magazine published a cover story entitled "Women Face the `90s," which examined the future of feminism. It featured poll results about public perceptions of the women's movement, finding that among women respondents, 94% answered TRUE to the statement "The movement has helped women become more independent," 86% responded TRUE to the statement "The movement has given women more control over their lives," and 82% responded TRUE to the statement "The movement is still improving the lives of women." Sixty-four percent did not believe the movement was anti-family and 62% did not think the movement was "out of date in its goals." (12/04)

Backlash

The
Moral
Majority
Is
Neither

The Rev. Jerry Falwell, best known as head of the now defunct right-wing Moral Majority, announced the demise of his monthly publication *Fundamentalist Journal*. The *Journal* was founded in September 1982 to present fundamentalism in a more positive light. (12)

YEAR	1990
U. S. President	George Bush
NOW President	Molly Yard

EVENTS

The Chief Cabinet Secretary of Japan, Mayumi Moriyama, withdrew her request to present a trophy to the winner of a sumo wrestling contest after she was besieged by protests. No woman had ever been permitted to enter the sacred center ring of sumo. (01)

After his re-election as Japanese Prime Minister, Toshiki Kaifu, a member of the Liberal Democratic Party, dropped the only two women members from his Cabinet. (02)

The District of Columbia Court of Appeals in a 7-1 ruling declared that a pregnant woman, even one who was terminally ill and whose fetus was probably viable, could not be forced to undergo a Caesarean delivery in an effort to save the fetus. In 1987 a judge ordered a a Caesarean section to be performed on Angela Carder, who was dying of cancer and was in her 26th week of pregnancy. Both the woman and the fetus died. (04/26)

ISSUES

Lifestyles
Education
Economic
Religion
Media
Legal
Political

**Anna Arnold Hedgeman
1900-1990**
Anna Arnold Hedgeman, 90, a NOW founder, an educator, author, civil rights advocate, and the first Black woman to serve on a mayoral cabinet in New York City, died on January 17 in Harlem Hospital, NYC. She was married for 54 years to the late Merritt A. Hedgeman, an interpreter of Black folk music and opera.

To commemorate the 17th anniversary of the U.S. Supreme Court's *Roe v. Wade* decision, NOW commissioned the Feminist Majority to create and erect a memorial to victims of illegal abortions. The memorial was inscribed with words written by Toni Carabillo: "In memory of the courageous women who died from illegal, unsafe abortions because they had no choice." NOW's national president, Molly Yard, presided over a memorial service which included the laying of wreaths, songs, and special guest speakers, including Bill and Karen Bell of Indianapolis, IN. In 1988, their 17-year-old daughter, Becky, died from an illegal abortion which she had sought in an effort to avoid using Indiana's parental consent/or judicial bypass law. (01/22)

Agreeing with the NOW LDEF, which filed an *amicus curiae* brief arguing that the secrecy of the academic tenure process can be a shield for discrimination, the U.S. Supreme Court unanimously ruled that the University of Pennsylvania must make relevant files available to federal investigators. NOW LDEF became involved in the case as counsel for Professor Rosalie Tung who had accused the university of discriminating on the basis of sex and national origin. (01)

A study by the Institute of Medicine reported that the United States had fallen significantly behind other countries in developing new methods of birth control. Approximately 750,000 of the abortions performed annually in this country resulted from contraceptive failure. (02)

Two male (Pittsburgh, PA), disk jockeys were ordered to pay a female news director nearly $700,000 in damages for making sexually explicit remarks about her on the air. The two were found liable for intentional infliction of emotional distress, defamation and invasion of privacy. (02).

NOW's Freedom Caravan for Women's Lives began a five-day tour of Pennsylvania to recruit challengers to incumbent anti-abortion state legislators. The tour began in Delaware County, home of Rep. Steven Freind, the chief sponsor of the 1989 Abortion Control Act, the most restrictive abortion law in the nation. Freind was also notorious for his declaration that female rape victims couldn't get pregnant because they secreted a body fluid that killed sperm. (02/28)

A lesbian, who jointly decided with her partner to have a child and who shared responsibility for the child's upbringing, had no legal rights to visitation after the couple split up, the New York Appellate Division, Second Department, ruled. The case, *Alison D. v. Virginia M.* was on appeal in the New York State Court of Appeals. In September, NOW LDEF filed an *amicus curiae* brief in the Court of Appeals in support of a definition of parenthood broad enough to include two parents of the same sex. (03)

NOW activists in Washington, D.C., began picketing the offices of the National Conference of Catholic Bishops and at least 12 lay Catholic women's organizations began organizing protests among their members and supporters protesting the $5 million contract with Hill & Knowlton and the Wirthlin Group to develop a campaign to end public support of legal abortion. (04)

NOW's Freedom Caravan for Women's Lives and the Feminist Majority campaign in Pennsylvania paid off. By the conclusion of the March 6 filing date for candidates for the 1990 elections, 91 women had filed for the state legislature. Only 17 women served in the legislature out of a total membership of 252. Many of the male candidates were also running on pro-abortion rights positions.(03/06)

NOW's Freedom Caravan for Women's Lives in a back-to-back, three-state tour, barnstormed Nevada, Oregon and Massachusetts in a successful quest for activist volunteers for the 1990 elections. The Nevada tour also worked to develop support for a ballot referendum to codify existing law that basically paralleled the *Roe v. Wade* U.S. Supreme Court decision. (04/05)

Backlash

The February issue of *Lear's* magazine, founded by Frances Lear, (ex-spouse of TV's Norman Lear), published a misinformation-packed and derogatory article on NOW by Margaret Carlson, a senior writer for *Time* magazine. (02)

Governor Cecil Andrus of Idaho vetoed the most restrictive state abortion law in the country. Andrus was the target of intense lobbying by both sides of the abortion issue that included 20,000 telephone calls, letters and messages. NOW and other women's groups threatened a national boycott of Idaho products. (03/30)

AT&T ended 25 years of contributions to Planned Parenthood because of "unprecedented concern" from employees, customers and shareholders that the money was being used to fund abortions. The Christian Action Council, based in Falls Church, VA, took credit for the AT&T decision. The funds were actually used for teen-pregnancy prevention. (03) **133**

YEAR	1990		
U. S. President	George Bush		
NOW President	Molly Yard		

EVENTS

President Bush signed legislation requiring the Federal government to collect hate crime statistics based on race, ethnic background, religion and sexual orientation. Excluded from this bill were crimes motivated by gender. (04)

President Bush vetoed the "Family and Medical Leave Act," a bill guaranteeing unpaid leave to workers who are seriously ill or who must care for sick relatives or newborn children. (06)

Charles Keating, who owned Lincoln Savings and Loan, was indicted in the savings and loan financial crisis for criminal fraud. (09/18)

The Federal Deposit Insurance Corporation sued Neil Bush, the President's son, and other officials of the defunct Silverado Banking, Savings and Loan Association for "gross negligence" that the FDIC said would cost taxpayers more then $1 billion. (09/22)

ISSUES

Lifestyles
Education
Economic
Religion
Media
Legal
Poltical

Some 550 pro-choice supporters turned out for a rally with the NOW Freedom Caravan in Grants Pass, OR, a strong-hold of survivalist and white supremist groups. An almost equal crowd of anti-abortion people surrounded the building where the rally was held to which only 250 abortion supporters could be admitted. While a face-off between the pros and antis outside was going on, inside the Mayor of Grants Pass and her daughter committed to fight for abortion rights both in their state and county. When the rally ended, some 25-30 anti-abortionists remained outside waiting for Molly Yard's departure. When police took Yard and Vice President-Action Sheri O'Dell to a waiting police car, the protestors surged forward, surrounded the car and began pounding on the top, sides and windows shouting and threatening until the police could drive away. The anti-abortion initiative was defeated in the county on May 15. (04)

Anne Pride
1942-90
Anne Pride, a former NOW National Board member from 1975-78 and longtime activist for women's issues, died in Pittsburgh, PA on April 24 of ovarian cancer. Pride was editor of NOW's national newspaper, then called *Do It NOW*, from 1976 to 1978. (04/24)

In a Washington state bookstore, Nikki Craft shredded four copies of *Esquire* magazine's June issue which was promoted as "An Owner's Manual" describing the American wife. Craft, arrested on charges of disorderly conduct, spent 23 days in jail because she refused to post bond. (06)

Derrick Bell, the first Black Professor at the Harvard Law School, announced he would take a leave of absence without pay until a Harvard appointed a tenured Black woman to its law faculty. It was a sacrifice he felt he had to make in good conscience. Of the schools 61 tenured faculty members, three are Black and five are women. Harvard Law School never had a tenured Black woman professor. though a spokesperson said they had been searching for one. Bell's salary, at the top of the Harvard scale was between $115,000 and $125,000. The expected loss of his health insurance would be another substantial sacrifice since his wife was seriously ill. (04/23)

About a third of Hill & Knowlton's headquarters staff signed a letter protesting the agency's contract with the Catholic Church to develop an anti-abortion campaign. Many others complained individually and one quit. The protest letter declared, "For management to seek out as well as accept an assignment whose ultimate goal is to limit our fundamental rights leaves us with a stinging sense of betrayal." The company announced that its employees were "not compelled to work on projects to which they object." (04/21)

Nora Dunn, an NBC "Saturday Night Live" (SNL) regular, and singer Sinead O'Connor boycotted the SNL show when comic Andrew Dice Clay, known for his misogynist brand of humor, was booked as guest host. (05)

Pauline Frederick, a pioneering broadcast journalist who helped open radio and television newsrooms to other women, died at age 84. (05/09)

The National Coalition for Women and Girls in Education published *Education For All: Women and Girls Speak Out on the National Education Goals* which declared that educational goals must ensure that women and girls are full partners in the pursuit of educational excellence. The publication was an attempt to prod the Bush Administration into action on sex equity, a goal it had virtually abandoned. (05)

A University of Pennsylvania study of over 1,000 children in divorced families nationwide from 1976 -1987 reported that the fathers of 42% of the children had neither seen nor contacted them at all in the previous year. Only one child in six saw her or his father once a week or more. (06)

Delegates to the 1990 NOW National Conference in San Francisco re-elected Molly Yard as National NOW President along with her ticket of Patricia Ireland, Vice-President-Executive; Rosemary Dempsey, Vice President-Action; and Kim Gandy, Secretary. The Yard ticket ran for a three-year term in which Yard and Ireland would split the presidency of the organization, with Yard retiring in December, 1991 when, under NOW's by-laws, she would be succeeded by Ireland. To fill the vacancy in the office of Vice President-Executive, the delegates passed a resolution calling on the National Board of Directors to elect Gandy to fill that vacancy, and to elect former Southeast Regional Board member Ginny Montes to succeed Gandy as National Secretary. The conference resolution was not binding on the board, because under NOW's by-laws, it was the board that had the power to fill vacancies in any office between national conferences. (06/29-07/01)

Backlash

Randall Terry, founder and director of Operation Rescue, resigned from running the day-to-day operations of the anti-choice organization to campaign, he said, against judges and district attorneys who enforce laws on behalf of woman denied access to clinics. (05)

Iron John, A Book About Men by Robert Bly was published and became the bible of a "men's movement." Bly used the Grimm fairy tale "Iron John," in which a mentor or "Wild Man" guides a young man through eight stages of male growth.

Since 1988 a network of 60 conservative student publications on college campuses was created by donations from the Olin Foundation, the Madison Center for Educational Affairs and the Leadership Institute, all far Right organizations. The publications campaign against affirmative action, women's studies and Black studies.

YEAR	1990
U. S. President	George Bush
NOW President	Molly Yard

EVENTS

In *Hodgson v. Minnesota*, the U.S. Supreme Court in a 5-4 decision ruled that states may require that pregnant teenage girls either notify both biological parents before having an abortion or seek a judicial authorization through "judicial bypass." In *Ohio v. Akron Center for Reproductive Health,* the Court upheld by a 6-3 vote the state's law requiring notification of one parent while also allowing the judicial bypass. (06/25)

David Duke, a former grand wizard in the Ku Klux Klan, campaigning for "equal rights for whites," made a strong but ultimately unsuccessful effort in Louisiana to win election to the U.S. Senate. However, he received 44% of the vote. (10/06)

After 45 years, West and East Germany were reunited as the Federal Republic of Germany. (10/02-03)

The highest ranking woman in the Bush Administration, Elizabeth Dole, resigned as Secretary of Labor. She planned to accept the presidency of the American Red Cross. (10/24)

ISSUES

Lifestyles

At the 1990 NOW National Conference in San Francisco, Sharon Kowalski and Karen Thompson, a lesbian couple, were honored by NOW's President Molly Yard with the Women of Courage Award. Thompson had been fighting a six-year court battle to become Kowalski's legal guardian, since she was seriously injured in an automobile accident. Kowalski's family provided only custodial care; Thompson was fighting for Kowalski's right to proper medical and rehabilitative care. (06/29-07/01)

Education

Mills College students' two-week protest against changing to a coed institution resulted in the trustees' reversal of their decision to abandon the school's all-women enrollment policy. (06)

Economic

The Feminist Majority produced a new video, *Abortion Denied: Shattering Young Women's Lives,* dramatizing the impact of parental consent and notification laws on young women's lives and telling the Becky Bell story. (07)

Media

Karen and Bill Bell

Karen and Bill Bell, whose daughter Becky died as a result of seeking an illegal abortion because of Indiana's parental consent law, joined forces with the Feminist Majority in a national campaign against parental consent/notification laws. (08)

Legal

Poltical

An internal Navy memo was leaked to the National NOW Action Center and to Rep. Gerry Studds (D-MA) by anonymous sources. The memo, written by Vice Admiral Joseph Donnell, urged intensified efforts to expel lesbians from the Navy while characterizing "the stereotypical female homosexual" as "hardworking, career-oriented, willing to put in long hours on the job and among the Command's top professionals." NOW President Molly Yard said of the memo, "Rarely is the public privy to such a clear example of the military's homophobic, sexist bigotry. . . . This directive uses the military's institutional homophobia to directly attack women in the Navy who are by the author's own admission, 'the Command's top professionals.'" (07)

Eleanor Smeal and Peg Yorkin of the Feminist Majority Foundation led a delegation of 10 scientists and feminist leaders, including Patricia Ireland, Vice President Executive of NOW, to meet with executives of Roussel-Uclaf in France and Hoechst, A.G. in Frankfurt. They presented the executives with 115,530 petitions urging the introduction of RU-486 in the United States. This was the first American group to meet with the manufacturers of RU-486, a safe medication for abortion. (07/23-25))

The NOW Commission on Responsive Democracy, created by a resolution at the 1989 National Conference, held its organizing meeting in Washington, D.C. (07/16)

The American Bar Association adopted a revised Code of Judicial Conduct, the model for most state codes, with many positive implications for women. The new code employed gender neutral language, cited sexual harassment as a form of judicial misconduct and barred judges from belonging to clubs and organizations that practiced discrimination. (08)

The Feminist Press celebrated its 20th Anniversary.

Ms. magazine was reborn as a bi-monthly with no advertisements with American feminist Robin Morgan as its editor. (08)

The Amateur Athletic Foundation released a study that found that women's sports received less air time than men's. In the six-week study, men's sports received 92% of the air time, while women's sports only received 5%, and gender neutral topics, just 3%. (08)

A federal district court held that a law passed in Guam, outlawing abortion except when the pregnancy endangered the life of a woman, and making it a felony to solicit a woman to have an abortion, was unconstitutional. Guam's Government vowed to appeal the ruling. (08)

The U.S. Senate Judiciary Committee held hearings on The Violence Against Women Act. If passed, the bill would establish new federal penalties for sexual assault and domestic violence, provide funding for battered women's shelters, rape crisis centers, and rape prevention education on college campuses and provide judges with training on violent crimes against women. (08)

Backlash

Seventeen members of Operation Rescue were convicted of trespassing during an anti-abortion protest at a Colorado Springs, CO, clinic. (08/23)

The American Bar Association (ABA) rescinded the policy it adopted in February opposing legislation that interfered with a woman's constitutional right to terminate a pregnancy at any time before viability or thereafter to protect her life or health. The ABA adopted a policy that it characterized as "neutral," taking no position on abortion. (08)

Pat Robertson formed the American Center for Law and Justice, a not-for-profit public interest law firm and educational organization to promote "pro-liberty, pro-life and pro-family causes."

135

YEAR	1990
U. S. President	George Bush
NOW President	Molly Yard

EVENTS

David H. Souter, only recently appointed to the Federal appeals court, was nominated by President Bush to replace retiring Justice William J. Brennan Jr. on the U.S. Supreme Court. (07/23) After NOW President Molly Yard and Feminist Majority President Eleanor Smeal gave eloquent testimony against his confirmation, (09/17), they were subjected to a patronizing tongue-lashing by Senator Alan Simpson (R-WY) because Molly Yard shrugged after Sen. Strom Thurmond commented on the presence of "lovely ladies" but had no questions for them. On the Judiciary Committee, only Senator Kennedy voted against Souter's confirmation. (09/27) The full Senate voted to confirm Souter 90-9. (10/02)

ISSUES

Lifestyles

The Civil Rights Act of 1990, a bill that would have protected women and minorities from discrimination in the workforce, was vetoed by President Bush. The Administration said it would lead to quotas in employment, although the legislation stated quotas were prohibited. (10)

Education

The first national conference to focus exclusively on clinic defense and the first in which providers and other activists met together to develop strategies to combat Operation Rescue and other anti-abortion extremists was sponsored by NOW and the Washington Area Clinic Defense Task Force in Washington, D.C. Attendees came from as far away as Alaska, California and Ontario, Canada. (10/19-21)

Economic

Network television continued to give women fewer leading roles, both on screen and off, than it did to men. The on-screen television portrayals of women depicted them as "half-witted and needing to be rescued by a man," reported the National Commission on Working Women. Also women made up 15% of producers, 25% of writers and only 9% of the directors in network television. (11)

Religion

Media

In Oregon, Ballot Measure 10, a parental notification provision, was defeated 52%-48%, and Ballot Measure 8, which would have banned abortion except in certain circumstances, was defeated 67%-33%. The Feminist Majority played a pivotal role in the defeat of these initiatives. Ellie Smeal toured campuses to register record numbers of students, and Bill and Karen Bell made a follow-up tour, telling the tragic story of their daughter's death (pg. 128). FFM staff members Lynda Tocci, Nancy Bowles, Jennifer Jackman, and FFM National Coordinator Katherine Spillar worked with local groups to achieve the victory. (11/08)

Legal

Poltical

In daring defiance of the Saudi tradition against women driving themselves, 50 Saudi women, some accompanied by daughters, dismissed their drivers in a supermarket parking lot, slipped behind the wheels of their cars, and drove off in a convoy for about half an hour before being stopped and detained by police. There was no written law that prohibited women from driving, but tradition required them to have a paid driver or a relative at the wheel. (11/06)

The California Judicial Advisory Committee on Gender Bias in the Courts published its report, bringing to 14 the number of state supreme court task forces on Gender Bias in the Courts that have published reports documenting serious bias against women as litigants, lawyers and court employees. The Colorado, Florida, Illinois and Utah task forces also published reports in 1990. More than 20 other states had task forces investigating gender bias in their court system. NOW LDEF's project, the National Judicial Education program to Promote Equality for Women and Men in the Courts, was the catalyst for and works closely with the national gender bias task force movement. (11)

On the basis of federal injunctions obtained by National NOW in D.C., Maryland and Northern Virginia, Federal District Court Judge Northrup found Operation Rescue guilty of contempt of court for its activities in Maryland over the past year and set fines of $50,000 for each future violation of the injunction. Previously, the court found Operation Rescue and several of its leaders guilty of contempt for their activities during 1989's "DC Project," and set fines of $25,000 for Operation Rescue and $5,000, doubled with each successive violation, for its leaders and those working with them. (11/08)

Democrat Ann Richards, 57, was elected governor of Texas, defeating Republican "Old Boy" Clayton Williams in a bruising campaign in which he outspent her $20 million to $11 million. Richards championed feminist issues throughout her campaign and won with a sizeable Gender Gap: she got 61% of her votes from women. In Oregon, Barbara Robert, 52, was elected governor. Exit polls showed that Roberts had captured 30% more votes from women than her Republican opponent, Attorney General David Frohnmayer. Sharon Pratt Dixon, 46, was elected the mayor of Washington, DC, the first Black woman to head the government of a major city. Anti-abortion Democrat Joan Finney, 65, was elected Governor of Kansas. In California, Democrat Dianne Feinstein narrowly lost the race for governor to Pete Wilson, 46%-49%. (11/08)

Eighty-five women ran for statewide office across the country this year, and 57 of them won. The result was three women governors, six lieutenant governors, 10 secretaries of state, three attorneys general and 12 state treasurers. On the national level, in the Senate there were only two women out of 100 members and 28 women out of 435 members in the House of Representatives. (11)

Backlash

A backlash against the Saudi women who drove their cars swept two women's university campuses, prompting the suspension of at least six professors who participated in the driving protest. Labeled "infidels" and "depraved women" by their students, the women were suspended by royal decree from their teaching jobs at the women's section of King Saud University after hundreds of students signed petitions asserting they did not want to be taught by them. The women in the demonstration had all been dressed conservatively in full abas (robes) and head scarves, but later rumors circulated that they had been wearing shorts and had burned their abas. (11/12)

As the conservative protests mounted, the Saudi government announced that women who drove automobiles in the kingdom were "portents of evil" and subject to appropriate punishment. (11/15)

YEAR	1990
U. S. President	George Bush
NOW President	Molly Yard

EVENTS

Gro Harlem Brundtland took power for the third time as Prime Minister of Norway, vowing to revive stalled talks on ties with the European Community, the issue that toppled the previous center-right government. Brundtland unveiled a 19-member Cabinet that included nine women. "Jobs, the environment and children," she said, would be the top domestic priorities. (11/03)

Junk bond king Michael Milken was sentenced to 10 years in prison for financial crimes committed to achieve more power and wealth for himself and his wealthy clients by Judge Kimba M. Wood. (11/21)

Mary Robinson, a 46-year-old lawyer, was sworn in as Ireland's first woman president. She was elected to the position in November with 52.8% of the vote. (12)

ISSUES

Lifestyles

Education

Economic

Religion

Media

Legal

Political

Members of NOW picketed the Saudi Embassy to protest the treatment of the Saudi women who drove their own cars to establish their right to drive; and the NOW Board passed a resolution demanding that President Bush "act immediately to make basic civil rights for Saudi and Kuwaiti women a pre-condition for continued U.S. support of these countries." (11/27)

The Vatican denied a German television report that its bank once held shares in a drug company that produced birth control pills. However, a spokesman at the Geneva headquarters of the pharmaceutical company Serono, said the Vatican did hold stock in its Rome subsidiary in the 1960s and possibly into the early 1970s, though he denied the company made birth control pills. (11/23)

Women at the publishing house of Simon and Schuster mounted a successful campaign against the publication of *American Psycho* by Bret Easton Ellis, a novel describing in graphic detail a young investment banker's obsession with the brutal killing of women. When the book was picked up for publication by Knopf, Tammy Bruce, president of Los Angeles NOW, led a nationwide boycott, arguing that while Knopf had the right to publish it, consumers had the right to express their outrage at a book condoning violence against women. (11)

In settlement of the case in which George Washington Medical Center subjected a terminally ill pregnant woman to a Caesarean section against her wishes and those of her husband, parents and physicians, the hospital adopted a policy to ensure that decisions about the treatment of seriously ill women and their fetuses would be made by the woman, her family and her own doctors, not the courts. (11)

Elizabeth Morgan, the woman who served 25 months in jail for contempt of court for refusing to disclose her daughter's whereabouts, won custody of her eight-year-old daughter in New Zealand. Her ex-husband, whom Dr. Morgan accused of incestuously abusing their daughter, announced he was giving up the custody fight. A New Zealand family court judge ruled that the child and Dr. Morgan must remain in New Zealand. (12)

IBM announced that it would spend $3 million in 1991 to build five child-care centers near its offices and plants around the country to serve 530 pre-school children. It said it would spend an additional $500,000 in communities with large populations of IBM workers to improve existing day-care centers and to recruit and train people who care for children in their homes. The company did not plan to operate the centers; that would be done by companies specializing in child care. (12/12)

A letter sent to Knopf and the press calling for a boycott of all books published by Knopf which, like *American Psycho*, celebrated violence against women was signed by Gloria Steinem, Andrea Dworkin, Phyllis Chesler, Charlotte Bunch, Sidney Abbott, Kate Millet, Brenda Feigen and others. (12/08)

More than 400 American Roman Catholic theologians charged that the Vatican had been throttling church reforms and imposing "an excessive Roman centralization." The theologians contended that the Vatican had undercut a greater role for women, violated rights of theologians, slowed the ecumenical drive for Christian unity and undermined the collegial functioning of national conferences of bishops. (12/15)

Norplant, a new form of contraception that uses implants that last for up to five years, was approved by the federal Food and Drug Administration. The small tubes planted under a woman's skin, slowly release the hormone progestin. When the tubes are removed, fertility is restored. (12)

The Olympic Club of San Francisco, CA, a 130-year-old refuge for moneyed white men, agreed to admit women after years of legal wrangling with the city. Several all male and all-female clubs endured in San Francisco despite a city ordinance that outlawed discrimination based on race or sex. (12/12)

Car dealers charge women and Blacks higher prices than they charge white men, according to a study done in Chicago by an arm of the American Bar Association. Black, white and female researchers posing as middle class car shoppers, using the same tactics, negotiated their best prices at 90 Chicago-area dealerships on a car that cost the dealer about $11,000. White men got a final price offer that averaged $11,363; white women got final offer that averaged $11,504; Black men's final prices averaged $11,783; and Black women's final prices averaged $12,237. Ironically, the worst deals were offered by sellers of the same race and sex as the "buyer." (12/14)

Ohio Governor Richard F. Celeste granted clemency to 25 women prisoners who he said had committed crimes because they were victims of battering or other forms of physical or emotional abuse. Celeste, a lame duck governor, said he had reviewed 105 cases in which "battered woman syndrome" was suspected. The Ohio Supreme Court and state legislature established the syndrome as a defense against murder and other crimes in March, 1990. (12/22)

Backlash

The Saudi Interior Minister announced that the monarchy had banned any new demonstrations or other demands for change by women. Prince Naif, a leading member of the royal family, asserted that some of the protesting women were not raised in Saudi Arabia and were "not brought up in an Islamic home," a statement that bordered on labeling the women blasphemers and foreigners. In fact, the women were from some of the most prominent families in the country and belonged to the small but highly influential Westernized professional class that was in direct conflict with the conservative Muslim establishment. (11/28)

During the year, *Mademoiselle* magazine asked, "Is Sisterhood Still Powerful?", *Newsweek* headlined "The Failure of Feminism," and the *New York Times* wrote on "Feminism, A Dirty-Word."

137

YEAR	1991
U. S. President	George Bush
NOW President	Molly Yard

EVENTS

In one of its most important sex discrimination rulings in recent years, the U.S. Supreme Court in *Automobile Workers v. Johnson Controls*, declared that employers could not exclude women from jobs in which exposure to toxic substances could harm a developing fetus. The ruling was a decisive victory for a broad coalition of labor unions and women's rights groups that challenged a "fetal protection" policy the country's biggest manufacturer of automobile batteries had adopted to prevent its female employees' being exposed to lead. All nine justices agreed the policy violated the Civil Rights Act of 1964. (03/20)

The U.S. Supreme Court ruled in *Rust v. Sullivan* that the government could regulate medical speech, women's speech and a woman's right to complete health information and care. In the decision, the Court ruled that it was constitutional for the government to restrict Title X funded clinics from counseling women on abortion, upholding a "gag rule," even if the continued pregnancy threatened a woman's life or health. (05/23)

ISSUES

Lifestyles

Members of the action staff of National NOW constructed and erected a "Wall of Names" to mark the 18th anniversary of *Roe v. Wade,* the U.S. Supreme Court decision that legalized abortion. The wall was filled completely with names garnered from all over the country of those who signed petitions in support of keeping abortion legal. The panels contained 25,000 names, just 4% of the 650,000 signatures NOW and the Fund for the Feminist Majority had gathered in support of abortion rights. (01/22)

Education

NOW joined other civil rights groups in demanding fair hiring and employment practices at the Cracker Barrel Country Store, Inc. in Atlanta, GA. Cracker Barrel had dismissed over 15 employees solely on the basis of sexual orientation or perceived orientation. Cracker Barrel gave no consideration to the length of employment or the quality of job performance. (01/19)

Economic

Religion

Utah NOW called for a worldwide boycott of Utah until the legislature repealed its restrictive abortion law and urged that the International Olympic Committee be lobbied not to choose Salt Lake City as the site of the 1998 Winter Olympics. (02/02)

Media

At the second in a series of hearings by the NOW Commission for Responsive Democracy, formation of a new political party won the overwhelming support of participants. By a vote of 2-1, the participants, many of whom had presented testimony during the day-long session, urged future political efforts be toward the formation of a new party and not just continuing to reform the present system. (01/19)

Legal

A NOW contingent was part of more than 200,000 patriotic Americans who marched for peace in the Middle East. NOW President Molly Yard was a speaker at the rally.(01/26)

Political

Frances Arick Kolb
1937-1991
On January 12 Fran Kolb died of breast cancer in Marlboro, MA. Kolb was a longtime activist in NOW. She was a founder of the South Hills (suburban Pittsburgh, PA) chapter of NOW, an activist in New Jersey NOW, a national board member, and the director of the Eastern Region from 1971 to 1974. As a Bunting fellow at Radcliffe College's Schlesinger Library in 1979, she was writing a history of the first 10 years of NOW.

The NOW Foundation's Commission on Responsive Democracy held a hearing, co-sponsored by Texas NOW, at the Thurgood Marshall School of Law of Texas Southern University. Among the highlights of the town meeting-style event was testimony by Molly Ivins, feminist columnist for the *Dallas Times Herald*, who regaled the audience with tales of "good old boy" politics in Texas; Sissy Farenthold, long time political activist, who discussed the growth and danger to democracy of "the National Security State;" and Billie Carr, Democratic National Committee person and author of *Organizing, Organizing,* who urged those attending to work from the grass roots and take over the party structure. (03/01)

Young feminists from all over he country converged on Akron, OH, for NOW's Young Feminist Conference that attracted 750 participants from 42 states. Conference participants attended workshops and issue hearings, discussed, debated, caucused and passed resolutions, signed up for campus action teams, internships and field organizing work and organized a zap action to demonstrate their opposition to the Persian Gulf War. (02/01-03)

In New York, feminists battled a new state law requiring liquor sellers to post alcohol-warning signs aimed at pregnant women. Molly Yard, president of the National Organization for Women, charged that the legislation was a first step in setting up "a pregnancy-police state." (03)

The NOW Commission on Responsive Democracy convened at the Tampa Bay Performing Arts Center with the help of Florida NOW and the Tampa Bay, FL, Chapters. There was a lively debate among commissioners on whether NOW should form a new party or work to reform the existing political system. (03/23)

The NOW Commission on Responsive Democracy held its Mid-West hearing at the Hubert H. Humphrey Institute Conference Center in Minneapolis, assisted by Minnesota NOW. After a welcome by Minneapolis Mayor Don Fraser, the morning session focussed on how citizens could reclaim politics, with specific discussion on the barriers to citizen action, including the lack of access to the media. In the afternoon, there was testimony from activists on the need to build an agenda for political change, including a proposal for the formation of a Women's Party by Polly Mann from Women Against Military Madness. (03/27)

Backlash

Governor Norm Bangerter of Utah signed into law the nation's most restrictive abortion legislation. The law stated that all abortions were illegal and made exceptions only for the mother's life, grave damage to the mother's medical health, grave fetal defects, and rape or incest during the first 20 weeks if reported to a law enforcement agency by the victim herself or someone acting on her behalf. Anyone who performed an illegal abortion would be subject to a $5,000 fine and/or five years in prison, though under the statute, the woman who had an abortion would not be charged with any crime. The bill was intentionally drafted to challenge the U.S. Supreme Court's decision in *Roe v. Wade* legalizing abortion. (01/25)

YEAR	1991		
U. S. President	George Bush		
NOW President	Molly Yard		

EVENTS

The U.S. Supreme Court, dealing another blow to abortion rights advocates, (*Planned Parenthood Federation v. Agency for International Development*, 90-1169), affirmed the federal government's right to deny foreign aid to overseas health care organizations that promote abortion as a means of family planning. Planned Parenthood had sought to overturn the Reagan Admin-

istration's Mexico City policy. (06/03)

Thurgood Marshall, the only Black ever to serve on the U.S. Supreme Court, announced his retirement. (06/27)

President Bush nominated Clarence Thomas, 43, a federal appeals court judge, to replace Thurgood Marshall on the Supreme Court. (07/01)

NOW urged the NIH, as the leading body on medical research, to design a long-term research agenda that strives to improve the health and lives of women in this country. (06/12)

ISSUES

Lifestyles

With the theme of "Diversity, Solidarity, Empowerment," the National Lesbian Conference convened in Atlanta, GA. NOW members from Maine to California were among the 2,500 women attending the conference and were visible and effective participants, facilitating workshops, mediating disputes and staffing a NOW table in the Market Place. (04/24-28)

Education

The growing shortage of physicians performing abortions in the United States prompted a group of doctors and public health experts to call for an overhaul of doctor-training programs and a nationwide push for physicians to include abortion in their practices. The group, organized by the American College of Obstetricians and Gynecologists and the National Abortion Federation, made the first concerted effort to bring embattled abortion services and providers into the mainstream of medical training and practice. (05/01)

Economic

Religion

CBS aired *Absolute Strangers*. The two-hour movie, starring Henry Winkler, was based on the 1989 court case of Martin Klein, a Long Island accountant faced with the dilemma of aborting his second child in order to enhance the chances of saving the life of his comatose wife. *Absolute Strangers* took its title from the idea that anti-abortion activists with no family or legal ties to the Kleins went to court in an effort to strip Martin Klein of his rights, as Nancy Klein's husband, to decide on her medical treatment. (04/10)

Media

Legal

For the first time in its 75 year history, Boys Town elected a girl for mayor. Sarah Williamson, 16, won a close four-way race in the village of about 550 students. Boys Town began admitting girls in 1980. (05/02)

Poltical

The Polish Government, which financed at least 70% of all medicines for its citizens, eliminated subsidies for birth control pills–more than tripling their price. But the Polish Parliament rejected legislation that would have banned abortions, dealing the Roman Catholic Church there its first political setback since 1989. (05/09)

New Hampshire offered to be a test site for the French abortion pill RU-486 in a resolution passed by the state legislature. Jennifer Jackman of the Feminist Majority Foundation, which backed the resolution, said it was part of a nationwide strategy to bring RU-486 into the country by demonstrating to its manufacturers that the climate was ripe for its introduction. (05)

A federal judge dismissed a NOW lawsuit alleging that anti-abortion protesters violated racketeering and antitrust laws by demonstrating at abortion clinics. The lawsuit sought an injunction against protests at abortion clinics around the country. NOW claimed that demonstrators engaged in extortion by threatening personnel, blocking clinic entrances, trespassing and damaging equipment. NOW appealed. (06/01)

The NOW Commission on Responsive Democracy convened at the State Public Utilities Building in San Francisco, co-sponsored by San Francisco NOW. Expert witnesses discussed campaign financing reform, term limitation proposals, gender and racial parity in elected office through redistricting and proportional representation. (05/04)

Abortion rights advocates won a victory in the House when the chamber voted to reverse Bush Administration policy denying foreign aid funds to private family planning groups that advocate abortion. The so-called "Mexico City policy," first promulgated in 1984 by then-President Ronald Reagan and supported by the House in votes twice before, was rejected on a 222-200 roll call, despite a White House warning that the legislation would be vetoed if the policy was reversed. (06/03)

Dr. Frances Conley, 50, one of the country's first female neurosurgeons, resigned her tenured professorship at Stanford Medical School after 25 years at the school because of sexual harassment. Only 15% of the medical school's faculty were women as against about 25% nationwide. (06/03) Conley later (09/04) withdrew her resignation when the school promised changes and did not promote the physician whom she believed was largely responsible for the harassment.

In the Gulf War, women were 35,000 of the 540,000 U.S. troops. Though technically not assigned to combat by law, they ferried fuel, food and troops into combat areas. They maintained equipment, operated communication equipment and developed intelligence information. Two women were taken prisoner and 11 lost their lives. (07/02/90-04/06/91)

Backlash

As part of a real estate transaction with the Roman Catholic Church, a hospital in Chicago agreed not to perform elective abortions. Supporters of a woman's right to choose abortion contended that the hospital, the Illinois Masonic Medical Center, bargained away a badly needed health service to obtain a parcel of land. The hospital

was one of the few in Chicago that offered abortions through the 20th week of pregnancy. (01/07)

The *Tidings* and the *National Catholic Reporter* began running advertisements from the National Conference of Catholic Bishops' $5 million public relations program orchestrated by the firm of Hill and Knowlton. The Bishops also enlisted a Latina lawyer, Helen Alvare, to be their spokesperson. (03-04)

139

YEAR	1991
U. S. President	George Bush
NOW President	Molly Yard

EVENTS

More than 2,000 activists from around the nation forged a dynamic plan of action for the 90's at the National NOW Conference in New York. A march and rally also brought 7,500 people to the streets of New York during the conference to protest the "gag rule." (07/05-07)

Allegations of sexual harassment against U.S. Supreme

Court nomineee Clarence Thomas by law professor Anita

Hill, which were quietly dismissed by the Senate Judiciary Committee, surfaced publicly in stories by *Newsday* and National Public Radio. (10/06) Though the full U.S. Senate was about to vote on the nomination, public pressure, primarily from women, including seven Congresswomen who stormed the Senate, forced reopening of the hearings. (10/08)

ISSUES

Lifestyles

NOW President Molly Yard walked out of the National Rehabilitation Hospital in Washington, D.C. with only a very stylish cane to assist her. Yard had suffered a stroke on May 15. (07/26)

Education

Male students at St. Kizito's co-ed boarding school in Kenya raped 71 teenage schoolgirls and 19 other girls died in a night of dormitory violence. The rampage began when the 271 girls at the school refused to join a strike planned by the boys. Women's organizations released a statement that declared "St. Kizito boys found legitimacy from the way the Kenyan society subordinates women and girls." (07)

Economic

The U. S. Senate voted overwhelmingly to open combat positions for women aviators. The measure, offered by Senator Roth (R-DE) and Senator Kennedy (D-MA), was an amendment to the Department of Defense Authorization bill. (07/31)

Media

Graduate of the Thelma & Louise Finishing School

Time magazine tried to explain why the movie *Thelma & Louise*, struck a nerve with women who made it a sleeper hit of the year. (06/24)

Legal

A letter hand-delivered to each Senator from Executive Vice President Patricia Ireland, expressed NOW's opposition to the White House /Danforth Compromise Civil Rights Act of 1991 with its caps on damages and other weakening amendments. However, the Senate voted overwhelmingly to accept it. (06/18)

Clinics that performed abortions in Wichita, KS, had been under siege by Operation Rescue (OR) since July 15. According to a poll by *The Wichita Eagle* and KAKE-TV, 78% of the city's residents disagreed with Operation Rescue's tactics, 75% approved of Judge Patrick Kelly's order to arrest protestors blocking clinic entrances, and 69% favored a law that did not restrict abortion. The U.S. Justice Department joined forces with Operation Rescue to fight Judge Kelly's injunction prohibiting OR from blocking access to the clinics. More than 2,000 arrests of OR protestors were made. (07/15-08/12)

The Fund for the Feminist Majority (FFM) launched a unique campaign to stop violence against women. Katherine Spillar, FFM National Coordinator, spearheaded a campaign for gender and racial balance in the Los Angeles Police Department after the Rodney King beating. Spillar and FFM President Eleanor Smeal held a news conference calling for gender balance in the special commission investigating the King beating as well as integration of the police force. Spillar also testified before both the special commission and the regular police commission with hardhitting, well-researched data on how women police dramatically reduce police violence and improve responsiveness to violence against women. (07)

A federal district judge ruled that Virginia's state-supported military college, Virginia Military Institute, could continue admitting only men, saying that the benefits of a single-sex education justified the college's 152-year-old policy of excluding women. (06/17)

Molly Yard testified at the Senate Judiciary Committee hearings on the Clarence Thomas nomination to the U.S. Supreme Court, opposing his appointment on behalf of NOW. She described the Thomas nomination as "a disaster for women." NOW was one of the first groups to oppose Thomas on the basis of his views on affirmative action and found his testimony on the issue of abortion as simply not credible. (09/01)

Five thousand people turned out for a pro-choice rally in Wichita, KS, where speakers such as Eleanor Smeal of the Feminist Majority and Kate Michelman of the National Abortion Rights Action League (NARAL) urged resistance to Operation Rescue tactics. (08/24)

More than 100 Filipino women, Sri Lankans and other foreign women reported being raped or badly beaten by Kuwaiti soldiers, police, and Kuwaiti citizens in whose homes they were supposed to have been hired for domestic service. (07/29)

A U.S. Labor Department year-long pilot study of nine *Fortune* 500 corporations, confirmed that women and minorities faced barriers in their careers–the "glass ceiling"–at a far earlier stage than previously believed. The study found that they were excluded from networking, mentoring, and participation in policymaking committees. But President Bush continued to oppose civil rights legislation. (08/12)

Political

NOW chapters all over the country shadowed President Bush, Vice President Quayle, and Secretary Sullivan wherever they spoke. At the public speaking events, NOW activists protested by wearing white gags on their mouths and holding signs that read "Overturn the Gag Rule." (06/25)

Backlash

Writing in the August/September issue of *Operation Rescue National Rescue*, Randall Terry asked "Why do Christians use birth control?" and urged his followers to stop. Describing the pill and IUD as abortifacients, he said,"At its core, birth control is anti-child. . . . why can't we simply trust God for how many children we have?"

A Michigan judge, who said he would grant permission for abortions only to white girls raped and impregnated by Black men, created a furor across the state. Judge Francis Bourisseau told the Ludington (MI) *Daily News* he didn't approve of abortion except in cases of rapes of whites by Blacks and for victims of incest. (04/26)

The Mississippi legislature voted to override the Governor's veto of legislation requiring a 24-hour waiting period for women who wanted abortions.

YEAR	1991
U. S. President	George Bush
NOW President	Molly Yard

EVENTS

The re-opened Senate Judiciary Committee hearings on Clarence Thomas were carried live on the major television networks. (10/11) Anita Hill gave a graphic description of Thomas' sexual comments.

Thomas was permitted to testify in his defense before, after and for six hours on the following day (Saturday). Hill spoke to 5 million people during the day on Friday; Thomas spoke to 30 million at night and on Saturday . Four people testified that Hill had told them several years before of Thomas' actions. Senators Specter, Simpson, and Hatch savaged Hill, accusing

her of fantasizing the events described in her testimony. The Committee finished its hearings with no decision. The full Senate voted 52-48 to confirm Thomas. (10/15)

ISSUES

Lifestyles
Economic
Media
Legal
Poltical

The Senate voted to overturn the Administration's "gag" rule that bars federally financed family planning clinics from giving women information about abortion. The prohibition against the rule was included in the $205 billion fiscal 1992 appropriations bill for the Department of Health and Human Services that passed 72-25 and was sent to the White House. The Senate vote was five more than would be needed to override an expected veto by President Bush. The 272-156 vote in the House was short of the required two-thirds mark for an override. Bush vetoed the legislation and the House was 12 votes short of the two-thirds needed to override. (08/03)

District Court Judge George Woods granted a preliminary injunction against the Detroit, MI, public schools' plan to open three male-only academies. Noting that Detroit's plan was illegal because girls had been denied access to those schools in violation of the equal protection clause of the U.S, Constitution, the Michigan State Constitution, Title IX, the Equal Education Opportunities Act, the Michigan Elliot Larsen Act, and the Michigan School Code, the judge ordered the parties involved to meet as soon as possible to work out an acceptable resolution of the issue. An interim agreement was reached which added 137 seats for girls, without eliminating any of the almost 600 seats for boys. That a crisis existed also for African-American girls was reflected in high rates of early pregnancy, drug abuse and victimization in crimes of violence–most often by the men of their community. ACLU joined NOW LDEF in a suit challenging the exclusion of girls from the proposed academies. (08/15)

Comic strip heroine Blondie got a job outside the home after six decades of homemaking, child-rearing (now grown to adolescent mall-hoppers), and managing her spouse, Dagwood. In her first week on the job, the children's sitter got sick so she had to take the kids to work with her , she experienced sexual harassment, suffered from a backache, head-ache and wris-tache from hours at the VDT, and learned she was only making 60% of what the men in her office made. (09/06)

A 200-page report by a task force studying gender bias in the Connecticut legal system, concluded that sex bias pervaded the system and included judges that whistled at women lawyers and made offensive remarks and sometimes sexual advances. Commissioned in 1987 by Chief Justice Ellen A. Peters of the Connecticut Supreme Court, the study, which took three years to complete, also showed that female lawyers were less likely than men to get lucrative case referrals or judicial appointments. Recommendations included making the language in judicial rule books and codes of conduct "gender neutral;" providing courses on sex bias for judges, lawyers and others in the judicial system, and condemning and punishing sexist conduct by judges, lawyers and court officials. (09/08)

The NOW Commission on Responsive Democracy, meeting in Washington, D.C., urged that NOW help launch a new political party, free from what it called the corruption and hypocrisy of the Democratic and Republican parties. (09/16)

The Senate Judiciary Committee deadlocked 7 to 7 on the nomination of Judge Clarence Thomas to the U.S. Supreme Court, refusing to endorse President Bush's choice. (09/27)

Feminist Peg Yorkin donated $10 million–the largest gift in women's rights history–to the Feminist Majority Foundation, half to endow the organization and half earmarked for the effort to bring RU-486 into this country. (10/02)

Twenty-five employees, most of whom were Black and female, died in a fire at the Imperial Food Products plant in Hamlet, NC. The fire started when an overhead hydraulic line ruptured spilling its flammable fluid on the floor where gas burners under the frying vats ignited the fumes. Panicked employees ran for the exits only to find some of them locked or blocked. The 11-year old plant had never been inspected. "The tragedy that occurred in Hamlet is a direct result of 10 years of the Reagan-Bush philosophy of letting industry police itself," said Deborah E. Berkowitz, top safety expert for the United Food and Commercial Workers International Union. (09)

Backlash , The Undeclared War on American Women by Susan Faludi, documenting the backlash against the feminist movement, was published by Crown and began climbing on the best-seller list where it remained through the rest of the year. (10)

Backlash

Operation Rescue declared November 17-23 the week of National Days of Rescue IV with 50 or 60 citiestargeted for attack. Less than half that number actually experienced blockades and in each city, clinics were kept open and scheduled appointments were kept.

NOW protested the Justice Department's unprecedented

action in filing a legal brief in court in Wichita, KS, supporting Operation Rescue's illegal attacks at abortion clinics in that city and even at the trial judge's home. The Justice Department argued that Judge Patrick Kelly had no power to see to it that the federal civil rights laws were obeyed in Kansas. (08/16)

Conservative William F. Buckley and other alumni members of Skull and Bones, a Yale University secret society whose membership includes President Bush, obtained a court order temporarily blocking the all-male club from admitting women. Six women were to be initiated into the 159-year old association. (09/05)

YEAR	1991		
U. S. President	George Bush		
NOW President		Molly Yard	Patricia Ireland
EVENTS	Women's police stations were part of a growing effort to end judicial immunity afforded men who attack women in Brazil. Brazil's criminal justice system failed to treat violence against women as a crime, and it was still possible in Brazil for a man to kill his allegedly unfaithful wife and be absolved on the grounds of honor, according to Americas Watch, a	New York-based human rights group. Rape was seldom investigated and rarely prosecuted. (11/17) In the worst wave of scandals to embarass the Roman Catholic Church in North America, dozens of priests were accused of sexually abusing underage boys in the U.S. and Canada. By one estimate, Catholic institutions paid $400 million in settle-	ments, with no end yet in sight. The accused included parish priests such as Father Gilbert Gauthe in Louisiana, who allegedly molested 35 boys, to the Rev. Bruce Ritter, the creator of Covenant House, a shelter for runaway boys, and Bishop Joseph Ferrario of Honolulu. William Kennedy Smith was acquitted of rape charges. (12/11)
ISSUES Lifestyles Education Economic Religion Media Legal Political	Four undergraduate women, current and former members of Texas A&M Corps of Cadets, came forward with claims of pervasive and systematic sexual harassment and sex discrimination of women in the Corps. Texas A&M NOW contacted Commandant Thomas Darling on behalf of the women asking for immediate remedial action. (10/06) Jockey Julie Krone, 28, ranked No. 3 in the jockey standing in New York. Krone had won purses totaling $37 million, much more than any other woman in racing, and earned more than $300,000 a year. (10/02) In 1990, according to the Director's Guild of America, women directed 23 of the 406 feature films produced under guild contracts. At roughly 5%, that was only a small rise from the 4.2% average they had maintained for the previous seven years. Of the 7,332 feature films made in Hollywood between 1939 and 1979, only 14 were directed by women, according to the Women's Steering Committee of the DGA, which was formed in 1981 when those statistics surfaced. (10/14) An episode of CBS' "Designing Women" dealt with the sexual harassment charges Anita Hill made against Clarence Thomas and came down clearly on the side of Anita Hill. The show placed second only to ABC Football and, along with other CBS comedies, helped CBS win the ratings war that night with very positive audience reaction. A memorial to the more than 10,000 women (most of them nurses) who served in Vietnam, eight of whom died, cleared its final bureaucratic hurdle in a seven-year campaign to honor the women. The model, by Santa Fe artist Glenna Goodacre, passed three federal commissions who review memorials. (11/11)	Cardinal Joseph Bernardin of Chicago, IL, issued an apology for his handling of a child sex abuse case involving a priest. He also appointed a three-member commission to review archdiocesan policies on handling priests accused of sexual misconduct with children. The Catholic Church reportedly spent hundreds of millions of dollars in legal fees and settlements, but often permitted such priests to be relocated in new parishes where they continued to have contact with children. (10/26) As a result of NOW's Women Elect 2000 project in Louisiana, coordinated by NOW 's Kim Gandy, the number of women in the legislature tripled from three to nine, defeating anti-abortion incumbents. An abortion rights supporter was elected Lt. Governor, a woman was re-elected State Treasurer and another was elected to the Senate, the only woman serving there. Among the sweetest victories was: the defeat of Senator Alan Bates, the Senate sponsor of Louisiana's harsh abortion law; the landslide defeat of an Eagle Forum standard bearer; and the trouncing of Rep. Carl Gunter who helped to defeat himself by his comment on incest– "That's how we get thoroughbred race horses." NOW activist Harriet Trudell served as Campaign Manager. (11/05) Attorneys for the ACLU and Planned Parenthood Federation filed an appeal to the U.S. Supreme Court asking it to rule directly in a Pennsylvania case on whether "a woman's right to choose abortion is a fundamental right protected by the U. S. Constitution." (11/07)	Molly Yard retired from the Presidency of NOW. Yard had announced in July 1990, when she was elected to a second term, that she would step down in December 1991, halfway through her term. She was succeeded by Executive Vice President Patricia Ireland. Despite the stroke suffered in May, Yard had steadily recovered and planned to continue to undertake feminist projects. (12/15) Culminating a seven-year effort by NOW Task Force Chair Dorothy Jonas and her daughter Bonnie Sloane, a landmark marital fiduciary duty bill with penalties was signed by Governor Pete Wilson, making California the first state to guarantee full protection of the law over the economic rights of spouses. Justice Donald King had opposed this bill even more vigorously than its 1989 predecessor; but Jonas and Sloane received support from over 50 statewide women's groups, law school deans and legal scholars, and a retired Appellate Court Justice, Betty Barry-Deal, who successfully neutralized King's opposition. Gloria Steinem's book, *Revolution From Within, A Book of Self-Esteem*, was published and made the best-seller list, where it stayed for the year. Anthony, Stanton and Gage, the nation's only feminist political and management consulting firm dedicated solely to advancing women's rights, was established. Peg Yorkin was president, Jeanne Clark, operating officer, Jan Welch, executive assistant, and with Eleanor Smeal as consultant. (12)
Backlash	Three researchers, described as radical feminists, held a news conference at Massachusetts Institute of Technology (MIT) to denounce RU-486 as a dangerous and cumbersome medication that should not be permitted to replace surgical abortions in the U.S. or elsewhere. The three were Lynette Dumble, a medical scientist at the Univer-	sity of Melbourne, Australia, Renate Klein, lecturer on women's studies at Deakin University in Victoria, Australia, and Janice Raymond, a medical ethicist at the University of Massachusetts at Amherst. "I think their perceptions are at odds with the data the French and others have collected about RU 486," said Dr. Philip Darney of the Univer-	sity of California, San Francisco, an expert on RU 486. (09/12) The Navy investigated charges by Lt. Paula Coughlin that drunken Navy officers fondled and harassed at least five women, including an Admiral's aide (Coughlin) and one who was stripped of her clothes, at the Tailhook Association's Convention in Las Vegas. (10/31)

YEAR	1992
U. S. President	George Bush
NOW President	Patricia Ireland

EVENTS

Members and delegates gathered in Washington, D.C. for NOW's Silver Anniversary and 25th annual conference, presided over by NOW's eighth national president, Patricia Ireland. Events included a gala dinner honoring past presidents of the organization at the French Embassy, an auction, and a women's comedy night produced by Robin Tyler. The centerpiece was a Global Feminist Conference, with representatives from 45 countries. It included workshops, and a general assembly session that called for a "global communications network so women could share information and react quickly to injustices around the world." The Women's Philharmonic, conducted by JoAnn Falletta, presented the first-ever women's concert at the Kennedy Center as the final event of the weekend. (01/10-12)

Heavyweight boxing champion Mike Tyson was convicted of rape. (02/10)

ISSUES

Lifestyles

Every day 15 to 20 Filipino, Sri Lankan and other foreign women brought to Kuwait as domestic servants sought refuge in their embassies, according to a report in the *New York Times*. The Philippine Embassy alone sheltered 130 of these refugees. They complained of beatings, sexual abuse, late or non-payment of salaries, no time off and being denied contact with the outside world. The Kuwaiti government would not issue exit visas without their employers' consent. Unless they could raise the $1,500 to cover their employers' cost in bringing them to Kuwait, they were trapped, unable to work and unable to leave. (01/03)

Education

Economic

NOW reported that anger over the Senate Judiciary Committee's treatment of Anita Hill at the Clarence Thomas confirmation hearings had translated into 13,000 new members in the final months of 1991. The Feminist Majority reported receiving an unsolicited contribution of $10,000 after the hearings and a 30% rise in contributions. Ellen Malcolm of EMILY's List disclosed a 52% rise in contributions to her organization in the seven weeks after the hearings. (01/07)

Legal

Working in coalition with abortion rights supporters from other organizations, NOW thwarted Operation Rescue's (OR) Capitol Project–an attempt to blockade four Washington, D.C. clinics and deny women access to them. The clinics were kept open by hundreds of defenders. In addition to this direct defense coordinated by the Washington Area Clinic Defense Task Force, 51st State NOW, working with National NOW, coordinated a series of events to exert pressure on government officials to protect women's rights. This pressure worked to significantly improve the city's response over previous years. (01/21-22)

Political

Saginaw NOW, Midland NOW and Bay County NOW, the three northern-most Michigan chapters, trained members and other volunteers in tactics of clinic defense when two area clinics became the target of anti-abortion fanatics. They were successful in keeping the clinics, located in a strip shopping mall, open.

Twenty years after the passage of Title IX prohibiting sex discrimination in education, a report issued by the National Collegiate Athletic Association (NCAA) documented the persistence of bias in favor of men. For every woman who got a chance to play Division I college sports, there were 2.24 men; for every woman who received a scholarship, 2.26 men did; and for every $1 paid to a men's basketball coach, the women's coach received 55 cents. In scholarship expenses men received $849,130 to women's $372,800. The gap in recruiting expenses was nearly 5-1. The breakdown of operating expenses showed $612,206 for men to $179,078 for women.

The Fund for the Feminist Majority predicted that 1992 would be a breakthrough year for women candidates. It launched its 1992 Feminization of Power Campaign, spearheaded by FM National Coordinator Katherine Spillar and the campaign's Southwest Coordinator, Dolores Huerta, to inspire record-breaking numbers of women to run for office. As part of the campaign, FFM released a new report, *The Feminization of Power: 50/50 by the Year 2000*, exploring the severe under-representation of women in government. Women were only 5% of the members of Congress and only 18.4% of all state legislative seats. "Our strategy is simple–the more women who run, the more women will win," said Spillar. (01)

The Feminist Majority Foundation (FMF) expanded its campaign to bring RU 486 into the country by focusing greater attention on Hoechst AG, the German corporation that was the majority owner of the French pharmaceutical company, Roussel Uclaf, that developed the drug. Hoechst was believed to be blocking distribution of RU 486 in the U.S. FMF President Eleanor Smeal traveled to New Jersey to target the Hoechst Celanese Corporation which now accounts for more than 50% of Hoechst AG profits. Said Smeal, "We want the women of New Jersey to know a company headquartered in Sommerville is pivotal in the fight to bring RU 486 into the country."(01/22)

The Anita Hill hearings stirred Mary Dorman, a lawyer, Ann Philbin, curator, Deb Kass, a visual artist and some 100 women in New York City to form the Women's Action Coalition (WAC) which soon spread to 35 other cities. (01)

A study of sexual harassment in the U.S. Navy by retired Navy Commander Kay Krohne confirmed yet again a widespread problem in the behavior of both male officers and enlisted men. Krohne, who retired in 1989 after a 21-year Navy career, interviewed 61 women officers, of whom 40–65.5%–had experienced harassment that ranged from being groped to officers exposing themselves. (02/10)

The Minnesota Supreme Court's refusal to hear an appeal on the guardianship of Sharon Kowalski finally ended the eight year struggle by Karen Thompson for the right to care for her life partner, Kowalski, who was severely disabled in an auto accident in 1983. A Minnesota Court of Appeals ruled in December 1991 that Thompson and Kowalski were ". . . a family of affinity, which ought to be accorded respect," naming Thompson as guardian. (02/12)

Backlash

Pope John Paul II called the use of contraceptives "a sign of grave moral degradation" and praised abstinence. (01/10)

"I'm out there with you in spirit," President Bush told some 70,000 anti-abortion marchers on the Mall in Washington, D.C. on the anniversary of the U.S. Supreme Court decision in *Roe v. Wade*, legalizing abortion. The March for Life was sponsored by the National Right to Life Committee. Meanwhile, Operation Rescue tried for the second consecutive day to block entrances at two Washington abortion clinics. Police arrested 140 persons for crossing police line, fined them $50 each, and released them. (01/22)

In a widely syndicated article entitled "Feminists Have Killed Feminism," Sally Quinn, third wife of Ben Bradlee, editor of the *Washington Post*, declared that "feminism as we have known it is dead." (01/23)

YEAR	1992
U. S. President	George Bush
NOW President	Patricia Ireland

EVENTS

Some 750,000 women, men and children turned out for a NOW-organized march in Washington, D.C. They massed behind a banner that declared "WE WON'T GO BACK! WE WILL FIGHT BACK!" It was the largest march and rally ever held in the nation's capital. In addition to the leadership and delegations from every pro-choice organization and hundreds of celebrities, thousands of students from 600 campuses across the country participated. (04/05)

ISSUES

Lifestyles
Economic
Religion
Media
Political

Feminist Majority President Eleanor Smeal set up an emergency Western Union HotLine and urged the public to flood the Kuwait Embassy and the U.S. State Department with letters urging immediate action on the widely reported accounts that hundreds of Asian women workers were being raped or beaten by their Kuwaiti employers and had taken refuge in their countries' embassies. The Pentagon had already denied a request by Rep. Pat Schroeder (D-CO) for use of a military plane to fly the women to their respective countries. Schroeder was also denied a visa to visit Kuwait to investigate the reports. (03/16)

Representatives from the Feminist Majority met with Hoechst in Frankfurt to discuss the licensing of RU-486 in the U.S. The delegation included Eleanor Smeal, Peg Yorkin and Jennifer Jackman. They were joined by Dr. Carolyn Motzel, secretary of the Women's Medical International Organization. The FM delegation separately met with Iris Blaul, the Minister of Health for the German State of Hessen. Blaul had led efforts to begin RU 486 clinical trials in Germany. (02/20)

The arrival in video stores of the women's "buddy" film, *Thelma and Louise*, knocked *Terminator 2: Judgement Day*, the Arnold Shwarzenegger macho action film, out of first place in rentals. (02/10)

The Girls in the Balcony by Nan Robertson, Pulitzer Prize winning former reporter with the *New York Times*, took its title from the balcony in the ballroom at the National Press Club, which did not admit women as members. Women reporters were relegated to this balcony to cover events. The book told the story of the landmark 1974 sex discrimination lawsuit known as *Elizabeth Boylan et al v. The New York Times*. (02)

In Illinois, Carol Moseley Braun defeated two-term incumbent Senator Alan J. Dixon in a stunning upset in the primary. Dixon's defeat was attributed to his vote in favor of confirming Clarence Thomas to the U.S. Supreme Court. NOW-PAC voted to endorse Braun before she had formally announced her candidacy and maxed out in financial contributions to her. NOW chapters and PACs in Illinois worked for her election statewide in a campaign called "One Million Women for Braun." (03/17)

The Feminist Majority (FM) sponsored a conference on domestic violence immediately after the March for Women's Lives. FM organizers met with the leadership of 48 state domestic violence coalitions and strategized to increase funding for programs to combat the mounting epidemic of violence against women. The conference was co-sponsored by the National Woman Abuse Prevention Center and focused on sharing information on legislation, developing a federal policy agenda and implementing the Feminist Majority's campaign to achieve gender balance in the police force. (04/06)

Senator Brock Adams (D-WA), 65, ended his campaign for re-election after allegations by eight women of 20 years of persistent physical assaults and sexual harassment. Adams, a former U.S. Secretary of Transportation elected to the U.S. Senate in 1986, was already in trouble as the result of allegations he drugged and molested a female aide in 1987. At his press conference, Adams said that "this is the saddest day of my life. I have never harmed anyone." (03/01)

The first successful legal action against sexual harassment in Japan came in a decision by a district court (in Fukuoka in Southern Japan) that ruled that a publishing company and one of its male employees had violated a woman's rights by crude remarks that drove her to quit her job. The feminist movement in Japan is small compared with those in other countries and has had few victories against entrenched sexism. Women said that sexual harassment–from suggestive comments to actual touching– was the norm in Japanese workplaces. Though women are about 40% of the workforce in Japan, most hold clerical jobs. (04/16)

The Feminist Majority Foundation launched the Web of Influence Campaign to intensify the economic pressure aimed at Roussel Uclaf, the French company that developed RU 486, and its parent company, Hoechst AG of Germany and Rhone-Poulence SA of France, the multi-national corporations that had refused to license the drug in the United States. The campaign identified companies, unions, and organizations in the U.S. that held stocks and bonds in, represented employees at, or bought products from these multi-national companies and their U.S. subsidiaries, Hoechst Celanese, Hoechst-Roussel Pharmaceuticals, and Rhone Poulenc Forer. (04)

In an upset victory, Lynn Yeakel of Philadelphia surged from behind to win the Pennsylvania Democratic primary to challenge incumbent Republican Senator Arlen Specter. Key to Yeakel's victory was a television ad showing Senator Spector's prosecutorial questioning of Anita Hill during the Clarence Thomas confirmation hearings, after which Yeakel appeared to asked, "Did this make you as angry as it made me?" (04/28)

Backlash

In Ireland, a 14-year old girl who became pregnant after being raped by the father of a friend after more than a year of sexual abuse by the man, was forbidden to seek an abortion in England by the Attorney General. Her case came to the attention of authorities when her family asked police whether they should preserve tissue

samples from the fetus for possible prosecution of the rapist. The family planned to appeal to the Irish Supreme Court. Ireland's abortion law was the most restrictive in Europe, permitting only the use of a "morning after" pill that terminated pregnancies in the first 72 hours. (02/20)

Barbra Streisand was passed over for an Academy Award

nomination as the director of the film *The Prince of Tides*, though both Nick Nolte and Kate Nelligan were nominated for their performances in the movie. In the 64-year history of the Academy Awards, no woman director had ever won an Oscar and only one–Lina Wertmuller in 1976–was ever nominated. (02)

YEAR	1992		
U. S. President	George Bush		
NOW President	Patricia Ireland		

EVENTS

In Los Angeles, rioting, looting, arson involving 600 buildings, and 52 deaths, followed the acquittal of four policemen on trial for the beating of Rodney King, a Black motorist. (04/29)

The Navy announced it had sent the names of 70 men to their commanding officers for possible disciplinary action for their roles in the 1991 sex abuse

incident at the Tailhook Convention in 1991. (06/03)

The U.S. Supreme Court postponed ruling on a case on whether federal judges have the power to protect abortion clinics from disruptive protests of Operation Rescue. (*Bray v. Alexandria Women's Health Clinic*). The issue had last arisen in Wichita, KS, when a federal judge called in U.S. marshalls to

prevent Operation Rescue from blockading the clinics. The widely used law was based on the Ku Klux Klan Act of 1871. Speculation was that the justices, who heard the arguments before Clarence Thomas joined the Court, were deadlocked 4-4 and that the arguments would have to be reheard with Justice Thomas casting the deciding vote. (06/08).

ISSUES

Lifestyles

Economic

Media

Legal

Political

The five major clinics in Buffalo, NY, became the target of another siege by Operation Rescue intended to duplicate their effort in Wichita. KS. But this time the Feminist Majority Foundation's National Coordinator Katherine Spillar, a specialist in clinic defense, was on hand with FMF's Clinic Defense Project organizers, Valerie Berman, Colleen Dermody, duVergne Gaines and Julie Schollenberger, to help Buffalo abortion rights groups organize and to train them in the tactics successfully used in other states. While hundreds of anti-abortion protestors came to Buffalo, not one clinic shut down because hundreds of abortion rights supporters formed a human barricade in front of the clinics and local police maintained tight control at the sites. Key leaders of the local effort included Dianne Mathiowetz, Val Colangelo, Cathy McGuire, Beverly Hiestand, Darcy France, Stephanie Foote, Lynn Rich, and Sharon Fawley. The local YWCA and its executive director, Sue Gaska, provided office and organizing space and support to the defense effort. NOW President Patricia Ireland moved the National Board meeting from Florida to Buffalo and local NOW chapters, as well as NOW volunteers from New York and Boston, all joined in the defense of the clinics. Operation Rescue ended its two-week campaign, suffering from a growing shortage of volunteers willing to risk arrest and overwhelmed by pro-choice forces. The media dubbed the failed effort "Operation Fizzle." Said Eleanor Smeal, president of the Feminist Majority Foundation, "There will never be another Wichita." (04/20-05/02)

State Farm Insurance Company agreed to pay $157 million to 814 women who were denied jobs as agents in the biggest sex discrimination settlement in U.S. history under the Civil Rights Act of 1964. The class action suit stemmed from a 1975 Equal Employment Opportunity Commission complaint by Muriel Kraszewski, a former secretary with State Farm who was rejected as an agent by eight State Farm offices despite 12 years experience in insurance sales. She went on to become a successful agent for Farmers Insurance Group, Los Angeles. The women received average payments of $193,000 each. The agreement settling the suit set up a system to allow other California women to file claims and forced State Farm to hire women for 50% of its agent jobs for 10 years. (04/29)

Vice President Dan Quayle charged that the Los Angeles riots were the result of "a poverty of values" and the breakdown of family structure, saying "It doesn't help matters when prime time TV has Murphy Brown–a character who supposedly epitomizes today's intelligent, highly paid, professional woman–mocking the importance of fathers, by bearing a child alone, and calling it just another 'life style choice.'" In the very popular television series, the character Murphy Brown chose to have the baby, fathered by her former husband, rather than have an abortion. (05/19)

Britain's House of Commons chose Betty Boothroyd as the first woman speaker in its 615-year history. Boothroyd, 62, won by a vote of 372-238 in what was only the third contested election for speaker in this century. There were only 59 women members of the 651-member chamber. (05)

The Northwest Women's Law Clinic planned to file suit on behalf of Colonel Margarethe Cammermeyer who was discharged from the Washington National Guard, (where she had served as chief nurse), because she was a lesbian. She joined the Army as a student nurse in 1961, was awarded a Bronze Star for her 14-month tour of duty in Vietnam in 1968, and in 1985, was chosen from among 34,000 candidates nationwide as the Veterans Administration's Nurse of the Year. Married to a career military man for 16 years, she has four sons, two of whom–a 15 and 17 year old–still live with her. (05/30)

Female officers in the North Atlantic Treaty Organization (NATO) pressed for wider combat roles for women in the services contending that the performance of women in the Persian Gulf War had shown their value. Five of the 15 NATO nations sent women to the Gulf combat zone: the United States, Britain, Canada, Norway and Denmark. Of the NATO forces, only Iceland and Italy had no women. (05/22)

California Superior Court Judge Maxine M. Chesney ruled unconstitutional a state law requiring unmarried minors to obtain parental or judicial consent for an abortion. Judge Chesney held that the law, passed in 1987 but not enforced while it was being challenged in court, violated a minor's right to privacy under the California Constitution. Anti-abortion forces were certain to appeal her decision to the State Supreme Court. (05/27)

In California, Barbara Boxer and Dianne Feinstein won their primary contests to become the Democratic candidates for the U.S. Senate. Political pundits predicted a tougher time for them in the November general election. (06/02)

Backlash

John Cardinal O'Connor led a 13 block march to a Manhattan abortion clinic, the Eastern Women's Services clinic, where he prayed. The rally was organized by Helpers of God's Precious Infants, a group that has organized vigils at abortion clinics in Brooklyn and Queens once a month for the last two years. These vigils were led by

Bishop Thomas V. Daily of Brooklyn, who marched with the Cardinal. Some 800 abortion rights supporters, including New York City NOW, the Women's Health Action Mobilization and the Women's Action Coalition were on hand to protect the clinic. (06/13)

In Maryland, 30 anti-abortion demonstrators were arrested

after they occupied Prince George's Reproductive Health Services clinic in Adelphi and refused to leave. (06/13)

In Milwaukee, police arrested 105 anti-abortion protestors, including 32 children, as they tried unsuccessfully to block an abortion clinic entrance in defiance of a court order. (06/16)

145

YEAR	1992
U. S. President	George Bush
NOW President	Patricia Ireland

EVENTS

The 1992 Tailhook Association convention in San Diego, CA was cancelled as the investigation of sexual misconduct by Navy officers at the 1991 convention continued and widened as a result of the disclosure that important documents were omitted from an official inquiry into the assaults. (06/17) Navy Secretary H. Lawrence Garrett III resigned, accepting responsi-bility for "a leadership failure" in the Tailhook scandal. (06/27)

President George Bush vetoed legislation overturning a federal ban on the use of transplanted fetal tissue from abortions in patients suffering from Parkinson's disease, Alzheimer's disease, diabetes, Huntington's disease, spinal cord injuries and other conditions. (06/23)

In *Planned Parenthood of South-eastern Pennsylvania v. Casey*, the Supreme Court reaffirmed what it called the "essential holdings" of Roe that women have a constitutional right to choose abortion prior to fetal viability, but declared that states also have a "compelling" interest in potential human life throughout pregnancy and upheld a series of restrictions. (06/29)

ISSUES

Lifestyles
Religion
Political

"Strength In Diversity" was the theme of the 1992 National NOW Conference held in Chicago, IL. Resolutions passed by the conference included: endorsement of NOW's "Elect Women For A Change" campaign; a strategy to step up non-violent civil disobedience actions in support of legal abortion; opposition to anti-lesbian and gay ballot measures such as those in Colorado and Oregon; and a campaign to pressure the Department of Defense to make a full investigation into the Tailhook incident. Conference delegates also voted to endorse the 21st Century party, the creation of which was proposed by NOW's Commission for Responsive Democracy in 1991. NOW President Patricia Ireland, Executive Vice President Kim Gandy, Secretary Ginny Montes and Action Vice President Rosemary Dempsey also led a NOW delegation of more than 250 activists in Chicago's Gay Pride March. (06/26-28)

Three states–Massachusetts, Rhode Island and Minnesota–were considering criminal charges against former Roman Catholic priest, Father James Robert Porter, accused of sexually abusing them as children 30 years ago by more than 50 men and women (though the actual total may be 300). The former priest, 58, who had married and fathered four children, was tracked down by Frank Fitzpatrick, one of his victims. The victims who came forward wanted acknowledgement from the church that it made serious mistakes in handling Father Porter's case; they wanted mechanisms put in place to prevent a recurrence; and financial compensation. Catholic journalist Jason Berry estimated that since 1985, the Catholic Church has paid more than $350 million in damages, health care and legal expenses coming from cases of pedophilia by priests. (06)

Roman Catholic Archbishop Joseph Cardinal Bernardin, the National Conference of Bishops' head of the Right to Life Committee, announced he would establish an independent board made up mostly of lay members to investigate accusations of sexual abuse of children by priests in his archdiocese. He was accepting the recommendation of a three-member commission which had been asked to review archdiocesan policies after it was revealed that several priests with histories of sexual abuse had been reassigned to parishes. The commission found that 57 archdiocesan priests and two visiting priests had been accused of sexual misconduct over the last three decades, and that the charges against 38 priests were substantiated. All but eight were no longer in parish ministry. (06/18)

At an illegal speakout in front of the White House protesting the U.S. Supreme Court decision in *Casey*, NOW President Patricia Ireland, Feminist Majority President Eleanor Smeal, and five other speakers were arrested. It was the kickoff of NOW's non-violent campaign of civil disobedience. Other feminist leaders arrested were Urvashi Vaid, Executive Director of the National Gay and Lesbian Task Force; Ruby Sales, National Chair of Women of All Colors; Kay Ostberg, Lesbian Rights Program Director at the Human Rights Campaign Fund; Aida Bound, Legal Director of Women's International League for Peace and Freedom; and Jane Tennington, Field Service Assistant of the Older Women's League. (06/30)

The German Parliament voted 357-284 to adopt a multi-party bill permitting abortion during the first trimester of pregnancy after counseling. Prior to this, in West Germany, only a doctor could decide whether a woman could terminate a pregnancy. (06/26)

In the first direct challenge to the Food and Drug Administration's (FDA) ban on importing RU 486, a pregnant woman, Leona Benten, attempted to bring in a prescription of RU 486 prescribed by her doctor, Louise Taylor, and filled in Europe. The pills were promptly seized by U.S. Customs at Kennedy International Airport. Her trip was arranged by Lawrence Lader of the Abortion Rights Mobilization (ARM), who planned to challenge the seizure in court because they said it was on the FDA's "import alert" list for political reasons. At the airport to greet Benten and Lader, were NOW President Patricia Ireland, and Feminist Majority President, Eleanor Smeal. (07/01)

A class-action lawsuit was filed challenging the constitutionality of the Food and Drug Administration's (FDA) ban on importing RU 486. The suit was filed by the newly established Center for Reproductive Law and Policy on behalf of Leona Benten. The suit alleged that the FDA ban on RU 486 violated the right of privacy of women who want a non-surgical abortion and interfered with the performance of doctors by preventing them from offering a treatment in the best interests of their patients. In 1988, the FDA issued guidelines permitting the importation of small quantities of unapproved drugs for the personal use of an individual bringing it into the country. Benten carried only enough pills to terminate her own pregnancy. (07/08)

Backlash

Harvard Law Professor Derrick Bell was dismissed when he was denied an extension of a two-year leave of absence he had taken to protest the school's failure to grant a woman of color tenure on its law school faculty. The school still had not appointed a Black woman. Of the 68 tenure or tenure-track positions at Har-vard Law, seven were held by white women and five by African-American men. (08)

According to the Christian Coalition's estimates, as many as 43% of the delegates to the Republican Convention in Houston were evangelicals; one in seven delegates was a member of the Christian Coalition. (08/17-21)

In Zinder, Niger, a mob attacked bars and bordellos, setting them on fire, after militant Muslim holy men declared that the indecent dress and immoral behavior of women were causing a drought, and urged the mob on. (07/18)

YEAR	1992
U. S. President	George Bush
NOW President	Patricia Ireland

EVENTS

House Minority Whip Newt Gingrich (R-GA) barely won renomination. Running in a new district in suburban Atlanta because of redistricting, Gingrich, who outspent his Republican challenger $1.1 million to $150,000, squeaked to victory with 50.7% of the vote. (07/21)

The Democratic Party nominated Gov. Bill Clinton of Arkansas and Sen. Albert Gore of Tennessee as its candidates for President and Vice President. (07/13-17) H. Ross Perot unexpectedly abandoned plans to run as an independent. (07/16) The Republicans renominated President George Bush and Vice President Dan Quayle. (08/19)

At the Republican Convention, the religious right captured the party platform as Pat Buchanan, Pat Robertson and Dan and Marilyn Quayle (who shared their box with right wing radio host Rush Limbaugh, Pat Robertson and Jerry Falwell) all but declared cultural civil war in harsh speeches that bashed feminists and gays. (08/17-21)

ISSUES

Lifestyles

Acting Navy Secretary J. Daniel Howard ordered a servicewide "stand-down" to give every member of the Navy training on sexual harassment and he announced that the Navy was permanently severing its ties to the Tailhook Association. He also announced the creation of a Standing Committee on Women in the Navy and the Marine Corps to review service sexual harassment policies and hear victims' complaints.(07/03)

Economic

Two days after Army Specialist Jacqueline Ortiz (see 06/30 below) said that she had been sexually assaulted by a superior while serving in Saudi Arabia during the Gulf War, the Army charged Reserve Sergeant David Martinez with one count of forcible sodomy, one count of indecent assault and four counts of falsifying official statements, charges that could result in 40 years of confinement. (07/03)

Muriel Siebert, the first woman permitted to buy a seat on the New York Stock Exchange in 1967, was honored for her efforts on behalf of Wall Street women. She was named the 1992 Veuve Clicquot Business Woman of the Year, one of only 13 women in the world to be so honored. The international award was established by Mme. Nicole-Barbe Clicquot, a widow who took over her husband's winery in 1805 and ran it for 60 years. Siebert warned, however, that "Firms are doing what they have to do, legally. But women are coming into Wall Street in large numbers– and they still are not making partner. . . ." Siebert said that equality would come only when the women who gained power on Wall Street used it on behalf of other women. "It will take the decided effort on the part of major firms to make sure that women are advanced according to their abilities. And it will be up to the women who rise to the top to see that they make that effort." (07/05)

Legal

Political

Operation Rescue targeted clinics in New York to disrupt the Democratic Convention, but advance teams from the Feminist Majority, led by Katherine Spillar went to New York weeks before the convention at the invitation of local groups who wanted to learn the successful tactics that had been used in Buffalo. Feminist Majority organizers worked with the New York Clinic Defense Task Force training and mobilizing thousands of clinic defenders. Constantly covering up to 35 of the city's 151 clinics at a time, up to 3,000 clinic defenders kept all clinic doors open during OR's attempted blockades. Feminist Majority President Eleanor Smeal personally served an injunction to OR's leader Randall Terry whose forces dwindled steadily. By the time it was over, Terry faced a potential prison term for violating an injunction and OR faced thousands of dollars in fines. NOW Action Vice President Rosemary Dempsey and National Secretary Ginny Montes and volunteers from the National NOW Action Center, NOW New York City, Bronx NOW, Brooklyn NOW, Long Island NOW, New York State NOW and the NOW LDEF were all part of the coalition. NOW Executive Vice President Kim Gandy joined the action in New York after a successful effort to stop OR from blockading clinics in Louisiana. (07/13-17)

Women from 53 countries attended an international four-day summit in Dublin, Ireland, organized by Irene Natividad, a former president of the National Women's Political Caucus (NWPC), and drafted resolutions about women and politics, labor, religion, health and the media. Speakers included Mary Robinson, Ireland's president; Vigdis Finnbogadottir, Iceland's president; former U.S. Rep. Bella Abzug, Tiananmen Square student leader Jingqing Cai, and author Betty Friedan. (07/13)

NOW Membership – 275,000
NOW PACs – $550,000

Federal District Court Judge Charles P. Sifton, ruled that the government acted illegally when it seized the RU 486 pills from Leona Benten when she re-entered the U.S. However, a panel of three judges of the Federal Appeals Court of the Second Circuit ordered a delay before the pills could be returned to her. Politics surrounding the issue of abortion were apparent in these decisions: Judge Sifton was appointed by President Jimmy Carter; the appeals court panel was composed of John M. Walker, appointed by President George Bush (in fact his cousin), Frank X. Altimari and Daniel J. Mahoney, both appointed by President Ronald Reagan. The appeal to the U.S. Supreme Court where it was scheduled to be taken up by President Bush's most recent appointee, Justice Clarence Thomas, was to determine if the Appeals Court was correct in stopping the order to return the pills to Benten. (07/14)

By a 7-2 vote, the U.S. Supreme Court refused to order the return of the RU 486 pills to Leona Benten, the woman from whom they had been seized by U.S. Customs. In an unsigned opinion, the Court said that Ms. Benten's lawyers had failed to show a substantial likelihood that the case could be won if it were argued before the U.S. Court of Appeals for the Second Circuit. Justices Harry A. Blackmun and John Paul Stevens dissented, arguing that the government's action placed an "undue burden" on Ms. Benten's right to an abortion. (07/17)

Backlash

Five Navy officers were relieved of command and 16 others counseled in disciplinary action that resulted after the "Tomcat Follies" at the Miramar officers club in San Diego, CA. A retired female Navy captain who saw the show protested a banner with a sexual message about Rep. Patricia Schroeder (D-CO). Schroeder's Congressional office

received an obscene message from a fax machine at the Marine Corps Air Station at New River, NC. Schroeder, who sits on Armed Services Committee in Congress, had been very critical of the Navy's investigation of the 1991 Tailhook scandal. (06/25)

Female veterans told the Senate Veterans Affairs Committee that

they had been sexually assaulted by male soldiers, their complaints to superiors were generally ignored or dismissed as untrue and veterans hospitals had been unresponsive. Jacqueline Ortiz, 29, an Army reservist who served in the Gulf War said she was "forcibly sodomized" by her sergeant. (06/30)

YEAR	1992
U. S. President	George Bush
NOW President	Patricia Ireland

EVENTS

John Schlafly, 41, the eldest son of anti-feminist Phyllis Schlafly, publicly acknowledged that he was gay. Schlafly's admission came two weeks after *QW*, a New York magazine, revealed his homosexuality without his consent. His mother, who fought ratification of the Equal Rights Amendment by suggesting there was a connection between the ERA and AIDS, denied that this and her opposition to extending civil rights protection to gays, was gay-bashing. (09/18)

Congress passed a Family Medical Leave bill which would grant workers up to 12 weeks a year of unpaid leave to obtain medical treatment for themselves or to care for a newborn, sick children, ill spouses or elderly parents. (09/10) Presi-dent Bush vetoed the bill. (09/22) Congress failed to override his veto.

The Senate Judiciary Committee reported that there were about a million attacks on women in the previous year by their husbands or lovers and another 3 million violent domestic crimes that went unreported. (10/02)

ISSUES

Economic

The largest single award in a sex discrimination case which was won against Texaco by an employee, Janella Sue Martin, was thrown out by Los Angeles Superior Court Judge Ronald E. Cappai, who had presided at the trial. A jury in 1991 had awarded Martin $20.3 million in damages and the same judge had ordered Texaco to promote her two grades. Cappai ruled that the promotion as well as the financial award must be retried, saying that the award was "so disproportionate. . . that it constitutes a manifest injustice and shocks the conscience of this court." Martin, 49, a credit supervisor, had worked for Texaco for more than 26 years and had agreed to move to Los Angeles from Houston in 1984 because Texaco promised to promote her to manager of credit. After she set up the Los Angeles credit department, Texaco transferred a male employee from Houston, to be her boss while she was on vacation. (07/20)

Legal

During the Republican Convention in Houston, TX, Operation Rescue and the Lambs of Christ attempted to blockade clinics but were outnumbered three to one by clinic defenders trained by Katherine Spillar, Feminist Majority National Coordinator, and an action team from NOW led by President Patricia Ireland. Texas NOW President Jenniffer Hudson joined the national team which included national board member Ellen Convisser, Project Stand Up for Women Director Loretta Kane, NOW's volunteer and intern coordinator Amy Tracy, Acting Press Secretary Susie Rodriques and field organizer Elizabeth McGee. Planned Parenthood provided resources for the defense of the clinics and the National Republican Coalition for Choice, led by Mary Dent Crisp, former co-chair of the Republican Party, joined the defense lines. (08/17-21)

Political

NOW President Patricia Ireland, Political Director Alice Cohan and Field Organizer Faith Evans were in Florida for NOW's "Elect Women For A Change" campaign, when Hurricane Andrew devastated the state. Working with Palm Beach, Broward and Dade NOW Chapters, they rounded up $200,000 in supplies and cash. Their 30 vehicle "Elect Women For A Change" caravan arrived at Homestead Hospital, where candidates Gwen Margolis for Congress, Elaine Gordon for the Florida House and Linda Singer Stein for County Judge, joined them to unload supplies with which the hospital was able to reopen. (08/24-28)

The founding convention of the 21st Century Party took place in Washington, D.C. with more than 230 members from 30 states in attendance to adopt a constitution and platform. Its founding principles called for women as 52% of the Party's candidates and officers who must reflect the racial and ethnic diversity of the nation; and also called for an *expanded* Bill of Rights for the 21st century. Dolores Huerta, co-founder and Vice President Emerita of the United Farm Workers of America, was elected National Chair. Eleanor Smeal, president of the Feminist Majority was elected National Secretary and Paula Craver, chief executive officer of Craver, Mathews, Smith and Company, was elected National Treasurer. Four of the original conveners of the Party were elected Vice Chairs: Patricia Ireland, president of NOW; Mel King, MIT professor and co-founder of the Rainbow Coalition; Sara Nelson, executive director of the Christic Institute; and Monica Faith Stewart, Black Women's Network, Chicago, IL. (08/29-30)

Retired Republican Congresswoman Millicent Fenwick, a champion of liberal causes and the model for the Representative Lacey Davenport character in Garry Trudeau's *Doonesbury* comic strip, died of heart failure at the age of 82. (09/16)

The Feminist Majority's campaign for gender balance broke new ground with the unanimous vote by the Los Angeles City Council in favor of proposals for gender balancing the Los Angeles Police Department (LAPD). The proposals, drafted by the Feminist Majority in conjunction with the California Women's Law Center and Los Angeles City Council member Zev Yaroslavsky, sought to increase the percentages of women in the LAPD from 14% of the force to 44%. Katherine Spillar, the Feminist Majority's National Coordinator who spearheaded the police project in Los Angeles, pointed out, "Well over half of all 911 calls are calls of violence against women. Research shows that women officers tend to respond more effectively to incidents of violence against women. And women officers are more convinced of the importance of responding to family fights as a crucial police duty." (09/09)

NOW's "Elect Women For A Change" campaign had projects running full force in Connecticut, Florida, Georgia and Tennessee, helping feminist candidates win Congressional, state and local primaries. Working with NOW President Patricia Ireland, were National Political Director Alice Cohan and Field Organizers Joan Monnig and Faith Evans. (08-11)

In Bosnia and Herzegovina, some 150 Muslim women and teenage girls, in advanced stages of pregnancy, said they were raped by Serbian nationalist fighters and imprisoned for months afterward to keep them from having abortions. (10/02)

Backlash

It was widely reported that the former leader of the Moral Majority, the Rev. Jerry Falwell, was clinging to an empire $73 million in debt and on the verge of collapse. The Thomas Road Baptist Church, used as collateral 11 times on loans and bond issues since 1981, was in the hands of the Resolution Trust Corp., the federal agency charged with salvaging the assets of failed savings and loans. A group of 2200 investors, who bought $18.8 million of now-defaulted church bonds in 1991, wanted to foreclose on the 160-acre Liberty University campus. An Arkansas Bank was collecting from Falwell's own paycheck for repayment of loans he personally secured. And his Liberty Home Studies Institute was more than $10 million in debt. As debts mounted, Falwell cut the number of stations carrying his "Old Time Gospel Hour" from 200 to 60. Falwell was planning to buy more air time to promote a new book he had written on traditional family values. (09)

148

YEAR	1992		
U. S. President	George Bush		
NOW President	Patricia Ireland		

EVENTS

Congress approved a budget of more than $400 million for breast cancer research, a three-fold increase over the previous year for the disease that hits one in every eight American women and kills 46,000 a year. The increase in funding came from the Pentagon budget. The federal budget for AIDS research was set at about $1.2 billion for 1993. (10)

President George Bush vetoed a bill to overturn the "gag rule"–the federal regulation prohibiting abortion counseling at federally financed family planning clinics–that had been upheld by the U.S. Supreme Court in 1991. The Senate voted to override the veto 73-26, (10/01) but the House failed to override with a vote of 266-148, 10 votes short. (10/02)

Democrat Bill Clinton was elected President, and Al Gore, Vice President, defeating incumbent Republican President George Bush and Vice President Dan Quayle. The electoral college vote was 370-168. (11/03)

ISSUES

Lifestyles

Education

Religion

Media

Legal

Political

On Election Day in Maryland voters endorsed by 57-43% a constitutional guarantee of a woman's right to have an abortion. In Arizona, voters rejected by 69-31% a measure that would have amended the state Constitution to ban abortion except to save a woman's life. In Iowa, voters narrowly rejected by 52% to 48% an initiative to put an Equal Rights Amendment in the state Constitution. (When the ERA was on the state ballot in 1980, it was defeated by 12%). According to exit polls, a majority of women voted for the ERA, but a larger majority of men voted against it. In fact the 1992 ERA lost because of massive gender gap–18 points: men denied women Constitutional equality. Pat Robertson and his Christian Coalition, Phyllis Schlafly and her Eagle Forum and Beverly LaHaye and Concerned Women for America, were the forces driving the campaign to defeat the amendment. In Oregon, an anti-homosexual ballot measure put up by Pat Robertson's Christian Coalition was soundly defeated, but in Colorado, a nationally-linked religious right coalition, Colorado for Family Values, succeeded in passing an initiative 54-46% that wrote discrimination against homosexuals into the state constitution. The measure allowed state agencies to discriminate against acknowledged lesbians and gay men or against those simply perceived to be homosexual. (11/03)

After nine years of debate over a pastoral letter on the role of women in society and the church, the National Conference of Catholic Bishops fell 53 votes short of a necessary two-thirds to adopt the statement that had ended by being dominated by traditional church views anyway. It was the first time that a proposed pastoral letter–an authoritative teaching of the bishops–had ever been defeated in the U.S. (11/18)

The Year of the Woman became a reality in the 1992 elections with victories across the country. The percentage of women in Congress doubled from 5% to 10% with the election.Women of color increased their representation in Congress from six seats to 14. The number of women in the Senate increased from two to six and 48 women were elected to the House of Representatives–all pro-choice. Women held more than 20% of statewide elected executive offices and increased their nationwide representation in state legislatures to 20%. A total of 224 women –141 Democrats and 83 Republicans– filed as candidates for House races this year, a record number. In many states (California, New York, Oregon, Tennessee, Florida and South Carolina) the Feminist Majority, NOW and other women's rights groups recruited feminist women to flood the ticket and run for public office. Carol Moseley Braun of Illinois became the first elected African-American woman senator; California made history by being the first state to elect two women to the U.S. Senate, Democrats Dianne Feinstein and Barbara Boxer and for the first time in many years, two senators from the same party; California also elected the first Mexican-American congresswoman, Los Angeles Democrat Lucille Roybal-Allard; Georgia and North Carolina both elected their first Black congresswomen; New York elected the first Puerto Rican woman in Congress; and Virginia elected a woman to Congress for the first time. Feminist Majority President Eleanor Smeal said, "If we keep this momentum throughout the decade, we will achieve the goal of 50% women in Congress by the year 2000. (11/03)

Audre Lorde, 58, black feminist writer and poet laureate of New York State in 1991, died of liver cancer at her home in St. Croix. (11/19)

The highest ecclesiastical court of the Presbyterian Church (USA) over-ruled a New York congregation's decision to hire an openly lesbian minister, ruling that no openly gay, sexually active person could serve as a minister of any of its 11,500 churches. The action barred the Rev. Jane Adams Spahr of San Anselmo, CA, from becoming co-pastor at the Downtown Presbyterian Church of Rochester, NY. Spahr 50, , a divorced mother of two adult sons, was ordained by the denomination four years before its General Assembly halted the ordination of gays and lesbians in 1978. (11/04)

Black women make up 35% of female seminary enrollment but when they seek a pulpit in Black Baptist churches, they find the ministry remains a bastion for Black men. Many have turned to mainline predominantly white denominations for a pulpit such as the United Methodist Church or Presbyterian Church (USA), where they still may find both sexism and racism. Rev. Claudia Copeland theorized that Black male preachers guard their pulpits because the church "has been the one place of authentic ownership for the Black male." (11/07)

Tammy Bruce, president of Los Angeles NOW, threatened a boycott of sponsors of E! Entertainment Television, because of its hiring of shock jock Howard Stern to host a weekly celebrity interview show. "When is this industry going to draw the line" she asked, adding that "through the hiring of Stern, E! was sending the message that misogyny and sexism pays and that the network was intent on perpetuating the hatred of women through Stern," E! agreed to consult with Bruce and other chapter representatives about programming ideas dealing with women's issues. (11)

Backlash

In a nationwide push for power, the Christian Coalition, a tax-exempt religious right organization founded by Pat Robertson, using covert methods, including fielding candidates who concealed their true beliefs, won hundreds of local races on Election Day. Said Ralph Reed, executive director of the Christian Coalition, "We

focused on where the real power is: in the states and in the precincts and in the neighborhoods where people live and work. . . . at school boards and at the state legislative level we had big, tremendous victories." As the Coalition gains power in local government, it will press its conservative agenda, opposing abortion and laws guaran-

teeing rights of women and homosexuals, seeking the removal of certain books from school libraries and pressing for school prayer, teaching abstinence in sex education classes and the teaching of creationism in schools. It was estimated that the Coalition had won 40% of the 500 races it had targeted. (11/03)

149

Epilogue 1993

Political power was the password for the women's rights movement at the beginning of 1993. Having closed 1992 pushing Clinton to honor his campaign promise of making his cabinet look like America, feminist leaders remained determined to shatter the political glass ceiling to regain the ground lost during the 1980's under the Reagan-Bush Administrations and the influence of the Radical Right.

The President lashed out at women's groups who were pressing him to appoint a historic Cabinet. At a year-end press conference naming Hazel O'Leary, an African-American woman to Secretary of Energy, Clinton called the women leaders "bean counters" and chastised them for promoting "quotas," not competence.

The Feminist Majority and *Ms.* Magazine immediately ordered buttons declaring, "Feminist Bean Counter and Proud of It," and feminist leaders continued to press for a woman attorney general.

The push for women in the Cabinet paid off. Clinton completed his Cabinet early in 1993 with the naming of veteran state prosecutor from Miami, Janet Reno, as the nation's first woman Attorney General. With Reno's confirmation, Clinton's Cabinet numbered five women for the highest of any presidential cabinet in United States history — Donna Shalala, Secretary of Health and Human Services; Hazel O'Leary, Secretary of the Department of Energy; Madeleine Albright, Ambassador to the United Nations;

Carol Browner, Director of the Environmental Protection Agency; and Janet Reno, Attorney General. These women, together with Laura D'Andrea Tyson, Chair of the National Council of Economic Advisors, clearly represented a political breakthrough at the top for women. Feminists were quick to point out, however, that the President's inner circle of advisers still remained primarily white and male.

Moreover, the struggle for a woman attorney general revealed that the double standard in appointments for women was still alive and well. The withdrawal of first Zoe Baird and then Kimba Wood as possible nominees for Attorney General signaled that the arrangements women appointees made for domestic workers are considered more crucial than for men appointees. In fact, Secretary of Commerce Ron Brown was permitted to quietly pay back taxes on Social Security for his domestic employees during the height of the controversy over Baird's late payment of Social Security taxes. Though Kimba Wood had followed the letter of the existing law on the employment of an undocumented immigrant worker, it did not spare her from the same fate of Zoe Baird, who improperly hired an undocumented worker.

The struggle for Cabinet appointments, behind the scenes and in the media, showed the depth and maturity of the feminist movement. Inside the White House, feminist Hillary Rodham Clinton and her colleague,

Susan Thomases, also an attorney, were front-and center advisors. Outside the White House, agitating for the appointment of more women were Judith Lichtman and Marcia Greenberg, both attorneys and Executive Directors of the Women's Legal Defense Fund and the National Women's Law Center, respectively. The National Women's Political Caucus Chair, Harriet Woods, released a daily score of Clinton appointments entitled "the mirror." Eleanor Smeal, President of the Feminist Majority, pushed with a high-visibility strategy in the media with the assistance of Jeanne Clark, Operating Officer of Anthony, Stanton & Gage, and coordinated a fax campaign to Little Rock from women activists. Patricia Ireland, attorney and President of NOW, Helen Neuborne, attorney and Executive Director of NOW LDEF, Ann Bryant, Executive Director of American Association of University Women, Gwendolyn Baker, Executive Director of the YWCA – all weighed in along with countless other women across the country invoking the ever-present power of the gender gap in voting.

The President's appointments broke another historical barrier with the naming of the second woman and the first self-described feminist to the United States Supreme Court, Judge Ruth Bader Ginsburg. Ginsburg, depicted widely as a moderate, was nevertheless not only the general counsel to the American Civil Liberties Union but also a board member of the National Organization for Women's Legal Defense and Education Fund in the 1970s. In that decade, Ginsburg won five landmark women's rights cases before the U.S. Slupreme Court and mapped a course for the inclusion of women in the equal protection clause of the 14th Amendment. During her confirmation hearings, she became the first Supreme Court appointee to clearly state to the Senate Judiciary Committee her position that the right to abortion is essential to women's equality. She condemned discrimination against homosexuals. She stated she believed that the 19th Amendment granting women the right to vote and full political citizenship, coupled with the 14th Amendment, already provided women with the basis for full legal equality under the law. But she said, in light of the long history of discrimination against women, the Equal Rights Amendment to the United States Constitution should be ratified in order to send a clarion call to the nation and to the world that women were full equal citizens in every respect.

The feminist euphoria on appointments for women continued with the announcement of Dr. Joycelyn Elders as Surgeon General of the United States. Dr. Elders, an unabashed supporter of abortion rights, sex education, family planning, AIDS prevention, school-based clinics, and preventive health care measures, was the first African-American woman named to the post.

Meanwhile, as Dr. Elders' confirmation moved forward, feminists and civil rights leaders decried the withdrawal by the President of Lani Guinier's nomination as Assistant Attorney General for Civil Rights. Guinier, considered by many to be the leading civil rights litigator in the nation, won 41 of 43 cases argued before the Supreme Court for the NAACP Legal Defense and Education Fund and was a member of the NOW Legal Defense and Education Fund board. Her nomination was withdrawn because her writings advocated a new look at the enforcement of the Voting Rights Act. Labeled by the right wing as a "quota queen" with views threatening to democracy, she was not even given a chance to defend her ideas and record before the Senate Judiciary Committee.

Her withdrawal, under a vicious attack by the radical right wing and lacking strong support from moderate Democrats in the Senate, provided a splash of cold water on feminist euphoria. It showed the power of the use of the word "quota" to stop any affirmative action proposal and the power of negative stereotyping of African-American women ("quota queen" as in "welfare queen"). Ironically, she fell victim to a post-Communist form of McCarthyism, which questioned her loyalty to democracy because she dared to vigorously enforce the Voting Rights Act and suggest new ways of solving the problem of underrepresentation of African-Americans and Latinos.

At the same time as the Ginsburg nomination was moving forward and Lani Guinier was being dropped, the backlash to affirmative action and the enforcement of the Voting Rights Act continued to be manifested in Supreme Court decisions. Early in 1993, the Supreme Court handed down two adverse decisions that sent the feminist and civil rights communities reeling.

In *Shaw v. Reno*, the Supreme Court ruled that a long, narrow North Carolina political district, designed to sufficiently represent blacks, could very well be considered unconstitutional. The district, created to comply with the Voting Rights Act of 1965, was challenged by five white North Carolina voters who claimed it amounted to racial gerry-

mandering. In Shaw, the Court claimed the new district was irregular and served to further segregate the races. Civil rights advocates feared the decision would cost racial minorities seats in Congress. Feminists feared the decision would cost the seats of the newly elected women of color. In 1993, 12 of the 48 women in the House of Representatives, or 25%, were women of color. U.S. Representative Eva Clayton (D-NC), elected president of the 1993 class of the House, was one of the two Blacks elected from North Carolina to seats created by enforcement of the Voting Rights Acts.

In a second case, the Court dramatically undermined Title VII of the Civil Rights Act of 1964, which prohibited discrimination in employment. In a 5-to-4 decision in *St. Mary's Honor Center v. Hicks,* the Supreme Court increased a worker's burden to prove employment discrimination. The Court said it was not enough for employees to show that their employer lied in dismissing the employee, but rather that the employee may also have to prove the real reason they were dismissed or denied a job or a promotion. In the past, if an employee could show that an employer's reasons were simply a pretense, they could win the case. Now, they must not only show that it was a pretense but also demonstrate the *intent* of the employer.

Meanwhile, the women in Congress, having been sworn in as the largest freshwoman class in Congress, departed from the tradition of being seen but not heard in their first year. The four newly-elected Democratic women of the Senate, led by incumbent Senator Barbara Mikulski, served notice that they would carry the flag of reproductive choice onto the floor of the senate, and that they would no longer permit poor women and federal employees to be denied abortion funding without a fierce fight. The day after this declaration, abortion rights supporters won their first Medicaid-funding vote in 10 years by a narrow 15-14 in the Senate Appropriations Committee.

Senator Carol Moseley-Braun, the first African-American woman to be elected to the Senate, interrupted Senator Orrin Hatch in committee on a point of personal privilege and told him that she could not tolerate the comparison of the *Dred Scott* decision with *Roe v. Wade.* In the same week, Senator Braun notified the entire Senate that the Daughters of the Confederacy symbol, which contained the Confederate flag, could not be provided the imprimatur of the United States Senate. In a shocking reversal, the Senate, which had previously indicated it would approve the symbol, actually defeated the proposal overwhelmingly. Senator Joseph Biden, Chair of the Judiciary Committee, said that he had rarely seen one speech on the Senate floor that so dramatically changed the outcome of a vote.

On the House side, the women reinforcements did not succeed in changing the vote on Medicaid funding for abortion. The House defeatedthat measure by a resounding 255 to 178. If *only* the women in the House had been able to vote on the Medicaid funding provision, it would have passed overwhelmingly. Seventy-five percent of the women *voted for* Medicaid funding, but 56% of the men *voted against* it, for a whopping 41% gender gap. Although the women of the House did not prevail, they were heard— as veteran Congresswoman Cardiss Collins (D-Ill) and first-year Congresswoman Cynthia

McKinney (D-GA), together with Representative Nita Lowey (D-NY), led the floor fight to provide abortion funding for poor women.

The outlook for abortion rights, however, improved dramatically in 1993 with President Clinton beginning the new year on the anniversary of *Roe v. Wade* (January 22nd) by announcing the repeal of the Mexico City policy that denied United States foreign aid to countries providing abortion funding to women; announcing a repeal of the Reagan-Bush Gag Rule that prohibited doctors in federally-funded clinics from providing abortion counseling; lifting the ban on fetal tissue research; and encouraging the research and development of RU-486 in this country.

Despite the political victories, the violence at abortion clinics continued. Americans were shocked to hear that Dr. David Gunn was murdered – shot three times in the back at close range – by a fanatic anti-abortion demonstrator outside an abortion clinic in Pensacola, Florida. While Gunn, at the rear of the clinic, was being shot, Rescue America demonstrators led by former Ku Klux Klan member John Burt demonstrated out front.

Throughout the spring of 1993, Operation Rescue trained an "Impact Team" in Central Florida to harass and intimidate abortion providers, health care workers and patients. Neither the State of Florida nor the federal government entered to protect the Florida clinics. The Feminist Majority Clinic Defense Project, in conjunction with the local NOW chapters and the Florida Abortion Council, trained hundreds of volunteer clinic defenders. In May, NOW led a Mother's Day March for Abortion Rights in Pensacola numbering some 3,000 participants to show the strong support for choice throughout the state.

At mid-year, feminists successfully defended abortion clinics against a "Seven Cities of Refuge" attack by Operation Rescue, which fizzled as pro-choice activists everywhere outnumbered and outmaneuvered Operation Rescue. Shortly after, feminists braced for Pope John Paul II's visit to Colorado amidst his railing that the ideology of some Catholic feminists led to "forms of nature worship and the celebration of myths and symbols."

The Catholic Church, under siege by charges of pedophilia against its priests and the attendant lawsuits, continued to grasp at the mantle of moral authority by preaching no abortion, no artificial contraception, and no sterilization. The Pope, looking desperately for an excuse in his first public statement on pedophilia, blamed an atmosphere of promiscuous sex in the United States, even though some charges dated back forty years. The worst case was in Canada – a one billion dollar lawsuit in Quebec against priests and nuns for sexual abuse and torture of children over a twenty-five year period.

The violence and intimidation at the abortion clinics continued: shots rang out from a drive-by shooting into abortion clinic windows and even, in one case, into the home of a physician who performed abortions. The number of butyric acid attacks on clinics increased and the death threats to physicians and health care providers continued to climb.

At the same time, the response of Congress, despite the 1992 election wins, was slow. At mid-year, the Freedom of Access to Clinics Act had only passed out of Senate and House committees. To date, the FBI has classified clinic violence not as domestic terrorism but simply as a "local" problem.

And the fight continued on other issues. The constitutionality of the "Don't Ask, Don't Tell" compromise on gay men and lesbians in the military was instantly challenged in court.

Feminists pushed the Violence Against Women Act in Congress. On the local and state levels, women initiated sex bias and sexual harassment cases in unprecedented numbers. Gender-balance bills mandating governors to appoint equal numbers of women and men to boards and commissions were introduced in some 16 states in 1993.

The stronger the forward advance by feminism, the more the backlash grew. Rush Limbaugh's book, *The Way Things Ought To Be,* was high on the best-seller list throughout much of 1992 and was among the top ten books in 1993.

Conservative forces and neoconservatives attempted to discredit Anita Hill. David Brock's *The Real Anita Hill: The Untold Story* also hit the best-seller list in 1993. Brock claimed that his "objective" and "unbiased" research and investigation uncovered evidence that Professor Hill had lied. But the real story revealed Brock had strong conservative credentials as a former fellow at the Heritage Foundation, a former editorial writer for *The Washington Times,* and a contributor to *The American Spectator.* But most importantly, both the Bradley Foundation and the Olin Foundation, organizations that promote right-wing causes, helped to bankroll Brock's book. Perhaps most interesting, the head of the Olin Foundation, William

Simon, also served as Finance Chair of the Citizens' Committee to Confirm Clarence Thomas. So much for an "objective and unbiased" orchestration of the backlash.

Feminists were not to be outdone on the best seller list, however. *Women Who Run With The Wolves* by Dr. Clarissa Pinkola Estes broke into the hard-cover best seller list in 1993, while Deborah Tannen's *You Just Don't Understand,* Gloria Steinem's *Revolution from Within,* and Susan Faludi's *Backlash: The Undeclared War on American Women,* remained high on the paperback best-seller list in 1993.

And the victories continued. Anti-clinic-violence bills were passed in several states. The unpaid Family and Medical Leave Act was finally passed into law by Congress and signed by the President.

And the "first woman" phenomena continued. The first woman ever to command a military base took charge of a base her father once commanded. Ground was broken on the first war memorial dedicated to women – the Vietnam Women's Memorial. The first woman jockey won the Belmont Stakes and was the first woman ever to win any of the Triple Crown races. Florence "Flo-Jo" Griffith Joyner replaced Arnold Schwarzenegger as head of the President's Commission on Fitness. The first woman baseball-park announcer was hired in California.

And the struggle for political power continued. A woman, Kim Campbell, became Prime Minister of Canada; Hanna Suchocka was serving as Prime Minister of Poland; even more surprisingly, Turkey's ruling party chose a woman, Tansu Ciller, as its leader, ensuring her designation as the nation's first woman Prime Minister.

Worldwide, six countries had female prime ministers, three had female presidents and three female governors-general. However, the United Nations Human Development Report for 1993 concluded, "No country treats its women as well as it treats its men, a disappointing result after so many years of debate on gender equality, so many struggles by women and so many changes in national laws."

"Women are the world's largest excluded group," the United Nations Report declared. "Even though they make up half the adult population. . . they make up just over 105 of the world's parliamentary representatives and consistently less than 4% of Cabinet ministers or other positions of executive authority."

Two-thirds of the world's illiterates are women. While the number of women in the workplace has risen dramatically to 42% in industrialized countries and 34% world wide, the jobs they can hold continue to be of lower status and lower pay. And in Russia, the collapse of communism has not improved women's lives but worsened them: over the past two years, some 70% of the lay-offs have been of female workers; Soviet women, who once made about 70% of what men made, now make 40%.

Furthermore, barbaric customs continue to jeopardize the very lives of women: female infanticide in China, genital mutilation in Africa, forced prostitution in Thailand and Vietnam, and wife-burning in India.

On June 15 in Vienna, a coalition of about 950 women's groups from around the world came together at the U.N. World Conference on Human Development and emerged as the strongest and most effective lobby. Their

Global Campaign for Women's Human Rights won major victories in several ways: in winning unusually strong wording in support of rights for women worldwide and in the call for the end of sexual harassment, exploitation, and gender-based violence. U.S. Secretary of State Warren Christopher pledged that Washington would press for the appointment of a U.N. Special Rapporteur on Violence Against Women and said the Clinton Administration would seek Senate approval of the *Convention on the Elimination of all Forms of Discrimination Against Women.*

In the United States, the fight goes on: the largest number of women ever filed as candidates for the state legislatures of New Jersey and Virginia, the only states to have races in 1993. Feminists fanned out all over the country to recruit more women than ever before to run for political office in 1994.

The pace of the feminist chronicles intensifies, as does the backlash. The stakes grow higher as women get closer and closer to real power. In every way, nearly every day, the feminist struggles affect the daily lives of American women and men. Even the harshest critics of feminism would say that the feminist journey of the last 40 years has made a difference.

Perhaps the best report card earned by feminists so far is the fact that one public opinion poll after another in the past 20 years indicated that most women in the United States believe the feminist movement had improved their lives.

August, 1993

PART III

THE EARLY
DOCUMENTS

NATIONAL ORGANIZATION FOR WOMEN
(N.O.W.)
Statement of Purpose

*(Adopted at the organizing conference in Washington, D. C.,
October 29, 1966)*

We, men and women, who hereby constitute ourselves as the National Organization for Women, believe that the time has come for a new movement toward true equality for all women in America, and toward a fully equal partnership of the sexes, as part of the world-wide revolution of human rights now taking place within and beyond our national borders.

The purpose of NOW is to take action to bring women into full participation in the mainstream of American society now, exercising all the privileges and responsibilities thereof in truly equal partnership with men.

We believe the time has come to move beyond the abstract argument, discussion and symposia over the status and special nature of women which has raged in America in recent years; the time has come to confront, with concrete action, the conditions that now prevent women from enjoying the equality of opportunity and freedom of which is their right, as individual Americans, and as human beings.

NOW is dedicated to the proposition that women, first and foremost, are human beings, who, like all other people in our society, must have the chance to develop their fullest human potential. We believe that women can achieve such equality only by accepting to the full the challenges and responsibilities they share with all other people in our society, as part of the decision-making mainstream of American political, economic and social life.

We organize to initiate or support action, nationally, or in any part of this nation, by individuals or organizations, to break through the silken curtain of prejudice and discrimination against women in government, industry, the professions, the churches, the political parties, the judiciary, the labor unions, in education, science, medicine, law, religion and every other field of importance in American society. Enormous changes taking place in our society make it both possible and urgently necessary to advance the unfinished revolution of women toward true equality, now. With a life span lengthened to nearly 75 years it is no longer either necessary or possible for women to devote the greater part of their lives to child-rearing; yet childbearing and rearing which continues to be a most important part of most women's lives—still is used to justify barring women from equal professional and economic participation and advance.

Today's technology has reduced most of the productive chores which women once performed in the home and in mass-production industries based upon routine unskilled labor. This same technology has virtually eliminated the quality of muscular strength as a criterion for filling most jobs, while intensifying American industry's need for creative intelligence. In view of this new industrial revolution created by automation in the mid-twentieth century, women can and must participate in old and new fields of society in full equality—or become permanent outsiders .

Despite all the talk about the status of American women in recent years, the actual position of women in the United States has declined, and is declining, to an alarming degree throughout the 1950's and '60s. Although 46.4% of all American women between the ages of 18 and 65 now work outside the home, the overwhelming majority—75%—are in routine clerical, sales, or factory jobs, or they are household workers, cleaning women, hospital attendants. About two-thirds of Negro women workers are in the lowest paid service occupations. Working women are becoming increasingl—not less—concentrated on the bottom of the job ladder. As a consequence full-time women workers today earn on the average only 60% of what men earn, and that wage gap has been increasing over the past twenty-five years in every major industry group. In 1964, of all women with a yearly income, 89% earned under $5,000 a year; half of all full-time year round women workers earned less than $3,690; only 1.4% of full- time year round women workers had an annual income of $10,000 or more.

Further, with higher education increasingly essential in today's society, too few women are entering and finishing college or going on to graduate or professional school. Today, women earn only one in three of the B.A.'s and M.A.'s granted, and one in ten of the Ph.D.'s .

In all the professions considered of importance to society, and in the executive ranks of industry and government, women are losing ground. Where they are present it is only a token handful. Women comprise less than 1% of federal judges; less than 4% of all lawyers; 7% of doctors. Yet women represent 51% of the U.S. population. And, increasingly men are replacing women in the top positions in secondary and elementary schools, in social work, and in libraries—once thought to be women's fields,

Official pronouncements of the advance in the status of women hide not only the reality of this dangerous decline, but the fact that nothing is being done to stop it. The excellent reports of the President's Commission on the Status of Women and of the State Commissions have not been fully implemented. Such Commissions have power only to advise. They have no power to enforce their recommendations; nor have they the freedom to organize American women and men to press for action on them. The reports of these commissions have, however created a basis upon which it is now possible to build.

Discrimination in employment on the basis of sex is now prohibited by federal law, in Title VII of the Civil Rights Act of 1964. But although nearly one-third of the cases brought before the Equal Employment Opportunity Commission during the first year dealt with sex discrimination and the proportion is increasing dramatically, the Commission has not made clear its intention to enforce the law with the same seriousness on behalf of women as of other victims of discrimination. Many of these cases were Negro women, who are the victims of the double discrimination of race and sex. Until now, too few women's organizations and official spokesmen have been willing to speak out against these dangers facing women. Too many women have been restrained by the fear of being called "feminist."

There is no civil rights movement to speak for women, as there has been for Negroes and other victims of discrimination. The National Organization for Women must therefore begin to speak.

WE BELIEVE that the power of American law, and the protection guaranteed by the U. S. Constitution to the civil rights of all individuals, must be effectively applied and enforced to isolate and remove patterns of sex discrimination, to ensure equality of opportunity in employment and education, and equality of civil and political rights and responsibilities on behalf of women, as well as for Negroes and other deprived groups.

We realize that women's problems are linked to many broader questions of social justice; their solution will require concerted action by many groups. Therefore, convinced that human rights for all are indivisible, we expect to give active support to the common cause of equal rights for all those who suffer discrimination and deprivation, and we call upon other organizations committed to such goals to support our efforts toward equality for women.

WE DO NOT ACCEPT the token appointment of a few women to high-level positions in government and industry as a substitute for a serious continuing effort to recruit and advance women according to their individual abilities. To this end, we urge American government and industry to mobilize the same resources of ingenuity and command with which they have solved problems of far greater difficulty than those now impeding the progress of women.

WE BELIEVE that this nation has a capacity at least as great as other nations, to innovate new social institutions which will enable women to enjoy true equality of opportunity and responsibility in society, without conflict with their responsibilities as mothers and homemakers. In such innovations, America does not lead the Western world, but lags by decades behind many European countries. We do not accept the traditional assumption that a woman has to choose between marriage and motherhood, on the one hand, and serious participation in industry or the professions on the other. We question the present expectation that all normal women will retire from job or profession for 10 or 15 years, to devote their full time to raising children, only to reenter the job market at a relatively minor level. This in itself, is a deterrent to the aspirations of women, to their acceptance into management or professional training courses, and to the very possibility of equality of opportunity or real choice, for all but a few women. Above all, we reject the assumption that these problems are the unique responsibility of each individual women, rather than a basic social dilemma which society must solve. True equality of opportunity and freedom of choice for women requires such practical, and possible innovations as a nationwide network of child-care center which will make it unnecessary for women to retire completely from society until their children are grown, and national programs to provide retraining for women who have chosen to care for their own children full-time.

WE BELIEVE that it is as essential for every girl to be educated to her full potential of human ability as it is for every boy—with the knowledge that such education is the key to effective participation in today's economy and that, for a girl as for boy, education can only be serious where there is expectation that it be used in society. We believe that American educators are capable of devising means of imparting such expectations to girl students. Moreover, we consider the decline in the proportion of women receiving higher and professional education to be evidence of discrimination. This discrimination may take the form of quotas against the admission of women to colleges, and professional schools; lack of encouragement by parents, counselors and educators; denial of loans or fellowships; or the traditional or arbitrary procedures in graduate and professional training geared in terms of men, which inadvertently discriminate against women. We believe that the same serious attention must be given to high school dropouts who are girls as to boys.

WE REJECT the current assumptions that a man must carry the sole burden of supporting himself, his wife, and family, and that a woman is automatically entitled to lifelong support by a man upon her marriage, or that marriage, home and family are primarily woman's world and responsibility—hers to dominate—his to support. We believe that a true partnership between the sexes demands a different concept of marriage an equitable sharing of the

162

responsibilities of home and children and of the economic burdens of their support. We believe that proper recognition should be given to the economic and social value of homemaking and child-care. To these ends we will seek to open a reexamination of laws and mores governing marriage and divorce, for we believe that the current state of "half-equality" between the sexes discriminates against both men and women, and is the cause of much unnecessary hostility between the sexes.

WE BELIEVE that women must now exercise their political rights and responsibility as American citizens. They must refuse to be segregated on the basis of sex into separate-and-not-equal ladies auxiliaries in the political parties, and they must demand representation according to their numbers in the regularly constituted part committees—at local, state, and national levels—and in the informal power structure, participating fully in the selection of candidates and political decision-making, and running for office themselves.

IN THE INTERESTS OF THE HUMAN DIGNITY OF WOMEN, we will protest, and endeavor to change, the false image of women now prevalent in the mass media, and in the texts, ceremonies, laws, and practices of our major social institutions. Such images perpetuate contempt for women by society and by women for themselves. We are similarly opposed to all policies and practices—in church, state, college, factory, or office—which, in the guise of protectiveness, not only deny opportunities but also foster in women self-denigration, dependence, and evasion of responsibility, undermine their confidence in their own abilities and foster contempt for women.

NOW WILL HOLD ITSELF INDEPENDENT OF ANY POLITICAL PARTY in order to mobilize the political power of all women and men intent on our goals. We will strive to ensure that no party, candidate, president, senator, governor, congressman, or any public official who betrays or ignores the principle of full equality between the sexes is elected or appointed to office. If it is necessary to mobilize the votes of men and women who believe in our cause, in order to win for women the final right to be fully free and equal human beings, we so commit ourselves.

WE BELIEVE THAT women will do most to create a new image of women by acting now, and by speaking out in behalf of their own equality, freedom, and human dignity—not in pleas for special privilege, nor in enmity toward men, who are also victims of the current, half-equality between the sexes—but in an active, self-respecting partnership with men. By so doing, women will develop confidence in their own ability to determine actively, in partnership with men, the conditions of their life, their choices, their future and their society.

NATIONAL ORGANIZATION FOR WOMEN (N.O.W.)

AN INVITATION TO JOIN - SEPTEMBER, 1966

N.O.W. is a new national organization being formed "To take action to bring women into full participation in the mainstream of American society NOW, assuming all the privileges and responsibilities thereof in truly equal partnership with men."

With so many Americans consciously concerned with full participation of all our citizens and with dramatic progress at many levels in recent years, the time is ripe for concerted directed national action. The report of the President's Commission on the Status of Women, "American Women" has laid out a broad field of action. Governor's Commissions in virtually every state in the union have studied or are studying the situation in their states and many are working to modernize their laws and practices. An Interdepartmental Committee, advised by the Citizens Advisory Council on the Status of Women, has responsibility for promoting full partnership within the federal government. The Civil Rights Act of 1964 prohibits discrimination in employment on the ground of sex, as well as of race, religion or national origin, and the Alabama jury case of 1966, *White vs. Crook*, brings women under the "equal protection of the law" as provided in the 5th and 14th amendments of the Constitution.

The basis has thus been laid for realizing the democratic American goal of full participation and equal partnership for all citizens. We are convinced, however, that only with continuing pressure and action by those most concerned can we assure the gains that are in sight and prevent the dilution of the goals.

Through its broad range of individual members, N.O.W. will build upon the work of and cooperate closely with other organizations with similar goals, action and non-action, private and public, women's organizations and organizations concerned with specific issues and fields of action. N.O.W. will identify areas in which action is needed and provide leadership in pursuing appropriate courses of action.

As an organization of individuals, not delegates or representatives, N.O.W. will be able to act promptly. It will not generally engage in independent research but will act on the basis of information and recommendations available from status of women commissions, government agencies and specialized organizations. As a private, voluntary, self-selected group it will establish its own procedures and not be limited in its targets for action or methods of operation by official protocol.

Membership is open to any individual who is committed to our purpose. Initial dues of $5.00 are payable to the Temporary Chairman. All who join prior to October 15, 1966, will be charter members and will participate in organizational and program decisions and in the election of officers.

Temporary Steering Committee
Dr. Kathryn F. Clarenbach, Temporary Chairman
2229 Eton Ridge, Madison, Wisconsin 53705
Miss Dorothy Haener, Michigan
Mrs. Esther Johnson, District of Columbia
Dr. Pauli Murray, New York
Mrs. Inka O'Hanrahan, California
Mrs. Betty Talkington, Iowa
Dr. Caroline Ware, Virginia

NOW's First Election Ballot

Attachment A

NOW 10/26/66

Nominees for National Officers and Executive Board 1966-67

Chairman of the Board:	Kathryn Clarenbach (Wis.)
President:	Betty Friedan (N. Y.)
Executive Vice President:	Aileen Hernandez (Calif.)*
Vice President:	Richard Graham (D.C.)
Secretary-Treasurer:	Caroline Davis (Mich.)

Other Board Members:
Boland, Colleen (Ill.)
Conroy, Catherine (Wis. and Ill.)
Degler, Carl (N. Y.)
Drews, Elizabeth (Ore.)
Fox, Muriel (N.Y.)
Furness, Betty (N.Y.)
Haener, Dorothy (Mich.)
Hart, Jane (D.C., Mich.)
Hedgeman, Anna (N.Y.)
Indritz, Phineas (Md., D.C.)
Lewis, Rev. Dean (Pa.)
O'Hanrahan, Inka (Calif.)
Plante, Patricia (N.Y.)
Purvis, Eve (Indiana)**
Roe, Charlotte (N.Y.)
Rossi, Alice (Ill.)
Schletzer, Vera (Minn.)**
Schwartz, Edna (Minn.)**
Simchak, Mora (D.C.)

* Subject to nominee's acceptance, following effective date of her resignation as Commissioner of EEOC.

** Subject to nominee's acceptance, not yet asked.

First Memo to National Board Members

November 29, 1966

MEMO TO: NOW Board Members

FROM: Kathryn F. Clarenbach, Chairman of the Board

By now you have all received a first mailing of materials and know that NOW is in business. The November 20th Board meeting in New York was well attended (18 members present) and we worked out temporary operating procedures to enable orderly functioning until the constitution is redrafted and approved. Minutes of that meeting as well as the October 29th and 30th meeting in Washington will be distributed by mail prior to the next Board meeting.

Will each of you please send me a letter of acceptance of your Board position? In the informality of getting organized this step was by-passed.

In the same letter will you also specify preference of dates of the next Board meeting? We agreed in New York to convene next in Chicago during the week of February 20, 1967. This will be a two-day meeting to consider constitution and task forces. As we want to accommodate schedules of the largest number of Board members, will you please indicate at least whether mid-week or week-end would be possible and which would be preferable. We will notify you as soon as possible of precise dates and place in Chicago.

At least two weeks prior to the February Board meeting you will receive a copy of the re-drafted constitution, and a short statement prepared by the temporary convener of each task force indicating philosophy, scope and possible implementation. We can all arrive at the meeting on somewhat the same wave length and make the best use of our time together.

Task force statements will be prepared by:

Education	- Elizabeth Drews
Employment	- Dorothy Haener
Legal and Political Rights	- Jane Hart
Family Life (Social Innovation)	- Sister Mary Joel Read
Poverty	- Anna A. Hedgeman
Mass Media Image	- Dean Lewis
NOW Membership	- Gretchen Squires
Finances	- to be assigned

A suggested outline for the brief presentation as been prepared by Sister Mary Joel Read and will go out tomorrow to each of the above.

The press conference in New York on November 21st was remarkably well-attended and handled. Muriel Fox and Betty Friedan gave an enormous amount of themselves in setting up the entire weekend.

On Tuesday, November 22nd, the three E.E.O.C. Commissioners received a NOW delegation for an hour and a half. Betty Friedan, Anna Hedgeman, Phineas Indritz, Marguerite Rawalt (our legal counsel) and I were all present. Prior to that Betty Friedan, Jane Hart and I were interviewed on television in D.C., and Betty and I had an inspection tour of our Washington headquarters — Courtesy Services. The Headquarters Committee is to be commended in its choice of this service and the smooth procedure it has set up.

The executive Committee (Betty Friedan, Anna Hedgeman, Richard Graham, Caroline Davis and I) will function between Board meetings Any steps beyond those which we five have been empowered to take will be referred to the entire Board.

I look forward to receipt of your response regarding Board position and February dates.

Thank you.

NOW TASK FORCE ON EDUCATION

(Background Comments of the Substitute Temporary Convener
Helen Schleman, May 1967)

I.   Composition of Task Force - We are dealing in an area where only the word of well-known experts gets much attention. It is therefore recommended that every effort be made to recruit a few well recognized persons for this group whose recommendations will carry weight. Suggestion: 1) Rosemary Park, who has spoken out frankly about women's lack of aspiration to achieve at top levels*, 2) Mary Keyserling, whose agency is also on record as believing that lack of aspiration is a critical factor in women's achievement**, 3) John Macy, who recognizes the importance of motivation and of changing fathers' expectation for their daughters***, 4) Alice Rossi, who is already active on another task force, but whose reputation for pinpointing needs for fundamental change is such that we need her support for any undertakings that focus on this effort, 5) Dr. Jean Paul Mather, Executive Vice President of University City Science Center at Philadelphia Pennsylvania who has appeared on various national programs, speaking of the necessity of using womanpower at top levels (e.g., Intercollegiate Associated Women Students, National Education Association), and 6) Eli Ginzberg, who is well known for his knowledge of womanpower and who is currently directing a national-scale study being undertaken by a research group of Columbia University. (The study, financed by a $235,000 grant from the Rockefeller Brothers Fund, is to evaluate counseling in areas of education and employment. It will undoubtedly include study of the influences which motivate young girls in junior high school and high school, were aspirations for high achievement begin to take form.)[1]

II.   Focus of Immediate Attention: There are undoubtedly many reasons why women do not hold influential leadership positions, at high levels of our national life, in proportion to their numbers in the populations, or to their numbers in the labor force. Two far-reaching and all-pervading attitudinal factors, however, seem to be among the chief culprits; 1) Women's own lack of aspirations to achieve levels commensurate with their intellectual ability and 2) the limiting sex-oriented self-concept and "other-sex" concepts taught to young children (and continuously expressed to them as expectations), which result in traditional ways of thinking about women by men in decision-making positions (and even make it difficult for many mature women to achieve a broad, inclusive self-concept).

Attitudes can be changed. It is suggested that the NOW Task Force on Education focus it efforts 1) on raising the aspirations of girls and women at all stages of education and 2) on combating the limiting influence of traditional sex-oriented self-concepts and expectations. This is no under-taking for amateurs. High aspiration must be preceded by motivation. Motivation in common sense terms, is made up of all of the factors that cause a person to want (to aspire) to do a certain thing, to reach (aspire to) a certain goal. These factors are legion.

III.   Specific Action To Be Undertaken: (Note: It is recognized that there will be overlap with the work of other task forces. Obviously, there must be good communication to avoid duplication of effort. For

168

instance, the work of the Task Force on the Mass Media Image of Women ties in directly in the aspirations and motivations of junior high school girls, high school girls, and women — not to say the image held by boys and men.) It is suggested that the NOW Education Task Force:

1. Make contact with Dr. Ginzberg regarding his current study for the following purposes: 1) to inform him of our interest and concern in the study as it pertains to the aspirations and motivations, or lack thereof, of girls and women toward high goals of achievement, and 2) to seek his counsel regarding useful steps we as a task force might take to raise the aspirations of girls and combat the traditional, limited self-concept so many of them hold.

2. Make contact with junior high school and high school counselors of both girls and boys to persuade them to try to inspire girls to aspire to educate themselves to the limit of their intellectual capacity and then to *use* their education fully.[2] We should place articles in their professional journals which will give specific information about scope of opportunities for both girls and boys, will discuss the current life-patterns of women and men that both boys and girls need to be familiar with, and will emphasize the importance to girls themselves, as well as to our whole society and economy, of their aspiring to use their full intellectual talents in top-level spots. Counselors need very much to adopt a new outlook and set of expectations for girls if the girls themselves are to develop higher aspirations and a new self-concept.[3] This is a crucial change that must be emphasized in every way possible.

3. Make contact with school administrators and try to persuade them of the importance of making successful-outside-the-home, loved and respected women models visible to boys and girls. Urge them to use them in the school system as well as to bring them in from the outside community to demonstrate that women are expected to participate at significant levels outside the home.

4. Make contact with parents, PTAs, any way possible to make known what the current situation is and to urge higher expectations for their daughters equal to those they hold for their sons

5. Make contact with men's service club. in a variety of ways - through their publications programs, etc., with particular emphasis on the father's role in rising the aspirations of his daughter by his own expectations of her.

The ways to effect change of the traditional self-concepts held by many girls that limit their aspirations are as many and varied as imagination will produce. The same holds for changing the traditional expectations held by others for girls and women, We need a working task force to agree on limited objectives and specific approaches.

Summary of Proposed Action
It is suggested that NOW name at least 3 or 4 members of the Task Force on Education at once to begin work in the areas indicated.
A.Specific objectives: 1) raise the aspirations of girls and women at all stages of education and 2) combat the limiting influence of traditional

sex-oriented self-concepts and expectations.

B. Some specific action programs:

1. Make contact with Dr. Ginzberg. . . .

2. Make contact with junior high school and high school counselors. . . .

3. Make contact with school administrators. . . .

4. Make contact with parents, PTAs. . . .

5. Make contact with men's service club. . . .

* "On the subject of women's education, Rosemary Park, in her final report as president of Barnard College, declared that the traditional lack of scope in women's aspirations is the factor most responsible for their absence in posts of leadership." (From Intercollegiate Press Bulletin; Vol. 31, #35, May 1, 1967.)

** "An important part of the answer to the disparity in women's educational attainment and earnings lies in the goals and aspirations of these women when they were girls." (U.S. Department of Labor, Women's Bureau, April l, 1967, WB67-281)

*** "This educational fallout is due largely to lack of motivation, but a negative attitude on the part of parents toward college for their daughters is an influential factor. I think that fathers are especially responsible in this. Fathers, in particular, need to abandon the assumption that their daughters really cannot learn math, or that it's not quite feminine to major in physics or chemistry, or that the engineering degree is strictly a male degree." (John W. Macy, Jr., "Unless We Begin Now," Vital Speeches of the Day, p. 680, September 1, 1966. Paper delivered at Atlanta, Georgia, July 25, 1966.)

[1] School and Society, Vol. 95, p. 286. Summer 1967. Columbia University Study.

[2] "Women also encounter manipulative counseling. 'A counselor will tell a woman that it really doesn't matter what she studies in college because she will get married and won't have to work. But studies show this is not true.'" Eli Ginzberg, "Study of Education and Job Counseling." School and Society, Vol. 95, p. 286. Summer, 1967. Columbia University study.)

TASK FORCE ON WOMEN IN POVERTY
(Task Force Report-1967)

A. We start with a concern for the plight of women who now live in poverty.The most serious victims of sex-discrimination in this country are the women at the bottom, including those who, unsupported, head a great percentage of families in poverty; those women who work at low-paying, marginal jobs, or who cannot find work; and the seriously increasing number of high school dropouts who are girls. No adequate attention is being given to these women by any of the existing poverty programs.

B. N.O.W. will work to insure that all federal poverty-related programs, including the Job Corps and the MDTA, shall be administered without discrimination on the basis of sex and shall provide serious training for disadvantaged girls and women, as well as boys and men, in order that they may take a rewarding and productive role in society. We will fight the current practice of ignoring women and girls in such government programs; of providing them with training, under the M.D.T.A. of only the beauty care or unskilled clerical sort that is not geared to the future or even to the hope of adequate pay.

C. Our concern with these problems leaves us to seek broader and more meaningful expansion of economic opportunities. There cannot be significant opportunities for women (especially those "at the bottom of the heap") unless there is room for them to move into. We cannot simply ask that women enter fierce competition for scarce opportunities, setting one group against another. The poverty program has brought to light serious inadequacies and the patchwork quality of some of the present approaches to job training, job creation, education for potential jobs, the lack of regional and city planning, the failure to identify and utilize the already existing experiences of women as well as men for whom the program is intended. Furthermore, full employment is essential to any decent plan for economic development that will meet the needs of all women. `This fact is especially true for women in poverty. We see the need for job innovation at every level of employment in which women are concentrated. Already existing skills of women (home nursing, teachers aides, day care and recreation work, foster parents, etc.) can be utilized to meet unmet needs in the areas of education and many other social services, including rewarding employment.

Submitted by: Dr. Anna Arnold Hedgeman, Chairman

TASK FORCE ON LEGAL AND POLITICAL RIGHTS
(1967)

Goals:

*A campaign for women to assume equal rights and responsibilities as American citizens, including full participation in political decision-making in the power structure of the political parties, in the selection of candidates and the formation of national policy, in the holding of public office, and in service to the nation, including military service and jury service.

*A campaign for the abolition of ladies' auxiliaries and any other separate-but-not-equal organizations which segregate women, or other forms of "special" representation of women, outside the decision-making mainstream in the Republican, Democratic or any other political party.

*A campaign to get women to run for political office and to run for membership in the regularly constituted party committees on all levels —local, state and national—and to seek assignments on committees concerned with all aspects of government — space, finance, and urban affairs—refusing to be segregated as "Chairman of Women's Division," or to be restricted to the kind of health and welfare post considered traditionally more suitable for women. On all other political issues, we may be quite divided among ourselves, nor will we campaign to elect any woman just because she is a woman—but we will campaign to support a woman, or man who actively fights for our basic interests, and to defeat any man or woman who betrays our interests, or gives mere lip service.

*We will do our best to awaken in the largest possible number of American voters an awareness of the basic interest of women's unfinished equality, and a candidate's record on it, as burning as we already know it to be in ourselves.

*Support federal civil rights legislation in 1967 which includes provisions prohibiting any distinction based on sex in selection of federal and state juries.

*Support and encourage women seeking to invoke their right to equal protection of the law under the United States Constitution, without discrimination based on sex, particularly in fields such as public employment, public education, laws and official practices which deny equal opportunity to women.

ACTION, FOLLOW THROUGH:

The continuing duty of the task force on legal and Political Rights

1. Review treatment of men and women in regard to their legal and political rights at the municipal, state and federal level.

2. Present the results of the review to the national executive committee of NOW for evaluation and plans for appropriate action.

Evidence of progress towards the stated goals of NOW should be given equal attention and credit should be given to appropriate authorities.

In 1963, it was noted in the Report of the Committee on Civil and Political Rights to the Presidents' Commission on the Status of Women that the bulk of the subject matter of this Task Force is in the jurisdiction of the State Legislatures. Therefore, members of the Task Force on the state level should accumulate and channel information from as many sources as are available to the national executive committee of NOW. That committee should plan appropriate action which can be effected through mobilization of all the members in the state in question.

The nature of the information to which the task force should address itself should include state laws and city ordinances which treat women differently from men in a manner wholly untenable in the light of present day multiple activities for which women are entirely qualified.

It is strongly advised that a realistic attitude be adopted in the matter of changing state and local laws to meet the goals of NOW. Our laws are expressions of cultural patterns which are no longer acceptable to us. Changing them, however, may require a great deal of time during which a process of education proceeds. This serves to change the pattern and, in turn, builds pressure that finally achieves the goal.

Political Rights

Evidence indicates that a poor percentage of eligible women voters actually do vote. The task force should update the data on this subject, (obligations and rights should balance). Further, the Task Force should investigate the status and treatment of women within State Political Party organizations. State Party policy is usually reflected at the local level. Determine the degree to which the political party utilizes women at the policy level. The pattern in both major parties has been male chairmen and female vice-chairmen. This is a device which serves to structure the division and stereotype the activities of women within the party structure. If possible it would be useful to determine the ratio of financial contributions of male and female who are active in a party organization on a percentage basis.

Greater participation within the party structure will produce more party activists, candidates for office and voters.

Submitted by: Mrs. Janey Hart, Chairman

TASK FORCE ON EQUAL OPPORTUNITY
IN EMPLOYMENT (1967)

GOALS:

A campaign for rigorous enforcement of Title VII of the Civil Rights Act of 1964, which will insist that all the tools of the law proved effective in eliminating racial discrimination be applied to the elimination of discrimination on the basis of sex in private employment.

1. Demand immediate amendment of the federal Executive Order No. 11246, to prohibit discrimination on the basis of sex in government employment, and in employment under government contract.

2. Active encouragement and assistance to women in bringing complaints against sex discrimination, under federal and state equal employment opportunity laws.

3. A campaign for enactment, in all states, of the model state civil rights act which includes a prohibition against employment discrimination based on sex.

4. Reexamination of the so-called state protective laws with the goal of extending to men the protections that are genuinely needed; and of the abolition of those obsolete restrictions that today operated to the economic disadvantage of women by depriving them of equal opportunity.

5. Assistance to women in any industry or profession in the organization of conferences or demonstrations to protest policies of(or?) conditions which discriminate against them; to open avenues of advancement to the decision-making power structure from which they are now barred, whether it be from executive training courses, the main line of promotion that leads to corporate presidencies or full professorships, or the road to union leadership.

6. A campaign to open new avenues of upgrading and on-the-job training for women now segregated in dead-end clerical, secretarial, and menial jobs in government, industry, hospitals, factories and offices — providing them training in new technological skills, equally with men, and new means of access to administrative and professional levels.

7. A campaign to eliminate, by federal and state law, discrimination on the basis of maternity — providing paid maternity leave as a form of social security for all working mothers, and the right to return to her job.

8. A campaign to permit the deduction of full child care expenses in income taxes of working parents. part

9. A campaign against age discrimination, which operates as a particularly serious handicap for women reentering the labor market after rearing children, and which is imbued with the denigrating image of women viewed solely as sex objects in instances such as the forcing of airline stewardesses to resign before the age of 32.

10. Urge enactment of equal pay legislation applicable to all public and private employment.

11. Drafting and enactment of a model state labor standards

174

law to protect health and economic well being of all workers, male and female.

12. Urge prompt appointment of the full number (5) of Commissioners of the Equal Employment Opportunity Commission authorized by the law. Support the appointment of persons to the Commission and to its top staff, who are committed to full enforcement of the law and who are dedicated to implementing the provisions against <u>all</u> prohibited forms of discrimination.

13. Demand replacement of the EEOC guideline on employment advertisements, which affirmatively permit discrimination based on sex with a guideline prohibiting such discriminatory job advertisements.

14. Support federal legislation to strengthen the authority of the EEOC to effectively implement equal employment opportunity in private employment and to extend the prohibitions against discrimination to public employment.

ACTION, FOLLOW THROUGH:

Recommendations of the Equal Opportunity in Employment task force were embodied in NOW letters to the President, EEOC Chairman and Attorney General and head of civil service commission; subsequent delegations to Washington and letters in behalf of the airline stewardesses will be sought to obtain cooperation between various government agencies in implementing laws to eliminate discrimination, such as the President's Committee on Government Contracts, EEOC, Manpower Training and Redevelopment Act, Wage & Hour Division, State Employment Commissions, etc.

Authorization given to the Legal Committee to file an amicus brief or otherwise assist the plaintiffs in the Mengelkoch case, and that the Committee also watch other sex discrimination cases with a view to entering amicus briefs where the Legal Committee deems it desirable.

A Brief was filed with the EEOC urging them to reconsider and change their earlier guidelines authorizing male and female help-wanted ads.

Submitted by: Dorothy Haener, Chairman

TASK FORCE ON IMAGE OF WOMEN
IN MASS MEDIA (1967)

Goals:

We will campaign to change the stereotyped image and the denigration of women in all the mass media, by all the forms of protest and pressure on networks, advertisers and editors which have been effective in abolishing the stereotyped images of Negroes and Jews. We will campaign for the inclusion of images of women which reflect, and thus encourage, the active participation of women in all fields of American society; images which are now completely absent from school books, as well as the media. "Look, Jane, Look" should have other pictures of women than the aproned mother, waving goodbye.

ACTION, FOLLOW THROUGH:

The New York Committee on Image was organized in February, 1967, under the chairmanship of Patricia Trainor, a computer programmer. Because of its geographical location in relation to the centers of the communications media, it will serve as the nucleus for a National Task Force on Image.

Twenty members have been active during the past month, setting up initial priorities, creating a structure for action, and initiating specific projects. Plans for action in the Mass Media have coalesced around three main focuses:

Monitor Subcommittee–

Under the direction of Dolores Alexander, reporter on *Newsday*, this committee will monitor media, assigning priorities and suggesting specific communications outlets as targets for NOW action. Plans have been drawn up for an Ad Hoc Committee of the general membership to visit various Equal Employment Agencies in New York City and newspapers during April, asking that the interpretation of Title VII of the Civil Rights Act of l964, which currently permits Help Wanted ads to be segregated by sex if a disclaimer is printed, be changed to require full integration of employment ads.

In addition to this project, plans are under way to approach specific TV networks and advertisers regarding the image of women they use to sell their air time and products.

Research subcommittee–

This Subcommittee, under the direction of Susanna Schad, sociologist at Rutgers, will perform services to the entire membership of the NOW organization, supplying facts about the role and contribution of women in the modern world. In addition, it will research the current image of women in the public mind, suggesting substitute images for NOW to foster. An In-House Education project, organizing lectures and seminars for members of NOW (and eventually the general public) is planned.

Creative Individual Participation–
We wish to combine the advantages of creative individual action with the power available to an organized group. Action by membership from all geographic areas is crucially important. Members of NOW are urged to write immediately in their own names to publishers and communications executives whenever a false image of women has been promulgated. This enables immediate action, without the delay which is necessary whenever we are going to speak as a group. Then, a copy of the letter is to be forwarded to Dolores Alexander (Monitor Subcommittee). Monitor will analyze all letters received from members with a view to a subsequent statement to the addressee in the name of the NOW organization.

Submitted by: Patricia Trainor, Chairman

NATIONAL ORGANIZATION FOR WOMEN

TO: All members of NOW

FROM: Betty Friedan, President   DATE: January 15 1968

For your information, and to guide your action in 1968 as a member of NOW the enclosed documents constitute the basic reports and policy positions adopted by the Second National Conference of the National Organization for Women (NOW) in Washington, D,C., November 18/19, 1967.

Of the total NOW membership of 1,122, the conference was attended by 105 women and men from California, Connecticut, the District of Columbia, Georgia, Illinois, Indiana, Maryland, Massachusetts, Michigan, Minnesota, Missouri, New Jersey, New York, Ohio, Pennsylvania, Virginia and Wisconsin.

The conference opened with the report of the president (Document I), detailing the progress of NOW in its first year of existence and proposing a Bill of Rights for Women in 1968 to be presented to all political parties and candidates as a touchstone for the coming election year.

The first article of NOW's Bill of Rights for Women in 1968 is the long-delayed Equal Rights Amendment to the Constitution. After a special all-conference discussion, the following resolution presented by the National Capital Area chapter of NOW was approved by a vote of 82 for, 3 against, with 12 abstentions:

"WHEREAS the National Organization for Women (NOW) is incorporated for the purpose of taking action to achieve equal rights and responsibilities in all aspects of citizenship, public service, employment, education, and family life; and

WHEREAS NOW is actively assisting women workers in seeking to invoke the protection of the United States Constitution to strike down statutes and official practices which deprive women of equal job opportunities; and

WHEREAS other classes of persons have been adjudged full recognition by the courts of complete equality without class distinction; and

WHEREAS the Equal Rights Amendment would unequivocally secure the right to equal treatment under the law without differentiation based on sex; and

WHEREAS opposition to the Equal Rights Amendment in the past was principally based on the presumed need for special "protective" labor legislation for women, the basis for which opposition Congress has removed by the enactment of the equal opportunity provisions of the Civil Rights Act of 1964; and

WHEREAS there are now pending in Congress various joint resolutions, such as S.J. Res.54 and H.J.Res.52, which would amend the U.S.Constitution to provide that "Equality of rights under the law shall not be denied or abridged by the United States or by any State on account of sex";

BE IT RESOLVED THAT NOW urge the House and Senate Judiciary Committees to immediately report favorably on the Equal Rights Amendment and call upon the Ninetieth Congress to approve this amendment, without qualification, for submission to the States for ratification."

Articles 2 through 6 of the Bill of Rights (see Document I, page 5) were approved at appropriate points by vote of the conference. Article 7 was approved with slightly different wording, following the second all-conference discussion on the question of abortion. By a vote of 57 for, 14 against, the conference approved the following resolution:

"NOW endorses the principle that it is a basic right of every woman to control her reproductive life, and therefore NOW supports the furthering of the sexual revolution of our century by pressing for widespread sex education, provision of birth control information and contraceptives, and urges that all laws penalizing abortion be repealed."

The position paper on which the all-conference discussion of the equal Rights Amendment was based was mailed to all members of NOW with the call to the national conference. The key section of the lengthy position paper on which the abortion discussion was based is included here as Document II. The other sections of the NOW position paper on abortion will be sent to chapter convenors and can also be obtained by writing to national headquarters. Copies of the entire NOW Bill of Rights for Women in 1968 will shortly be printed in final form and will be available in bulk to carry out the following resolution also adopted by the conference:

"BE IT RESOLVED THAT the national officers be directed to implement the Bill of Rights for Women in 1968 by urging support by appropriate officials of the executive and legislative branches of Government and other organization specifically the President of the United States and members of Congress and the State Commissions on the Status of women, and by the Republican and Democratic parties by inclusion in their party platforms."

Document III details legal procedures to be used in job discrimination ease a blank to be used by individual victims of job discrimination or by NOW chapters aiding such victims, and certain economic facts about job discrimination as presented— and discussed at the Training Session on Fighting Job Discrimination which was conducted by the NOW Legal Committee and Aileen Hernandez NOW Vice President-East, formerly a member of the Equal Employment Opportunity Commission. The report of the Legal Committee was dramatized by the appearance before the conference of three victims of job discrimination, Georgiana Sellers, Anna Casey and Lena Moore, who were denied higher paying jobs with the Colgate Palmolive company in Indiana because of new weight limit restrictions imposed on women workers. With long-distance guidance from NOW's Legal Committee, these women were able to act as their own lawyers in appealing pernicious court decisions on job discrimination which threatened to nullify Title VII of the Civil Rights Act of 1964 as far as women are concerned. The conference urged the utmost haste in setting up and raising money for the tax exempt NOW Legal Defense and Educational Fund to help fight the increasing number of such cases seeking help from NOW. A major resolution later voted by the conference reads as follows:

WHEREAS NOW is vitally concerned with the existing and continuing disadvantages to working women raising out of state protective laws applicable only to women,

THEREFORE BE IT RESOLVED that chapters of NOW in states having protective labor laws applicable only to women,

on a priority basis, seek to:
     (1) amend these laws to include men under those
protections which establish fair labor standards, and
     (2) repeal those laws which raise barriers to employment
based on sex.

Document IV comprises the reports of the NOW Task Forces on the Family, Discrimination in Education, Equal Employment Opportunity, Political Rights and Responsibilities, Women in Religion, Women in Poverty, and the Image of Women, as well as the report of the NOW Campus Coordinating Committee. Each one of the reports was approved by the conference, with separate votes also taken on the specific action resolutions recommended for NOW priority in 1968.

Every member of NOW is urged to read carefully all of these documents, for they comprise in total the national policy of NOW for 1968, implementing our Statement of Purpose in terms of the most urgent needs for our action during the crucial year ahead. Not every member or chapter of NOW will be equally interested in every aspect of our national program. Every chapter and member of NOW is urged to be creative in proposing and carrying out actions that will be most effective achieving any or all parts of this program in accordance with your own local situation. On the issues of our greatest national priority we shall continue to devise concerted national demonstrations, as we did most successfully in our National Day of Demonstration, December 14, 1967, against EEOC laxity in the matter of sex- segregated Help Wanted ads. This day of demonstration, which was voted as one of the final acts of the national conference, saw concerted activity of NOW members in New York, Washington, Atlanta, San Francisco and Chicago, joined by Milwaukee, Madison, Indiana and Iowa. On some issues, not the same kind of action may be appropriate in every state, For instance, NOW members in New York, where Governor Rockefeller has called for immediate reform of the abortion laws, may wish to take action on the abortion question which members in some other states where this has not even been publicly discussed might not consider appropriate at this time. In such states NOW members are urged first to educate themselves, in order to begin educating the public, by studying NOW position papers on the policy adopted by NOW, which is the first public expression of the voice of women, as well as men, on this. NOW's stand, as set forth in the enclosed position papers, is not the same so-called "abortion reform" position, and in fact is a new position in the United States.

Document V consists of the press release issued at the press conference held Monday morning in Washington following the close of the national conference, and the report of the NOW Public Relations Committee. Local chapters or NOW leaders might use some local action endorsing this program or pinpointing a local target for it, as a lead in issuing this same press release to your own newspapers, radio, and TV. You will find in the press release a list of the officers and board members elected for the coming year.

Dedicated as we are to action and not just words in NOW, many of those attending the conference stayed over in Washington to go to Capitol Hill on Monday to present our Bill of Rights for women in 1968, and our sentiments about the failure of the Administration to adequately enforce the sex discrimination provisions of the Civil Rights Act, to John Macy, who met with us on behalf of President Johnson and to the offices of Senators Eugene McCarthy, Robert Kennedy, Charles Percy, and our own Senators and Congressmen. Now it is up to every member and chapter of NOW to act to bring our Bill of Rights for Women in 1968 to the attention of local political representatives and

Candidates as well as to your representatives in Washington, and to devise new ways of exposing and combating sex discrimination in employment, education, the political parties, churches, and mass media. In a year when women will represent at least 51% of the vote, we can, if we begin to act now, direct major national attention to our unfinished revolution of full equality for women in truly equal partnership with men.

Finally, the Financial Report of the Secretary/Treasurer, indicates that although we have over 1,100 members of NOW our bank balance at the end of 1967 was only $1,062.35 and that, with this mailing, will be close to the vanishing point. In order to implement the goals we have agreed upon for 1968, it is urgently necessary that every member use the enclosed envelope to pay their dues and make any further contribution possible.

Happy New Year for NOW!

Betty Friedan
President
National Organization for Women

ERA POSITION PAPER (1967)
CONSTITUTIONAL PROTECTION AGAINST SEX DISCRIMINATION
An informational memorandum prepared for the National Organization for Women (NOW) regarding the Equal Rights Amendment and similar proposals.

NOW's Statement of Purpose endorses the principle that women should exercise all the privileges and responsibilities of American society in equal partnership with men and states that:

> "the power of American law, and the protection guaranteed b the U. S. Constitution to the civil rights of all individuals, must be effectively applied and enforced to isolate and remove patterns of sex discrimination, to ensure equality of opportunity in employment and education, and equality of civil and political rights and responsibilities on behalf of women, as well as for Negroes and other deprived groups."

The Fourteenth Amendment to the United States Constitution provides that no State shall "deprive any person of life, liberty or property, without due process of law; nor deny to any person with its jurisdiction the equal protection of the laws." The Fourteenth Amendment restricts the <u>States</u> and the "due process" clause of the Fifth Amendment similarly restricts the Federal Government from interfering with these individual rights. These are the constitutional provisions under which much of the civil rights for Negroes litigation has been brought and it is now clear that any radical distinction in law or official practice is unconstitutional.

The President's commission on the Status of Women recommendation.

The issue of constitutionality of sex distinctions in the law has been raised in a number of cases under the 5th and 14th Amendments. However, the Civil and Political Rights Committee of the President's Commission found in 1963 (Report, p. 34):

> "The courts have consistently upheld laws providing different treatment for women than for men, usually on the basis of the State's special interest in protecting the health and welfare of women. In no 14th Amendment case alleging discrimination on account of sex has the United States Supreme Court held that a law classifying persons on the basis of sex is unreasonable and therefore unconstitutional. Until such time as the Supreme Court reexamines the doctrine of 'sex as a basis for legislative classification' and promulgates the standards determining which types of laws and official practices treating men and women differently are reasonable and which are not, it will remain unclear whether women can enforce their rights under the 14th amendment or whether there is a constitutional gap which can only be filled by a Federal constitutional amendment."

The President's Commission on the Status of Women in its report to President Kennedy in October, 1963, declared:

> "Equality of rights under the law for all persons, male

or female, is so basic to democracy and its commitment to the ultimate value of the individual that it must be reflected in the fundamental law of the land."

The Commission went on to say that it believed that the principle of equal rights for men and women was embodied in the 5th and 14th amendments, and accordingly, "a constitutional amendment need not now be sought in order to establish this principle." The Commission stated further:

"Early and definitive court pronouncement, particularly by the U.S. Supreme Court, is urgently needed with regard to the validity under the 5th and 14th amendments of laws and official practices discriminating against women, to the end that the principle of equality become firmly established in constitutional doctrine."
(*American Women*, pages 44-45)

The Commission report optimistically does not include any recognition of the possibility that the Court might rule against women seeking to invoke the protection of the Constitution.

History of the Equal Rights Amendment

The constitutional amendment which the Commission stated it did not deem necessary to endorse in 1963 was the proposed Equal Rights Amendment. That amendment, which has been introduced in every Congress since 1923, in its present form would provide (see S.J. Res. 54, 90th Congress. 1st Sess.):

"Equality of Rights under the law shall not be denied or abridged by the United States or by any State on account of sex."

Congress has in the past held hearings on the Equal Rights Amendment, most recently in 1948 and in 1956, and the amendment has twice passed the Senate, but with a provision added that the amendment "shall not be construed to impair any rights, benefits, or exemptions now or hereafter conferred by law, upon persons of the female sex." The effect of the added provision, known as the "Hayden rider", has been to kill the Equal Rights Amendment, since proponents of the amendment obviously would not wish to support the addition. The Senate Judiciary Committee has frequently reported favorably on the amendment and the recent reports specifically oppose the "Hayden rider" pointing out that the qualification "is not acceptable to women who want equal rights under the law. It is under the guise of so-called 'rights' or 'benefits' that women have been treated unequally and denied opportunities which are available to men".

Effect of the Equal Rights Amendment

Constitutional amendments, like statutes, are interpreted by the courts in light of intent of Congress. Committee reports on a proposal are regarded by the courts as the most persuasive evidence of the intended meaning of a provision. Therefore, the probable meaning and effect of the Equal Rights Amendment can be ascertained from the Senate Judiciary Committee reports (which have been the same in recent years):

1. The amendment would restrict only governmental action, and would not apply to purely private action. What constitutes "State action" would be the same as under the 14th amendment and as developed in the 14th amendment litigation on other subjects.
2. Special restrictions on property rights of married women would be unconstitutional; married women could engage in business as freely as a member of the male sex; inheritance rights of widows would be the

same as for widowers.

3. Women would be equally subject to jury service and to military service, but women would not be required to serve (in the Armed Forces) where they are not fitted any more than men are required to so serve.

4. Restrictive work laws for women only would be unconstitutional.

5. Alimony laws would not favor women solely because of their sex, but a divorce decree could award support to a mother if she was granted custody of the children. Matters concerning custody and support of children would be determined in accordance with the welfare of the children and without favoring either parent because of sex.

6. Laws granting maternity benefits to mothers would not be affected by the amendment, nor would criminal laws governing sexual offenses become unconstitutional.

Support of and opposition to the Equal Rights Amendment

The National Woman's Party, which continued to carry on the feminist movement following the adoption of the Nineteenth Amendment, has led the fight for an Equal Rights Amendment. Other organizations which have supported the amendment include the National Federation of Business and Professional Women's Clubs, the General Federation of Women's Clubs, National Association of Women Lawyers, National Association of Colored Business and Professional Women, St. Joan's Alliance, American Federation of Soroptimist Clubs, and various women's professional and civic organizations. Strong opposition to the amendment has come from the labor unions. Other organizations opposing the amendment have included the Americans for Democratic Action, National Council of Jewish Women, National Council of Catholic Women, National Council of Negro Women.

The most recent Congressional hearings on the amendment were held in 1956. There does not appear to be any record which would indicate that any of the opponents of the amendment who objected to the amendment's effect of eliminating special labor laws for women, have re-examined their position since the enactment of Title VII of the Civil Rights Act of 1964. Some of the organizations opposed to the amendment have urged the Equal Employment Opportunity Commission not to enforce Title VII in a manner which would affect State laws restricting the employment of women. On the other hand, some labor unions, notably the U.A.W., Chemical Workers and Typographical Workers, have urged the EEOC to rule that the equal employment opportunity provisions of the Federal law supersede special hours and weight lifting restrictions on women workers.

Current sex discrimination cases

In a 1966 case, *White v. Crook,* a three judge federal court in Alabama held the Alabama law excluding women from serving on juries violate the 14th amendment. The court said that "the plain effect (of the equal protection clause of the 14th amendment) is to prohibit prejudicial disparities before the law. This means prejudicial disparities for all citizens — including women." The State did not appeal to the U.S. Supreme Court and the Alabama legislature amended its law to permit women to serve on juries on the same basis as men. A similar case challenging the constitutionality of a Mississippi jury law excluding women is currently pending before a three judge federal court in Mississippi. *(Willis v. Carson)* The Mississippi jury law is also at issue in *Bass v. Mississippi,* pending before the Fifth Circuit U.S. Court of Appeals. The Mississippi Supreme Court, in the case of *Hall v. Mississippi,* declined to apply the doctrine of *White v. Crook* and held that the Mississippi law did not violate the 14th amendment. The U.S. Supreme Court dismissed the appeal in that case on jurisdictional grounds and did not hear the case.

The exclusion of women from draft boards under selective service regulations (which have recently been amended to permit women to serve) is at issue in a conscientious objector case in Georgia.

In *Mengelkoch v. Industrial Welfare Commission* the constitutionality of the California hours restriction law for women workers is being challenged. This case is pending before a three judge federal court in Los Angeles. NOW attorneys Marguerite Rawalt and Evelyn Whitlow are representing the plaintiff women workers. A Federal court in Indiana recently ruled in *Bowe v. Colgate-Palmolive Co.* that Title VII does not prohibit an employer from excluding women from jobs which require the lifting of more than 35 pounds. Although Indiana does not have a weight lifting restriction law for women, the court reasoned that some States do and this justifies employers in other States in adopting the same "protective" practices. A California weight lifting limitation on women workers is alleged as violating their right to equal employment opportunity under Title VII in *Regguinti v. Rocketdyne and North American Aviation*, pending in a Federal court in that State. However, plaintiff's attorney did not raise the issue of a violation of the 14th amendment. There may be other Title VII cases as well which could involve testing the validity under the 14th amendment of State restrictive laws, but in which the attorneys have failed to raise the issue.

A Pennsylvania State court held that a statute providing longer prison sentences for women than for men does not deny to women the equal protection of the laws under the 14th amendment. *(Commonwealth v. Daniels).* This case is currently being appealed to the Pennsylvania Supreme Court. A county court in Oregon held, in January, 1967, that a city ordinance providing for punishment of female prostitutes is unconstitutional because it does not apply equally to males.

This listing of pending litigation does not, of course, purport to be exhaustive.

Suggested new interpretations of the 5th and 14th amendment

In "Jane Crow and the Law" (34 G.W. Law Rev. 232 (1965) authors Murray and Eastwood suggest that the doctrine that sex is a reasonable basis for classifying persons under the law, which has been used to justify upholding the constitutionality of laws which treat women differently from men, should be discarded by the courts. They point out that it could be argued that *any sex* differentiation in law or official practice today is inherently unreasonable and discriminatory and therefore violates the Constitution. The prospective effect of such an interpretation of the Constitution by the courts is outlined on pages 240 and 241 of that article.

NOW's brief in the *Mengelkoch* case asserts that the doctrine that sex is a valid basis for classifying persons does not even apply where there is involved the right to pursue lawful employment, since this is an *individual* right and a liberty and property which the State cannot restrict.

If these suggested constitutional interpretations are adopted by the courts in all areas of sex discrimination, the principle of equality set forth in the Equal Rights Amendment might in effect be "read into" the 5th and 14th amendments.

Analysis of Arguments Against the Equal Rights Amendment

Reasons which have been given for opposing the Equal Rights Amendment are as follows:
1. The amendment would be difficult to interpret and would result in a great deal of litigation.
2. The amendment is not necessary because women can achieve

constitutional equality through litigation under the 5th and 14th amendments.

3. Any constitutional requirement of equal treatment of the sexes is undesirable because it would require equal treatment of men and women in (a) state labor laws, (b) family law, (c) criminal laws, (d) social benefits law, and (e) obligations to the State and to the Nation.

* * *

(1)"The amendment would be difficult to interpret and would result in a great deal of litigation."

The meaning of "equality of rights under the law" would be a question for interpretation by the courts. The language of the Equal Rights Amendment is patterned after the 19th Amendment:

ERA: "Equality of rights under the law   shall not be denied
19th: "The right of citizens of the United States to vote shall not be denied or abridged by the United States or by any State on account of sex."

However, the 19th amendment is specific and applies only to the right to vote. Its meaning is therefore more clear than the Equal Rights Amendment, which applies to all "rights." Excessive litigation (and possible undesirable decisions) under the Equal Rights Amendment might be avoided if "equality of rights" were more clearly defined in the legislative history of the amendment as meaning *the right to equal treatment without differentiation based on sex.*

As noted in the cases mentioned above, women are now seeking to invoke the protection of the 14th amendment in the courts. In part because of the enactment of Title VII of the Civil Rights Act of 1964., it is likely that litigation under the 14th amendment will increase. It is possible that the adoption of the Equal Rights Amendment would actually have the effect of reducing the amount of litigation necessary to secure equal treatment of the sexes under the law. Of course, litigation is not necessarily bad. Indeed under our legal system litigation is a proper means for correcting discriminatory treatment.

(2) The amendment is not necessary because women can achieve constitutional equality through litigation under the 5th and 14th amendments.

Women have been seeking equal rights under these amendments since 1872. (For a summary of the cases see the Report of the Committee on Civil and Political Rights, Appendix B, President's Commission on the Status of Women.) Women can and should continue to do so until discrimination in laws and official practices is eliminated. In "Jane Crow and the Law" (op. cit. supra) Murray and Eastwood state (page 237):

"Although the Supreme Court has in no case found a law distinguishing on the basis of sex to be a violation of the fourteenth amendment, the amendment may nevertheless be applicable to sex discrimination. The genius of the American Constitution is its capacity, through judicial interpretation, for growth and adaptation to changing conditions and human values. Recent Supreme Court decisions in cases involving school desegregation, reapportionment, the right to counsel, and the extension of the concept of state action illustrate the modern trend towards insuring equality of status and recognizing individual rights. Courts have not yet fully realized that women's rights are a part of human rights; but the climate appears favorable to renewed judicial attacks on sex discrimination..."

Supporters of the Equal Rights Amendment believe that the potential of the 14th amendment is too unclear and that women's constitutional rights to equality are too insecure to rely exclusively on the possibility of getting more enlightened court decisions under that amendment.

In a 1963 case, the Supreme Court stated:

"The Fifteenth Amendment prohibits a State from denying or abridging a Negro's right to vote. The Nineteenth Amendment does the same for women....Once a geographical unit for which a representative is to be chosen is designated, all who participate in the election are to have an equal vote— whatever their race, whatever their sex. . . . This is required by the Equal Protection Clause of the Fourteenth Amendment." *Gray v. Sanders, 372 U.S. 368,379.*

This interpretation of the 14th amendment reinforced and made doubly secure the right to vote. There are numerous cases in which the Supreme Court has interpreted the 14th amendment to reinforce or to extend rights guaranteed by earlier or, as in the above case, later amendments to the Constitution. For example, the more general due process and equal protection concepts of the Fifth and Fourteenth Amendments have been used to strengthen more specific rights of individuals to freedom of speech, assembly and religion guaranteed by the First Amendment; and the right to a speedy trial and right to counsel guaranteed by the Sixth. If the Equal Rights Amendment is adopted, the courts might well subsequently interpret the Fourteenth Amendment as reinforcing constitutional equality for women.

A question might be asked as to why there should be a special equality guarantee for women and not for Negroes or for the aged. As a result of successful litigation under the Fifth and Fourteenth Amendments, Negroes today *have* the constitutional right to equal treatment and both the Federal Government and the States are absolutely prohibited from treating persons differently because of race. The same is true as to national origin and religion. With respect to age, absolute equality of rights and responsibilities is *not* desirable. If age were added to the Equal Rights Amendment, child labor laws would be rendered void, as would social security and government retirement systems. Selective service laws could not place the responsibility to serve in military service on a certain age group, and state requirements that children attend school could not be based on age.

If the Fourteenth Amendment had been drafted so as to absolutely and unequivocally require equal treatment without differentiation based on race, Negroes would not have had to painstakingly, step by step, achieve equality of rights under the law through litigation and legislation. The general language of the 14th amendment guarantees of due process and equal protection of the law for all persons has enabled the courts to give recognition to important human rights concepts of freedom of speech and religion and protection of the rights of persons accused of crimes. These are unrelated to race and it is not suggested that the 14th amendment should have been limited to requiring racial equality. Nevertheless, one might ask those who oppose the Equal Rights Amendment on the ground that equality of rights for women might ultimately be achieved under the present constitutional framework whether, at this day in history, women should be asked to repeat the painful, costly and uncertain course of litigation which Negro Americans had to endure.

> 3. Any constitutional requirement of equal treatment of the sexes is undesirable because it would require equal treatment of men and women in (a) state labor laws, (b) family law, (c) criminal laws, (d) social benefits law, and (e) obligations to the State and to the Nation.

At the time of the last Congressional hearings on the amendment (1956) it was assumed by both proponents and opponents of the amendment that there is no existing constitutional requirement that women be accorded equal rights and responsibilities under the law. The debate centered on whether the constitution *should* require equal treatment of the sexes. Those who opposed the amendment simply opposed equal treatment of men and women.

It is assumed that all members of NOW favor equal rights and responsibilities for women. Nevertheless, before endorsing or rejecting the Equal Rights Amendment one would want to know the consequences and effects of the amendment.

The precise effect in a particular case alleging denial of equal rights under the amendment would be a question for the courts. As noted above, the courts, in making their determinations, would be guided by the intended meaning or the "legislative history" of the amendment. Organizations such as NOW could help in shaping the legislative history and in clarifying the effect the amendment is intended to have.

The President's Commission on the Status of Women and the various State Commissions have outlined the areas of law and official practice which treat men and women differently. All of these studies have been made *since* the last hearings on the amendment.

The Equal Rights Amendment would require equal treatment without differentiation based on sex. Purely private discrimination, whether based on race, religion, sex or national origin, is not reached and is not prohibited by the U.S. Constitution. Laws and actions of agents of the Government are clearly reached. The question in each instance would be whether the right to equal treatment is denied or abridged the State or Federal Government.

The precise effect of the amendment in a given situation can not be predicted with absolute certainty since this would be determined by the courts. The following discussion indicates how the amendment might affect various laws and practices which treat men and women differently.

(a) *State labor laws*

(1) Minimum wage laws and other laws giving rights to women workers. If the State guarantees to women workers a minimum wage, men workers would be entitled to equal treatment by virtue of the Equal Rights Amendment. The same reasoning applies as to any state protected guarantees of seating facilities, lunch periods, or similar benefits provided for women workers. These laws or regulations would be automatically extended to persons of both sexes in the same way the State voting laws which applied only to men were automatically extended to women by virtue of the 19th amendment.

(2) State laws limiting and restricting the hiring and employment of female workers—hours restrictions, night work restrictions and weight lifting limitations. These laws are all limitations on the freedom of women workers because of their sex. They limit the right to pursue lawful employment and to work when and how long they choose. They confer <u>no</u> rights on women. Both men and women are, of course, free to not work longer than they so choose or at such times as they choose, by virtue of the 13th amendment's prohibition against slavery and forced labor. State restrictive laws would not be extended to men; they would be nullified by the Equal Rights Amendment because they

place restrictions on women not placed on men.

(3) Laws totally prohibiting the employment of women in certain occupations, such as bar tending and mining, likewise would be void, because they clearly deprive women, because of their sex, of the right to employment in these occupations. State laws providing a higher minimum age for employment for girls would be affected by the amendment by reducing the age to that provided for boys.

(4) Maternity laws would not be affected by the amendment because such laws are not based on sex; they do not apply women as a class. (See "Jane Crow and the Law," pages 239-240.)

(b) *Family law.*

(1) Both mothers and fathers are now generally responsible for the support of children under state laws. This would not be changed by the Equal Rights Amendment. In case of divorce or separation, where the mother (or father, as the case may be) has custody and care of the children, courts could continue to require the other parent, be it mother or father, to contribute to the financial support of the children .Present laws do not give recognition to the financial worth of homemaking and child care. The Equal Rights Amendment would probably not require that such worth be recognized in determining the relative responsibilities of parents in case of divorce. However, recognizing the value of child care and homemaking would be consistent with the principle of equality of rights under the amendment.

(2)Alimony for wives solely because they are female would be prohibited by the Equal Rights Amendment. However, continued support by one spouse for the other after divorce or separation based on actual necessary economic dependency, relative ability to provide family support or past relationships and obligations of the particular parties would not be prohibited by the amendment because the alimony or support would not be based on sex but upon some other criteria. The states would continue to be free to establish these values and criteria; they would simply be prohibited from discriminating against either men or women because of sex.

(3) Minimum age for marriage. Some states provide a lower minimum age for marriage for women that for men. The amendment would prohibit treating men and women differently in regard to age for marriage. If under state law women have the right to marry at age 18 and men at age 21, the amendment would give men the right to marry at 18. The state could, of course, amend its law to provide that the age be 21 for both sexes.

(4) Age of right to parental support. Some states give girls a right to be supported to age 18 and boys to age 21. Since the girls would have the right to be treated equally under the amendment, their right in these states would be automatically extended to age 21. The states would be free, of course, to provide a different age, so long as it is the same for boys and girls.

(5) State laws placing special limitations and restrictions on married women but not on married men would be nullified by the amendment.

(c) *Criminal law.* States would be prohibited from providing greater penalties for female law violators than for males. There are certain sex crimes, such as rape, which apply only to males. These would not be affected by the the Equal Rights Amendment since the state in enacting these laws has not made any classification of persons by sex; if these laws were drafted so as to refer to persons instead of males, their meaning would be the same. (see "Jane Crow and the Law," page 240.)

(d) *Social benefits laws.* There are certain differences in benefits which men and women receive under the social security and government retirement laws. There may be similar state retirement systems which give greater or lesser benefits to women. Legislation is currently pending in Congress to correct some of the inequities in the Federal law (see, e.g., H.R.643, 90th Congress, to eliminate differences in government employees' fringe benefits.). It could reasonably be expected that by the time an Equal Rights Amendment became effective, differences between the sexes in these laws would have been corrected. However, insofar as differences remained, the State or Federal Government, as the case may be, would be obligated by the Equal Rights Amendment to give the same benefits to both sexes.

(e) *Service to the State and to the Nation.* (Government employment, jury service and military service.) The Equal Rights Amendment would prohibit discrimination against women in public employment at all levels of government. The Administration's Civil Rights Bill would prohibit any sex discrimination in juror qualification or in selection of jurors. This would eliminate laws excluding or discouraging women from serving on juries. It is generally agreed that a state law relieving women from jury service responsibilities relegated them to second class citizenship and should be forbidden. The Equal Rights Amendment would make women eligible to serve on all juries on the same basis as men. With regard to military service the same reasoning might apply. It could be argued that failure of a nation to give its women the same responsibilities as it requires of its men makes women second class citizens. The Military Selective Service Act of 1967 requires men but not women to register for military service. The Equal Rights Amendment would have the effect of extending this requirement to women and make women eligible for selection just as women would be eligible for jury selection on the same basis as men. The present selective service law will automatically expire on July 1, 1971.

***

Some lawyers might disagree that the Equal Rights Amendment would have the effects outlined above. However, to the extent that supporters of the amendment can agree on the desired effects of the amendment on existing laws, such effects could be made more certain if they are carefully set forth and made a part of the amendment's legislative history.

NATIONAL ORGANIZATION FOR WOMEN

THE RIGHT OF A WOMAN TO DETERMINE HER OWN REPRODUCTIVE PROCESS (1967)

The following proposals are offered for purposes of discussion by the 1967 NOW Membership Conference.

1. Constitutional Amendment

There is perhaps no more fundamental human right, save the right to life itself, than the right to one's own physical person, a basic part of which is the right to determine whether or not one will give birth to another human being. An egg, a sperm, a zygote or a fetus is not a person or a human being and does not have "rights" as a person or a human being. Whatever "rights" these may have are necessarily because of biological fact completely dependent upon and subordinate to the human bodies which house them.

Constitutional rights are accorded to human beings solely in terms of *restrictions on governments*. It is the government's interference with the right of women to control their own reproductive process that we are concerned with here. All of the states have laws restricting this right of a woman to her own physical person. New York NOW has urged that that state adopt a constitutional provision prohibiting governmental interference with this right. The following suggested amendment to the United States Constitution would protect this right of women in all the states:

> THE RIGHT OF A WOMAN TO PREVENT
> CONCEPTION AND WITH PROPER
> MEDICAL SAFEGUARDS TO TERMINATE
> HER PREGNANCY SHALL NOT BE DENIED
> OR ABRIDGED BY THE UNITED STATES OR
> BY ANY STATE.

The effect of this amendment would be to nullify all existing state criminal abortion laws, leaving the question of whether or not to have an abortion a matter for the woman herself, rather than the government, to decide.

2. Revision of State Laws

Criminal abortion laws in 42 states prohibit the performance of abortions unless necessary to save the life of the pregnant woman. In the other eight states — Alabama, California, Colorado, Maryland, Mississippi, New Mexico, North Carolina, and Oregon — and in the District of Columbia, abortions are permitted in certain other additional circumstance, such as where pregnancy results from rape, incest, or where the physical or mental health of the woman is endangered.

Bills to make abortion laws restrictive were introduced in 28 state legislatures in 1967. The Colorado and North Carolina laws, enacted in 1967, are patterned after the American Law Institute's Model Penal Code.

They permit abortions where continuance of the pregnancy would gravely impair the physical or mental health of the woman, the child would be born with grave physical or mental defect, or the pregnancy resulted from rape, incest or other felonious intercourse. (It may be noted that the definition of "human being" in the ALI Model Penal Code criminal homicide provisions is "a person who has been born and is alive.")

In spite of the state criminal abortion laws, it is estimated that between 200,000 and over a million illegal abortions are performed in this country each year, and at least 4 out of 5 of them on married women.

Abortion is not a desirable method of birth control and other means should be made available to everyone who wishes to use them. However, criminal abortion laws clearly have proven to be ineffectual in eliminating the use of abortion as a means of birth control, and have driven women to unskilled practitioners, handicapped doctors in practicing their profession, and have made a mockery of the law.

State criminal abortion laws could, of course, simply be repealed or they could be replaced with statutes which give a pregnant woman a right of *civil* action against any government official who requires or attempts to require her to have an abortion or who prevents or attempts to prevent her from having an abortion. In other words, the statute would recognize her civil right to determine her own reproductive process by giving her a right to sue the particular agent of the state who deprives or attempts to deprive her of that right.

This kind of civil rights protection giving a right to sue for damages is similar to that provided in one of the post Civil War federal civil rights statutes (42 U.S.C. 1983):

> "Every person who, under color of any statute, ordinance, regulation, custom, or usage, of any State or Territory, subjects, or causes to be subjected any citizen of the United States or other person within the jurisdiction thereof to the deprivation of any rights, privileges, or immunities secured by the Constitution and laws, shall be liable to the party injured in an action at law, suit in equity, or other proper proceeding for redress."

Under such a replacement statute, a doctor would be free to perform an abortion without fear of any criminal prosecution. But if a state or local welfare official tried to force a woman to have (or not have) an abortion, she could sue him for damages or get a court order restraining him from pressuring her or cutting off her welfare funds if she refused to comply with his wishes.

The following is a proposed model state law to prevent governmental interference in a woman's reproductive process:

ANY PERSON WHO, UNDER COLOR OF ANY FEDERAL, STATE OR LOCAL LAW, REGULATION OR CUSTOM, REQUIRES OR

ATTEMPTS TO REQUIRE ANY PREGNANT
WOMAN IN THIS STATE TO HAVE AN
ABORTION, OR PREVENTS OR ATTEMPTS TO
PREVENT ANY PREGNANT WOMAN IN THIS
STATE FROM HAVING AN ABORTION
PERFORMED BY A LICENSED MEDICAL
PRACTITIONER SHALL BE LIABLE TO SUCH
WOMAN IN AN ACTION AT LAW, SUIT IN
EQUITY, OR OTHER PROPER PROCEEDING FOR
REDRESS.

SECTION *(reference to criminal abortion law)* OF
(state statutes) IS HEREBY REPEALED.

It is not the function of government to determine who shall and who shall not give birth to a child. The first paragraph of the above model law, with the deletion of the words "in this state" might also be appropriate for a federal law.

REPORT... OF THE LEGAL COMMITTEE OF THE NATIONAL ORGANIZATION FOR WOMEN

TO: The Board of Directors and the members of the National Organization for Women, at the First Annual Conference, Washington, D.C. November 18-19, 1967.

The organizing Conference of the National Organization for Women, at its October, 1966 meeting, authorized a Legal Committee to assist in litigation involving discrimination based on sex. The organizing conference was particularly concerned about the Mengelkoch case which had just been filed in the U.S. District Court, Southern District, California, by women factory workers who were denied promotions to better paying jobs, and denied opportunity to earn time and a half for overtime because of a California law prohibiting women (but not men) from working more than 8 hours per day or 48 hours per week.

The Committee. There are at least 30 members in NOW who are attorneys and judges. We would like to regard every one of them as a member of the Legal Committee and to count upon each of them to serve as court attorney or as consultant, according to their circumstances. My Memorandum to all these members of the bar November 9, 1967 invited them to indicate whether they could serve as an attorney of record and enter appearance and conduct a case when one arose in their home jurisdiction; and whether they would be willing to take a case from beginning, either without fee as a NOW representative, or by referral, for a woman alleging sex discrimination, if the litigant is able to pay reasonable fees.

Because of geographical separation over the country, there have been no meetings of the full committee. Moreover, communication by correspondence has had the handicap of working without operating headquarters and staff. The attorneys in Washington area have met when developments in pending litigation demanded. It has been a single individual, or two or three together, who has carried the burden in each piece of litigation and in other assignments carried out by this Committee. Positions taken in litigation must be correlated through the Chairman so that the Organization might avoid being placed in irreconcilable positions in our efforts to achieve legal equality. It would be my pleasure to name each attorney and give individual credit for his or her efforts. Attorneys from California to New York to Washington, D.C. have worked without fee. However, this report will be made in the impersonal term of "Legal Committee" leaving individual laurels to other channels.

In one short year of existence, remarkable progress has resulted from the devotion and skill of attorney members who have worked in their "Leisure Hours" to contribute to NOW's drive toward full partnership of women. Within such time, the Legal Committee has served as summarized below.

Bylaws. The Legal Committee hammered out the final draft of national bylaws which was then presented to and approved by the

Board of Directors at its February 22-23, 1967 meeting in Chicago as correctly implementing the organizational conference directives and actions. These bylaws were then officially adopted by the corporation as the bylaws of the incorporated NOW.

The Committee was then called upon by the Board to draft standard bylaws for chapters, a task carried out through considerable correspondence. Standard bylaws were ordered and approved to simplify tax exemptions as well as to provide good framework for an organization to grow. After thorough discussion and refinement by the Board of Directors, it adopted a Standard Bylaws for Chapters consisting of 15 Sections. Provision is made therein for the chapter to adopt additional chapter bylaws to implement this necessary framework, and to meet the particular needs of the individual chapter, it being required only that there by no conflict with the standard and required sections. This will now pave the way for needed tax exemptions.

Incorporation. The legal services and drafting of necessary papers together with secretarial services involved, to bring about incorporation of the organization were the work of two members, acting under authority of the Board. A Certificate of Incorporation was issued February 10, 1967 by the Recorder of Deeds, District of Columbia, Washington, D.C. to the National Organization for Women under the provisions of the District of Columbia Non-profit Corporation Act.

Legal Defense and Educational Fund. Members of this Committee have from the beginning approved and urged the establishment of a Legal Defense and Educational Fund within the provisions of Section 501 (c)(3) Internal Revenue Code, which would thus be equipped to attract contributions which would be tax deductible, the fund designed to serve as the medium of giving legal assistance in court litigation. The Board of Directors, meeting in Madison, Wisconsin September 17, 1967 unanimously approved this recommendation of the Committee and authorized and directed the officers of NOW to "proceed forthwith to incorporate such legal and education fund" in New York. One of our prominent attorneys of New York is handling this matter.

Individual requests for legal aid. The Chairman has had aid and assistance of members in processing and replying to some 25 individual appeals for assistance or legal advice in cases of alleged discrimination. This requires the reading and analysis of pages of records and weighing the presented evidence against the law. The cases which seemed to have merit were answered as carefully as possible with our recommendations as to possible courses. We have not been in position of course to undertake to be counsel for these persons from widely separated areas of our country. As chapters grow in number, these instances can have better and more effective action there. We simply did our best on our own time and expense. A funded Legal Defense Fund is needed as the number of reported cases increases.

Court decisions. To the knowledge of this Chairman, there has not been a single court decision which has enforced the sex-discrimination provisions of Title VII. Nor, to our knowledge, has there been a single instance in which the Attorney General of the United States has intervened, as he may do under Title VII, on grounds of sex discrimination. Nor, has there come to knowledge or attention of this Committee, any instance of the Equal Employment Opportunity Commission entering or assisting in litigation where sex discrimination was at issue.

On the other hand, there have been adverse court decisions under Title VII. In *Thelma Bowe et al v. Colgate-Palmolive Co.* the U.S. District Court Southern District Indiana, handed down a decision on June 30, 1967 upholding company policy regulations under which women factory workers were confined to lower paid "finishing" jobs on the ground that it is proper to "protect" women from jobs requiring the lifting of more than 35 pounds. There was no state law involved; the decision is a limitation on the Federal statute, Title VII in its alleged ban on sex-discrimination which can be broadly expanded to many other restrictions upon women employees. The NOW Board has authorized the Legal Committee to assist plaintiffs on appeal. Three of the plaintiffs only have sought the assistance of our organization.

The case of *Mengelkoch v. State of California* filed in Federal Court in October 1966, is still undecided. The pleadings therein challenge the maximum hours law of California as a violation of Title VII, and as unconstitutional under the 14th amendment, by denying the right to pursue lawful employment without due process of law and in violation of equal protection of the laws. As authorized, NOW members of the Legal Committee prepared a brief sustaining plaintiffs, which was proffered to the Court as an amicus curiae brief. The brief was later filed as the brief of plaintiff, Velma Mengelkoch, when her original attorney was superseded by a California attorney and member of NOW, the brief being signed by the Chairman of the Legal Committee, and the California attorney. The original attorneys in the case failed to argue and support the 14th amendment issue when the case was heard on a motion to dismiss. This case seeks a special three-judge court on the ground of constitutional issue. If upheld, appeal would lie direct to the U.S. Supreme Court.

Advertising guidelines under Title VII. The Committee prepared a petition filed in December 1966, urging that the discriminatory guidelines on sex-segregated classified advertising in newspapers be rescinded, and that the Equal Employment Opportunity Commission substitute clear and unequivocal guidelines suggested by Congresswoman Martha Griffiths, the wording of which was included. This led to public hearings in May, 1967 by the EEOC on several issues under Title VII, including advertising, state labor laws, and pension and retirement plans. In connection with the May hearings, NOW submitted proposed *guidelines on state labor laws as well.*

Participation in interviews with officials. The Chairman and other Committee members have participated in face to face interviews by NOW delegations headed by President Friedan, insisting upon serious enforcement of the Sex-discrimination provisions of Title VII: On November 26, 1966 with all members of the Equal Employment Opportunity Commission; on January 12, 1967 with Attorney General Ramsey Clark; on January 13, 1967 with Chairman John Macy, Jr. and all other members of the Civil Service Commission, Mr. Macy being also Special Presidential Assistant.

The Committee has one recommendation: it urges the officers to take such action as will at the earliest possible moment set up and activate a Legal Defense and Education Fund as a means of furthering the most urgent needs of the organization.

In behalf of a loyal group, the Legal Committee:

Marguerite Rawalt, Chairman
1801 16th St. N.W.
Washington, D.C. 20009

NATIONAL ORGANIZATION FOR WOMEN (NOW)

Legal Procedures in Job Discrimination Cases (1967)

Discrimination by private employer or labor union

1. If your state (or municipality) has a fair employment law including sex, write to the state agency which enforces the law, by registered mail, giving all the facts of the discrimination. (State FEP laws)

2. If your state (or municipality) does <u>not</u> have such a law, file a complaint directly with the Equal Employment Opportunity Commission field office (find address in current *Government Organization Manual* at your public library), or at the EEOC, 1800 G Street, N.W., Washington, D.C. Complaint forms are available from the EEOC. Title VII covers employers having 50 or more employees and labor unions with 50 or more members (or which operate a hiring hall); as of next July 2, 25 or more employees or members. *Note:* charges must be filed within 90 days after the discriminatory practice occurred. (Title VII)

3. If in a case under (1) above, the state agency is unable to stop the discrimination within 60 days of the registered letter, or if the state agency terminates the proceedings before then, you may file with the EEOC as in (2) above, but you must file within 210 days of the discriminatory practice or 30 days after receiving notice that State proceedings have terminated, whichever is earlier.

4. If the EEOC notifies the complainant that it is unable to obtain compliance with Title VII, the complainant may, within 30 days, file a civil action against the employer or union in the Federal district court. (Title VII)

5. In cases of sex discrimination in pay, you may also simply write or telephone the U.S. Labor Department Wage and Hour and Public Contracts Division regional office (see *Government Organization Manual*) or write to that Division of the Labor Department in Washington, D.C. (FLSA Equal Pay Act). Note: there are some exceptions to this law but unless you are sure the law does not apply, notify the Labor Department.

6. If an employer or union has a general practice of widespread sex discrimination, send the information to the Attorney General of the United States and ask him to bring an action. Title VII gives the Attorney General this authority.

7. In all cases where complaints are filed with the EEOC or where any court action is take, immediately notify the chairman of the NOW legal committee, Suite 500, 1629 K Street N.W., Washington, D.C.

Discrimination by a state or local governmental agency (e.g., civil service, public schools and institutions)

1. These cases are not covered by Title VII. However, some of the State fair employment or civil service laws apply to sex discrimination in governmental employment. If your state (or city) has such a law,

proceed as in (1) above.

2. Whether or not your state has such a law, a court action, in Federal or State court, can be filed against the agency or official which discriminates, on the ground that such discrimination violates due process of law and equal protection of the laws under the 14th amendment of the United States Constitution (and in some States, the State Constitution).

Discrimination caused by a State law or regulation (e.g. a law prohibiting employment of women in certain work, maximum hours restrictions on women only and weight lifting restrictions applying only to women)

An action can be filed in a three-judge Federal court to restrain the State officials from enforcing the discriminatory law, on the ground that the law is unconstitutional.

Discrimination in Federal employment

File a complaint with the equal employment opportunity officer of the particular agency. If the case is not satisfactorily resolved within the agency, a complainant may appeal to the United States Civil Service Commission.

Discrimination by labor union

A suit may be filed in Federal court to enjoin a labor union from discriminating against women workers and for damages for such discrimination. The Supreme Court has held that under the Fifth Amendment to the United States Constitution, labor unions must represent all workers fairly and equally and without arbitrary discrimination.

Note: In all types of cases, the facts supporting the charge of sex discrimination are important. In some cases, more than one of the above procedures may be applicable.

If you are in doubt as to what to do in a particular case, write to the NOW legal committee at the national headquarters giving as much information as possible on the case.

Other Techniques

1. A NOW chapter delegation can ask to meet with and persuade an employer, union, or government agency to change its discriminatory policy.

2. Have a press conference to dramatize and give publicity, and elicit public support, for a case.

3. Picket.

4. Try to get state legislatures to equalize all state labor laws or repeal special restrictions on women.

5. If your state has an FEP law which does not include sex, get sex added; if no FEP law, get one passed with sex in it, such as the model state civil rights law, which includes a prohibition against sex discrimination in employment.

If you are in doubt as to what laws your state has, ask an attorney member to look it up, or write to the NOW legal committee at the national headquarters.

INFORMATION CONCERNING ALLEGED
DISCRIMINATION BASED ON SEX

(MR.)
NAME (MISS)
(MRS.)

ADDRESS:
(Including City,
State, Zip Code)

Male   Female   Area Code
Phone Number

When did the alleged
discriminatory act
take place?   (Day)
(Month)   (Year)

Who discriminated?
(Name of company, union,
etc. —include address

Describe briefly what happened that leads you to believe that you were discriminated against because of your sex?

Have you filed a charge of this discriminatory act with any agency? If yes, specify which agency and when?

Have you taken any court action in regards to this alleged discrimination? If yes, specify where and when.

****

I would like the National Organization for Women to take appropriate action to process the foregoing charge of discrimination in my behalf.

TASK FORCE ON THE FAMILY (1967)

Guiding Ideology:

The basic ideological goal of NOW is a society in which men and women have an equitable balance in the time and interest with which they participate in work, family and community. NOW should seek and advocate personal and institutional measures which would reduce the disproportionate involvement of men in work at the expense of meaningful participation in family and community, and the disproportionate involvement of women in family at the expense of participation in work and community.

SUGGESTED MEASURES TO IMPLEMENT THIS GOAL:

Section 1 -

Cultivation of a wide spectrum of interests and skills among both girls and boys. If men and women are to participate as equal partners in adult life, boys must be encouraged to develop broad non-vocational interests, domestic skills and eagerness for community service, and young girls must be exposed to a wide range of career possibilities and encouraged to make career choices consistent with their true interests rather than social expectations of appropriate female fields. Only by changes in childhood experience and exposure can we counteract the work-achievement-science-money focus of American men, and the narrow home-nurturance-culture-beauty focus of American women.

Section 2 -

Later age at marriage and first pregnancy. If more women finished their educational training and acquired work experience relevant to their long range occupational goal before marriage and maternity, they would acquire more of the motivation, self-confidence and independence necessary for a balanced pattern of work and family life involvement after marriage. NOW should encourage wider opportunity of choice as to when or whether a person should marry or remarry, have or not have children.

Section 3 -

Individual control of reproductive life. NOW endorses the principle that it is a basic right of every woman to control her reproductive life, and therefore NOW supports the furthering of the sexual revolution of our century by pressing for widespread sex education, provision of birth control information and contraceptives, and urges that all laws penalizing abortion be repealed.

Section 4 -

Expansion and change in home maintenance services. NOW urges the upgrading of the status and competence of domestic service occupations. This is a necessary change both to improve the social and economic lot of household employees, and to enable women who have to work or wish to work, to minimize the length of time they withdraw from the labor force due to family and home responsibilities.

Section 5 -

Expansion and change in child care services. If women are to participate on an equitable basis with men in the world of work and of community service, child-care facilities must become as much a part of our community facilities as parks and libraries are, to be used or not used at the discretion of individual parents. NOW encourages the development of a variety of child-care facilities available on an all-day, all-year basis, adequate to the needs of children from the preschool years through early adolescence. This can be accomplished by the upgrading of skills and licensing of "mother substitutes" similar to the development of practical nursing, as well as by child-care centers administered as an added employee facility by private or public employers at the place of work, as a logical extension of the local educational system. Standards for facilities and personnel should be established by law.

Section 6 -

Revision of divorce laws and alimony arrangements so that unsuccessful marriages may be terminated without hypocrisy, and new marriages contracted without undue financial hardship to either man or woman

Section 7 -

Loosening of nepotism rulings and practices so that husbands and wives can work for the same enterprise in business, government or the educational system.

Section 8 -

Revision of tax laws to permit the deduction of full home and child-care expenses in income taxes of working parents.

Section 9 -

Revision of social security laws to assure equitable coverage for married and widowed women who have worked, as they now do for married women who did not work, and to eliminate discrimination based on sex or marital status in the conferring of benefits thereunder. (The question of divorced women was raised and was referred to the Legal Committee for clarification.)

Section 10 -

Maternity Benefits. Since bearing and rearing of children is an important and valued contribution to the perpetuation of our society, maternity should not involve any penalties to women who have to or wish to work. NOW encourages a campaign to eliminate discrimination on the basis of maternity by the protection of a woman's right to return to her job within a reasonable time after childbirth, determined by the woman herself, without loss of her disability credits or seniority.

Section 11 -

Expansion of "sick leave" to family members of employees. Men and women should be able to use sick leave to cover illnesses of children or spouses, not merely themselves. This is a needed social change both to revise our thinking from the needs of the individual to the needs of the family unit and to facilitate the sharing by men and women of their parental and marital responsibilities. Permit the deduction of full home and child-care expenses in income taxes of working parents.

Section 12 -

Employment laws designed to shorten hours of work should be revised to require equal treatment of male and female workers. As a current example, many women cannot work overtime if they wish to and many men feel compelled to work more overtime than they wish to. State employment laws should be reviewed and revised to assure that male and female employees have the right to refuse overtime work beyond a specified legal limit on overtime hours per week. Only by such equitable treatment can working fathers and mother participate equally in the pleasures and responsibilities of home care and child rearing.

RECOMMENDATIONS FOR PRIORITY:

(1) CHILD CARE

(a) Everyone opposes H.R. 12080 as passed by the House of Representatives. Urge support of the Kennedy amendment.

(b) NOW should take vigorous action to disassociate child care centers from "poor children of welfare cases." Child care facilities should be community resources like parks and libraries, to be used or not at the discretion of individual citizens.

(2) Cultivation of wide spectrum of interests and skills among young boys and girls. Urge Image and Education Task Forces to concern themselves with books in elementary schools re image of what women do.

(3) Urge all members of NOW to affiliate with National Committee for Day Care of Children, 114 East 32nd St., New York, NY 10016.

(4) Urge and recommend that NOW have more detailed discussion of maternity benefit issue before taking any action on this issue.

MOTIONS:

Propose the motion that 4 articles be approved to the Bill of Rights of 1968:

(1)   Right of women who have to or want to work by protecting her right to remain on the job during pregnancy and return to her job after childbirth without loss of disability credits or seniority.

(2)   Revision of tax laws to make child care and home maintenance tax deductible.

(3)   Encourage the development of child care facilities for all preschool children and older children for hours they are not in school, to be used or not used at the discretion of individual citizens, much as parks and libraries are.

(4)   NOW endorses the human right of every woman to control her reproductive life.

* * *

TASK FORCE ON EDUCATION (1967)

GOALS:

1.   To revise the systematic and deliberate mis-education with respect to sex roles which prevails in the American school system.

2.   Enforcement of Title VII of the Civil Rights Act of 1964 - and the inclusion of sex in Title VI of the Civil Rights Act of 1964.

3.   The elimination of restrictive quotas on the basis of sex, written or unwritten in colleges, universities, graduate and professional schools.

4.   All schools should offer an identical curriculum for boys and girls. Neither men nor women should be discouraged from pursuing those professions which traditionally were restricted to the opposite sex.

5.   All schools should provide a realistic education which includes instruction in contraceptive devices and family planning.

6.   Sufficient funds should be made available so that self-supporting mothers, mothers on welfare and those whose income is essential to family survival can afford to complete their education without the triple burden of child-care, work and school.

7.   A substantial number of high schools and universities should provide day care facilities to enable mothers of preschool children to complete their education.

REPORT OF THE TASK FORCE
ON EMPLOYMENT (1967)

Discussion was had of the attitudes of newspapers towards the interests of working women, and of industry opposition to women workers in certain areas.

Examples were given by various individuals of discrimination against women in union jobs, as well as jobs in education, government, libraries, the hard sciences, medical arts, law and the space affiliated field, which women are being discouraged from entering.

We suggest a study and research item as a long range effort, that NOW collect and compile existing data on women's employment, such as salaries, promotion levels and other data, which would be more detailed and penetrating than the compilations now available.

Resolution 1: (As an action item of first priority)
We urge that NOW set a day of national action on sex-segregated help-wanted advertising. This could be the mailing to the EEOC, or possibly to the President himself, of marked help-wanted sections from all over the country, or possibly picketing of the newspapers, on a set day.

Resolution 2: (As another high priority item)
We urge that facts regarding discrimination against women workers, women's need to work and their reasons for working, women's median salary levels and similar data be constantly furnished in brief, concise, graphic form to NOW members. This hard data would make our members more effective recruiters, persuaders, speakers, and members of panels. This data could also be distributed by our members to other interested groups at strategic times.

Resolution 3:
Press for day care centers for all working mothers.

Resolution 4:
That local chapters endeavor to recruit as NOW members those women who have effective influence on the nation's newspapers. These women might include advertisers and wives of advertisers, owners and wives of owners, advertising and public relations women, department store executives who place advertising, and employment agencies which place advertising.

Resolution 5:
That local chapters endeavor to recruit into NOW more guidance counselors, elementary through college level, to change the image now prevalent of counseling girls into "safe" fields, rather than into more challenging ones. We also believe that NOW should provide speakers to work towards this end.

Resolution 6:

In order to implement our judgements on the effectiveness of government bureaus and of our elected officials in serving the needs of working women, we urge that NOW appoint ARCHIVISTS to search the voting and committee records of elected officials and government bureaus whose work affects working women.

We urge that their findings of fact be briefly tabulated and widely disseminated. These could be sent out just before elections to each elected official's constituency, to NOW chapters, which would then inform all women's organizations willing to publicize the data among their membership. Similar action could be taken at time of appointment of officials and other strategic times.

This action would be possible with our presently existing membership. It would have immediate impact on Capitol Hill when it was observed that our workers were tabulating this data on our elected representatives.

It would have a salutary effect on the voting of our representatives who vote our way in Washington and talk another way when back at home campaigning.

It would make it possible for us to stiffen up our own spines to cross party lines in voting and working for candidates, when confronted with their actual tabulated voting records.

It would make us influential far beyond the numbers of our membership in enforcing more favorable legislation for working women, both on the national and the state level if we have archivists both in Washington and in state capitals.

Resolution 7:

Incorporate and continue to work on the Equal Employment Task Force report adopted last year.

Resolution 8:

Urge the U.S. Civil Rights Commission to include the word "sex" in the study it is doing on discrimination.

Resolution 9:

Write a letter to the appropriate government official or agency urging them to undertake the study of restrictive laws affecting women workers recommended by the President's Commission on the Status of Women in 1963 immediately and asking for an explanation of why it has not been done. This letter should probably go to the President, Labor Department, Women's Bureau, etc.

REPORT OF THE TASK FORCE ON
POLITICAL RIGHTS AND RESPONSIBILITIES (1967)

1. It is recommended that the Bill of Rights for Women, including the amendment to Section VII, be adopted.

2. NOW members should not only register and vote but become active in a political party at local, state and national levels. NOW members should be willing to cross party lines in order to elect candidates who have accepted our goals.

3. Immediate priority should be given to getting the Bill of Rights for Women into the hands of the platform committees and the leading candidates of the major political parties. Each NOW chapter should endeavor to get women elected to the party conventions.

4. NOW should encourage women who hold elected offices to join our organization and/or to advocate the Bill of Rights for Women. The Bill should be distributed to other women's organizations, to civil rights groups and to the churches for their support.

5. The task force strongly urges that women in NOW who work within the Women's divisions of the major political parties refrain from doing the traditional menial work of sealing envelopes, ringing doorbells and raising pin money through cocktail parties and "kaffee klatches" unless men do their share and women are proportionately represented on all committees. It is felt that this strategy could be the starting point for women's political bargaining.

6. The task force recommends that the women's divisions of the major political parties be eliminated and integrated fully in the party structure in the future.

7. Politicians and other public figures should be challenged to produce results in terms of NOW's Bill of Rights for Women.

8. NOW believes that women should be equitably represented on all policy-making boards, committees, and commissions of governmental, political and tax-free quasi-

public non-governmental organizations which have a bearing on the overall well-being of people.

Action Resolutions From The Task Force On Political Rights and Responsibilities

A. The task force on political rights and responsibilities recommends the adoption of the Bill of Rights for Women including the amendment to Section VII.

B. NOW members should not only register and vote, but become active in a political party at the local, state and national levels. NOW members should be willing to cross party lines in order to elect candidates who have accepted our goals.

C. Immediate priority should be given to getting the Bill of Rights for Women into the hands of the platform committees and the leading candidates of the major political parties. Each NOW chapter should endeavor to get women elected to the party conventions,

D. NOW should encourage women who hold elected office to join our organization and/or advocate the Bill of Rights for Women. The Bill should be distributed to other women's organizations, to civil rights groups and to the churches for their support.

E. It is recommended that the women's divisions of the political parties should be eliminated and fully integrated into the parties in the future.

F. NOW believes that women should be equitably represented on all policy-making boards, committees, and commissions of governmental, political and tax-free quasi-public non-governmental organizations which have a bearing on the overall well-being of people.

Task Force on Women and Religion (1967)

All Conference Resolution:

Be it resolved that NOW recognizes that it is the right of women to participate fully on an equal basis with men at all levels and in all areas of church life and practice.

Task Force Statement
Tenet: We hold that discrimination based on sex is destructive of religious values. We oppose discrimination based on sex and the religious teachings and laws which cause or reinforce it.

Action: 1. Encourage woman to enter professional theological fields and work to ensure job opportunities for women.

2. Strive to open the priesthood and ministry to women in religious groups where it is now forbidden.

3. Strive to integrate religious organizations and societies which are segregated solely on the basis of sex.

4. Promote the principle of equal pay for equal work in all institutions conducted by religious groups.

5. Integrate religious-sponsored institutions such as schools, colleges and seminaries.

Task Force on Women In Poverty (1967)

The Task Force on Women in Poverty urged the board of NOW to call a national conference on "Women in Poverty" to deal with special problems of women in poverty and urged women to attend such conferences held by other groups to speak directly for the rights and needs of women. Discriminatory practices within the Job Corps and other poverty programs were deplored. Action was urged of the membership to correct unequal representation of women on policy-making bodies of poverty programs

REPORT OF THE TASK FORCE ON
THE IMAGE OF WOMEN (1967)

"Stronger than a hundred armies is the force of an idea whose time has come."
"You cannot reason a man out of a position he didn't reason himself into."

The first thing that comes up in all meetings on the image of women is that we certainly do not yet know everything there is to know about the nature, origins, and force of the image of women presented to our society by its mass media, This is an honest concern. Nevertheless, this task force has resolved that, while we don't know everything there is to know, we know enough to begin to take action. We know at least that the mass media's image of woman is not realistic, and that we have ideas about more realistic images to supersede the current ones.

The Image Committee will probably function as a two-pronged force: immediate action and continuing research. Because of limited resources we set a priority on action now.

The mass media are defined as TV and Radio; commercial advertising; newspapers, news services and national magazines; textbooks; and language itself.

The audience is all of society: men, women, girl children, boy children, and institutions and communities.We wish to reach all these people, but in particular we wish to reach women and girls with models which will enable them to form a new self-image; one which more closely matches their reality as independent, rational, vital, growing, curious, inquiring homo sapiens (or perhaps I should say mulier sapiens).

We would conclude that our most powerful potential tool for myth-shattering is the mass medium of TV. Accordingly, we outline specific goals and initial recommendations for their accomplishment in this area,

1. **Goal** - Increase the number of models of healthy, happy women with expertise and contributions to make in areas which may include but are not restricted to home-making and child-rearing,
   Method-Local chapters assemble lists of the female resources of the community, approach the producers of local public affairs shows requesting a real effort to find women to appear on these shows as experts (e.g. in air pollution, city planning, the arts, not just the role of woman) and be prepared to aid the local media outlets in finding such people.
2. **Goal** - The entertainment shows which are based on the facts of daily life more accurately reflect the many roles which women fill in our present society.
   Method-This must be developed by the task force as a top priority in 1968,

3. **Goal** - Personal models of mulier sapiens for young girls.
   Method-establishment of speakers' bureaus on the local and national levels.

Miscellaneous Comments:

We feel that we must be able to present a plethora of new images of women to supplement the aproned mother. The vital career woman is one. There are many more.

There are single women who are home-makers. There are women who work primarily because they are breadwinners, rather than because they have profession or are seeking stimulations outside the family circle. And concurrently with presenting new images of women, we must develop and present new images of men.

Our numbers are small but our potential power may be relatively large. Some techniques which we may use are consumer pressure, pressure on one medium through another (i.e. letters to the editor criticizing TV shows) both techniques in which one articulate individual can accomplish virtually as much as a hundred silent armies.

In conclusion, we request approval of the following two resolutions for immediate action:

1. We urge that all local NOW chapters will have approached local TV outlets to stimulate the greater representation of women on public affairs shows by the end of the first quarter of 1968, having previously prepared themselves to provide, where necessary, the names of such women.

2. We urge that all local chapters and the national structure have formally organized a speakers bureau by spring of 1968.

3. We request that our report with its awareness of needs which must be further explored and for which specific modi operandi must be further developed be adopted by this conference.

Campus Coordinating Committee Report (1967)

The purpose of NOW is to bring women into full participation in the mainstream of American society, to share equally with men the rights and responsibilities necessary for the full development of human potential. To achieve this goal, occupational and educational benefits must be made equal and young women must be encouraged to take advantage of their increasing opportunities. NOW should therefore oppose those policies of schools, colleges and universities which discriminate against women economically, unfairly limiting their chances for career and financial advancement, and socially inhibiting their development of confidence and personal responsibility. The Campus Coordinating Committee hopes to spearhead such opposition by recruiting students, faculty and university employees and by forming campus chapters of NOW. Although it is anticipated that such chapters will become deeply concerned with other aspects of the unfinished revolution of women, they will be uniquely adapted to working towards such goals as:

1. **Dual educational opportunities:** Abolition of discrimination against women in undergraduate and graduate school admissions and in the granting of scholarships, fellowships and other types of assistance.

2. **Dual employment benefits:** Abolition of discrimination in pay, consideration for hiring and opportunities for job advancement in all branches of university employment.

3. **Establishment of University-run nurseries** where parents may leave their children while at work or study.

4. **Abolition of nepotism rules,** written and unwritten, which deprive faculty wives of jobs by forbidding both husband and wife to hold faculty appointments simultaneously in the same academic department.

5. **Academic reform:** (a) Abolition or revision of all psychology, homemaking and other courses which present a subservient and degraded image of women; (b) opening up to members of both sexes, courses, such as home economics courses, previously offered to one sex only; (c) establishment of courses dealing with women, their problems, and their fight for equality in psychology, sociology and history departments.

6. **Equalization of all dormitory hours, sign-out requirements and social regulations** which discriminate against women on assumption that they require more protection than men and are not equally endowed with self-control, responsibility and common sense.

7. **Integration of student facilities,** in order to promote healthy social contact between men and women without artificial barriers, and thereby combat the stereotyping of individuals by members of the opposite sex. Such integration by sex could be achieved by providing common dining halls, study rooms and recreational facilities for men and women and by providing alternation of the sexes by dormitory wing, floor or segment of floor.

8. **Equality of initiative and responsibility in dating:** Alteration of the rigid pattern by which dating and other social contact between men and women is initiated, planned, paid for and controlled by men.

9. **Sex equalization or abolition of the draft.**

10. **Birth control:** Student health services should be encouraged to make birth control information and methods available to all students over the age of consent who want them.

NATIONAL ORGANIZATION FOR WOMEN
BILL OF RIGHTS IN 1968
(Adopted at the 1967 National Conference)

   I.   Equal Rights Constitutional Amendment
   II. Enforce Law Banning Sex Discrimination in Employment
   III. Maternity Leave Rights in Employment and in Social Security
        Benefits
   IV. Tax Deduction for Home and Child Care Expenses for Working
        Parents
   V.   Child Day Care Centers
   VI. Equal and Unsegregated Education
   VII. Equal Job Training Opportunities and Allowances for Women
        in Poverty
   VIII. The Right of Women to Control their Reproductive Lives

We Demand:

I. That the United States Congress immediately pass the Equal Rights Amendment to the Constitution to provide that "Equality of rights under the law shall not be denied or abridged by the United States or by any State on account of sex" and that such then be immediately ratified by the several States.

II. That equal employment opportunity be guaranteed to all women, as well as men by insisting that the Equal Employment Opportunity Commission enforce the prohibitions against sex discrimination in employment under Title VII of the Civil Rights Act of 1964 with the same vigor as it enforces the prohibitions against racial discrimination.

III. That women be protected by law to insure their rights to return to their jobs within a reasonable time after childbirth without loss of seniority or other accrued benefits and be paid maternity leave as a form of social security and/or employee benefit.

IV. Immediate revision of tax laws to permit the deduction of home and child care expenses for working parents.

V. That child care facilities be established by law on the same basis as parks, libraries and public schools adequate to the needs of children, from the pre-school years through adolescence, as a community resource to be used by all citizens from all income levels.

VI. That the right of women to be educated to their full potential equally with men be secured by Federal and State legislation, eliminating all discrimination and segregation by sex, written and unwritten, at all levels of education including college, graduate and professional schools, loans and fellowships and Federal and State training programs, such as the job Corps.

VII. The right of women in poverty to secure job training, housing and family allowances on equal terms with men, but without prejudice to a parent's right to remain at home to care for his or her children; revision of welfare legislation and poverty programs which deny women dignity, privacy and self respect.

VIII. The right of women to control their own reproductive lives by removing from penal codes the laws limiting access to contraceptive information and devices and laws governing abortion.

PUBLIC RELATIONS COMMITTEE REPORT
November 18, 1967

Our public relations efforts in NOW's first year of life have pursued three main goals: 1.) To educate the public and public officials on the prevalence of discrimination based upon sex–with emphasis on the *illegality* of such discrimination under Title VII of the Civil Rights Act of 1964. 2.) To tell the world about NOW as an organization, and to publicize NOW campaigns. 3.) To help create a dignified *new image* of American women, and to help revise long-established cliches in the communications media that foster "self-denigration, dependence, and evasion of responsibility" among women. We trust that our efforts have achieved some success toward those three goals.

On the whole, NOW has been treated by the press with respect and fairness. Press conferences have been well attended; and although certain newspapers restrict NOW coverage to the woman's page, most papers carry our stories in the general *news* section. Thanks to coverage by Associated Press, NOW has appeared on the front page of many leading American newspapers.

Television and radio have been especially generous, with networks and local stations carrying NOW stories on their top night-time newscasts. The NBC-TV network TODAY show presented a two-hour program on discrimination against women; largely as a result of a NOW memorandum; Betty Friedan appeared on this program with Senator Maurine Neuberger and Dr. Bruno Bettelheim. The NBC radio network then produced a three-program series on the same subject with the same three experts.

This Week magazine carried a three-page picture story about NOW, titled "Sex and Civil Rights," to its 26 million readers. The *National Observer* and *True* magazine did features– the former on page One. Major stories quoting NOW in sex discrimination are currently in the works at five other leading magazines. Although most women's magazines (*Mademoiselle, Vogue; Glamour, McCall's, Redbook,* etc.) have written about NOW, some were critical. (*Vogue's* comments might be summarized thus: Girls, why settle for job equality, when it's more fun to dream about finding a rich husband to support you.)

Local NOW chapters and individual NOW members might profit from this brief summary of NOW's main news stories thus far:

> l) Our organizing conference in Washington. (Local Chapters: How about local publicity when you become an official chapter, or when you elect officers? Good-quality news pictures of your officers should be welcome at the newspapers and TV stations. Ask your radio and TV stations if they'd like to interview your chapter officers.)
> 2) NOW's first press conference, stating its immediate goals. (Local Chapters: *Your* press conference could reveal your state and local objectives.)

3) NOW's petition to the EEOC regarding sex-segregated "Help Wanted" ads. (Local Chapters: Any local issues worthy of a NOW-sponsored petition?)

4) A press conference in Washington following meetings between representatives and key Washington officials. (Local Chapters: When you have a solid, newsworthy issue, how about a call on your Mayor, and Governor, perhaps followed by a press conference?)

5) Interviews with prominent men and women who are members of NOW. (Prominent members, don't be modest. Your local press is interested.)

6) Press conferences following NOW national board meetings in certain cities.

7) Press conferences and news releases expressing NOW support for victims of sex discrimination. For example, NOW has received nationwide publicity for its assistance to Pauline Dziob, who was denied a yeoman (clerk-typist) job aboard ship on the grounds that this was "man's work," and for its intervention in the "Mengelkoch case" protesting a California state labor law which restricts women (but not men) in hours of overtime work in factories. (Dramatic case histories are always welcomed by the press. But check all the facts carefully first! The national NOW legal committee can advise you.)

A FEW WORDS OF CAUTION: Don't let the press lure you into a battle-of-the-sexes approach. Emphasize that NOW has many men members, and that we are working for equal *partnership* between men and women—with no discrimination against either sex. . . . Don't participate in a discussion that pokes fun at women. Sure we all have a good sense of humor; but let's try to promote the image of American woman as a serious, responsible person–not a helpless object for ridicule. . . . When you are interviewed as a NOW representative, use good judgment if the press tries to draw you out on controversial issues not covered by NOW policy. Remember, the public might erroneously get the impression that you are stating NOW policy, rather than your own personal opinions as an individual. Also, if your local NOW chapter has taken a certain stand which is not the policy of the national NOW organization, please be sure to emphasize in press interviews that you are speaking for your *local* chapter only. If in doubt about a future statement or interview, please check first with your local NOW chapter president or with a NOW national officer.

NOW keeps a scrapbook of national and local publicity. This helps us tell our story to prospective members, financial supporters and allies. Would you kindly send any and all NOW clippings you come across to Muriel Fox, 43 East 83rd St. New York City 10028. If you wish, we will xerox your clippings and return the originals to you In the next mail.

A special word of thanks to Patricia Perry, Barbara Ireton, Linda Waring and Bette Jerome for their publicity work in Washington; and to Marsha Lane and Dolores Alexander for their work in New York.

Respectfully submitted
Muriel Fox, Public Relations Chairman

From: NOW (National Organization for Women) FOR
IMMEDIATE RELEASE

PRESS CONTACTS: Barbara Ireton, 202-DU 7-3200
                         Betty Friedan, 212-874-1658
                         Muriel Fox- 212-YU 8-1124

NOTE: The latter two may be reached Monday, Nov. 20,
            through the Mayflower Hotel.

WASHINGTON, D. C. November 20 - - The National Organization for Women (NOW) announced today that its second annual National Conference has adopted a Bill of Rights for Women in 1968 to be presented to all political parties and candidates in the coming election year, and that candidates for office would be judged by their assistance to its proposals.

NOW, which was founded in Washington one year ago by men and women pledged to work actively for full equality for women in truly equal partnership with men, re-elected Dr. Kathryn Clarenbach of the University of Wisconsin as chairman of the board and author Betty Friedan of New York as president. Re-elected as vice presidents were two former Commissioners of the Equal Employment Opportunity commission, Mrs. Aileen Hernandez of San Francisco and National Teacher Corps director Richard Graham. San Francisco biologist Inka O'Hanrahan was elected secretary-treasurer.

The Conference called for abolition of the women's divisions of the major political parties and their integration into the parties' main structures; and NOW advised women to "refrain from merely doing the traditional menial work of sealing envelopes, ringing doorbells, raising pin money and holding koffee klatches unless they are also admitted to the policy-making mainstream of the political parties." More than a dozen Conference resolutions regarding political action included one suggesting that NOW members "cross party lines to elect candidates who support equality for women, and to defeat its enemies.

Although many sections of the NOW Bill of Rights for women were passed unanimously, two sections engendered heated discussion before passage by the Conference. One resulted in NOW support for the Equal Rights Constitutional Amendment, currently before Congress, providing that "Equality of rights under the law shall not be denied or abridged by the United States or by any State on account of sex." This language became the first item in NOW's "Bill of Rights for Women."

The second controversy ended in a strong NOW stand on birth control and abortion: "NOW endorses the principle that it is a basic right of every woman to control her reproductive life; and therefore NOW supports the furthering of the sexual revolution of our century by pressing for widespread sex education and provision of birth control information and contraceptives, and by urging that all laws penalizing abortion be repealed." This too was incorporated in the NOW Bill of Rights for Women.

Another section in the NOW Bill of Rights stressed the right of women to be accorded equal treatment with other victims of discrimination in all decisions by governmental officials and agencies regarding employment discrimination. This includes the right to "immediate relief from governmental rulings permitting sex-segregated Help Wanted ads, which perpetuate and tolerate discrimination." NOW has repeatedly urged the Equal Employment Opportunity Commission to outlaw sex-segregated classified ads as violating Title VII of the Civil Rights Act of 1964 which prohibits employment discrimination based upon sex as well as race, religion, or national origin.

Sounding a battle cry for the election year ahead, NOW president Betty Friedan urged "the organization of women and men committed to our goals into a true voting power block. I will not call it `woman power' for it includes men. We must find a synonym for 'sexual equality power.'" This "New Woman" power block, Mrs. Friedan said includes "28 million American working women, the millions of women emerging from our colleges each year who are intent on full participation in the mainstream of our society, and mothers who are emerging from their homes to go back to school or work. This New Woman could prove a significant factor in the presidential election."

The "Bill of Rights for Women also states: "The rights of women in poverty to secure job training, housing and family allowances in equal terms with men must be secured by revision of welfare legislation and poverty programs which today deny women of dignity privacy and self-respect." A separate NOW resolution deplored "discrimination against women within the Job Corps and other poverty programs" and called for appointment of more women to policy-making posts in poverty programs and agencies. NOW also passed a resolution regarding H.R.12080, the Social Security bill passed by the House of Representatives and currently before the Senate, which makes it possible for women receiving Aid to Dependent Children welfare payments to be forced to take jobs or job training, and to place their children in child care centers. NOW has previously written the Senate Finance Committee in strong opposition to this requirement, stating it would be "punitive, undemocratic and un-American to deny welfare mothers of the *option* of choosing whether to work or stay home with their children." NOW supported the language of the amendment to this bill proposed by Senator Robert Kennedy of New York.

In reference to child care centers, The NOW Bill of Rights for Women states: "To ensure the right of women to participate on an equal basis with men in the world of work, education and political service, fully adequate child care facilities be established by Federal law on the same basis as parks, libraries and public schools, as a community resource to be used at the option of citizens from all income levels."

The NOW Bill of Rights for Woman continues: "The right of women to equal opportunities in employment must be implemented by immediate revision of income tax laws ensuring the right to permit the deduction of full home and and child care expenses for working parents.

Another plank in the NOW Bill of Rights states: "Since bearing and rearing children is important to society, the right of women who want to, or have to work not to suffer because of maternity, must be protected by laws ensuring their right to return to the job within a reasonable time after childbirth, without loss of disability credits or seniority."

Finally, the NOW Bill of Rights for women urges: "The right of every man and woman to be educated to the fullest potential should be secured by federal and state laws to eliminate quotas and discrimination on the basis of sex on all levels of education, discrimination in loans and fellowships, segregation of educational facilities including dropout programs, and education which develops passivity and inferior aspirations among women while encouraging abdication of responsibility for home and children among men."

At a press conference this morning In the Mayflower Hotel, NOW officers revealed the new "Bill of Rights for Women" and announced NOW support for music teacher Cindy Hill in her fight against the school district of Chartiers Valley Pennsylvania, a suburb of Pittsburgh. Mrs. Hill was deprived of sabbatical study pay, and subsequently fired, after she gave birth to a baby while on sabbatical leave obtaining her master's degree at Duquesne University. NOW charged the school district has "violated the rights of motherhood, the rights of a married couple to manage its own family, and the basic individual rights of a teacher"and called Mrs. Hill's case "a serious example of employment discrimination based on sex." Introduced at the press conference, Mrs. Hill stressed that she had fulfilled all requirements of her sabbatical study leave, and had won her master degree "with accolades," taking off only one week to have her baby.

The NOW Conference also heard three women from Indiana who were denied higher paying jobs with the Colgate-Palmolive Company because of new weight-limit restrictions imposed by the company on women workers only. One of the women, Mrs. Georgianna Sellers, was elected to the NOW board of directors.

The Conference unanimously adopted a resolution stating "Women should be equitably represented on all policy-making boards, committees and commissions of governmental, political and tax-free quasi-public organizations which have a bearing on the over-all well being of people."

The Conference resolved: "It is the right of women to participate on an equal basis with men at all levels and in all areas of church life and practice" and approved the report of NOW's Task Force on Religion calling for removal of sex segregational religious organizations and church-sponsored schools. This report said NOW members must "strive to open the priesthood and ministry to women in religious groups where it is now forbidden." And it called for "equal pay for equal work" for women employed by religious institutions.

Delegates at the NOW conference included several veterans of the early movement for women's right to vote, and also many students–young men and young women alike–from NOW groups on college campuses. The Conference adopted a 10-point report of its Campus Coordinating Committee urging a drive for equality in university employment, admissions, curricula, dormitory regulations, student loans, scholarships and all other phases of campus life. The report also urged integration of dormitory facilities, dining halls, study rooms and recreation facilities.

The NOW "Image of Woman" committee report adopted at the convention, called upon members and chapters to fight for "more realistic and varied images of women" in the mass media including textbooks and it stressed, especially, the need for television programs to depict more examples of women who are experts in many fields "to supplement the all-pervasive image of the aproned mother."

The NOW Board of Directors for the following year includes: Julia Arri, California clothing company executive, past president of the California Federation of Business and Professional Women's Clubs; art historian Ti-Grace Atkinson of New York; Ernesta D. Ballard, Philadelphia horticulturist and author; Elizabeth Boyer, attorney, past president of the Ohio League of Women Voters; Grace D. Cox, New York City attorney, president of the National Association of Women Lawyers; Professor Carl Degler of Stanford University, prominent historian and author; Alisson Drucker, student at the University of Chicago; Sister Mary Austin Doherty, a Catholic nun, teacher at Alverno College; Dr. Elizabeth Jane Farians, Catholic theologian from New Jersey; Frances Flores of Riverside, California, consultant to the Food and Drug Administration; Muriel Fox of New York City, vice-president of one of the country's largest public relations agencies; Ruth Gage-Colby of Minnesota and New York, journalist, and board member of the women's International League for Peace and Freedom; Jane Hart, wife of the Senator from Michigan, herself a professional pilot who campaigned for admission of women as astronauts; Claire Hatch, Connecticut teacher and industrial artist; Wilma Heide, Pittsburgh sociologist and journalist; Dr. Anna Arnold Hedgeman, coordinator of the Commission on Religion and Race of the National Council of Churches; Barbara Ireton, Washington public relations executive; Lucy Jarvis, prize-winning NBC Television network producer; Coretta King, Atlanta civic leader and concert singer, wife of Dr. Martin Luther King; Reverend Dean Lewis of Philadelphia, Secretary of the Office of Social Education and Evangelism, United Presbyterian Church in the U.S.A.; Ollie Butler-Moore of Baton Rouge, dean of women at Louisiana State College; Eliza Paschall, Atlanta community relations official and member of the Unitarian Universalist Association Commission on Religion and Race; Marguerite Rawalt, Washington attorney and past president of the National Federation of Business and Professional Women's Clubs; Sylvia Radyx, Washington research consultant in information sciences; Dollie Robinson, New York attorney, official with the Hotel and Allied Service Union; Dr. Alice S. Rossi, prominent sociologist at Johns Hopkins University; Aaron Scheinfeld of Milwaukee and Chicago, chairman of Manpower, Inc.; Susanne Schad-Somers, Rutgers University sociologist; Georgianna Sellers, the Indiana worker mentioned previously; and Los Angeles attorney, Evelyn Whitlow.

Lesbian Rights (1971)

WHEREAS the first wave of feminist anger in this Country recognized the fundamental issue of women's liberation as "the most sacred right of all—a woman's right to her own person." This is the right that NOW reaffirmed a century later when it took up the banner and dedicated itself to changing those conditions in society, the laws, the practices, the attitudes — that prevented women from realizing their full human potential. Recognizing that a woman cannot reach this potential if she is denied the basic right to control her own body, NOW has demanded the dissemination of birth control information and contraceptives and the repeal of all laws against abortion. It has stopped short, however, of clarifying its position on every woman's right to define—and express —her own sexuality, to choose her own lifestyle. Specifically, NOW has been silent on the issue of lesbianism. Yet no other woman suffers more abuse and discrimination for the right to be her own person than does the lesbian, and

WHEREAS, the lesbian is doubly oppressed, both as a woman and as a homosexual, she must face the injustices and degradation common to all women, plus endure additional social, economic, legal, and psychological abuse as well. In education and employment, the lesbian confronts more than discrimination or tokenism. She can be arbitrarily rejected or dismissed from many professions, even those—such as teaching—traditionally relegated to women. Married women are denied equality under laws that decree men as head of the household, but a wife is nonetheless allowed some legal protection. A lesbian, however, who shares her home with another woman—regardless of her income or responsibilities—forgoes all the economic and legal compensations granted to the married woman, including the tax deductions, insurance benefits, inheritance rights, etc., and

WHEREAS, this prejudice against the lesbian is manifested in the courts as well, and

WHEREAS, most divorced women are conceded the right to their children, a lesbian is automatically presumed unfit for motherhood, and can have her children taken from her, and

WHEREAS, these are but a few of the laws and practices in our society that reflect irrational assumptions about lesbians. Just as the false and demeaning image of all women provides the rationale to keep them subjugated, so does the distorted stereotype of the lesbian sanction her persecution. Not only is she assumed to be unstable or sick or immoral; but because she defines herself independently of men, the lesbian is considered unnatural, incomplete, not quite a woman—as though the essence of womanhood were to be identified with men. Obviously, this *Playboy* image of the lesbian reduces her to an abject sexual object, deprived of the most basic civil and human rights due every person, and

WHEREAS, because she is so oppressed and so exploited, the lesbian has been referred to as "the rage of all women condensed to the point of explosion." This rage found a natural outlet in the women's liberation movement that seemed to view women in a new way and promised a new pride and sisterhood for every woman in search of equality and independence. Lesbians became active in NOW and in other groups, fighting for all the feminist goals, including child care centers and abortion repeal. As a result of their activism in the movement, lesbians

—as did all feminists—reached a new consciousness, a new sense of their worth and dignity as women and human beings. They began to rebel against the intolerance of a society that condemned their lifestyle, but instead of finding support from their sisters, lesbians discovered that NOW and other liberation groups reflected some of the same prejudices and policies of the sexist society they were striving to change, and

WHEREAS, lesbians were never excluded from NOW, but we have been evasive or apologetic about their presence within the organization. Afraid of alienating public support, we have often treated lesbians as the step-sisters of the movement, allowed to work with us, but then expected to hide in the upstairs closet when company comes. Lesbians are now telling us that this attitude is no longer acceptable. Asking women to disguise their identities so they will not "embarrass" the group is an intolerable form of oppression, like asking black women to join us in white face. Furthermore, this discrimination is inconsistent with NOW's stated goal to "recognize our sisterhood" and to help women "overcome self-degradation." If this pledge is to be anything more than idle rhetoric, NOW must reassess the priorities that sacrifice principle to "image," and

WHEREAS, some members of NOW object that the lesbian question is too controversial to confront right now, that we will weaken the movement by alienating potential and current members who are comfortable with NOW's "respectable" image. The same argument, that women would be frightened away, was raised a few years ago when NOW took a bold stand on the controversial abortion issue. The argument did not prove prophetic then, and we do not believe it is valid now. We are, after all, a reform movement, with revolutionary goals. The D.A.R. can be "respectable," but as Susan B. Anthony pointed out::

> "Cautious, careful people always casting about
> to preserve their reputation or social standards,
> can never bring about a reform. . ."

WHEREAS, it is encouraging to note that feminists are not so easily frightened. Since the resolution supporting lesbians was passed in Los Angeles NOW two months ago, the chapter has increased, not decreased, in membership. If a few cautious, careful people scurried away, the loss was imperceptible. And we are stronger now because many women feel more relaxed and are freer to work with us towards NOW goals, and

WHEREAS, another objection to the resolution contends that lesbian oppression is simply not "relevant" to the concerns of NOW; "the movement will be weakened or even destroyed" if we diffuse our energies on non-feminist issues. This is a curious argument, since all one has to do is read the NOW Bill of Rights to find that we have pledged support to the cause of "equal rights for all those who suffer discrimination and deprivation;" further, we have recognized a "common oppression that affects all women." If lesbians are women, and if lesbians suffer discrimination and deprivation, then the conclusion is inescapable: their oppression is not only relevant, but an integral part of the women's liberation movement, and

WHEREAS, we are affected by society's prejudices against the lesbian, whether we acknowledge it or not; as feminists we are all subject to lesbian-baiting by opponents who use the tactic of labeling us the worst thing they can think of, "lesbians," in order to divide and discredit the movement and bring women to heel. Even within NOW, regrettably, this tactic is employed by some members who conjure up the sexist-image of lesbians and shout "lavender menace" at anyone who opposes their views. NOW is inevitably weakened by these attempts to undermine the spirit and efforts of its members; we can no longer afford to ignore the problem; and

WHEREAS, the resolution does not mean that we are changing our emphasis and concentrating on specific lesbian issues, however. We have not been asked, nor do we intend, to diffuse our energies in any way. The resolution, in itself, is an action—the first step towards breaking down the barriers between women that have kept them weak and suppressed. We are giving notice that we recognize our sisterhood with all women and that we are fighting for every woman's "sacred right to her own person." As feminists, we can do no less;

THEREFORE, BE IT RESOLVED: That NOW recognizes the double oppression of women who are lesbians, and

BE IT FURTHER RESOLVED: That a woman's right to her own person includes the right to define and express her own sexuality and to choose her own lifestyle, and

BE IT FURTHER RESOLVED: That NOW acknowledge the oppression of lesbians as a legitimate concern of feminism.

Resolution on Establishing a Task Force on
The Masculine Mystique (1971)

WHEREAS the ideal of NOW is truly equal partnership for men and women, and

WHEREAS the reality is that many women continue to find men a stumbling block to their own development and many men are still not free to develop in ways other than those considered typically "male," and

WHEREAS the pervasive effects of "privileges" for women and "prerogatives" for men are equally injurious to their mutual growth and maturation, and

WHEREAS human liberation necessarily involves the critical examination, vigorous analysis and daily reacceptance of themselves as women and men, and

WHEREAS consciousness-raising groups of a continuing nature provide both the time and framework within which such an examination can occur,

THEREFORE BE IT RESOLVED: That NOW create a task force on the Masculine Mystique charged with suggesting the best methods in which women and men can successfully raise their consciousness to make truly equal partnership a reality.

Equal Rights Amendment
Declaration of State of Emergency
(February, 1978)

We declare a State of Emergency for the National Organization for Women in which we turn all our resources to the ratification effort and to extension of the deadline for ratification an additional seven years.

There comes a time when the harsh political realities must be recognized: the major interests of our country have hypocritically given lip service to the ERA while sabotaging its ratification by political deals, tradeoffs and do-nothingness.

There comes a time when a movement must decide its own destiny—when it must determine on what line it will stand and fight.

The ERA is the foundation on which all our gains rest. If the ERA is defeated, it will be perceived as a vote against equality for women. The gains women have made in the past 15 years will be eroded and erased. Worse yet, every future effort we make will be dismissed with the excuse that when the ERA failed, it proved that the women of this country didn't want equality.

Never mind that only 7% of those voting on the ERA in their state legislatures - where it counts—have been women.

Never mind that 80% of those women at the National Women's Conference—where it could have no binding effect—voted for the ERA.

Never mind that public opinion polls have time again proved majority support.

Never mind that 2/3 of the states with 3/4 of the population have ratified the ERA.

Political leaders do not want to be diverted by the truth or confused by the facts. And an indifferent national press refuses to consider the life and death issues facing women as hard news.

The burden on those of us who know the truth is to explode the myths, to confront the realities.

There comes a time to stand and fight and it is NOW.

The ERA is the last best hope in this century of committing this country to the principle of human equality—regardless of sex. It has been 55 years since the ERA was first introduced in Congress as the second step in guaranteeing full citizenship to women.

Two generations of women have now struggled for its ratification. If it fails, it will take 2 more generations to recover from the loss. There comes a time when we must have the courage to declare "This ABOVE ALL."

If we do not say this, *who will?*

If we who believe most passionately that all women and men are created equal are not willing to fight when the last chance to realize that dream in our lifetime is in dire peril, *who will?*
If we who know the hypocrisy that has almost turned our victory into defeat will not expose it, *who will?*

If we do not rise to the challenge of going the extra mile, of giving all that we can in the last critical days, *who will?*

If we back away from a last ditch, all-out fight for the ERA today, what compromise of our convictions will we tolerate tomorrow?

WE MUST NOT REFUSE THIS CHALLENGE.

We must not deceive ourselves into believing that we can proceed with business as usual while the victory we have so nearly won is stolen from us.

Most of the traitors who switched votes and sold us out cannot be held accountable until after March, 1979 because they are not up for election until 1980. There is no longer one full legislative session left before the deadline is reached and our opposition is stalling with parliamentary delaying tactics and is prepared to stonewall it until time runs out. We cannot fool ourselves. We have done less than the best. We cannot fail to recognize that we in fact have not adequately alerted our own membership and indeed the nation to the peril to those of us who dream of full equality for women.

Therefore we declare a State of Emergency for the National Organization for Women in which we turn all our resources to the ratification effort and to extension of the deadline for ratification of the ERA an additional 7 years.

That we emphatically state that the extension of the deadline is necessary. Necessary for the real impact of the ERA boycott of convention business in unratified states; necessary for an electoral strategy to have full impact; necessary to remove time as the issue and to place the ERA before the public in an atmosphere in which the merits of the ERA itself are the only issue, necessary to erase the half-truths and distortions of the opposition and that we state emphatically that we are not willing to accept the false hope of reintroduction on March 23, 1979 that erases 55 years of work.

Rather we recognize that a vote against extension of the deadline is a vote *against* equality for women in this century.

There comes a time to gather the courage of our convictions, the strength of our unity, the passion of our commitment and declare we are pledged to do all that is humanly possible to pass H.J. Res. 638 - the extension of the time line in this session of Congress. We are determined to be victorious because we will not tolerate the possibility of living lives in which there is no realistic hope of sisters and brothers, wives and husbands, mothers and fathers, women and men, living together, working together as equals.

WE HAVE PASSED THE POINT OF NO RETURN!

NOW urges Congress to hold hearings during the 96th session on legislation establishing a Homemakers' Bill of Rights. Following are the major provisions which should be included in the Bill.

HOMEMAKERS' BILL OF RIGHTS (1979)

I. Educational Rights for Homemakers

A. A tax policy which enables homemakers to deduct all educational expenses, including transportation costs and child care over the entire period of their schooling;

B. Revision of AFDC to cover all educational expenses and full costs of transportation and child care for homemakers who resume their schooling;

C. Provision of loans at modest rates of interest to homemakers who wish to pursue vocational, professional, or graduate training;

D. Incentives to businesses to train and hire homemakers, including a massive educational effort alerting corporations, organizations, and the government to the need to give special consideration to homemakers.

II. Economic Rights for Homemakers

A. Rights for Women in the Home

1. Revision of federal income tax forms to clearly indicate that all income listed on a joint income tax return is equally shared.

2. Elimination of gift taxes on interspousal transfers.

3. Inclusion in the GNP of the value of goods and services produced and provided by homemakers.

4. Provision of independent Social Security coverage, including disability, in the homemakers own name, portable in and out of marriage, and continuing as the homemaker leaves and re-enters the paid workforce.

5. Reform of the welfare system, including setting a Federal floor at the Bureau of Labor Statistics lower-living standard, and extension of coverage to all persons in need.

6. Increase and expansion of flex-time and part-time employment and job sharing opportunities. Twenty-four hour child care facilities must be made available so that parents of young children can be free to work varied hours. All flex- and part-time jobs must offer full fringe benefits.

7. Reform of civil and criminal laws to protect homemakers from spousal and domestic abuse.

B. Economic Rights for Homemakers in Transition

1. Equitable division of property and assets, including pensions and annuities, in recognition of the unpaid contributions of the homemaker in acquiring and maintaining the family's assets;

2. Vigorous enforcement of maintenance (alimony) orders to assure compensation for the loss of educational opportunities, seniority, advancement, benefits and accrued protection the homemaker would have had if s/he had been in the paid workforce during the years of homemaking;

3. Funding of programs to provide displaced homemakers with job entry education, training, counselling and placement, and supportive service;

4. Eligibility of homemakers for unemployment compensation;

5. Revision of pension and Social Security laws so that divorced homemakers are entitled to retirement and disability benefits for their years of service, and so widowed homemakers are provided with special transition payments if they are not eligible for parent's or retirement benefits;

6. Assurance of widows' right to continued access to the family savings accounts, checking accounts, securities and safety deposit boxes and continuation of pensions, family insurance coverage, and other employment-related benefits.

Many of the provisions outlined in the Homemakers Bill of Rights must be extended to benefit other midlife women as well. Congress must take immediate action to provide short-term relief for women currently in midlife and at the same time develop long-term legislation, monitor and enforce existing laws and programs, and initiate mass public education efforts. Other measures needed to accomplish these goals are:

1. **Ratification of the Equal Rights Amendment,** and strengthened enforcement of existing sex and age discrimination laws. Passage of the ERA would guarantee justice on the job for women both in the marketplace and in the home, and assure that government regulated and funded programs in areas such as education and training, insurance, pensions, credit, etc., cannot discriminate on the basis of sex.

2. **Increased education, training, and employment opportunities** for women of all ages. For midlife women, special emphasis should be placed on short-term vocational training. Skills developed in volunteer jobs and homemaking should be identified and recognized as qualification for paid employment.

3. **Development and enactment of a National Retirement Program,** so that all citizens are assured a decent income in their later years. Comprehensive Social Security and Pension reform is needed which recognizes the value of homemaking, and which does not tie pension benefits to one locality or employer. Under current policies, pension plans are not transferable between employers, and pensions are provided mainly to reward workers for long years of loyal service. This results in age discrimination, when companies are reluctant to hire older workers who are likely to retire soon, and also restricts mobility and freedom of workers.

4. **Passage of Comprehensive Child Care legislation,** which enables all parents to obtain affordable, quality, 24-hour child care, and encourages schools to have supervised lunch hours, and before and after school programs.

5. **Passage of Comprehensive Welfare Reform,** instituting a decent federal floor, and allowing full deduction of all work-related and education expenses, including child care and transportation. Training, job-placement, and supportive services must be provided to give women a realistic option to work inside or outside the home.

6. **Enactment of National Health Insurance** which includes comprehensive coverage, especially in reproductive health areas, and provides rehabilitation for drug and alcohol abuse and depression.

I. NOW's Position on the Current Proposal to Institute a Compulsory Registration of Young People (1980)

Statement From Eleanor Smeal, President

"We are opposed to reinstatement of compulsory registration. As the first step toward reinstatement of the draft, registration is a return to the sexist and racist Selective Service System which gave us discrimination against the poor, minorities, and women while it lowered the quality of our military forces. Our long standing position against violence combined with our determination to end discrimination makes us unable to support registration.

"The voluntary armed service is of higher quality than the draft service and would be even more so if it were free of discrimination against women and minorities. Discrimination against women and minorities produces in the armed services exactly what it produces in the society as a whole—wasted skills, talents and potential and inevitable reliance on lower quality because of the refusal to recruit and select the best qualified regardless of sex or race."

The drive to reinstate compulsory registration of young people and to ultimately reinstate the draft was begun almost immediately after the draft was ended and the All-Volunteer Force (AVF) was created in 1973 (registration of young American males ended in 1976). Four reasons generally appear in arguments to reinstate the draft: (1) It would be required in the case of a major war; (2) the declining youth population will create serious problems in meeting personnel requirements; (3) should a national youth training and work program be instituted military service would be part of the program; and (4) considerable savings in costs could be realized. Underneath the surface of these arguments are the racist and sexist attitudes which pervade our society, coupled with undisguised economic exploitation.

A fear frequently expressed is that the army is rapidly becoming a black man's army—34% of Army recruits in 1978 were black—with the unstated racist views that blacks are inferior "raw material" and therefore inferior soldiers. Hand-in-glove with these racist attitudes are the sexist attitudes towards women in the military. Female participation in the military has increased dramatically under the AVF to a projected 13% of the active forces in 1983. Women constituted less than 1% of the draft army.

Poverty has always been one of the features of military life, especially in the lower ranks. This situation has been somewhat mitigated in the

AVF by the pay increases required to attract volunteers with the result that personnel costs, in the view of some, have made serious dents in funds available for hardware. A return to the draft is viewed, again by some, as the easiest way to reverse this trend.

Myths about the All-Volunteer Force are abundant. Contrary to myth, the active forces of the AVF have been within 1.5% of the congressionally authorized limits since 1974. The AVF has superior mental ability, is better educated, has less discipline problems, and has proportionally the same number of people from the lower economic levels, but a higher percentage of minorities, compared to the old conscripted service of the Vietnam War period. The Department of Defense itself in a December 1978 report stated in unequivocal terms that the AVF was superior to the drafted force.

Why then the need to register? We are told it will show the USSR that we mean business, and that it will increase our ability to mobilize. Actually, registration saves only a few days. And although it sounds strong to Americans who want to show that we are serious, in reality it proves nothing to the USSR which appreciates fully how little names on a list actually mean. NOW is against the registration of young people precisely because it is a response which stimulates the environment of preparation for war. Too many of us still remember the senseless killing and destruction in Vietnam—which we also protested—and believe that violence is the "ultimate solution" taught most typically to males in our society. We reject that solution, and believe that too many are willing to wage war with others' lives. National defense and self defense is one thing; aggression for economic self-interest is quite another. To fight a war for oil is to deny that the inherent rights of all human beings must take precedence over the economic self-interest of a very few. We are committed to working for the day when our nation and our world priorities will be people—a day when our domestic problems are not solved by military aggression.

If the objective is really to increase the number of people capable of being mobilized in a short period of time and to improve the quality of the national defense, the easiest way to accomplish this without increasing the war atmosphere in the world and without involuntarily disrupting the lives of young people is to remove the sex discriminatory restrictions on women in the military. Without these discriminatory practices, women recruits would be in far greater supply and of a higher caliber than additional male recruits. Under existing practices, female numbers are depressed to a current 8% of the armed forces (programmed to increase to about 13% by 1983). The current discriminatory practices are based upon outmoded concepts of both women's role and combat. Today's military is highly technological. The military is more in need of brains than brawn.

Moreover, physiological limitations go both ways: a small, agile person is more advantageous than a large, heavy person in many situations. What Is the impact of sex discrimination on women in the current military? Women are given fewer educational, training and advancement opportunities than men in the largest single vocational training institution in our country, the military. Approximately 83% of enlisted women are in the four lowest pay grades as compared to 68% of men. The four highest pay grades hold 23% of enlisted men and only 3% of enlisted women. Officer training programs and many specialties are closed to women except in token numbers. Using even the most inclusive measures, 75% of the positions in the military are unavailable to women because they are defined as combat-related or because they are reserved to provide rotational and career progression slots for men.

What would be the impact on women and the nation if women were excluded from the registration or ultimately from a draft? Currently, more women are capable and willing to serve than are recruited. Many more will be turned away to the detriment of women and the military if the limited progress toward equality in the armed forces is halted. Female numbers in the military would decrease or be held to current projections. During the last draft, women were held to 2% of the armed services. A signal would be sent to the armed services that women do not have to be treated equally. Women serving in combat areas would simply be classified once again as non-combatants or civilians and asked to serve for fewer benefits and lesser training, as was done in the past.

Women have always served. The question is whether they will serve equally or at greater risk to themselves. In modern warfare, the front line and combat zone are difficult to determine. People behind the so-called front lines are nevertheless serving at great risk. Women are serving at even greater risk because they have less combat training.

The modern military depends upon a high degree of technology. Not only in the modern civilian labor force do women fill many of the technically trained positions, but also in the current military. Women are simply necessary and the need for women is increasing as the supply of men decreases and the need for highly qualified and trained or trainable people increases.

The current debate over foxholes in Korea and the trenches of World War I is as obsolete to warfare in 1980 as the structured lines of' the British Redcoats in the American wilderness. Warfare has changed and so has the position of women in education, training and the labor force.

We will serve. We will serve, for one reason, because the military has difficulty attracting sufficient numbers of people who are educated and technically trainable. One half of the pool of talented and trained youth of our country is women. Moreover, many personnel categories required by the modern armed services—clerical workers, keypunch operators, computer specialists, communications experts, administrative personnel—are more readily found already trained in the female population. If there is a true national emergency we will serve and we will do so in all capacities. The myth that we are not needed and not first class citizens must end right now.

Those who oppose the registration and draft for females say they seek to protect women. But omission from the registration and draft ultimately robs women of the right to first class citizenship and paves the way to underpaying women all the remaining days of our lives. Moreover, because men exclude women here, they justify excluding women from the decision-making of our nation.

When the word "protection" is used, we know it costs women a great deal. In this case, it fortifies a pattern of sex discrimination in our nation which manifests itself in many ways. One rape occurs every eight minutes. One out of every four American married women is a victim of wife beating. Eight out of ten murder victims in the United States are female. Women earn $.59 for every $1 a man earns in the same 40-hour week. The 13 million American women 65 years of age and over have an average income of less than $3000 a year.

Do women know violence? Yes: women are the most frequent victims of violence. We must not forget that the great wars in Europe have visited far greater hardship upon the civilian population, largely untrained and unprotected women and children, than upon the military forces of the combatants.

Do women know hardships? Yes: the cost of discrimination to women is too dear—we pay with our lives. War is senseless. Neither the lives of young men nor young women should be wasted. But if we cannot stop the killing, we know we cannot choose between our sons or daughters. The choice robs women as well as men. In the long and short run, it injures us all.

II. The Current Role of Women In the Military
Background

WORLD WAR II: 350,000 women served in many traditional roles and in non-traditional roles as pilots, truck drivers, airplane mechanics, gunnery instructors, air traffic controllers, naval air navigators, etc.

1948-1967: Woman were limited by law to 2% of the total enlisted services. Women officers were limited by law to 10% of total enlisted women.

1968-1972: As the result of military regulations severely restricting the positions available to them, women remained less than 2% of the armed services.

1973-1980: The draft terminated and the All-Volunteer Force was established. The armed forces began to increasingly utilize women as a factor in making the All Volunteer Force work. The number of women increased from 2% to approximately 8% of the total armed services today. Despite these increases, women continue to be restricted by law, regulations, practices and policies to a small fraction of the military. The restrictions are based largely on the exclusion of women from jobs defined as combat-related and the reservation of numerous slots for men for career progression and rotation purposes.

Present Status of Women
Quantity and Diversity

Women comprise approximately 8% of the total armed services. Women are projected by the Department of Defense to be 13% of the armed services by 1983.

Increased participation for women in the military has also meant increased participation for minority women although the only group of minority women currently fairly well represented is black women who comprise 19% of total enlisted women. Hispanic women are a little more than 3% of enlisted women and Native American and Asian American women are less than $2 1/2$%.

The restricted number of women officers and the token number of women promoted to truly significant rank is especially apparent when it comes to minority women who have not even reached the level of tokenism.

Women recruits are performing well in diverse military occupational groups including electrical equipment repair, communications and intelligence, other technical, administrative and clerical, crafts, service and supply, and medical and dental.

Quality

Higher Educational Level: With the growing complexity of the modern technological military, high school completion is the best single measure of potential to succeed in the armed services, according to the Department of Defense. A significantly greater percentage of women recruits have high school diplomas.

% Recruits H.S. Grads	1971	1972	1973	1974	1975	1976	1977	1978
Female	93.9	94.4	95.2	91.7	90.6	91.1	NOT	91.0
Male	68.3	66.8	66.5	58.1	62.5	66.7	AVAIL.	75.0

Equal or Better Performance at Military Service Academies: Women have been admitted to the Army, Navy and Air Force Academies since 1978. In this year's first graduating classes with women, the women's performance has equaled and often surpassed that of their male counterparts.

Fewer Disciplinary Problems: The average woman recruit is much less likely than a male recruit to become a discipline problem. Women lose far less time than men for absence without leave, desertion, alcoholism and drug abuse.

Physiological Differences

On the average, American men are taller, heavier and stronger than American women. This fact is cited as proof that men should dominate the military and be the only ones in combat roles. This unwarranted assumption ignores four major points:

1. Size is Not Always a Factor: Technological advances continue to diminish the importance of brute strength. The "person who pushes the button" may be in a combat role, but does not require extraordinary strength to carry out her/his duties.

Even many of the "traditional" combat roles, such as those in the Air Force and Navy, do not now and never have required the brute strength allegedly associated with combat.

If the truth be known, in most close combat, a gun is the great equalizer. And our experience in ground combat with Asian men (who are on the average smaller than American women) in Korea and Vietnam demonstrated that smaller men can be the victor because of skill or training.

2. Size Can Be Factor—A Plus for Women: There is no reason behind the blanket assumption that "bigger is always better" in the military arena.

The proliferation of advanced equipment installed in planes, ships, tanks and other land vehicles is turning "elbow room" into a scarce commodity. A soldier with a smaller physique becomes a valuable asset in these situations. In many cases, it is the small, lithe and agile soldier who can do the job more proficiently, escape the space more easily, and better fit the needs of today's (and tomorrow's) armed forces.

3. Weaponry and Equipment Can Be Adapted to Fit the Needs of the Average Female Soldier: Our military has already faced similar needs in adapting U.S. military equipment for use by allied forces whose average sized male is smaller than the average American male. American industry has made great strides in adapting equipment and clothing originally designed for use by men in the construction and telecommunications fields to fit the needs of the highly productive female worker in non-traditional occupations.

4. Finally, the Fact That the Average Man Is Stronger Than the Average Women Does Not Mean That All Men Are Stronger Than All Women: First, it has been proven that the differences narrow or disappear when women receive adequate training. And, more significantly, no one disputes that some women are stronger than some men. Assigning jobs by gender instead of by ability simply does not make sense. What it does make is a less qualified military. If the armed services are to operate to their fullest capacity, they must classify people by their ability to do the job—not by their gender.

Combat Effectiveness

The first myth to be dispelled is that women have not been in combat. According to the Women's Equity Action League Educational and Legal Defense Fund:

"During World War II, 200,000 military women in the Army, Navy, Marine Corps and Coast Guard served as nurses, mechanics, truck drivers, parachute riggers, typists, radio operators, technicians and air traffic controllers. They performed bravely and competently under hostile fire.

"American military women landed on the beaches at Normandy, France as part of the 'D-Day' allies invasion. Army women traveled with the Fifth Army close to the front lines during the invasion of Italy. Army women also served in the South Pacific and North Africa. They received many military decorations for bravery; including the Purple Heart—awarded to those wounded by enemy fire.

"Nearly 100 Army and Navy nurses were prisoners of war for three years in the Philippines during World War II. "Over 7,000 women served their country in Southeast Asia during the Vietnam War and received combat pay. Some of these military women died as a result of enemy action."

Women have served and will continue to serve in combat environments under the same conditions, suffering the same risks and the same injuries as men. Playing the language game of classifying an army nurse or a Women's Air Service Pilot as non-combatant does not change the fact that they are in combat. The reality is that women have served and died for their country and will continue to do so. The question is whether they will do so with the same training, benefits and salary as men.

In contrast to emotionalism and unsubstantiated generalities, many tests have been done *by the armed forces* in the late 1970s to assess the capabilities of women in combat roles:

Women Content in Units Force Development Test (MAX WAC)
Purpose: To test the effect of placing women in combat support and combat service support units.
Exercise: 72 hours under normal field conditions.
Results: The performance of men and women with no prior civilian experience and equal military training was equal.

The units effectiveness was not impaired by the presence of up to 35% women soldiers.

Note: 35% was the maximum tested in this particular exercise; there is no evidence it is the actual "maximum."

Reforger Exercises (Return of Forces to Germany Exercise)

Purpose: To test the performance of enlisted women in extended field situations.

Exercise: A 30 day field exercise involving 1 1/2 weeks of war games in Germany. Ten percent of the combat support and combat service support units were comprised of women.

Results: Women's skills were as good or better than the males. Women had the stamina and endurance to maintain performance standards in the field equal to those of men. Women were highly proficient. Women were highly motivated.

Navy U.S.S. Sanctuary

Purpose: To test the effectiveness of women at sea.

Exercise: 60 enlisted women served on board the U.S.S. Sanctuary.

Results: Women performed every shipboard function with the same ease, expertise and dedication as men. Morale was high. Response of male and female sailors was favorable.

Operation Bold Eagle

Purpose: A guerrilla warfare and airborne assault exercise.

Exercise: 150 women and 4000 men participated.

Results: Women were exposed to the same hardships in the field as men and they performed very well.

Army Human Engineering Lab Test

Purpose: To test the ability of women to operate 105 and 155mm artillery howitzers.

Exercise: 13 women office workers participated in a three-week physical training program and were then assigned to the "heaviest, noisiest job in the army." They loaded and fired the howitzers and met a tough rate-of-fire test of four rounds a minute for three minutes, then one round a minute for the 155mm and ten rounds a minute for three minutes for the 105, followed by three rounds a minute on the same weapon.

Results: The women were rated "professional, outstanding, and phenomenal."

The above tests demonstrate that women are capable of performing satisfactory or better in combat-related positions. Those who would restrict women from combat based on the fear that the quality of our military could be adversely affected should rather advocate women in the armed forces. Selection and training of soldiers based on ability rather than gender would result in a better quality military than could be achieved by arbitrary exclusion of one-half the potential pool.

Women Soldiers Lose Less Active Duty Time Than Men.

Myth: Women, because of pregnancy and menstruation, will lose more active duty time than men.

Reality: The evidence is that there is little difference in the time lost by women and men and that, in fact, it appears that less time is lost by women. This is true even when pregnancy, the largest single factor in

Comparison of Lost Time for Enlisted Men and Women in the Navy		
	Lost Days as % of Total Days Available	
Lost Time Category	Women	Men
Alcohol Abuse	.09	.12
Drug Use	.02	.12
Unauthorized Absence (AWOL)	.05	.24
Returned Deserters	.07	.62
Abortion	.03	0
Pregnancy	.37	0
TOTAL	.63	1.10

lost time for women, is included. The only definitive lost time study was done in the Navy and it shows that men lose twice as much time as women.

The Retention Rate of Women Soldiers is Higher

Myth: Women are more likely to drop out of the service (because of pregnancy, marriage, or alleged lack of ability) thereby wasting valuable training invested in them.

Reality: Women are being retained in the services at higher rates than men.

Of those recruited in 1973-1976, 64% of the men remained on active duty as of June 1978 compared with 70% of the women.

Percentage of 1971-76 Enterees Still on Active Duty as of 06/76		
Year of Entry	Female	Male
1971	22.8	17.6
1972	28.0	23.4
1973	43.1	37.5
1974	61.6	58.3
1975	75.9	74.6
1976	87.7	87.4

Economics of Women in the Military

Opening the doors to more women in the military would prove cost-effective. The simple fact is that it costs far less to recruit high quality women than to recruit high quality men. Because of the restrictions on the number of women the services will accept, highly qualified women are recruited without effort while less qualified men are sought with incentives and high cost advertising campaigns. Excluding enlistment bonuses, the costs for an Army recruit are:

High Quality Men	**$3,700**
High Quality Women	**$150**
Low Quality Men	**$150**

Many people believe that the Military spends more money per female recruit because of "difficulties" in training, housing, clothing

Characteristics of Male & Female Recruits*		
Characteristics	Male	Female
Average Age	18.9	20.0
Percent Married	11.6	11.6
Percent Black	18.5	16.1
Percent Hispanic	Not Avail.	3.1**
Percent High School Grads.	62.9	91.7
Percent Still on Active Duty, 30 June 1978	64.0	70.0
Marginal Recruiting Cost for High Quality Army Recruit	$3,700	$150

*Fiscal Years 1973-1976   **1977 Data
Department of Defense Statistics

and recruiting women. This is simply not true. The average woman in the military costs the Defense Department about 8% less than the average man according to an often quoted study on Women and the Military by Binkin and Bach for the Brookings Institution. The average annual per capita costs of providing medical care, housing and transportation are approximately $982 less for women than for men.

Despite the sex discrimination which restricts them to few and truncated career paths, the military is attractive monetarily to many women. Especially for those women who pursue traditional careers, the average pay for enlisted military personnel far surpasses the average pay for civilian women who earn 59¢ for every $1 earned by men. The services, unlike the private sector, do pay men and women equally if they are of the same grade, longevity, and skills. Like the private sector, however, enlisted women are clustered in the lower pay grades and are under-represented in the higher pay grades.

III. Registration and the Draft

Registration means simply compiling a list of all people (male, female, or both) who happen to fall within a certain age category, e.g., 18 to 22 year-olds. It does not mean classifying these people as to suitability for military service. Thus registration is only a crude first step in generating an effective military force. Registration at the present time would save only 13 days of the months required to produce military personnel with even minimal training if a draft were to actually follow registratIon. This is the real effect of registration and its relevance to our military preparedness.

A draft subsequent to registration would mean the classification, induction and training for military service of a large fraction of all young people in a certain age group. It is important to remember that every draft has included exemptions and deferments. Although one can no longer openly buy one's way out of the draft as during the Civil War, large numbers of men are exempted because of their physical or mental condition, because they support more than a certain (arbitrary) number of family members, or because they possess critical skills. Deferments have been granted for completion of education and training and for employment in fields deemed vItal to the war effort. Since our armed forces have been staffed on an all-volunteer basis since

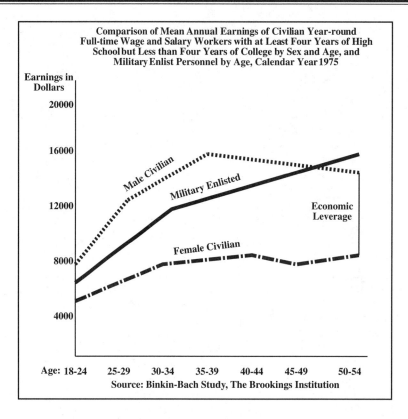

Comparison of Mean Annual Earnings of Civilian Year-round Full-time Wage and Salary Workers with at Least Four Years of High School but Less than Four Years of College by Sex and Age, and Military Enlist Personnel by Age, Calendar Year 1975

Earnings in Dollars

Male Civilian

Military Enlisted

Female Civilian

Economic Leverage

Age: 18-24   25-29   30-34   35-39   40-44   45-49   50-54

Source: Binkin-Bach Study, The Brookings Institution

1973 a draft represents a complete reversal in policy.

Some would have us believe that the shortcomings of the All Volunteer Force have been so serious that the draft is the only recourse. How does the AVF compare to the pre-1973 draft military? A 1978 Department of Defense study of the AVF showed it to be superior to the draft military with respect to:

1. Educational Level: One measure of the increased educational level is the percentage of high school graduates. This has increased from 88% of those entering the services in 1972, the last year of the draft, to 77% of all recruits in 1978. Other measures, such as the percentage of the enlisted force with some college education, also show an increased education level in the AVF.

2. Mental Quality: Written test scores show that mental quality of recruits in the AVF is better than that in the draft era forces. One illustration of this improvement is the decrease from 14% to 5% of personnel in the lowest mental quality category during the years the AVF has been in existence.

3. Discipline: Military discipline as measured by court-martial rates, non-judicial punishment rates and desertion rates has steadily improved since the inception of the AVF. For example, desertion rates have dropped from 25 per 1000 in 1973 to 18 per 1000 in 1977.

Initial concerns that the AVF would be less representative of society as a whole than the draft forces have not materialized. Geographic representation and family income profiles almost precisely duplicate those of the draft. In both, the very rich and the very poor are under-represented.

Since the inception of the AVF, however, minority participation in the military has increased significantly. The 1978 study of the Department of Defense on the AVF did not publish statistics on percentages of all minority service persons, but did publish this data for blacks. In the AVF, the percentage of blacks continues to increase, both in officer and enlisted ranks. By the end of 1978, blacks comprised 17% of total active duty armed forces personnel, 19% of enlisted personnel and 4% of officers. In the Army, blacks comprised 7% of officers, 29% of enlisted personnel, and 34% of new recruits, an all-time high. In fiscal years 1964 to 1972, before the AVF came into existence, blacks comprised an average of 10.8% of total enlisted active duty forces.

The disproportionate numbers of black volunteers are partially the result of job discrimination and blocked mobility patterns in the larger society. Indeed, many civil rights leaders believe that a return to the draft would in fact threaten job opportunities for blacks in the military.

As to cost savings, in contrast to the claims that a draft force would be far less expensive, it was estimated in the 1978 Department of Defense study that the savings in returning to a draft force would be only about 0.2% of the Department of Defense budget. According to the 1978 Department of Defense study: "Considering that the career force has always been (staffed) by volunteers, the only savings one should anticipate are those associated with recruiting, paying, and training the first-term members." Those savings would be partially offset by the cost of operating the conscription system.

Draft advocates may be planning to "save" money in personnel by freezing or reducing pay at lower enlistment levels. The point is that the major way the draft could result in significant cost savings would be through gross economic exploitation of draftees considering that junior pay is barely at minimum wage today.

Considerable concern was expressed during planning for the AVF that recruitment alone could not maintain the required staffing levels. This has not proved to be the case. Since 1974 staffing levels in the AVF have been within 1.5% of those authorized by Congress.

Other arguments for resuming the draft focus on the understaffed reserve forces. Department of Defense statements indicate that the origin of this problem lies in the initial assumption by the military that the major problems in the All-Volunteer Force would be with the active components. These therefore received most of the management attention and the reserves were left to languish. Defense spokesmen have stated that increased attention to the reserves will undoubtedly yield better results and that until such efforts are made it would be reckless to advocate conscription to fill vacancies in the reserve.

The establishment of the All-Volunteer Force is in line with our tradition of using the draft only in time of war. Since no case can be made for any deficiency in the All-Volunteer Force, it is legitimate to question the motivation of those pushing for a return to the draft.It is even more difficult to argue for the wasted expenditures and efforts of registration without a draft.

IV. The Registration and Drafting of Women

NOW opposes the registration and drafting of anyone. The elimination of sex discrimination in the military would, in and of itself, markedly improve our national defense. However, to adequately utilize women, as volunteers or as draftees, sex discriminatory practices must be eliminated. In fact, if the current restrictive legislation, regulations, policies and procedures are maintained in the military, the percentage of women cannot increase much beyond 15% whether or not there is a draft of women.

If a draft and registration is instituted, NOW believes it must include women. As a matter of fairness and equity, no draft or registration that excludes one half of the population in 1980 simply on the basis of gender could be deemed fair. Young people who have common aspirations, hopes and education will resent women being excluded. Women will pay with more limited opportunities and rights. Our nation will pay by limiting its resources. All will pay by the constant exclusion of females and their priorities from the nation's decision-making.

Any registration or draft that excluded females would be challenged as an unconstitutional denial of rights under the Fifth Amendment. Two developments since the termination of the Vietnam-era draft weigh heavily on the question of women's inclusion in any future registration and draft and lead to the conclusion that excluding women would be found unconstitutional.

The first of these was the establishment in 1978 by the Supreme Court of a more stringent review standard for sex-based classification and the subsequent application of this standard to legislatIon containing sex-based classifications. The second development is the consistently high performance of women in all military categorIes to which they have been admitted as the result of recent changes in military policy.

There is no doubt that any attempt to institute registration and a draft excluding women would result in legal action. There are also very substantial grounds for believing that the courts would find any such attempt in violation of the Equal Protection Clause of the Fifth Amendment.

Between 1980 and 1992 the pool of young males will decrease by almost 25 percent. This drop, coupled with the increasing complexity of modern weapons and the even more limited pool of technically trained or trainable youth, leaves little room for rational argument against women's increasing participation in the military, on either a voluntary or involuntary basis. The military simply will not be able to operate without utilizing women.

Any draft, whether it includes women or not, will have deferments and exemptions based upon such matters as physical and mental health, specialized skills, or family dependents and obligations. The draft has usually been applied to young people, the overwhelming majority of whom are not married and do not as yet have family responsibilities. In any case, if women were included, such exemptions would have to be written to be applicable to either sex. Congress would retain the power to define the exemptions from compulsory service which then would be applied to both men and women.

The issues of fairness, legality and need not withstanding, the full integration of women in the military cannot occur until sex discrimination is routed out. The April 1977 report of the U.S. Commission on Civil Rights found 140 provisions relating to the armed forces under Title 10 of the U.S. Code which contained sex-based references. Not until discriminatory regulatIons, laws, practices and policies are off the books will women gain equal access to the opportunities available in the military.

Sex Discrimination In the Military

Sex discrimination is rampant in the military. The single largest reason given is the exclusion of women from combat roles. In reality, sex discrimination in the military serves to protect male career lives and is based on stereotypic assumptions about the inferiority of women.

In considering women in combat there have been two basic questions:

1) Should women be exposed to the conditions of combat and war, and

2) Will women in combat adversely affect the proficiency of the combat force?

Clearly, neither men nor women should be exposed to war. It is obvious, however, that without the establishment of a war-free society it is impossible to shield women from the violence of war either as civilians, soldiers, or as relatives or loved ones or both.

Women, as members of the civilian population have always suffered great damage as the front lines of war merge with their homes. If civilian women have been unable to escape from war, it is surely evident that women in the military have been repeatedly exposed to combat conditions. Although women have been barred from combat on paper, they have often served in the midst of it, and been exposed to the same dangers and hardships as their male counterparts. Women's Air Service Pilots, nurses, medical technicians, and many more have served and died for their country. Women are assigned to combat support and combat service support units, and function side by side with men. "Behind the lines"' jobs are hardly safe in a world where there are fewer and fewer known "lines."

Moreover, the hysteria at the thought of sending women into combat must be placed in its proper perspective. In the last draft, less than 1% of the men eligible were inducted and subsequently assigned to a combat unit. If women were added to the pool, the statistical chance of an individual being drafted and assigned to a combat unit— whether or not there was a female combat exclusion—would be negligible.

The second question that is inherent in any plea to keep women out of combat is whether the presence of women soldiers will lower the fighting quality of the military. Again, clearly, women soldiers who have been trained have demonstrated their capabilities. The numerous tests cited herein are proof that those persons who serve in

Service Data Submission on Potential Use of Women		
Positions		**Percentage**
A	Total Positions	100%
B/C	Combat & Combat Support	43%
D	Net = A - (B/C)	57%
E	Rotation Base	7%
F	Physiological Limits	0%
G	Other Limits	23%
H	Open to Women H = D- (E + F + G)	27%
I	Women Utilized 1977	6%

241

combat must be chosen on the basis of ability rather than gender if the military is to be as proficient as possible. Thus, it is clear that there are no genuine reasons to exclude women from combat. There are, however, grave effects on the opportunities available to military women based on the unnecessary combat restrictions. The chart on the preceding page, entitled "Service Data Submission on Potential Use of Women," indicates the Department of Defense's explanation of restricted positions for women. The single largest reason for closing positions to women is indicated in line B/C—combat and combat support. Combat restrictions do not now and never have "protected" women. They do assure that military women can never reach the same posts as men or follow unlimited career paths. They do serve to restrict women from 43% of the total military positions.

Aside from combat restrictions, however, the chart tells a shocking story about discrimination against women in the military. Line E indicates that an additional 7% of positions are reserved for men to provide a base for sea/shore and overseas/continental U.S. rotations. Line G shows that yet another 23% of positions are reserved for other reasons. What are the other reasons? Slots reserved to provide career progression opportunities for men. Limitations on the concentration of women in various units. Lack of available housing—the Air Force, for example, excludes women from 45% of its overseas positions because of "unacceptable" facilities. The Air Force considers it "unacceptable" for men and women to share a common hall.

Perhaps the most revealing line is line F. The military there states that no additional positions are excluded for physiological reasons. The armed forces are saying that aside from those positions restricted unnecessarily because of their "combat" nature, there are no jobs in the military which women cannot perform because of size, or strength. The bottom line, using even this most liberal of measures, is dismal—a total potential of only 27% of military positions open to women, and women today comprise even less at 8% (6% in 1977).

		Maximum Weight for 72"	Difference
Army	Male	227	56
	Female	171	
Navy	Male	227	52
	Female	175	
Marine Corps	Male	203	32
	Female	171	
Air Force	Male	196	29
	Female	167	

Women's entry into the military is hampered by physiological restrictions. Height and weight restrictions serve to assure that women remain frailer than men by imposing lower weight limitations on women regardless of their bone structure or muscularity. The maximum weights for men and women six feet tall in the various branches of the military are indicated above.

There are clear inequities in the different limitations. Women are not allowed to weigh the same or even near the same as men regardless of their bone structure. An Air Force regulation even allows further adjustment of the maximum weight allowance for men with large bone structure, but women with large bone structure are not granted any adjustment.

To illustrate the problems that these restrictions can cause beyond the initial problem of being allowed to enlist, there is the regulation that provides that if a male or female in the Air Force wants to be a firefighter, he or she must be at least 5'6" and weigh at least 140 pounds. The maximum allowable weight, however, for a 5'6" woman in the Air Force is 141 pounds. In other words, an Air Force woman 5'6" must be within one pound of her maximum weight allowance to be a firefighter.

Yet another source of discrimination is the failure of the armed forces to provide equipment and clothing adapted for use by women and men of small stature. The Defense Advisory Committee on Women In the Services (DACOWITS) recommended in the fall of 1979 the adaptation of military clothing to suit women's needs. During visitations to military installations, DACOWITS found that there were "items of present field work and organizational clothing for women that fit women so poorly that they constitute health and safety hazards and are inappropriate and non-functional."

Finally, there is the problem of sexual harassment of women in the military which has assumed epidemic proportions. The entire range from verbal abuse to physical attack can be found at any military installation. The attitude of some men is often one of resentment—that "this man's army" is being invaded by women who have no place in it.

Some service men look upon service women as a sexual convenience and freely use rank to proposition them. Official response to reports of sexual harassment is often non-response, the product of a "boys will be boys" mentality. Refusals on the part of women are often countered with charges of lesbianism, redeemable for a less than honorable discharge. Discharge may result regardless of the veracity of the charge.

Suspected homosexuality on the part of male and female military personnel constitutes grounds for discharge, with female personnel generally prosecuted more harshly than males. The waste of human talent and potential that results from the military's irrational discrimination against lesbians and gay men is oppressive to the individuals involved and is not in the national interest.

Beyond the discrimination against women who are actually in the military, there is lifelong discrimination against those women who are excluded from the military through no fault of their own. They suffer discrimination in the pursuit of governmental civilian jobs because of veterans preference. Veterans are, by law, given preferential treatment in federal jobs and most state jobs, both in hiring and promotions. Currently, because of past discrimination in the military, only 2% of our nation's veterans are females. Considering that the federal government alone has three times as many civilian positions as American Telephone and Telegraph (AT&T), the nation's number one private employer, this results in massive discrimination against females. There are more than 28 million federal jobs. More civilians work for the Department of Defense than for General Motors. And the Veterans Administration has almost as many jobs as Exxon and Dupont Corporation combined. Discrimination against women in the military serves to injure all women in governmental employment and in salaries for their entire lives.

The effects of discrimination against women in the military cannot be measured in dollars and cents alone. Being told they are unfit for combat training, that they need "protection," women are more readily victims of violence of every kind. Without training and the confidence that they can defend themselves, women live in daily fear of physical assault. One must ask, also, whether a would-be rapist might be less likely to attack a woman if he thought she had been trained as a Marine.

VI. Registration, Draft and the ERA

The present discussion about the registering and drafting of women is without an Equal Rights Amendment and without our nation being at war. For the past several years, without any international crisis, the discussion of registering and drafting women has been a serious part of the drive to return to a drafted military. Whatever happens about registering or drafting women in the short run, in the event of a real national crisis or war, women will be drafted (if men are) and will serve.

Why? Because they are needed. Women today are an essential part of our nation's work force and are a key part of the trained and trainable technical pool of young people required to operate a modern military. Moreover, because of sex segregation in our labor force, certain work categories, which are essential to the military, are overwhelmingly female. Women are a vital part of the administrative, computer, communications, medical and other technical personnel of this nation.

Discrimination against women in the military costs this nation literally billions of dollars a year because better qualified women are not recruited while less qualified males are and at much higher enlistment bonuses and costs.

The combat restrictions serve to bar an entire sex from a wide range of career opportunities and to deprive our national security of vital personnel resources. Women in combat-related categories have been in combat, wounded and killed. But they have served at greater risk to themselves because they have not had adequate combat training.

Discrimination against women in the military depresses opportunities, career paths, training and benefits for women. The military provides thousands of jobs, training programs and educational opportunities which are, for the most part, presently closed to women. Military pay which is, on the average, some 40% higher than female civilian pay, could be the only way out of poverty for countless young women. Restrictions on women in the military, far from protecting them, serve to continue their second class citizenship, pay and opportunity. And this discrimination exercised by the military affects women's employment opportunities and wages throughout their entire work lives because of veterans preference.

The inarguable need for women in the military, coupled with the blatant and crippling discrimination against women in the military, dramatically demonstrates the need for the ERA. Women in the military have just as much right to adequate equipment, training, clothing, benefits and career progression as men do. The Equal Rights Amendment will guarantee women equal rights and would serve as the basis to eliminate sex discrimination in the military.

Under the Equal Rights Amendment, the military's practices,

regulations, statutes and policies that discriminate on the basis of sex would be held unconstitutional. People would serve in the armed forces according to their own abilities. The national defense would gain by increasing the size of the talented personnel pool at lower recruiting posts while women would have an increased number of jobs, training programs, and financial benefits.

In the event of registratIon, or draft under the ERA, men and women would register and be drafted according to their ability. Exemptions would be determined along equitable and necessary lines, e.g. physical or mental fitness, sole parent of dependent child, etc.— but not upon the basis of gender alone. Under the ERA, the very possibility of a need for a draft or registration would be reduced because the numbers in the available pool of recruits for the All-Volunteer Forces would double.

The debate about whether women will, serve in the military is over. They must serve, but at what cost to themselves?

The debate over registering or drafting women only serves to underline the dramatic necessity for the immediate ratification of the Equal Rights Amendment.

Major Sources

America's Volunteers: A Report on the All-Volunteer Armed Forces, Office of the Assistant Secretary of Defense. (Manpower, Reserve Affairs, and Logistics), second edition, September 1978.

Hearings on Women in the Military, U.S. House of Representatives, Armed Services Committee, Subcommittee on Military Personnel, November 1979.

The Role of Women in the Military. Hearings before the Subcommittee on Priorities and Economy in Government of the Joint Economic Committee, Congress of the United States, July 22 and September 1, 1977.

Use of Women In the Military. Office of the Assistant Secretary of Defense (Manpower, Reserve Affairs, and Logistics), second edition, September 1978.

Women and the Military. Binkin, Martin and Bach, Shirley; The Brookings Institution, Washington, D.C.; 1977.

Women Content in the Army: REFORGER (REF-WAC 77). U.S. Army Research Institute for the Behavioral and Social Sciences; Alexandria, VA; May 30, 1978.

Women Content in Units Force Development Test (MAX WAC). U.S. Army Research Institute for the Behavioral and Social Sciences: Alexandria, VA; October 3, 1977.

Women and the Military: A WEAL Fund Kit. Women's Equity Action League Educational & Legal Defense Fund, Washington, D.C.; 1979.

Women in the Armed Forces. (Issue Brief B79045); Collier, Ellen C.; Foreign Affairs and National Defense Division of the Library of Congress, Congressional Research Service; October 25, 1979.

Women In the Military: Topics for Discussion—1979. Gilden, Nina; Legislative Assistant for Military Affairs to Congresswoman Patricia Schroeder (D-CO)

Social Security - September, 1984

WHEREAS, 91% of older women receive Social Security payments; and

WHEREAS, women receive approximately 62% of the dollars men receive at the time of retirement and beyond; and

WHEREAS, the age for receipt of Social Security benefits will be raised from age 65 starting in the year 2000; and

WHEREAS, the U.S. Commission on Civil Rights reports that nearly all the poor of this country will he women and children by the year 2000;

THEREFORE BE IT RESOLVED that the National Organization for Women work to implement the earnings sharing concept to Social Security allowing all women to live with adequate income above the poverty level during their retirement years;

BE IT FURTHER RESOLVED that one half the earning credit for all families be paid out equally and automatically to each partner;

BE IT FURTHER RESOLVED that the National Organization for Women shall work to implement this policy with adequate funding in order to educate the public, NOW members and members of Congress concerning the drastic needs of women as they reach the retirement years.

Expanded Bill of Rights
for the 21st Century (1989)

Whereas, we are determined that an Equal Rights Amendment that bans sex discrimination in the United States Constitution is ratified; and

Whereas, the Supreme Court has begun to dismantle women's reproductive rights; and

Whereas, the Supreme Court has refused to grant the right to privacy on the basis of sexual preference; and

Whereas, the Supreme Court has dismantled affirmative action plans that fight institutional practices of race and sex discrimination; and

Whereas, the original Bill of Rights was passed in the year 1789 at a time when slavery was legal and women were considered legal chattel by our revolutionary founders; and

Whereas, it is time to complete the promise of liberty and justice under the law for all; and

Whereas, our nation faces new problems of catastrophic environmental conditions which could not have been conceived of by the country's founders;

Therefore be it resolved that it is time for an expanded Bill of Rights for the 21st Century which will ensure that all of the citizens of the United States enjoy basic, inalienable and indivisible human rights to which must be added:

1. the right to freedom from sex discrimination;
2. the right to freedom from race discrimination;
3. the right of all women to freedom from government interference in abortion, birth control and pregnancy and the right of indigent women to public funds for abortion, birth control and pregnancy services;
4. the right to freedom from discrimination on the basis of sexual orientation;
5. the right to freedom from discrimination based on religion, age, ongoing health condition, or a differently abled situation;
6. a right to a decent standard of living, including adequate food, housing, health care and education;
7. the right to clean air, clean water, safe toxic waste disposal and environmental protection; and
8. the right to be free from violence, including freedom from the threat of nuclear war.

Notes To
Part I

NOTES TO PART I

[1] Doris Stevens to Betty Gram Swing, January 8, 1946, Stevens papers, Schlesinger Library.

[2] Columbia University Press, 1957.

[3] "Support To Eliminate Sex Bias In Education," by Dr. Kathryn G. Heath, Assistant for Special Studies, Office of Education, Department of Health, Education and Welfare; paper presented at University of South Carolina, April 29, 1972.

[4] Rupp, Leila, and Verta Taylor, *Survival in the Doldrums: The American Women's Rights Movement, 1945 to the 1960s.* New York, Oxford University Press, 1987. pg. 172.

[5] Rupp, Leila, and Verta Taylor, *Survival in the Doldrums: The American Women's Rights Movement, 1945 to the 1960s.* New York, Oxford University Press, 1987. Harrison, Cynthia, *On Account of Sex, The Politics of Women's Issues,* California, University of California Press. pg. 135.

[6] *American Women, Report of the President's Commission on the Status of Women,* 1963, U.S. Government Printing Office; 1965 edition edited by Margaret Mead, New York, Charles Scribner's Sons.

[7] *Wall Street Journal,* November 6, 1963.

[8] Executive Order 11126, November 1, 1963.

[9] Rupp, Leila, and Verta Taylor, *Survival in the Doldrums: The American Women's Rights Movement, 1945 to the 1960s.* New York, Oxford University Press, 1987, pg. 174; Harrison, Cynthia, *On Account of Sex, The Politics of Women's Issues,* California, University of California Press. pgs. 160-161.

[10] *Washington Star,* February 13, 1962.

[11] Harrison, Cynthia, *On Account of Sex, The Politics of Women's Issues,* California, University of California Press. pg. 96

[12] *Washington Post,* June 11, 1963.

[13] Lifton, Robert Jay, *The Woman In America,* Boston, Beacon Press, 1964, 1965; originally published in the Spring, 1964 issue of *Daedalus,* the Journal of the American Academy of Arts and Sciences.

[14] Ibid.

[15] Harrison, Cynthia, *On Account of Sex, The Politics of Women's Issues,* California, University of California Press. pg. 176.

[16] Bird, Caroline, *Born Female, The High Cost of Keeping Women Down,* New York, David McKay Company, Inc., 1968. p. 4. Transcript, *Meet the Press,* January 26, 1964.

[17] The Congressional Record, February 8, 1964.

[18] Bird, Caroline, *Born Female, The High Cost of Keeping Women Down,* New York, David McKay Company, Inc., 1968. pg. 8.

[19] Harrison, Cynthia, *On Account of Sex, The Politics of Women's Issues,* California, University of California Press. pg. 184.

[20] Hernandez, Aileen C., *The Women's Movement: 1965-1975,* paper for the Symposium on the Tenth Anniversary of the U.S. Equal Employment Opportunity Commission, sponsored by Rutgers University Law School, November 28-29, 1975. pg. 6.

[21] Ibid.

[22] Ibid.

[23] *Wall Street Journal,* June 22, 1965

[24] Hernandez, Aileen C., The Women's Movement: 1965-1975, pgs. 6-7.

[25] Ibid. pg. 6.

[26] Ibid. pgs. 7-8.

[27] Ibid. pg. 10.

[28] *New Republic,* September 4, 1965.

[29] Hernandez, Aileen C., The Women's Movement: 1965-1975, pg. 11.

[30] Ibid. pg. 12.

[31] Murray, Pauli and Mary O. Eastwood, "Jane Crow and the Law: Sex Discrimination and Title VII, *The George Washington Law Review,* December 1965, pg. 235.

[32] Ibid. pg. 256

[33] Degler, Dr. Carl N., "American Women in Social and Political Affairs—Change and Challenge," presented January 27, 1966, at a symposium at Southern Methodist University, Dallas, Texas.

[34] Friedan, Betty, "How NOW Began," NOW document, 1967.

[35] Ibid.

[36] Hole, Judith and Ellen Levine, *Rebirth of Feminism,* Quadrangle Books, a New York Times Company, 1971. Pg. 82.

[37] Friedan, Betty, *It Changed My Life, Writings on the Women's Movement,* Random House, 1976, pg. 81

[38] Ibid.

[39] Ibid.

[40] *NOW Acts,* Vol. 4, No. 3, Fall, 1971. Pg. 9

[41] Knaak, Nancy, Memoir, 1973.

[42] Interview with Rosalind Loring, 1976.

[43] Ibid.

[44] Knaak, Nancy, Memoir, 1973.

[45] Ibid.

[46] Interview with Rosalind Loring, 1976.

[47] Friedan, Betty, *It Changed My Life, Writings on the Women's Movement,* Random House, 1976, pg. 82

[48] NOW document, 1971, and *NOW Acts,* Vol. 4, No. 3, Fall, 1971, pg. 6.

[49] Hernandez, Aileen C., *The Women's Movement: 1965-1975,* pgs. 22-24.

[50] Hernandez, Aileen C., *The Women's Movement: 1965-1975,* pg. 24.

[51] Hernandez, Aileen C., *The Women's Movement: 1965-1975,* pg. 25.

[52] Hernandez, Aileen C., *The Women's Movement: 1965-1975,* pg. 25.

[53] Friedan, Betty, *It Changed My Life, Writings on the Women's Movement,* Random House, 1976, pg. 85.

[54] Hole, Judith and Ellen Levine, *Rebirth of Feminism,* Quadrangle Books, a New York Times Company, 1971, pg. 84

BIBLIOGRAPHY

BIBLIOGRAPHY

American Women, Report of the President's Commission on the Status of Women, 1963, U.S. Government Printing Office; 1965 edition edited by Margaret Mead, New York, Charles Scribner's Sons.

Anderson, David E., *Newsroom Guide to Abortion and Family Planning,* A Project of the Reproductive Rights Task Force of the Citizens' Commission on Civil Rights, Communications Consortium Media Center, 1993.

Bellant, Russ, *The Coors Connection, How Coors Family Philanthropy Undermines Democratic Pluralism,* South End Press, 1991

Bellant, Russ, *Old Nazis, the New Right and the Republican Party,* South End Press, 1991.

Berger, Margaret A., *Litigation on Behalf of Women, A Review for the Ford Foundation,* Ford Foundation, May 1980.

Bird, Caroline, *Born Female, The High Cost of Keeping Women Down,* New York, David McKay Company, Inc., 1968.

Blumenthal, Sidney, *The Rise of the Counter-Establishment, From Conservative Ideology to Political Power,* Times Books, Random House, 1986.

Caroli, Betty Boyd, *First Ladies,* Oxford University Press, 1987.

Conway, Flo and Siegelman, Jim, *Holy Terror, The Fundamentalist War on America's Freedoms in Religion, Politics and Our Private Lives,* Doubleday, 1982.

Crawford, Alan, *Thunder on the Right, The "New Right" Politics of Resentment,* Pantheon, 1980.

Daniel, Clifton, Editor, *Chronicle of America,* Chronicle Publications.

Daniel, Clifton, Editor, *Chronicle of the 20th Century,* Chronicle Publications, 1987.

Delsman, Mary A., *Everything You Need To Know About ERA,* Meranza Press, 1975.

Flake, Carol, *Redemptorama, Culture, Politics, and the New Evangelicalism,* Doubleday, 1984.

Faludi, Susan, *Backlash, The Undeclared War Against American Women,* Crown Publishers, 1991.

Friedan, Betty, *It Changed My Life, Writings on the Women's Movement,* Random House, 1976.

Harrison, Cynthia, *On Account of Sex, The Politics of Women's Issues,* California, University of California Press.

Hernandez, Aileen C., *The Women's Movement: 1965-1975,* paper for the Symposium on the Tenth Anniversary of the U.S. Equal Employment Opportunity Commission, sponsored by Rutgers University Law School, November 28-29, 1975.

Hole, Judith and Ellen Levine, *Rebirth of Feminism,* Quadrangle Books, a New York Times Company, 1971.

Hymowitz, Carol, and Weissman, Michaele, *A History of Women in America,* Bantam Books, 1978.

Kaledin, Eugenia, *Mothers and More, American Women in the 1950s,* Twayne Publishers, 1984.

Levine, Suzanne and Lyons, Harriet, *The Decade of Women, A Ms. History of the Seventies in Words and Pictures,* Paragon Books, 1980.

Macdonald, Anne L., *Feminine Ingenuity,* Ballantine, 1992.

Macguire, Daniel C., *The New Subversives, Anti-Americanism of the Religious Right,* Continuum, 1982.

McIntyre, Thomas J., *The Fear Brokers, Peddling the Hate Politics of the New Right,* Beacon Press, 1979.

Mills, Kay, *A Place in the News, from the Women's Pages to the Front Page,* Dodd Mead and Co., 1988.

Morris, Richard B., *Encyclopedia of American History,* Harper and Row, 1965.

O'Neill, Lois Decker, *The Women's Book of World Records and Achievements,* Anchor Press/Doubleday, 1979.

Robertson, Nan, *The Girls In The Balcony, Women, Men and the New York Times,* Random House, 1992.

Rose, Marjorie, *Popcorn Venus,* Avon Books, 1973.

Rupp, Leila, and Verta Taylor, *Survival in the Doldrums: The American Women's Rights Movement, 1945 to the 1960s.* New York, Oxford University Press, 1987.

Smeal, Eleanor, *Why and How Women Will Elect the Next President,* Harper and Row, 1984.

Wallechinsky, David and Wallace, Irving, *The Peoples Almanac I and II*, Doubleday, 1975.

Wandersee, Winifred D., *On the Move, American Women in the 1970s*, Twayne Publishers, 1988

World Book Encyclopedia and The World Book Year Books, various issues, Field Enterprises Educational Corporation.

Yallop, David A., *In God's Name, An Investigation Into The Murder of Pope John Paul I*, Bantam, 1984.

Young, Perry Deane, *God's Bullies, Power Politics and Religious Tyranny*, Holt, Rinehart and Winston, 1982.

Los Angeles Times
New York Times
USA Today

Washington Post
Wall Street Journal
Ms. Magazine,
Newsweek Magazine
Time Magazine
U.S. News & World Report

Miscellaneous other newspapers and magazines.

National NOW Times, 1977-1993
NOW Acts, 1968 - 1973
Do It NOW, 1971 -1977
NOW National Board Meeting Minutes
The Smeal Report, 1983-1989
The Spokeswoman, 1970-1973

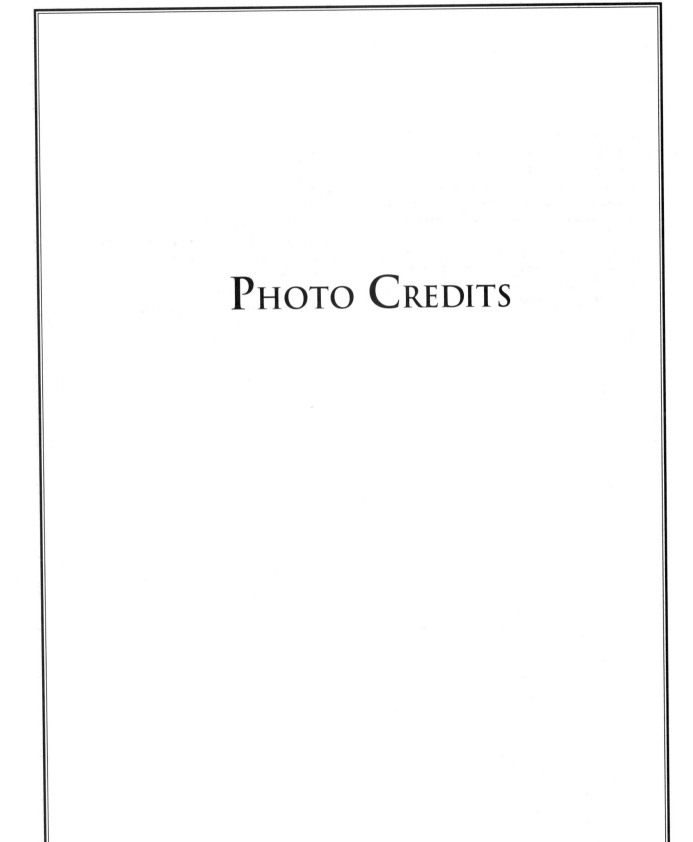

PHOTO CREDITS

PHOTO CREDITS

Cover. Photo by Bettye Lane: the Hoboken Little League

Cover. Photo by Diane Mullikin: Coreta Scott King, with First Lady Rosalyn Carter, former First Ladies Betty Ford and Ladybird Johnson, at the National Women's Conference in Houston, November 18, 1977

Cover. Photo by Peter Banks: the Los Angeles 1981 "Last Walk for ERA"

Cover. Photo Courtesy of the the Fund for the Feminist Majority: Feminist Majority President, Eleanor Smeal, 1990

Cover. Photo by Matt McVay, *Seattle Times* Co: six-year-old Alicia Jacot, Tacoma, Washington in Seattle's International Women's Day March, 1982

Cover. Photo courtesy of NOW, National Organization for Women: President Patricia Ireland, 1992

Cover. Photo courtesy of Feminist Majority Foundation, Rosie Jiminez, died of illegal abortion due to the Hyde Amendment which mandated the elimination of abortion funding for poor women

Cover. Photo by Byron J. Cohen: " We Won't Go Back March," Washington, D.C., 1992

Cover. Photo courtesy of Feminist Majority Foundation: former NOW President, Molly Yard, 1991

Cover. Photo courtesy of U.S. House of Representatives: Bella Abzug

Cover. Photo courtesy of U.S. House of Representatives: Patricia Schroeder

Cover. Photo by Robert L. Knudsen: Aileen Hernandez at NOW's Minority Women Conference in Washington, D.C., 1982

Cover. Photo by Toni Carabillo: Betty Friedan at NOW's National Conference in Des Plaines, Illinois, March 1970

Cover. Book Jacket, *Song In A Weary Throat* , Dr. Pauli Murray

Cover. Photo by Sheldon Machlin, courtesy of the Franklin D. Roosevelt Library: Eleanor Roosevelt

Cover. Photo courtesy of the Office of U.S. Senator Carol Mosely Braun

Cover. Photo by G. Jean Holtz: Gloria Steinem as MC at 1978 NOW Conference

39.   Photo by Elliott Erwitt, Magnum Photos, Inc.: Simone De Beauvoir

    Photo by UPI: Rosa Parks

    Photo: Historical Pictures Service, Mary McLeod Bethune

    Photo courtesy of the Franklin D. Roosevelt Library: Lorena Hickok

    Photo by Sheldon Machlin, courtesy of the Franklin D. Roosevelt Library: Eleanor Roosevelt

42.   Photo courtesy of Allan K. Jonas: President John F. Kennedy

43.   Photo courtesy of the Franklin D. Roosevelt Library: Eleanor Roosevelt with President John F. Kennedy

Photoy courtesy of the Department of Labor: Esther Peterson

    Official White House photo: First Lady Jacqueline Kennedy

44.   Photo courtesy of the Franklin D. Roosevelt Library: Eleanor Roosevelt

45.   Photo by Toni Carabillo: Betty Friedan at NOW's board meeting in San Francisco, 1969

    Photo by Judith Meuli: Alice Rossi speaking at the first women's conference held at UCLA, under the aegis of the UCLA Extension program for Continuing Education headed by Rosalind Loring, early 1969

46.   Campaign photo: President Lyndon B. Johnson

    Photo courtesy of U.S. Senate Historical Office: Margaret Chase Smith

47.   Photo by Toni Carabillo: Aileen C. Hernandez at NOW's board meeting in San Francisco, 1969

    Book Jacket, *Song In A Weary Throat* : Dr. Pauli Murray

    Photo courtesy of the Franklin D. Roosevelt Library: Frances Perkins with President Franklin D. Roosevelt

48.   Photo by *New York Daily News:* three of the NOW founders, Betty Friedan, Kathryn Clarenbach, and Anna Arnold Hedgeman at the first executive board meeting in New York, November, 1966

    National Organization for Women Commemorative Medallion struck in 1976 for NOW's tenth anniversary: Toni Carabillo and Judith Meuli

    Photo by Jay Sternberg: Margaret Sanger

49.   Photo by Sylvia Cary (Hartman): Southern California NOW protest at Los Angeles Times, Mary Gale carrying the sign

50.   Photo by Morton Waters Co.,: protest at EEOC office in San Francisco, 1967

51.   Photo by Bettye Lane: Kate Millett, 1971

    Publicity photo: Caroline Bird

52.   Photo by Wide World: "Miss America Cattle Auction," 1968

53.   Photo by Jurate Kazickas: Biltmore Men's Bar (NY) circa 1969

    Photo by Toni Carabillo: Dolores Alexander, NOW's first executive director, at the NOW board meeting in San Francisco, February 11, 1969

54.   Photo by Andrea Jacobson: NOW attorney Sylvia Roberts

55.   Photo by Visual Impact/Rosalind Bossette: Aileen Hernandez at 1970 NOW Conference in Des Plaines, Illinois

    Photo by *Washington Post:* twenty NOW members, led by Wilma Scott Heide, Joanne Evansgardner and Jean Witter, disrupt the Senate to demand hearings on the ERA, February 17, 1970

    Photo by Nexus/Vickie Hochberg: *Ladies Home Journal* sit-in, March 18, 1970

Equal Justice Medallion: Judith Meuli, struck for NOW LDEF's tenth anniversary in 1980

56. Graphic: Poster WOMEN OF THE WORLD UNITE by Toni Carabillo and Judith Meuli circa 1970

Graphic: Ivy Bottini, the logo for the National Organization for Women (NOW), 1970

57. Photo by Lenore Youngman: NOW demonstration against National Association of Manufacturers and Department of Labor at Los Angeles conference site, the Biltmore Hotel, July 31, 1970

58 Photo by Wide World Photo: Ti-Grace Atkinson is slapped by Patricia Buckley Bozell, March 5, 1971

Photo by Sylvia Cary (Hartman): *Los Angeles Times* protest, 1971

59. Photo by Wide World Photo: NWPC founders Gloria Steinem, Bella Abzug, Shirley Chisholm, Betty Friedan, July 10, 1971

Photo by Judith Meuli: demonstration against AT&T and in support of Lorena Weeks at the Pacific Bell Telephone headquarters in Los Angeles, March 29, 1971

Photo by Jean Stapleton: at the NOW Conference in Los Angeles, Western Regional Director Shirley Bernard talks with outgoing President Aileen Hernandez, standing, and incoming President Wilma Scott Heide talks with outgoing VP Public Relations Lucy Komisar (seated), 1971

Photo by Sylvia Cary (Hartman): protest at trial of Dr. Leon Belous, Los Angeles, 1970

60. Photo by *NOW Acts*, photographer not identified: Wilma Scott Heide, 1973

Photo by Frank Altschul: Margaret Bourke-White, late 1950s

Photo by Walter Bennett: U.S. Representative Martha Griffiths

61. Photo courtesy of U.S. House of Representatives: Shirley Chisholm

Photo by G. Jean Holtz: Gloria Steinem at 1978 NOW conference

62. Book jacket: *Eleanor and Franklin* by Joseph P. Lash

63. Photo by Alan Berliner: Bea Arthur as she appeared at NOW's twentieth anniversary event, December 1, 1986

Photo courtesy of U.S. House of Representatives: Elizabeth Holtzman

Photo by Lucy Komisar: New York NOW members march to Brooklyn apartment of Representative Emanuel Cellar to ask him to hold hearings on the Equal Rights Amendment, May 9, 1970

64. Photo courtesy of the *National Geographic Society:* Justice Harry A. Blackmun, 1992

Photo by *NOW Acts:* demonstration at the Supreme Court, February 16, 1973

65. Button: Jo Ann Evansgardner 1973

66. Photo by Jeanette Calmette: Los Angeles NOW Coordinator Rose Greene passes out Women's Equality awards in Rancho Park, Los Angeles, August 26, 1973

Photo by Alan Berliner: Helen Reddy as she appeared at NOW's twentieth anniversary event, December 1, 1986

67. Photo by Pontifica Photographs/V. Babuino, courtesy of Betty Friedan: Friedan presents the Pope with the "Brassy" (women's equality symbol), October 24, 1973

Photo by Gail Bryan: author and theologian, Mary Daly

68. Photo by Ruth Putter: NOW president Karen DeCrow at the NOW conference in Philadelphia, May 25, 1974

Advertisement: AT&T, woman telephone worker

Photo by UPI: White House reporter Helen Thomas

69. Photo by Bettye Lane: Hoboken Little League

70. Photo by *Washington Post*,: "Gridiron studs are sexist bigots" March 14, 1970

71. Photo: Margaret Thatcher

Photo courtesy of *NOW Acts;* Dr. Ann London Scott, 1974

72. Graphic: Official emblem for International Women's Year designed by Valerie Pettis to illustrate the themes of IWY: Equality, Development, Peace. The design employs the mathematical symbol for equality, the woman's symbol and the dove of peace.

Photo: from collection of Judith Meuli and Toni Carabillo, Tish Sommers and Laurie Shields, April, 1979

73. Photo by *NOW Acts;* Ellie Smeal and Karen DeCrow after Majority Caucus Victory, October 27, 1975

Photo by Bettye Lane: Majority Caucus campaign poster at 1975 NOW convention

Photo courtesy of *NOW Times:* "Take Back The Night" in Bloomington, IN.

Photo courtesy of The London Museum: Emmeline Pankhurst, leader in the British Suffrage movement, October 17, 1912, and subject of the documentary *Shoulder to Shoulder* by Midge Mackenzie, award-winning film director and producer who has worked extensively in both America and Europe.

Photo by Marilyn Zimmerman: ERA demonstration, Jefferson City, Missouri, May 25, 1975

74. Bicentennial Medallion, Toni Carabillo and Judith Meuli, 1976

Photo by Drew Stephens: Karen Silkwood and her children, early 1970s

Photo by Laura Wilensky: Del Martin, author of *Battered Wives*

Photo by Sylvia Johnson: 100-mile ERA march of Virginia NOW to Washington, D.C., January 14, 1976

75. Graphic: *NOW Times,* ERA Train, May 15, 1976

Photo by Flo Gaskill: 16,000 chanted at Springfield, Illinois ERA demonstration, front line is Clare de Miha (77 year-old feminist from New York), Ellie Smeal (Chairone of the Board) and Karen De Crow (NOW President) May 16, 1976

Photo: ABC publicity photo, Barbara Walters

76. Photo by Reed Stevens: President Jimmy Carter

Photo courtesy of *NOW Times:* first woman to be officially admitted to the priesthood in the Episcopal Church in America, Jacqueline Means, a 40-year-old nurse and prison chaplain

77. Photo by Diane C. Mullikin: Ellie Smeal at press conference during National Women's Conference conference in Houston, November 20, 1977

Photo by G. Jean Holtz: Catherine Timlin and

Alice Bennett, October 6, 1978

Photo by Bettye Lane: Nuns picket in front of St. Patricks Cathedral, New York City on February 27, 1977

78. Photo by Richard J. Muzzrole: Dr. Alice Paul, founder and later National Chairman of the National Woman's Party, 1970s

Photo: The only woman among 3,000 Medal of Honor winners in American history, Dr. Mary Edwards Walker

79. Photo by Janice Rubin: torch carried by runners arrives in Houston to start the National Women's Conference, November 19, 1977

Photo by Flo Gaskill: Southwest Council Pennsylvania NOW Walkathon, August 29, 1977

Photo by Dr. Douglas Roth: the first ERA march in D.C., on the 57th anniversary of the 19th Amendment (Suffrage for women), August 26, 1977

Photo by Bettye Lane: Janet Guthrie, the first woman to race in the Indianapolis 500, shown here in the Trentonian 200 Car Race, New Jersey, April 23, 1976

80. Photo by Diane C. Mullikin: National Women's Conference attendees included Coretta Scott King, Rosalyn Carter, Betty Ford, and Ladybird Johnson, November 18, 1977

Photo by Diane C. Mullikin: Phyllis Schlafly holds press conference at National Women's Conference, November 20, 1977

Photo by California Newsreel: women from Wilmar, Minnesota, dubbed the Wilmar 8, shown protesting the discrimination at the bank where they had been employed. Their heroic struggle was the subject of a documentary by Lee Grant, 1977

81. Photo by Sussman and Fiore: largest Virginia ERA march was organized by LERN, a coalition of the state's labor groups, January 22, 1978

Photo by Richmond Newspapers, Inc. with special thanks to Pat Petro: the Virginia NOW State Coordinator and registered lobbyist, Jean Marshall Clark, February 9, 1978

82. Photo courtesy of the Kentucky Lt. Governor, Thelma Stoval

Photo by Jane Wells Schooley: U.S. Senator Birch Bayh

Photo courtesy of U.S. House of Representatives: Elizabeth Holtzman

Photo courtesy of U.S. House of Representatives: Don Edwards

83. Photo by Carol Hindson: NOW-organized ERA March and Extension rally in Washington, D.C., July 9, 1978

Commemorative ERA March medallion: Judith Meuli, July 9, 1978

Photo by *NOW Times*: culminating an intensive 3-year lobby effort, Massachusetts NOW members watch Governor Dukakis sign the Displaced Homemakers Act into law, July 26, 1978

Photo by Dr. Douglas Roth: caught his cat with the right button, 1978

84. Photo by G. Jean Holtz: Senator Edward Brooke and NOW President Ellie Smeal celebrate in the Dirksen Room after the ERA time extension passes the Senate, October 7, 1978

Photo courtesy of U.S. House of Representatives: Elizabeth Holtzman

Photo courtesy of Grand Rapids (MI) NOW

85. Photo by John Danicic Jr.,: firefighter Linda Eaton with baby, Ian, is denied right to breast-feed infant during personal time while at the firehouse, January 22, 1979

86. Photo courtesy of U.S. House of Representatives: Bella Abzug

Photo courtesy of U.S. Mint: Susan B. Anthony dollar, February 2, 1979

87. ERA Medallion: Toni Carabillo and Judith Meuli

Photo by Kelly Copeland: women pilots are honored at reception after the *Silver Wings and Santiago Blue* screening, 1981

Photo by Richard Bright: Dorothy Jonas in 1981

Photo by Diane C. Mullikin: actor Jean Stapleton taken at the Women's Conference in Houston, November 20, 1977

Photo by G. Jean Holtz: Norman Lear, Frances Lear, Ellie Smeal, Joan Hackett and Maureen Reagan give a "thumbs up" for the ERA, March 24, 1979

88. Photo courtesy of *NOW Times*,: Lily Tomlin and her mother at Los Angeles NOW's second annual Mother's Day Brunch, 1979

Photo courtesy of *NOW Times*,: Florida ERA demonstration, May 17, 1979

Photo by Eleanor Self: Senator Edward Kennedy speaks for the ERA, June 25, 1979

89. Photo by Maggi Cage, Fox Cities (WI): NOW ERA Walkathon, August 26, 1979

90. Photo by Bettye Lane: anti-ponography demonstration in Times Square, October 20, 1979

Photo by Joe Kennedy, *Los Angeles Times:* Sister Mary Theresa Kane and Pope John Paul II, October 7, 1979

Publicity photo, Margaret Sanger and her sons

91. Photo by Reed Stevens: President Jimmy Carter with Presidential Assistant Midge Costanza

Photo by Jan Holden: NOW demonstrators call for the disqualification of Judge Marion J. Callister, December 13, 1979

Photo by Jill Nash,: demonstration in support of Sonja Johnson at the Mormon Temple in Los Angeles, December 20, 1979

Photo by Jeff Lynn Schumann: Sonja Johnson after she was tried by her Church of the Latter Day Saints for the "crime"of supporting the ERA, December 1, 1979

92. Photo by Alan Kamuda: Detroit NOW protests the program,"Three's A Crowd," at their local TV station, January 15, 1980

93. Photo by Eleanor Self: NOW attorneys Donna Kohansky and John Vanderstar with National NOW Secretary, Sandra Roth, March 28, 1980

94. Photo by Dr. Douglas Roth: front line of 90,000 ERA marchers in Chicago, May 10, 1980

Photo by Dr. Douglas Roth: Joan Hackett, taken in Chicago at the ERA march and rally, May 10, 1980

Photo by G. Jean Holtz: Norman Lear and Frances Lear with NOW President Ellie Smeal, 1979

95. Photo by Cynthia Foster: Nan M. Johnson protests

the removal of the ERA from Republican platform, August 26, 1980

Photo by Beth Leopold: ERA floatathon in West Virginia, August 26, 1980

96. Photo by Joe Holly, Union-Tribune Publishing Co: San Diego NOW led protest at appearance of candidate for President, Ronald Reagan, because he opposed the ERA, September 23, 1980

97. Photo by Positive Images: thousands lined inauguration route with ERA YES banners, January 20, 1981

98. Photo by Eleanor Self: NOW demonstrators at the White House protesting Judge Marion Callister's refusal to recuse himself from hearing the case on ERA extension/recision lawsuit, Jean Conger carries a sign asking President Carter to disqualify Callister, March 6, 1981

99. Photo by Richard Bright: Eleanor Smeal announces that Alan Alda and former First Lady Betty Ford would be National Honorary Co-Chairs of the ERA Countdown events, June 10, 1981

Photo by Jeanne Marklin: Alan Alda speaking at ERA Countdown rally in Washington, D.C., June 30, 1981

100. Photo by *National Geographic Society*: Justice Sandra Day O'Conner

Photo by Dori Jacobson: NOW President Ellie Smeal and former First Lady, Betty Ford, October 12, 1981

Photo by Dori Jacobson: former First Lady, Lady Bird Johnson, October 12, 1981

Poster: Jane Guthrie, "The Last Walk for ERA," 1981

Photo by Richard Bright, "The Last Walk for ERA," Los Angeles,1981

101. Photo by Cooper Zale: David M. Dismore leaves Los Angeles for his 4,482 mile ERA bikeathon to Tallahassee, Florida, January 9, 1982

102. Photo of Ellie Spikes, courtesy of Aileen Hernandez.

Photo courtesy of Esther Rolle

103. Photo by *Birmingham NEWS*: one of 13 billboards the Birmingham NOW chapter produced, July, 1982

104. Photo by *NOW Times:* NOW President Judy Goldsmith, November 10, 1982

105. Photo courtesy of KEYT, Santa Barbara: Christine Craft, 1982

107. Photo by Virginia Kalhianes: NYC NOW pickets the Metropolitan Life Insurance Co.'s home office, June 8, 1983

Photo by NASA: Sally Ride

108. Photo by Matt McVay, *Seattle Times Co,*: six-year-old Alicia Jacot, Tacoma, Washington in the International Women's Day March 1982

109. Photo by Dr. Douglas Roth: Joan Hackett when she spoke for the ERA in Chicago, May 10, 1980

112. Photo by Richard Bright: Barbra Streisand and Jane Fonda at the Woman of Courage Award dinner orga-

nized by the Los Angeles NOW Education Fund, June 6, 1984

113. Photo courtesy of the Geraldine Ferraro for Vice President campaign, 1984

115. Photo by *NOW Times:* former NOW President Wilma Scott Heide

Photo by *NOW Times:* NOW President Judy Goldsmith

116. Photo courtesy of the Feminist Majority: NOW President, Eleanor Smeal

Photo by Pamela Valois: Tish Sommers
Book jacket, Dr. Pauli Murray

118. Photo by Arthur Shay: Oprah Winfrey

119. Photo by *National Geographic Society*: Justice William Rehnquist

Photo by Jeff Lynn Schumann: U.S. Representative Patricia Schroeder speaks to NOW at their 1983 National Conference

Photo by *National Geographic Society*: Justice Antonin Scalia

120. Graphic: NOW's Twentieth Anniversary, December 1, 1986

Photo by Office of U.S. Senator Barbara Mikulski

122. Photo courtesy of U.S. House of Representatives: Nancy Pelosi

Photo courtesy of U.S. House of Representatives: Edith Green

123. Photo from *NOW Times* archives: NOW President Molly Yard

Photo by Wally McNamee, *Newsweek*: Judge Robert Bork

Photo by David Vita: NOW-organized anti-Bork rally on opening day of Judge Bork's confirmation hearing in Washington, D.C., September 15, 1987

124. Graphic: Judith Meuli, elect women or AKA "Feminization of Power" designed in 1984

Photo by Jim Richardson, *Denver Post*: courtesy of Schroeder for President campaign, 1987

Photo courtesy of the U.S. Senate, Howard Metzebaum

125. Photo by *National Geographic Society*: Justice Anthony Kennedy

126. Photo by Bettye Lane: Betty Friedan shown with her book, *The Feminine Mystique*

127. Photo by *Ms.* magazine: Benazir Bhutto, 1988

128. Photo courtesy of the Bell family: Becky Bell, 1987

129. Photo by Bettye Lane: Catherine MacKinnon, March 24, 1985

Photo by David Dismore: highly visible among the Los Angeles Operation Rescue demonstration were catholic priests and fundamentalist ministers, February 11, 1989

130. Photo by *NOW Times:*: Abortion rights supporters over 600,000 strong march, April 15, 1989

132. Photo by Paula MacKenzie: Dr. Elizabeth Morgan

is released, September 9, 1989

Photo by Richard Bright: Dorothy Jonas, 1981

Photographer unidentified: Bonnie Sloane

133.   Photo by *New York Daily News*: Anna Arnold Hedgeman in 1966

Photo by Margot Ingoldsby, courtesy of the Feminist Majority Foundation: Memorial commissioned by NOW for the 17th anniversary of the *Roe v. Wade* decision, January 22, 1990

134.   Photo by Lee Silvian: Pauline Frederick, circa 1940

135.   Graphic: *Ms.* magazine, August 1990

Photo by Feminist Majority: delegation led by the Feminist Majority officers, Peg Yorkin and Eleanor Smeal, present 115,530 petitions to Russell-Uclaf urging the introduction of RU-486, July 29, 1990

Photo courtesy of Karen and Bill Bell, 1990

136.   Photo *Newsweek*: Senator Alan Simpson, 1990

Photo courtesy of Governor Ann Richards

Photo courtesy of U.S. Representative Barbara Roberts

Photo courtesy of U.S. Senator Dianne Feinstein

137.   Photographer not identified: Gro Harlem Brundtland

138.   Photo by Dr. Douglas Roth: former NOW Eastern Region Director and board member Fran Kolb at the Women's Conference in Houston, November 20, 1977

139.   Photo by *National Geographic Society*: Justice Thurgood Marshall

Photo by David Dismore: clinic defenders in Los Angeles, 1991

Photo by Bettye Lane: woman soldier

140.   Photo by Wide World: seven Congresswomen storm the Senate to reopen the Clarence Thomas hearings, October 8, 1991

Photo courtesy of the Fund for the Feminist Majority: FFM National Coordinator Katherine Spillar, 1991

141.   Photographer not identified: Anita Hill testifies in the Senate hearing on the appointment of Clarence Thomas, October 11, 1991

Photo by Judith Meuli: Feminist Majority chair of the board Peg Yorkin, 1991

Book jacket: *Backlash* by Susan Faludi, 1991

142.   Photo by *NOW Times:* NOW President Molly Yard

Book jacket: *Revolution From Within* by Gloria Steinem

143.   Photo courtesy of National Organization for Women: President Patricia Ireland

144.   Photo by Byron J. Cohen: "We Won't Go Back" NOW organized march in Washington D.C. April 5, 1992

Photo courtesy of the office of U. S. Senator Carol Mosely-Braun

145.   Photo courtesy of the Fund For The Feminist Majority: national coordinator Katherine Spillar

146.   Photo by Rebecca Cooney: flanked by Dr. Louise Tyrer, Patricia Ireland and Ellie Smeal, Leona Benten addresses reporters after bringing RU-486 into the United States for personal use on July 1, 1992

148.   Photo by Judith Meuli: Dolores Huerta, 1992

149.   Photo by White House: President Bill Clinton, 1993

AUTHORS' BIOGRAPHIES

TONI CARABILLO

Toni Carabillo is currently the national vice president of the Feminist Majority, an organization she founded with Eleanor Smeal, Peg Yorkin, Judith Meuli, and Katherine Spillar in 1987 to encourage women's empowerment. In 1988, she co-authored a book with Judith Meuli entitled *The Feminization of Power.*

She has been deeply involved in the feminist movement since she joined the National Organization for Women in 1966.

In 1967, she helped found the California Chapters of NOW. She has served as President of the Los Angeles Chapter from 1968 to 1970 and from 1980 through 1982. She was a member of NOW's National Board of Directors almost continuously from 1968 to 1977, served as a National Vice President from 1971 through 1974, and chaired NOW's National Advisory Committee from 1975 until 1977.

It was during her second tenure as president of Los Angeles NOW that the memorable "Last Walk for the ERA" in August 1981 was organized and more than 10,000 people marched on the Avenue of the Stars and more than $300,000 was raised for the ERA Countdown Campaign. She was simultaneously director of the NOW ERA Countdown Office in Los Angeles during the final ratification drive, which raised an additional $155,000 in six months through nightly phone banks and home parties for a total of nearly half a million dollars.

She was co-editor of NOW's national newsletter, *NOW Acts* , from 1970 to 1973 and co-editor of its national newspaper, the *National NOW Times* , from 1977 until 1985. She was an associate editor of *The Eleanor Smeal Report,* a national "insiders" newsletter with a feminist perspective, which was published from 1983 to 1990.

She developed a chronology of the feminist movement of the 20th century as a computerized data base, using this as the basis for the book *The Feminist Chronicles, 1953-1993.* The data base was used as the source for NOW's 25th Anniversary Show in Los Angeles in December 1986, subsequently released as a two-hour video tape. With the Feminist Majority, she participated in the production of two video tapes, *Abortion: For Survival* and *Abortion Denied: Shattering Young Women's Lives.*

In 1969, she co-founded the Women's Heritage Corporation, a publishing company that produced the *Women's Heritage Calendar and Almanac* and a series of paperbacks on such figures as Elizabeth Cady Stanton and Lucy Stone. In 1970, she formed a graphic arts firm with Ms. Meuli in Los Angeles.

Professionally, Ms. Carabillo is a writer and graphic designer. She earned an A.B. degree from Middlebury College, Vermont, and an M.A. from Columbia University.

Prior to 1970, she was assistant manager of Corporate Communications for System Development Corporation (SDC), a think tank working on national defense systems. At SDC, she supervised a corporate publications unit of writers, a graphic design department, an employee publications unit, and corporate exhibits staff, in addition to editing a ground-breaking, award-winning magazine explaining computer technology and applications.

Her eleven-year career with SDC ended not long after she was involved in an unauthorized survey of women employees that revealed a pattern of sex discrimination in salaries and career opportunities.

As a feminist advocate, Ms. Carabillo has appeared on both national and local television and radio. She is the author of many Op-Ed articles, a number of which were nationally syndicated. Her biography appears in *Who's Who In America* and *Who's Who of American Women.*

JUDITH MEULI

Judith Meuli is currently the national secretary of the Feminist Majority, an organization she founded with Eleanor Smeal, Toni Carabillo, Peg Yorkin, and Katherine Spillar in 1987 to encourage women to become involved in public affairs and the electoral process.

In 1988, she co-authored a book with Toni Carabillo entitled *The Feminization of Power.* The book grew out of a traveling exhibit that Meuli and Carabillo created for a twelve-city Feminization of Power campaign tour to empower women to run for office in 1988.

She has been an activist and an organizer in the feminist movement since she joined the National Organization for Women in 1967.

In 1968, she was elected to serve for two years as secretary of the Los Angeles Chapter of NOW. From 1971 to 1977, she served almost continuously as a member of NOW's National Board of Directors. From 1971 through 1974, she served as Chair of the National Membership Committee, instituting reforms for the fast-growing organization such as central dues collection and an anniversary payment system. In 1974, she also chaired NOW's National Nominating Committee. In 1976, she was elected coordinator of the Hollywood chapter.

She was co-editor of NOW's national newsletter, *NOW Acts*, from 1970 to 1973, editor of *Financing the Revolution*, a catalog of fund-raising tips, in 1973, and co-editor of NOW's national newspaper, the *National NOW Times*, with a circulation of 250,000, from 1977 until 1985.

For the major part of her professional life, Ms. Meuli has pursued both a career as a writer, graphic designer and jewelry designer and a career as a real estate broker and developer. In the latter role, in 1990, she designed and constructed a building to house the media center and archives for the Feminist Majority.

Ms. Meuli holds a bachelor of science degree from the University of Minnesota. For 10 years after graduating, she was a research scientist at the University of Minnesota, Minneapolis, and the University of California, Los Angeles, where she studied renal physiology.

Her career as a scientist ended when Ms. Meuli discovered that although she taught medical students research and surgical techniques, she was discouraged from entering medical school because she was female and, at thirty years old, she was considered too old.

In 1969, she co-founded the Women's Heritage Corporation, a publishing company that produced the *Women's Heritage Calendar and Almanac* and a series of paperbacks on such figures as Elizabeth Cady Stanton and Lucy Stone. In 1970, she formed a graphic arts firm with Ms. Carabillo in Los Angeles. Women's Graphic Communications produces and distributes books, newspapers, political buttons, and pins.

Ms. Meuli designed many of the symbols and logos of the women's movement, such as the designs for Woman's Equality, Human Liberation, Sisterhood, Matriarchy Lives, Woman's Peace, Older Women's League, Equal Rights Amendment, Woman Thinker, Failure Is Impossible, NOW's Commemorative medallion, and many feminist issue pins in cloisonné enamel.

Her biography appears in *Who's Who In America* and *Who's Who of American Women.*

JUNE BUNDY CSIDA

June Bundy Csida has been a member of Los Angeles NOW since 1970 when she coordinated a search for surviving pre-World War I suffragists to participate in NOW's historic Women's Strike for Equality celebration on August 26. The event marked the 50th anniversary of the day women won the right to vote.

Inspired by those gallant pioneer feminists, one of whom, Ernestine Kettler, served a jail sentence for picketing the Wilson White House, Ms. Csida became active in Los Angeles NOW and filled various chapter offices (vice president, secretary, public relations officer) throughout the '70s. Also during those years she assisted NOW's National Vice President Toni Carabillo with media relations and was a contributor and columnist for the *National NOW Times*.. In 1971, she persuaded several Los Angeles TV and radio stations—including two network outlets—to create and air public service spots for NOW, a first for the organization.

In 1972, she set up a special public forum on the then- startling theme *Rape — the Number One Crime Against Women*. The following year she and her husband, Joseph Csida, also a long-time NOW member, wrote *Rape (How To Avoid It And What To Do About It If You Can't)*, the first book-length feminist treatment of the shocking facts about the under-reported, under-prosecuted crime against women and children.

Ms. Csida is also the author of: *Elizabeth Cady Stanton, The 19th Century Renaissance Woman; American Entertainment, a Unique History of Popular Show Business* (with Joseph Csida), a chronological history of events in music, theatre, films, television, radio, dance, vaudeville, circus, fairs and carnivals since Colonial days; and *A Complete Guide to Healthy Pets*.

As a contributor to the *World Book Encyclopedia Year Book* for 14 years, Ms. Csida wrote annual reports on radio and television and many special features, including a special report on *The Second Feminist Revolt*, tracing the history of women's fight for equality from its origin in Seneca Falls, N.Y., in 1848 through 1972. She was also a contributor to *The People's Almanac #1* and *#2*, writing on rape, murder, and animals.

As a writer-reporter for *Billboard* magazine for 15 years, Ms. Csida wrote record, night club, theatre, radio, and television reviews, eventually serving as TV-radio programming editor.

Ms. Csida scripted and researched the syndicated TV series *Movie Museum*, a history of silent cinema featuring the film library of D.W. Griffith's and other silent movie classics; a syndicated radio series, *Show Ms!*, a feminist tribute to women musical stars from the '20s to the '80s; and *Billboard* magazine's annual *Yearbook*, a syndicated radio series covering current events and best-selling records for rock, middle of the road, and country.

In 1986, she wrote a tribute to male feminists which was delivered by actor Ed Asner at NOW's 20th anniversary show.

At the age of 20, in an era when most women stayed at home or worked as secretaries, Ms. Csida went out on the road as advance agent for the top novelty band of the day, Spike Jones and His City Slickers. Prior to joining *Billboard*, she ran her own publicity agency in partnership with Auriel Macfie.

INDEX

INDEX

Bethune, Mary McLeod: 39, 89
Bevilaqua, Anthony: 117
BFOQ (Bona Fide Occupational Qualification):
    13, 14, 17, 26, 28, 34, 47, 48, 51
Bhutto, Benazir: 127
Bielenson, Anthony: 46
Biden, Joseph: 154
Bike-a-thon (NOW): 101
Billboard campaign: 103
Billings, Robert: 86
Biltmore Hotel, NY: 47, 78
Birch Society: 54, 76
Bird, Caroline: 51
Birmingham (AL) NOW: 103
Birth control (see also Contraception): 39, 45,
    133, 137, 139, 140, 146
Birth Control Institute: 113, 115
Bitch Manifesto: 53
Blackmun, Harry A.: 64, 72, 102, 147
Blacks and car dealers: 137
Black studies: 134
Blackwell, Elizabeth: 89
Black Women's Network: 148
Black Women Organized for Action: 102
Blaul, Iris: 144
Blondie: 141
Bly, Robert: 134
Boggs, Corrine C. (Lindy): 65
Boisseau, Deborah: 58
Boland, Colleen: 30
Bolton, Doe v.: 64
Bonk, Kathy (Kathleen): 63, 71, 91, 110
Boston Marathon: 49
Book-banning: 104
Boothroyd, Betty: 145
Bork, Robert: 123, 125
Bosnia: 148
Boston: 145
Boston Firefighters Union, Local 718 v.
    Boston Chapter, NAACP: 105
Bottini, Ivy: 54, 56, 57
Bound, Aida: 146
Bourke-White, Margaret: 60
Bourisseau, Judge Francis: 140
Bowe v. Colgate-Palmolive: 50
Bowers v. Hardwick: 118
Bowles, Nancy: 136
Boxer, Barbara: 121, 145, 149
Boycott:
    Bus: (Rosa Parks): 39
    Colgate-Palmolive: 52
    E! Entertainment Television sponsor
        boycott:149
    ERA boycott of unratified states:
        93, 96, 97-99, 101,102, 106
    Farah: 65, 66
    Idaho potato boycott: 133
    J. P. Stevens: 77
    Knopf (American Psycho) boycott: 137
    Roe v. Wade movie boycott: 130

    Utah boycott: 138
Boyer, Gene: 24
Boylan, Elizabeth et al. v. The New York Times: 144
Bozell, Patricia Buckley: 58
BPW (Federation of Business and Professional
    Women): 2, 5, 11, 39, 50, 61, 66, 70, 106, 121,
    129
Bra-burning myth: 52
Bradlee, Ben: 143
Bradley Foundation: 155
Brassy, The: 54, 67
Bray v. Alexandria Women's Health Center: 145
Brazil, women's police stations: 142
Breast cancer: 139, 149
Bremer, Arthur: 62
Brennan Jr., William J.: 47, 64, 102, 113, 136
Brennan, Kate Pfister: 114
Brigade, Jeannette Rankin: 51
Brigham Young University: 73
Britain's abortion law: 93
Brock, David, conservative credentials: 155
Bronx (NY) NOW: 147
Bronze Star: 145
Brooklyn (NY) NOW: 147
Brooks, Gayle: 114
Broward (FL) NOW: 111, 148
Brown, Jan: 106
Brown, Jennifer: 114
Brown, Judith: 51
Brown, Jr., Edmund (Jerry): 100
Brown, Murphy: 145
Brown, Paul: 78
Brown, Ron: 151
Browner, Carol: 151
Brownmiller, Susan: 57
Bruce, Tammy: 137, 149
Brundtland, Gro Harlem: 118, 137
Bryan, Richard H.: 128
Bryant, Anita: 77, 78
Bryant, Ann: 152
Bryn Mawr: 100
Buchanan, Pat: 60, 147
Buck, Pearl: 66, 89
Buckley, William F.: 42, 141
Bucks County (PA) NOW: 111
Buffalo (NY) NOW: 145, 147
Bunch, Charlotte: 137
Bunker, Edith Memorial Fund: 94
Bunnies, *Playboy:* 47
Bureau of Alcohol, Tobacco, and Firearms: 113, 117
Burger, Warren E.: 75, 85, 100
Burke, Yvonne Braithwaite: 84
Burnett, Andrew: 127
Burnett, Carol: 104
Burnett, Patricia: 65
Burns, Ellen: 84
Burrell, Maryedith: 104
Burt, John: 154
Burton, John: 88
Burton, Sala: 122

Monroe, Marilyn: 40, 44
Montana: 70, 88, 98, 106, 114, 115
Montana Women's Political Caucus: 106
Montes, Ginny: 134, 146, 147
Montgomery, AL: 39, 47
Montgomery County (MD) NOW: 106
Montreal (Canada) Massacre: 131
Moore, Anne: 43
Moorman, Jeanne: 119
Morgan, Elizabeth: 132, 137
Morgan, Robin: 55, 135
Moriyama, Mayumi: 133
Mormon Church: 64, 77, 78, 79, 89
Mormon Bishops: 77
Mormon Missionary Project: 98-99
Mormons: 97, 98, 102
Mormon Temple demonstrations: 94, 96, 97, 106
Morristown (NJ) NOW: 86
Morse, Wayne: 41
Mortz, Monica: 55
Mory's Tavern: 61, 68
Moscone, George: 82, 84, 88
Moseley-Braun, Carol : X, 144, 149, 154
Moses, Grandma: 43
Mother Courage Restaurant: 62
Motherhood: 99, 111, 122, 128
Mothers' Day of Outrage: 73
Mother's Day March for Abortion Rights, NOW, Florida:154
Mott, Lucretia: 89
Motzel, Carolyn: 144
Movement to Restore Decency (MOTOREDE): 54
Ms. magazine : 62, 65, 135
Ms. Foundation for Education and
    Communication, Inc.: 82, 124
Ms. magazine: 61, 62, 67, 123, 124, 127
Mt. Pleasant (MI) NOW Chapter: 74
Mulhauser, Karen: 86
Muller v. Oregon: 16
Muncy Law: 52
Murray, Pauli: 11, 15, 19, 20, 22, 23, 33, 47,
    116, 127
Murrin, Barbara:85
Mutual of Omaha lawsuit: 113
Myers, Gary: 80, 81
Myers, Mary Lynn:76

N:
NAACP (National Association for the Advancement
    of Colored People): 63, 92, 105,125
Naif, Prince: 137
Nairobi, Kenya, "Forum '85": 116
NASA (National Aeronautices and Space Administra-
tion): 41, 43, 52, 67, 68, 98
Nashville Gas Company v. Satty: 80, 84
Nathanson, Bernard: 114
National Abortion Federation (NAF): 111-112, 118
National Abortion Rights Action League (NARAL):
    VII, 53, 96, 130, 140
National Academy of Sciences: 99

National Airlines: 60
National American Woman Suffrage Association
    (NAWSA): VII, VIII
National Association for Girls and Women in
    Sport: 123
National Association for the Repeal of Abortion Laws
    (NARAL): VII
National Association of Broadcasters (NAB): 67
National Association of Insurance Commissioners:
    106
National Black Women's Health Project: 122
National Collegiate Athletic Association
    (NCAA): 143
National Commission on Working Women: 127
National Conference of Catholic Bishops: 95, 116, 118,
    133, 137, 139, 149
National Conference of Puerto Rican Women: 82
National Conference for a New Politics (NCNP): 50
National Council of Negro Women (NCNW): 39
National Conservative Political Action Committee
    (NCPAC): 42, 70, 96, 120, 126, 131
National Consumers League: 8
National Council of Women of the United States: 14
National Federation of Business and Professional
    Women (BPW): 2, 5, 11, 39, 50, 61, 66,
    70, 106, 121
National Gay Task Force (NGTF) v.
    Oklahoma Board of Education: 114
National Gay and Lesbian Task Force:
National Institute for Women of Color: 122
National Insurance Consumer Organization
    (NICO): 107
National Lawyers Guild: 103
National Lesbian Conference (1991): 139
National Manpower Council (NMC): 2, 40
National Museum for Women in the Arts: 122
National NOW Times: 96
National Observer: 48
National Organization for Women, see NOW
National Press Club: 57, 144
National Right to Life PAC: 71
National Woman's Party (NWP): VII, VIII, 3, 8, 11
National Women's Law Center: 152
National Women's Political Caucus
    (NWPC): VII, 59, 70, 94, 105, 106, 109
    121, 123, 125, 147, 152
Natividad, Irene: 147
Natrona County (WY) NOW: 110
Naval Academy: 112
Navy: 64, 94, 103, 104, 108, 124, 125
NBC (National Broadcasting Company): 44, 62, 134,
    101, 130,
       "Today Show": 5
Nebraska: 63, 77, 114
Needham, Thomas: 79
Nehru, Jawaharlal: 41
Nelligan, Kate: 144
Nelson, Sara: 73, 88, 148
Neo-conservatism: 62
Neuborne, Helen: 152

Roth, Sandra Reeves: 90, 93
Roth, William: 140
Roybal-Allard, Lucille: 149
Rowe, Charlotte: 31
RU-486: 120, 127,128,130,131, 135, 139, 141, 142, 144,
        154
        Roussel Uclaf: 128, 131, 135, 143, 144
Rubbins, Mrs. Sheldon: 39
Rubella, Epidemic (German Measles): 46
Rubin, Carl: 81
Ruckelshaus, Jill: 65
Rural America, Task Force on Feminism in: 74
Rural women: 84
Russia: 156
Ryan, George: 101, 102
Ryan, John: 118, 128

S:
Sabin, Florence: 89
Sabourin, Debra:107
Sacramento (CA): 92
Saginaw (MI) NOW: 143
Sailors: 103, 125
Salem (OR) NOW:111
Sales, Ruby: 146
Salt Lake City: 106, 138
Sanders, Marion K.: 47
Sandler, Bernice R: 114
San Diego, CA: 146, 147
San Diego (CA) NOW: 68, 72
San Fernando Valley (CA) NOW: 87, 97
San Francisco, CA: 137, 142
San Francisco (CA) NOW: 139
San Joaquin (CA) NOW: 93, 111
Sanger, Margaret: 39, 48, 90
Sassower, Doris: 55
SAT (Scholastice Achievement Test): 120, 122
Satty v. Nashville Gas Company: 80, 84
Saturday Night Live (SNL): 134
Saudi Arabia: 136, 137, 147
Saudi women: 136, 137
Sawhill, John: 93
Saxon-Perry, Carrie: 125
Scaife Foundation: 70
Scalia, Antonin: 119
Schallert, William: 104
Scheidler, Joseph: 85, 94, 110, 118, 128
Schellman, Debbie: 65
Schiess, Betty Bone: 69, 76
Schlafly, Phyllis: 39, 40, 46, 49, 61, 71,
        77, 78, 80, 87, 89, 148, 149
        Phyllis Schlafly Report: 61
Schlafly, John: 148
Schleman, Helen: 49
Schlesinger Library: 138
Schneider, Claudine: 110
Scholarships: 101, 122, 123, 127
Schollenberger, Julie: 145
Schooley, Terry: 102
Schreiber, Lee Anne: 84

Schuchman Foundation, Robert: 61
Schultz, George P.: 60
Schletzer, Vera: 31
Schroeder, Patricia: 108, 124, 144, 147
Schwartz, Edna: 31
Schwartz, Felice: 129, 132
Schwarzenegger, Arnold: 143, 156
Schweiker Richard S.: 99, 101, 105
Science, American Women in: 70
Science Digest: 103
Scientists, women: 42
Scott, Ann: 56, 63, 71
Scouts, Girl:72
Screen Actors Guild (SAG): 79, 90, 126
S.C.U.M. (Society for Cutting Up Men) Manifesto: 52
SDS (Students for a Democratic Society): VII, 41, 44,
        47
Searle Pharmaceutical Co: 41
Sears, Roebuck: 71, 73, 117, 126
Seattle (WA): 58, 94, 96, 97, 117, 119
Seattle-King County (WA) NOW: 94
Seattle (WA) NOW: 58
Second Sex: 39
Secretaries Week: 111
Secular Humanism: 95
Sedey, Mary Ann: 92
Segal, Phyllis N.: 96
Segregation: 39, 40, 42, 45, 47, 48
Seidenberg, Faith: 61
Seidenberg v. McSorley's Old Ale House: 54, 56
Self-defense: 73, 74, 78
Self-examination, vaginal: 62
Seneca Falls (NY): 66, 89, 92, 99
Senate: 7, 39, 41, 42, 45, 46, 49, 52, 55, 57
        First all female race, 43
Seniority rights: 61, 75, 80
Service Academies: 69, 73, 76
"Sesame Street": 54
"Seven Cities of Refuge," Operation Rescue plan: 155
Sex-based admission policy: 105
Sex-based auto insurance rates: 114
Sex-based wage discrimination: 112, 123
"Sex Bias in the Public Schools": 59
Sex-bias in standardized tests: 122
Sex-segregated:
        employment ads: 14, 47-50, 51-54, 58, 66, 115
        school courses: 67
Sexism: 54, 55, 61-64, 70, 72, 75, 78, 79, 85, 89, 92, 106,
        110, 114, 118, 127, 131, 135, 141, 144, 149
"Sexism on Capitol Hill" study: 57
Sexual Behavior in the Human Female,
        (Kinsey Report):39
Sexual harassment: VIII, 72, 74, 84, 95, 98-100, 104, 116,
        118, 124, 125, 128, 131, 135, 139-142, 143, 144,
        147
Sex Information and Education Council of the U.S.
        (SIECUS): 46, 54
Sexual Suicide by George Gilder: 67, 98
Shalala, Donna: 151
Shamrock Broadcasting Company: 97

CONTRIBUTOR & ORDER FORMS

LAST CALL FOR INPUT

Did you or someone you know initiate or carry out an action for justice for women and girls that has not been documented here?

If you could take a few minutes and copy and/or fill out the form on the right we can add the event to the archives and possibly include it in the next edition or other future feminist movement documentation.

NAME: _____

ADDRESS: _____

_____

PHONE: _____

Do you have photos of the action(s) described? If yes, please complete the form on the next page, too.

Please send the completed form to the authors c/o:
Women's Graphics
1126 Hi-Point Street
Los Angeles, CA 90035

WHEN: _____

_____

_____

WHO: _____

_____

_____

WHAT: _____

_____

_____

_____

_____

_____

_____

_____

_____

_____

_____

_____

_____

_____

WHERE: _____

_____

_____

_____

PHOTO CALL

In our photo search, we found that many of our major events were undocumented by accessible photos. Did you or someone you know take photos of an action for justice for women and girls that has not been documented here? Do you have photos (or negatives) of an action(s) documented in this book but not accompanied by a photo?

If you would like to make photos of the event available to us, we can add them to the archives for possible inclusion in the next edition of the *Feminist Chronicles* or other future feminist movement publi-cations.

Please send the completed form with photos and/or negatives to the authors c/o: Women's Graphics
1126 Hi-Point Street
Los Angeles, CA 90035

WHEN: _____

_____

_____

WHO: _____

_____

_____

WHAT: _____

_____

_____

_____

_____

_____

_____

_____

_____

_____

WHERE: _____

_____

_____

I release the enclosed prints and/or negatives for reprint with the following credit:

Name of Photographer: _____

Address of Photographer: _____

Photo Courtesy of (if not the same as above): _____

Address: _____

Phone: _____

ORDER FORM

NAME: _____

ADDRESS: _____
(UPS to street address, Priority Mail to P.O. Boxes)

Quantity	Item	Unit Price	Total
	Feminist Chronicles: 1953-1993	$24.95	
	Women's Graphics Catalog	No Charge	
	Sales Tax (CA residents only)		
	Shipping		
	Total		

To be sure our history endures, I wish to donate a copy to:

LIBRARY OR RECIPIENT'S NAME: _____

ADDRESS: _____
    I understand that you will enclose a donor's gift card with each book I donate and that I will receive a receipt from you for my records.

SHIPPING TABLE
$5   1   Book
$7   2-3   Books
$1   Each Additional Book

IN A HURRY?
UPS 2nd day delivery is available: add $3.00 (contiguous states) or $5.00 Alaska & Hawaii) to your regular shipping and handling charges.

SALES TAX

METHOD OF PAYMENT
☐ Check enclosed
☐ Mastercard
☐ VISA

_____
Account #   Expiration Date

_____
Signature Authorizing

_____
Phone

WOMEN'S GRAPHICS • 1126 HI-POINT STREET • LOS ANGELES, CA90035